SOCIAL JUSTICE & ADVOCACY IN HUMAN SERVICES

Cailyn F. Green; Bernadet DeJonge; Nikki Golden; Kim Brayton; Carrie Steinman; and Shannon Raybold

Milne Open Textbooks
Geneseo

Social Justice & Advocacy in Human Services Copyright © 2025 by Cailyn Green and Bernadette DeJonge is licensed under a Creative Commons Attribution 4.0 International License, except where otherwise noted.

ISBN: 978-1-956862-15-7

Published by Milne Open Textbooks, Milne Library
State University of New York at Geneseo,
Geneseo, NY 14454

CONTENTS

	Preface	v
	Cailyn F. Green	
	Overview, Framing, and Definitions	vii
	Bernadet DeJonge and Cailyn F. Green	
1.	Historical Concepts of Social Justice	1
	Cailyn F. Green; Kim Brayton; and Bernadet DeJonge	
2.	Theories of Social Justice	14
	Cailyn F. Green; Kim Brayton; and Bernadet DeJonge	
3.	Human Rights and the Equitable Distribution of Resources	31
	Cailyn F. Green; Kim Brayton; and Bernadet DeJonge	
4.	Power, Privilege, Oppression, and Bias	43
	Cailyn F. Green; Kim Brayton; and Bernadet DeJonge	
5.	Legislation and Policy	59
	Bernadet DeJonge; Nikki Golden; and Cailyn F. Green	
6.	Race, Racism, and Being Black in the United States	84
	Nikki Golden and Bernadet DeJonge	
7.	Race: Being Asian, Indigenous, and Latinx in the United States	143
	Bernadet DeJonge and Nikki Golden	
8.	Being a Woman in the United States	231
	Nikki Golden and Bernadet DeJonge	
9.	Gender and Sexuality in the United States	274
	Nikki Golden and Bernadet DeJonge	
10.	Poverty in the United States	322
	Bernadet DeJonge	
11.	Religion in the United States	340
	Bernadet DeJonge; Nikki Golden; and Cailyn F. Green	

12. Ability in the United States — 374
    Bernadet DeJonge and Shannon Raybold
13. Community Action and Activism — 427
    Bernadet DeJonge; Nikki Golden; and Cailyn F. Green
14. Social Justice Practice in Human Services: An Individual Approach — 438
    Cailyn F. Green; Kim Brayton; Carrie Steinman; and Bernadet DeJonge
15. Social Justice Practice in Human Services: A Systems Approach — 462
    Cailyn F. Green; Kim Brayton; Carrie Steinman; and Bernadet DeJonge

Peer Reviewer Statement — 478
Acknowledgements — 480
About the Authors — 481

Preface

Cailyn F. Green

There is a noticeable disparity in the educational field when it comes to affordable resources on topics associated with social justice. Creating this open educational resource (OER) allowed us to "practice what we preach" when teaching a class about social justice and diversity. By offering a free, peer-reviewed resource for instructors, we can offer inclusivity and equity for students. Our goal is to disrupt the high cost of textbooks and to create space for students in the social justice movement.

Throughout the writing process of this OER, our team traveled and presented at national conferences all over the country. By presenting at different venues, we were able not only to share the idea of OER and how they benefit students, but also to share the specific content of this textbook. During our presentation at the National Conference on Race and Ethnicity (NCORE) in 2023, we asked the audience to share words or concepts that come to mind when they think about "social justice." The words they shared are listed below:

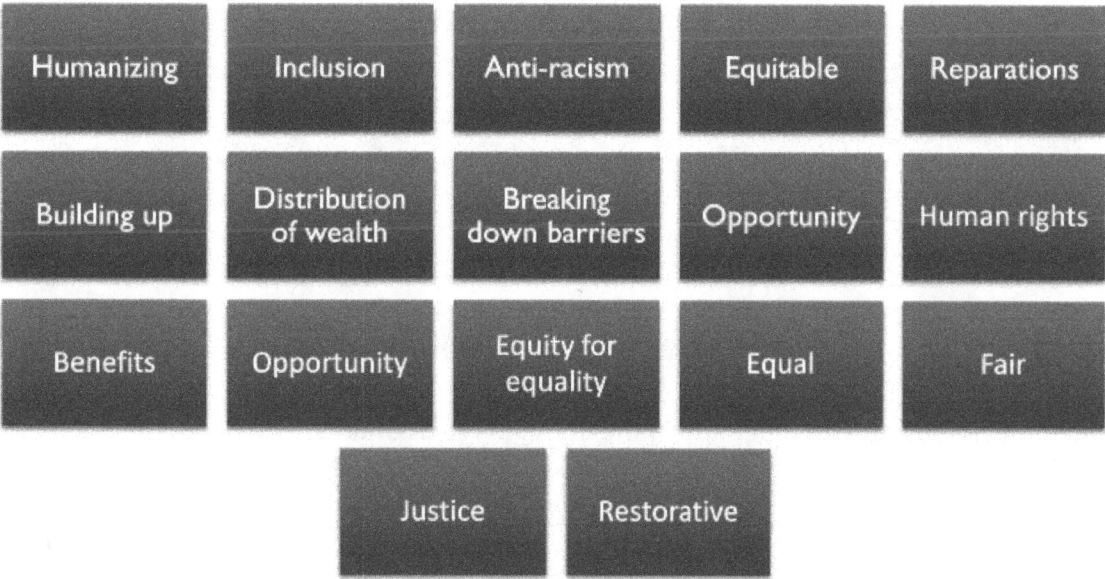

This collection of words was an inspirational message. It showed us that the work we are doing is necessary, important, and desired. The long-term plan for this OER is to update it on a yearly basis. We aim to maintain a current and up-to-date resource for instructors teaching social justice. If, after reading this OER, you have feedback to share regarding concepts, theories, facts, or ideas that you would like to see in the next updated version, please let us know.

Just as social justice will only grow if society remains vigilant, this OER will only remain strong if our community engages and supports this project.

Contact information for this project:

Cailyn Green

Cailyn.green@sunyempire.edu

518-581-5353

Bernadet DeJonge

bernadet.dejonge@yu.edu

315-460-3166

Overview, Framing, and Definitions

Bernadet DeJonge and Cailyn F. Green

> **Learning Objectives**
>
> 1. The reader will identify the framing used in this text.
> 2. The reader will define key terms used throughout this text.

Writing about social justice is a daunting task. Social justice cannot, by definition, be neutral. As writers on this project, we did not aim for neutrality. Our goal in writing this text is to advocate to change the systems of oppression that divide us. We believe social justice is important and salient in today's world and acknowledge the systems of power that permeate the content of this book. We also acknowledge that not every experience of injustice is the same and recognize that intersectionality is important in discussing social justice issues. And yet, we also had to organize this text to make it useful in the classroom setting and beyond. Thus, we have woven intersectionality in where we can while acknowledging the inherent difficulties in choosing to address populations individually. In addition, the authors acknowledge that this text is written by mostly White-identifying women who, while impassioned by the topic, also have not experienced all the marginalization discussed.

This text is written from the perspective that many marginalized identities are social constructs. As people, we sort ourselves into categories of race, ethnicity, gender, sexual orientation, and ability. However, these categories are constructed and maintained by the status quo and thus change and shift over time. Race is not a biological construct but a social one. Our chapters address race, gender, and ability from this perspective.

This text is also framed through a lens of social constructivism, which means that we learn from each other. In this vein, we have intentionally branched out from peer-reviewed sources to add real-world stories to supplement our research and work. This includes personal stories, voices found online, interviews, and the generation of real-world examples for the reader to learn from.

Overview of Chapters

This text is intentionally organized to be used in full in a human services context, or in pieces for any other subject. It is meant to be a broad overview with cues to encourage student exploration and depth. Our intent is to provide students and instructors the opportunity to use content that is useful for teaching social justice in any context.

This overview reviews the general themes and topics of the text, the framing of the text, and the definitions used throughout. Chapter 1 provides historical foundations for social justice concepts and explores how people have historically viewed and regulated morality and justice. Chapter 2 examines theories of social justice from ancient to modern times. Chapter 3 starts to frame social justice issues in the language of human rights and equitable distribution of resources. Chapter 4 examines and defines power, privilege, bias, and oppression. Chapter 5 examines the impact of law and policy on social justice issues.

Chapters 6 and 7 starts the discussion of racism, and examines the history and experience of specific populations. Chapter 8 examines women in the United States. Chapter 9 reviews sexuality and gender issues in the United States. Chapter 10 discusses the experience of poverty in the United States. Chapter 11 examines religion. Chapter 12 discusses disability.

Chapter 13 outlines political action and activism and gives readers some actionable steps they can take to impact social justice in various ways.

Chapter 14 starts the section of the text that is human services-specific. Chapter 14 revisits power, privilege, and bias in the human services context. Chapter 15 discusses equitable distribution and human rights in human services, as well as human services systems and entry points.

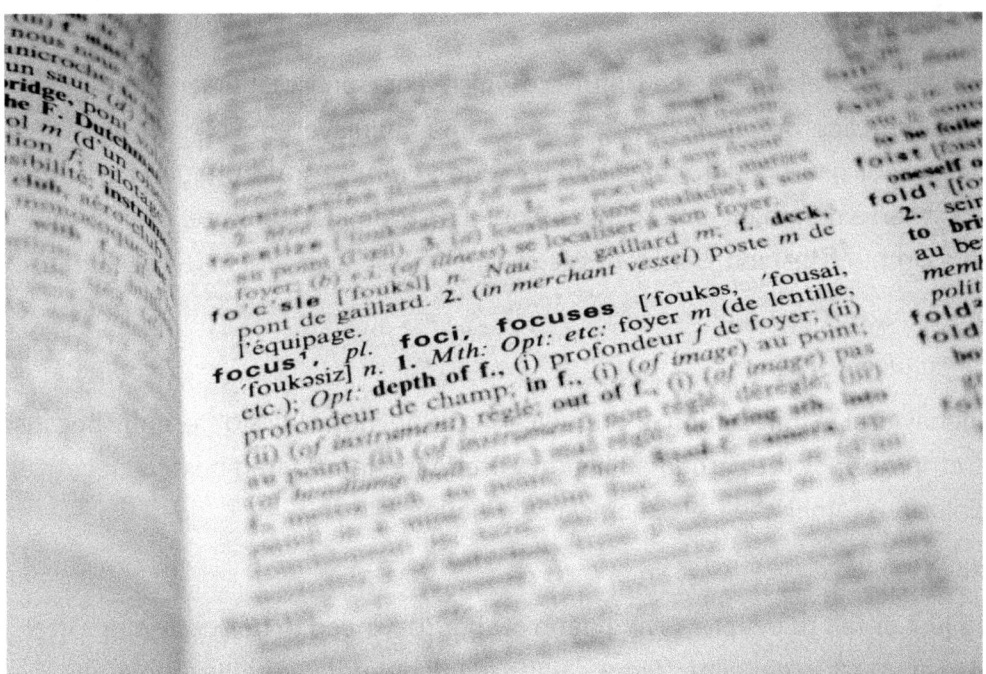

Definitions

Below, we provide the definitions of some of the overarching constructs used in this text.

Bias

A cognitive shortcut that leads a person to have a tendency, inclination, or prejudice toward another. Some biases are positive, and some are negative (Psychology Today, n.d.). Biases can be conscious or unconscious.

Cultural appreciation

Often used in contrast to cultural appropriation, cultural appreciation is the respectful sharing of cultural elements. Cultural appreciation includes asking for permission, giving credit, learning from, and elevating marginalized voices and experiences (Cuncic, 2022).

Cultural appropriation

Using objects or elements of a culture of which a person is not a part without permission. Cultural appropriation can be complex and multilayered. However, it often does not respect or give credit to the original culture. Cultural appropriation almost always occurs when a dominant culture takes from a nondominant culture. Examples include clothing, fashion, dance, music, wellness practices, and hairstyles (Cuncic, 2022).

Discrimination

The behavioral manifestation of prejudice. Treating individuals differently because of race, ethnicity, or other group affiliation. Discrimination is often hostile, negative, and injurious (American Psychological Association, n.d.).

Equity

Being just or fair to people. Giving people what they need to be successful. Often used in contrast to equality. Things can be equal but not equitable (The Annie E. Casey Foundation, 2021).

Equality

Providing everyone the same thing. Equality does not guarantee equity, as people's needs often differ (The Annie E. Casey Foundation, 2021).

Human rights

The United Nations (n.d.) defines "human rights" as follows:

> Human rights are rights inherent to all human beings, regardless of race, sex, nationality, ethnicity, language, religion, or any other status. Human rights include the right to life and liberty, freedom from slavery and torture, freedom of opinion and expression, the right to work and education, and many more. Everyone is entitled to these rights, without discrimination. (para 1)

Implicit bias

The unconscious negative evaluation of someone else based on race, gender, or other socially constructed group (FitzGerald & Hurst, 2017).

Individual racism

When someone acts negatively towards another based on their race or ethnic background (Meadows-Fernandez, 2019).

Internalized racism

Racist beliefs or stereotypes an individual holds about their own racial group (The Annie E. Casey Foundation, 2021).

Marginalization

Treating a person or a group as if they are less than others, unimportant, or powerless by isolating them or taking away their power (Hall & Carlson, 2016). Putting someone on the "margins" of society due to their race, gender, ethnicity, or other social construct (Pratt & Fowler, 2022).

Oppression

The combination of prejudice and institutional power that results in systemic discrimination against some groups (Dover-Taylor et al., 2017). When one group of people pushes down and limits another group of people from accessing resources or development (Marti & Fernández, 2013). Unjust or cruel exercise of authority or power.

Personal bias

A learned inclination for or against an object, group, individual, or person (Dover-Taylor et al., 2017).

Power

Possession or control, authority, or influence over others (Dover-Taylor et al., 2017).

Prejudice

An assumption about another individual based on their membership in a particular group. Groups may include race, gender, ethnicity, and LGBTGEQIAP+ status. Racism, sexism, disability, ageism, classism, and homophobia are all examples of prejudice (Gould, 2022).

Privilege

A benefit, advantage, or favor members of the dominant group have over those in non-dominant groups. Privilege can happen at individual, cultural, and institutional levels and usually occurs at the expense of the nondominant group (Dover-Taylor et al., 2017).

Race

A socially constructed way of identifying other people based on physical characteristics, generally skin color. There is no biological distinction between racial categories, and it is not scientifically based (The Annie E. Casey Foundation, 2021).

Racism

A form of prejudice based on race. Racism assumes that people have certain characteristics based on their race. Racism often assumes that there are dominant and inferior races (American Psychological Association, n.d.).

Social justice

The fair and equitable distribution of resources amongst people. Sometimes referred to as distributive justice. Principles of social justice include access, equity, diversity, participation, inclusion, and human rights (Mollenkamp, 2022).

Stereotyping

A generalized, fixed belief about someone based on their appearance. Stereotypes can be positive or negative (McLeod, 2023).

Systemic racism

When racism exists in systems that hold power. Examples include unequal treatment in health care, education, employment, media, housing, and legislation. Systemic racism limits oppressed groups from accessing resources that other groups are freely accessing (Meadows-Fernandez, 2019).

Unconscious bias

Bias that people have which they are unaware of. An example of an unconscious bias would be when someone decides based on their "gut" feeling (Suveren, 2022).

Author Disclosure Statements

Cailyn Green, Ph.D., CASAC-M, is female-identifying and of Irish and Italian descent. She has been teaching in higher education for 10 years. She has worked in the field of substance use with the recently incarcerated and those with mental health issues for 13 years. Through this community-involved work, she has gained insight into the social justice imbalances that exist between populations. She understands that her perspectives are unique to her and her personal and professional experiences and that her work impacts her view of many social justice topics.

Bernadet (Bernie) DeJonge, Ph.D., CRC is an assistant professor at SUNY Empire State University. She identifies with she/her pronouns and is mixed race. She has many years of experience working in the Medicaid field and specializes in working with individuals with disabilities. Issues of social justice have permeated that fieldwork and continue to impact the experience of teaching.

References

American Psychological Association. (n.d.). *Racism, bias, and discrimination.* https://www.apa.org/topics/racism-bias-discrimination

The Annie E. Casey Foundation. (2021, April 14). *Equity, inclusion and other racial justice definitions.* https://www.aecf.org/blog/racial-justice-definitions

Cuncic, A. (2024, May 24). *The differences between appreciating and appropriating culture.* Verywell Mind. https://www.verywellmind.com/what-is-cultural-appropriation-5070458

Dover-Taylor, K., Gray, J., & Lonial, A. (2017, December 5). *Understanding power, identity, and oppression.* https://www.ala.org/sites/default/files/pla/content/onlinelearning/webinars/Understanding-Power-Identity-and-Oppression-Webinar-Handout.pdf

FitzGerald, C., & Hurst, S. (2017). Implicit bias in healthcare professionals: A systematic review. *BMC Medical Ethics, 18*(19). https://doi.org/10.1186/s12910-017-0179-8

Gould, W. R. (2022, November 8). *What is the psychology behind prejudice?* Verywell Mind. https://www.verywellmind.com/what-is-prejudice-5092657

Hall, J. M., & Carlson, K. (2016). Marginalization: A revisitation with integration of scholarship on globalization, intersectionality, privilege, microaggressions, and implicit biases. *Advanced Nursing Science, 39*(3), 200-215. https://doi.org/10.1097/ANS.0000000000000123

Marti, I., & Fernández, P. (2013). The institutional work of oppression and resistance: Learning from the Holocaust. *Organization Studies, 34*(8), 1195-1223. https://doi.org/10.1177/0170840613492078

McLeod, S. (2023, November 10). *Stereotypes in psychology: Definitions and examples.* Simply Psychology. https://www.simplypsychology.org/katz-braly.html

Meadows-Fernandez, A. R. (2019). *Investigating institutional racism.* Enslow.

Mollencamp, D. T. (2024, April 2). *Social justice meaning and main principles explained.* Investopedia. https://www.investopedia.com/terms/s/social-justice.asp

Psychology Today. (n.d.). *Bias.* https://www.psychologytoday.com/us/basics/bias

Pratt, A., & Fowler, T. (2022, June 10). *Deconstructing bias: Marginalization.* Eunice Kennedy Shriver National Institute of Child Health and Human Development.

Suveren, Y. (2022). Unconscious bias: Definition and significance. *Psikiyatride Güncel Yaklaşımlar, 14*(3), 414–426. https://doi.org/10.18863/pgy.1026607

United Nations. (n.d.). *Human rights.* https://www.un.org/en/global-issues/human-rights

Media Attributions

- Yellow iron framework © Ashkan Forouzani is licensed under a CC BY-ND (Attribution NoDerivatives) license
- Focus Dictionary Page © Romain Vignes is licensed under a CC BY-ND (Attribution NoDerivatives) license

1.
Historical Concepts of Social Justice

Cailyn F. Green; Kim Brayton; and Bernadet DeJonge

> **Learning Objectives**
>
> 1. The reader will identify how historical concepts have impacted the experience of social justice, diversity, and equity in the United States today.
> 2. The reader will identify historical legal codes that have impacted the experience of social justice, diversity, and equity in the United States today.

Many societies today have established what they believe to be an equitable distribution of opportunities, wealth, control, power, and privilege—but how did these approaches come about? Historical context provides an important framework for current social justice concepts. This chapter reviews historical attempts to define social justice, from Hammurabi of Babylon to the Founding Fathers of the United States, and lays the foundation for ongoing development and discussion of contemporary and current social justice topics. This chapter is not exhaustive of all historical social justice concepts, as this is not the primary focus of this text. However, some understanding of the history which leads to current day social justice constructs is necessary.

Code of Hammurabi

The Code of Hammurabi was created by Hammurabi, the King of Babylon, in the Middle East, around 1790 BCE. It is recognized as one of the first legal codes, predating other well known written codes, such as the Jewish Ten Commandments (around 1000 BCE), the Hindu Vedas (around 800 BCE), and the writings of the philosopher Confucius (around 500 BCE) (Finucane, 2017). Not only was it the first of its kind, but also unique to later codes in that it was a formally written legal code enforced by the government. This may reflect an expectation from lawmakers in this period (1790 BCE) for people to treat their fellow community members with respect and dignity.

2 | HISTORICAL CONCEPTS OF SOCIAL JUSTICE

> **Activity 1.1 – Digging Deeper: Hammurabi's Code**
>
> Visit the Avalon Project website to read through some of Hammurabi's laws: The Avalon Project: Code of Hammurabi. (https://avalon.law.yale.edu/ancient/hamframe.asp)
>
> **Discussion Questions**
>
> - What values were the lawmakers attempting to legislate?
> - Discuss how Hammurabi's code is still in use today. What current laws or policies exist that may be grounded in this historical code?

The prelude to the Code of Hammurabi includes the justifications and purpose for creating the code. It begins with Hammurabi explaining his royal status and undeniable authority. He explains: one of their gods has given him the right to protect the people of Babylon, and he is doing this righteously by creating a set of laws that everyone must live by. These laws encompass family laws, tax laws, and contractual laws, and include punishment by death and/or mutilation (Pyrcz, 2019). One of the most well-known tenets of the Code of Hammurabi is "an eye for an eye"; essentially, "whatever I did to you, you should be able to do to me." However, the implementation was not always equal. This may be one of the earliest forms of documented discrimination. If a free man were to punch a slave in the face, the free man might be fined, as the individuals during this time considered a slave's life to be worth less than the life of the free man. However, if a slave were to punch a free man in the face, the slave could lose their hand altogether (Pyrcz, 2019). This injustice reflects societal attempts, even in some of the earliest recorded human history, to balance individual human value with a community of social justice.

That the Code of Hammurabi was developed and written in stone acted as a form of societal control. These laws were written physically and irreversibly to show community members that they would not waver, regardless of who committed the crime. Inscribed on a black stone pillar, the laws included the belief that if someone was accused of a crime, they were presumed innocent. On the other hand, the Code of Hammurabi also treated individual lives as having varying levels of worth. For example, a pregnant slave was only considered to have a third of the value held by a free man's eyeball (Pyrcz, 2019).

> **Activity 1.2 – The Code of Hammurabi**
>
> Watch Dr. Paul Raha dive deeper into Hammurabi's Code: The Code of Hammurabi & the Rule of Law: Why Written Law Matters (https://www.youtube.com/watch?v=_rC5V5vEprs)

HISTORICAL CONCEPTS OF SOCIAL JUSTICE | 3

Stele of Hammurabi

 One or more interactive elements has been excluded from this version of the text. You can view them online here: https://milnepublishing.geneseo.edu/social-justice-in-human-services/?p=39#oembed-1 (#oembed-1)

Discussion Question

- Why is it important that laws evolve as society changes?

The Golden Rule

The next historical group of ideas that can be connected to early social justice concepts are found in religious books and religious followings. These include what is commonly referred to as the Golden Rule in the Abrahamic faiths (Finucane, 2017). This Golden Rule, in its more basic form, means to treat others as you would want to be treated. The Golden Rule in the Christian holy book, the Bible, is found in the book of Matthew, as a part of the Sermon on the Mount. It states: "Therefore all things whatsoever ye would that men should do to you, do ye even so to them: for this is the law and the prophets" (King James Bible, 1769/2017, Matthew, 7:12). This is often translated into the concept: "Do unto others as you would have them do unto you". The Muslim holy book, the Qur'an, states a similar idea: "Love your neighbor as yourself" (Finucane, 2017).

The essence of the Golden Rule is seen throughout history in various religious contexts. These variations of a Golden Rule helped to guide the reciprocal nature of interaction between individuals by focusing on what *to* do, instead of what not to do. It is important to note, however, that the Golden Rule can be very subjective. As the "rule" is open to interpretation, it may be manipulated for ill intention. The Golden Rule works due to social consequence; it provides a socially acceptable outcome if an individual engages in a certain behavior or action. With the Golden Rule heavily influencing many social norms and laws throughout history, its subjectivity is essential to recognise. Does the Golden Rule, for example, allow society members to do good to others because they themselves believe it to be good, even though the other parties may not (Green, 2008)?

Discussion Questions

- Did you grow up with some version of the Golden Rule? Why do you think that this concept has been sustained throughout history into the present day?
- Can you think of an example when the Golden Rule might not work?
- What about doing good even if others don't think it is good? Can you think of an example of this?
- How might your personal bias come into play with the Golden Rule?
- How do your religious beliefs work (or not) with the Golden Rule?

Magna Carta

The Magna Carta is a document that was written by King John of England in 1215. It defined who held power over the English people. At the time, the English people argued over the King's extreme level and misuse of authority. This document contains basic principles of human rights and stated that even the King was not above the law (Turner, 2014). With the monarchy having been previously seen as all-powerful and unchallengeable, this represented a large shift in power.

At the time, the Magna Carta was seen as a solution to all of England's political problems. It contained laws ensuring personal freedom, and supported the idea of equity under the law. The Magna Carta contained rules which have been interpreted and used as a foundation for the development of laws throughout history. This includes rules regarding the freedom of individuals, particularly around imprisonment. The Magna Carta significantly influenced the systems of justice now seen in the United States. Concepts of a fair and impartial judge and a jury of one's peers can be traced back to this historical document. Eventually, the Magna Carta was brought to the United States by English settlers who felt they were the king's free subjects as they settled into the New World (Turner, 2014).

> **Activity 1.3 – Digging Deeper: Magna Carta**
>
> Read through the National Archives Magna Carta (https://www.archives.gov/exhibits/featured-documents/magna-carta/translation.html) translation in its entirety.
>
> Discussion Questions
>
> - What do you think is interesting in the Magna Carta? Why?
> - How does the Magna Carta relate to life today?

The Declaration of Independence

John Trumbull's painting, Declaration of Independence, being represented to the Congress. The original hangs in the US Capitol rotunda. It does not represent a real ceremony; the individuals portrayed were never in the same room at the same time.

The Declaration of Independence was signed by the Continental Congress on July 4th, 1776. It declared the separation of the thirteen North American colonies from England following the American Revolution between 1775 and 1776, creating the United States of America (Britannica, 2022). The Declaration of Independence included principles such as that "all men are created equal," and that all men have "inalienable rights...of life, liberty, and the pursuit of happiness." It is important to note that this doctrine was initially designed to be applied only to certain men; it did not include people who were enslaved, or women. The Declaration of Independence has been the foundation of many of the social justice arguments throughout American history.

The theological context behind the Declaration of Independence was the notion that God had instilled all people with basic human rights, and that no one person in power has the right to revoke power from others (Britannica, 2022). The Declaration of Independence states that the people will choose who holds power, and that those given power cannot give it to someone else (Jayne, 1998). This concept stems from the mentality that since God is the creator of all things, only He has the power to instill this type of power (Beck, 2016).

The Declaration of Independence also valued, what they considered to be, basic moral judgement, relying on the idea that the government and those chosen to run it would be morally judged by its citizens. This places the responsibility of choosing a morally sound government in the hands of the people, including the decision of how to define morality (Jayne, 1998). It cannot be forgotten that during this time, the same people who were writing the Declaration of Independence owned slaves, and considered this morally right (Sandefur, 2018). It is important to remember the subjectivity of moral values.

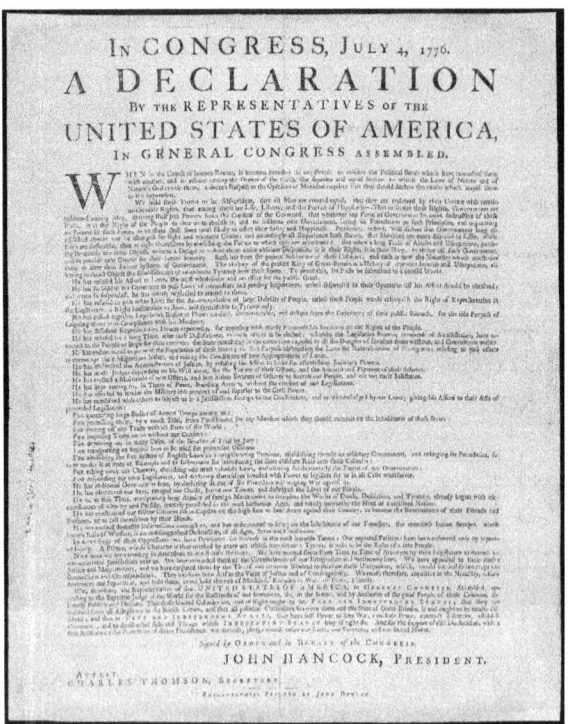

Declaration of Independence, printed by John Dunlap in Philadelphia

Activity 1.4 – Digging Deeper: Declaration of Independence

Read through the Declaration of Independence as reproduced on Harvard's Declaration Resources Project website. (https://declaration.fas.harvard.edu/resources/text)

Video: Declaration of Independence (https://www.youtube.com/watch?v=BVctfLkuUxk).

 One or more interactive elements has been excluded from this version of the text. You can view them online here: https://milnepublishing.geneseo.edu/social-justice-in-human-services/?p=39#oembed-2 (#oembed-2)

Discussion Questions

- Why did the colonists feel that they needed to include the line "The right to life, liberty, and pursuit of happiness?"
- Does this line still apply to us today? Why or why not? Please provide examples for either argument.

The Constitution

The United States Constitution was written in 1787 and has been in operation since 1789. The Constitution was written to connect the United States by a common thread of laws and interests (National Archives, 2022). By promoting a general sense of welfare and unity, the United States Constitution organized the government branches and explained the responsibilities of each. It outlined the powers that each branch held and how they were expected to practice and work together as a cohesive entity (National Constitution Center, 2023).

Activity 1.5 – The US Constitution

Read through the entire United States Constitution with helpful annotations through the National Constitution Center's website. (https://constitutioncenter.org/the-constitution/full-text)

Discussion Questions

- Does the United States Constitution still work? Why or why not?
- If you had the power to do so, what would you change about the Constitution?

Bill of Rights 1791

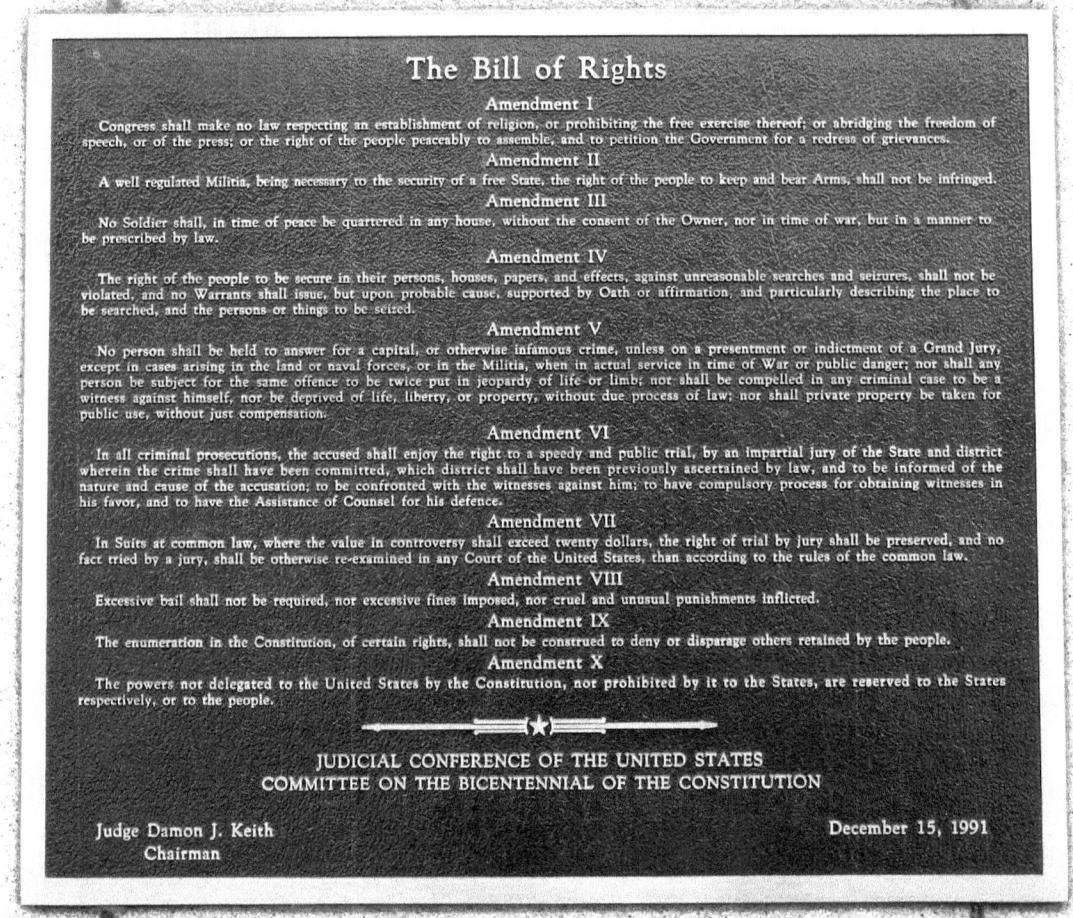

The Bill of Rights are amendments written in 1791 to address objections to the Constitution. These amendments were intentionally written to guarantee United States citizens freedoms and rights. The federalists, including James Madison, studied the United States Constitution and identified several important issues which they felt had been overlooked in the initial Constitution. The Federalist Party designed 12 amendments and sent them to Congress for 'ratification': the process to formally change the United States Constitution. For an amendment to be ratified, it must be proposed by Congress with a two-thirds majority vote and then by three-fourths of the states. Another way an amendment can be ratified is through the legislatures in two-thirds of the states being in agreement to move in this direction. Congress ended up ratifying points three through 12, which became the first 10 amendments of the United States Constitution, titled the Bill of Rights (National Archives, 2016).

The Bill of Rights evolved as a response to the treatment of the English monarchy towards the colonists before the American Revolution. The newly formed United States government wanted to clearly outline the rights that the new government could not infringe upon. They wanted to give the new government a vital role in protecting citizens from abusive governments (Amar, 1998). Examples of these rights include the right to freedom of speech, the right to bear arms, and the right to not allow the government or soldiers to requisition their homes. The latter is a practical example of a pervasive issue during the period, as the British soldiers had the right to go into any home and take it for their own use during the Revolutionary War. Similarly, each of these ten amendments is connected to, and derived from, an intentional process of regulating government overreach in an effort to prevent future treatment of citizens like that of the colonists by the English monarchy.

Today, there are 27 amendments to the United States Constitution (National Archives, 2016). That means that 17 amendments have been added since the Bill of Rights was created. Thus, the United States government is founded on the idea that *the people* have the power to adjust and add to the Constitution as society changes. Eighteenth century politicians saw the need for citizens to be able to evolve their government, and this is the process they established to facilitate this (National Archives, 2016).

Activity 1.6 – Digging Deeper: Bill of Rights

Read the first 10 amendments that compose the Bill of Rights via the National Archives. (https://www.archives.gov/founding-docs/bill-of-rights-transcript#toc-the-u-s-bill-of-rights)

Discussion Questions

- How do you connect the Bill of Rights to your life today?
- How does the Bill of Rights hold up in today's society?

Activity 1.7 – An Alphabet of World Problems in Achieving Social Justice

Considering its history and foundation, how has social justice developed over time, and what has aided in its creation? An exploration of some examples of world problems that exist today and hinder society from fully achieving social justice follows. Examination of these concepts throughout this textbook is not meant to be comprehensive, but rather to introduce the reader to areas of interest and concern and encourage independent research.

- **A**geism, anti-democracy, arms race, autocracy (the authors would like to add ableism to this list)
- **B**reaches of human rights, breakdown of public services and public goods, burnout
- **C**hauvinism, classism, climate change, consumerism, consumption of resources to the point of global destruction, commodification and monetization of human life, conflicts

across the world, crimes against humanity, criminal activity
- Despotism, dictatorships, discrimination, disease, disproportionate wealth in the hands of the few, dominatory ideology, drought
- Economic hegemony, energy costs, environmental decay and degradation, exclusion, exploitation, extremism
- Fake news, false imprisonment, fascism, financialization of life, food shortages
- Gender, genocide, global pestilence, greed
- Hatred, health and health care problems, hegemony, homophobia, hopelessness, hunger
- Identity, ideology, individualism, inequality, inhumanity, injustice, intolerance
- Justice as a purchasable commodity
- Klepto-autocracy
- Lawlessness, legitimation crises
- Mass media, materialism, migrants, militarization, misrecognition, monetization of life, motivation crises
- Narrow utilitarianism, nationalism, nationalistic populism, neglect of humanity, neo-colonialism, neoliberalism, New right
- Oppression, othering
- Political hegemony, pollution, population explosion, poverty, power, pragmatism, prejudice, privatization of public goods, profiteering, pursuit of profit at all costs
- Questioning of legitimacy and rights, quiescence in the face of injustices
- Racism, recognition, refugees, relativism, rentiers, repression
- Sexism, social exclusion, social injustice, sovereign debt crises, species extinction, starvation, steering media, stigmatization, surveillance society
- Theft, threats to democracy and emancipation, torture, totalitarianism, transphobia
- Unemployment, unequal opportunity, underinvestment for the public good, unfreedoms
- Violence, virus control for health, volatile food prices
- War, water shortages, wealth, wealth distribution
- Xenophobia
- Youth unemployment
- Zero-sum economic analysis (Bramley & Morrison, 2023, pg. 152).

Discussion Questions

- Choose one of the world's problems in achieving social justice and explain how/who is working to correct this issue. What forward movement has been made in this matter? What is stopping the forward movement?

- From your perspective or experience, what is missing from this list?

Thoughts from the Authors

Understanding the history behind how today's social justice has come to be is an important place to start. It is vital to remember that social justice is ever-changing and adapting to the world around us. We must be aware that by the time this textbook gets into your hands, there may be more to add to this list. It is the job of the authors to update this textbook to keep it current and relevant. This is also where, if you, the student or instructor, are aware of an important component of history that you feel has shaped today's social justice climate, please reach out and tell us!

Sincerely,
Dr. Green

History is certainly critical. Understanding many of the underlying philosophies that have led to the present-day principles we see represented in social justice approaches helps us to adapt as our world changes. Adapting while not losing sight of principles linked to long-fought human rights is a significant challenge. Just think about the changes that may come about because of the many events and experiences in just the past 5-10 years, including COVID, the #MeToo movement, and the war in Ukraine, just to name a few.

Sincerely,
Dr. Brayton

Chapter Summary Questions

1. In exploring ancient laws, what do you see that translated or was brought over into the development of the United States government? Why is this important when learning about the history of social justice?
2. What historical events influenced the creation of the Bill of Rights? Why is this impor-

> tant in learning about the history of social justice?
> 3. How do the 10 original Bill of Rights translate into today's society?
> 4. Which historical social justice concepts are still in use today? Which ones have been left behind? Why do you think some have lasted and some have not?
> 5. What is the significance of laws being written in stone?
> 6. Talk about laws written in stone versus the ability of a government to make changes or adapt laws. How does this flexibility impact social justice? Why do you think it might be important?

References

Amar, A. R. (1998). *The Bill of Rights creation and reconstruction*. Yale University Press. https://doi.org/10.12987/9780300127089

Beck, R. (2016). [Review of the book *The Declaration of Independence and God: Self-evident truths in American law*, by O. Anderson]. *Journal of Church and State, 58*(4), 779–781. https://doi.org/10.1093/jcs/csw093

Bramley, C., & Morrison, K. (2023). *Student engagement, higher education, and social justice: Beyond neoliberalism and the market*. Routledge. https://doi.org/10.4324/9781003331292

Britannica. (2022, December 3). Declaration of Independence. In *Encyclopedia Britannica*. https://www.britannica.com/search?query=Declaration+of+Independence

Finucane, B. (2017). *Human rights*. Mason Crest.

Green, W. S. (2008). Parsing reciprocity: Questions for the golden rule. In J. Neusner & B. Chilton (Eds.), *The golden rule: The ethics of reciprocity in world religions* (pp. 1-8). Continuum. https://doi.org/10.5040/9781472549440

Jayne, A. (1998). *Jefferson's Declaration of Independence: Origins, philosophy, and theology*. The University Press of Kentucky.

King James Bible. (2017). King James Bible Online. https://www.kingjamesbibleonline.org/ (Original work published 1769).

National Archives. (2016). *Amending America: Records from the National Archives*. https://www.archives.gov/files/amending-america/explore/aa-the-ebook-med-res.pdf

National Archives. (2022). *The Constitution of the United States*. https://www.archives.gov/founding-docs/constitution

National Constitution Center. (2023). *The United States Constitution*. https://constitutioncenter.org/the-constitution

Pyrcz, A. A. (2019). Set in stone: The ancient Babylonian law code of King Hammurabi. *Agora, 54*(1), 11–18.

Sandefur, T. (2018). The Declaration of Independence is the moral and legal foundation of America. *The Objective Standard, 13*(3), 107–110.

Turner, R. V. (2014). *Magna Carta: Through the ages.* Routledge. https://doi.org/10.4324/9781315837468

Media Attributions

- Stele of Hammurabi © Hammurabi/anonymous, Photo: Mbzt is licensed under a CC BY (Attribution) license
- "Declaration of Independence" © John Trumbull is licensed under a Public Domain license
- Declaration of Independence Broadside © Author: Thomas Jefferson; printed by John Dunlap is licensed under a Public Domain license
- The Bill of Rights Plaque © Photo by: Davy Jones is licensed under a CC BY (Attribution) license

2.

Theories of Social Justice

Cailyn F. Green; Kim Brayton; and Bernadet DeJonge

> **Learning Objectives**
>
> 1. The reader will distinguish between philosophers who shaped social justice theories.
> 2. The reader will evaluate how historical social justice theories have developed through history.

This chapter introduces students to social justice theories, covering classical, modern, and postmodern perspectives. Classical theories are distinct in focusing on the questions "What is there?" or "What sort of things exist?" (Tillman, 2021). Modern theories focus on the question of "How do we know?" Most of these were developed during the Renaissance era and are based on how we use our senses to understand things or concepts around us. Postmodern theories are based on the question "What should we do about it?", which is a much more practical approach (Tillman, 2021). Social justice theories provide unique motives for why individuals act the way they do with respect to social justice. While many of these theories are rooted in similar concepts, they vary in explaining how individuals react and work together or against each other. Through time, social justice theory has continued to evolve, and the linear progression of this chapter allows the theories to build upon each other.

Classical Theories

Plato's (427-347 BC) theory of social justice was one of the first on record. Plato speaks to both mythical and religious concepts of social justice (Capeheart & Milovanovic, 2007) and argues that social justice is a necessary component of happiness (Kamtekar, 2001). Plato believed that the mythical gods Zeus and Apollo were held responsible for making the local rules that people lived by. Plato also believed that people themselves are not able to determine social justice equity and that a larger governing body is required to teach people what is right and wrong. Some of Plato's drawings have been interpreted to express that fairness is

Herma of Plato, Musei Capitolini, Rome

embedded in every person's character. These foundational beliefs are then expressed through a person's behavior and actions (Capeheart & Milovanovic, 2007).

Aristotle's (384-322 BC) theory of social justice emulates Plato, as Plato was his professor and teacher. However, there are some differences. These differences may be rooted in Aristotle's middle-class background, which differed from Plato's upper-class, aristocratic upbringing. While Aristotle spoke of the concept of equity being necessary for justice, he did not argue for absolute equality; he focused on proportionate equality (Capeheart & Milovanovic, 2007). Proportionate equality is the idea that equals must be treated equally and unequals must be treated unequally. An example that Aristotle gives to explain this concept is the idea of monetary exchange. If there is a shoemaker and a house builder, how many shoes would the shoemaker have to make to pay for the house builder to build them a house? These are not equal. However, all shoes can be compared as equals. So, we can identify how many shoes in general, can equal a house. Equal must be equal, for example, shoes to shoes. Unequal must be unequal, for example, shoes to house (Capeheart & Milovanovic, 2007).

Activity 2.1 – Digging Deeper: Knowledge Check

1. Why is the concept of equality important when thinking about social justice?

Bust of Aristotle. Marble, Roman copy after a Greek bronze original by Lysippos from 330 BC.

2. Do you think that these ancient philosophers were really talking about social justice in their philosophies? Why or why not?

St. Thomas Aquinas' (**384-322 BC**) theory of social justice is grounded in the concept that justice is a natural law. This is then cut into two sections. The first is general justice, which is roughly the concept of legal justice and the rules and laws the state or governing entities create for people to live by. The second section is particular justice, which explains how people distribute goods and relate to one another (Capeheart & Milovanovic, 2007). Aquinas believed that a law that is unjust or not equal is not a law. Aquinas also spoke about the distribution of goods and believed that society must monitor how goods are divided. He recognized that a person's rank in the community impacts the goods that are distributed to them (Capeheart & Milovanovic, 2007). St. Thomas Aquinas also considered consequences for civil disobedience to be just and necessary to maintain social justice (Scholz, 2006).

Modern Theories

Thomas Hobbes' (**1588-1679**) theory of social justice was one of the first theories that did not rely on religion (Capeheart & Milovanovic, 2007). Hobbes viewed people as pessimistic and negative. Hobbes espoused that if people did not have a system of checks and balances to account for their negative behaviors, they would live in a constant warlike state, always against each other (Capeheart & Milovanovic, 2007). Hobbes believed that people would never choose to work together without an obligation or unless forced to do so. Hobbes felt that if society had a set of rules to abide by, people would follow those rules and live in harmony. The key to this theory is that people need a larger entity to make these rules, govern their interactions, and work together (Capeheart & Milovanovic, 2007).

Thomas Hobbes (1588-1679), Social philosopher.

Activity 2.2 – Digging Deeper: Choosing Sides

Hobbes included the theory of equity in his law of nature as well (Sorell, 2016). Hobbes tells us that people have two impressions of what equity means. The first type of equity is where a governing body determines what is fair and equal. This looks like a judge having a decision to make regarding which person in a situation is equal and just: they would follow the stated purpose of the law. The other type of equity is when people submit to using the theory of personal judgment when placed in a controversy (Sorell). This means people will favor one side of a controversy over another based on their personal biases and feelings. These different definitions of equity, as explained by Hobbes, are the foundation for his social justice theory.

Discussion Questions

> - Can you think of a time when you were forced to choose a side?
> - How did your personal bias play into the choice you made?
> - Looking back, was your choice equitable?

John Locke's (1632-1704) theory of social justice is similar in nature to Hobbes' theory in that social justice is seen as a type of social contract between people. The difference is that Locke's theory does not have the same negative view of society. Locke explains that while people need some type of contract and agreement to work together, they are obliged by their moral foundations, which are rooted in their belief in God, to respect each other (Capeheart & Milovanovic, 2007). A larger governing entity can support this, but Locke focused on a person's internal moral compass. This moral compass leads people to healthy interactions with fellow community members. An example given by Locke is as follows: God has given people the earth and the use of its resources for survival and comfort. When a person mixes their own personal labor with the God-given resource of land, they have made it their privately owned property (Munger et al., 2016). An example of this philosophy would be homesteading during westward expansion in the United States. Homesteaders put labor into their land and, thus, believed that God granted them this resource (Riddle, 2010). Locke suggests limiting the act of turning resources into property to ensure equity over distribution (Munger et al., 2016).

Activity 2.3 – Digging Deeper

Both Hobbes' and Locke's theories identify the importance of having a third party to determine if an inequity or imbalance exists. Thus, when an individual feels deprived of a right, they can take this dispute to a larger governing entity for resolution (Crawford, 2020). Both philosophers advocate for government as a part of moral decision-making.

Discussion Questions

- How might this kind of philosophy work in the current world?
- How might this kind of philosophy not work in the current world?
- What are the risks of assigning the government to make decisions about morality?

David Hume's (1711-1776) theory of social justice argued that the only real form of justice is guaranteed by having a larger entity, like a government, have power over the balance (Munger et al., 2016). Hume focused on politicians and rules as the driving factors behind what makes people treat each other morally. If a person is unwilling to follow the rules set forth by the government or politicians, that person is at risk of damaging their reputation. This is part of what Hume believed is necessary or drives people to follow the government-set rules. He identified justice as a "sense of common interest" that people feel in their moral self and how others view them (Coventry & Sager, 2013).

Jean Jacques Rousseau's (1712-1778) theory of social justice is rooted in the idea that community is what creates the action of social justice (Munger et al., 2016). Living and being a part of a community creates an unspoken social contract between the members. This social contract gears people to act as though they need to oblige each other and share living resources. This is the opposite of basic human nature, which, according to Rousseau, is to survive and focus on self-preservation (Munger et al., 2016). The existence of a social contract is when people consider the well-being of others and then distribute goods in a manner that will benefit others. Rousseau's theory is very similar to that of Locke in their understanding of a social contract existing between people (Capeheart & Milovanovic, 2007)

John Stuart Mill's (1806-1873) theory of social justice stems from a belief that people's sense of justice is rooted in our internal consciousness (Capeheart & Milovanovic, 2007). This internal consciousness guides our actions and beliefs in how we interact with each other. Mill believed that people behave in ways that bring them happiness. If this behavior does not impact anyone, people have the right to act on their wishes and wants. However, if the behaviors or actions people want to engage in may negatively impact another person, people do not have the right to engage in this behavior. Mill stated that when a conflict exists between the behavior we want to engage in and its potential consequences, society needs to follow a utility principle of following a just path (Capeheart & Milovanovic, 2007). This means respecting the happiness of others and allowing them to perform such acts that bring them happiness, until it harms others.

Activity 2.4 – Digging Deeper: Distribution of goods

Mill had three principles of justice when it came to the distribution of goods. The first was that a person has a right to the goods produced by their labor. The second is that people deserve compensation when they invest their own money, as they are benefiting society on a larger scale. Mill's third principle of equal distribution is that people have a right to property gifted to them (Nathanson, 2012).

Discussion Questions

- How do these three principles apply today?
- What would you add to Mill's three principles of justice regarding the distribution of goods?
- Where might individuals who struggle with poverty fit into this definition?

Karl Marx's (1818-1883) theory of social justice had similar approaches, with social justice being strongly connected to the economy and its structure (Capeheart & Milovanovic,

2007). Marx believed that justice was a tool used by the ruling upper class of society to hide the true missions of the capitalistic economy (Munger et al., 2016). He believed that rather than the existing market creating and producing justice naturally, the market itself (and those who controlled it) produced injustices regarding goods and their distribution (Capeheart & Milovanovic, 2007). Marx believed that the only way to do away with these injustices and unequal distribution of goods was to do away with the concept of a capitalist market. This did not mean that capitalism was fully unnecessary, rather he believed that capitalism was a necessary part of our development as a human race. It meant he believed it should be seen as a phase of our growth and be left behind for a more equitable system to take its place. This more equitable social justice system would turn away the ideals that material goods are the basis of society (Munger et al., 2016).

Postmodern Theories

Friedrich Nietzsche's (1844-1900) theory of social justice is rooted in class and power. Nietzsche believed that laws and rules were created by a particular set of people who held societal power (Capeheart & Milovanovic, 2007) and believed that the concepts of morals and ethics reflected an artificially created set of rules. He believed that pure justice exists only between two groups of equal power. According to Nietzsche, the development of social justice rules is done in two parts. In the first part, competing power groups create rules over the weaker groups. Inequalities then develop as the powerful group sets societal rules. The second part is focused on pity towards weaker groups stemming from Christian ideals. The weaker, less powerful groups then need to organize and create conflict with the stronger, more powerful groups to balance out power (Capeheart & Milovanovic, 2007).

John Rawls' (1921-2002) theory of social justice focuses on social disparities. The Rawlsian theory believes that large institutions perpetuate deep-seated inequalities that offer certain individuals privileges over others (Munger et al., 2016). This theory states that for justice to be present, there must be an equal distribution of goods, opportunity, and money in society. Without this equal distribution, social justice does not exist. Rawls created two principles to ensure social justice. The first principle is the Fair Equality Principle. This principle gives equal rights and basic liberties to all society members. The second principle is the Different Principle. This principle calls for a fair distribution of social goods, avoiding exchanges between economic/social gains and basic human liberties (Munger et al., 2016).

> ### Activity 2.5 – Digging Deeper: Affirmative Action
>
> An example of Rawls' second principle also applies today. Consider affirmative action. It was identified that there were disparities in who could receive education based on ethnic background, and affirmative action was enacted to create a fair distribution of education.
>
> Video: Is Affirmative Action Fair? (https://www.youtube.com/watch?v=ZhUOw0KidZg) by Above The Noise.
>
> > *One or more interactive elements has been excluded from this version of the text. You can view them online here: https://milnepublishing.geneseo.edu/social-justice-in-human-services/?p=44#oembed-1 (#oembed-1)*
>
> **Discussion Questions**
>
> - What are the goods involved when discussing affirmative action?
> - Does affirmative action create a fair distribution of goods? How?
> - Now that affirmative action has been overturned, how are college admission processes going to change? What can they do to maintain equity in the admission process?

Current Theories

Roy Wilkins' (**1901-1981**) theory of social justice. Roy Wilkins held leadership roles in the National Association for the Advancement of Colored People (NAACP) as the Executive Secretary and Executive Director from 1955 until 1977 (Ryan, 2014). Wilkins often spoke on instilling racial pride, supporting Black history, and integrating education, which differs from state to state (Robert Penn Warren Center for the Humanities, n.d.). While Wilkins is best known as a civil rights advocate, he used his journalism career to advance social justice as well. Wilkins was the first Black newspaper columnist in the syndicated, mainstream press. Wilkins used his platform for journalism to spread information regarding "denouncing black criminal acts and to encourage Black Americans to support law enforcement" (Bedingfield, 2019, para. 4).

Dr. Martin Luther King Jr.'s (**1929-1968**) theory of social justice focused on mass civil disobedience. This theory came about due to the White backlash of Black Power movements and from issues that arose when attempting to move forward with acts of liberation and taking back power (Livingston, 2020). Dr. King often referred to justice as a concept that "ought" to be rather than "is." He viewed the civil rights movement as a morally focused attempt to adjust and fix an unjust relationship (Lee, 1984). Dr. King's work paved the way for many modern-day social justice activists.

Roger Wilkins

Roger Wilkins' (1932-2017) social justice theory. Roger Wilkins was a lawyer, civil rights leader, journalist, and professor who served as the Assistant Attorney General of the United States from 1966-1969. He brought the Black Power movement to the presidential office during this time. The goals of the Black Power movement were focused on Black politics and economic power. Wilkins believed in promoting racial pride and Black economic empowerment and promoted the Black Power movement as a positive and necessary strategy to continue the forward movement of civil rights. Wilkins fought for Black Power to show the country how "black middle class success and growing disadvantage for power and working-class African Americans" (Davies, 2017, p. 3) reveal the power and strength of White interest.

Kimberlé Crenshaw's (1959- living) theory of social justice is heavily influenced by contemporary feminist and antiracist concepts. Crenshaw states that to overcome racist and patriarchal shadows, the victims of political and social crimes must make their circumstances known (Crenshaw, 2005). Crenshaw's theory relies heavily on the construct of intersectionality.

> The concept of intersectionality describes the ways in which systems of inequality based on gender, race, ethnicity, sexual orientation, gender identity, disability, class and other forms of discrimination intersect to create unique dynamics and effects. For example, when a Muslim woman wearing the Hijab is being discriminated, it

President Lyndon B. Johnson meets with civil rights activist Roy Wilkins in the Oval Office, 1963.

Kimberlé Crenshaw in Berlin, 2018

would be impossible to dissociate her female from her Muslim identity and to isolate the dimension(s) causing her discrimination. (Lawrence Hall, 2022, para 4)

24 | THEORIES OF SOCIAL JUSTICE

In an interview with Crenshaw at Columbia Law School in 2017, she identified intersectionality as "a lens through which you can see where power comes and collides, where it interlocks and intersects" (Columbia Law School, 2017, para. 4). Other examples of this include how transgender people of color report increased experiences of abuse in our medical system compared to patients who identify as White and straight, or how Latinx women earn lower wages and are overrepresented in jobs that are known to offer lower wages, especially when compared to White women (Heyl, 2023).

Activity 2.6 – Intersectionality

Video: The urgency of intersectionality (https://www.youtube.com/watch?v=akOe5-UsQ2o&t=511s) by Kimberlé Crenshaw.

 One or more interactive elements has been excluded from this version of the text. You can view them online here: https://milnepublishing.geneseo.edu/social-justice-in-human-services/?p=44#oembed-2 (#oembed-2)

Discussion Questions

- How do you see intersectionality represented in your community?
- How do you see intersectionality represented in your classes?

Activity 2.7 – Digging Deeper: Interview Dr. John Watts

Dr. Green here. I spoke with Dr. John Watts about the concept of intersectionality for the purpose of this chapter so I could learn more about it. Dr. Watts is a former probation supervisor for the State of Connecticut and currently an Assistant Professor and the Program Director for the Criminal Justice and Restorative Justice Program at the University of Saint Joseph in West Hartford, Connecticut, and a Certified Criminal Justice Addictions Counselor. Dr. Watts explained:

> When I think about intersectionality, the first thing that comes to mind is the overlapping systems of oppression. For instance, someone can be African American and identify as gay or lesbian; that particular individual can be exposed to societal racism based on their skin color and homophobia based on their sexual orientation at times from their own race or culture. As a response to those overlapping systems of discrimination/oppression, many marginalized groups learn how to "code switch." Code switch is a way to navigate those overlapping systems of discrimination/oppression. Code-switching can be very exhausting because the marginalized individual is constantly trying to assimilate in and out of different situations/systems, thus losing a part of their identities.

> In my profession, I had to learn how to code-switch in order to be promoted to a Chief Probation Officer. Currently, I'm one of only four Black male supervisors in the entire probation department. Even in our probation department, Black males are seen as over-aggressive, angry, and lacking the skills to be in a leadership position. So, in order to move up in the department, I knew I needed to work to offset those negative stereotypes of Black males, which propelled me right into my doctoral degree (J. Watts, personal communication, July 25th, 2023).

Discussion Questions

- What type of intersectionality do you see in your career?
- How do you navigate intersectionality in the workplace?
- How does intersectionality impact your ability to do your job?
- How is intersectionality reflected in today's politics? Supreme Court decisions?

Rose Braz's (1961-2017) theory on social justice stemmed from a grassroots movement to connect climate, environment, social justice, labor, and faith in working together to better serve the people (Center for Biological Diversity, 2023). She believed the first step in making any change is to name it clearly (Bennett, 2008). Much of Braz's social justice work centered around prison reform and challenging the currently existing criminal justice structure (Braz et al, 2000). Braz and her supporters followed specific, intentional steps to impact social justice reform. They started with gathering members, then moved on to having regular meetings, choosing a focus, seeking publications to support the cause, and working together on steps toward the right direction (Braz et al., 2000).

Critical Race Theory (CRT)

Critical Race Theory (CRT) is a newer concept in the field of social justice. CRT began in the 1970s in the wake of the civil rights era. Many people attribute the beginning of CRT to Malcolm X (Rabaka, 2002). Malcolm X, originally named Malcolm Little, was born in 1925 and died in 1965 (Assensoh & Alex-Assensoh, 2014). Malcolm X expressed that our society was "undergoing a radical process of change and development" (Rabaka, 2002, p. 146). Some of the points that he focused on included the fact that Black Americans have been impacted, influenced, and corrupted by imperialism, which interrupted Black history. An essential aspect associated with the evolution of CRT is the utilization of the lived experiences of Black people to criticize the discrimination they face, which can serve as a basis for striving toward liberation (Rabaka, 2002).

Many individuals played significant roles in the continued growth and development of CRT. Writers and theorists such as Derrick Bell, Alan Freeman, and Richard Delgado saw a need for a new movement to continue forward progression. CRT is a movement supported by activists and scholars, which is focused on transforming the relationship between race, racism, and power (Delgado & Stefancic, 2017). CRT speaks to concepts from the civil rights movement and ethnic studies and then adds a broader perspective that "includes economics, history, setting, group and self-interest, and emotions and the unconscious" (Delgado & Stefancic, 2017, p. 3).

Racism has been created systematically in the United States. It has been embedded in society, laws, policy, and institutions for hundreds of years and continues to be a struggle today. CRT posits that racism is normal and the usual way our society behaves, and it is a regular, everyday experience for people of color. In addition, society is geared towards supporting the White population as the dominant group. CRT believes in social constructivism, which means that they see race as the product of social thought, not as a fixed, scientific construct. Today, CRT can be seen in multiple ways: the Latinx-critical movement, queer-crit (LGBTGEQIAP+) studies, and thinkers challenging how we conceptualize equality, civil rights, and national security (Delgado & Stefancic, 2017). These movements challenge the status quo to make forward-moving change.

Activity 2.8 – History & Social Justice

Video: *"Indigenous in Plain Sight* (https://www.youtube.com/watch?v=s3FL9uhTH_s)" by Gregg Deal.

One or more interactive elements has been excluded from this version of the text. You can view them online here: https://milnepublishing.geneseo.edu/social-justice-in-human-services/?p=44#oembed-3 (#oembed-3)

Discussion Questions

- How do or can we use history to support and move forward in social justice?
- What theories can explain Gregg's experiences? Where does his story fit into the content you learned in this chapter?

DisCrit Theory

DisCrit Theory, or Disability Critical Theory, provides insight into where racism and ableism intersect (Love & Beneke, 2021). It focuses on how the forces and power of racism and ableism exist independently and are often neutralized for the public to upload a certain sense of normalcy (Connor, et al., 2021). The goal of DisCrit theory is to support people in valuing their multidimensional identities. By considering the legal and historical aspects of disability/ability and race, people can better understand how the Western cultural norms have oppressed individuals living in this crosshair (Connor et al., 2021).

> ### Activity 2.9
>
> Video: Changing the way we talk about disability (https://www.youtube.com/watch?v=4WIP1VgPnco) by Amy Oulton.
>
> *One or more interactive elements has been excluded from this version of the text. You can view them online here: https://milnepublishing.geneseo.edu/social-justice-in-human-services/?p=44#oembed-4 (#oembed-4)*
>
> **Discussion Questions**
>
> - After watching the TedTalk by Amy Oulton, what is one way you can change the way you react to or talk about disability/ability?
> - Why is it important that we work to change the way we think and talk about disability/ability?

Thoughts from the Authors

I wanted to share my personal experience with writing this chapter. After my first draft, I felt this chapter was the easiest for me to write. All I had to do was search through history and summarize some past social justice theorists...that is, until my wonderful colleagues and peer reviewers alerted me to the Whitewashed history that I was sticking to. Once I was made aware of this, something that I was so used to reading, I really had to dive deep to uncover and share crucial theories of social justice that are not shared in mainstream history books. This is a perfect example of the vital importance of peer review and collaboration. History is written by the winners and those who take the time to put pen to paper. If we want to change what we read in history books, we need to be the ones to write our ideas and concepts down to save them for future generations to read. This is also a place where I would like to invite you to connect with me and share other theorists and theories that you feel should be discussed. I would love to update this chapter to reflect how social justice has developed and played out over time.

Sincerely,

Dr. Green

For me, the theories begin by defining what social justice is and evolve into recognizing what social *injustice* is. That seems to be the driving force behind change. As a psychologist, change is a desired result. My clients come to me because they desire some kind of change, whether it be changing how they feel about something, how they think about something, or how they do things. Frequently, it is that they want someone around them to change. I tell them all that *without distress, there is no change*. So, even if they've come to me in distress and want to do something new or different, wanting to change for someone else is quite challenging. If that person feels no distress about what they are doing, they won't change or do anything differently. I think that is what makes it so interesting to look at how these theories develop. What is the distress that leads to the shift? How does that distress get identified in others so that change occurs? Important questions that we all grow from.

Sincerely,

Dr. Brayton

> **Chapter Summary Questions**
>
> 1. Which theorists are most relevant to today's social justice climate? Provide examples to support your choice.
> 2. What are some common themes amongst the theorists outlined? Why do you think these common themes have lasted into today?
> 3. The more modern theories address how change occurs. How is this supported by or different from the earlier theories, such as social justice being based on natural law (Aquinas) or social contract (Locke)?
> 4. What are some of the stressors that have led to the development of modern theories?
> 5. We see a repeated theme of God and church in historical theories; why do you think this is? Where does religion fit into a discussion of social justice theories?

References

Assensoh, A. B., & Alex-Assensoh, Y. M. (2014). *Malcolm X: A biography*. Greenwood.

Bedingfield, S. (2019). The journalism of Roy Wilkins and the rise of law-and-order rhetoric, 1964-1968. *Journalism History*, 45(3), 250-269. https://doi.org/10.1080/00947679.2019.1631082

Bennett, H. (2008, July 11). *Organizing to abolish the prison-industrial complex*. Dissident Voice. https://dissidentvoice.org/2008/07/organizing-to-abolish-the-prison-industrial-complex/

Braz, R., Brown, B., DiBenedetto, L., Gilmore, C., Hunter, D., Parenti, C., Rodriguez, D., Shaylor, C., Stoller, N., & Sudbury, J. (2000). The history of critical resistance. *Social Justice*, 27(3), 6-10.

Capeheart, L., & Milovanovic, D. (2007). *Social justice: Theories, issues, and movements*. Rutgers University Press. https://doi.org/10.36019/9780813541686

Center for Biological Diversity. (2023). *Rose Braz in memoriam*. https://biologicaldiversity.org/about/staff/rose_braz.html

Columbia Law School. (2017). *Kimberle Crenshaw on intersectionality, more than two decades later*. https://www.law.columbia.edu/news/archive/kimberle-crenshaw-intersectionality-more-two-decades-later

Connor, D. J., Ferri, B. A., & Annamma, S. A. (2021). From the personal to the global: Engaging with and enacting DisCrit Theory across multiple spaces. *Race, Ethnicity and Education*, 24(5), 597-606. https://doi.org/10.1080/13613324.2021.1918400

Coventry, A., & Sager, A. (2013). Hume and contemporary political philosophy. *The European Legacy*, 18(5), 588-602. https://doi.org/10.1080/10848770.2013.804709

Crawford, C. (2020). Access to justice for collective and diffuse rights: Theoretical challenges and opportunities for social contract theory. *Indiana Journal of Global Legal Studies*, 27(1), 59-86. https://doi.org/10.2979/indjglolegstu.27.1.0059

Crenshaw, K. W. (2005). Mapping the margins: Intersectionality, identity politics, and violence against women of color. *Cahiers du genre*, 39, 51-82.

Davies, T. A. (2017). *Mainstreaming Black Power*. University of California Press.

Delgado, R., & Stefancic, J. (2017). *Critical race theory: An introduction* (3rd ed.). New York University Press. https://doi.org/10.2307/j.ctt1ggjjn3

Heyl, J. C. (2023). *What is intersectionality? Race and social justice*. Verywell Mind. https://www.verywellmind.com/what-is-intersectionality-7097945

Kamtekar, R. (2001). Social justice and happiness in the republic: Plato's two principles. *History of political thought*, 22(2),189-220.

Lawrence Hall. 2022. The Intersectionality of Race, Sexuality and Gender. retrieved from https://lawrencehall.org/news/brave-conversations-intersection-of-race-sexuality-and-gender

Lee, S.-H. (1984). The concept of justice in the political thought of Martin Luther King, Jr. *Journal of East and West Studies*, 8(2), 43-64.

Livingston, A. (2020). Power for the powerless: Martin Luther King, Jr.'s late theory of civil disobedience. *The Journal of Politics*, 82(2), 700-713. https://doi.org/10.1086/706982

Love, H. R., & Beneke, M. R. (2021). Pursuing justice-driven inclusive education research: Disability Critical Race Theory (DisCrit) in early childhood. *Topics in Early Childhood Special Education, 41*(1), 31-44. https://doi.org/10.1177/0271121421990833

Munger, F., MacLeod, T., & Loomis, C. (2016). Social change: Toward an informed and critical understanding of social justice and the capabilities approach in community psychology. *American Journal Community Psychology, 57*(1-2), 171-180. https://doi.org/10.1002/ajcp.12034

Nathanson, S. (2012). John Stuart Mill on economic justice and poverty. *Journal of Social Philosophy, 43*(2), 161-176. https://doi.org/10.1111/j.1467-9833.2012.01556.x

Rabaka, R. (2002). Malcolm X and/as critical theory: Philosophy, radical politics, and the African American search for social justice. *Journal of Black Studies, 33*(2), 145-165. https://doi.org/10.1177/002193402237222

Riddle, M. (2010). *Donation Land Claim Act, spur to American settlement of Oregon Territory, takes effect on September 27, 1850*. History Link. https://www.historylink.org/file/9501

Robert Penn Warren Center for the Humanities. (n.d.). *Roy Wilkins*. Who Speaks for the Negro: An Archival Collection, Vanderbilt University, Nashville, TN. https://whospeaks.library.vanderbilt.edu/interview/roy-wilkins

Ryan, Y. (2014). Roy Wilkins and the civil rights "crisis of unity." *Social Policy, 44*(1), 46-53.

Scholz, S. J. (2006). *Civil disobedience in the social theory of Thomas Aquinas*. Routledge.

Sorell, T. (2016). Law and equity in Hobbes. *Critical Review of International Social and Political Philosophy, 19*(1), 29-46. https://doi.org/10.1080/13698230.2015.1122353

Tillman, M. (2021, November 12). What's the difference between classical, modern and postmodern philosophy? *Friendly Philosophy*. https://micahtillman.com/clasicalmodernpostmodern

Media Attributions

- Plato © Photo by: Ricardo André Frantz is licensed under a CC BY-SA (Attribution ShareAlike) license
- Aristotle © After Lysippos is licensed under a Public Domain license
- Thomas Hobbes © John Michael Wright / NPG is licensed under a CC BY-NC-ND (Attribution NonCommercial NoDerivatives) license
- Roger Wilkins © Photo by Lonnie Tague for The Department of Justice is licensed under a Public Domain license
- LBJ with Roy Wilkins © LBJ Library is licensed under a Public Domain license
- Kimberlé Crenshaw © Mohamed Badarne is licensed under a CC BY-SA (Attribution ShareAlike) license

3.

Human Rights and the Equitable Distribution of Resources

Cailyn F. Green; Kim Brayton; and Bernadet DeJonge

Learning Objectives

1. The reader will analyze the words equitable, distribution, and resources.
2. The reader will distinguish the difference between equality and equity.
3. The reader will identify the connection between human rights and equity.

"A right delayed is a right denied."
-Martin Luther King Jr. (True Justice Has Been Delayed and Thus it is Still Being Denied, 1994).

The well-known quote by Martin Luther King, Jr. highlights the critical significance of human rights. In this chapter, we will explore the concepts of human rights and fair distribution of resources as they are essential to social justice.

Human Rights

Human rights are the rights that society has deemed every person is entitled to. These rights include freedom, justice, and equality in various aspects of life. Examples include being free to travel, leaving your country of origin, marrying, having a family, and owning property. Human rights include respect for all humanity and are connected to beliefs about how all people should be treated, regardless of the community in which they live (Finucane, 2017).

Before the term human rights was internationally recognized and defined in 1948, it was regulated by social relationships and interactions. Thus, every community, religion, society, or country has different views on human rights. For example, some ancient communities viewed human sacrifice as the ultimate way of showing something sacred. To be chosen for a human sacrifice meant you were chosen as the most sacred, highest person in that community (Woodiwiss, 2005). In contrast, in other communities, killing a person in the name of a deity or god would be viewed as a violation of human rights. This term was, and still is, dependent on how the community views human rights and the role in their lives.

> **Discussion Questions**
>
> - Why do you think we are talking about human rights in a text on social justice?
> - Is social justice a human right? Why or why not?

Universal Declaration of Human Rights 1948

Eleanor Roosevelt holding poster of the Universal Declaration of Human Rights (in English), Lake Success, New York. November 1949.

The Universal Declaration of Human Rights (UDHR) was proclaimed by the United Nations (UN) General Assembly in December 1948 (United Nations, n.d.). This was the first document to be internationally agreed upon regarding human rights. The UDHR is still used today as an important document, particularly in times of war and conflict between countries. The UDHR was written to protect the human rights of all, but directs particular attention to racial minorities, children, women, migrants, and people with disabilities (United Nations, n.d.).

The team who wrote the UDHR was composed of 18 members from various political, religious, and cultural backgrounds. These members included Eleanor Roosevelt (United States), Rene Cassin (France), Charles Malik (Lebanon), Peng Chung Chang (China), and

John Humphrey (Canada). After finishing this document, this diverse team decided it was so important that they released it as a declaration instead of a treaty. The UDHR was meant to inform humanity that everyone had these rights, even if their government did not provide them (Global Citizenship Commission, 2016). It published a set of fundamental human rights universally protected in all parts of the world. The UDHR has been translated into over 500 languages and has paved the way for human rights treaties worldwide (United Nations, n.d.).

The UDHR opens with a preamble introducing the reader to the idea that disregard for human rights has resulted in "barbarous acts which have outraged the conscience of mankind" (United Nations, n.d., para. 2). An example is the horrific historical event of the Holocaust. The UDHR argues that all people must have fundamental rights that should be protected. If these rights are not protected, people can rebel against tyranny and oppression. This document includes human rights such as "all humans are born free and equal" (United Nations, n.d., para. 9), "everyone is entitled to all rights and freedoms set forth in this declaration" (United Nations, n.d., para. 10), and "no one shall be held in slavery" (United Nations, n.d., para. 12).

The writers of the UDHR document established three sections in the document: (1) a set of general principles, (2) the actual codification of those principles into laws, and (3) the practical and actual means of implementation (Global Citizenship Commission, 2016). Writing a declaration was one thing, but the team tasked with writing the UDHR wanted to convey a clear expectation of action regarding human rights. They believed it was important for governments to act on their declaration to create communities free of oppression and dangerous or harmful situations.

The UDHR was written in 1948. Since then, society has changed and evolved. Understanding the UDHR through the lens of today's world is an important part of maintaining human rights worldwide. The UDHR is not merely a document to be taken at face value; it is meant to be applied in the context of our world as it currently exists. For example, when the UDHR was first written in 1948, women had limited rights. However, today, the UDHR has been interpreted more broadly to encompass rights for women, children, the disabled, and prisoners, as well as the right to sexual orientation (Global Citizenship Commission, 2016). Our government must adapt to our changing and evolving world by applying the UDHR appropriately.

Activity 3.1 – Digging Deeper: Universal Declaration of Human Rights

Read through the UN's Universal Declaration of Human Rights. (https://www.un.org/en/about-us/universal-declaration-of-human-rights)

Video: Human rights and technology (https://www.youtube.com/watch?v=Gcs6gX-sfsU) by Flynn Coleman.

> *One or more interactive elements has been excluded from this version of the text. You can view them online here: https://milnepublishing.geneseo.edu/social-justice-in-human-services/?p=48#oembed-1 (#oembed-1)*

Discussion Questions

- Talk about your experience of reading the Universal Declaration of Human Rights.
- Do human rights change over time? Why or why not?
- What values do you want to see incorporated into artificial intelligence in the future?

Protecting Human Rights

Even though international government agencies agree on this set of rules, human rights continue to be violated on both small and large scales. Some of this is severe in the form of governments, such as dictatorships, where one ruler decides what rights society members have (Finucane, 2017). These types of governments violate human rights by killing their people, unlawful imprisonment, and engaging in rape and other acts of violence against women. However, in some countries, human rights violations remain unclear. For example, consider the Flint, Michigan, water crisis in 2016, which denied access to clean, drinkable water to most of the city's population. Many do not think of this as a human rights issue; however, this experience for the community of Flint violates the UDHR (Goldblum & Shaddox, 2021).

The most important aspect of upholding human rights is the ability to protect them. One way to protect human rights is through laws and policies. This is not always easy because there are often disagreements on the interpretation of the UDHR. Not everyone agrees on what actions or behaviors should be protected. That said, a just government must create laws and generate policies that protect and uphold human rights (University of Michigan, 2023).

The United States has generated multiple laws that protect human rights. An example is *Brown v. Board of Education*, where, in 1954, the Supreme Court determined that racial segregation in public schools was unconstitutional and violated the human right to be treated with dignity and equality (Premdas, 2013). Another example is *Griffin v. Illinois* in 1956. This Supreme Court ruling stated that a criminal defendant cannot be denied the right to appeal to court cases because of their inability to pay for a trial transcript (Woodiwiss, 2005). These court rulings exemplify how government laws and policies can be used to protect human rights.

The United Nations continues to work tirelessly to promote and protect human rights worldwide. One way they do this is through the Human Rights Treaty Bodies. These are committees of independent experts who monitor how countries implement the core values as expressed in the UDHR (United Nations, n.d.). The United Nations also has working groups that focus on mainstreaming these basic human rights in countries and governments.

> **Discussion Questions**
>
> - What do human rights have to do with social justice?
> - Explain, in your own words, why human rights should be protected. How can they be protected?
> - How have we utilized the concept of human rights to create policies and laws in the United States?
> - How can we further use policies and laws to uphold human rights in the United States?
> - Do some research: What human rights are currently being violated in the world?
> - Do some research: What human rights are currently being violated in the United States?

Distribution of Resources

Social justice movements focus on achieving a fair and equitable distribution of resources. To understand what equitable distribution of resources means, it is important to first clarify some definitions. It is important to note that equality and equity are not the same things. Equity refers to finding a balance between being equal and being fair. The word "equitable" describes how something can be just and impartial to all parties involved, taking into account each party's unique needs (Gomez & Premdas, 2013). However, this does not imply that everything is the same for everybody.

Imagine a classroom full of students. The teacher comes in and tells them that they are all getting a new pair of sneakers this year. Equal would be giving each student the exact same pair, including the same size. But, not every student in the classroom wears the same size. To make this *equitable*, the shoe size must be considered. This is the difference between being equal and being equitable.

> **Activity 3.2 – Digging Deeper: What is Equitable?**
>
> Video: Equality, Equity, and Social Justice (https://www.youtube.com/watch?v=Uvoios7frIs) by Southern Illinois Professional Development Center.
>
> > *One or more interactive elements has been excluded from this version of the text. You can view them online here: https://milnepublishing.geneseo.edu/social-justice-in-human-services/?p=48#oembed-2 (#oembed-2)*
>
> **Discussion Questions**

> - In your own words, describe the difference between equality and equity.
> - Provide two real world examples of the difference between equality and equity.

Distribution means to split something and share it amongst the parties involved. The number of parties involved is not defined as part of the word, nor does the word "distribution" give us any glimpse into how the splitting will occur. The methods by which resources can be split include percentages, weights, and numbers.

The *Markov Decision Process* is a distribution model that considers supply, demand, and equity-based objectives (Fianu & Davis, 2018). The goal is to use the supply to maximize the equity in the distribution of the goods to benefit as many people as possible. Thus, goods are allocated proportionally to poorer populations who report the need for resources. The difficulty in this construct is deciding where the resources go. The entity determining where to allocate the goods must consider who needs them and determine how to distribute them equitably (Fianu & Davis, 2018).

When there is uncertainty about the goods that will be available for distribution, the method of allocating them becomes more complex. For example, consider a food bank that relies on the ebb and flow of donations. One way to compensate for an unsteady supply of goods is to treat the demand as steady and plan backward (Orgut et al., 2018). By keeping the demand the same over a year, one stable factor remains. With this one stable factor, we can then compensate for the ebb and flow of supply and allocate it equitably throughout the year (Orgut et al., 2018).

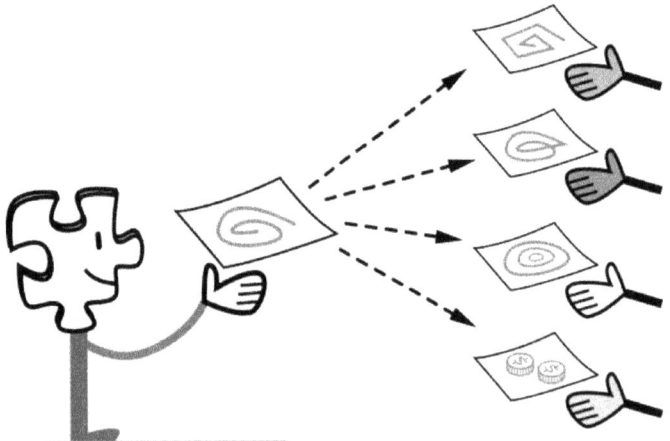

Resource is a word used to describe a supply of something currently existing. Resources can be physical, mental, actionable, emotional, or ideas. Resources include things like diamonds, food, money, mental health, mental bandwidth, emotional and physical energy, healthcare, and volunteers (Orgut et al., 2018).

In summary, equitable distribution of resources is defined as the act of sharing a supply of something in a way that is fair and based on what the parties involved need. To be able to distribute resources equitably, the needs of the parties involved must be considered. The distribution of resources should be proportional to the needs and number of parties involved (Capeheart & Milovanovic, 2007). However, this is not always the case. Food distribution is often used as an example to highlight inequitable distribution. Food is a good that is needed for human survival. While all people need food, not everyone has access to the food supply they need. Thus, food is often not equitably distributed. When this happens, government agencies and nonprofit entities, such as food banks, often step in to try and fill that need (Fianu & Davis, 2018). Other resources relevant to the social justice context include housing, food, education, jobs, community resources, health care, social support, language, literacy, representation, and political involvement (Shaw et al., 2017).

Activity 3.3 – Digging Deeper: Resource Distribution in Action

Interview with Susan Lintner, the Director of Community Impact at the Regional Food Bank of Northeastern New York

I interviewed Susan Lintner, the Director of Community Impact at the Regional Food Bank of Northeastern New York, to talk about how her agency distributes resources. Susan explained that, traditionally, they respond to requests made by food bank managers. If one food bank said they regularly had 20 people walk through their doors on a weekly basis, they would provide that food bank with food to accommodate that specific number. However, this did not accommodate those in the community who did not walk through the

> agency doors. The team determined that this was not equitable or "fair" as not everyone in the community who had need was being funded.
>
> Susan informed me that the Regional Food Bank of Northeastern New York recently went through a strategic planning process to correct this previous approach. They identified that many of the 23 counties they served were not receiving enough food. The team came up with a plan to change their methods to ensure that individuals who were food insecure were able to get access to the same amount of food regardless of what county they lived in. This was done through mobile pantries, which brought food to those who did not have access to it previously. Through such efforts, food resources were made physically available for people who did not have access in the past with the intent of being more equitable in resource distribution (S. Lintner, personal communication, December 8, 2023).
>
> If you want to learn more about the work of the Regional Food Bank of Northeastern New York (https://regionalfoodbank.net/), please visit their website.
>
> **Discussion Questions**
>
> - Find out how your local food bank decides to allocate resources. In your opinion, is this fair? How might it be improved?

Equitability

Who decides what is equitable? This is placed on the shoulders of whoever controls the supply of goods or resources. The entity that has the power to decide what an equitable distribution is should have an unbiased connection to both the supply holder and the population that is going to receive the goods. When the decider (e.g., the food bank manager) has a connection that can sway their decision, an equitable distribution is less likely. An example of this is if the person in charge of the food bank's distribution has a personal or professional connection to one local mayor among the many areas his food bank serves. If the food bank manager (the decider) is swayed by this connection, such as the mayor offering them money or appealing to their personal relationship, the allocation of food may not be equitable.

Research has shown that when people are given a choice in allocating goods, they often choose what they think is the "morally right" thing to do. Generally, this is to act in an equitable manner. People are driven by engaging in prosocial behavior (Huang et al., 2019). Prosocial behavior is behavior or actions that benefit others and do not benefit the person performing the behavior. Examples of prosocial behavior throughout history include multiple ancient warriors fighting a bear to save one community member, and, more currently, cities with volunteer firefighting stations. People choose to engage in these types of behaviors, which will benefit the community or others over themselves (Huang et al., 2019).

HUMAN RIGHTS AND THE EQUITABLE DISTRIBUTION OF RESOURCES | 39

The office of City Council President Darrell L. Clarke (5th District), the Office and Children and Families (OCF), the Philadelphia Housing Authority (PHA) and Philabundance partnered to provide food to North Philadelphians experiencing food insecurity in the 2021 holiday season.

Activity 3.4 – Digging Deeper

Video: Innovation in human rights by Mallika Dutt (https://www.youtube.com/watch?v=U9v_f_dJ1TA).

 One or more interactive elements has been excluded from this version of the text. You can view them online here: https://milnepublishing.geneseo.edu/social-justice-in-human-services/?p=48#oembed-3 (#oembed-3)

Discussion Questions

- How can you advocate for human rights in your job?
- How do you practice human rights in your daily life?

Activity 3.5 – Case Study: Trayvon Jackson

Trayvon Jackson, the executive director of the African American Cultural Center, opened a nonprofit grocery store in Albany, New York in 2022. By working with 75 different organizations to open this grocery store location, the African American Cultural Center turned a previous McDonald's location into a grocery store in an area that once only had convenience stores, bodegas (stores selling little fresh food marked up at high prices), and fast food options. Prior to this, the southern end of Albany was identified as a food desert for many years.

Discussion Questions

- Describe what a food desert is in your own words.
- What do food deserts have to do with equitability of resources?
- Who decides when and where a grocery store opens? Why is this important?
- Why might people struggle to access groceries? Why might they choose a convenience store or bodega over a grocery store?
- How do we solve the problem of food deserts?

Thoughts from the Authors

I'd like to provide a little background on me and why this chapter was so important for me to write. I went to a predominantly White undergraduate university and a predominantly White graduate school. My experience in higher education was mostly with individuals similar to myself: middle class, using financial aid, but having a supportive family to help out when needed. When I moved to Portland, Oregon, and began working as an instructor at Portland Community College (PCC), I quickly learned that my higher education experience was not the only one. Portland Community College had an extremely high percentage of not only first-generation college students, but also first-generation English speakers. My Department Chair, Adrian Rodriguez, shared with me the example I shared with all of you regarding sneaker size. This was how he explained equality versus equity to me, and this example really resonated. I have been able to use this example in most of my counseling courses, as well as keeping it in mind during my role as an academic mentor.

Sincerely,
Cailyn Green

When I think about this topic, I always remember the warning given by one of my early bosses/mentors, a gentleman named George Bennett. He worked with a number of companies spanning numerous industries, and he liked to raise awareness of the challenges of equitable distribution. One story he would tell is of a company executive who had a million dollars to give away to his employees. By not considering equitable distribution, he offended everyone he gave that money to. While one moral of his story was that you can never make everyone happy, the more important understanding is about identifying what is equitable and recognizing how different people are affected.

Sincerely,
Kim Brayton

Chapter Summary Questions

1. Provide your own example of something being equal versus equitable.
2. How would you define human rights in your own words? What rights do all people have]? What about those who do not have those rights?
3. How can bias impact the equitable distribution of goods? What other factors might impact the equitable distribution of goods?
4. Thinking back to the case study regarding the food desert in Albany, New York, can you think of other ways discrimination has led to or could lead to inequitable distribution of resources?

References

Capeheart, L., & Milovanovic, D. (2007). *Social justice: Theories, issues, and movements.* Rutgers University Press. https://doi.org/10.36019/9780813541686

Fianu, S., & Davis, L. B. (2018). A Markov decision process model for equitable distribution of supplies under uncertainty. *European Journal of Operational Research, 264*(3), 1101–1115. https://doi.org/10.1016/j.ejor.2017.07.017

Finucane, B. (2017). *Human rights.* Mason Crest.

Goldblum, J. S., & Shaddox, C. (2021). *Broke in America: Seeing, understanding, and ending US poverty*. BenBella Books.

Gomez, E. T., & Premdas, R. (Eds.). (2013). Affirmative action, horizontal inequalities, and equitable development. *Affirmative action, ethnicity, and conflict* (pp. 1-27). Routledge. https://doi.org/10.4324/9780203078839

Global Citizenship Commission. (2016). *The universal declaration of human rights in the 21st century: A living document in a changing world*. G. Brown (Ed.). Open Book Publishers. http://www.jstor.org/stable/j.ctt1bpmb7v

Huang, L., Lei, W., Xu, F., Yu, L., & Shi, F. (2019). Choosing an equitable or efficient option: A distribution dilemma. *Social Behavior and Personality, 47*(10), 1-10. https://doi.org/10.2224/sbp.8559

Orgut, I. S., Ivy, J. S., Uzsoy, R., & Hale, C. (2018). Robust optimization approaches for the equitable and effective distribution of donated food. *European Journal of Operational Research, 269*(2), 516–531. https://doi.org/10.1016/j.ejor.2018.02.017

Premdas, R. (2013). The struggle for equality and justice: Affirmative action in the United States of America. In E. T. Gomez & R. R. Premdas (Eds.), *Affirmative action, ethnicity, and conflict* (pp. 43-66). Routledge. https://doi.org/10.4324/9780203078839

True Justice Has Been Delayed And Thus Is Still Being Denied. (1994). *The Philadelphia Tribune (1884), 111*(11).

Shaw, L. J., Pepine, C. J., Xie, J., Mehta, P. K., Morris, A. A., Dickert, N. W., Ferdinand, K. C., Gulati, M., Reynolds, H., Hayes, S. N., Itchhaporia, D., Mieres, J. H., Ofili, E., Wenger, N. K., & Bairey Merz, C. N. (2017). Quality and equitable health care gaps for women: Attributions to sex differences in cardiovascular medicine. *Journal of the American College of Cardiology, 70*(3), 373–388. https://doi.org/10.1016/j.jacc.2017.05.051

United Nations. (n.d.). *Universal declaration of human rights*. United Nations Office of the High Commissioner for Human Rights. https://www.un.org/en/about-us/universal-declaration-of-human-rights

University of Michigan. (2023). *Government obligations*. https://humanrightshistory.umich.edu/accountability/obligationr-of-governments/

Woodiwiss, A. (2005). *Human rights*. Routledge.

Media Attributions

- Eleanor Roosevelt UDHR © FDR Presidential Library & Museum is licensed under a CC BY (Attribution) license
- Sharing Character © Wikimedia Foundation adapted by Yuriy Bulka is licensed under a CC BY-SA (Attribution ShareAlike) license
- Street Food © brainbox tamil is licensed under a CC BY-SA (Attribution ShareAlike) license
- Council President Clarke hosts Holiday Food Distribution © Jared Piper/PHLCouncil is licensed under a CC BY (Attribution) license

4.

Power, Privilege, Oppression, and Bias

Cailyn F. Green; Kim Brayton; and Bernadet DeJonge

Learning Objectives

1. The reader will define power, privilege, oppression, and unconscious bias.
2. The reader will understand what constitutes power, privilege, oppression, and unconscious bias.
3. The reader will analyze how power, privilege, oppression, and bias impact the forward movement of social justice.

Social justice has many definitions. However, all definitions of social justice have three common concepts: equitability of rights, opportunity, and treatment. Social justice examines how wealth is distributed and what kind of political and social power individuals have (San Diego Foundation, 2022). Social justice has been defined as the fairness that manifests itself in a community. This fairness, or lack of it, is created by roles taken in society, which include positions of hierarchy and differences in power (van Ham, 2010).

Power is the capacity to influence and make decisions that impact others. Power allows an individual or group the capacity to influence and impact someone else's behaviors, choices, or actions (Joshi & Fast, 2013). When one person has power over another, they can impact the lives of others, often in a negative way. A key example of this power is the government. A government is an entity that has the power to create a structured set of rules that the population follows. Today, these rules take the form of laws and policies that maintain social order. The underlying idea is that the community agrees with the government to which they grant the power. They trust that those in charge will make decisions that will benefit the community (Judicial Learning Center, 2019).

In every relationship, there exists a balance of power. Examples include the power relationships that exist within families, between coworkers, voters, consumers, and all other social relationships. This power balance may be positive or negative, and only through examining who has power and what they are doing with that power can it be determined if the balance of power is healthy or not (van Ham, 2010).

When individuals or groups are part of a healthy balance of power, both parties are satisfied with the power split and responsibilities shared (van Ham, 2010). However, there are also often inequitable balances of power, which is where social justice issues frequently arise. An example of inequitable power is socioeconomic status—the rich and the poor. If individuals with money have power, then they also make policy decisions. These decisions may negatively impact those with less power—the poor. These individuals may not agree with the decisions made by the people in power. However, because they do not have the power, they often do not have the resources to influence the decision making. So, what do they do in this case? Do they go along with the decisions being made? Do they fight back? These are the inequitable power scenarios fuelling the social justice movements we see today.

Power is not always about numbers. Instead, it is often the group with more resources, such as money, that ends up being the stronger, more powerful group, irrespective of size and numbers (Capeheart & Milovanovic, 2007).

Activity 4.1 – Digging Deeper: The Citizens United v. FEC Supreme Court decision

In this case, the Supreme Court of the United States overturned earlier precedent banning/prohibiting independent expenditures by corporations toward political campaigns. The Court ultimately determined that such a prohibition amounted to a ban on speech. Critics of this ruling have often pointed to the fact that corporations are owned and run by individuals, who have their own political agendas. By utilizing the funds of their corporations, these owners generally would have far greater ability to finance and otherwise support campaigns than the average, every-day citizen. Thus, the phrase "money equals speech" was born.

See The Federal Election Commission's website (https://www.fec.gov/legal-resources/court-cases/citizens-united-v-fec/) for a summary of the case.

Discussion Question

- What kind of power balance, if any, did this decision create or support?

When power differentials become significant and severe, those not in power often fight back. Examples of this in United States history include the Slave Rebellion, Women's Suffrage movement, the civil rights movements of the 1960s, and the disability rights movement. Revolts are a part of history in many countries and often amplify issues of power. One example is the American Revolution, which happened from 1765-1781. In this case, the American colonists did not agree with Great Britain taxing them on the goods they were importing. The American colonists disagreed with the rules put in place by Great Britain and decided to revolt. They fought for their freedom and won in 1781 (Lowery, 2016).

Activity 4.2 – Activism

Video: Power and Promise of Social Justice Activism by Zohra Moosa (https://www.youtube.com/watch?v=2SW-r0UtVms)

 One or more interactive elements has been excluded from this version of the text. You can view them online here: https://milnepublishing.geneseo.edu/social-justice-in-human-services/?p=77#oembed-1 (#oembed-1)

Discussion Questions

- How do people get together to begin to make change?
- What unites them/us?

Power is often used by the group that has power to attain goals, particularly surrounding money and social capital. Large power-holding entities, such as governments, have been known throughout history to utilize power in political pursuits. Power is used to persuade those with less power to give, make, or accomplish the goals of the power holder. Thus, power is often used to take advantage of and oppress those not in power (Bramley & Morrison, 2023).

Activity 4.3 – Propaganda

Video: A Guide to Propaganda by Shawn Grenier (https://www.youtube.com/watch?v=8i_Zw1Itv40)

 One or more interactive elements has been excluded from this version of the text. You can view them online here: https://milnepublishing.geneseo.edu/social-justice-in-human-services/?p=77#oembed-2 (#oembed-2)

Discussion Questions

- How does propaganda fit into a discussion of power?
- Have you ever observed propaganda? If so, who was in power and how were they trying to wield their power over others?

Power can be used to influence people in a variety of ways, including information and education provided by governmental entities. A concrete example of this would be government-created mental health resources and websites, such as the Substance Abuse and Mental Health Services Administration (SAMHSA), which provide resources and educational information to the public about addiction and mental health concerns. The government in power is using its money, influence, and time to provide educational materials and interventions for those needing assistance (Bramley & Morrison, 2023). Some non-governmental examples include UNICEF, Habitat for Humanity, and other charities run by religious or nonreligious organizations that focus on using their power to support others.

There are many ways in which a group acquires power, from military means and money to influence and coercion. This may occur naturally over a course of evolution and time. However, when a group acquires power, it is never stagnant. Power is a fluid concept based on communication, interactions, knowledge, goods, institutions, and relationships (van Ham,

Propaganda poster shows a terrifying gorilla with a helmet labeled "militarism" holding a bloody club labeled "kultur" and a half-naked woman as he stomps onto the shore of America.

2010). Understanding power is essential to understanding concepts of social justice, as power influences justice in all forms. Unqual distributions of power often lead to conflict.

Privilege

When one group has more power than another, a form of privilege often arises. Privilege refers to specific advantages, benefits, and respect that someone may have due to being associated with a certain social group. In Western society, privilege is often reflected in the social identities of people who have historically held dominance over others. For example, those who are cisgender, heterosexual, Christian or financially affluent have benefitted from privileges that others have not (Garcia, 2018). Other forms of privilege that exist may be related to someone's abilities or education level. While an individual cannot rid themselves of their privilege, it is their responsibility to be aware of this and to ensure it does not lead to the oppression of others.

> ### Activity 4.4 – Digging Deeper into Privilege
>
> Imagine a classroom with rows of students. The teacher places a garbage can at the front of the classroom, directly in front of the first row of students. Next, the teacher hands a tennis ball to every student in every row. They then inform the students that whoever gets their tennis ball in the garbage will get an automatic A on their next quiz. However, they must throw it from their seat to do so. Students in the first row have an advantage in getting their tennis balls in the garbage can compared to the students in the back row. Therefore, the students in the front row have a privilege that others in the class do not (Glass, 2019).

In the context of social justice, certain groups of people receive privileges or unfair advantages to acquire benefits such as jobs, money, housing, and land. Those groups receive privilege without having earned it. Generational wealth, for example, money earned in a previous generation and passed down through a family. Research has shown that slavery severely impacted the generational wealth of Black people in America, thus individuals who are Black have less privilege than those who are White (Baker & Addo, 2023). Privilege rises and is created fundamentally through the oppression and/or suppression of minority groups. Thus, understanding and acknowledging privilege is an essential part of the social justice movement. We will explore one of the outcomes of privilege, oppression, in the next section.

Oppression

Oppression is what happens to weaker groups who do not hold power or who do not have privilege. It is the "unfair process of aiding some people while harming others and the resulting condition of inequality between people" (David & Derthick, 2018, p. 3). Oppression is created purposely when the stronger group, who has current power, decides that another group, who has less power, should not be given power. Thus, the weaker group is constantly prevented from rising in power by the stronger, more powerful group.

A historical example of this is the ownership of slaves by American people. When one group of people, slave owners, dehumanized the life of another group of people, such as slaves, they created a climate in which the powerful oppressed the weaker group. In the example of slavery, the oppression was such that the enslaved group had no rights or power and lived their lives at the slave owner's whim. In this, the smaller group is unable to flourish as the strong group does not allow them to do so (David & Derthick, 2018).

Activity 4.5 – The Language of Social Justice

Video: The language of social justice by Alexandra Campion (https://www.youtube.com/watch?v=FJkEDpWw45c)

 One or more interactive elements has been excluded from this version of the text. You can view them online here: https://milnepublishing.geneseo.edu/social-justice-in-human-services/?p=77#oembed-3 (#oembed-3)

Discussion Questions

- Why is it important that we verbalize our social justice issues?
- What can you do to make more noise about social justice issues that are impacting your life?

Oppression is not inevitable or natural. Community members engage in behaviors that create oppression through socially constructed norms (Adams, 2023). Choices made by community members, even unconsciously or without malicious intent, may create an environment of oppression. An example is when a community has a surplus of tax money. Instead of deciding to put that money into the local homeless shelter to support those in need, the voting community members decide to repave Main Street. The community members in charge of the financial resources have made a decision that will benefit themselves but not the community population, who could use additional support.

When an oppressive environment is created, labeling theory becomes significant. The labeling theory posits that people will begin acting as the society and community around them expect them to act (Becker, 2016). Thus, members of an oppressed group may begin to assimilate the negative stereotypes and expectations that others have about them into their everyday lives (Bell, 2023).

Activity 4.6 – Defining Oppression

Video: Unpacking the Meaning of Oppression by Ayesha Haq (https://www.youtube.com/watch?v=bUQqhl-Fjwk)

 One or more interactive elements has been excluded from this version of the text. You can view them online here: https://milnepublishing.geneseo.edu/social-justice-in-human-services/?p=77#oembed-4 (#oembed-4)

Discussion Questions

- How do you define oppression?
- Who decides what oppression is?

How These Concepts Impact Our Social Interactions

Power, privilege, and oppression are a part of every life, whether consciously or not. Some individuals are extremely aware of these experiences, while others have the privilege of not being aware of them at all. It is the responsibility of every individual to remain conscious of what may cause inequity among people. Examples include upbringing, location, peers, income, assets, trauma experiences, religion, and ethnicity (Gordon, 2019). Only as individuals remain conscious of their privilege may they move forward to engage and support others not afforded the same privileges.

Bias

Bias describes the way we feel about an individual or a group of people without any evidence or reason to support it. Biases are generally unconscious, however often have a significant impact on behavior. It is common for people to have biases, both positive and negative. Negative bias occurs when people tend to give more significance to negative information, events, or situations when evaluating an individual or group of people. On the other hand, positive bias occurs when people tend to judge someone or a group of people favorably (Kiken & Shook, 2011). Biases may be influenced by anything around an individual, including family, friends, environment, politics, culture and news. It is therefore a collective responsibility to be aware of emotive responses to and interpretations of everyday experiences.

Unconscious Bias

Activity 4.7 – Case Study: Brenda

Brenda comes into the boardroom prepared for her morning meeting. Her male colleagues file in around her. As the meeting starts, her supervisor asks who would be willing to take notes for the meeting. No one says anything. Brenda sighs inside because she knows what is coming. Her supervisor then assigns her to take notes for the meeting. This happens every meeting.

Discussion Question

- Why might Brenda being asked to take notes in a meeting be problematic?

Brenda being asked to take notes in the meeting may or may not be problematic. However, it also might reflect the unconscious bias in the room. Brenda is the only woman in a room full of men and, without thinking, they ascribe the task of note-taking to her because they perceive this as her role as a woman. This may occur even despite her work role being equivalent to theirs. This is an example of unconscious bias.

Unconscious or implicit bias occurs when an individual makes unconscious decisions about someone else. In its most basic form, unconscious bias can be described as the cultural lens through which we view the world. This lens then creates biases or stereotypes that are applied to individuals and impact our experience of certain people. Unconscious bias can impede our ability to treat and think of others fairly. That said, unconscious bias differs from overt racism and bigotry because it happens without intent (Veesart, 2020).

Some suggest that unconscious bias can even be good. An example of this may be if you are biased against junk food so you only eat fresh fruits and vegetables. However, when privilege and oppression exist as part of everyday interactions, unconscious bias can reflect this power and privilege, causing harm to individuals who have historically been marginalized.

Biases are universal and often deeply ingrained. Most individuals are unconscious of these biases. Yet biases can significantly influence the attitudes and behaviors of an individual towards others. Biases are easily quantifiable, which allows them to be tested empirically (Noon, 2018). Understanding individual bias is essential for the eventual mitigation of this.

Activity 4.8 – Digging Deeper: Implicit Bias

Complete Harvard's online Implicit Bias Test (https://implicit.harvard.edu/implicit/takeatest.html)

Discussion Questions

- What was the outcome of your assessment?
- Were you surprised by the outcome of your assessment? Why or why not?
- Do you think that this assessment is accurate? Why or why not?

Unconscious bias often stems from individuals unconsciously believing that their race, background, culture, education, etc. is superior to others. In addition, individuals may be influenced by external factors, such as their family of origin, their history of interaction with people different from them, social mores, and the media. When individuals or systems have these unconscious biases, they create environments in which oppression and privilege thrive (Noon, 2018).

Personal unconscious biases also significantly influence interactions between people. Biases have the capacity to influence the way individuals see, think, act, and speak to others. When individuals enter relationships (professional, personal, and academic) with preconceived notions or biases, the relationship cannot develop to its fullest potential because it is restricted by unconscious biases (Tate & Page, 2018).

Sometimes, the impact of biases can come in the form of an ethical lapse of judgment. Many individuals assume that their moral compasses are accurate and reliable, unaware of the impact of unconscious biases (Perez, 2019). When moral dilemmas are influenced by these biases, the decisions made may be adversely affected. The ramifications of this occurring are significant.

Activity 4.9 – Case Study: Positive Unconscious Bias

Ken and Sharon are walking into the meeting room and talking about the new manager position.

Ken: "Did you hear who applied?"

Sharon: "Kind of, they did interviews while I was in the office. Amy interviewed for sure. You know she went to Harvard."

Ken: "Yeah, can you imagine what that was like? Totally different from my lowly state school degree."

As the meeting starts, it is announced that Amy has been offered and accepted the management position. One of the things that is said about her in her intro is that she is "Harvard-educated."

While Amy did nothing wrong by going to Harvard for her degree, this scenario exemplifies what might be considered a positive unconscious bias. Even if considered positive, biases manifest themselves in Amy's promotion to a position of power and may marginalize individuals who are just as qualified but do not have the status that Amy does with her Harvard degree. This "halo effect" identifies only that she is Harvard-educated, and that becomes the overarching idea of who she is within the workplace.

Another example of this could be the current Supreme Court. In 2024, 8 out of the 9 Supreme Court justices were from either Harvard or Yale. The one outlier, Amy Coney Barrett, went to Notre Dame.

Discussion Questions

- What role did unconscious bias play in this scenario?
- What are your thoughts on the fact that 8 out of 9 of our current Supreme Court justices went to not just Ivy Leagues schools but one of two?

Activity 4.10 – Checking Unconscious Bias

Video: How to check your unconscious bias by Dr Jennifer Eberhardt (https://www.youtube.com/watch?v=egw-iheD1Mc).

 One or more interactive elements has been excluded from this version of the text. You can view them online here: https://milnepublishing.geneseo.edu/social-justice-in-human-services/?p=77#oembed-5 (#oembed-5)

Discussion Questions

- What can you do to be more aware of your unconscious biases?
- How do your unconscious biases impact your day-to-day interactions?

Identifying Unconscious Bias

Identifying unconscious biases may be difficult. It is often assumed that we treat each other equally, but research has shown otherwise (Tate & Page, 2018). The best way to manage unconscious bias is to identify our own personal biases. This process begins with recognizing our background, experiences, ethnicity, socioeconomic status, education level, sexuality, gender identity, and religion. Identifying unconscious bias starts with being honest with ourselves about how these factors may have influenced our unconscious biases. Only when we acknowledge and disengage from our personal biases can we interact with others on a more level playing field.

Disengaging from Unconscious Bias

To begin the process of separating our unconscious personal biases, we must first make a conscious decision to do so. One effective way to reduce our personal biases is to educate ourselves about differences between people. This may be achieved by exploring the struggles, challenges, and daily experiences of individuals who are different from ourselves. By doing so, we may reduce our tendency to judge others based on our unconscious biases. The ultimate goal is to interact with others based on the information they share over our own preconceptions. (Veesart, 2020).

Changing unconscious bias takes time, patience, and commitment. Unconscious bias must be considered, discussed, and exercised daily. Moreover, this work needs to be done for the sake of actual change in real-life situations, rather than just to avoid being challenged. Change arises from incorporating new thought patterns into everyday, real-life situations (Perez, 2019). This requires effort and practice. However, individuals can better manage their unconscious bias and its effect on their interactions and relationships by doing this work.

Conscious Bias

Conscious bias, similar to unconscious bias, refers to the way individuals feel about certain things or groups of people. The difference is that in conscious bias, individuals are aware of these feelings. Researchers believe that labeling bias as "unconscious" has allowed many people to continue practicing discrimination without taking responsibility for their actions. While many organizations offer mandatory training on recognizing unconscious biases, conscious bias training is essentially non-existent (Tate & Page, 2018). Examples of conscious bias in everyday life include preferring to work with men over women, refusing to listen to opposing viewpoints, and only engaging with people and content on social media that aligns with one's own beliefs. This may be dangerous as it prevents individuals from learning and growing beyond their own comfort zones.

Activity 4.11 – Digging Deeper

Discussion Questions

- What are some of your conscious biases?
- How do these impact our day-to-day life?
- What are the pros and cons to having your personal conscious biases?

Thoughts from the Authors

While I was an instructor at a college, my department was in an eight-hour long training on unconscious bias. Before we broke for lunch, my department chair stood up to make an announcement: "One of our instructors recently completed their dissertation, earned their Ph.D., and is now a doctor! Let's all give them a round of applause." I stood up, as this was regarding my recent doctoral graduation. A colleague of mine raised their hand and stated "I want to share an unconscious bias that I just discovered. When you said someone here had earned their Ph.D., I expected a man to stand up. When Dr. Green stood up, I was very surprised. This is an unconscious bias that I am now aware that I have regarding people who have earned their Ph.D.s." This was such a wonderful learning moment for this instructor to identify this bias in themselves, but also for the entire room to see how we can be aware of our biases and adjust so we can work more efficiently with those around us.

Sincerely,
Cailyn Green

Sometimes there is a fine line between having privilege and being oppressed. My undergraduate degree is in engineering, a field that in the 80s did not have many women represented. During my internship, I worked at a steel processing plant. When I walked on the floor, I wore a white hat, indicating my position in management as an engineer. This indicator meant that the people on the floor would stop things they were doing and answer questions for me, defer to my decisions, and step back letting me take the lead when going onto elevators or walking through the facility. However, when we went into the boardroom, I was the only woman in the room. There I was treated in a more guarded fashion and was not invited into the same conversations because of my gender. In the same setting, I experienced both privilege and oppression. As Dr. Green said above, this is something we can all relate to in varying degrees. What is important is our awareness of these positions and how they are being wielded or abused.

Sincerely,
Kim Brayton

Chapter Summary Questions

1. Who currently holds power in current society? How did they obtain this power? Why do they continue to hold this power?
2. List the intersecting groups you belong to (e.g., I am a woman, Caucasian, PhD, work-

ing mother, and Pittsburgh Steeler fan). As you consider that list, what groupings do you recognize as ones with privilege versus ones that experience oppression?
3. What is an example of your unconscious bias? How does this impact your interactions with people around you?
4. There are many expressions in our culture that reinforce biases. For example: "You throw like a girl!" Can you think of other expressions or words that may indicate a conscious or unconscious bias?

References

Baker, R. S., & Addo, F. R. (2023). Barriers to racial wealth equality. *Human Rights, 48*(2), 2-5.

Becker, H. S. (2016). Relativism: Labeling theory. In P. Adler & P. Adler (Eds.), Construction of deviance: Social power, context, and interaction (8th ed., pp.40-44). Cengage.

Bell, A. B. (2023). Theoretical foundation for social justice. In M. Adams, L. A. Bell, D. J. Goodman, D. Shlasko, R. R. Briggs, & R. Pacheco (Eds.) *Teaching for diversity and social justice* (4th ed., pp. 2-25). Routledge. https://doi.org/10.4324/9781003005759

Bramley, C., & Morrison, K. (2023). *Student engagement, higher education, and social justice: Beyond neoliberalism and the market.* Routledge. https://doi.org/10.4324/9781003331292

Capeheart, L., & Milovanovic, D. (2007). *Social justice: Theories, issues, and movements.* Rutgers University Press. https://doi.org/10.36019/9780813541686

David, E. J. R., & Derthick, A. O. (2018). *The psychology of oppression.* Springer.

García, J. D. (2018). *Privilege (social inequality).* Salem Press.

Glass, K. (2019). *Looking at privilege and power.* Enslow.

Gordon, A. (2019). Medical students: Privilege faced with poverty. *British Journal of General Practice, 69*(687), 502. https://doi.org/10.3399/bjgp19X705785

Joshi, P. D., & Fast, N. J. (2013). I am my (high-power) role: Power and role identification. *Personality and Social Psychology Bulletin, 39*(7), 898-910. https://doi.org/10.1177/0146167213485443

Judicial Learning Center. (2019). Law and the rule of law. https://judiciallearningcenter.org/law-and-the-rule-of-law/

Kiken, L. G., & Shook, N. J. (2011). Looking up: Mindfulness increases positive judgements and reduces negativity bias. *Social Psychological and Personality Science, 2*(4), 425-431. https://doi.org/10.1177/1948550610396585

Lowery, Z. (2016). *The American revolution.* Rosen.

Noon, M. (2018). Pointless diversity training: Unconscious bias, new racism and agency. *Work, Employment and Society, 32*(1), 198–209. https://doi.org/10.1177/0950017017719841

Perez, P. (2019). *The drama-free workplace: How you can prevent unconscious bias, sexual harassment, ethics lapses, and inspire a healthy culture.* Wiley.

San Diego Foundation. 2022. What is social justice? https://www.sdfoundation.org/news-events/sdf-news/what-is-social-justice/

Tate, S. A., & Page, D. (2018). Whiteliness and institutional racism: Hiding behind (un)conscious bias. *Ethics and Education, 13*(1), 141–155. https://doi.org/10.1080/17449642.2018.1428718

van Ham, P. (2010). *Social power in international politics.* Routledge. https://doi.org/10.4324/9780203857847

Veesart, A., & Barron, A. (2020). Unconscious bias. *Nursing Made Incredibly Easy, 18*(2), 47-49. https://doi.org/10.1097/01.NME.0000653208.69994.12

Williamson, S., & Foley, M. (2018). Unconscious bias training: The "silver bullet" for gender equity? *Australian Journal of Public Administration, 77*(3), 355-359. https://doi.org/10.1111/1467-8500.12313

Media Attributions

- Balance scale © Nikodem Nijaki is licensed under a CC BY-SA (Attribution ShareAlike) license
- Destroy this mad brute Enlist – U.S. Army. © Harry R. Hopps is licensed under a Public Domain license
- Classroom © University of Texas at Arlington Photograph Collection is licensed under a CC BY (Attribution) license
- Group of people © Jr Korpa is licensed under a CC BY-ND (Attribution NoDerivatives) license

5.

Legislation and Policy

Bernadet DeJonge; Nikki Golden; and Cailyn F. Green

> **Learning Objectives**
>
> - The reader will understand the history of discriminatory laws and policies in the United States.
> - The reader will analyze how legislation and policy impact current socioeconomic trends for communities of color.
> - The reader will describe how discriminatory legislation and policy continue to reinforce the stereotyping of marginalized populations.

Many scholars have stated that social change occurs at the intersection of personal behavior change and policy change. That said, policy is often cited as having more influence on social change than personal activism (Hébert-Dufrense et al., 2022). There have been ongoing perspective shifts in understanding racism and marginalization. With this, discussions of social justice now focus on systemic issues of power, privilege, and oppression.

Systems of power have existed since the first settlers arrived in the United States and continue to exist today. Throughout the complex history of the United States, division around religion, slavery, race, immigration, gender, sexual orientation, and colonization has been cemented in discriminatory law and policy. While it is important to understand history, it is also important to be aware of how the complicated past of discriminatory laws has resulted in lasting consequences. This chapter examines these discriminatory laws and policies and outlines the long-term effects they have had on marginalized communities in the United States.

> **Activity 5.1 – Digging Deeper: An Analogy of Racism**
>
> Imagine two runners running a race against one another. Each is equally fast, but the first runner is given a mile head start. Because of this advantage, the second runner will never

be able to catch up even though they have equal skill. This is systemic racism in a world where racial equality, *not equity*, has been achieved.

Now imagine that the second runner, who is already a mile behind the first, must periodically jump over hurdles. These hurdles slow them down even further. Those hurdles are the many issues described in this chapter that disproportionately impact people of color. In the end, that second runner will never be able to catch up.

Discussion Questions

- How does the running analogy fit into your current understanding of racism?
- What does the analogy teach us about the historical and generational impacts of racism?
- How do we create a scenario where the second runner catches up?

Historical Laws and Policy

The United States has a history of racist laws and policies that continue to impact people of color today (Best & Meja, 2022; Rothstein, 2017; Yearby et al., 2022). Slavery was, clearly, one of the first. However, even after the end of slavery, Jim Crow laws continued to enforce segregation in the United States, particularly in the southern states. Jim Crow laws, based on the legal doctrine of "separate but equal," segregated Black Americans in the United States for decades (PBS, n.d.). Some examples of Jim Crow laws include illegal interracial marriage, division in transportation systems, burial segregation, and segregation of sports teams. Other examples of discriminatory laws in the 19th and 20th centuries included the Page Act of 1875, The Chinese Exclusion Act, and The Dawes Act (Bowling Green State University, n.d.).

After World War II, Jim Crow laws were challenged by the civil rights movement. In 1948, the United States military was racially integrated by President Harry S. Truman, and in 1954, the famous Brown v. Board of Education case ended racial segregation in schools (History.com, 2023). Ten years later, in 1964, the Civil Rights Act marked the legal end of Jim Crow laws. The Voting Rights Act of 1965 and the Fair Housing Act of 1968 followed. Despite these legal wins, some argue that, in the United States, laws and policies continue to be racist and separatist, particularly in southern states (History.com, 2023).

Activity 5.2 – Digging Deeper: Historical Law and Policy

Video: Plessy v. Ferguson and Segregation: Crash Course Black American History #21 (https://www.youtube.com/watch?v=nbZUQGPMTjk)

 One or more interactive elements has been excluded from this version of the text. You can view them online here: https://milnepublishing.geneseo.edu/social-justice-in-human-services/?p=90#oembed-1 (#oembed-1)

Learning Link: The Enforcement Act of 1870 (1870-1871) (https://www.blackpast.org/african-american-history/the-enforcement-act-of-1870-1870-1871/)

Discussion Questions

- How did court cases like *Plessy v. Ferguson* and policies like the Enforcement Act contribute to systemic racism in the United States?
- What did the Enforcement Act mean for Black people in America? How does the Act impact Black Americans today?
- Why is it relevant that the Enforcement Act was taken to the Supreme Court and dismissed as a states' rights issue? What did this mean for Black Americans at the time? What does it mean for Black Americans today?

Redlining

The term redlining stems from the 1930s, post-Depression era when the New Deal Legislation was introduced in the United States. One of the New Deal provisions offered government-insured mortgages intended to stop people in the United States from losing their homes. As these mortgage programs grew into the mortgage industry, policies about who was eligible for mortgage loans were developed. Eligibility practices included property risk ratings. If someone lived in a high-risk neighborhood, they were not eligible for government-insured loans. People of color, who were often poor, often lived in neighborhoods that were rated high risk. Color-coded maps ranked neighborhoods, and houses that fell within a red area were deemed ineligible for government-insured mortgages. This practice is now referred to as redlining (Jackson, 2021).

Redlining maps were government-issued, but private lenders used them as well. Because of redlining practices, home values in numerous Black neighborhoods plummeted. Many potential homeowners, who were people of color and lived in the redlined districts, could not secure funding for a home. Those who did were given high-interest loans, which were virtually impossible to pay off (Rothstein, 2017). During this time, housing prices were at a premium and many Black families could only afford substandard and crowded housing. This housing was the foundation for what is often referred to as ghetto housing projects (Rothstein, 2017).

> **Activity 5.3 – Digging Deeper: Color-Coded Maps**
>
> In 1976, historian Kenneth T. Jackson discovered one of the color-coded maps when searching other housing records, and this was the first time that the official government practice of redlining came to public light (Jackson, 2021).
>
> Website: Mapping Inequality: Redlining in the New Deal America (https://dsl.richmond.edu/panorama/redlining/)
>
> Discussion Questions
>
> - Do you think Kenneth T. Jackson understood what he had found when he found the redline maps? Why or why not?
> - Explore the mapping inequality website. What did redlining look like in the community where you live? How does that continue to impact the community you live in today?

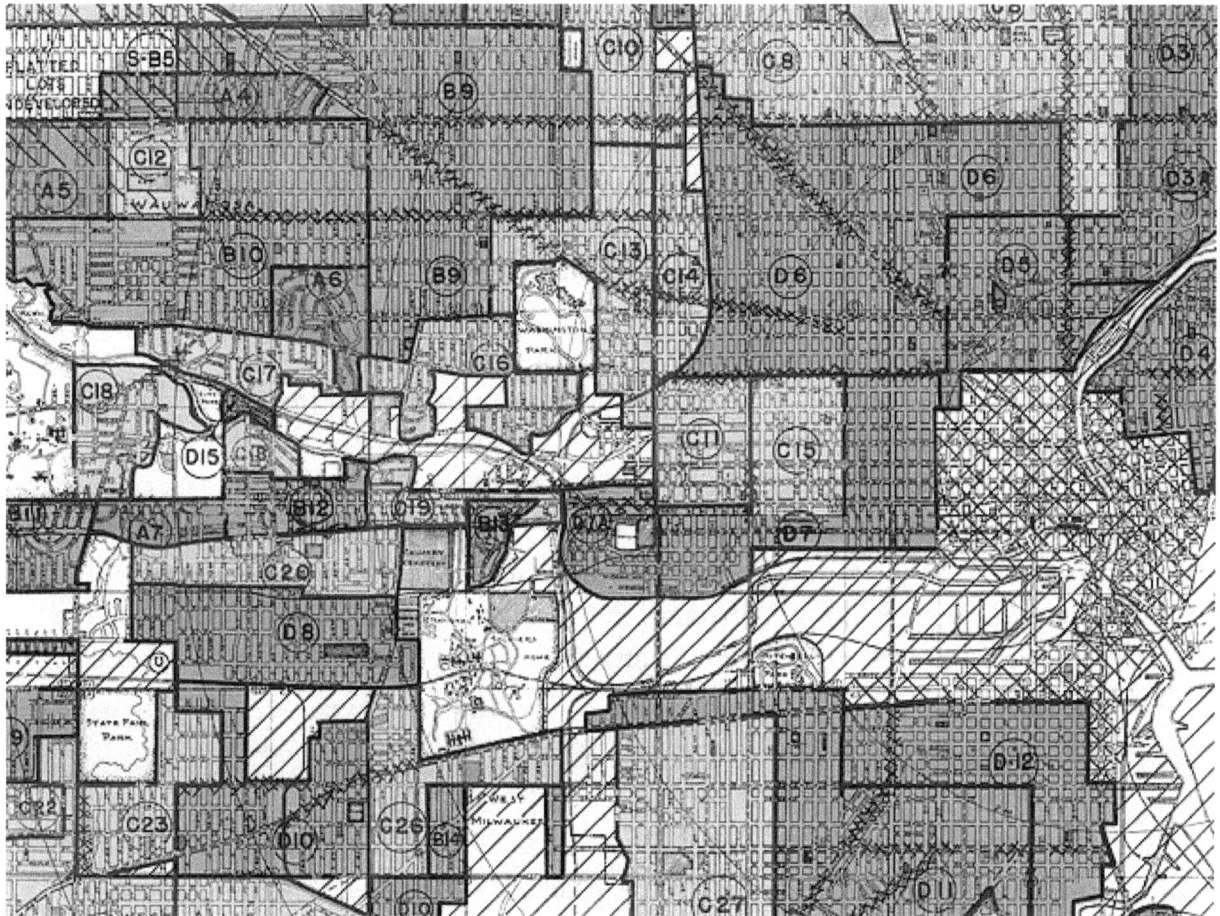

Redlining in Milwaukee, WI

Activity 5.4 – Digging Deeper: Redlining

Video: Redlining and Racial Covenants: Jim Crow of the North (https://www.youtube.com/watch?v=ymOaiWla3DU)

 One or more interactive elements has been excluded from this version of the text. You can view them online here: https://milnepublishing.geneseo.edu/social-justice-in-human-services/?p=90#oembed-2 (#oembed-2)

Discussion Questions

- How was redlining associated with Jim Crow legislation and policy?
- How does Jim Crow legislation and policy impact people of color in the United States today?
- How does redlining impact people of color in the United States today?
- How do Jim Crow legislation and redlining connect to each other?

In 1968, following the assassination of Martin Luther King Jr., the Civil Rights Act was passed. One of the bills included was the Fair Housing Act, which outlawed discrimination in housing and ended the formal practice of redlining (Jackson, 2021). However, despite the Fair Housing Act, racist practices have continued to be rampant in the housing industry. Best and Mejia (2022) reviewed 138 cities that had redlining maps and found that, overwhelmingly, neighborhoods that were redlined in the 1930s continue to be primarily Black, Latinx, or Asian, while neighborhoods that were greenlined (deemed worthy of lending) are still predominantly White.

Redlining practices had a significant impact on a Black family's ability to accumulate wealth. Policies such as redlining have contributed significantly to the statistical wage and wealth gaps commonly seen between races in the United States.

The legacy of redlining extends far beyond housing segregation, too. Its impact can be seen today in minority neighborhoods' access to health care, poorer educational opportunities, and increased risk of climate change, as many of these areas are more prone to flooding and extreme heat. Without a serious confrontation of its lasting generational damage, the racial segregation caused by redlining isn't going anywhere either. (Best & Mejia, 2022, para. 48)

Activity 5.5 – Digging Deeper: Redlining Today

I (Dr. DeJonge) moved to Syracuse in 2021 from the Seattle area. I was referred to a realtor who I enjoyed working with. I really wanted to be in the more urban center of the city, but he kept steering me away toward the suburbs. I remember feeling a bit uncomfortable with it. It felt wrong somehow. As housing was a challenge to find, I did end up in the suburbs. Now that I am establishing a community here, I hear a lot about how lucky I was to have a good realtor who steered me in the "right" direction. I hear a lot about how there is a lot of crime in certain areas and a lot of racism that is masked as "safety" and "property values."

Discussion Questions

- Is what my realtor did illegal? Why or why not? Is it ok to steer someone to more affluent areas when they are buying a home?
- What kinds of things might impact a realtor steering people to predominantly White neighborhoods?
- Is what my local friends tell me about being lucky true? Are they redlining? If yes, how?
- How do we balance out home values, safety, and other factors when looking at housing and historically redlined areas? What can we do to combat this segregation in the housing market?

In examining the long-term impacts of redlining and housing discrimination, two phenomena permeate the literature (Best & Mejia, 2022). The first phenomenon is the concept of White flight. White flight refers to White people moving from urban to suburban areas in response to people of color moving into previously White neighborhoods. Best and Mejia cited the city of Detroit as an example of White flight.

The second phenomenon is gentrification. As White people move into formerly redlined areas, property values increase and lower-income people, many of whom are people of color, cannot afford to stay. Gentrification is the direct result of federal tax reform intended to infuse the inner-city areas with money. Federal tax breaks, taken advantage of by White people who had the financial capacity to restore historic areas, led to low-income families of color having to leave their homes. An example of this phenomenon is the inner-city areas of Philadelphia (Best & Mejia, 2022).

As homeownership is the most common form of wealth accumulation in the United States, policies such as these increase the wealth gap between White people and people of color. According to Best and Mejia (2022),

> simply encouraging homeownership…where the housing stock is old and dilapidated, could saddle Black Americans with debt. Without being able to fund repairs or escape long, predatory mortgages, these programs could exacerbate the housing crisis and push more Black people out of their neighborhoods. (para. 45)

Activity 5.6 – Knowledge Check: Legislation Policy and Race

Discussion Questions

- How have policy and legislation impacted communities of color?
- Talk about White flight and gentrification—how can we impact these behaviors?
- Do we still "redline?" How?

United States Tax Structures

Another set of policies that impact wealth equity in the United States are tax structures. Although, in general, federal income tax is a progressive tax structure, meaning people pay more if they earn more, state tax structures, such as consumption taxes, disproportionately impact low-income communities of color. The impact of these taxes varies from state to state, and less progressive states often have more inequitable tax structures. According to Davis, Hill, and Wiehe (2021), sales and excise taxes (often referred to as consumption taxes) impact wealth equality the most because low and middle-income families spend a larger percentage of their income on consumption goods compared to high-income families.

Property tax structures can also be discriminatory. Homes owned by White people in predominantly White neighborhoods continue to have higher value due to historical redlining practices. Higher home values lead to higher property taxes, which is how most public schools are funded. Thus, public schools in predominantly White neighborhoods are often better funded than those in predominately Black neighborhoods. Early advantages of attending well-funded public schools, many of which impact future wage earning, continue to disproportionately benefit White students. Think back to the running example—poorly funded public schools are one of the hurdles people of color face. This is a current, concrete example of the impact of redlining.

In some areas, assessment and property tax structures continue to be discriminatory as homes in lower-income areas are inappropriately assessed with inflated values. Thus, some Black and Latinx homeowners end up with assessment values on their homes that are significantly more than the realistic selling price. This leads to tax bills that are 10 to 13 percent higher than White homeowners who own homes with the same market value (Hill et al., 2021).

People of color earn lower wages than their White counterparts and experience poverty at higher rates due to both individual and systemic racism (Hill et al., 2021). Tax codes in the United States increase this wealth gap by disproportionately taxing consumer goods, which are consumed more by people of lower income. While these issues are complex and nuanced, it makes sense to advocate for them to be examined and remedied as issues of inequity (Infanti, 2019). "Years of racism and discrimination across all segments of society—the housing market, labor market, financial industry, education systems, criminal justice, and other areas—have prevented people of color from building wealth on the same level as white families" (Hill et al., 2021, p. 7).

> ### Activity 5.7 – Knowledge Check: Taxes in the United States
>
> **Discussion Questions**
>
> - Do you think the United States tax system is fair? Why or why not?
> - Do you think the United States tax system perpetuates racism? Why or why not?
> - How would you propose we make the United States tax system more equitable for people of color?

Predatory Lending

Subprime Mortgages

In the early 2000s, the United States experienced a housing bubble. A housing bubble is when housing prices increase due to increased demand. Prices continue to increase until the bubble "bursts" (Investopedia, 2020, para. 1). The early to mid-2000s housing bubble was particularly severe, brought on by an economic boom in the technology sector, which subsequently crashed. When this happened, many investors moved their money into the housing market. This sudden surge in the housing market was reinforced by governmental policies to encourage homeownership, including offering exceptionally low interest rates (Investopedia, 2020).

During the housing bubble, it was easy to obtain a mortgage. If an individual or family was not eligible for a standard or prime mortgage, they were often offered subprime mortgages. Subprime mortgages generally have a higher interest or a variable interest rate that fluctuates. This is often referred to as an adjustable-rate mortgage or ARM loan (Consumer Financial Protection Bureau, 2017). Subprime mortgages may have higher closing costs, higher interest rates when fixed, longer payment periods, or interest-only options (Akin, 2022). These subprime mortgages are often offered to individuals who do not qualify for a standard mortgage—usually people with low socioeconomic status and disproportionately people of color.

Studies show that during the housing bubble in the 2000s, predatory subprime loans were targeted towards people of color. Even when credit risk was controlled, Black people were almost four times more likely and Latinxs were almost three times more likely to receive subprime loans than their White counterparts. Compared to prime lending, people who take out subprime loans are eight times more likely to default. Thus, when the housing bubble burst and interest rates started to rise, people of color were disproportionately affected by the subsequent increase in home foreclosures as their house payments became unaffordable.

In addition, many argue that these subprime loans were offered with the intention that they would default. This is because mortgage defaults equated to profits for lenders. As housing turned over repeatedly, lenders continued to profit, while people of color lost their housing. According to Mehkeri (2014),

> These mortgages were made to default. By using this fraudulent tactic, financial institutions were able to obtain big, short-term gains at the expense of homeowners. This was an exploitation of the most disempowered communities of the U.S. by the most powerful companies in finance. Despite the financial collapse of 2008, minority communities can still feel the expense of such exploitation today. (p. 1)

Foreclosure has multiple repercussions. It impacts credit scores and impacts an individual's ability to rent or buy a home again. Finding housing with a foreclosure on a credit report is difficult (Mehkeri, 2014). Beyond personal financial repercussions, foreclosures also impact communities of color. Many communities affected by the housing bubble crash were the same communities impacted by redlining. The compounding of racial injustices has led to increased violence, decreased property values, and decreased funding for essential services in affected communities of color. It has been argued that generations will feel the effects of these racist and unjust policies for years (Mehkeri, 2014).

Activity 5.8 – Knowledge Check: Subprime Lending

Discussion Questions

- How does subprime lending intersect with social justice?
- How do subprime mortgages disproportionately impact communities of color?
- Is there a place in our financial marketplace for subprime lending? Why or why not?
- Should subprime lending have more oversight/laws/policies? Why or why not? What kind of policies?

Short-Term Loans

Predatory loan lenders rely on an "information advantage" over their consumers (Cyrus, 2023, para. 6). Lenders know how to manipulate loans so that people keep coming back to borrow. In 2010, in response to the housing bubble and crash, the Dodd-Frank Act was passed by the United States Congress to address issues of predatory lending and to create the Consumer Financial Protection Bureau (CFPB). Despite the protections in place, predatory lending in Black and Latinx communities continues to be rampant, often through short-term or payday loans (Cyrus, 2023).

Many short-term loans have exceptionally high interest rates and hidden fees. They often roll over into new loans, which traps people in a cycle of debt (Cyrus, 2023). According to the St. Louis Fed, in 2019, the average interest rate on payday loans was 391%. This contrasts with 17.8% for the average credit card and 10.3% for the average personal loan from a commercial bank (Broady et al., 2021). Cyrus goes on to say: "The key components of the industry, from geography to marketing, take aim at Black and Latinx borrowers in need. Low wages, generational poverty, and a lack of traditional financial services funnel people to predatory lenders" (para. 9).

Front Window of a financial institution in Illinois which offers payday loans.

Activity 5.9 – Digging Deeper: Short-Term Loans

Video: Interest Rates (https://www.youtube.com/watch?v=GHHesANT6OM)

 One or more interactive elements has been excluded from this version of the text. You can view them online here: https://milnepublishing.geneseo.edu/social-justice-in-human-services/?p=90#oembed-3 (#oembed-3)

Video: How Expensive is Credit Card Interest? (https://www.youtube.com/watch?v=vUT0zLgKoOc)

> *One or more interactive elements has been excluded from this version of the text. You can view them online here: https://milnepublishing.geneseo.edu/social-justice-in-human-services/?p=90#oembed-4 (#oembed-4)*

Video: Payday Loan Interest Rates (https://www.youtube.com/watch?v=SKSVAwN_GXM)

> *One or more interactive elements has been excluded from this version of the text. You can view them online here: https://milnepublishing.geneseo.edu/social-justice-in-human-services/?p=90#oembed-5 (#oembed-5)*

Discussion Questions

- If Lorin has a credit card at 17.8% interest and borrows 1000 dollars for a year, how much will they pay in interest in a year?
- If Lorin has a payday loan at 391% interest and borrows 1000 dollars, and it continues to roll over for a year, how much will they pay in interest in a year?
- Which loan would you rather take out after doing the math? Why?
- Why might Lorin have to choose the payday loan instead of the credit card?
- How might the difference between these loans impact how Lorin accumulates wealth?
- How might each loan impact Lorin's children and grandchildren in the future?

Often, payday lending, pawn shops, and check cashing centers are conveniently located in communities of color that do not have other banking options (Broady et al., 2021; Cyrus, 2023). As online banking becomes more prevalent, many brick-and-mortar banks are closing, and bank deserts are forming (Cyrus, 2023). Of the banks that closed between 2017 and 2021, a third were in minority communities, leaving many without traditional banking options (Broady et al., 2021).

High-cost lending services purport to serve communities that traditional banking leaves out. However, those services are often predatory and contribute significantly to the wealth gap between White people and people of color. Mortgages continue to be challenging to obtain both in communities of color due to historical redlining practices and for people of color due to racist practices by individual banks (Broady et al., 2021). While the CFPB was established to address predatory lending, the actual impact of this agency has been negligible (Cyrus, 2023). Thus, communities of color continue to fall prey to predatory lending practices.

Activity 5.10 – Knowledge Check: Predatory Lending

Discussion Questions

- How is short-term, high interest lending an issue of social justice?
- How does predatory lending continue the racist legacy of redlining?

> - What kinds of solutions are there to predatory lending practices?
> - How responsible should banks and short-term lenders be in providing fair and equitable access to credit and loans? How do we reinforce their responsibility to the communities they serve?

Student Loans

Generational wealth plays a significant role in student loan statistics. Students of color often have more student loan debt. This is because they statistically start with fewer financial resources. Think back to the running example—this is the runner who starts a mile behind. For these individuals, parents and grandparents have less wealth due to historical inequities that affect wealth building. Thus, students of color acquire more debt when attempting to get ahead. The wage gap then negatively impacts student loan payments as people of color are statistically likely to earn less than their White counterparts. Because these students are not earning the same as their White counterparts, making payments on their loans is more difficult for them (Grabenstein & Khan, 2022). This is another hurdle in our running example as people of color struggle to succeed following graduation.

Statistics show that students of color have more student debt than White students and owe, on average, $25,000 more (Hanson, 2023; Perry et al., 2021). This disparity increases throughout the life of the loans due to the compounding interest (Hanson, 2023). Students of color with student loan debt are less likely to own a home, less likely to pay off their student loans, and are more likely to be behind on their student loan payments. This leads to an increased number of students of color defaulting on their student loans, which impacts credit and the ability to accumulate wealth in the future (Grabenstein & Khan, 2022).

In response to the student loan crisis, the United States government developed the income-driven repayment plan (IDR). The IDR plan allows students to make student loan payments based on their income. However, with interest on the total student loan debt continuing to accrue, the result of the IDR plan is perpetual payments towards a debt that continues to increase. Thus, many students will never be able to pay their student loan debt in full (Perry et al., 2021). This perpetual balance of student loan debt, often throughout a lifetime, contributes negatively to the mental health of students of color (Mustaffa & Davis, 2021).

Scholars have suggested that student loan debt forgiveness is a form of racial justice (Grabenstein & Khan, 2022). Mustaffa and Davis (2021) reported that student loans both perpetuate and are perpetuated by structural racism and that framing the experience of student loan debt as good debt ignores the lived experience of students of color. Perry et al. (2021) stated:

Wealth is not a direct result of hard work and determination in college. And racial wealth disparities are not a direct result of differences in college completion rates. Anti-Black policies across multiple sectors have diminished wealth-building opportunities that accelerate economic and social mobility. To ignore wealth disparities in the search for solutions to the student debt crisis is to turn a blind eye to the systemic racism that created the crisis itself. (para. 31)

Activity 5.11 – Knowledge Check: Student Loans and Race

Discussion Questions

- Discuss how generational wealth impacts the experience of student loans for students of color.
- Many have claimed that student loan forgiveness is a form of racial justice. Why might this be? Do you agree? Why or why not?

Healthcare Policy

Structurally racist policy has consistently impacted the implementation of social safety net programs such as Medicare and Medicaid. Assumptions based on stereotypes of Black people being lazy and the "Welfare Queen" rhetoric permeates legislative discussion and policy around the funding for social safety net programs (Levin, 2019; Yearby et al., 2022). It has been argued that the 20% Medicare service co-pay was implemented to discourage access to communities of color. TikTok influencer Goddess Mia (2023) said it best: "We have to pay 20% because of racism!" (1:43). Healthcare policy decisions are grounded in White culture, with most policy decisions being made by White people (Yearby et al., 2022). These policy decisions are rife with marginalization, oppression, racism, and bias, which negatively impact communities of color.

Medicaid

As of 2023, there were 86.7 million people on Medicaid programs in the United States (Medicaid.gov, 2023). Medicaid receives funding from both federal and state budgets and is administered by the state in which an individual lives. Thus, an individual with the same income and/or situation may receive different benefits depending on which state they reside in (Center on Budget and Policy Priorities, 2020). Medicaid recipients are mainly people of color, older adults, and disabled people (Alio et al., 2022).

Research shows that, statistically, people of color are in worse health than their White counterparts. This is often attributed to social determinants of health. Social determinants of health are the environmental conditions people are born in and live in that can have an impact on their health. Examples include socioeconomic status, access to and quality of education, access to and quality of healthcare, where people live, and the social context in which people live (Office of Disease Prevention and Health Promotion, n.d.). Many negative social determinants of health are rooted in racism and marginalization, and can be traced back to segregation, Jim Crow Laws, and redlining (Haldar et al., 2023).

One of the compounding pieces of social determinants of health is access to Medicaid-funded services. Access to Medicaid services is often discriminatory, and Medicaid-funded patients often struggle with access to appropriate and timely medical care. Physicians are less likely to take Medicaid patients and when they do, their services are often not timely. This is even more significant with patients of color and could be considered continued structural racism in medical practice. Alio et al. (2022) suggested multiple avenues to address these inequities. These suggestions included clear policies from medical centers that outline their Medicaid acceptance policies, a commitment to addressing issues of structural racism in healthcare, and federal and state governments incentivizing Medicaid acceptance.

> ### Activity 5.12 – Digging Deeper: Black Maternal Mortality in the United States
>
> Video: Black Maternal Mortality in the US and its Slave (https://www.youtube.com/watch?v=FAPT8ywaCvA)Origins (https://www.youtube.com/watch?v=FAPT8ywaCvA)
>
> *One or more interactive elements has been excluded from this version of the text. You can view them online here: https://milnepublishing.geneseo.edu/social-justice-in-human-services/?p=90#oembed-6 (#oembed-6)*
>
> **Discussion Questions**
>
> - What kind of ideas do you have about how to remedy the statistics on Black maternal mortality?
> - How does Black maternal health relate to the history of slavery and Black marginalization?
> - The Black maternal mortality rate has been called a silent crisis—why do you think that is?

Medicare

Medicare is federally funded health insurance for people over 65 and those under 65 who are disabled. Medicare covers a portion of most healthcare services, including hospitalization, physician services, and prescription drugs. Part A is for inpatient hospitalization, Part B is for outpatient services such as doctor visits and home health, Part C is the advantage plans, which turn benefits over to a health maintenance organization (HMO), and Part D is for prescription drug coverage (KFF, 2019).

While Medicare provides insurance to older adults and disabled people, there are also coverage gaps that impact low-income recipients. For example, Medicare does not cover eyeglasses, hearing aids, dental work, in-home care, or long-term care (KFF, 2019). Medicare coverage also significantly limits substance use and mental health treatment (Medicare.gov, n.d.; Steinberg et al., 2021). As mentioned above, Medicare has a 20% co-pay for most services (Medicare.gov, n.d.). In addition, if an individual is under 65 with an approved disability, there is generally a two-year waiting period between when the disability is determined and when coverage begins, depending on the diagnosis (KFF, 2019). For example, if you have end-stage renal disease or amyotrophic lateral sclerosis (ALS), you can receive Medicare immediately after disability status is obtained. However, if you have a condition such as paralysis from an accident or are approved based on a mental health diagnosis, there is a two-year waiting period for coverage (Srakocic, 2021).

Private Insurance

Many people in the United States obtain health insurance through employment. That said, Collins et al. (2022) found that 23% of working adults are underinsured, meaning they have insurance, but access to medical care is still not affordable. Often, these individuals are not eligible to switch to the Affordable Care Act (ACA) Marketplace due to a "firewall" (Yearby et al., 2022, p. 189) in the ACA. Yearby et al. (2022) refer to a policy that prevents specific individuals from accessing ACA Marketplace subsidies if they have access to employer-sponsored health insurance. Many cannot afford this option despite it being touted as affordable.

Lower-paying jobs are disproportionately filled with Black and Brown Americans; thus, those being most impacted by inadequate healthcare coverage are those who have been traditionally marginalized in the United States. Marginalized people are left struggling to manage insurance premiums, high deductibles, and coverage limitations. In addition, the cost of medication is often prohibitive. Collins et al. (2022) found that up to a quarter of people surveyed who struggled with a chronic health condition had chosen not to fill a medication prescription in the last year due to cost.

> **Activity 5.13 – Digging Deeper: Health Insurance**
>
> I (Dr. DeJonge) had a conversation with a friend recently about health insurance. They told me they were going to take a year off from their health insurance and go uncovered. I was horrified by this, but for them, it is an issue of cost. They pay a large monthly premium so they and their child can be covered—and they still have a $15,000 deductible. They said they never hit their deductible, so why pay the premiums on top of their already high out-of-pocket expenses?
>
> **Discussion Questions**
>
> - What would you do as the person making this decision in this situation?
> - What would you say as the friend hearing about this decision?
> - Discuss the policy and personal elements of this scenario. How much is policy, and how much is personal choice?

The Uninsured

Despite the ACA and Medicaid expansion, many remain uninsured in the United States. Of those uninsured, many are people of color (Young, 2020). The uninsured population in the United States is more likely to be poor, sicker, and reside in the southern states (Collins et al., 2022). Collins et al. found that 79% of those surveyed had been without health insurance

76 | LEGISLATION AND POLICY

for a year or more. The main reason for the lack of healthcare is premium costs. Yearby et al. (2022) stated:

> Among those who fall into the Medicaid coverage gap—people too poor to afford insurance but who do not meet the narrow eligibility categories of traditional Medicaid—about 60 percent are people of color, who disproportionately live in Southern states that choose not to expand Medicaid. Black people are more than twice as likely as White people and Latino people to fall in the coverage gap. (p. 189)

Activity 5.14

Video: Michael Moore Takes 9/11 First Responders to Cuba for Free Healthcare, a scene from his film, "SiCKO" (https://www.youtube.com/watch?v=j7cME3lCdwE)

Discussion Questions

- What are your initial thoughts on this clip?
- What should we do for these first responders?

Incarceration

The United States has more people incarcerated than any other country in the world, many of whom are people of color. Discrimination in the United States justice system is rampant. It begins with the school-to-prison pipeline and continues through policing, arrest, jury selection, sentencing disparities, resources for defense, incarceration, and parole (Nembhard & Robin, 2021; Wiley, 2022). Nembhard and Robin reported that laws and policies have always been written and enforced by people in power and that the definition of what is criminal in the United States is rooted in racist practice and structural inequity. Examples of historical discriminatory policy include vagrancy laws, Jim Crow laws, labeling civil rights activists as violent, and the war on drugs (Nembhard & Robin, 2021).

Activity 5.15 – Digging Deeper

Podcast Series: In the Dark: Season Two (https://features.apmreports.org/in-the-dark/season-two/)

Article: Mississippi to pay Curtis Flowers $500,000 after 23 years of wrongful imprisonment (https://www.revolt.tv/article/2021-03-05/58421/mississippi-to-pay-curtis-flowers-500000-after-23-years-of-wrongful-imprisonment)

Discussion Questions

- What discriminatory practices occurred in the Curtis Flowers case?
- How does this case tie into a discussion of incarceration and racism?
- How does local versus Supreme Court play a role in this case? How does it play a role in creating an equitable justice system?
- Is $500,000 enough money to compensate Mr. Flowers? Why or why not? How do we compensate for something like this?

School-to-Prison Pipeline

In 2012, the United States Department of Justice sued a school district in Mississippi for running a "school to prison pipeline" (Blitzman, 2021, para. 1). This lawsuit began a national conversation about the criminalization of children of color, especially Black children, in the school system. The school-to-prison pipeline is a set of school system policies that push students out of the classroom and into the justice system.

School systems have implemented policies such as zero tolerance, police presence, physical restraint, and automatic punishment (Blitzman, 2021; Elias, 2013). However, these policies have had a disproportionate impact on children of color and children with disabilities

(Elias, 2013). Studies indicate that students of color are three to five times more likely to be suspended or arrested compared to White students (Blitzman, 2021).

The school-to-prison pipeline is fed from underfunded, under-resourced schools that are often in low-income districts. Students from these schools are more likely to be labeled as having behavioral issues. They are also less likely to graduate, increasing the likelihood of contact with the justice system (Blitzman, 2021). Thus, the school-to-prison pipeline is a direct result of historical racism and segregation, particularly the practice of redlining. Blitzman suggests that we are not struggling with a school-to-prison pipeline, but a "...cradle to prison pipeline" (para. 4).

Racism and the Criminal Justice System

The Sentencing Project (2018) reported that Black Americans are almost six times and Latinx Americans are about three times as likely to be arrested than their White counterparts. Additionally, Black people are twice as likely as White people to be killed by the police (Nembhard & Robin, 2021).

The above disparaging statistics begin with the school-to-prison pipeline and continue throughout the lives of marginalized people. In addition, it is relevant to note that these statistics perpetuate the stereotype that Black people are dangerous while discounting issues of systemic racism, discrimination, and bias throughout the criminal justice system (The Sentencing Project, 2018). The criminal justice system then traps low-income people into an endless cycle of debt and criminal activity. Fees accrue while behind bars, which can impact economic well-being for generations (Huang & Taylor, 2019). Roth (2022) gives an example from a 2015 Department of Justice report:

> An African American woman who in 2007 was fined $151 for parking illegally. In a little more than three years' time, the woman, who had experienced homelessness, was charged with seven offenses for failing to appear in court and missing fine payments, each offense then leading to an arrest warrant and additional fees and fines. Over a period of seven years—for the same parking offense—the woman was arrested twice, spent six days in jail, and paid $550 to the court. Despite initially owing a $151 fine and already paying $550, the woman still owed $541 when the Department of Justice report was written. (para. 1)

Activity 5.16 – Knowledge Check: The school-to-prison pipeline

Discussion Questions

- How is the school-to-prison pipeline racist?

- What alternatives are there to zero-tolerance policies in schools?
- What are the disadvantages to changing zero-tolerance policies in schools?
- How does the school-to-prison pipeline and, later, the criminal justice system perpetuate racial stereotypes?
- How does the school-to-prison pipeline and, later, the criminal justice system perpetuate the racial wealth gap?

Chapter Summary Questions

1. What historical laws and policies have impacted people of color in the United States?
2. If you were explaining redlining to a friend, how would you describe it?
3. In what ways can you still see the impacts of redlining today?
4. How does completing your annual tax return impact your experience of financial stability? How might this be different for others?
5. Identify the three main kinds of loans outlined in this chapter. Why are they relevant in a discussion of social justice? Are there other financial policies or laws relevant in a discussion of social justice?
6. Discuss safety net priorities in the context of healthcare. How do we provide care to the most vulnerable?
7. Discuss the school-to-prison pipeline as an issue of social justice. What can we do to

impact this?
8. What laws or policies are missing in this chapter that also impact the experience of marginalization in the United States?

Thoughts from the Author

I spent so much time on this chapter and want to acknowledge that there are still things missing. There is just so much out there—I could probably write a book on each. I have tried to highlight legislation and policy that is useful and relevant and frames social justice in useful, impactful ways. I have so much passion around policy and the impact that bad policy has on people—it is a passion that has grown through the writing of this chapter, and passion I hope to pass on to you too!

Sincerely,
Bernadet DeJonge

References

Akin, J. (2022, July 2). *What is a subprime mortgage?* Experian. https://www.experian.com/blogs/ask-experian/what-is-a-subprime-mortgage/

Alio, A. P., Wharton, M. J., & Fiscella, K. (2022). Structural racism and inequities in access to Medicaid-funded quality cancer care in the United States. *JAMA Network Open, 5*(7). https://doi.org/10.1001/jamanetworkopen.2022.22220

Batchelder, L., & Leierson, G. (2023, January 20). *Disparities in the benefits of tax expenditures by race and ethnicity.* US Department of the Treasury. https://home.treasury.gov/news/featured-stories/disparities-in-the-benefits-of-tax-expenditures-by-race-and-ethnicity

Best, R., & Mejia, E. (2022, February 9). *The lasting legacy of redlining.* FiveThirtyEight. https://projects.fivethirtyeight.com/redlining/

Blitzman, J. (2021, October 12). Shutting down the school-to-prison pipeline. *Human Rights Magazine, 47*(1). https://www.americanbar.org/groups/crsj/publications/human_rights_magazine_home/empowering-youth-at-risk/shutting-down-the-school-to-prison-pipeline/

Bowling Green State University. (n.d.). *Laws and race*. Race in the United States, 1880-1940, Student Digital Gallery, Bowling Green State University, Bowling Green, OH, United States. https://digitalgallery.bgsu.edu/student/exhibits/show/race-in-us/laws-and-race

Broady, K., McComas, M., & Quazad, A. (2021, November 2). *An analysis of financial institutions in Black majority communities: Black borrowers and depositors face considerable challenges in accessing banking services*. Brookings. https://www.brookings.edu/articles/an-analysis-of-financial-institutions-in-black-majority-communities-black-borrowers-and-depositors-face-considerable-challenges-in-accessing-banking-services/

Center on Budget and Policy Priorities. (2020). *Policy basics: Introduction to Medicaid*. https://www.cbpp.org/research/health/introduction-to-medicaid

Collins, S. R., Haynes, L. A., & Masitha, R. (2022, September 29). *The state of U.S. health insurance in 2022: Findings from the Commonwealth Fund biennial health insurance survey*. Commonwealth Fund. https://www.commonwealthfund.org/publications/issue-briefs/2022/sep/state-us-health-insurance-2022-biennial-survey

Consumer Financial Protection Bureau. (2017). *What is a subprime mortgage?* https://www.consumerfinance.gov/ask-cfpb/what-is-a-subprime-mortgage-en-110/

Cyrus, R. (2023, June 5). Predatory lending's prey of color. *The American Prospect*. https://prospect.org/economy/2023-06-05-predatory-lendings-prey-of-color/

Davis, C., Hill, M., & Wiehe. (2021, April 2). Sales taxes widen the racial wealth divide. States and cities have far better options. *Inequality.org*. https://inequality.org/research/taxes-racial-equity/

Elias, M. (2013, Spring). The school-to-prison pipeline. *Learning for Justice*. https://www.learningforjustice.org/magazine/spring-2013/the-school-to-prison-pipeline

Goddess Mia [@evelrooted]. (2023, August 10). *Racism is the reason healthcare is not an American right* [Video]. Tik Tok. https://www.tiktok.com/@evelrooted/video/7262512583071042858

Grabenstein, H., & Khan, S. (2022, April 11). *Student loan debt has a lasting effect on Black borrowers, despite the latest payment freeze*. PBS News Hour. https://www.pbs.org/newshour/economy/student-loan-debt-has-a-lasting-effect-on-black-borrowers-despite-the-latest-freeze-in-payments

Haldar, S., Rudowitz, R., & Artiga, S. (2023, June 2). *Medicaid and racial health equity*. KFF. https://www.kff.org/medicaid/issue-brief/medicaid-efforts-to-address-racial-health-disparities/

Hanson, M. (2023, September 3). *Student loan debt by race*. Education Data Initiative. https://educationdata.org/student-loan-debt-by-race

Hébert-Dufrense, L., Waring, T. M., St-Onge, G., Niles, M. T., Corlew, L. K., Dube, M. P., Miller, S. J., Gotelli, N., & McGill, B. J. (2022). Source-sink behavioural dynamics limit institutional evolution in a group-structured society. *Royal Society Open Science*, *9*(3). https://doi.org/10.1098/rsos.211743

Hill, M., Davis, C., & Wiehe, M. (2021, March 31). *Taxes and racial equity: An overview of state and local policy impacts.* Institute on Taxation and Economic Policy. https://itep.org/taxes-and-racial-equity/

History.com. (2023). *Jim Crow laws.* https://www.history.com/topics/early-20th-century-us/jim-crow-laws

Huang, C-C., & Taylor, R. (2019, July 25). *How the federal tax code can better advance racial equity: 2017 tax law took step backward.* Center on Budget and Policy Priorities. https://www.cbpp.org/research/federal-tax/how-the-federal-tax-code-can-better-advance-racial-equity

Infanti, A. C. (2019, April 11). *How US tax laws discriminate against women, gays and people of color.* The Conversation. https://theconversation.com/how-us-tax-laws-discriminate-against-women-gays-and-people-of-color-115283

Investopedia. (2020). *What is a housing bubble? Definition, causes, and recent examples.* https://www.investopedia.com/terms/h/housing_bubble.asp

Jackson, C. (2021, August 17). What is redlining? *The New York Times.* https://www.nytimes.com/2021/08/17/realestate/what-is-redlining.html

KFF. (2019, February 13). *An overview of Medicare.* https://www.kff.org/medicare/issue-brief/an-overview-of-medicare/

Levin, L. (2019). *The Queen: The forgotten life behind an American myth.* Back Bay Books.

Medicare.gov. (n.d.). *Mental health care (outpatient).* https://www.medicare.gov/coverage/mental-health-care-outpatient

Mehkeri, Z. A. (2014). Predatory lending: What's race got to do with it. *Public Interest Law Reporter, 20*(1), Article 9. http://lawcommons.luc.edu/pilr/vol20/iss1/9

Mustaffa, J. B., & Davis, J. C. W. (2021, October 20). *Jim Crow debt: How Black borrowers experience student loans.* The Education Trust. https://edtrust.org/wp-content/uploads/2014/09/Jim-Crow-Debt_How-Black-Borrowers-Experience-Student-Loans_October-2021.pdf

Nembhard, S., & Robin, L. (2021, August). *Racial and ethnic disparities throughout the criminal legal system: A result of racist policies and discretionary practices.* Urban Institute. https://www.urban.org/sites/default/files/publication/104687/racial-and-ethnic-disparities-throughout-the-criminal-legal-system.pdf

Office of Disease Prevention and Health Promotion. (n.d.). Social determinants of health. https://health.gov/healthypeople/priority-areas/social-determinants-health

PBS. (n.d.). *Jim Crow laws.* American Experience. https://www.pbs.org/wgbh/americanexperience/features/freedom-riders-jim-crow-laws/

Perry, A. M., Steinbaum, M., & Romer, C. (2021, June 23). *Student loans, the racial wealth divide, and why we need full student debt cancellation.* Brookings. https://www.brookings.edu/articles/student-loans-the-racial-wealth-divide-and-why-we-need-full-student-debt-cancellation/

Roth, M.S. (2022, February 15). The debt trap: How court debt widens the racial wealth gap. *Shelterforce*. https://shelterforce.org/2022/02/15/the-debt-trap-how-court-debt-widens-the-racial-wealth-gap/

Rothstein, R. (2017). *The color of law: A forgotten history of how our government segregated America*. Liveright.

The Sentencing Project. (2018, April 19). *Report to the United Nations on racial disparities in the U.S. criminal justice system*. https://www.sentencingproject.org/reports/report-to-the-united-nations-on-racial-disparities-in-the-u-s-criminal-justice-system/

Srakocic, S. (2021, June 8). *When is the Medicare waiting period waived?* Healthline. https://www.healthline.com/health/medicare/medicare-waiting-period-waived

Steinberg, D., Weber, E., & Woodworth, A. (2021, June 22). *Medicare's discriminatory coverage policies for substance use disorders*. Health Affairs. https://www.healthaffairs.org/content/forefront/medicare-s-discriminatory-coverage-policies-substance-use-disorders

Wiley, E. (2022, July 20). *How racism in the courtroom produces wrongful convictions and mass incarceration*. Legal Defense Fund. https://www.naacpldf.org/judicial-process-failures/

Yearby, R., Clark, B., & Figueroa, J. F. (2022). Structural racism in historical and modern US health care policy. *Health Equity*, 41(2), 187-194. https://doi.org/10.1377/hlthaff.2021.01466

Young, C. L. (2020, February 19). *There are clear, race-based inequalities in health insurance and health outcomes*. Brookings. https://www.brookings.edu/articles/there-are-clear-race-based-inequalities-in-health-insurance-and-health-outcomes/

Media Attributions

- Silhouettes © Fitsum Admasu is licensed under a CC BY-ND (Attribution NoDerivatives) license
- Milwaukee Redlining © National Archives is licensed under a Public Domain license
- Graffiti protesting gentrification © Shiraz Chakera is licensed under a CC BY-SA (Attribution ShareAlike) license
- Payday Loans © swanksalot is licensed under a CC BY-SA (Attribution ShareAlike) license
- Man in gray crew-neck shirt © Mubarak Showole is licensed under a CC BY-ND (Attribution NoDerivatives) license
- Medical consultation © National Cancer Institute is licensed under a CC BY-NC (Attribution NonCommercial) license
- Razor wire © Hédi Benyounes is licensed under a CC BY-NC (Attribution NonCommercial) license

6.

Race, Racism, and Being Black in the United States

Nikki Golden and Bernadet DeJonge

> **Learning Objectives**
>
> - The reader will be able to explain race as a social construct.
> - The reader will be able to discuss racial identity theories and models.
> - The reader will be able to identify the impacts of anti-Black racism in the United States.
> - The reader will be able to connect systemic racism and current social justice movements.
> - The reader will be able to identify historical events that continue to impact the lived experiences of Black/African American people in the United States.

Introduction

Addressing social justice requires persons living in the United States to acknowledge and confront systemic racism, which has played a significant role in perpetuating social injustice throughout the country's history. The legacy of racial injustice, which stems from the genocide of Indigenous groups and the chattel enslavement of Africans, continues to affect people in the United States today. This chapter explores the social constructs of race and racism and examines the historical evolution of race in the United States from the perspective of people with African ancestry.

Throughout the chapter, we use the terms "Black" and "African American" interchangeably to honor how people of African descent choose to self-identify. "African American" typically refers to persons who have ancestral ties to Africa through the history of slavery and colonization in the United States. This term emphasizes geography and history: people whose ancestors were forcibly brought to the Americas as part of the Transatlantic Slave Trade and who have since developed a distinct cultural identity within the United States.

"Black" is a broader racial and cultural identifier that can include African Americans, immigrants from Africa or the Caribbean, and people from other countries around the world associated with Africa either phenotypically, culturally, or both—regardless of specific national or ethnic background.

Race as a Social Construct

Race is not biologically determined; instead, it is a social construct created by humans based on characteristics such as skin color, with specific value-laden categories emerging relatively recently in human history (Kendi, 2016). These categories carry profound social and political consequences shaped by historical power dynamics and cultural interpretations. In the early English colonies, before the establishment of fixed racial categories, religious affiliation often dictated social status (Wilkerson, 2023). Today, racial classifications are based on observable yet arbitrary physical characteristics, genetics, or cultural differences (Bonham, 2024; Burton et al., 2010). According to the National Human Genome Research Institute, race is defined as "a social construct used to group people" and "was constructed as a hierarchical system for classifying human groups, creating racial classifications that identify, distinguish, and marginalize certain groups across nations and globally" (Bonham, 2024, para 1). Despite the socially-constructed nature of race, racial categories in the United States are deeply ingrained, to the extent that even in the face of scientific evidence, "some human beings continue to perceive other human beings as excluded from the moral order of personhood" (Zimbardo, 2008, p. 307).

Furthermore, racial hierarchy in the United States can be explained as politically constructed, where "Whiteness" is deliberately positioned at the top of the hierarchy through laws, policies, and social practices designed to concentrate power, wealth, and privilege among those classified as White. This system was historically codified through slavery, segregation, discriminatory housing policies, unequal education, and biased criminal justice practices. This hierarchy was not natural or inevitable, but was deliberately created to justify exploitation and maintain power imbalances (Coates, 2015). In its simplest form, this hierarchy in the United States is typically framed in two distinct parts understood to be mutually exclusive and opposing: White and not White (Rosenblum & Travis, 2016). While significant legal progress has occurred, this historical ordering continues to shape contemporary society through persistent wealth gaps, residential segregation, educational disparities, and implicit biases in institutions.

Because race is a social construct, categorical definitions have been fluid, with determining factors based on need versus fact (Burton et al., 2010). An example is the Latinx population, which was considered White well into the 20th century. The category of "Hispanic" was adopted by the United States government for the first time in 1980 (Simon, 2024). But Hispanic or Latinx is considered an ethnicity, not a race. Thus, one can be Hispanic on the

United States Census and be of another race, such as White or Asian (U.S. Census Bureau, 2022). Kendi (2016) argues that racial categories in the United States were created for political and economic gain: "European cultural values and traits, and hierarchy-making was wielded in the service of a political project: enslavement" (p. 83).

Racial Identity in the United States

Racial identity is how individuals understand and define themselves in relation to their racial group. It also incorporates how society assigns meaning to these groups. Racial identity is shaped by historical, cultural, and social contexts and influenced by experiences of discrimination, privilege, and power. For racialized groups, identity often forms through encounters with prejudice and societal expectations, leading individuals to develop coping or resistance strategies (Tatum, 2017). In contrast, individuals from dominant racial groups may experience their racial identity with less awareness of its influence, recognizing it primarily in moments of racialized tension (DiAngelo, 2018). Racial identity is not static; it evolves over time and can shift based on personal experiences and social interactions. Socially constructed identities such as race are critical factors in predicting life outcomes, including education, income levels, health and healthcare, and access to other resources. Understanding how people form and express their racial identity is crucial to addressing racism, inequality, and social justice.

Racial Identity Theories

Theories such as Social Identity Theory, Critical Race Theory, and Racial Identity Development models provide frameworks for understanding how individuals understand and negotiate their racial identity within society. The concept of Double Consciousness and the framework of Intersectionality further enrich our understanding by highlighting the internal and multifaceted nature of racial identity. These theories collectively emphasize that racial identity is not just about how individuals see themselves, but also about how they are perceived and navigate a society deeply influenced by race and racism.

Double Consciousness

Double Consciousness was introduced by W. E. B. Du Bois in his seminal work *The Souls of Black Folk* (1903). It is a critical historical concept in any discussion of racial identity. Double Consciousness refers to the internal conflict that African Americans (and, by extension, other marginalized racial groups) experience as they negotiate their identity in a society that devalues their race. Du Bois describes it as a kind of psychological division where individuals are constantly aware of how they are perceived by the dominant, often oppressive, group and how they view themselves (Gingras, 2010).

Double Consciousness encompasses several key points. First, the concept of a dual identity involves racialized individuals' awareness of themselves from both their personal perspective and the perspective imposed by a society dominated by Whiteness. This awareness often leads to internal conflict and tension, as individuals struggle to balance their personal sense of identity with the need to conform to or negotiate societal expectations and stereotypes. Additionally, the struggle of Self-Perception vs. External Perception captures the difficulty of reconciling one's self-view with how one is perceived and judged by others. This complex interplay highlights the internal and external struggles inherent in managing dual aspects of racial identity in a society organized around race (Du Bois, 1903).

W. E. B. Du Bois in 1918

Social Identity Theory

Henri Tajfel and John Turner proposed Social Identity Theory in the 1970s. According to this theory, individuals derive part of their self-concept from membership in various groups, including racial groups. Tajfel and Turner argued that social identity provides individuals with a sense of belonging, purpose, self-worth, and identity. Additionally, the tendency to categorize, identify, and compare with other groups influences an individual's experience of social identity (McLeod, 2023). Social Identity Theory is responsible for introducing the concepts of in-group and out-group, which are frequently used in psychology to explain biased behavior. Criticisms of Social Identity Theory include an overemphasis on group identity, overly simplistic study environments, lack of focus on individual differences, neglect of power and structural factors, and insufficient explanations for why people sometimes favor out-groups (Brown, 2000; Ellemers et al., 2002; Hogg & Abrams, 1990; Jost & Banaji, 1994; Reicher & Haslam, 2006).

Critical Race Theory

Critical Race Theory (CRT) explores the intersections of race and racism with other forms of social stratification, such as social, legal, and institutional structures. Originating in the late 1970s and 1980s from the work of legal scholars like Derrick Bell, Kimberlé Crenshaw, and Richard Delgado, CRT emerged as a response to the inadequacies of traditional legal approaches in addressing racial injustice. CRT recognizes racism as systemic and underscores that racism is embedded in United States law, policy, and practice. CRT emphasizes intersectionality and the social construction of race, and it places value on the lived experiences of those subject to racism. Additionally, CRT challenges colorblindness and gradualist change, instead advocating for large-scale systemic power shifts through a social justice lens (Delgado & Stefancic, 2017).

Activity 6.1 – Critical Race Theory (CRT) and Religion

While some view CRT as a critical tool for understanding and dismantling systemic racism, others argue that it is incompatible with traditional religious or ideological beliefs, as exemplified by a statement issued by Southern Baptist church leaders in 2020. The six White male presidents of the Southern Baptist seminaries issued a joint statement against CRT as "incompatible with the denomination's confession of faith" (Jones, 2023, p. 268).

However, in 2021, the Catholic order of the Jesuits "announced an initiative to raise $100 million to atone for their role in slavery and to benefit the descendants of the enslaved people they had once owned" (p. 267), with all funds placed in a foundation to be co-facilitated by direct descendants of enslaved people (as cited in Jones, 2023).

Discussion Questions

- What are the potential impacts of rejecting or embracing CRT on religious and educational institutions?
- What role should religious organizations play in addressing the legacy of slavery and systemic racism in the United States?
- How has the backlash against CRT from 2020 onward influenced broader discussions on race, history, and education in the United States?
- Given the racial tensions and protests of 2020, how should institutions, both secular and religious, approach the teaching of history and race in ways that promote healing

> and understanding?

Racial Identity Development Models

Racial Identity Development models seek to explain how individuals come to understand and internalize their racial identities. These models describe the stages that individuals experience as they grapple with the meanings, implications, and significance of race in their lives. They help explain how people move from racial unawareness to a more nuanced understanding of where their racial identity fits in societal power structures. Most models follow a pattern of a trigger event, exploration and searching, and internalization and acceptance. More recently, researchers have begun to study White identity and its development (Project Ready, 2016).

White Racial Identity Model: Janet Helms (1990)

This model describes the racial identity development of White individuals in the context of a racially stratified society. The stages are:

- Contact: Lack of awareness about racism and White privilege.
- Disintegration: Growing awareness of racial inequalities, leading to discomfort.
- Reintegration: Reaffirmation of racial privilege or denial of racism to reduce discomfort.
- Pseudo-Independence: Intellectual recognition of racism without fully confronting personal privilege.
- Immersion/Emersion: Active exploration of one's own racial privilege and racism.
- Autonomy: Full acknowledgment of White privilege and active commitment to dismantling racism.

Biracial Identity Development Model: Walker S. Carlos Poston (1990)

This model accounts for the unique experiences of biracial or multiracial individuals. The stages are:

- Personal Identity: The basis for identity emphasizes personal characteristics rather than race.
- Choice of Group Categorization: Choice to identify with one racial group, typically due to external pressures.

- Enmeshment/Denial: Confusion or guilt about selecting one racial group over another.
- Appreciation: Increasing awareness and appreciation of the multiple racial heritages.
- Integration: Full integration and acceptance of a biracial or multiracial identity.

Nigrescence Model: William E. Cross (1991)

Focuses on African American racial identity and describes a process called *nigrescence* (the process of becoming Black), in which individuals move from a state of unawareness or devaluation of their Black identity to one of affirmation and pride. The stages include:

- Pre-Encounter: Lack of awareness of race or preference for dominant White culture.
- Encounter: Personal or social event that triggers awareness of racism.
- Immersion/Emersion: Immersion in Black culture and often a rejection of anything related to White culture.
- Internalization: Development of a balanced, secure sense of Black identity.
- Internalization-Commitment: Commitment to racial justice and Black empowerment.

Model of Ethnic Identity Development: Jean Phinney (1992)

Describes the ethnic identity development process for all racial/ethnic groups, including both minority and majority individuals. It outlines the following stages:

- Unexamined Ethnic Identity: Lack of interest in or awareness of one's ethnic identity.
- Ethnic Identity Search: A triggering event that leads to active exploration of one's ethnic background.
- Achieved Ethnic Identity: Formation of a clear, secure sense of one's ethnic identity.

Discussion Questions

- How do Cross's Nigrescence Model and Helms's White Racial Identity Model compare in their depiction of identity development in relation to systemic racism? What are the similarities and differences in how each model addresses the impact of racial awareness on individual identity?
- How do the stages of racial identity development in Helms's White Racial Identity Model and Cross's Nigrescence Model reflect different aspects of privilege and oppression? What insights can be gained by comparing the processes through which White individuals and African American individuals come to understand their racial identities?

- In examining how individuals move through stages of identity development, how might Cross's Nigrescence Model and Poston's Biracial Identity Development Model provide complementary perspectives on forming racial identity in response to social and personal experiences?
- Most of these models were generated in the 1990s. Why might that be? What current theories or movements are out there that describe racial identity development?

Activity 6.2 – White Racial Identity Development

Video: How Can I Have a Positive Racial Identity? I'm White! (https://www.youtube.com/watch?v=hxXMf5K1W6E&t=1s)

 One or more interactive elements has been excluded from this version of the text. You can view them online here: https://milnepublishing.geneseo.edu/social-justice-in-human-services/?p=369#oembed-1 (#oembed-1)

Discussion Questions

- What are the central themes explored in the video regarding White identity? How does the video define or conceptualize what it means to be White?
- What insights does the video offer about the role of White individuals in challenging racism? How are these insights connected to broader social justice efforts?
- How does the video challenge viewers to reflect on their own experiences and identities in relation to Whiteness? What questions or prompts does it provide for personal reflection?
- What connections can you make between the video's content and other discussions or materials on race and identity? How does this video contribute to or enhance your understanding of these topics?

Intersectionality

Intersectionality is a framework developed by Kimberlé Crenshaw to understand how various social identities intersect and create unique experiences of oppression and privilege. When applied to racial identity, intersectionality explores how race interacts with other aspects of identity, such as gender, class, sexuality, and disability, to shape an individual's experiences and social realities. Intersectionality acknowledges that individuals possess multiple overlapping identities that cannot always be separated (e.g., the experience of being a Black queer woman). One cannot examine race, gender, or sexuality alone; all dimensions of identity must be acknowledged in the individual's experience. Thus, individuals may have both marginalized and privileged identities in various situations. Intersectionality has become a crucial concept in social justice movements because it emphasizes the necessity of acknowledging the intricate and overlapping nature of oppression. This approach promotes the creation of fairer policies and practices by examining how different forms of discrimination intersect and impact people in diverse ways (Carbado et al., 2013).

Racism in the United States

Racism is a system of beliefs, behaviors, and institutional structures that perpetuate unequal power relations based on racial or ethnic identity. It encompasses prejudice, discrimination, and antagonism directed against individuals or groups based on their race, rooted in the belief that some races are inherently superior or inferior to others (American Psychological Association [APA], 2023). Racism operates on multiple levels, including individual, institutional, and structural levels.

Prejudice and discrimination are both forms of racism. Prejudice involves making assumptions about individuals based on their association with a particular group, which can result in biased attitudes and behaviors. Discrimination is the act of treating individuals differently based on prejudice related to race, ethnicity, or other affiliations (APA, 2023). Discrimination comes in various forms, such as sexism, disability discrimination, ageism, classism, homophobia, and racism. Targeted groups may be defined by race, gender, ethnicity, or LGBTGEQIAP+ status.

Activity 6.3 – Scientific Racism

Scientific racism misuses scientific methods to justify the belief in the inherent superiority or inferiority of different racial groups. Scientific racism typically involves the manipulation of anthropological, biological, and genetic data to create a pseudoscientific basis for racial discrimination. Examples of the impacts of scientific racism include social hierarchies, colonialism, slavery, and discriminatory policies. Despite being widely discredited by modern science (attribution here), the legacy of scientific racism continues to influence social attitudes and institutional practices today.

Video: Darwin, Africa, and Genocide: The Horror of Scientific Racism (https://www.youtube.com/watch?v=IQPrvPM38Ws)

 One or more interactive elements has been excluded from this version of the text. You can view them online here: https://milnepublishing.geneseo.edu/social-justice-in-human-services/?p=369#oembed-2 (#oembed-2)

Video: Human Zoos: America's Forgotten History of Scientific Racism (https://www.youtube.com/watch?v=nY6Zrol5QEk)

One or more interactive elements has been excluded from this version of the text. You can view them online here: https://milnepublishing.geneseo.edu/social-justice-in-human-services/?p=369#oembed-3 (#oembed-3)

Discussion Questions

- What is scientific racism, and how has it historically been used to justify social hierarchies and discriminatory policies?
- In what ways did scientific racism influence public policy, education, and social norms in the 19th and 20th centuries? How do these influences persist in current societal structures or beliefs?
- How has scientific racism affected marginalized communities? What are the long-term impacts on these groups?
- How do the concepts of eugenics and biological determinism relate to scientific racism? In what ways have these concepts resurfaced in modern discussions about race, genetics, and intelligence?

The impacts of racism operate at multiple levels throughout society. Racism can be covert and systemic as well as overt and individualized. The former appears in institutional policies and practices, while the latter emerges in personal interactions and implicit biases. Individual racism occurs when someone treats another individual negatively based on their race or ethnic background (Meadows-Fernandez, 2019). Structural racism (sometimes referred to as systemic racism), on the other hand, refers to the existence of racism in systems that hold power. Examples include unequal treatment of racialized people in healthcare, education, employment, media, housing, and legislation. Systemic racism restricts oppressed groups from accessing resources that other groups can freely access (Meadows-Fernandez, 2019).

Activity 6.4 – Structural, Systemic, and Individual Racism

Video: Types of Racism (https://www.youtube.com/watch?v=YEOxgbqPUCQ)

One or more interactive elements has been excluded from this version of the text. You can view them online here: https://milnepublishing.geneseo.edu/social-justice-in-human-services/?p=369#oembed-4 (#oembed-4)

Video: What Is Systemic Racism in America? (https://www.youtube.com/watch?v=AjQBg-BcbOyQ)

One or more interactive elements has been excluded from this version of the text. You can view them online here: https://milnepublishing.geneseo.edu/social-justice-in-human-services/?p=369#oembed-5 (#oembed-5)

Video: Structural Racism Explained (https://www.youtube.com/watch?v=IQ_8eOaiz8o)

One or more interactive elements has been excluded from this version of the text. You can view them online here: https://milnepublishing.geneseo.edu/social-justice-in-human-services/?p=369#oembed-6 (#oembed-6)

Discussion Questions

- How do individual racism and systemic racism interact to perpetuate racial inequality?
- What are some examples of structural racism? How do these structures reinforce racial disparities in areas like education, healthcare, housing, or employment?
- In what ways might the concept of colorblindness contribute to the perpetuation of structural and systemic racism?
- What role does individual racism play in maintaining or challenging structural and systemic racism?
- Why is it important to differentiate between individual, structural, and systemic racism when discussing racial inequality? How can understanding these different forms of racism lead to more effective strategies for social justice?

Anti-Black Racism in the United States

It is worth emphasizing that although race is a social construct, its construction has "created racial realities with real effects" (Burton et al., 2010, p. 444). These effects manifest in tangible ways across society, influencing how people are perceived and treated. While race has no biological basis, it has been historically used to stratify society and impact access to resources. Stratification based on race has led to oppressive systems and significant issues with racism in the United States and beyond.

The complexity of racial dynamics requires thoughtful examination across different contexts and communities. While acknowledging that there are many other stories and experiences in the United States around race, we have chosen to focus this chapter on people of African descent in the United States. We use the racial descriptors of African, African American, and Black somewhat interchangeably, but primarily chronologically. This approach reflects the evolving nature of racial identity and self-identification over time and acknowledges and respects "that Africans forced to come to this country did not racialize themselves as Black in their homelands; they had their own indigenous roots and tribal beliefs; they were connected to lands, customs, and cosmologies" (Mays, 2021, p. 4).

Slavery

The history of African-descended people in the Americas does not begin with enslavement. Still, to understand the full impact of racial construction in the United States, we must confront the foundational role that the institution of slavery played in establishing and reinforcing a race-based social hierarchy. Human slavery has existed for centuries across all regions of the world (Stevenson, 2018). To justify the Greek practice of slavery, Aristotle wrote, "Humanity is divided into two: the masters and the slaves, or if one prefers it, the Greeks and the Barbarians, those who have the right to command and those who are born to obey" (Kendi, 2016, p. 17). However, "American slavery, which lasted from 1619 to 1865, was not the slavery of ancient Greece" (Wilkerson, 2023, p. 44).

Unlike historical forms of bondage that sometimes allowed for eventual freedom or a measure of social mobility, slavery was uniquely cruel in the United States. Enslaved Africans were treated not as temporary servants but as permanent property to be bought, sold, and inherited across generations. Further, the institution of slavery established a rigid binary social system, where "slave" and "free" became the fundamental categories determining one's rights and humanity (Berlin, 1998). Over time, this stratification became increasingly racialized, with "slave" becoming synonymous with African ancestry while "free" status was protected for and associated with Whiteness. This racial codification was formalized through laws like Virginia's 1662 statute decreeing that a child's status followed the mother's condition, ensuring that children born to enslaved African women remained enslaved regardless of their father's race or status, thereby cementing the economic and social equation of Blackness with bondage and Whiteness with freedom.

The United States would not have gained status as a global power as quickly as it did without its created system of slavery (Wilkerson, 2023). Baptist (2014) points out that "Enslaved African Americans built the modern United States, and indeed the entire modern world…"(p. xxv). This economic system required ideological justification, leading to the deliberate construction of "race" as a concept that positioned Africans as inherently inferior and thus suited for enslavement. Pseudo-scientific theories emerged to rationalize this hierarchy, with scholars, physicians, and religious leaders generating "evidence" of Black inferiority to defend the institution (Davis, 2006). These fabricated racial distinctions served to dehumanize enslaved people, making their brutal treatment appear natural and necessary within the American economic system.[1]

---

1. It is important to note that not all African or Black people in the United States were enslaved, and not all enslaved people were African or Black. Although the enslavement of Africans dominated the slave industry in the United States, other groups of enslaved people existed as well.

Colonization

Slavery was a significant part of everyday life during colonial times (Warren, 2016; Wilkerson, 2023). In the mid-1600s, England entered the African slave trade to provide labor for its island colonies. The first enslaved Africans arrived in North America's English colonies in 1619. By the end of the 1600s, English slave traders "carried more than a quarter of a million men, women, and children across the ocean, shackled in ships' holds" (Lepore, 2018, p. 47). Enslaved Africans were the source of free labor on plantations, mostly in the Southern states. This was because the Northern states did not cultivate large-scale agrarian crops like cotton or sugar. In the Northern Colonies, enslaved Africans were often used for domestic labor. Domestic labor, although valuable, did not have the same market value as slave labor that produced exportable crops (Warren, 2016). Therefore, "enslaved people never made up for more than 5 or 10 percent of the population…" in Northern Colonies (Warren, 2016, p. 133).

English colonists created laws to justify and protect their use of enslaved people, especially Africans, for labor. "With each new charter, with each new constitution, with each new slave code, England's American colonists upended assumptions and rewrote laws governing the relationship between the rulers and the ruled" (Lepore, 2018, p. 52). English colonists established a caste system with "only two colors, black and white, and two statuses, slave and free" (Lepore, p. 70).

In 1638, the first rebellion of enslaved people occurred at an English colony on Providence Island (Warren, 2016). It was not the last. After a series of rebellions by enslaved people, including the Stono Rebellion in South Carolina, colonists created increasingly dehumanizing laws to ensure complete control over enslaved people (Lepore, 2018). For example, South Carolina passed *An Act for the Better Ordering and Governing of Negroes*, which "restricted the movement of slaves, set standards for their treatment, established punishments for their crimes," and "made it a crime for anyone to teach a slave to write" (Lepore, p. 59). According to Kendi (2016):

> No matter what African people did, they were barbaric beasts or brutalized like beasts. If they did not clamor for freedom, then their obedience showed they were naturally beasts of burden. If they nonviolently resisted enslavement, they were brutalized. If they killed for their freedom, they were barbaric murderers. (p. 70)

American Revolution

The American Revolutionary War was not fought for or against slavery, but slavery was still an issue. English colonists instigated the revolution for various reasons. Many of the colonists resented the control and oversight of the English government. However, as with many other wars, this one had much to do with greed (Lepore, 2018). Taxes imposed on the

English colonists by the English crown, including the American Revenue Act and the Stamp Act, provoked anger among colonists. The colonists argued that "taxation without representation...is rule by force, and rule by force is slavery" (Lepore, p. 81). John Adams, who opposed the Stamp Act, wrote that "[we] won't be their negroes" (Lepore, p. 82).

> **Activity 6.5 – Digging Deeper: Taxation and Slavery**
>
> As author Jill Lepore (2018) stated: "It was lost on no one that the loudest calls for liberty in the early modern world came from a part of the world that was wholly dependent on slavery" (p. 64). In 1775, English colonist Samuel Johnson wrote in his *Taxation Not Tyranny* pamphlet, "How is it that we hear the loudest yelps for liberty among the drivers of Negroes?" (as cited in Lepore, 2018, p. 92).
>
> Discussion Questions
>
> - How do the quotes from Jill Lepore and Samuel Johnson illustrate the paradox of liberty and slavery in the early modern world?
> - Reflect on the moral implications of advocating for liberty while simultaneously participating in or benefiting from the enslavement of others.
> - How might these historical perspectives inform contemporary discussions about freedom, justice, and human rights?

Post-Revolutionary War

After the Revolutionary War, the concept of race became incredibly powerful across the colonies. Beliefs about race and White American supremacy were used to justify capitalist greed and slavery, and these beliefs influenced the governing principles of the developing United States (Baptist, 2014; Jones, 2023). Debts owed to domestic creditors and foreign allies as obligations from financing the war became a major political challenge in the early republic. The newly formed federal government was in an economic crisis, and the Articles of Confederation gave it no power to raise money. The new United States government had to decide how to tax individual states, particularly whether they should pay based on population or property. This question became more complicated by the fact that enslaved people were considered property. In addition, this issue reinforced the distinction between the Northern and Southern states around slavery. While the enslaved population had grown in the Southern states, it had decreased in the Northern states during the Revolutionary War (Lepore, 2018).

In 1787 at the Constitutional Convention, delegates from each state gathered to deliberate on what would become the Constitution of the United States. Four significant compromises, all related to slavery, were negotiated during the convention: the Northwest Ordinance, the Connecticut Compromise, the Three-Fifths Compromise, and the Compromise on the Importance of Slaves. The consequences of the four compromises proved devastating to the United States.

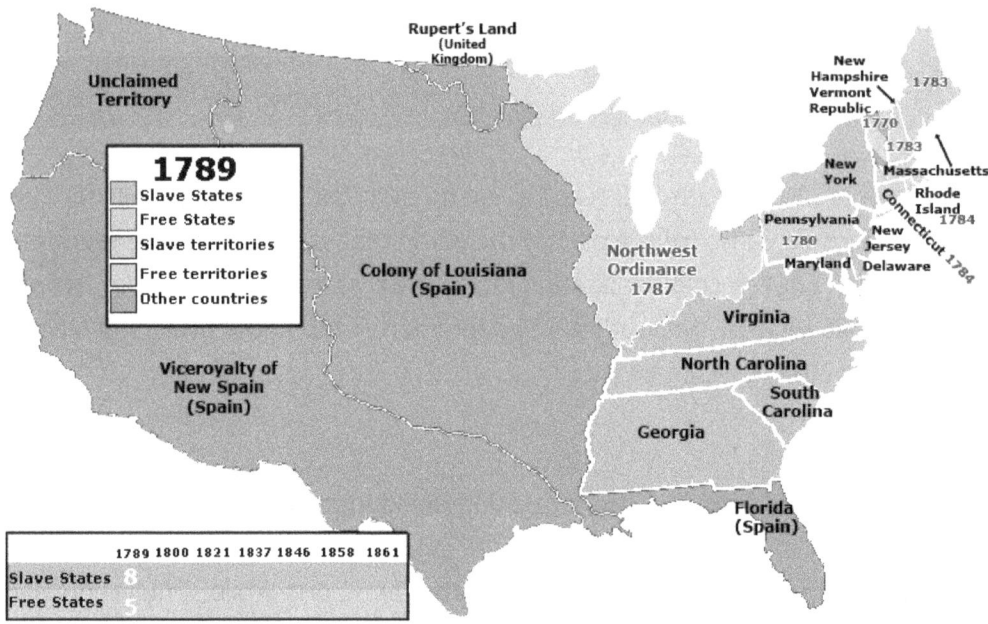

Map showing which areas of the United States did and did not allow slavery between 1789 and Lincoln's inauguration in 1861. The online animation includes a 5 second frame on 1789, 1800, 1821, 1837, The unrealized 1846 Wilmot Proviso, 1846, 1858, and 1861. The map colorings of some areas require further comment. New York (1799) and New Jersey (1804) adopted laws gradually freeing enslaved people, but some people in these states remained enslaved until 1824 (NY) and 1865 (NJ).

The first compromise was the Northwest Ordinance, which decreed that any new states established north of the Ohio River would be free states, and any new states established south of the Ohio River would be slave states (Lepore, 2018).

The second compromise was the Connecticut Compromise. The Connecticut Compromise ensured that each state would have an equal voice in the Senate, granting each state two senators. Meanwhile, in the House of Representatives, the number of representatives for each state would be determined by population, allowing for representation based on the demographic size of each state.

Related to the Connecticut Compromise, the third compromise, known as the Three-Fifths Compromise, established that enslaved people would be counted as three-fifths of a person. This addressed the issue of how individual states would be represented in the House of Representatives. The Three-Fifths Compromise gave slave states more representation in Congress, providing the Southern states with a political advantage. In addition, this compromise resulted in Southern states having greater representation in the Electoral College (Lepore, 2018).

The final compromise was between those who were against the slave trade and those who supported it. This clause in the United States Constitution prevented the new government from restricting the importation of people for 20 years. While it did not specify slavery, this compromise was aimed at continuing to allow slave importation while the newly formed government was established. The clause expired in 1808 (Lloyd & Martinez, n.d.). By 1816, the United States' two political parties were almost equally divided between anti-slavery and pro-slavery (Lepore, 2018).

Activity 6.6 – Digging Deeper: The Three-Fifths Compromise

The Three-Fifths Compromise was the result of the disagreement between the Northern and Southern states over how slaves should be counted for representation and taxation in the United States. Southern states wanted slaves to be counted as part of their population to increase their representation in the House of Representatives. In contrast, Northern states objected, arguing that slaves should not be counted as they were considered property. As a compromise, it was agreed that three-fifths of the total slave population would be counted for both representation and taxation purposes. This compromise had significant implications for the distribution of political power in the forming United States.

Discussion Questions

- Analyze the causes and consequences of the Three-Fifths Compromise. How did this agreement reflect the political and economic tensions between the Northern and Southern states?
- What were the lasting implications of the Three-Fifths Compromise for the distribution of political power and the institution of slavery in the United States?
- What might the long-term consequences of the Three-Fifths Compromise be? How might this impact how we view race today?

Abolitionists

Many free Black people, some formerly enslaved, fought against the slavery of African and Black people. "It must be noted that long before white people established formal antislavery societies, Black people had been resisting their enslavement" (Herschthal, 2021, p. 11). Black people such as Harriet Tubman, David Walker, Frederick Douglass, and Sojourner Truth risked their freedom and lives to fight for social justice.

During the mid-1700s, a small minority of Quakers had begun to question the morality of slavery (Kendi, 2016; Lepore, 2018). Quakers such as John Woolman, Anthony Benezet, and Benjamin Lay believed that slavery contradicted Christian principles (Kendi, 2016). By 1775,

Quakers had already banned slavery and excluded enslavers from their membership (Herschthal, 2021; Lepore, 2018).

Activity 6.7 – Friends in History

Video: John Woolman – Friends in History (https://www.youtube.com/watch?v=owD-SkR6Omec)

 One or more interactive elements has been excluded from this version of the text. You can view them online here: https://milnepublishing.geneseo.edu/social-justice-in-human-services/?p=369#oembed-7 (#oembed-7)

In the English colonies, Christianity was used to both justify and denounce slavery. When many others participated in slavery, both actively and passively, John Woolman chose a different path and was an active abolitionist.

Discussion Questions

- Discuss the dual role of Christianity in the context of slavery in the English colonies. How was religion used to both justify and oppose the institution of slavery?
- What do you think makes it possible for some, like John Woolman, to choose to advocate for social justice?

By the end of the 1700s, formal abolitionist and anti-slavery societies formed in the United States. Many of the earliest White members of anti-slavery societies supported a gradual approach to ending slavery. They advocated banning the transatlantic slave trade and enacting emancipation laws (Herschthal, 2021). However, even while some claimed to be against slavery, they continued to view Black people as naturally inferior to White people (Kendi, 2016; Warren, 2016). Others, such as Benjamin Rush, believed being enslaved was what made Black people inferior to White people (Kendi, 2016). Anti-slavery sentiments did not equate to racial egalitarianism beliefs.

By the 1820s, some White people who supported the end of slavery "came to believe that gradual emancipation would occur only if freed Black people were voluntarily resettled outside of the United States" (Herschthal, 2021, p. 13). The American Colonization Society (ACS) was founded in 1816 and was a mix of pro- and anti-slavery elite White men. It was initially formed to remove free Black people from the United States. The underlying belief was that Black people would never be accepted as equals in society and should be sent somewhere else to colonize their own country. In the early 1820s, delegates from the ACS traveled to West Africa and purchased land for colonization. A small number of emigrants were even sent to West Africa. However, the colonization failed due to objections from Black Americans, financial concerns, high mortality for the emigrants, and hostility from the Indigenous people of West Africa towards colonization (Robinson, 2022).

In the 1830s, abolitionist societies started becoming racially integrated and allowing female members: a significant change from earlier efforts led mainly by White men. This shift brought new perspectives and energy to the movement. Additionally, abolitionist movements began to demand an immediate end to slavery, moving away from earlier ideas of gradual abolition (Herschthal, 2021).

The West

As westward expansion progressed, the United States government grappled with the issue of slavery in new territories and states. Indiana (1816) entered the United States as a free state, whereas Louisiana (1812) and Mississippi (1816) entered as slave states. Slavery was expanding into the western part of the United States (Lepore, 2018).

In 1819, Missouri became the first territory acquired through the Louisiana Purchase to seek admission to the Union as a state. Missouri's application for statehood raised critical questions about whether Missouri would enter the Union as a free or slave state, highlighting the growing tensions between the North and South. In 1820, after much political debate, Congress negotiated the Missouri Compromise. The Missouri Compromise was the Northwest Ordinance but with new boundary lines. The Missouri Compromise declared that any state north of a certain latitude would enter the Union as a free state, and any state south of that point would enter the Union as a slave state (Lepore, 2018).

The Compromise of 1850 was a series of legislative measures passed by the United States Congress aimed at resolving conflicts between the North and South over the issue of slavery. The Compromise of 1850 was intended to appease both Northern and Southern states. This compromise included California becoming a state, not restricting slavery in either of the territories of Utah or New Mexico, and creating a stronger law regarding fugitive slaves. In addition, the Compromise of 1850 abolished slavery in Washington, D.C. (Murray & Hsieh, 2016).

The strengthened Fugitive Slave Law outlined in the Compromise of 1850 "gave slavery a dark face throughout the North that had not existed before" (Murray & Hsieh, 2016, p. 22). Northerners became aware of and resentful of the federal resources being used to capture escaped enslaved people. For example, in 1854, President Franklin Pierce "sent the marines, cavalry, artillery, and a revenue cutter to hold and then ship a single escaped slave back to bondage" (Murray & Hsieh, p. 22). Many Northerners felt this was a waste of valuable government funds.

In 1854, Congress passed the Kansas-Nebraska Act, which created two new territories, Kansas and Nebraska, west of Missouri. Under the 1820 Missouri Compromise, both territories should have joined the Union as free states. However, the Kansas-Nebraska Act repealed the Missouri Compromise and decreed that the new states' free or slave status would be determined by the voters (Lepore, 2018). "The battle that followed the introduction and simultaneous denunciation of the Kansas-Nebraska Act was the most thunderous in the history of congressional debate over the expansion of slavery" (Baptist, 2014, p. 371).

The Kansas-Nebraska Act outraged Americans living in the Northern states and abolitionists (Lepore, 2018). This led to a period of violent conflict known as "bleeding Kansas" (Cowie, 2022, p. 106), as settlers on both sides of the slavery debate rushed into Kansas to impact the vote. Conflict erupted in the streets: "Bands of free-soil guerrillas, known as Jayhawkers, battled with militant bands of border ruffians interested in making Kansas a slave state by whatever means they could. The open clash between free and slave forces turned the territory into Bleeding Kansas" (Cowie, p. 106). The violence following the Kansas-Nebraska Act is known to have been a critical step toward the Civil War.

The Three-Fifths Compromise and the Kansas-Nebraska Act further deepened the political disparity between Northern and Southern states. The Southern states exploited these agreements to bolster their political power by inflating their population through the increased numbers of enslaved people. This strategic manipulation allowed them to exert significant influence over the political landscape of the United States, tipping the balance in their favor (Lepore, 2018).

Justification for Secession

In the 1850s, Americans were still divided on the issue of slavery, and the United States was on the brink of a crisis. Even though Congress had banned discussions about slavery, it was a topic of debate across the country. Many Americans believed that the United States could not remain both anti-slavery and pro-slavery (Lepore, 2018). New York Senator William H. Seward stated, "It is an irrepressible conflict between opposing and enduring forces, and it means that the United States must and will, sooner or later, become either entirely a slaveholding nation, or entirely a free-labor nation" (Lepore, p. 282).

King Cotton

In 1793, Eli Whitney invented the cotton gin (Hamalainen, 2019). By the mid-1800s, the Southern states produced approximately half of the world's cotton; by 1820, Southern cotton was the most widely traded commodity in the world (Baptist, 2014). By 1936, "more than $600 million, or almost half of the economic activity in the United States...derived directly or indirectly from cotton produced by the million-odd slaves–6 percent of the total U.S. population" (Baptist, 2014, p. 322).

By the 1850s, cotton production in the Southern states had doubled, and after a short dip in the 1840s, the Southern economy was again booming (Baptist, 2014). More importantly, Southerners were not ready or willing to surrender their political power. They would soon prove their willingness to fight to retain it (Hamalainen, 2019; Lepore, 2018).

The Price of Humanity

In 1807, the United States Congress enacted the Act Prohibiting the Importation of Slaves, which barred the importation of enslaved individuals to the United States. This legislative measure directly challenged the institution of slavery in the United States. Despite this challenge, the Act did not abolish slavery, nor did it forbid the procreation of enslaved individuals. Exploiting this loophole in the Act, slaveholders intensified the practice of coerced breeding. If an enslaved woman was unable to conceive with one man, she was compelled to bear children through forced unions with others (Faderman, 2022).

> ### Activity 6.8 – Digging Deeper: The Forced Breeding of Slaves
>
> As early as 1662, the Colony of Virginia assembly created a law that "defined slavery by the status of the mother, reflected in the Latin phrase *partus sequitur ventrem*" (Berry & Gross, 2020, p. 33). The law decreed that any child born to a slave would be born into slavery. This meant that White male enslavers could profit from their own children born to enslaved Black people (Kendi, 2016). By 1663, the Province of Maryland passed the same law (Berry & Gross, 2020). When the Act Prohibiting the Importation of Slaves passed, forced breeding became a way to continue the practice of slavery without importing new slaves.
>
> **Discussion Questions**
>
> - What were the economic and social implications of the law requiring children born to enslaved mothers to inherit their mother's enslaved status?
> - In what ways did the laws in Virginia and Maryland reflect the attitudes and practices regarding race and slavery in the 17th-century American colonies? How were these attitudes perpetuated into the 1800s when the Act Prohibiting the Importation of Slaves was passed?
> - What was the impact of the Act Prohibiting the Importation of Slaves on the practice of slavery in the United States?
> - Discuss the moral and ethical implications of forced breeding to continue slavery after the importation of slaves was banned.

By the 1830s, ownership of enslaved people was deeply intertwined with the United States economy, and slaves were considered an investment that could have significant returns for their owners. This was particularly true in the South, where the economy relied on slavery to cultivate cash crops. Southern banks accepted slaves as collateral on loans, and in 1859, enslavers in the state of Louisiana raised $25.7 million by mortgaging enslaved people (Baptist, 2014).

In the 1850s, there was a marked rise in opposition to slavery in the free states, while simultaneously, there was a surge in support for pro-slavery views in the slave states. This shift was influenced by the rising price of slaves, which soared from an average of $900 in 1850 to $1,600 a decade later. Due to the increasing purchase prices for enslaved people, some enslavers suggested re-establishing the transatlantic slave trade. Pro-slavery groups like the African Labor Supply Association (ALSA) justified this idea using the principle of free trade (Lepore, 2018). By 1860, "the United States had become the largest slaveholding nation in the world" (Herschthal, 2021, p. 12).

Slave Stampede

During the early to mid-1800s, many Americans were dissatisfied with the government's attempt at compromise regarding slavery. Enslavers felt that free states threatened their way of life and feared there would be a "slave stampede" to the free states (Lepore, 2018, p. 280). On the other hand, many abolitionists and residents of free states believed that the compromises allowed the perpetuation and expansion of an immoral and inhumane institution, which they wanted to see abolished entirely.

On October 16, 1859, the fears of enslavers were realized when abolitionist John Brown and 21 other men launched a raid on the United States Armory at Harper's Ferry, Virginia. Brown planned to incite a massive uprising among enslaved people, arming them with weapons seized from the armory. However, Brown's mission was unsuccessful, as enslaved people were unaware of Brown's intentions and did not join the insurrection (Herschthal, 2021). Colonel Robert E. Lee and the United States Marines quickly stopped Brown and his group. "Barely twelve hours after the raid had begun, headlines were being telegraphed across the continent: *INSURRECTION...at Harper's Ferry...GENERAL STAMPEDE OF SLAVES*" (Lepore, 2018, p. 283). Brown was found guilty of conspiracy, murder, and treason, and was executed on December 2, 1859 (Lepore, 2018).

After Brown's raid, Southern enslavers' fears increased. Six days after Brown's execution, Mississippi Congressperson Reuben Davis stated in a speech to Congress that the federal government had betrayed the South and, therefore, "to secure our rights and protect our honor we will dissever the ties that bind us together, even if it rushes us into a sea of blood" (Lepore, 2018, p. 285). In preparation for the 1860 presidential election, Southern states' legislatures stockpiled arms and began plotting a coup (Baptist, 2014). The South was preparing for war.

Secession

In 1860, Abraham Lincoln was elected President of the United States on an anti-slavery platform (Baptist, 2014). As expected, Lincoln did not win any slave states (Lepore, 2018). Within six weeks of Lincoln's election, South Carolina's legislation voted to repeal their ratification of the United States Constitution. Alabama, Florida, Georgia, Louisiana, Mississippi, and finally, Texas, followed South Carolina's lead (Lepore, 2018). By February of 1861, the seven Southern states formed the Confederate States of America, with former Mississippi senator Jefferson Davis as president (Lepore, 2018).

Civil War (1861-1865)

At its core, the American Civil War was a conflict over slavery. With Lincoln elected president, the Confederacy identified the institution of slavery as the cornerstone of its decision to secede from the United States of America. In April of 1861, President Lincoln "raised the Union Army to put down the insurrection" (Kendi, 2016, p. 215).

The original goal of the Union Army was to preserve the Union. However, in 1863, President Lincoln issued the Emancipation Proclamation, which intensified the debate over the institution of slavery. After four years of brutal battle, "some 750,000 soldiers plus an unknown number of civilians" died (McPherson, 2015, p. 2). The Union ultimately won the war in 1865, resulting in the abolition of slavery and laying the groundwork for the ongoing struggle for racial equality in the United States.

Activity 6.9 – Sanitizing History: Confederate Apologists

Video: Confederate Reckoning: Teaching the history of the Confederacy (https://www.youtube.com/watch?v=fVFV8Vi3cwA)

 One or more interactive elements has been excluded from this version of the text. You can view them online here: https://milnepublishing.geneseo.edu/social-justice-in-human-services/?p=369#oembed-8 (#oembed-8)

Confederate apologists are individuals who defend the actions of the Confederacy during the Civil War by minimizing the issue of slavery and emphasizing other political factors, such as states' rights and constitutional principles. Baptist (2014) states:

> Ever since the end of the Civil War, Confederate apologists have put out the lie that the southern states seceded and southerners fought to defend an abstract constitutional principle of "states' rights." That falsehood attempts to sanitize the past. Every convention's participants made it explicit they were seceding because they thought secession would protect the future of slavery. (p. 390)

Discussion Questions

- What are the main arguments put forth by Confederate apologists regarding the causes of the Civil War? How do these arguments compare with historical evidence?
- Why is it important that Confederate apologists attempt to downplay or minimize the

> role of slavery in the Civil War? How might this impact Black people in the United States today?
> - What role do Confederate monuments, symbols, and memorials play in perpetuating or challenging the narratives promoted by Confederate apologists?

The Emancipation Proclamation

On September 22, 1862, Lincoln issued the preliminary Emancipation Proclamation (Lepore, 2018). Lincoln used the preliminary Proclamation to issue an ultimatum to the Confederate States: "On the first day of January...all persons held as slaves within any State, or designated part of a State, the people whereof shall then be in rebellion against the United States shall be then, thenceforward, and forever free" (National Archives, n.d.). The Confederate states refused to comply.

As promised, Lincoln issued the official Emancipation Proclamation on January 1, 1863. As Lincoln signed the Proclamation, he said, "I never, in my life, felt more certain that I was doing the right thing than I do in signing this paper" (Lepore, 2018, p. 299). With his signature, Lincoln declared that all persons held as slaves within the rebellious states "are, and henceforward shall be free" (National Archives, n.d.).

The Proclamation granted Black Americans the right to serve in the Union Army, and it is estimated that over 200,000 chose to do so (Baptist, 2014). This was significant for Black Americans, as Frederick Douglass stated:

> Let the Black man get upon his person the brass letters US...a musket on his shoulder, and bullets in his pocket, and there is no power on earth or under the earth which can deny that he has earned the right of citizenship in the United States. (as cited in Baptist, 2014, p. 401)

The Emancipation Proclamation was a noteworthy step toward freeing enslaved people in the seceded Confederate States. However, it was also a political tactic of war and did not declare the entire population of slaves in the United States to be freed. The Emancipation Proclamation only freed Southern slaves of the Confederacy and did not include those enslaved in Northern or Union states. It also did not apply to enslaved people in certain Southern states, like parts of Louisiana and West Virginia, that were pro-Union or working with the Union. Additionally, enslaved people in border states and Union-held territories such as Delaware, Maryland, Kentucky, and Missouri were not granted freedom under the Proclamation. In total, about 3.9 million enslaved people remained in bondage after the Proclamation was issued (Baptist, 2014).

African American soldiers mustered out at Little Rock, Arkansas, Harper's Weekly, May 19, 1866.

Reconstruction (1865-1877)

The Emancipation Proclamation laid the groundwork for Reconstruction, which began in 1865 and ended in 1877 with the recall of federal troops from the Southern states (Alexander, 2020). The end of the Civil War brought immense and immediate changes to the United States. Four million enslaved people were freed (White, 2017), federal income taxes were implemented, and "for the first time in U.S. history, voting directly impacted people's pocketbooks" (Richardson, 2023, p. 27).

On April 15, 1865, President Abraham Lincoln was assassinated. On the same day, Vice President Andrew Johnson was sworn into the office of the President of the United States. Most Americans believed that Johnson would follow in Lincoln's footsteps regarding Reconstruction. However, during his presidency, Johnson's only pro-Black Americans act was to support the ratification of the Thirteenth Amendment (Levine, 2021). In the early months of his presidency, Johnson made it clear that he only planned for "restoration without a plan for reconstruction" (Levine, 2021, p. 55).

On May 29, 1865, Johnson enacted the *Amnesty Proclamation*, which declared "that he pardon most rebel leaders and just about all male citizens of the ex-Confederate states" (Levine, 2021, p. 54). During the second year of his presidency, Johnson refused to continue to fund the

Freedmen's Bureau, which was "a radical agency that challenged the racial hierarchies and exclusions that had been central to slave culture" (Levine, 2021, p. 106). Johnson also vetoed the *Civil Rights Act*, which would have granted citizenship to all native-born people except Indigenous people (Levine, 2021). Johnson claimed the Civil Rights Act favored Black people over White people.

Any progress in Black people's rights was perceived by White Southerners as a threat to White people's rights (Cowie, 2022), and President Johnson's veto of the Civil Rights Act reinforced this belief (Levine, 2021). White Southerners saw themselves as victims of an oppressive federal government. They were determined "to restore the power dynamics of the master-slave hierarchy…using all tools at their disposal: political, religious, social, and economic" (Jones, 2023, p. 47). The only protection that Black Americans had from the systemic oppression of the South was federal protection (Levine, 2021). Many Black Americans believed that "federal power—especially the military—was the key source of leverage against the rebuilding of unrestrained white power" (Cowie, 2022, pp. 118-119). However, the farther away that protection was, the more danger Black Americans faced (Cowie, 2022). For example, federal troops were far away when, in 1865, Mississippi's State Legislature passed what was known as the Black Codes. These were "racially based laws that effectively continued slavery by way of indentures, sharecropping, and other forms of service" (Lepore, 2018, p. 318). Black Mississippians "were prevented from carrying weapons, consuming alcohol, and from having any stand in a court of law" (Jones, 2023, p. 47). They were banned from congregating for religious worship, and Black ministers had to be licensed to preach (Jones, 2023). Mississippi's Black Codes even went as far as controlling the lives of Black children. If a Black child was an orphan, they "could be forcibly apprenticed to any competent white person" (Jones, 2023, p. 48).

Other challenges during Reconstruction also affected the United States government's ability to protect Black citizens. Soldiers wanted to return home after being deployed throughout the Civil War, and the financial burden of keeping the Union Army stationed in the South was substantial. Other regions of the country were also grappling with instability, and the resources of the United States government were wearing thin. Meanwhile, the United States was also engaged in conflicts with Indigenous tribes, leading to further deployment of federal troops to monitor borders in the West and Southwest. As a result, Black Americans in the Southern states were especially vulnerable (Lepore, 2018).

During the Reconstruction era, Black individuals and their White allies continued to advocate for Black rights. They recognized the need for collective action and formed organizations such as Union Leagues, Republican clubs, and Equal Rights Leagues. They called for recognition of their inherent dignity and humanity and fought for legal equality and access to the privileges and protections afforded to all citizens of the United States. Organizations addressed education, employment, housing, and public accommodations. Furthermore, these organizations advocated for suffrage rights. They mobilized voters, campaigned for voting rights legislation, and fought against voter suppression tactics aimed at disenfranchising Black voters (Lepore, 2018).

Reconstruction Amendments

Three amendments to the United States Constitution—the Thirteenth, Fourteenth, and Fifteenth Amendments—were ratified during the Reconstruction era.

The Thirteenth Amendment

On December 6, 1865, the ratification of the Thirteenth Amendment changed the trajectory of the United States. The Thirteenth Amendment ended slavery by forbidding chattel slavery across the United States, except as punishment for a crime. When the Thirteenth Amendment was presented for a congressional vote, the Confederate States, having declared their independence and formed their own government, were not represented in the United States Congress. Despite this, the Thirteenth Amendment passed by only two votes (Cowie, 2022). Thus, "a third of those who remained in the union refused to vote for a constitutional amendment to end slavery" (Cowie, 2022, p. 123). Confederate States were later required to ratify the Thirteenth Amendment if they wanted to rejoin the Union (Cowie, 2022).

The Fourteenth Amendment

In 1868, Congress ratified the Fourteenth Amendment, although only one Southern state, Tennessee, voted for ratification. The Fourteenth Amendment declared that anyone born on United States soil, except Indigenous people, was automatically granted citizenship. The Fourteenth Amendment was designed to safeguard the rights of all citizens of the United States and restrain the authority of individual states by expanding the power of the federal government (Cowie, 2022).

The Fifteenth Amendment

In 1870, the Fifteenth Amendment was ratified, giving all men, except Indigenous men, the right to vote. This was one of the most critical issues during Reconstruction. However:

> As everyone would learn and many knew...the Fifteenth was the weakest of the Reconstruction amendments. By banning a denial of the right to vote on the grounds of race, color, or previous condition of servitude, it left out the fact that a state could deny the right to vote for just about any other reason it selected (Cowie, 2022, p. 132).

Former slave and prominent abolitionist Frederick Douglass believed that without Black men having the right to vote, "the war was not really over and not completely won" (Levine, 2021, p. 62).

Southern Backlash

While slavery officially ended in 1865, the racial categories it had established remained deeply embedded in the national consciousness of the United States. The ideology of White supremacy that had justified slavery transformed into new systems of oppression—such as Jim Crow segregation, sharecropping, convict leasing, and systematic disenfranchisement—all designed to maintain racial hierarchy without the legal institution of slavery itself. These systems were further reinforced through cultural representations, discriminatory policies, and both legal and extralegal violence against Black communities.

By 1873, White Southerners had employed various tactics and strategies to reclaim political, social, and economic dominance in the United States. At the beginning of the Reconstruction era, many White Southerners believed that they could continue to control free Black people "based on the old model of plantation paternalism" (Cowie, 2022, p. 141). When that failed, White Southerners engaged in any means necessary to regain power and subjugate Southern Blacks.

Activity 6.10 – Digging Deeper: The Ku Klux Klan

The Ku Klux Klan (KKK) was founded in Pulaski, Tennessee, in December 1865. Initially a social club for Confederate veterans, it quickly turned into a clandestine group resisting Reconstruction efforts and terrorizing newly freed Black citizens. Operating mainly at night in white robes and hoods to hide their identities, Klan members carried out violent acts like lynchings and arson, targeting Black individuals and allies of civil rights. In response, Congress passed Enforcement Acts in 1870-71 to suppress Klan activities and protect Black rights. By the mid-1870s, Klan influence waned due to federal intervention, internal disputes, and the decline of Reconstruction policies. However, the KKK significantly influenced the American racial landscape, and its revival in 1915 has continued, even into modern times (Stewart, 2016).

Video: The KKK: Its History and Lasting Legacy (https://www.youtube.com/watch?v=yyGZISG134Q)

 One or more interactive elements has been excluded from this version of the text. You can view them online here: https://milnepublishing.geneseo.edu/social-justice-in-human-services/?p=369#oembed-9 (#oembed-9)

Discussion Questions

> - What are the lasting impacts of the Klan's actions during Reconstruction on race relations and civil rights in the United States?
> - How have the tactics and ideologies of the KKK evolved over time? What challenges do they present to efforts to achieve racial equality?
> - What strategies can be employed to counteract the influence of hate groups like the Ku Klux Klan and promote societal inclusivity and tolerance?

By the fall of 1873, brutal attacks on Black people by groups known as White Leagues or White Lines occurred in Southern states like Mississippi and Louisiana. White Line groups employed terror tactics, including murders, beatings, and intimidation, to suppress Black political participation. These groups were well organized and consisted of former Confederate soldiers, White Southern elites, and poor White citizens who saw the United States government as a threat to the Southern way of life. These White supremacists framed their violent actions as "redemption," portraying themselves as saving the South from corruption and Black incapacity. This narrative was perpetuated for generations and continues to impact racial attitudes today (Cowie, 2022).

Reconstruction Failure

Many factors led to the ultimate failure of Reconstruction. One key issue was land redistribution, which was rejected, leaving Black people with no means of economic support. In addition, factionalism and corruption among Republicans undermined governmental reconstruction efforts. In the North, people were tired of war. Public sentiment had shifted, leaving people indifferent to the struggles of Black people in the South. The Northern interest in Southern politics also waned. In the South, there was an aggressive drive for redemption and to recreate the Southern systems that had existed pre-Civil War, including slavery. Widespread violence towards Black people erupted regularly (Cowie, 2022).

The United States government's financial crisis depleted resources, leaving Black Southerners without federal protection (Cowie, 2022). By "the end of Reconstruction, a wave of terror had descended on the South... [and] the national government abandoned Blacks to state control" (Horowitz & Theoharis, 2021, p. 14). As the federal government abandoned Black Southerners, White Southerners found new ways to abuse and terrorize Black Americans, such as convict leasing, sharecropping, and lynching (Cowie, 2022).

Convict Leasing

The *Thirteenth Amendment* legally abolished slavery "except as a punishment for crime whereof the party shall have been duly convicted" (Cowie, 2022, p. 196.) This clause, known as the exception clause, allowed White Southerners to create a system known as convict leasing. In this system, White labor contractors paid the fines of Black prisoners and bought out their prison sentences. Then, the White labor contractors presented Black prisoners with contracts, which they had no power to refuse, leasing them to mining operators, farmers, and plantation owners (Cowie, 2022).

Convict leasing was often more deadly than enslavement for Black convicts. Although technically Black convicts could gain their freedom, "their overseers had no investment in keeping them healthy or even alive," as "convicts were disposable, cheap, and in near infinite supply" (Cowie, 2022, p. 192). Black convicts, kept in inhumane cells, were often beaten and whipped (Cowie, 2022). They were also charged for food, medical treatment, and other incidentals. "Under the lease system, the convicts could then work off their growing debt by adding additional time onto the sentence they received for their alleged crimes" (Cowie, 2022, p. 195).

The convict leasing system generated labor and a "substantial financial incentive to increase the number of local prisoners in the system" (Cowie, 2022, pp. 195-196). It was so profitable that it continued until World War II (Cowie, 2022). "Meantime, for well over half a century, convict labor afforded whites the freedom…to take out their unrestrained rage on their African American neighbors, for profit and politics alike" (Cowie, 2022, p. 209).

Sharecropping

After the Civil War, sharecropping emerged as a labor system in which formerly enslaved people worked land owned by others, typically White plantation owners. This system became widespread in the South during the Reconstruction era and persisted well into the 20th century. Under this arrangement, tenant farmers leased small plots of land and paid landowners a portion of their harvested crops. Although sharecropping initially appeared to offer a degree of independence, it effectively served as a mechanism to control Black labor, replicating many aspects of slavery (Foner, 2014).

The system of sharecropping subjected formerly enslaved individuals to exploitative economic practices, often trapping them in cycles of debt. These individuals received little legal protection, and the contracts they entered were frequently unfair and heavily biased in favor of White landowners. In addition, the legal system at the time overwhelmingly favored the interests of landowners. Sharecropping functioned to keep Black families economically dependent and socially subordinate. It sustained the racial hierarchy in the post-Civil War South and continued to perpetuate a system of racial and economic inequality (Foner, 2014).

Lynching

White Southerners believed that they had the right to kill Black Americans without cause or consequence (Cowie, 2022). Often, this was done through lynching. By definition, lynching is "to put to death (as by hanging) by mob action without legal approval or permission" (Merriam-Webster, 2025). Lynching is a practice that is in direct conflict with the United States judicial system and has roots in the institution of slavery.

The lynching of Black Americans, both men and women, was justified under many pretenses. One of the most common justifications was the "myth of having to protect white womanhood against Black bestiality" (Cowie, 2022, p. 236). Black men accused of sexually assaulting White women were burned, castrated, dismembered, and hung by White mobs. Ida B. Wells, a former enslaved Black woman, wrote, "White men used their ownership of the body of the white female as a terrain on which to lynch the black male" (as cited in Cowie, 2022, p. 236).

A journalist and anti-lynching activist, Wells launched an investigation into the practice of lynching in the South after three of her friends were lynched in Memphis, Tennessee. In 1892, she published her findings about lynching in the pamphlet *Southern Horrors: Lynch Law in All Its Phases* (Lepore, 2018). A few years later, in 1895, Wells published *The Red Record*, which was the first statistical report on lynching in the United States. Wells' publications made her a national expert on the practice of lynching. In 1898, when Wells met with President McKinley, she gave him a petition, where she wrote:

> For nearly twenty years lynching crimes…have been committed and permitted by this Christian nation. Nowhere in the civilized world save the U.S. of America do men, possessing all civil and political power, go out in bands of 50 and 5,000 to hunt down, shoot, hang or burn to death a single individual, unarmed and absolutely powerless. Statistics show that nearly 10,000 American citizens have been lynched in the past 20 years. (as cited in Mobley, 2021, para. 7)

However, President McKinley did not support a federal anti-lynching law. In 1900, when Congressman George White presented a federal anti-lynching bill to Congress, it did not pass, nor did the "nearly two hundred attempts to pass anti-lynching legislation" that followed (as cited in Mobley, para. 8).

During the early 1900s, some estimated that a Black American "in the South was hanged or burned alive every four days" (Lepore, 2018, p. 369). Lynching had become so normalized that incidents were written in newspapers like sporting events (Cowie, 2022). The terrorism of lynching Black Americans continued well into the mid-20th century.

> ### Activity 6.11 – Digging Deeper: Emmett Till
>
> In 1955, 14-year-old Emmett Till was lynched in Mississippi for allegedly committing the crime of flirting with a White woman. When one of Emmett Till's murderers was brought to trial, the White jury found him not guilty after 30 minutes of deliberation. Emmett Till and his family never received justice. It took the United States government 67 years after Emmett Till was murdered to pass federal anti-lynching legislation.
>
> According to Kendi (2016), between 1979 and 1982, 28 young Black Americans were lynched in Atlanta. In 1980 alone, 12 Black Americans were lynched in the state of Mississippi.
>
> On March 29, 2022, President Joe Biden signed the Emmett Till Antilynching Act, which made lynching a federal hate crime. The Emmett Till Antilynching Act was the result of over 200 efforts by lawmakers to make lynching a federal crime.
>
> **Discussion Questions**
>
> - How did the murder of Emmett Till influence the Civil Rights Movement in the United States?
> - How does the Emmett Till Antilynching Act of 2022 address historical injustices?
> - Compare the public and legal responses to Emmett Till's lynching in 1955 with the responses to racially motivated violence in recent years. What has changed, and what has remained the same?
> - How does the signing of the Emmett Till Antilynching Act by President Joe Biden signify progress in addressing hate crimes in the United States?

Jim Crow Laws

Jim Crow laws, enacted in the late 19th and early 20th centuries, institutionalized racial segregation and discrimination across the American South. These laws, named after a derogatory minstrel character, mandated the separation of Black people from White people in public spaces, including schools, transportation, and housing. The Jim Crow era was characterized by a systematic effort to enforce racial hierarchy and disenfranchise Black citizens through legal means. This legislative framework not only perpetuated racial inequality but also entrenched social and economic disadvantages for Black citizens, creating a pervasive environment of inequality in the United States. Understanding the origins, impacts, and resistance to Jim Crow laws is crucial for comprehending the broader struggle for civil rights and social justice in the United States history.

RACE, RACISM, AND BEING BLACK IN THE UNITED STATES | 115

The Great Migration

In the 1900s, life had become increasingly difficult and dangerous for Black Southerners. The oppressive conditions and constant threats of violence, including lynching and discriminatory practices, created an unbearable and hostile environment. In response, many Black Americans embarked on a mass exodus known as the Great Migration. This movement, which started in the early 1900s and continued until the late 1960s, saw millions of Black Americans leave the South in search of greater opportunities and safer living conditions in the North and West. Before it began, only 10% of Black Americans lived outside of the South. By the end of the Great Migration, 37% of Black Americans had left the South (Wilkerson, 2023).

There were two waves of the Great Migration. The first wave started in 1910. "Between 1910 and 1920, 300,000 left; over the next ten years, 1.3 million; in the 1930s, 1.5 million left; and in the 1940s, 2.5 million" (Horowitz & Theoharis, 2021, p. 16). The second wave of the Great Migration occurred between 1940 and 1945 (Horowitz & Theoharis, 2021). Both waves were influenced by war and industrialization; however, at its core, the Great Migration was about the safety of millions of Black people. The Great Migration was a pivotal moment in American history, reflecting a profound quest for freedom and equality amidst the harsh realities of Jim Crow-era America (Wilkerson, 2023).

Activity 6.12 – The Great Migration

Video: The Great Migration: Crash Course in Black American History #24 (https://www.youtube.com/watch?v=Woh63FlFDBk)

One or more interactive elements has been excluded from this version of the text. You can view them online here: https://milnepublishing.geneseo.edu/social-justice-in-human-services/?p=369#oembed-10 (#oembed-10)

Video: The Great Migration and the Power of a Single Decision (https://www.youtube.com/watch?v=n3qA8DNc2Ss)

One or more interactive elements has been excluded from this version of the text. You can view them online here: https://milnepublishing.geneseo.edu/social-justice-in-human-services/?p=369#oembed-11 (#oembed-11)

Discussion Questions

- What were the primary factors that made life increasingly difficult and dangerous for Black Southerners in the early 1900s?
- What were some of the significant social, economic, and cultural impacts of the Great

> Migration on the regions Black Americans moved from?
> - What were some of the significant social, economic, and cultural impacts of the Great Migration on the regions Black Americans moved to?
> - How does the Great Migration continue to influence contemporary issues of race, migration, and urban development in the United States?

Collective Activism and Social Change

The National Association for the Advancement of Colored People

In 1908 in Springfield, Illinois, a mob of over 5,000 White citizens violently attacked Black neighborhoods in attempts to seek out and lynch two Black men, one accused of murder and the other rape. At least 17 people died, Black property and businesses were targeted and destroyed, and the state militia was called in. In the aftermath of few legal repercussions and fleeing Black citizens, it was clear that action and organization were necessary. In 1909, the National Association for the Advancement of Colored People (NAACP) was founded by White journalists and social reformers in response to the Springfield Riot. The organization was established to advance civil rights and combat racial discrimination through legal challenges and advocacy. Over time, it became a leading force in the fight for racial justice, playing a crucial role in pivotal civil rights milestones and shaping national policy (Horowitz & Theoharis, 2021; Richardson, 2023). Initially, W. E. B. Du Bois was the only Black officer in the organization, but his presence drew more Black leaders and activists to the NAACP. By 1919, the NAACP had grown to include approximately 100,000 members. By the 1920s and 1930s, the organization had a diverse leadership and membership, reflecting broad engagement from the Black community (Horowitz & Theoharis, 2021).

The NAACP forced attention on what was happening to Black Americans that would otherwise have gone unnoticed by the majority of White Americans. "The NAACP had long focused on challenging racial inequality by calling popular attention to racial atrocities and demanding that officials enforce laws already on the books" (Richardson, 2023, pp. 14-15). In 1940, attorney Thurgood Marshall founded the NAACP Legal Defense and Educational Fund (Richardson, 2023). During the 1940s, the NAACP Legal Defense and Educational Fund sponsored many lawsuits that rose through the legal system to the United States Supreme Court. Some of those lawsuits, *Smith v. Allwright* (1944), *Morgan v. Virginia* (1946), and *Shelley v. Kraemer* (1948), were wins for Black Americans (Horowitz & Theoharis, 2021). These victories advanced civil rights and laid the groundwork for the landmark cases of the 1950s and 1960s, further dismantling legalized segregation and discrimination in the United States.

Activity 6.13 – Digging Deeper: The Springfield Race Riots

Video: The Springfield Race Riots (https://www.youtube.com/watch?v=As8WbSGKpcM)

One or more interactive elements has been excluded from this version of the text. You can view them online here: https://milnepublishing.geneseo.edu/social-justice-in-human-services/?p=369#oembed-12 (#oembed-12)

Discussion Questions

- What were the underlying social, economic, and political factors that contributed to the Springfield Race Riot?
- How did the riot impact the perception of racial violence in Northern states compared to the South?
- In what ways did the riot contribute to the formation of the NAACP, and what were the organization's initial goals?
- What do you think of the actions in current-day Springfield, Illinois, to acknowledge the Springfield Race Riots? Is it enough? Why or why not?

World War II

The poet Langston Hughes wrote in his poem, *Beaumont to Detroit: 1943:*

>You tell me that hitler
>Is a mighty bad man.
>I guess he took lessons
>From the ku klux klan
>(As cited in Nordell, 2021, p. 21)

During World War II, approximately one million African Americans served in the United States military, despite the segregation and discrimination they faced both within the armed forces and on the home front. Black soldiers were often relegated to non-combat roles such as cooks, laborers, and drivers, but many also distinguished themselves in battle. Though they fought for democracy abroad, Black servicemen were denied fundamental rights at home, highlighting the hypocrisy of segregation. Their participation in the war contributed to the growing momentum of the Civil Rights Movement, as many returned determined to challenge the racial injustices they had endured. The experience of African Americans in World War II laid the foundation for increased activism and the eventual desegregation of the military in 1948 (Hine et al., 2010).

Enlistment in World War II

During World War II, many Black men showed reluctance to enlist. Consequently, in the early 1940s, the United States government took an interest for the first time in the perspectives of Black Americans regarding race (Nordell, 2021). The refusal of Black Americans to participate in the war effort highlighted the glaring contradictions between America's democratic ideals and the reality of racial injustice. "Racism ...undermined the legitimacy of the fight. Black Americans were being asked to crush the Nazi ideology of racial supremacy on behalf of a country whose racism enforced their own second-class citizenship" (Nordell, 2021, p. 20). As a result, the government realized that addressing these grievances was crucial to maintaining a robust military force and upholding national unity. This period marked a critical moment in civil rights history, underscoring the interconnectedness of domestic policies and racial justice.

In 1942 and again in 1944, the Office of War Information commissioned surveys of thousands of Black and White Americans about their racial beliefs (Nordell, 2021). The results of the two surveys demonstrated that "racism...flourished in the minds of individual White Americans" (Nordell, 2021, p. 21). The results further showed that "Black Americans are deeply devoted to American ideals, asking only that these ideals be realized in relation to themselves" (Nordell, 2021, p. 21).

Post-World War II

After World War II, violence against Black Americans again rose in the South (Horowitz & Theoharis, 2021). In February of 1946, Isaac Woodard, a Black soldier who had served in World War II, was brutally attacked by a police officer in South Carolina. Woodard had been riding a public bus when he was arrested. The police officer "beat him, plunging a billy club into each of his eyes" (Richardson, 2023, p. 18). The attack left Woodard permanently blind. The South Carolina justice system refused to charge the officer. The NAACP immediately got involved and eventually met with President Harry S. Truman to discuss the case (Richardson, 2023).

Under Truman's directive, the Department of Justice investigated Woodard's case, and within a week, a federal district court indicted the police officer (Richardson, 2023). Truman later stated, "When a Mayor and City Marshal can take a...Sergeant off a bus in South Carolina, beat him up and put out...his eyes, and nothing is done about it by the State authorities, something is radically wrong with the system" (Richardson, 2023, p. 18). However, an all-White jury acquitted the police officer, who claimed self-defense, after deliberating for only a half hour. Those present in the courtroom applauded the decision (Richardson, 2023).

In response to increasing violence in the South, representatives from 46 civil rights, religious, and labor organizations formed the National Emergency Committee Against Mob

Violence (NECMV). In 1946, leaders of the NECMV met with President Truman to ask for federal intervention in Southern violence against Black Americans (Horowitz & Theoharis, 2021). After the NECMV leaders described the severity of the violence in the South, "Truman rose from his chair and said, 'My God! I had no idea that it was as terrible as that! We've got to do something!'" (As cited in Horowitz & Theoharis, 2021, p. 32). In response, Truman created the President's Committee on Civil Rights to investigate racial violence (Horowitz & Theoharis, 2021).

In 1947, the NAACP submitted a landmark petition to the United Nations Human Rights Commission on behalf of Black Americans. Titled *An Appeal to the World*, the petition sought to highlight the systemic racial discrimination and violations of human rights Black Americans faced in the United States. By appealing to an international body, the NAACP sought to draw global attention to the injustices occurring under Jim Crow laws and to pressure the United States government to address these inequalities. This petition marked a significant moment in the civil rights struggle, as it framed the fight for racial equality in America as not just a national issue, but a matter of global human rights (Horowitz & Theoharis, 2021).

Later that same year, the President's Committee on Civil Rights released its findings and recommendations, which "codified the demands of the then Civil Rights movement and gave them presidential approval" (Horowitz & Theoharis, 2021, p. 34). For the first time, a United States President sent Congress a message about the importance of civil rights for all Americans.

Despite these actions, by the 1950s, Black Americans in the South continued to face widespread oppression on economic, political, and personal levels. This oppressive system sparked a climate of protest and collective strength among Black Americans, particularly in urban areas of the South (Horowitz & Theoharis, 2021). As tensions grew, the South was once again primed for violence.

The Civil Rights Movement

Most historians mark the Civil Rights Movement as beginning in the 1950s and ending in the 1970s. Many Black Americans tirelessly advocated for their civil rights during this period, and prominent figures such as Rosa Parks and Dr. Martin Luther King Jr. emerged as national icons. Countless Black Americans fought for their rights, facing racism and violence. The brutal murder of 14-year-old Emmett Till was a particularly galvanizing event, inciting widespread outrage among Black Americans. The lack of consequences for Till's murderer and the denial of justice for his family intensified this fury, fueling mass demonstrations across the United States (Richardson, 2023).

Nonviolence

During the Civil Rights Movement, many Black-led activist groups practiced nonviolence. The idea of nonviolence was often misinterpreted and, at times, mocked. This nonviolent stance, frequently attributed to Dr. Martin Luther King Jr., was influenced by one of his close advisors, Bayard Rustin (Eig, 2023). Dr. King believed nonviolence was "an alternative to wanton violence; …It was active resistance to evil… It attacked an evil system, not the evildoers themselves" (Horowitz & Theoharis, 2021, p. 301).

In his Letter from Birmingham Jail, Dr. King wrote, "In any nonviolent campaign there are four basic steps: collection of the facts to determine whether injustices are alive, negotiation, self-purification, and direct action" (King, 1963). Many civil rights organizations, such as the Congress of Racial Equality (CORE), the Student Nonviolent Coordinating Committee (SNCC), and the Southern Christian Leadership Council (SCLC), engaged in nonviolent strategies—including boycotts, sit-ins, and freedom rides (Lepore, 2018).

Activity 6.14 – The Medical Committee for Human Rights

Video – The Medical Committee for Human Rights (https://www.youtube.com/watch?v=9AWpRLQ0RXo)

One or more interactive elements has been excluded from this version of the text. You can view them online here: https://milnepublishing.geneseo.edu/social-justice-in-human-services/?p=369#oembed-13 (#oembed-13)

Another nonviolent organization established during the Civil Rights Movement was the Medical Committee for Human Rights (MCHR). Comprised of medical professionals who believed the United States healthcare system was "racist, unjust, and inadequate," members of this group provided medical care to frontline activists and protestors (Horowitz & Theoharis, 2021, p. 275).

Discussion Questions

- How did the establishment of MCHR contribute to the Civil Rights Movement?
- In what ways did the organization's mission to address the "racist, unjust, and inadequate" healthcare system impact frontline activists and protestors?
- In what ways can the mission and efforts of the MCHR during the Civil Rights Movement inform current efforts to address disparities in today's healthcare system? How can medical professionals continue to support social justice and provide care to activists and marginalized communities in contemporary movements?

Montgomery Bus Boycott

There is a long history of Black Americans protesting their treatment on public transportation in the United States. For example, in 1900 in Montgomery, Alabama, Black Americans "conducted a two-year boycott of the city's streetcars" due to the abusive treatment they received (Horowitz & Theoharis, 2021, p. 55). However, even with boycotts and protests in the 1950s, Black Americans continued to face abuse on the public bus transportation system across the South (Horowitz & Theoharis, 2021). "Buses in the South were rolling theaters of degradation, with daily drama acted out for all to see" (Eig, 2023, p. 129). This was especially true in Montgomery, Alabama (Eig, 2023).

In 1955, 62 buses traveled 14 routes, many segregated by race, and carried over 60,000 people in Montgomery, Alabama (Horowitz & Theoharis, 2021). The first 10 rows of each bus were reserved for White people, even if no White people were onboard (Eig, 2023). The last 10 rows of each bus were reserved for Black people, even when there were more Black riders than seats (Horowitz & Theoharis, 2021). "Additionally, Black passengers were required to buy their tickets at the front and then disembark and board the bus through the rear door. Frequently drivers would speed away leaving the Black passenger who had paid standing on the street" (Horowitz & Theoharis, 2021, p. 54).

In Montgomery, numerous incidents of violence against Black Americans occurred on buses. "Of all the nightmares of living under segregation in Montgomery, riding the buses was perhaps the most vivid and widely shared" (Eig, 2023, p. 130). Black people were tired of the chronic abuse. On December 1, 1955, Rosa Parks, a longtime member of the NAACP, left her job and boarded her regular bus (Horowitz & Theoharis, 2021). The seats on the bus reserved for White people were full when a White man boarded the bus. The driver instructed four Black people, including Parks, to empty the row for the White man because "the law did not permit Blacks and whites to occupy separate seats in the same row" (Horowitz & Theoharis, 2021, p. 63). Three Black people moved, but Parks, who was in the aisle seat, refused to do so. The bus driver called the police, and Parks was arrested.

The day after Parks was arrested, on December 2, a brand-new, 26-year-old local church minister was drafted to lead a protest of Parks' arrest (Lepore, 2018). That minister was Dr. Martin Luther King Jr. "Parks had been arrested on a Thursday; by Monday, 90 percent of the city's Blacks were boycotting the buses. Over 381 days, Blacks in Montgomery, led by Parks and Dr. King, boycotted the city's buses" (Lepore, 2018, p. 584). The Montgomery Bus Boycott only ended after the United States Supreme Court ruled that segregation on intrastate transportation was against the law (Eig, 2023).

Dr. King and other local Black leaders led the Montgomery Bus Boycott. However, it was sustained by the thousands of Black Americans who refused to ride a bus at significant cost to themselves (Eig, 2023). Additionally, the Montgomery "bus boycott caused collateral damage. Rosa Parks lost her department store job five months after her fateful bus ride. Her husband, a barber at Maxwell Air Force Base, lost his position soon afterward" (Eig, 2023, p. 172).

Rosa Parks being fingerprinted on February 22, 1956, by Lieutenant D.H. Lackey as one of the people indicted as leaders of the Montgomery bus boycott. She was one of 73 people rounded up by deputies that day after a grand jury charged 113 African Americans for organizing the boycott. This was a few months after her arrest on December 1, 1955, for refusing to give up her seat to a white passenger on a segregated municipal bus in Montgomery, Alabama.

However, the bus boycott also created "a new state of mind, a new sense of power" for many Black Americans (Eig, 2023, p. 173). It also gave the Civil Rights Movement and all Americans Dr. Martin Luther King Jr.

Sit-In Movement

But young Black Americans were tired of waiting for the older establishment and the United States government to move forward on civil rights. "With no national organization backing them, with no national leader speaking for them, with no overarching set of demands, a new grassroots movement began, aimed at one of the most glaring symbols of segregation, the humble lunch counter" (Eig, 2023, p. 220). In two years, from 1960 to 1962, lunch counter sit-ins occurred in more than 100 Southern cities in the United States, with over 7,000 arrests (Horowitz & Theoharis, 2021).

During this period, on February 1, 1960, four Black college freshmen, Ezell Blair Jr., David Richmond, Franklin McCain, and Joseph McNeil, nonviolently declined to give up their seats at a Woolworth's lunch counter in Greensboro, North Carolina. They attracted national media attention and started a student revolution. The following week, 400 more young college students joined the lunch counter sit-ins in Greensboro. Soon after, sit-ins occurred in Arkansas, Georgia, Texas, and West Virginia. In March 1960, sit-ins occurred in 40 more cities, with thousands of college students participating (Lepore, 2018).

Activity 6.15 – Digging Deeper: Sit-Ins

Video: Reflections on the Greensboro Lunch Counter (https://www.youtube.com/watch?v=uFQ3ZCAgAA0)

One or more interactive elements has been excluded from this version of the text. You can view them online here: https://milnepublishing.geneseo.edu/social-justice-in-human-services/?p=369#oembed-14 (#oembed-14)

Discussion Questions

- How did the Greensboro sit-ins fit into the broader strategy and goals of the Civil Rights Movement?
- How do the tactics used in the Greensboro sit-ins compare to those used in contemporary social justice movements, such as Black Lives Matter?
- In what ways can the principles and tactics of the Greensboro sit-ins be applied to current efforts to combat racial and social injustice?

Freedom Riders

In May of 1961, the Congress of Racial Equality (CORE) decided to test the progress of desegregation in the South, specifically in interstate transit (Lepore, 2018). Thirteen Black and White men and women volunteered to ride two commercial buses from Washington, D.C., to New Orleans (Gage, 2023). The riders, mostly young college students, became known as the Freedom Riders. Two weeks before the Freedom Ride's start date, "CORE sent letters to the FBI, the Justice Department, and the White House outlining the Freedom Riders itinerary and asking for federal protection" (Gage, 2023, p. 499). CORE did not receive a reply (Gage, 2023). The two commercial buses left Washington, D.C. on May 4, 1961. On May 13, in Anniston, Alabama, "a white mob attacked the Greyhound bus on which one group of the Freedom Riders had been riding, shattering the windows, slashing the tires, and, finally, burning it" (Lepore, 2018, p. 605). The second bus, which had fallen behind, was attacked by the KKK when it arrived in Birmingham, Alabama (Lepore, 2018). The attack lasted "a full fifteen minutes during which the unarmed passengers…were beaten, kicked, and punched, sometimes by half a dozen men at a time" (Gage, 2023, p. 503). Birmingham police failed to intervene promptly (Gage, 2023).

Two days later, CORE continued its test with new volunteers (Gage, 2023; Lepore, 2018). Attorney General Robert Kennedy pressured the governor of Alabama to provide a police escort for the Freedom Riders during their journey from Birmingham to Montgomery (Lepore, 2018). The new group of Freedom Riders only made it to Montgomery before they were attacked. The police in Montgomery "held back for several minutes before even attempting to intervene" (Gage, 2023, p. 505).

The following night, the Freedom Riders and over 1,000 Black Montgomery residents gathered at the First Baptist Church in Montgomery, Alabama (Gage, 2023; Lepore, 2018). In response, more than 2,000 White Montgomery residents, armed with torches, rocks, and chains, surrounded the church, threatening to burn it down and attack anyone who tried to flee (Gage, 2023). The situation escalated until the Alabama National Guard intervened, dispersing the mob (Lepore, 2018).

Not only did the original Freedom Riders continue their ride, but other Freedom Rides also formed across the United States (Harriot, 2023). "The racist opposition to the simple act of sitting down on a bus had become a national story. All across the country, people…boarded buses, sat down in segregated restaurants, protested injustice, and developed a multicultural coalition" (Harriot, 2023, p. 296). The Freedom Riders' pain and suffering, which had been exposed to the American public by the media, resulted in the Interstate Commerce Commission banning segregation in all interstate transit facilities (Gage, 2023).

Activity 6.16 – Freedom Riders

Video: Who Were the Freedom Riders? | The Civil Rights Movement (https://www.youtube.com/watch?v=E1smGpGSa14)

One or more interactive elements has been excluded from this version of the text. You can view them online here: https://milnepublishing.geneseo.edu/social-justice-in-human-services/?p=369#oembed-15 (#oembed-15)

Video: "Who the Hell is Diane Nash?" From Freedom Riders (https://www.youtube.com/watch?v=GIffL6KplzQ)

One or more interactive elements has been excluded from this version of the text. You can view them online here: https://milnepublishing.geneseo.edu/social-justice-in-human-services/?p=369#oembed-16 (#oembed-16)

Discussion Questions

- What were the goals and strategies of the Freedom Riders, and how did they differ from other civil rights tactics of the time?
- What were the immediate and long-term effects of the Freedom Rides on the Civil Rights Movement and the broader struggle for racial equality in the United States?
- What lessons can be learned from the Freedom Rides about the power of nonviolent resistance, grassroots organizing, and collective action in effecting social change?

March on Washington for Jobs and Freedom

In August 1963, Bayard Rustin organized the March on Washington for Jobs and Freedom to celebrate the 100th anniversary of the *Emancipation Proclamation* (Lepore, 2018). Approximately 300,000 people arrived at the Lincoln Memorial. The speeches were televised, and Americans across the country heard Dr. Martin Luther King Jr. speak for the first time. Dr. King delivered his renowned and powerful "I Have a Dream" speech at this historic event.

Activity 6.17 – "I Have a Dream"

Video: Martin Luther King I Have A Dream Speech (https://youtu.be/AUv2EIrAhv4)

 One or more interactive elements has been excluded from this version of the text. You can view them online here: https://milnepublishing.geneseo.edu/social-justice-in-human-services/?p=369#oembed-17 (#oembed-17)

Discussion Questions

- What is the significance of the "I Have a Dream" speech in the context of American history?
- How does Dr. Martin Luther King Jr.'s "I Have a Dream" speech resonate with current social justice movements?
- In what ways do you think the message of the "I Have a Dream" speech is relevant today?

Freedom Summer

In 1964, activists took on voter rights in the state of Mississippi. Mississippi was one of the most segregated states in the South, with regular, systemic violence against Black Americans. In addition, only 6% of Black Americans in the state of Mississippi were registered to vote. The primary goal of Freedom Summer was to send volunteers to register as many Black Americans to vote as possible. Over 1,000 predominantly young, White college students and activists from across the United States volunteered for Freedom Summer, working alongside local African American activists and community members (Richardson, 2023).

SNCC sent three civil rights activists, James Chaney (Black, age 21), Michael Schwerner (White, age 24), and Andrew Goodman (White, age 20), to participate in Freedom Summer. On June 21, Chaney, Schwerner, and Goodman disappeared (Richardson, 2023). President Johnson and Attorney General Kennedy asked the FBI to investigate their disappearance. On August 4, 1964, three months after their disappearance, the bodies of Chaney, Schwerner, and Goodman were discovered. Ku Klux Klan members had murdered them. A total of six civil rights activists, including Chaney, Schwerner, and Goodman, were killed that summer. "Thirty-five more would be shot, eighty would be beaten, and more than a thousand would be arrested" during Freedom Summer (Harriott, 2023, p. 297).

Bloody Sunday

During the early 1960s, SNCC was embroiled in the fight for Black Americans' right to vote in Selma, Alabama. The White Citizens' Council dominated politics in Selma, and only 0.9% of Black people eligible to vote were registered (Horowitz & Theoharis, 2021). On September 25, 1964, SNCC Chairman John Lewis led a picket line to protest that Black people in Selma had the right to vote. Lewis and 25 other picketers were arrested and sentenced to 100 days in jail (Horowitz & Theoharis, 2021).

On October 7, 1964, SNCC organized Freedom Day to assist Black people in registering to vote. While providing food and water to 200 Black Americans waiting in line to vote, SNCC members were arrested and beaten by Selma police (Horowitz & Theoharis, 2021). By November 1964, SCLC had joined SNCC to secure voting rights for Black Americans in Selma (Horowitz & Theoharis, 2021).

In January of 1965, Dr. Martin Luther King Jr. announced SCLC's campaign to support voter registration in Selma, Alabama (Horowitz & Theoharis, 2021). On February 1, 1965, Dr. King led a group of nonviolent protesters to the courthouse in Selma. Dr. King, along with 700 of those protesters, was arrested (Horowitz & Theoharis, 2021). Although the protest ended with an arrest, Dr. King and SCLC brought national attention to Selma as racial tensions continued to rise in the state of Alabama.

On February 10, 1965, Selma police officers riding horses "used cattle prods to drive 165 protestors into the country on a forced march at top speed" (Horowitz & Theoharis, 2021, p. 282). Local Black people, exhausted and terrified, were ready for a truce if they were allowed to register to vote. However, SCLC and Dr. King were unwilling to concede, as their goal was to achieve change on a federal level, using Selma as an example (Horowitz & Theoharis, 2021).

On February 18, 1965, during a night march to the courthouse, Jimmie Lee Jackson attempted to protect his mother from being beaten by an Alabama State Trooper. The

Alabama State Trooper shot the unarmed Jimmie Lee Jackson; he died from his wounds on February 26, 1965 (Lepore, 2018). To "defuse the community's anger, Black leaders in Selma planned a march" (Richardson, 2023, p. 37). On March 7, 1965, in memory of Jimmie Lee Jackson, 600 protestors attempted to march from Selma to the Alabama Capitol building in Montgomery (Horowitz & Theoharis, 2021). As the protestors crossed the Edmund Pettus Bridge, they were met by over 500 law enforcement officers (Lepore, 2018). The police ordered the protestors to disperse, but they did not.

Alabama State Trooper Major John Cloud ordered his officers to advance, using their billy clubs and tear gas, on the protestors. John Lewis' skull was fractured, and voting rights leader Amanda Boynton was beaten unconscious (Richardson, 2023). Another 80 people were injured, with an additional 17 people sent to the hospital. Video evidence of police brutality was televised across the United States (Horowitz & Theoharis, 2021; Richardson, 2023). This day would later be dubbed Bloody Sunday.

On March 9, Dr. Martin Luther King Jr led 2,000 protesters on the same march they had attempted two days earlier (Lepore, 2018). Once again, the protesters were met by Alabama State Troopers and a United States Marshall, who read a court order mandating that the march end. Dr. King agreed to stop the march (Horowitz & Theoharis, 2021).

Activity 6.18 – Marches

Video: John Lewis: The Selma to Montgomery Marches (https://www.youtube.com/watch?v=DRwnXUbJdfg)

One or more interactive elements has been excluded from this version of the text. You can view them online here: https://milnepublishing.geneseo.edu/social-justice-in-human-services/?p=369#oembed-18 (#oembed-18)

Video: Rare Video Footage of Historic Alabama 1965 Civil Rights Marches, MLK's Famous Montgomery Speech (https://www.youtube.com/watch?v=CBm48Scju9E)

One or more interactive elements has been excluded from this version of the text. You can view them online here: https://milnepublishing.geneseo.edu/social-justice-in-human-services/?p=369#oembed-19 (#oembed-19)

Discussion Questions

- How did the fight for voting rights in Selma fit into the larger context of the Civil Rights Movement of the 1960s?
- What role did the Edmund Pettus Bridge play in the confrontation, and why was it a significant symbol in the Civil Rights Movement?
- What parallels can be drawn between the struggles for voting rights and racial justice

> in the 1960s and contemporary efforts to combat voter suppression and systemic racism?

On March 15, 1965, in a speech to the United States Congress, President Lyndon Johnson addressed the violence in Selma and the ongoing racism that denied Black Americans voting access. He denounced the ongoing racial violence and urged Congress to pass voting rights legislation to protect all Americans' right to vote. Finally, on March 25, 1965, accompanied by "nineteen hundred Alabama National Guardsmen, two thousand army personnel, and US marshals" 300 people marched from Selma to Montgomery. Twenty-five thousand people were at the Montgomery Capitol building to hear Rosa Parks, Dr. Martin Luther King Jr., and others speak. Congress passed the *Voting Rights Act* on August 6, 1965 (Horowitz & Theoharis, 2021).

Activity 6.19 – The American Promise

Video: Special Message to the Congress: The American Promise (https://www.youtube.com/watch?v=5NvPhiuGZ6I)

 One or more interactive elements has been excluded from this version of the text. You can view them online here: https://milnepublishing.geneseo.edu/social-justice-in-human-services/?p=369#oembed-20 (#oembed-20)

Discussion Questions

- What are the main points of President Lyndon B. Johnson's speech on the American promise?
- How effective was the speech in persuading lawmakers to pass the Voting Rights Act? What about the general public?
- What is the significance of the term "American promise" in the context of Johnson's speech and the Voting Rights Act?
- How does the video connect the achievements of the Voting Rights Act to current discussions about voting rights and electoral reforms? Are there parallels between the issues addressed in 1965 and those happening today?

Black Power

Not everyone in the Civil Rights Movement agreed with the stance of nonviolence advocated by Dr. Martin Luther King Jr. By 1962, many Black Americans "called for armed self-defense" (Lepore, 2018, p. 607). In the mid-1960s, some SNCC leaders became increasingly frustrated with Dr. Martin Luther King Jr. and SCLC (Horowitz & Theoharis, 2021). These young Black activists believed that the Civil Rights Movement's focus should shift from established political strategies and coalitions toward creating Black power for Black people (Harriott, 2023). One of these activists was Stokely Carmichael.

Stokely Carmichael became disillusioned after witnessing the brutalization of peaceful protesters in the Southern states. He is credited with first using the phrase "Black Power" and creating the Black Panther mascot (Harriott, 2023). During his time in Alabama helping Black people register to vote, Carmichael organized the Lowndes County Freedom Party (LCFP), which became the Black Panther Party in 1965 (Horowitz & Theoharis, 2021). Carmichael, who eventually served as SNCC chairman in 1966, defined Black Power as "a call for black people in this country to unite, to recognize their heritage, to build a sense of community" (Horowitz & Theoharis, 2021, p. 299). In 1966, SNCC "officially voted to expel its white staff members" (Horowitz & Theoharis, 2021, p. 308).

Lowndes County Freedom Organization flyer. Alabama original Black Panther party 1966.

Laws During the Civil Rights Movement

Brown v. Board of Education[2]

Segregation based on race had long existed in the United States. However, in the post-Reconstruction decades, segregation was the primary tool of oppression and White supremacy in the United States (Eig, 2023). The landmark United States Supreme Court case, *Brown v. Board of Education* in 1954, challenged the constitutionality of racial segregation in public schools, declaring that "separate but equal" facilities were inherently unequal. Despite the monumental nature of the *Brown v. Board* of Education decision, the ruling also highlighted the limitations of the federal government in fully addressing segregation. Although this legislation technically ended segregation, the United States Supreme Court's decision in *Brown v. Board of Education* did not provide a means of enforcing desegregation. Segregation in public spaces continues to be a conversation, even in current times (Cowie, 2022).

Civil Rights Act

President Lyndon Johnson was not a perfect president, but during his time in office he did more for civil rights than any other president. A Texan, Johnson was sworn into the office of the President of the United States after the assassination of President John F. Kennedy. He was determined to make civil rights a reality for all Americans (Lepore, 2018).

On July 2, 1964, Johnson signed the Civil Rights Act, which "outlawed discrimination based on race, color, religion, sex, or national origin; gave the attorney general power to enforce desegregation; allowed for civil rights cases to move from state to federal courts; and expanded the Civil Rights Commission" (Lepore, 2018, p. 612). It passed with a bipartisan vote in both the Senate and the House (Richardson, 2023).

Post-Civil Rights Movement

In 1968, the Southern strategy emerged as a political approach used by the Republican Party to gain support from White voters in the South. This strategy involved appealing to racial anxieties and resistance to civil rights reforms, subtly signaling opposition to desegregation and promoting 'law and order' policies, which resonated with many White Southerners disaffected by the Democratic Party's support for civil rights. This strategy represented a shift in party positions on racial issues, with the Republican Party increasingly adopt-

---

[2]. Much has been written about the landmark United States Supreme Court decision in Brown v. Board of Education, including in other chapters of this text. For this section, the Brown case indicates the need for the federal government to enforce laws pertaining to civil rights.

ing conservative stances and the Democratic Party embracing more liberal views on race (Richardson, 2023). As a result, the two major political parties became more polarized, with conservatives aligning with the Republicans and liberals with the Democrats (Cowie, 2022). The first to use the Southern strategy on a national level, presidential candidate Richard M. Nixon became a permanent member of the Republican Party to win the votes of White Southerners (Richardson, 2023). As part of his Southern strategy, Nixon appealed to White supremacists by fanning their fears of Black Americans as well as "liberals, intellectuals, radicals, and defiant youngsters"(Richardson, 2023, p. 42). To do so, Nixon's political team created an image of bad Americans and "had an obvious foil not only in Black activism but also in the rise of the New Left in the 1960s" (Richardson, 2023, p. 42).

During the 1980 presidential election, Ronald Reagan "built upon the success of earlier conservatives who developed a strategy of exploiting racial hostility...without making explicit reference to race" (Alexander, 2020, p. 61). During his campaign, Reagan created the image of the welfare queen, which was a racist code "for lazy, greedy, black ghetto mother" (Alexander, 2020, p. 62). "The truth did not matter to the Reagan campaign as much as feeding the White backlash to Black Power" (Kendi, 2016, p. 424).

However, Reagan's "absence of explicitly racist rhetoric afforded the racial nature of his coded appeals a certain plausible deniability" (Alexander, 2020, p. 61). For example, when incumbent President Jimmy Carter accurately "called out racism in Reagan's states' rights speech, the press attacked him for being mean" to Reagan (Richardson, 2023, p. 52).

War on Black Americans

In 1982, President Ronald Reagan launched the War on Drugs, even though only 2% of Americans considered drug use to be the nation's most pressing issue at the time (Kendi, 2016). At the same time, many inner-city communities, often primarily Black, were in economic crisis. Industrial jobs had left urban cities, and technology had changed the jobs that were still available. Many Black Americans, especially men, struggled with unemployment (Alexander, 2020). As unemployment and economic turmoil deepened in Black urban communities, the emergence of crack cocaine provided a new target for media and political rhetoric.

By 1985, crack cocaine became the focus of racial stereotypes about Black Americans, as media coverage sensationalized the drug's impact on urban communities. News outlets and politicians repeatedly emphasized the presence of crack in these areas, reinforcing negative perceptions. The portrayal of crack use was often exaggerated, depicting Black neighborhoods as crime-ridden and dangerous, while framing Black Americans as inherently prone to drug abuse and violence. This narrative not only fueled public fear but also shaped punitive policies that disproportionately targeted Black communities (Alexander, 2020).

Regan signed one of these policies into law in 1986. Called the Anti-Drug Abuse Act, it mandated minimum sentences for selling cocaine and more severe penalties for anyone caught selling crack cocaine. In 1988, Reagan's administration increased the scope of the

Anti-Drug Abuse Act. This authorized government officials to evict public housing tenants engaged in any drug-related activity. Anyone convicted of a drug-related crime became ineligible for certain federal benefits, including financial aid for school. While the Anti-Drug Act claimed to address the growing drug crisis, its mandatory minimum sentences and harsh stance on benefits disproportionately impacted Black communities already struggling with an economic crisis and reinforced harmful stereotypes about Black urban communities (Alexander, 2020).

Rodney King Assault

In 1991, four White Los Angeles Police Department (LAPD) officers were caught on video "beating and tasering Rodney King, an unarmed Black man, while more than a dozen watched" (Nordell, 2021, p. 145). The following year, a California State Jury found the four White LAPD officers not guilty of excessive force and assault. The verdict sparked widespread outrage. After the decision was announced, uprisings erupted, leading to widespread destruction in Black, Hispanic, and Korean communities (Nordell, 2021). During the uprisings, which became known as the 1992 LA Uprising or 1992 Los Angeles Riots, more than 50 people died and over 2,000 were injured.

Activity 6.20 – "Uprising" Versus "Riot"

What's in a term? Many members of the Black community choose to use the term "uprisings" instead of "riots" to emphasize the community's response to systemic injustices rather than framing the events solely as criminal acts. Both terms are used, but "uprisings" reflect a broader understanding of the underlying causes related to racial inequality and police violence.

Discussion Questions

- How do the terms "uprising" and "riot" shape our understanding of historical events? What are the implications of using one term over the other?
- How do the media and political leaders' use of the terms "riot" or "uprising" influence public reactions and policy responses to civil unrest?
- Think about an example of civil unrest from history or recent events. How might the framing of the event as either a "riot" or an "uprising" affect its long-term legacy?

The 1992 LA Uprising highlighted the long-standing racial tensions and systemic racism within law enforcement that Black communities had endured for decades. It symbolized the deep-rooted inequality and lack of accountability that Black individuals and communities faced in the justice system. A post-uprising investigation found that in the aftermath of the Rodney King verdict LAPD officers used the code NHI (no humans involved) to refer "to calls from Black and other marginalized communities" (Nordell, 2021, p. 146). The uprisings were a collective outcry against the broader patterns of police violence and racial discrimination. They became a pivotal turning point in raising national awareness about police brutality, prompting ongoing discussions about racial justice and reform that continue to resonate today.

President Barack Obama

In 2008, Barack Obama was elected 44th President of the United States, making history as the first African American to hold the office. Obama's first campaign, energized by his message of hope and change, ran with the slogan, "Yes We Can." Obama's campaign inspired millions of new and young voters, and voter turnout surged to unprecedented levels. Obama won decisively, securing over 9 million more votes than his opponent, Senator John McCain—a remarkable victory reflecting the nation's desire for a new direction during economic crisis and disillusionment with traditional politics (Lepore, 2018).

Once elected, President Obama represented a lot of things to a lot of people. For many, he represented hope for change; for others, a chance for the United States to redeem itself; and for others, he was a Black man who had become the most powerful person in the world. For Black Americans, his election was particularly significant, marking a historic breakthrough in a country with a long history of slavery, segregation, and systemic racism. Obama's presidency symbolized the culmination of decades of civil rights struggles, offering a vision of progress that had once seemed unattainable. However, despite the hope his election inspired, Obama immediately found himself facing a wall of systemic racism. "On the night of Obama's inauguration, Republican leaders…agreed over dinner to oppose anything that the new president proposed, regardless of whether they agreed with it" (Richardson, 2023, p. 78). This opposition highlighted the persistent racial divisions in America and underscored the ongoing challenges Black leaders face, even at the highest levels of power.

Black Lives Matter

Black Lives Matter (BLM) is a decentralized social and political movement that advocates for Black people's rights, dignity, and equality. In 2013, three Black women, Alicia Garza, Patrisse Cullors, and Opal Tometi, started BLM in response to the acquittal of George Zimmerman, a neighborhood watch volunteer in Sanford, Florida, who fatally shot Trayvon Martin, an unarmed Black teenager. The movement seeks to address and dismantle systemic racism, mainly focusing on police brutality, racial profiling, and the disproportionate rates of violence against Black people. At its core, Black Lives Matter calls attention to the systemic inequalities embedded in the criminal justice system and beyond, while advocating for policy changes that promote racial justice and equality (Garza, 2014).

The slogan "Black Lives Matter" is a response to the devaluation of Black lives throughout American history. It asserts that Black human beings deserve the same protection and rights as others. BLM has since grown into a global movement, sparking protests and discussions about racial injustice in many parts of the world. The BLM movement used personal devices and social media to bring attention to Black Americans' daily experiences of racism (Lepore, 2018). By doing so, it "captured the experiences of young black men who for generations had been singled out by police, pulled over in cars, stopped on street corners, pushed, frisked, punched, kicked, and even killed" (Lepore, 2018, p. 767).

Activity 6.21 – Black Lives Matter

Video: 8 Years Strong (https://www.youtube.com/watch?v=WW8JlOcS19Q)

One or more interactive elements has been excluded from this version of the text. You can view them online here: https://milnepublishing.geneseo.edu/social-justice-in-human-services/?p=369#oembed-21 (#oembed-21)

Video: Now, We Transform (https://www.youtube.com/watch?v=Mv3XmmQOOao)

One or more interactive elements has been excluded from this version of the text. You can view them online here: https://milnepublishing.geneseo.edu/social-justice-in-human-services/?p=369#oembed-22 (#oembed-22)

Discussion Questions

- What key themes and messages about the Black Lives Matter movement are highlighted in the videos? How do these themes resonate with the movement's objectives?
- What roles do community organizing and grassroots activism play in the BLM movement, as portrayed in the videos? How does this compare to traditional forms of political engagement?
- What does the phrase "Black Lives Matter" signify to you, and how does it resonate within the broader context of social justice?
- How has the Black Lives Matter movement influenced conversations about race and racism in the United States and globally?

In 2014, the murder of 18-year-old Michael Brown by a White police officer in Ferguson, Missouri, marked a critical turning point in the ongoing struggle against police violence and systemic racism. Eyewitnesses recorded the events, capturing public attention and fueling widespread outrage. This incident, along with others where brutal attacks against Black

Americans were filmed, underscored a pattern. Officers involved in these killings were frequently being acquitted or exonerated in court and were not being held accountable for their racist actions (Lepore, 2018).

It was in the summer of 2020 that BLM became a national and international movement. On May 25, 2020, George Floyd, a Black American, was murdered by Minneapolis police officers (Richardson, 2023). George Floyd's murder, captured on video by someone in the crowd, "revealed a casual savagery so dehumanizing and horrific it shook the world" (Nordell, 2021, p. 5). Protests sprung up across the United States. Protesters in Minneapolis and other cities such as Los Angeles, Seattle, Portland, and New York chanted, "Black Lives Matter" (Richardson, 2023). In response, President Donald Trump tweeted, "When the looting starts, the shooting starts" (Richardson, 2023, p. 138).

Trump's blatantly racist stance, in combination with George Floyd's brutal murder, brought a new spotlight to systemic racism in the United States. In response, "a wave of leaders from the U.S. Air Force, Army, and Navy spoke up to call for justice for Black Americans" along with the four living former presidents, Barack Obama, Bill Clinton, George W. Bush, and Jimmy Carter, and numerous other former members of the Department of Justice, and Democratic lawmakers (Richardson, 2023, p. 139).

Activity 6.22 – Confederate Monuments

In 2020, following the murder of George Floyd, a significant wave of social justice activism led to the removal of 168 Confederate monuments across the United States. This action reflected a broader reckoning with the legacy of racism and White supremacy in American history, as communities sought to dismantle symbols that many viewed as oppressive and divisive (Jones, 2023).

In June 2021, a bill was introduced in the United States House of Representatives that aimed to remove statues commemorating Confederate leaders and figures associated with White supremacy from the United States Capitol. The proposed legislation sought to address the historical legacy of racism and ensure that America's Capitol reflects its values of equality and justice, in keeping with a growing national movement to reevaluate and dismantle symbols of oppression. One hundred and twenty Republican representatives opposed the bill; it died on the Senate floor. As of 2023, 2,100 Confederate symbols and over 700 Confederate monuments remain on United States public property (Jones, 2023).

Discussion Questions

- What do the presence of Confederate statues in public spaces symbolize in terms of American history and identity?
- How does the removal of these statues contribute to the ongoing conversation about

> racial justice and equality in the United States?
> - How do the recent actions surrounding Confederate monuments reflect changes in social attitudes toward race and history?
> - Should there be a process for determining which historical figures are commemorated in public spaces? If so, what criteria should be used?

Conclusion

In 1965, Malcolm X said, "White means free, boss" (as cited in Cowie, 2022, p. 411). He was right. Some people and lawmakers continue to prioritize states' rights over federal government power to uphold racist power structures. Although "mobs of people may not have directly stormed the voting booths and shot Black voters en masse as they had in 1874, American political power has been aggressively beaten back to the local, more controllable, level of the compound republic since the 1970s" (Cowie, 2022, p. 409).

Throughout the 20th century and into the present day, this legacy continues to shape social institutions, and racism in the United States continues to be insidious. "The racial bias of today, whether stealthy or overt" is a disease that rots the soul of each individual as well as the soul of the United States (Nordell, 2021, p. 7). While it may be tempting to assert that conditions for Black Americans in the United States have improved, it is neither appropriate nor possible for those outside of the Black community to judge or define their experiences fully. The complexities of systemic racism, coupled with the subjective nature of lived experiences, make it essential to approach such claims with humility and recognition of the ongoing challenges Black Americans continue to face.

In fact, many things have not gotten better for Black Americans. While explicit racial discrimination has been outlawed through civil rights legislation and progress has been made in certain areas, the structures built upon centuries of racial hierarchy remain. Disparities in wealth, healthcare, education, and criminal justice remain pervasive, and the Black community continues to bear the brunt of systemic inequalities that are deeply entrenched in American society. The enduring power of racism in the United States lies precisely in how thoroughly the concept of race was embedded into the nation's foundation. What began as an economic justification for slavery evolved into a comprehensive worldview that structured all aspects of American society. The persistence of racial violence, voter suppression efforts, and the disproportionate impact of mass incarceration serve as stark reminders that true "liberty and justice for all" is still far from realized. These inequities underscore the need for continued advocacy, systemic reform, and an honest reckoning with the history of racial injustice in the United States.

A highlighted memorial photo of Geraldine Talley, one of many killed at the 2022 Buffalo shooting, on the website sayevery.name

Chapter Summary Questions

1. What does it mean to say that race is a social construct? Provide examples that illustrate how this concept has been used to justify social hierarchies in U.S. history.
2. Describe one or more racial identity development models. How might these models help explain the experiences of Black individuals navigating predominantly white spaces?
3. How has anti-Black racism been maintained through laws, policies, and cultural narratives in the U.S.?
4. In what ways have events like slavery, Jim Crow laws, and redlining shaped the contemporary experiences of Black communities?
5. Reflect on the persistence of colorblind ideologies in the U.S. How might these ideologies hinder efforts toward racial justice?
6. How does intersectionality deepen our understanding of what it means to be Black in the United States?
7. What are the implications of acknowledging that U.S. systems (such as housing, education, or criminal justice) were built on and continue to reflect anti-Blackness? How might this recognition change how we pursue equity?
8. What is your understanding of your own racial identity? How does this shape the way you engage with the issues of anti-Black racism and social justice?

9. How can non-Black individuals serve as allies in dismantling systemic racism? What are some common missteps or challenges that might arise in this work?

Thoughts From the Author

Writing this chapter was one of the most challenging tasks I've undertaken. As someone who is not Black, I found it difficult even to begin, knowing the immense responsibility that came with addressing such a complex and painful subject. I am incredibly grateful to Dr. Golden for stepping in and taking the lead—her work on this chapter was invaluable, and she deserves full credit and more. The history of racism in this country is both staggering and deeply troubling, especially given the persistence of systemic racism in the United States today. Despite the weight of these issues, I found inspiration in learning about the voices advocating for change. Watching impactful videos and exploring narratives from Black authors and philosophers was eye-opening and enriching. The depth of my learning throughout this process was immense, and for that, I am truly grateful.

Sincerely,

Dr. DeJonge (Bernie)

References

Alexander, M. (2020). *The new Jim Crow: Mass incarceration in the age of colorblindness.* (10th-anniversary ed.). The New Press.

American Psychological Association (APA). (2023). *Racism, bias, and discrimination.* https://www.apa.org/topics/racism-bias-discrimination

Baptist, E. E. (2014). *The half that has never been told: Slavery and the making of American capitalism.* Basic Books.

Berlin, I. (1998). *Many thousands gone : The first two centuries of slavery in North America.* Harvard University Press.

Berry, D. W., & Gross, A. (2020). *A Black women's history of the United States.* University of Beacon Press.

Bonham, V. L. (2024, September 26). *Race*. National Human Genome Research Institute. https://www.genome.gov/genetics-glossary/Race

Brown, R. J. (2000). Social identity theory: Past achievements, current problems, and future challenges. *European Journal of Social Psychology, 30*(6), 745-778. https://doi.org/10.1002/1099-0992(200011/12)30:6%3C745::AID-EJSP24%3E3.0.CO;2-O

Burton, L. M., Bonilla-Silva, E., Ray, V., Buckelew, R., & Freeman, E. H. (2010). Critical race theories, colorism, and the decade's research on families of color. *Journal of Marriage and Family, 72*, 440-459. https://doi.org/10.1111/j.1741-3737.2010.00712.x

Carbado D. W., Crenshaw K. W., Mays V. M., Tomlinson B. (2013). Intersectionality: Mapping the movements of a theory. *Du Bois Review: Social Science Research on Race,10*(2), 303-312. https://doi.org/10.1017/s1742058x13000349

Coates, T. (2015). *Between the world and me*. One World.

Cowie, J. (2022). *Freedom's dominion: A saga of white resistance to federal power*. Basic Books.

Cross, W. E. (1991). *Shades of Black: Diversity in African American identity*. Temple University Press.

Davis, D. B. (2006). *Inhuman bondage : The rise and fall of slavery in the new world*. Oxford University Press, Inc.

Delgado, R., & Stefancic, J. (2017). *Critical race theory: An introduction* (3rd ed.). New York University Press.

DiAngelo, R. (2018). *White fragility: Why it's so hard for white people to talk about racism*. Beacon Press.

Du Bois, W. E. B. (1903). *The souls of black folk*. A. C. McClurg & Co.

Eig, J. (2023). *King: A life*. Farrar, Straus, and Giroux.

Ellemers, N., Spears, R., & Doosje, B. (2002). Self and social identity. *Annual Review of Psychology, 53*(1), 161-186. https://doi.org/10.1146/annurev.psych.53.100901.135228

Faderman, L. (2022). *Women: The American history of an idea*. Yale University Press.

Foner, E. (2014). *Reconstruction: America's unfinished revolution, 1863–1877*. Harper Perennial.

Gage, B. (2022). *G-Man: J. Edgar Hoover and the making of the American century*. Penguin Books.

Garza, A. (2014, October 7). *A herstory of the #BlackLivesMatter movement*. The Feminist Wire. https://thefeministwire.com/2014/10/blacklivesmatter-2/

Gingras, B. (2010). "Double consciousness" and the racial self in Zitkala-Ša's American Indian stories. *Undergraduate Review, 6*, 83-86.

Hamalainen, P. (2019). *Lakota America: A new history of Indigenous power*. Yale University Press.

Harriot, M. (2023). *Black AF history: The un-whitewashed story of America*. HarperCollins Books.

Helms, J. E. (1990). *Black and White racial identity: Theory, research, and practice*. Greenwood Press.

Herschthal, E. (2021). *The science of abolition: How slaveholders became the enemies of progress.* Yale University Press.

Hine, D. C., Hine, W. C., & Harrold, S. (2010). *African Americans: A concise history* (4th ed.). Prentice Hall.

Hogg, M. A., & Abrams, D. (1990). Social motivation, self-esteem, and social identity. *Social identity theory: Constructive and critical advances* (pp. 28-47). Springer-Verlag.

Horowitz, P., & Theoharis, J. (Eds.). (2021). *Julian Bond's time to teach: A history of the Southern Civil Rights movement.* Beacon Press.

Jones, R. P. (2023). *The hidden roots of white supremacy and the path to a shared American future.* Simon & Schuster.

Jost, J. T., & Banaji, M. R. (1994). The role of stereotyping in system-justification and the production of false consciousness. *British Journal of Social Psychology, 33*(1), 1-27. https://doi.org/10.1111/j.2044-8309.1994.tb01008.x

Kendi, I. X. (2016). *Stamped from the beginning: The definitive history of racist ideas in America.* Bold Type Books.

Lepore, J. (2018). *These truths: A history of the United States.* W. W. Norton & Company, Inc.

Levine, R.S. (2021). *The failed promise: Reconstruction, Frederick Douglass, and the impeachment of Andrew Johnson.* W. W. Norton & Company.

Lloyd, G. & Martinez, J. S. (n.d.). *The slave trade clause.* National Constitution Center. https://constitutioncenter.org/the-constitution/articles/article-i/clauses/761

Lynching. (2011.) In Merriam-Webster.com. Retrieved DATE HERE, from https://www.merriam-webster.com/dictionary/lynching

Mays, K. T. (2021). *An Afro-Indigenous history of the United States.* Beacon Press.

McLeod, S. (2023). *Social identity theory.* Simply Psychology. https://www.simplypsychology.org/social-identity-theory.html

McPherson, J. (2015). *The war that forged a nation: Why the Civil War still matters.* Oxford University Press.

Meadows-Fernandez, A. R. (2019). *Investigating institutional racism.* Enslow Publishing, LLC.

Mobley, T. (2021). *Ida B. Wells-Barnett: Anti-lynching and the White House.* The White House Historical Association.https://www.whitehousehistory.org/ida-b-wells-barnett-anti-lynching-and-the-white-house

Murray, W. & Hsieh, W. W. (2016). *A savage war: A military history of the Civil War.* Princeton University Press.

National Archives. (2022, January 28). The Emancipation Proclamation. In NationalArchives.gov online exhibit. Retrieved DATE HERE, from https://www.archives.gov/exhibits/featured-documents/emancipation-proclamation#:~:text=President%20Abraham%20Lincoln%20issued%20the,and%20henceforward%20shall%20be%20free.%22

Nordell, J. (2021). *The end of bias: A beginning: The science and practice of overcoming unconscious bias.* Metropolitan Books.

Phinney, J. S. (1992). The multigroup ethnic identity measure: A new scale for use with adolescents and young adults from diverse groups. *Journal of Adolescent Research, 7*(2), 156-176. https://doi.org/10.1177/074355489272003

Poston, W. S. (1990). The biracial identity development model: A needed addition. *Journal of Counseling & Development, 69*(2), 152-155. https://doi.org/10.1002/j.1556-6676.1990.tb01477.x

Project Ready. (2016). *Module 9: Racial and ethnic identity development.* Reimagining Equity and Access for Diverse Youth.https://ready.web.unc.edu/section-1-foundations/module-9-racial-and-ethnic-identity-development/

Reicher, S., & Haslam, S. A. (2006). Rethinking the psychology of tyranny: The BBC prison study. *British Journal of Social Psychology, 45*(1), 1-40.https://doi.org/10.1348/014466605X48998

Richardson, H.C. (2023). *Democracy awakening: Notes on the state of America.* Viking Press.

Robinson, C. (2022). *The American Colonization Society.* The White House Historical Association. https://www.whitehousehistory.org/the-american-colonization-society

Simon, Y. (2024, August 20). *Latino, Hispanic, Latinx, Chicano: The history behind the terms.* The History Channel. https://www.history.com/news/hispanic-latino-latinx-chicano-background

Stevenson, B. E. (2018). What's love got to do with it?: Concubinage and enslaved women and girls in the antebellum south. In D. R. Berry & L. M. Harris (Eds.), *Sexuality & Slavery: Reclaiming intimate histories in the Americas* (pp. 109-123). The University of Georgia Press.

Stewart, M. (2016). *The Ku Klux Klan: A history of racism and violence.* Southern Poverty Law Center.https://www.splcenter.org/sites/default/files/Ku-Klux-Klan-A-History-of-Racism.pdf

Tatum, B. D. (2017). *Why are all the Black kids sitting together in the cafeteria? And other conversations about race.* Basic Books.

United States Census Bureau. (2024, December 20). About the topic of race. https://www.census.gov/topics/population/race/about.html#:~:text=People%20who%20identify%20their%20origin,Hawaiian%20or%20Other%20Pacific%20Islander.

Warren, W. (2016). *New England bound: Slavery and colonization in early America.* Liveright Publishing Corporation.

White, R. (2017). *The republic for which it stands: The United States during Reconstruction and the Gilded Age, 1865-1896.* Oxford University Press.

Wilkerson, I. (2023). *Caste: The origins of our discontent.* Random House.

Zimbardo, P. G. (2008). *The Lucifer effect: Understanding how good people turn evil.* Random House.

Media Attributions

- WEB_DuBois_1918 is licensed under a Public Domain license
- US_Slave_Free_1789-1861 © Kenmayer is licensed under a CC BY (Attribution) license
- Mustered out is licensed under a Public Domain license

- Rosa Parks being fingerprinted is licensed under a Public Domain license
- Lowndes County Freedom_Organization flyer © SNCC Political Education Materials by Courtland Cox and Jennifer Lawson is licensed under a CC0 (Creative Commons Zero) license
- Say their names website is licensed under a All Rights Reserved license

7.

Race: Being Asian, Indigenous, and Latinx in the United States

Bernadet DeJonge and Nikki Golden

> **Learning Objectives**
>
> - The reader will be able to describe race as a social construct.
> - The reader will be able to identify historical events that have impacted the experience of being Asian, Indigenous, and Latinx in the United States.
> - The reader will be able to connect systemic racism to current social justice movements.

It is essential to understand that systemic racism plays a significant role in contributing to social injustice in the United States. Racial injustice, which has roots in slavery and genocide, remains an essential issue in the United States today. Achieving social justice requires Americans to recognize and address systemic racism. This chapter explores the social concept of race, examining its historical evolution and impact in the United States through the lens of three racial populations.

Race as a Social Construct

Race is not rooted in biology; it is a social construct created by humans. The current concept of racial categories is a relatively recent development in human history (Kendi, 2016). In the English colonies, before racial categories had solidified, religious beliefs often determined people's social status (Wilkerson, 2023). However, "the foundations of race and racist ideas were laid" (Kendi, 2016, p. 18). In the United States, racial categories are so deeply embedded in humans' collective consciousness that even when confronted with science, "some human beings continue to perceive other human beings as excluded from the moral order of personhood" (Zimbardo, 2008, p. 307).

The National Human Genome Research Institute defines race as "a social construct used to group people. Race was constructed as a hierarchical human-grouping system, generating racial classifications to identify, distinguish, and marginalize some groups across nations and the world" (Bonham, 2024, para. 1). Categories of race, as used today, classify people into different groups based on observable and arbitrary physical characteristics, genetics, or other cultural differences (Bonham, 2024; Burton et al., 2010). Additionally, because race is a social construct, categorical definitions have been fluid, with determining factors based on need versus fact (Burton et al., 2010). In the United States, racial categories were created based on "European cultural values and traits, and hierarchy-making was wielded in the service of a political project: enslavement" (Kendi, 2016, p. 83).

Activity 7.1 – Digging Deeper: Race

The U.S. Census Bureau (2022) uses five categories to define race:

White – A person originating in any of the original peoples of Europe, the Middle East, or North Africa.

Black or African American – A person who originates in any of the Black racial groups of Africa.

American Indian or Alaska Native – A person who originates in any of the original peoples of North and South America (including Central America) and maintains tribal affiliation or community attachment.

Asian—A person having origins in any of the original peoples of the Far East, Southeast Asia, or the Indian subcontinent, including, for example, Cambodia, China, India, Japan, Korea, Malaysia, Pakistan, the Philippine islands, Thailand, and Vietnam.

Native Hawaiian or Other Pacific Islander—A person having origins in any of the original peoples of Hawaii, Guam, Samoa, or other Pacific Islands (para. 1).

Discussion Questions

- Why do we track racial data in the United States? How might the data be used?
- Who is missing from the five categories? How do we account for those who do not strongly identify with a particular category?
- Latinx is identified as an ethnicity rather than a race. What is the difference between ethnicity and race? Where does Latinx fit in a discussion of race?

Populations

Racism permeates the experiences of those living in the United States. Although race is a social construct, its construction has "created racial realities with real effects" (Burton et al., 2010, p. 444). While race has no biological basis, it has historically been used to stratify society and impact access to resources. Socially constructed identities such as race are critical factors in predicting life experiences, including education, income levels, health and healthcare access, and access to other resources. Stratification based on race has led to oppressive systems and significant issues with racism in the United States and throughout the world (Grzanka et al., 2019).

Racism can be overt and systemic as well as covert and individualized. An entire book could be written dissecting these issues, and many have been. While acknowledging that there are stories and experiences from all racial groups in the United States, we have chosen to focus this chapter on those of Asian, Indigenous, and Latinx people in the country.

Being Asian in the United States

Historically, the term Asian has been used to broadly define people from East, South, Central, and West Asia. Examples include people from China, Vietnam, Japan, and Malaysia. People from the Asian continent have been immigrating to the United States since colonial times, bringing their culture and religious beliefs with them (Ling, 2023). Being Asian in the United States is complicated by historical events, including Westward Expansion, legislation, the Japanese attack on Pearl Harbor, Japanese internment, racism, and recent events such as anti-Asian hate associated with the COVID-19 pandemic. As with other sections of this textbook, entire books can be written on this topic. We have chosen to highlight four dominant Asian groups in the United States: Chinese, Japanese, Filipino, and Indian.

Historical Aspects of Being Chinese in the United States

In the late 1700s and early 1800s, both Europeans and colonists wanted Chinese goods. Tea, silk, and porcelain were all status symbols, and demand was high. As soon as America became independent, the government began direct trade with China. "Trade routes between the United States and China were well established by the 1830s" (Ling, 2023, p. 11). Asian immigration, however, is generally seen as more of a trickle until the 1850s, when gold was discovered in California.

The gold rush of the 1850s brought large numbers of Chinese immigrants to the United States. Most were men, and most arrived in California, specifically San Francisco (Lepore, 2018). "In the early 1850s, the number of Chinese in America increased dramatically—2,716 in 1851 and 20,026 in 1852. By 1882, when the passage of the Chinese Exclusion Act ended large-scale Chinese immigration, there were about 300,000 Chinese living in the United States" (Ling, 2023, p. 18).

Activity 7.2 – The Gold Rush

Video: The Untold Story of Chinese Immigrants in the California Gold Rush (https://www.youtube.com/watch?v=yPN9-fLm_h0)

 One or more interactive elements has been excluded from this version of the text. You can view them online here: https://milnepublishing.geneseo.edu/social-justice-in-human-services/?p=409#oembed-1 (#oembed-1)

Discussion Questions

- How did systemic racism and legal discrimination manifest against Chinese immigrants during the Gold Rush era?
- How did Chinese immigrants create and sustain their communities despite facing significant adversity and exclusion?
- What forms of resistance and advocacy did Chinese immigrants and their allies engage in to fight against discrimination and injustice?
- How did the experiences of Chinese immigrants intersect with those of other marginalized groups during this time in United States history?

As with other ethnic and racial populations, stereotypes and rumors accompanied the Chinese men to the United States. Many saw Chinese laborers as a replacement for White laborers, and the term "yellow peril" came into fashion to describe this fear (Ling, 2023, p. 32).

"Yellow peril" referred to Western anxieties that Asians, particularly the Chinese, would take their land and undermine Western morals and values such as fairness, religion, and innovation. Additionally, stereotypes brought back from China by merchants, diplomats, and missionaries fueled anti-Chinese sentiment in the United States. These stereotypes portrayed the Chinese as peculiar, eating dogs, cats, and rats, being dirty and arrogant, practicing infanticide, and being un-Christian.

Activity 7.3 – The Chinese Slave Trade

Video: Chinese Slaves in America-Forgotten History (https://www.youtube.com/watch?v=d805nNq_CBE)

 One or more interactive elements has been excluded from this version of the text. You can view them online here: https://milnepublishing.geneseo.edu/social-justice-in-human-services/?p=409#oembed-2 (#oembed-2)

> **Discussion Questions**
>
> - Compare and contrast the experiences of Chinese laborers with those of African slaves. What was similar? What was different? What led to these differences?
> - What methods were used to coerce Chinese individuals into labor, and how did these methods differ from other forms of slavery?
> - What challenges exist in documenting and acknowledging the history of Chinese slavery in the United States? How do we address these challenges?
> - What steps can be taken to acknowledge and rectify the historical injustices faced by Chinese laborers in the United States?

The marginalization of the Chinese during the 1800s and 1900s involved more than just discrimination and slavery. Laws, policies, and taxes aimed at Chinese immigrants also impacted their experience in the United States. The first was a tax levied in California called The Foreign Miners' License Tax. This tax required foreign miners to pay $2.50 a month to the government of California. While originally meant to exclude all foreign miners, this tax ended up becoming directed specifically against Chinese immigrants. "Between 1850 and 1970, the state collected five billion dollars, with nearly 95 percent paid by the Chinese" (Ling, 2023, p. 34). Nevada also taxed foreign miners, and Ling (2023) estimates as much as 96% of Chinese immigrants' income was used to pay taxes during that time.

In 1860, inspired by the Foreign Miners' Tax, a tax on Chinese immigrant fishermen was levied in California. Following this, other taxes targeting Chinese immigrants continued to be levied, such as taxes on small mass shrimp nets and laundromats, and head taxes, which taxed Chinese people coming into the harbor. In addition, alien land laws discouraged Chinese immigrants from settling in rural Western and Midwestern areas. California enacted the Alien Land Law in 1913, and many Chinese farmers had to put land in their children's names or form a corporation under White attorneys to own land. Some scholars speculate that this may be why many Chinese immigrants ended up in more urban areas (Ling, 2023).

In addition to racist tax policy, exclusionary legal precedent also occurred during this time in United States history. Ling (2023) points out that hundreds of Chinese men were murdered during the first five years of the gold rush. One of those was Ling Sing. On August 9, 1853, a White miner named George Hall shot and killed Ling Sing, who was also a miner. Hall was convicted of the murder. Hall appealed his conviction, and the California Supreme Court ruled in *People v. Hall* that "Asiatics" could not testify against White citizens in court (Ling, 2023, p. 36). The California Supreme Court then overturned Hall's conviction. This decision was based on existing law that prevented both Black and Indigenous people from testifying in court (Blakemore, 2024, April 23).

People v. Hall set the stage for violence without consequence against Chinese immigrants. Tax collectors would tie up Chinese miners, often with their hair, and steal their tools, boots, and belongings. White miners would assault and murder Chinese men without consequences and often resorted to arson. Violence erupted in many Western cities, including Los Angeles, Denver, Tacoma, Seattle, and Bellingham (Washington), and Rock Springs (Wyoming) (Ling, 2023).

Racist attitudes soon spread to the urban areas of California as well, and Chinese immigrants were often forced to live outside city limits.

In 1858, the mayor of Mariposa, California, ordered that no one rent to the Chinese, as they cooked over open fires, lit firecrackers on holidays, and burned joss sticks before their gods. He declared Chinatown a fire hazard and that it should be demolished (Ling, 2023, p. 36).

Activity 7.4 – The Chinese Massacre of 1871

Video: Los Angeles Chinese Massacre of 1871 (https://www.youtube.com/watch?v=nauaI-bOXaYo)

 One or more interactive elements has been excluded from this version of the text. You can view them online here: https://milnepublishing.geneseo.edu/social-justice-in-human-services/?p=409#oembed-3 (#oembed-3)

Discussion Questions

- What were the short-term and long-term effects of the massacre on the Chinese community in Los Angeles and the United States?
- How did racial tensions and xenophobia against Chinese immigrants manifest in Los Angeles before and after the massacre?
- How does the Chinese Massacre of 1871 compare to other acts of racial violence in United States history, such as the Tulsa Race Massacre or the internment of Japanese Americans during World War II?
- What lessons can be drawn from the Chinese Massacre of 1871 in addressing contemporary issues of racism, xenophobia, and violence against minority communities?

Immigration Policy and Exclusion

The first national exclusion law aimed at Asian immigration was the Page Act of 1875. The Page Act was aimed at preventing both laborers and women from entering the United States from the Asian continent, but was primarily enforced against Chinese immigrants. It was commonly believed that most Chinese women coming into the United States did so as prostitutes. The Page Act required all women entering the United States to prove they were not prostitutes, and this often led to invasive and humiliating questions from United States immigration officials, who were given the power to admit or deny immigrants. The Page Act was relatively effective, and the gender imbalance in Chinese communities continued to skew male in the late 1800s. In addition, Chinese men were often discouraged from marrying outside their race, so many remained unmarried or returned to China (Rotondi, 2024).

In 1882, Congress passed the Chinese Exclusion Act. This was the first law to ban a specific ethnic group from entering the United States, barring the entry of Chinese laborers for 10 years. Merchants, diplomats, students, teachers, and travelers were exempt. Under this law, Chinese laborers were required to get certification to enter the United States, and Chinese immigrants were excluded from United States citizenship (Ling, 2023).

On October 1, 1888, Congress passed the Scott Act, which expanded the Chinese Exclusion Act. The Scott Act suspended the system of reentry for Chinese laborers who had left the United States and wanted to return, establishing a system where Chinese laborers had to get a certificate from the United States government to return. Many struggled to gain reentry, even with the certificates, and it is estimated that the racist implementation of this law prevented the reentry of 20,000 Chinese laborers.

The Geary Act of 1892 expanded the Chinese Exclusion Act even further, extending the exclusion of Chinese immigrants for 10 more years. It mandated that all Chinese residents in the United States carry their certificates, and thus placed the burden of proof to remain in the United States on them. The Geary Act continued to target Chinese women under the assumption that they were coming to the United States to engage in prostitution. The 1882 Exclusion Act was renewed in 1892 with the Geary Act, and again in 1902 when the restrictions on Chinese immigration were renewed indefinitely. The Geary Act regulated Chinese immigration well into the 20th century (Ling, 2023).

Following World War I, Congress established a new immigration policy based on the 1890 census, utilizing quotas based on national origin. The limit for new immigrants was 2% of the nationality already living in the United States. In 1943, the Magnuson Act repealed all the Chinese Exclusion Acts, as China was a member of the Allied Nations during World War II. However, the quotas remained unchanged, and the annual limit for Chinese immigrants to the United States at that time was 105 (National Archives, 2023).

The Immigration Act of 1965 changed the quota system. Instead of focusing on Chinese immigrants, the United States set a limit of 170,000 immigrants from outside the Western Hemisphere, with a maximum of 20,000 from any one country. Factors that influenced approval included needed skills and the need for political asylum. In 2011 and 2012, the House and Congress condemned the Chinese Exclusion Act (National Archives, 2023).

Resistance to exclusionary law and policy came both officially from Asian governments and unofficially from protests of those affected. To protest the Chinese exclusion laws and the violence against people of Chinese descent in the United States, China began a nationwide anti-American boycott. Millions of Chinese in China and abroad responded to the call to boycott American goods. On September 22, 1892, nearly 200 English-speaking Chinese from the East Coast rallied at the Cooper Union in East Village in lower Manhattan to form the Chinese Equal Rights League (Ling, 2023).

Activity 7.5 – Wong Chin Foo: Chinese Civil Rights Activist

Video: Who Was Wong Chin Foo? (https://www.youtube.com/watch?v=m4B5Gr8ohG0)

 One or more interactive elements has been excluded from this version of the text. You can view them online here: https://milnepublishing.geneseo.edu/social-justice-in-human-services/?p=409#oembed-4 (#oembed-4)

Discussion Questions

- Wong Chin Foo is often described as one of the first Chinese American civil rights activists. What does this mean in the context of United States history?
- Wong Chin Foo believed education was a form of activism. How did this show in the work he did? Was this an effective strategy? Why or why not?
- How does Wong Chin Foo's activism compare to that of other civil rights leaders of his time? In what ways did his approach differ from or align with the strategies used by other marginalized groups seeking justice?
- How did Wong Chin Foo's activism intersect with other social justice issues of his time?

Wong Chin Fu in Harper's Weekly

Wong Chin Foo was not the only person voicing opposition. There were a multitude of court cases filed in response to the exclusionary legislation. Two cases often cited in the literature are *Takao Ozawa v. the United States* in 1922 and the *US v. Bhagat Singh Thind* in 1923. Takao Ozawa was born in Japan but grew up in California. He was Christian, spoke English, and fully integrated into the culture of the United States. Ozawa filed for citizenship in 1922, arguing that he should be considered White because of his acculturation. The United States government argued that White refers specifically to those who are Caucasian, which does not include people from Japan. The Supreme Court unanimously ruled against Ozawa and held that White people and Caucasians were the same (Tanaka, n.d.).

In 1923, Bhagat Singh Thind applied for United States citizenship. Thind was an Indian Sikh living in the United States who had served in World War I for the United States. Thind argued in the *US v. Bhagat Singh Thind* that he was scientifically part of the Caucasian race as the racial classification at the time considered Aryan individuals to be Caucasian, and Thind identified as Aryan. The government countered with the argument that Whiteness should be interpreted as the common understanding of White in American culture, not the scientific classification. The United States Supreme Court unanimously ruled against Thind (Tanaka, n.d.).

Activity 7.6 – Knowledge Check

- What were Takao Ozawa and Bhagat Singh Thind's main legal arguments in their respective cases? How did each of them attempt to qualify as "White"?
- How did these two cases (*Takao Ozawa v. the United States and the US v. Bhagat Singh Thind*) contradict each other? Why are these contradictions important in understanding the history of race in the United States?
- What do the outcomes of these cases reveal about the role of the legal system in perpetuating racial exclusion and discrimination?
- In what ways are the issues raised in the Ozawa and Thind cases still relevant today? How do these historical cases inform current debates about race, citizenship, and immigration?

Historical Aspects of Being Japanese in the United States

The Japanese population in the United States experienced discrimination to their Chinese counterparts in the late 19th century. However, there were significantly fewer Japanese people in the mainland United States during that time. That said, between 1850 and 1920, more than 300,000 Asians emigrated to the Hawaiian Islands, most of them Japanese. Sugar production demanded labor, and much of that need was met by Japanese and other Asian workers. In the late 19th century, going to Hawaii to earn money to pay off debt became popular amongst Japanese farmers. Many Japanese people went to Hawaii and, in lesser numbers, the mainland United States as contract workers. Between 1895 and 1908, private companies brought more than 130,000 Japanese workers to the United States. Most of these workers, 85%, were male (Ling, 2023).

In 1908, after one and a half years of negotiation, the Japanese and American governments came to a gentleman's agreement on immigration. This non-binding, non-legal agreement stated that the Japanese government would control emigration and would no longer send laborers to the United States. It could, however, send business professionals, students, and family members of people already residing in the United States. The United States agreed to ensure better treatment of Japanese immigrants already living in the United States and promised to address discriminatory practices impacting Japanese immigrants (Ling, 2023).

Activity 7.7 – Japanese Segregation in San Fransisco

Website: Segregation of Japanese School Kids in San Francisco Sparks an International Incident (https://celebratecalifornia.library.ca.gov/japanese-segregation/)

Discussion Questions

- What were the long-term effects of the gentleman's agreement on Japanese immigration and Japanese American communities in the United States?
- What role did local, state, and federal governments play in either perpetuating or challenging racial segregation and discrimination against Japanese Americans?
- How did the segregation of Japanese schoolchildren reflect broader racial inequalities in the United States education system during the early 20th century?

One consequence of the gentleman's agreement was the practice of bringing a picture bride to the United States. To enter the United States, a Japanese woman would marry her future husband in Japan by proxy and then join him in the United States as his wife. By 1908, more than 20,000 Japanese women had come to the United States as a picture bride. Starting in 1920, the Japanese government stopped issuing passports to picture brides (Ling, 2023).

Activity 7.8 – Picture Brides

Video: Rice & Roses Excerpts Picture Brides (https://www.youtube.com/watch?v=kHf9ol71Dn4)

> *One or more interactive elements has been excluded from this version of the text. You can view them online here: https://milnepublishing.geneseo.edu/social-justice-in-human-services/?p=409#oembed-5 (#oembed-5)*

Discussion Questions

- Why are personal stories about immigration essential to our understanding of history?
- How did United States policy and legislation impact the experience of picture brides and other Japanese immigrants?

Despite the gentleman's agreement, life on the sugar plantations was hard. The living and working conditions were poor, and pay was low. By the 1870s, Japanese laborers significantly outnumbered the native Hawaiian and Chinese workers and were paid $10 to $15 a month. This contrasted with the average of $50 a month on the mainland. Plantation workers also lost wages to fines that were established to "discipline" them (Ling, 2023, p. 65). Drinking, gambling, fighting, insubordination, refusing work, trespassing, and breaking materials were all behaviors that could be fined. In addition to fines, Japanese workers faced whippings, beatings, and interethnic inequities intended to cause strife among workers as a form of control (Ling, 2023).

While systemic racism was used to control Japanese workers on sugar plantations, many still protested. Some resisted by calling in sick, minimizing their workload, or deserting their work before their contracts expired. Many Japanese workers also engaged in collective action, including multiple strikes. Generally, the strikes were organized by Japanese workers; however, at times, they collaborated with other Asian workers, including Chinese and Filipino workers. In response, plantation owners began to import workers from Korea. Korean workers did not engage with the Japanese workers due to animosity from Japan's recent colonization of Korea, and the plantation owners took advantage of this (Ling, 2023).

Many Japanese workers moved to the mainland United States when their sugar plantation contracts expired. Between 1902 and 1906, almost 34,000 left Hawaii and settled in California and the Pacific Northwest. To support themselves, they sold fresh vegetables and fruit, engaged in retail work, or provided domestic service (Ling, 2023).

Activity 7.9 – 20th Century Immigrant Experience

Video: The Japanese Immigrant Experience in America: First Half of 20th Century (https://www.youtube.com/watch?v=91b3V0FsuPs)

> *One or more interactive elements has been excluded from this version of the text. You can view them online here: https://milnepublishing.geneseo.edu/social-justice-in-human-services/?p=409#oembed-6 (#oembed-6)*

Discussion Questions

- What were some key laws or policies that affected Japanese immigrants in the early 20th century? How did these policies impact their lives and communities?
- The video talks about Japanese immigrants dressing in Western-style clothing to fit into American culture. Did this work? Why or why not?
- How does the Japanese immigrant experience compare to other immigrant groups in the United States during the same period? What similarities and differences can be observed?

Japan entered World War I on the side of the Allied powers and became a global power due to its involvement in the war (Kiilleen, 2021). Japan and the United States had a history of diplomatic conflict over China and immigration; however, they came together for World War I. Once the war was won, however, conflict again erupted between the two nations (Office of the Historian, n.d.).

World War II began in 1939 with Germany's invasion of Poland. While the United States did not immediately enter the war, it supported the Allied powers politically and financially. Tensions with Japan continued due to the Japanese invasion of Manchuria in 1931 and their full-scale invasion of China in 1937. In July of 1941, the United States imposed an embargo on oil exports to Japan in response to their aggression in Southeast Asia. On December 7, 1941, Japan attacked Pearl Harbor, a United States Navy base in Honolulu, Hawaii. The next day, the United States entered World War II by declaring war on Japan (History.com, 2010).

Activity 7.10 – Pearl Harbor

Video: The Attack on Pearl Harbor (https://www.youtube.com/watch?v=DNV8enpVwok)

> *One or more interactive elements has been excluded from this version of the text. You can view them online here: https://milnepublishing.geneseo.edu/social-justice-in-human-services/?p=409#oembed-7 (#oembed-7)*

Discussion Questions

- Why was the attack on Pearl Harbor a significant event in World War II history? What immediate and long-term impacts did it have on the United States and the world?
- Were there any efforts to hold individuals accountable for the attack on Pearl Harbor? Discuss the concept of justice in the context of this event.

> - How has the historical interpretation of the attack on Pearl Harbor evolved over time? What are some of the differing perspectives among historians?

Ling (2023) points out that all Asian immigrants had faced discrimination in the United States; however, with the onset of World War II, public perceptions changed. "Chinese were now viewed as brave, heroic, honest, and hardworking allies, whereas Japanese were scorned as cowardly, conniving, and despicable enemies" (Ling, 2023, p. 107). Anti-Japanese sentiment reached "hysterical" levels (Ling, 2023, p. 108) following the attack on Pearl Harbor. Japanese American communities were subjected to government searches and confiscation of personal belongings in the name of national security.

On February 19, 1942, President Roosevelt signed Executive Order 9066, which authorized the internment of Japanese Americans. With Executive Order 9066, more than 40,000 Japanese people living on the West Coast of the United States and 70,000 of their American-born children were forced from their homes into internment camps. This event occurred under the guise of military necessity; however, it was heavily influenced by both political and public pressure (Ling, 2023).

In March of 1942, the military declared that all enemy aliens in Washington, Oregon, California, and part of Arizona had to move. This included people who were German, Italian, and Japanese. The Japanese order also included anyone with Japanese ancestry. In practice, few Germans and Italians were forced to move. However, the Wartime Civil Control Authority forced the evacuation of more than 100,000 people of Japanese ancestry (Ling, 2023).

Japanese Americans who were removed from the West Coast were given a week to prepare for evacuation and internment. They were only allowed to take what they could carry with them. The military moved them on buses and trains to assembly centers, often racetracks or fairgrounds, to be sorted into camps. Ten permanent internment camps were established, mainly in the desert and mountain areas of the West (Ling, 2023). Two camps were also located in Arkansas (The National WWII Museum, n.d.). Each camp was built to accommodate an average of 10,000 people (Ling, 2023).

Life at the camps was brutal. The camps were surrounded by barbed wire and armed guards. Internees lived in army-style barracks, which offered little privacy or protection from the elements. Food and bathroom facilities were communal. Some Japanese men had jobs, including outside the camps, as farm workers. However, their compensation was significantly less than standard wages. As time went on, internees lost their homes and farms back home as they defaulted on mortgages (Ling, 2023).

While the Japanese internees had initially been cooperative with internment, resentment built over time. Protests erupted at the camps. The first occurred in November 1942, at Poston, Arizona. As internees performed most labor in the camps, the protest and subsequent

Photograph of Members of the Mochida Family Awaiting Evacuation. Original caption: "Hayward, California. Members of the Mochida family awaiting evacuation bus. Identification tags are used to aid in keeping the family unit intact during all phases of evacuation. Mochida operated a nursery and five greenhouses on a two-acre site in Eden Township. He raised snapdragons and sweet peas. Evacuees of Japanese ancestry will be housed in War Relocation Authority centers for the duration."

strike were impactful. A larger mass protest broke out at Manzanar, California, on December 6, 1942 (Ling, 2023).

Interestingly, internment only occurred where Japanese people lived in small numbers. Japanese people in Hawaii did not face internment, as their removal would have devastated the Hawaiian economy. Ling (2023) also points out that

> there were over a million unnaturalized natives of the Axis powers resident in the United States…all of whom were potential internees. However, Japanese people, two-thirds of them native-born citizens, were the only ones singled out for mass internment because of their smaller population and racial background. (p. 114)

Activity 7.11 – Japanese Internment Camps

Video: Ugly History: Japanese-American Incarceration Camps (https://www.youtube.com/watch?v=hI4NoVWq87M)

One or more interactive elements has been excluded from this version of the text. You can view them online here: https://milnepublishing.geneseo.edu/social-justice-in-human-services/?p=409#oembed-8 (#oembed-8)

Video: Why I Love a Country That Once Betrayed Me (https://www.youtube.com/watch?v=LeBKBFAPwNc)

One or more interactive elements has been excluded from this version of the text. You can view them online here: https://milnepublishing.geneseo.edu/social-justice-in-human-services/?p=409#oembed-9 (#oembed-9)

Discussion Questions

- How can we evaluate the internment of Japanese Americans during World War II in terms of civil rights and constitutional protections? Discuss the balance between national security and individual freedoms.
- What were the psychological and social impacts of internment on Japanese Americans? Consider factors such as identity, trauma, and resilience.
- How did the internment affect Japanese American communities after the war ended? Discuss the challenges they faced in rebuilding their lives and reintegrating into American society.
- How does the internment of Japanese Americans compare to the treatment of other minority groups during times of national crisis? Consider similar instances in United States history or in other countries.
- How do personal narratives and testimonies from interned Japanese Americans contribute to our understanding of this period? What insights do they provide that might be missing from official records and histories?

In 1943, Japanese internees were subjected to loyalty tests. They were asked to renounce the Japanese emperor and state whether they would serve in the United States military. Many American-born Japanese people resented these tests and refused to cooperate, saying no to both questions. Those who did so, usually under protest, were labeled as disloyal and separated further from their families. As time went on, questions began to arise about why those who were deemed to be loyal were still interned. Pressure mounted for President Roosevelt to end the internment programs. He did so in December 1944 (The National WWII Museum, n.d.).

Activity 7.12 – Japanese Internment and Modern Day

Video: Why Japanese Internment Still Matters Today (https://www.youtube.com/watch?v=oG_0VukXtLo)

One or more interactive elements has been excluded from this version of the text. You can view them online here: https://milnepublishing.geneseo.edu/social-justice-in-human-services/?p=409#oembed-10 (#oembed-10)

Discussion Questions

- Why do you think Japanese internment still matters today?
- What actions can individuals take to advocate for the rights of marginalized communities today, inspired by the lessons from Japanese American internment?
- What long-term effects did the internment have on Japanese American communities? How are these effects still felt today?

Most people released from the internment camps returned to the West Coast of the United States. When they returned, many had lost everything. Homes had been looted, businesses and farms seized. Anti-Japanese racism continued, and the newly released internees faced daily harassment and abuse, including violence. In addition, many were turned away at local businesses. In response, many Japanese Americans resettled again, building communities in Salt Lake City, Chicago, Cleveland, and Detroit (Ling, 2023).

Activity 7.13 – The Redress Movement

Video: The Redress Movement: Reclaiming Civil Liberties (https://www.youtube.com/watch?v=8j-qHDMGMh8)

One or more interactive elements has been excluded from this version of the text. You can view them online here: https://milnepublishing.geneseo.edu/social-justice-in-human-services/?p=409#oembed-11 (#oembed-11)

Discussion Questions

- How significant was the formal apology from the United States government in the context of the Japanese Redress Movement? What impact did it have on the Japanese American community and American society as a whole?
- Compare the Japanese Redress Movement to other movements for reparations or justice for marginalized groups. What similarities and differences can you identify?

- What actions can individuals and communities take today to support similar movements for justice and redress for other marginalized groups? How can we ensure that past injustices are not forgotten and repeated?

On April 12, 1945, President Roosevelt died, and Harry Truman became his successor. In May 1945, Nazi Germany surrendered. However, Japan continued fighting and continued to inflict significant casualties on United States troops (History.com, 2010). In July 1945, the United States, the United Kingdom, and China met in Potsdam, Germany to discuss the terms for the end of the war. As part of these discussions, they called for Japanese to surrender in the Potsdam Declaration. When Japan rejected the declaration, the United States retaliated with two atomic bombs (Atomic Heritage Foundation, n.d.)

On August 6, 1945, the United States dropped the first atomic bomb on Hiroshima. On August 9, 1945, the United States dropped the second atomic bomb on Nagasaki. Japan surrendered to the United States on August 15, 1945. Estimates suggest that more than 210,000 people were killed, either immediately or in the aftermath of the bombings (History.com, 2010). Following the bombs on Nagasaki and Hiroshima, the United States occupied Japan until 1952 (Ling, 2023).

Activity 7.14 – The Atomic Bomb

Video: Remembering the Hiroshima and Nagasaki Bombings, 75 Years Later
(https://www.youtube.com/watch?v=5DG4Kxt3MpE)

 One or more interactive elements has been excluded from this version of the text. You can view them online here: https://milnepublishing.geneseo.edu/social-justice-in-human-services/?p=409#oembed-12 (#oembed-12)

Discussion Questions

- What ethical arguments can be made for and against the use of atomic bombs on Hiroshima and Nagasaki? What are the ethical implications of targeting civilians in military conflict?
- How can we evaluate the bombings of Hiroshima and Nagasaki in terms of international law and wartime conduct? Discuss the relevance of the Geneva Conventions and other legal frameworks.
- What lessons can be learned from Hiroshima and Nagasaki regarding the ethics and future of warfare? How do these events inform contemporary discussions on the use of military force and weapons of mass destruction?

- How do the bombings of Hiroshima and Nagasaki compare to other acts of mass violence?

Historical Aspects of Being Indian in the United States

The initial emigrants from India to the United States came from the Punjab region. When the British annexed Punjab in 1849, they levied cash taxes on the local population, and many farmers lost their land. In response, people from Punjab either joined the British army or became migrant workers. Some of these migrants made the long journey from Punjab to the United States, where early Sikh migrants worked in lumber and railroads in California. Later, they turned to agriculture (Ling, 2023).

Activity 7.15 – Sikhism

Video: What Is Sikhism? (https://www.youtube.com/watch?v=MWsClPXLApA)

One or more interactive elements has been excluded from this version of the text. You can view them online here: https://milnepublishing.geneseo.edu/social-justice-in-human-services/?p=409#oembed-13 (#oembed-13)

Discussion Questions

- What is the difference between Punjabi and Sikhism?
- What Sikh traditions impact their experience of living in the United States? How do their religious beliefs impact acculturation?

Activity 7.16 – Punjabi-Mexican Culture

Video: The Punjabi-Mexicans of California: The Unlikely Union of Two Communities (https://www.youtube.com/watch?v=99BTIGWjxhQ)

One or more interactive elements has been excluded from this version of the text. You can view them online here: https://milnepublishing.geneseo.edu/social-justice-in-human-services/?p=409#oembed-14 (#oembed-14)

Discussion Questions

- How has Punjabi-Mexican heritage influenced the cultural landscape of California

> today? The United States?
> - How does this story challenge or reinforce your understanding of American immigration and multiculturalism?
> - How have the descendants of Punjabi-Mexican families contributed to American society?

Much like other Asian populations, migrants from the Punjab region were primarily men. Due to racial marriage laws and the lack of Sikh women in the United States, many Sikhs married Mexican women (Ling 2023).

Valentina Alarez and Rullia Singh posing for their wedding photo in 1917. They were among the thousands of Punjabi-Mexican unions that sprouted up in the Southwest of the United States.

Many Sikh men worked in railroad construction at the turn of the century. Between 1903 and 1908, 2,000 Punjabi laborers worked on the Western Pacific Railroad in Northern California, building the section between Oakland and Salt Lake City. Most of these laborers were single men who lived in bunkhouses and provided their own food in collective cookhouses (Ling, 2023).

Prior to 1965, there was a very small population of Sikh or Punjabi immigrants in the United States. Post-World War II, most immigrants from India were professionals or students, and fewer were laborers. When Congress abolished national origin quotas in 1965, Indian immigration to the United States increased rapidly. As of 2022, Indian immigrants are the second largest immigration group, following Mexicans. Interestingly, the United States has recently seen a significant jump in unauthorized Indian arrivals at the United States-Mexico border (Hoffman & Batalova, 2022).

Historical Aspects of Being Filipino in the United States

One of the oldest Asian American communities in North America was a Filipino community established in the 1760s, when a group of Filipino sailors established a settlement in St. Bernard Parish, Louisiana (Ling, 2023). In 1898, the United States annexed the Philippines from the Spanish for $20 million at the Treaty of Paris. The Filipinos objected to this and rebelled. This led to the Philippine Insurrection, or the Philippine-American War, which lasted three years. In 1916, Congress promised the Philippines would have eventual independence and, in 1946, the United States granted the Philippines independence (Naval History and Heritage Command, 2023).

Because the Philippines was an American territory, Filipinos were considered American nationals. As racist immigration policy took hold at the turn of the century, Japanese, Korean, and Chinese laborers were no longer coming to the United States. Hawaiian sugar plantations saw Filipinos as affordable labor and began to recruit Filipino workers. By the 1930s, more than 20,000 Filipinos had emigrated to Hawaii and more than 30,000 Filipinos re-emigrated from Hawaii to the mainland in the 1920s and 1930s after their initial labor contracts ended (Ling, 2023).

In 1934, Congress passed the Tydings-McDuffie Act, otherwise known as the Philippine Independence Act. This act began the process of Filipino independence and reclassified all Filipinos as aliens. It also established a quota of 50 Filipino immigrants per year to the United States. This loss of national status for people from the Philippines led to a significant decrease in Filipino immigration. In 1935, the Filipino Repatriation Act offered free passage for Filipinos back to the Philippines. More than 2,000 Filipinos returned to their homeland this way (Ling, 2023).

Activity 7.17 – Filipino Repatriation Act

Video: Filipino Repatriation Act (https://www.youtube.com/watch?v=0HVoN_ORpGs)

"Gintong Kasaysayan, Gintong Pamana"("Filipino Americans: A Glorious History, A Golden legacy") mural in Unidad Park, Los Angeles promoting ethnic solidarity and the fight for historical inclusion of the 'forgotten' or 'invisible' Filipinos in American history.

 One or more interactive elements has been excluded from this version of the text. You can view them online here: https://milnepublishing.geneseo.edu/social-justice-in-human-services/?p=409#oembed-15 (#oembed-15)

Discussion Questions

- What were the primary motivations behind the enactment of the Filipino Repatriation Act of 1935? How do these motivations fit into a conversation about social justice?
- How can the Filipino Repatriation Act be evaluated in terms of its impact on the Filipino population in the United States?
- What lessons can modern policymakers learn from the Filipino Repatriation Act when designing immigration policies today?

The Contemporary Experience of Being Asian in the United States

Currently, the Asian population continues to grow in the United States. Between 2000 and 2019, Asian populations doubled, and the Pew Research Center states that by 2060, there will be more than 46 million people of Asian descent in the United States. Of these, the largest group is Chinese, followed by Indian Americans, Filipinos, Vietnamese, Koreans, and Japanese. Nearly half live in the Western half of the United States, with a third living in California. Asian immigrants, in general, are younger, less likely to live in poverty, and more likely than the average United States citizen to have a bachelor's degree (Budiman & Ruiz, 2021).

Activity 7.18 – Asian Adoption

One of the ways Asian populations have immigrated to the United States is through transnational, transracial adoption. This began following the Korean War and continues today. Most adoptions come from Korea and China. However, there is also a history of adoption from other countries—particularly for children of United States servicemen in Vietnam.

Video: Adoptees Speak Out: A Mini Documentary (https://www.youtube.com/watch?v=EFR-WmmBvnqA)

One or more interactive elements has been excluded from this version of the text. You can view them online here: https://milnepublishing.geneseo.edu/social-justice-in-human-services/?p=409#oembed-16 (#oembed-16)

Discussion Questions

- What historical events or factors have contributed to the rise of Asian transnational, transracial adoption?
- How do adoptees navigate their cultural identity, and what challenges do they face in balancing their heritage with their adoptive culture?
- How can adoptive parents effectively educate themselves and their children about the adoptee's racial and cultural background?
- How might the trends in Asian transnational, transracial adoption change in the coming years, and what factors will influence these changes?

Stereotypes and the Model Minority Myth

Since the 1960s, Asian Americans have been quite successful in the United States. Many have achieved educational, political, and occupational success. This was first noted in the press in 1966 with two articles detailing the socioeconomic achievements of Asian Americans, and this press coverage continued well into the 1980s (Ling, 2023). This success and the press response to it resulted in the stereotype of the "model minority" to describe Asian Americans. Ling states "Promoted by the popular press, the model minority image has since become a stereotype describing the socioeconomic success achieved by Asian Americans through hard work, respect for traditional values, and accommodation" (p. 181).

Ruiz et al. (2023) state that the model minority stereotype characterizes Asian Americans as high achieving, deferential to authority, intelligent, economically successful, and good at math and science. That said, many Asian people living in the United States do not identify or align with these characteristics, and many find this myth to impact both mental health and academic performance. Of the Asian Americans surveyed by Ruiz et al., only 44% of those surveyed had heard of the term "model minority" (p. 2). However, 63% stated that they have experienced someone thinking they were good at math or science in their day-to-day life. Many expressed that the stereotype has been harmful. Reasons include social pressure to succeed, all Asians being lumped into a monolithic culture, and stereotyping in the school environment.

The model minority stereotype also impacts other marginalized communities. This stereotype surfaced during the civil rights movement in direct contrast to Black and Latinx individuals fighting for equality (Ruiz et al., 2023). Often, the story of Asian American success in the United States is used to contrast the lack of success in Latinx and Black people in the United States, thus pitting different racial groups against each other (Ling, 2023; Ruiz et al., 2023). Ling (2023) states "The model minority theory has proven to be a useful and effective tool to triangulate race politics in America" (p. 182).

Activity 7.19 – The Model Minority

Video: Why Do We Call Asian Americans the Model Minority? (https://www.youtube.com/watch?v=PrDbvSSbxk8)

 One or more interactive elements has been excluded from this version of the text. You can view them online here: https://milnepublishing.geneseo.edu/social-justice-in-human-services/?p=409#oembed-17 (#oembed-17)

Discussion Questions

- In what ways has the "model minority" stereotype positively and negatively affected Asian American individuals and communities? How does the stereotype mask the diversity within the Asian American community?
- How is the "model minority" stereotype perpetuated in modern media and popular culture?
- What steps can be taken to challenge and dismantle the "model minority" stereotype in society today?

While seen as a model minority, Asian Americans also experience significant discrimination in the United States. Ruiz et al. (2023) state that 57% of Asian adults say discrimination is a major problem, and 33% say it is a minor problem. Examples of discrimination include offensive name-calling, suspicion of dishonesty, housing discrimination, workplace discrimination, and intimidation. In addition, participants discussed being bullied and harassed. Indian and Muslim Asians also report racial profiling regarding terrorism both by day-to-day people and airport security. They report this racial profiling has significantly increased since the September 11th terrorist attacks (Ruiz et al., 2023).

> **Activity 7.20 – Asian Racism**
>
> **Video: Asian Americans Share Their Experiences with Racism** (https://www.youtube.com/watch?v=pJuSkI-n6-8)
>
> *One or more interactive elements has been excluded from this version of the text. You can view them online here: https://milnepublishing.geneseo.edu/social-justice-in-human-services/?p=409#oembed-18 (#oembed-18)*
>
> **Discussion Questions**
>
> - What personal experiences with racism do the individuals in the video share, and how do these stories reflect broader societal issues?
> - In what ways do the experiences shared in the video connect to historical patterns of discrimination against Asian Americans?
> - Based on the video's discussions, what actions can society take to create a more inclusive and equitable environment for Asian Americans?

The COVID-19 Pandemic

Asian Americans were affected by the COVID-19 pandemic in a multitude of ways. One survey found that 51% of Chinese restaurants closed due to the pandemic, a significantly higher percentage than other types of restaurants. Much of this has been attributed to stereotypes about Chinese Americans and the origin of the COVID-19 virus (Ling, 2023). According to federal statistics, there has been a spike in hate crimes against Asian Americans since the onset of the COVID-19 pandemic, peaking in 2021 (U.S. Commission on Civil Rights, 2023). Ling states "On February 9, 2021, Stop AAPI Hate reported over 2,808 cases of hate crimes against Asian Americans from March 19 to December 2020 in forty-seven states and Washington, D.C." (p. 243). Incidents included bullying, shunning, physical assault, spitting, and using terminology such as the "Chinese Virus" or "Wuhan Flu" to describe COVID-19 (Ling, 2023; Ruiz et al., 2023). In addition, Asian Americans reported being targeted because they were perceived as Chinese, even if they were not (Ruiz et al., 2023).

BEING ASIAN, INDIGENOUS, AND LATINX IN THE US | 167

Stop AAPI Hate is an American nonprofit organization that runs the Stop AAPI Hate Reporting Center, which tracks self-reported incidents of hate and discrimination against Asian Americans and Pacific Islanders (AAPI) living in the United States.

Activity 7.21 – COVID-19 and Asian Hate

Video: Asian American community battles surge in hate crimes stirred from COVID-19 (https://www.youtube.com/watch?v=sJCactTaEfY)

 One or more interactive elements has been excluded from this version of the text. You can view them online here: https://milnepublishing.geneseo.edu/social-justice-in-human-services/?p=409#oembed-19 (#oembed-19)

Discussion Questions

- How have Asian hate crimes affected the lives of Asian American individuals?
- How has media coverage influenced public perception and awareness of the hate crimes against Asian Americans?
- How has rhetoric from public figures and leaders impacted the increase in hate crimes against Asian Americans?
- What historical parallels exist for the discrimination faced by Asian Americans during the COVID-19 pandemic?

Being Indigenous in the United States

Acknowledging the complex history of the Indigenous peoples of North America can help us fully understand the history of the United States. Indigenous peoples have rich, independent histories that predate colonization and the formation of the United States. Despite this, Indigenous people are often reduced to "one-dimensional stock figures, their complexity and differences pressed flat for dramatic purposes" (Hämäläinen, 2022, p. xi). While many lump Indigenous people into one homogeneous group, there are actually 574 federally recognized, distinct tribes. The United States is home to a little over four million people who identify as American Indian (AI) or Alaska Native (AN) (U.S. Census Bureau, 2023a, 2023b).

The attempted genocide of the Indigenous people of North America is one of the most shameful chapters in United States history. "America did not conquer the West through superior technology, nor did it demonstrate the advantages of democracy. America 'won' the West by blood, brutality, and terror" (Treuer, 2019, p. 94). That said, portraying Indigenous history solely as one of loss undermines the resilience and agency of Indigenous peoples (Blackhawk, 2023). Despite the United States government's attempts at genocide, Indigenous communities not only survived but continue to thrive and resist today. This section aims to intertwine aspects of Indigenous histories with key moments in United States history, providing a more nuanced understanding of both through a social justice lens.

Activity 7.22 – Genocide

The United Nations (1951) has defined genocide as:

...any of the following acts committed with intent to destroy, in whole or in part, a national, ethnical, racial or religious groups, as such: (a) Killing members of the group; (b) Causing serious bodily or mental harm to members of the group; (c) Deliberately inflicting on the group conditions of life calculated to bring about its physical destruction in whole or in part; (d) Imposing measures intended to prevent births within the group; (e) Forcibly transferring children of the group to another group. (Article II)

Discussion Questions

- What are the key criteria for determining if an act qualifies as genocide? How do historical events involving Indigenous peoples align with these criteria?
- What are the arguments for and against using the term "genocide" to describe the treatment of Indigenous populations in the United States?
- How does recognizing the treatment of Indigenous populations as genocide affect contemporary Indigenous rights and sovereignty movements? What role does this

> recognition play in ongoing efforts to address historical injustices?

Initial Contact between Colonists and Indigenous Peoples of North America

Initial contact between Indigenous people of the Americas and European colonists occurred in the Caribbean Islands in 1492, where Christopher Columbus and 88 other people encountered the Taino. The Taino welcomed Columbus and his men with gifts and food. However, Columbus and his men sought gold, silk, and spices, not kinship. This initial meeting started the colonization of the Caribbean and, in time, the Americas. In the 1400s and 1500s, Spain dominated the Caribbean. Spanish colonists exploited Indigenous goods and people, often brutally (Hämäläinen, 2022).

From the Caribbean Islands, Spanish colonists continued north, and in the 1500s, they arrived in Florida to a coordinated and successful resistance. They also moved into what is the modern-day Southwest region of the United States from Central and South America. Again, they were met with effective resistance. By the late 16th century, the Spanish continued to be unsuccessful in colonizing North America, and the continent remained primarily Indigenous (Hämäläinen, 2022).

Colonization of the East Coast

In the 1500s, many European traders regularly arrived along the East Coast of what is now the United States and Canada to fish and trade. Occasionally, they would come ashore and attempt to establish colonies. However, the Indigenous population was often not receptive to this, preferring to keep the Europeans at arm's length. Skirmishes between the French and Spanish colonists in Florida started to manifest over land disputes, even though none seemed to be able to colonize the Indigenous space successfully (Hämäläinen, 2022).

In 1607, three ships anchored off the coast of what is now Virginia. One hundred men came ashore and built a fort in what is now considered to be the first permanent English settlement in North America. They called their settlement Jamestown. The colonists at Jamestown had a tumultuous relationship with the Indigenous people of the area. The local Indigenous leaders tried to incorporate the colonists into their vast empire but were met with brutal resistance (Hämäläinen, 2022).

In addition to losing lives in conflict with Indigenous people, the colonists suffered from malaria, starvation, and the elements. By 1615, tobacco began to be exported from Virginia. Tobacco was widely popular in England, and the colonies' economic value began to grow. In 1619, the first enslaved Africans arrived in Virginia, and tobacco production surged (Hämäläinen, 2022).

During the 1600s and 1700s, interactions between Indigenous populations and European colonists remained complex. Conflicts with the colonists and the diseases they brought with them affected Indigenous populations' demographics. Additionally, Indigenous populations participated in trade and formed alliances with European colonies, resulting in frequent cultural clashes and conflicts (Hämäläinen, 2022).

The Revolutionary War

At first, Indigenous populations opted to remain neutral in the conflicts between the colonists and England, perceiving their conflict as infighting between a king and his subjects. However, as tensions increased and the war began, indigenous populations took sides (Makos, 2021). Many took the side of the British in hopes that it would send colonists back to England (Hämäläinen, 2022). For example,

> The Cherokee nation was split between a faction that supported the colonists and another that sided with Britain. The Iroquois Confederacy, an alliance of six Native American nations in New York, was divided by the Revolutionary War. Two of the nations, the Oneida and Tuscarora, chose to side with the Americans while the other nations, including the Mohawk, fought with the British. Hundreds of years of peaceful coexistence and cooperation between the Six Nations came to an end, as warriors from the different nations fought one another on Revolutionary War battlefields. (Makos, 2021, para. 4)

After the Revolutionary War, the British gave the new United States all British territory located east of the Mississippi and south of Canada. This decision did not elicit the input of the Indigenous tribes who had fought on their side and lived on those lands. As Westward expansion began, many Indigenous populations faced White—and often brutal—colonists who believed all Indigenous people had sided with the British coming into their territories. When Indigenous people resisted or fought back, they found no support from their supposed allies in England (Makos, 2021).

Activity 7.23 – Battles and Wars with Indigenous Populations

While numerous conflicts occurred between Indigenous populations and colonists — and later the United States government — specific battles and wars are particularly noteworthy due to their significant impact on history and their profound effects on Indigenous communities. Below, find a brief overview of some of those early conflicts.

Battle of Horseshoe Bend: In 1814, Andrew Jackson led a group of United States soldiers and a group of Cherokee soldiers in a war known as the Battle of Horseshoe Bend against the Creeks (Cowie, 2022). The battle resulted in the Creek Nation surrendering more than 20 million acres of land to the United States government (Lepore, 2018).

United States and Dakota War: In 1862, the Dakota nation, already removed from their sacred lands and placed onto a reservation, were tired of the continued encroachment and abuse of White settlers. Some of the Dakota people were starving, and the local Bureau of Indian Affairs (BIA) agent, Andrew Myrick, refused to sell them food on credit (Hämäläinen, 2019). Additionally, the Dakota nation was angry that the BIA "failed to investigate charges of…mistreatment of Indian women by white men" (Deer, 2015, p. 33). In retaliation, "Dakota warriors killed hundreds of settlers, burned farms, raided stores, and took hostages" (Hämäläinen, 2019, p. 254).

The United States military captured approximately 2,000 Dakota people, including women and children, and held them as prisoners of war (Hämäläinen, 2019). Initially, 303 Dakota warriors were sentenced to death. However, President Lincoln intervened. Lincoln reported he would only authorize the death of those Dakota warriors guilty of rape or "perpetrating massacres" (Hämäläinen, 2019, p. 254). On December 26, 1862, 38 Dakota warriors were executed by hanging. "It was and remains the largest mass execution in American history and is a source of enduring trauma for Dakota people" (Hämäläinen, 2019, p. 254).

Sand Creek Massacre: In 1864, Colonel Chivington led the First Colorado Infantry Regiment of Volunteers and the Third Regiment of Colorado Cavalry Volunteers who murdered approximately 150 Cheyenne and Arapaho people. Chivington and his volunteer forces

> killed and scalped pregnant women and cut one of them open, ripped out the fetus and scalped it. They had destroyed bodies, cutting out arms, legs, fingers, noses, breasts, genitals, and hearts, decorating their hats and uniforms with pieces of humans. (Hämäläinen, 2019, p. 264)

Wounded Knee Massacre: In 1890, one of the most infamous massacres on United States soil occurred in South Dakota (Richardson, 2010). On December 29, 1890, the Cavalry Regiment, led by Colonel James W. Forsyth, surrounded a group of Lakota Sioux at Wounded Knee Creek. The soldiers demanded that the Lakota surrender their weapons. While disarming the Indigenous people, a shot was fired by an unknown party, and violence erupted. The cavalry opened fire on the unarmed Lakota people, including women and children. Estimates are that somewhere between 150 and 300 Lakota people were killed. The Wounded Knee Massacre is often cited as an example of the extreme violence and injustices experienced by Indigenous peoples in the United States. It signified the outcome of oppressive measures against Native American tribes and the tragic ramifications of policies of displacement and cultural suppression (Klein, 2023).

Discussion Questions

- What common factors contributed to the conflicts represented by the Battle of Horseshoe Bend, the Dakota War, the Sand Creek Massacre, and the Wounded Knee Massacre? How did issues such as land, resources, and treaty violations drive these events?
- How did each of these events impact the Indigenous communities involved, both immediately following the conflicts and in the longer term? What were the specific repercussions for the Creek Nation, Dakota Sioux, Cheyenne, Arapaho, and Lakota Sioux?
- How have historical interpretations of these events evolved over time? What are the challenges in reconciling different perspectives on these conflicts?
- How are these events interconnected in the broader history of the expansion of the United States and Indigenous resistance? How do they collectively contribute to the understanding of the history of Indigenous relations with the United States?
- How do these events continue to influence discussions about Indigenous rights, historical injustices, and the policies of the United States? What lessons can be drawn from these events for contemporary issues facing Indigenous peoples?

Reservation Era

The United States government had various justifications for its genocidal campaign against Indigenous nations. However, the primary reason was greed. Indigenous nations occupied the land that the United States wanted for westward expansion. Two specific governmental policies ensured that the United States would take possession of Indigenous lands. These were *the Doctrine of Discovery* and the establishment of reservations (Blackhawk, 2023).

Doctrine of Discovery – Part 1

Pope Alexander VI issued the *Doctrine of Discovery* on May 4, 1492, for the Catholic Church. It stated that any land not inhabited by Christians was available for discovery and claim. The *Doctrine of Discovery* was intended to overthrow pagan nations and spread Christianity worldwide. In 1823, the United States Supreme Court ruled in *Johnson v. M'Intosh* that the discovery doctrine gave the United States the right to own the land on which Indigenous people lived (Charles & Rah, 2019). The case arose from a land dispute in which Thomas Johnson bought land from the Piankeshaw Nation, and William M'Intosh claimed the same land through a United States governmental grant. *Johnson v. M'Intosh* established the rights of Indigenous tribes to live on their lands, but not to sell or transfer land without the approval of the United States Government (Blackhawk, 2023).

> **Activity 7.24 – Knowledge Check: The Doctrine of Discovery**
>
> - In what ways did the *Doctrine of Discovery* dehumanize Indigenous populations and justify their subjugation?
> - How did the U.S. Supreme Court's ruling in *Johnson v. M'Intosh* (1823) perpetuate the principles of the *Doctrine of Discovery*?
> - What were the immediate and long-term effects of the *Doctrine of Discovery* on Indigenous communities in North America?
> - How did the *Johnson v. M'Intosh* ruling affect Indigenous land rights and sovereignty?
> - Why is it important to critically examine and understand historical doctrines like the *Doctrine of Discovery* in the context of social justice?
> - How can acknowledging the impacts of such doctrines contribute to reconciliation and justice for Indigenous peoples?

In 1823, President James Monroe stated in his annual speech to Congress that the Western Hemisphere was off-limits to further European colonization. This declaration later became known as the *Monroe Doctrine*. Monroe declared that the United States would not tolerate interference from any European nation and that any interference would be seen as a sign of aggression toward the United States. This also meant that Indigenous nations could no longer rely on their European allies against the United States (Blackhawk, 2023).

By the late 1820s, many White Americans, especially in the South, viewed Indigenous nations as "simply in the way" (Blackhawk, 2023, p. 186) of westward expansion and Southern states needed Indigenous land to continue expanding cotton production. The United States government saw the Indigenous populations as a problem and sought a solution. That solution was to remove Indigenous people from their land and establish reservations (Hämäläinen, 2019).

Indian Removal Act

In the 1820s and 1830s, Georgia passed a series of legislation aimed at the Cherokee Nation. These laws invalidated Cherokee law, took Cherokee land, banned Cherokee people from testifying in court against White people, and banned Cherokee people from meeting in groups (Brown, 2022). In response, the Cherokee Nation appealed to the federal government for protection.

Activity 7.25 – Indigenous Sovereignty

Cherokee Nation v. Georgia and *Worcester v. Georgia*

In 1831, in *Cherokee Nation v. Georgia*, the United States Supreme Court reaffirmed Indigenous tribes were, in fact, nations. However, according to Chief Justice Marshall, they were not foreign nations but "domestic dependent" nations (Mays, 2021, p. 95).

In 1832, in *Worcester v. Georgia*, the Court ruled that Georgia's laws had no authority within Cherokee territory, affirming the sovereignty of the Cherokee Nation and recognizing their right to self-governance (Mays, 2021).

Video: *Cherokee Nation v. Georgia* (https://www.youtube.com/watch?v=sObuS-scoww)

One or more interactive elements has been excluded from this version of the text. You can view them online here: https://milnepublishing.geneseo.edu/social-justice-in-human-services/?p=409#oembed-20 (#oembed-20)

Video: *Worcester v. Georgia* (https://www.youtube.com/watch?v=C-iBhamdgdg)

One or more interactive elements has been excluded from this version of the text. You can view them online here: https://milnepublishing.geneseo.edu/social-justice-in-human-services/?p=409#oembed-21 (#oembed-21)

Discussion Questions

- How did the Supreme Court's ruling in *Cherokee Nation v. Georgia* impact the legal status of Native American tribes in relation to state and federal governments? What did Justice John Marshall mean by describing tribes as "domestic dependent nations?"
- How does the lack of enforcement of the *Worcester v. Georgia* decision illustrate the challenges of implementing Supreme Court rulings? What does this case reveal about the limits of judicial authority in the face of political pressures?
- In what ways did the rulings in *Cherokee Nation v. Georgia* and *Worcester v. Georgia* influence subsequent legal and political developments regarding Native American rights and state-federal relations? How did this case set a precedent for future Supreme Court decisions?

Instead of protection, President Andrew Jackson signed the Indian Removal Act in 1830. The Indian Removal Act authorized the relocation of Indigenous tribes from their current land to land further west in current-day Oklahoma. The federal government claimed the power to exchange Indigenous land east of the Mississippi for land in the West. While the Indian Removal Act authorized negotiations and voluntary relocation, relocation was often achieved through coercion, deception, and force (Kiel, 2017). The Indian Removal Act proved to be a "brutal, sustained campaign of ethnic cleansing executed by often corrupt and inept patronage government employees" (Hämäläinen, 2019, p. 210) and had long standing consequences for multiple Indigenous tribes. In the years between 1830 and 1850, "more than 125,000 Indians…were forcibly removed to territory west of the Mississippi, mostly on foot and in wintertime. At least 3,500 Creek and 5,000 Cherokee and many from other tribes died along the way" (Treuer, 2019, p. 35).

Activity 7.26 – Trail of Tears

Video: What Life On the Trail of Tears Was Like (https://www.youtube.com/watch?v=x54xhAcpS8c)

 One or more interactive elements has been excluded from this version of the text. You can view them online here: https://milnepublishing.geneseo.edu/social-justice-in-human-services/?p=409#oembed-22 (#oembed-22)

Reading: Two Accounts of the Trail of Tears: Wahnenauhi and Private John G. Burnett (https://www.digitalhistory.uh.edu/disp_textbook.cfm?smtID=3&psid=1147)

Discussion Questions

- What were the immediate and long-term effects of the Trail of Tears on the Cherokee Nation? How did the forced relocation affect the tribe's social structure, culture, and economy?
- What do personal accounts or testimonies from individuals who experienced the Trail of Tears reveal about the human impact of the forced relocation? Why are these stories important?
- How does the Trail of Tears compare to other instances of forced migration in history? What similarities and differences can be observed in terms of causes, processes, and consequences?
- How do the events of the Trail of Tears continue to influence contemporary Native American policy and relations between tribal nations and the U.S. government?

Post Civil War

Between the Civil War and constant fighting with Indigenous tribes, the cost for the United States government to continue "an extended campaign of genocide" (Native American Rights Fund [NARF], 2019, p. 6) against Indigenous populations was no longer feasible.

The United States had already spent over $750 million on war since 1840 (Hämäläinen, 2019). In addition, Americans were tired of war, both with each other and Indigenous tribes.

By the late 1800s, the sentiment of the American public shifted from fear and hatred to sympathy for Indigenous people. Even members of the United States military struggled with continued physical aggression towards a seemingly defeated Indigenous population (Cozzens, 2016). General George Cook stated:

> when Indians see their wives and children starving and their last source of supplies cut off, they go to war. And then we are sent out there to kill them. It is an outrage. All tribes tell the same story. They are surrounded on all sides, the game is destroyed or driven away, they are left to starve, and there remains one thing for them to do-fight while they can. Our treatment of the Indian is an outrage (Cozzens, 2016, p. 7).

Although the United States government's ultimate objective to acquire Indigenous lands remained unchanged, its strategy evolved. According to Hämäläinen (2019), this shift represented an attempt by the federal government to adopt a more refined approach to imperialism. Rather than resorting to violence and conflict, it aimed to manage and reshape Indigenous peoples (Adams, 2020).

President Ulysses S. Grant recognized the failures of previous policies around Indigenous tribes and introduced a new strategy known as the Peace Policy. This initiative, which spanned the late 1860s and early 1870s, aimed to reform relations with Indigenous communities and address the shortcomings of earlier approaches. Grant's approach aimed to shift from aggressive expansion to a more humane interaction with Indigenous populations. In addition, the policy included an intentional effort to assimilate Indigenous populations into mainstream American culture. As part of this, indigenous agents would be appointed to the BIA. Grant appointed Ely S. Parker of the Seneca Nation to head the BIA. He served from 1869-1871 and advocated for Indigenous rights (National Park Service, n.d.).

After the Civil War ended, White nationalism was at an all-time high and westward expansion in the United States continued. While the Supreme Court case *Worcester v. Georgia* had established that Indigenous nations were sovereign, many in the United States felt that Indigenous people were now, with the advent of reservations, reliant on the United States government and should no longer be sovereign. In 1871, the Indian Appropriations Act was passed with a rider, which invalidated Indigenous sovereignty. Thus, the United States government would not negotiate further treaties with Indigenous tribes. The Indian Appropriations Act also gave the United States Congress more power to establish policies regarding Indigenous people. "This new phase of federal Indian policy was known as assimilation, and as bad as the years of warfare and treaty making had been, assimilation would be immeasurably worse" (Treuer, 2019, p. 114). The new policies were built upon three fundamental pillars: Christianization, education, and the promotion of private property (Grinde, 2004).

Christianization

The American public's sentiment shift was partly influenced by the rise of social reform movements in the United States. During the 1880s, "a chorus of voices from the pulpit, press, and Congress were again calling for a major overhaul of Indian policy" (Adams, 2020, p. 10). Social reform organizations, such as the Women's National Indian Association (WNIA) and the Indian Rights Association (IRA), focused on the plight of the Indigenous people. According to these social reformers, the only way to save the Indigenous people was to civilize them through Christianization (Adams, 2020).

Education

Education was a vital component of the United States government's assimilation strategy (Adams, 2020). The Secretary of the Interior, Carl Schurz, "estimated it cost nearly a million dollars to kill an Indian in warfare, whereas it cost only $1,200 to give an Indian child eight years of schooling" (Adams, 2020, p. 23). Education made economic sense and complied with the federal government's needs.

During the 1800s, the common school movement increased Americans' appreciation for education (Adams, 2020). Social reformers, such as Horace Mann, believed government-supported education created "a more useful citizen in the community" (Vinovskis, 1970, p. 562). Many social reformers viewed education "as a seedbed of republican virtues and democratic freedoms, a promulgator of individual opportunity and national prosperity, and an instrument for social progress and harmony" (Adams, 2020, p. 21). Therefore, social reformers believed that education was the most efficient route to civilizing Indigenous people, specifically Indigenous children. Three education models were employed in attempts to assimilate Indigenous children. These were the reservation day school, the reservation boarding school, and the off-reservation boarding school (Adams, 2020).

Activity 7.27 – The Common School Movement

Video: Who Were the Common School Reformers?: A Short History of Education (https://www.youtube.com/watch?v=ejAT3EAdC5w)

 One or more interactive elements has been excluded from this version of the text. You can view them online here: https://milnepublishing.geneseo.edu/social-justice-in-human-services/?p=409#oembed-23 (#oembed-23)

Video: The Origins of the American Public Education System (https://www.youtube.com/watch?v=HZp7eVJNJuw)

The Genoa U.S. Indian Industrial School in Genoa, Nebraska, which the United States eventually converted into the Genoa School. During its fifty years of operation from 1884 to 1934, the school enrolled over 4,300 children representing over forty Indian Nations.

 One or more interactive elements has been excluded from this version of the text. You can view them online here: https://milnepublishing.geneseo.edu/social-justice-in-human-services/?p=409#oembed-24 (#oembed-24)

Discussion Questions

- How did the common school reforms and the origins of the public school system influence Indigenous populations in the United States? Consider both the direct and indirect consequences.
- How did the goals of the United States public education system align or conflict with Indigenous cultural values and education systems?
- In what ways did the history of public schooling in the United States contribute to the assimilation policies that targeted Indigenous populations? Discuss the implications for cultural preservation.

Reservation Day School Model

The first educational model used to assimilate Indigenous children was the reservation day school. Initially popular, 48 reservation day schools were in operation in the United States by the 1860s. Typically located near or on Indigenous reservations, reservation day schools allowed Indigenous children to arrive in the early morning and go home to their families at the end of the day. The reservation day schools provided elementary-level education and focused on English language instruction and vocational training (Adams, 2020). Additionally, "the day school curriculum also provided for lighter activities such as singing and calisthenics, the former offering a perfect opportunity to introduce the Christian message in the form of hymns" (Adams, 2020, p. 33).

Some of the advantages of the reservation day school model were that the schools were inexpensive to operate and that Indigenous parents were less resistant to them. In addition, social reformers hoped that Indigenous children would bring what they learned home to their parents (Adams, 2020). However, this was not the case. The reservation day school model was eventually deemed an ineffective "instrument of assimilation" (Adams, 2020, p. 34).

Reservation Boarding School Model

The failure of the reservation day school model led to the idea that "sustained confinement was…the key element in the civilization process" (Adams, 2020, p. 36). As part of President Grant's Peace Policy in 1869, boarding school policies were implemented as a model to assimilate Indigenous children (NARF, 2019). The Boarding School Policy "authorized the voluntary and coerced removal of Native American children from their families for placement in boarding schools run by the government and Christian missionaries" (NARF, 2019, p. 7). By the late 1870s, with the reinforcement of the Boarding School Policy, the reservation day school model was replaced by the reservation boarding school model (Adams, 2020).

Reservation boarding schools were typically located near BIA offices on the reservation and were under the domain of the local BIA agents. Reservation boarding schools included four elementary grades and four advanced grades. Like the reservation day schools, the curriculum at the reservation boarding schools focused on instruction in the English language and vocational training. Indigenous children were required to remain at school for nine months a year and only allowed to visit their families during summer vacations. For government officials and social reformers, the primary advantage of the reservation boarding school model was the increased control over Indigenous children's lives (Adams, 2020).

BIA agents, government officials, and social reformers expressed concern that reservation boarding schools allowed Indigenous children too much access to their culture due to the schools' proximity to Indigenous reservations (Adams, 2020). BIA agents were frustrated that when Indigenous children went home for the summer, they reverted to their "savage mode of life" (Adams, 2020, p. 37). NARF (2019) points out that "mere education was not enough…Separating children from their family, their tribe, their culture, and their homes on the reservations was necessary to [sic] larger goal of assimilating them into the majority culture" (p. 6). BIA agents, government officials, and social reformers concluded that the only path to complete assimilation of Indigenous children was to remove all influence of their cultures. This conclusion led to the rise of the third educational model, the off-reservation boarding school (Adams, 2020).

Off-Reservation Boarding School Model

The first off-reservation boarding school, the Carlisle Indian School (Carlisle), was founded in 1879 by Captain Richard Pratt (Adams, 2020; Treuer, 2019). Pratt's military style of education became the model for Indigenous education across the United States (Treuer, 2019). "In fact, for several years philanthropists looked upon Pratt as a sort of Moses for the Indians" (Adams, 2020, p. 60). Pratt's success at Carlisle proved that the off-reservation boarding school model solved the United States government's Indian problem. By 1894, approximately 100 off-reservation boarding schools existed in the United States (Treuer, 2019). Unfortunately, not all boarding schools were the same. Carlisle "under Pratt's supervision and congressional scrutiny…was better staffed and better run than others around the country, which seem hellish in comparison" (Treuer, 2019, p. 137).

Although Pratt believed Indigenous people were "capable in all respects as we are, and that he only needs the opportunities and privileges which we possess to enable him to assert his humanity and manhood" (Treuer, 2019, p. 134), he also believed that they were culturally inferior to White Americans. Pratt's educational philosophy was based on his famous phrase, "Kill the Indian in him and save the man" (Adams, 2020, p. 56). Pratt believed, like so many other White Americans, that cultural erasure was the only way for Indigenous people to assimilate into society (Adams, 2020; Treuer, 2019).

Cultural Erasure

The boarding school model was designed to erase all traces of Indigenous identity from Indigenous children (Adams, 2020). "From the policymakers' point of view, the civilization process required a twofold assault on Indian children's identity" (Adams, 2020, p. 109). The first identity assault was the removal of any outward Indigenous cultural markers. The second identity assault was instruction on how to assimilate into White American culture. Pratt believed that complete immersion into White American culture would transform Indigenous children. According to Pratt, "We make our greatest mistake in feeding our civilization to the Indians instead of feeding the Indians to our civilization" (Adams, 2020, p. 57).

Activity 7.28 – Cultural Genocide

The United States government used a multitude of strategies for its campaign of cultural genocide of the Indigenous people of North America. Assimilation required that Indigenous people change everything about their identities and their cultures. Carasik and Bachman (2019) define cultural genocide as:

> any attempt to destroy a group as such by eliminating the group's culture. Acts that constitute cultural genocide include criminalization or de facto prohibition of a group's language, religious practices, customs, and traditions; destruction of heritage sites, artifacts, artwork, historical records, and books; and indoctrination and forced assimilation of a group's children into another group. (p. 98)

Discussion Questions

- How have government policies aimed at assimilating Indigenous peoples—such as residential schools, land allotment, and anti-cultural legislation—contributed to the erosion of Indigenous cultures? What were the intended and unintended consequences of these policies?
- How do contemporary assimilation policies and practices affect current Indigenous cultures? Are there current examples of assimilation or cultural erosion, and how are Indigenous communities responding to these challenges today?
- What are some potential strategies for preventing cultural genocide and supporting the cultural sovereignty of Indigenous peoples moving forward? How can policies be reformed to ensure the protection and flourishing of Indigenous cultures?

Indigenous children were sent far from their tribal lands to their assigned boarding schools. They traveled on trains, steamers, and wagons to cover great distances. Their journeys were unaccompanied, without their families, and often without knowing the other children they traveled with. Remarkably, some of these children were as young as 4 years old, and many had little to no prior exposure to White American culture (Adams, 2020).

Indigenous children experienced a dramatic cultural shift at the boarding schools. Everything from their clothing, religious beliefs and practices, and concepts of nature, time, and space were expected to change (Adams, 2020). Immediately upon their arrival at a boarding school, Indigenous children were required to bathe "to scrub away the filth that whites ascribed to Native home life" (Adams, 2020, p. 109). The children's traditional clothing was replaced with school uniforms, suits for the boys and dresses for the girls. "No child was permitted to blend gender roles, cross-dress, or alter their physical appearance to resemble that of the opposite gender" (Smithers, 2022, p. 94).

Indigenous boys were required to submit to short haircuts because of the "belief that the children's long hair was symbolic of savagism; removing it was central to the new identification with civilization" (Adams, 2020, p. 110). However, hair had sacred meaning for some

Indigenous cultures, such as the Sioux. For many of the Indigenous boys, it was traumatic to have their hair cut, and some older boys chose to run away rather than submit (Adams, 2020).

Indigenous children's identity was also removed. Children with traditional Indigenous names were renamed by the BIA agents serving as boarding school superintendents (Adams, 2020). For many Indigenous cultures, traditional names had significant meaning, and "the fact remains that it constituted a grave assault on Indian identity" (Adams, 2020, p. 119) to change them. However, renaming was seen as necessary to assimilate Indigenous people into White America.

Activity 7.29 – Boarding Schools

Video: The Dawes Act and Residential Boarding Schools: Assimilation or Annihilation (https://www.youtube.com/watch?v=jAcu-2QYgQU)

 One or more interactive elements has been excluded from this version of the text. You can view them online here: https://milnepublishing.geneseo.edu/social-justice-in-human-services/?p=409#oembed-25 (#oembed-25)

Audio/Website: No More Silence: Boarding School Survivor Anita Yellowhair Shares her Story (https://cronkitenews.azpbs.org/2023/05/08/indian-boarding-school-survivor-anita-yellowhair/)

Discussion Questions

- What were the cultural impacts of the Dawes Act and boarding schools on Indigenous communities? How did these policies contribute to the erosion of traditional practices and languages?
- What are the long-term social, economic, and psychological effects of the Dawes Act and residential boarding schools on Indigenous populations? How do these historical policies continue to influence Indigenous communities today?
- How have the Dawes Act and residential boarding schools been evaluated in terms of legal and moral responsibility? What role should the U.S. government play in addressing the harms caused by these policies?

Failed System

By 1900, the United States government had spent over $45 million, primarily on boarding schools, to assimilate 20,000 Indigenous children. By 1901, the Commissioner of Indian Affairs, William Jones, reported that the last 20 years of policies regarding Indigenous education were a failure. This began the campaign to end boarding schools (Adams, 2020).

Instead of just eradicating the boarding school system, education officials attempted to modify the operation of the boarding schools. The first change attempted was to adjust the boarding schools' curriculum (Adams, 2020). By 1916, almost all boarding school curricula shifted from, at least theoretically, a balance of academic and vocational focus to nearly all vocational. The next change was integrating small amounts of Indigenous culture into the boarding school programs. This included allowing Indigenous children to sing songs in their own languages, draw pictures of some Indigenous legends, and engage in Indigenous arts and crafts (Adams, 2020).

Further changes to the indoctrination of Indigenous children included re-engaging with on-reservation schools and transferring the responsibility for Indian public education to public schools. These changes substantially impacted the boarding school system. By 1918, the first off-reservation boarding school, the Carlisle School, was closed, and by 1925, the number of federal off-reservation boarding schools decreased from 25 to 18 (Adams, 2020).

In 1928, the Secretary of the Interior, Hubert Work, commissioned an investigation into the Indigenous policies of the United States. The investigation produced *The Problem of Indian Administration* report, also known as the *Meriam Report*. Included in the *Meriam Report* was a section on the Indigenous education policies of the United States as well as the current status of the education system. The *Meriam Report's* recommendations included a complete overhaul of the education system and its pedagogy (Adams, 2020). "For the first time in fifty years, the possibility for a new era in Indian policy... had been put forward as official policy" (Adams, 2020, p. 364).

Activity 7.30 – *The Meriam Report*

Reading: The Problem of Indian Administration (https://www.narf.org/nill/resources/meriam.html)

Discussion Questions

- What were the primary findings of the *Meriam Report*, and how did they contrast with the prevailing perceptions of Native American life at the time? What critiques did it offer?
- In what ways did the *Meriam Report* address the conditions within Indian boarding schools? What recommendations did it make for reforming the education of Native American children?
- What lessons can be drawn from the *Meriam Report* regarding the role of government reports and commissions in driving social and policy change?

Consequences of Boarding Schools

In 1967, the United States government acknowledged concerns about Indigenous education, and Congress established a subcommittee to investigate the Indigenous education system. In 1969, they delivered their report (Treuer, 2019). "The verdict was dismal: Indian education was a tragedy" (Treuer, 2019, p. 333). In response to the report, Congress passed the Indian Education Act of 1972 to overhaul the Indigenous education system. The Indian Education Act of 1972 included funding and required local education agencies (LEAs) to consult with Indigenous parents and educators. "At the same time, the scope of the legislation was broad enough to deal with many issues that extended beyond cultural differences and curricular sensitivity: transportation, nutrition, providing eyeglasses, and dental work" (Treuer, 2019, p. 334), all necessities for children to learn.

On June 22, 2021, the Secretary of the Interior, Deb Haaland, directed the Department of Interior agencies to investigate "the Federal Indian boarding school system to examine the scope of the system, with a focus on the location of the schools, burial sites, and identification of children who attended the schools" (Newland, 2022, para. 1). On April 1, 2022, Bryan Newland delivered the *Federal Indian Boarding School Initiative Investigative Report* to Haaland. In his cover letter, Newland (2022) wrote, "This report confirms that the United States directly targeted American Indian...children in the pursuit of a policy of cultural assimilation that coincided with Indian territorial dispossession" (para. 4).

The report confirmed that Indigenous children were forced to do manual labor that left them "with employment options often irrelevant to the industrial U.S. economy, further disrupting Tribal economies" (Newland, 2022, p. 8). Additionally, the report highlighted that boarding schools enforced rules "through punishment including corporal punishment such as solitary confinement; flogging; withholding food; whipping; slapping; and cuffing" (Newland, 2022, p. 8). The report went on to state that "approximately 19 Federal Indian boarding schools accounted for over 500 American Indian, Alaska Native, and Native Hawaiian child deaths. As the investigation continues, the Department expects the number of recorded deaths to increase" (Newland, 2022, p. 9).

The off-reservation boarding school model had extensive and far-reaching detrimental consequences for Indigenous tribes. One significant impact was the spread of the myth that Indigenous people had disappeared from the United States, erasing their presence and contributions from the national consciousness (Mays, 2021). This narrative not only undermines the visibility of Indigenous communities but also contributes to erasing their cultural identities, traditions, and ongoing struggles. Additionally, the boarding school system's efforts to assimilate Indigenous children further worsened the marginalization and disenfranchisement of Indigenous populations, and the consequences of this are still felt by Indigenous people today.

Activity 7.31: Intergenerational Trauma and Residential Schools

Video: What is Generational Trauma? (https://www.youtube.com/watch?v=sxiT7Ddd2Ts)

One or more interactive elements has been excluded from this version of the text. You can view them online here: https://milnepublishing.geneseo.edu/social-justice-in-human-services/?p=409#oembed-26 (#oembed-26)

Video: How Does the Boarding School Era Impact Native Youth Today? (https://www.youtube.com/watch?v=FsXKsCbNkQI)

One or more interactive elements has been excluded from this version of the text. You can view them online here: https://milnepublishing.geneseo.edu/social-justice-in-human-services/?p=409#oembed-27 (#oembed-27)

Discussion Question

- What is generational trauma? In what ways might Indigenous people experience generational trauma?
- What strategies for healing and resilience are out there for Indigenous communities dealing with generational trauma? How do these strategies balance the need for cultural preservation with the realities of past and ongoing trauma?
- How do we connect generational trauma and assimilation with broader social justice movements? What role should social justice play in addressing the historical and ongoing harms experienced by Indigenous people?

Legislation Impacting Indigenous Populations

From the late 19th century to the present day, many governmental policies and legislative actions have impacted the experience of being Indigenous in the United States. Relevant legislation includes the 1885 Major Crimes Act, the 1887 Dawes Act (General Allotment Act), the 1924 Indian Citizenship Act, the Meriam Report in 1928 (as discussed earlier in this chapter), the Indian Reorganization Act of 1934, the 1953 Public Law 280, and the Indian Civil Rights Act of 1968.

The 1885 Major Crimes Act

The 1885 Major Crimes Act changed how major criminal offenses on tribal lands are prosecuted. Before this, tribal courts had primary jurisdiction over criminal offenses committed by Indigenous people on reservations. However, the Major Crimes Act granted the United States federal jurisdiction over serious crimes committed by Indigenous people on reservations (Office for Victims of Crime, n.d.). This changed the power dynamic on the reservations and in tribal courts. The Major Crimes Act remains a topic of discussion and controversy, particularly in debates about the balance of federal and tribal authority, the rights of Native Americans, and the effectiveness of the federal criminal justice system in addressing crime on reservation land.

> ### Activity 7.32 – The Major Crimes Act of 1885
>
> **Video: What is the Major Crimes Act?** (https://www.youtube.com/watch?v=a62ar39rAYo)
>
> *One or more interactive elements has been excluded from this version of the text. You can view them online here: https://milnepublishing.geneseo.edu/social-justice-in-human-services/?p=409#oembed-28 (#oembed-28)*
>
> **Discussion Questions**
>
> - Is it fair that only Indigenous people in the United States can be tried twice for the same crime because of the Major Crimes Act? Why or why not?
> - How does the Major Crimes Act continue to impact Native American communities today? Are there ongoing debates or legal challenges related to the Act or its modern implications?
> - In what ways did the Major Crimes Act contribute to the erosion of tribal sovereignty and self-governance? How did it affect the authority and role of tribal courts in handling criminal matters?

The 1887 Dawes Act (General Allotment Act)

Signed into law on February 8th, 1887, the Dawes Act, or the General Allotment Act, exemplified the shift towards assimilating Indigenous people. The Dawes Act focused on breaking up reservations and allotting reservation land to Indigenous individuals instead of tribes. The Act encouraged Indigenous individuals who were allotted land to start farms as a first step to assimilation into White culture. Many tribes were excluded from the Act; however, as time went by, subsequent events extended the provisions of the Dawes Act (National Archives, n.d.).

> ### Activity 7.33 – The Dawes Act
>
> **Video: The Dawes Act** (https://www.youtube.com/watch?v=HrUv9XbQhbo)

One or more interactive elements has been excluded from this version of the text. You can view them online here: https://milnepublishing.geneseo.edu/social-justice-in-human-services/?p=409#oembed-29 (#oembed-29)

Discussion Questions

- How did the Dawes Act affect the social and cultural structure of Native American tribes?
- What were the main criticisms of the Dawes Act from contemporary Native American leaders and advocates? How did Native American communities resist or respond to the Dawes Act?
- In what ways does the impact of the Dawes Act still resonate in Native American communities today?

The 1924 Indian Citizenship Act

The 1924 Indian Citizenship Act, or the Snyder Act, granted citizenship to all Indigenous people born in the United States. While this was a step towards inclusion, many Indigenous people still faced discrimination, particularly around the right to vote, which was managed by the states until 1957 (Library of Congress, n.d.-b).

Activity 7.34 – The 1924 Indian Citizenship Act

Video: Echoes Extra: The 1924 Indian Citizenship Act (https://www.youtube.com/watch?v=5ocvDDGeVfw)

 One or more interactive elements has been excluded from this version of the text. You can view them online here: https://milnepublishing.geneseo.edu/social-justice-in-human-services/?p=409#oembed-30 (#oembed-30)

Further Reading: David Dry's Article "Unnatural Naturalization" (https://cdr.lib.unc.edu/concern/dissertations/z603r759q)

Discussion Questions

- What does it mean to be a ward of the government versus a citizen?
- How did the 1924 Indian Citizenship Act fit into the broader context of assimilation policies aimed at Native Americans? In what ways did it both support and conflict with efforts to preserve Native American cultures and tribal sovereignty?
- How did the Indian Citizenship Act of 1924 influence subsequent federal policies

towards Native Americans? What were the long-term implications for Native American rights and sovereignty?
- How is the Indian Citizenship Act of 1924 viewed today by Native American communities and scholars? Discuss the ongoing debates about its legacy.

The Indian Reorganization Act of 1934

The Indian Reorganization Act (IRA) of 1934, or the Wheeler-Howard Act, ended allotment and encouraged tribal governments to develop and instill United States-style governance on reservations. During reservation, boarding schools, and allotment, many tribes struggled to maintain their traditional style of governance. The IRA encouraged tribes to organize governmental systems and adopt constitutions (National Library of Medicine, n.d.).

Activity 7.35 – The Indian Reorganization Act (IRA)

Video: 1934 Indian Reorganization Act and its effect on Leadership (https://www.youtube.com/watch?v=Z8z5L7Z-0sU)

One or more interactive elements has been excluded from this version of the text. You can view them online here: https://milnepublishing.geneseo.edu/social-justice-in-human-services/?p=409#oembed-31 (#oembed-31)

Discussion Questions

- How did the IRA of 1934 impact traditional leadership structures within Native American tribes? What were the long-term consequences of this?
- In what ways did the introduction of tribal councils under the IRA both empower and challenge Native communities?
- How does the video suggest that the IRA's focus on written constitutions affected oral traditions and the passing down of leadership roles in Native communities?

The 1953 Public Law 280

The 1953 Public Law 280 allowed certain states to assume the authority once held by the federal government in prosecuting major crimes. Initially, this authority was given to six states: California, Minnesota, Nebraska, Oregon, Wisconsin, and Alaska. Other states were later allowed to choose to opt into the law. This law again impacted the power balance on reservations and increased state presence on tribal lands. Later amendments allowed states to return cases to federal courts if needed and allowed the tribal government to request the Attorney General intercede on cases (Office for Victims of Crime, n.d.).

The Indian Civil Rights Act of 1968

The Indian Civil Rights Act (ICRA) of 1968 limits tribal governments from creating or enforcing laws that violate certain individual rights. It is often compared to the Bill of Rights in the United States Constitution. Specifically, the ICRA protects freedoms such as religion and speech, prohibits double jeopardy, and prevents self-incrimination in criminal proceedings. Additionally, the law allows federal courts to get involved in disputes within tribes to ensure that these rights are respected, thereby balancing individual rights with tribal sovereignty (Library of Congress, n.d.-c).

Indigenous Activism

Since colonial times, Indigenous peoples have fought for their right to exist and resisted oppressive systems in the United States. People such as Arthur Parker (Seneca), Laura Cornelius Kellogg (Oneida), Charles Eastman (Dakota), and Annie Mae Aquash (Mi'kmaq) have all been involved in Indigenous activism (Blackhawk, 2023).

> ### Activity 7.36 – Indigenous Organizations
>
> **Society of American Indians (SAI)**
>
> - Established in 1911 by both Indigenous and non-Indigenous people.
> - Mission: To advocate for the rights of Indigenous people as sovereign nations (Mays, 2021).
> - Controversy: SAI also promoted U.S. citizenship for Indigenous people, seen by some as a tool of assimilation (Gillio-Whitaker, 2019).
> - Dissolved in 1923 due to internal conflicts, including disagreements over peyote use in spiritual practices.
>
> **National Council of American Indians**
>
> - Founded in 1923 after SAI's dissolution.
> - Mission: To continue advocacy for Indigenous rights.
> - Dissolved in 1944 when the National Congress of American Indians was formed.
>
> **National Congress of American Indians (NCAI)**

- Established in 1944 by 80 delegates from 50 tribes to combat treaty rights violations and the threat of termination (Gillio-Whitaker, 2019). The NCAI is still active today.
- Mission: To provide a unified voice for Indigenous people.
- Voice: The NCAI was a strong voice in the Indigenous civil rights movement and often represented tribes in court.

Discussion Questions

- How did the push for U.S. citizenship by early Native American rights organizations, such as SAI, reflect broader tensions between assimilation and sovereignty?
- Compare the approaches of the SAI, National Council of American Indians, and NCAI in addressing federal policies. How did their strategies evolve over time?
- Discuss the impact of the NCAI on the Native American civil rights movement and its role in shaping federal policies related to Indigenous rights.

During the 1960s, many Indigenous people participated in the Civil Rights Movement. In 1968, Indigenous leaders of the National Indian Youth Council, including Hank Adams (Assiniboine), Mel Thom (Walker River Paiute), and Tillie Walker (Mandan-Hidatsa), participated in the Poor People's Campaign initiated by Dr. Martin Luther King Jr. and the Southern Christian Leadership Conference (Mays, 2021). For many Indigenous activists, "fighting for the basic needs of Native people, especially the poor, did not stand in contradiction to their goals of tribal sovereignty" (Mays, 2021, p. 119). On May 1, 1968, Hank Adams stated:

> We have joined the Poor People's Campaign because most of us know that our families, tribes, and communities number among those suffering most in this country. We are not begging, we are demanding what is rightfully ours...Our chief spokesman in the Federal Government, the Department of the Interior has failed us...The Interior Department began failing because it was built and operates under a racist and immoral and paternalistic and colonialistic system. There is no way to improve racism, immorality, and colonialism. It can only be done away with. (Mays, 2021, p. 119)

Activity 7.37 – Digging Deeper: Fishing Rights

In 1968, Hank Adams and Tillie Walker joined members of the Nisqually and Puyallup tribes in Washington, D.C. The tribes had been fighting for their fishing rights, which were guaranteed by treaties with the United States government since the 1950s.

> **Video: The Civil Rights Struggle of the Pacific Northwest-The Fish Wars**
> (https://www.youtube.com/watch?v=9U5zTalWaxs)
>
> *One or more interactive elements has been excluded from this version of the text. You can view them online here: https://milnepublishing.geneseo.edu/social-justice-in-human-services/?p=409#oembed-32 (#oembed-32)*
>
> **Discussion Questions**
>
> - How did the Fish Wars reflect the broader struggle between Native American treaty rights and state regulations in the United States?
> - In what ways did the outcomes of the Fish Wars impact future legal and environmental battles for Native American communities?
> - How did the Fish Wars highlight the intersection between Indigenous rights and environmental conservation efforts?

Red Power

During the late 1960s and throughout the 1970s, Indigenous people struggled to establish themselves as American citizens and as members of sovereign nations. Like the experiences of young Black Americans and the formation of the Black Power movement, young Indigenous people became "disenchanted with the conservative values of their parents' generation" (Gillio-Whitaker, 2019, p. 103).

For Indigenous activists, the call for Red Power was "an assertion of Indigenous sovereignty, a declaration that Native people were there to stress to the white settlers that they were reclaiming their right to sovereignty" (Mays, 2021, p. 110). Some Indigenous groups, such as the American Indian Movement (AIM), used strategies similar to those of the Black Panther Party (Mays, 2021).

American Indian Movement (AIM)

In 1968, Dennis Banks (Ojibwe), Clyde Bellecourt (Ojibwe), Vernon Bellecourt (Ojibwe), George Mitchell (Ojibwe), and Harold Powless (Oneida) established AIM in Minneapolis, Minnesota. AIM was modeled, in part, on the Black Panther Party and its militant style. AIM members, like Black Panther Party members, believed in self-defense, and members often carried weapons to protect themselves. AIM patrols, like the Black Panther Party patrols, followed Minneapolis police and documented any indication of unwarranted brutality (Treuer, 2019).

Activity 7.38 – AIM

Video: Storied 1968: American Indian Movement (https://www.youtube.com/watch?v=LLh3gw0kVhQ)

 One or more interactive elements has been excluded from this version of the text. You can view them online here: https://milnepublishing.geneseo.edu/social-justice-in-human-services/?p=409#oembed-33 (#oembed-33)

Discussion Questions

- How did the political and social climate of the 1960s contribute to the emergence of AIM?
- What tactics did AIM use to draw attention to Native American issues, and how effective were these methods in achieving their goals?
- How did AIM's goals intersect with other civil rights movements of the 1960s?

In 1970, AIM occupied an abandoned naval air station and a Lac Courte Oreilles Reservation dam. The first occupation was to bring attention to the need for improved Indigenous education, and the second occupation was to recoup reparations for the illegal flooding that had affected the Lac Courte Oreilles Reservation (Treuer, 2019). The following year, AIM occupied the BIA headquarters in Washington D.C. "to protest BIA policies and paternalism" (Treuer, 2019, p. 301). Although AIM's occupation efforts produced little tangible results, they gained some national attention.

In 1972, AIM took part in the Trail of Broken Treaties caravan sponsored by Robert Burnette, the chairperson of the Rosebud Reservation (Treuer, 2019).

> [Burnette] gave voice to the idea of a caravan that would travel from reservation to reservation across the country in order to draw media attention to the struggles of Indians there and to the federal government's failure to address them or to meet its treaty obligations to sovereign Indian nations. (Treuer, 2019, p. 301)

Once again, AIM gained national attention and even some support from other national organizations such as the Native American Rights Fund and the National Council on Indian Opportunity.

The Trail of Broken Treaties caravan ended its journey in Washington, D.C. When they arrived, AIM members found that they had no place to stay and that the protest permits they had applied for had been denied (Treuer, 2019). AIM members went to the BIA's office and held a press conference. Russell Means (Oglala) gave a speech in which he stated, "You can see the frustration here, in the young people, and even in the old. Our full-bloods, the chiefs of our tribes, are saying it's time to pick up guns" (Treuer, 2019, p. 303).

AIM members refused to leave the BIA's office and, at first, demanded to meet with a representative of President Richard Nixon. Eventually, the AIM members demanded to meet with Nixon himself (Treuer, 2019). Protestors gathered outside of the BIA in support of AIM, and although the United States marshals were also present, they did not engage in any violence.

The protest continued for a few more days until Nixon's administration obtained a court order to evict the AIM members. When they learned of the court order, they vandalized the BIA office. The damages cost over $2 million (Treuer, 2019). Although furious, Nixon conceded to the AIM members and gave them $66,650 to return home. Once again, although accomplishing nothing, AIM gained national attention. And, more importantly, they encourage pride in their heritage.

> [AIM showed] Indians around the country that they were proud of being Indian, and in the most uncomfortable ways possible for the mainstream. Indians from reservations and cities alike were, for the first time, pushing back against the acculturation machine that was a part of America's domestic imperial agenda, and doing it loud and proud. (Treuer, 2019, p. 307)

Pine Ridge – Part 1

In 1972, Dick Wilson (Oglala) was elected to be the chairperson of the Pine Ridge Reservation in South Dakota. Wilson, like many other Pine Ridge Reservation chairs, used his power to engage in nefarious dealings (Treuer, 2019). Wilson had his own "ever-growing private security force, who was aided and advised by Nixon's domestic commando force, the Special Operations Group" (Treuer, 2019, p. 320), known as the Guardians of the Oglala Nation or GOONs. Members of the Oglala tribe requested AIM to intervene.

In 1973, Wilson was impeached, but the charges were dismissed due to technicalities. "Wilson remained in office and the village of Pine Ridge became increasingly militarized, packed with GOONs, Special Operation Group forces, U.S. marshals, and FBI agents. Tribal headquarters were sandbagged and crowned with a .50 caliber machine gun" (Treuer, 2019, p. 321).

On February 27, 1973, Russell Means (Oglala) along with other AIM members and approximately 200 members of the Oglala tribe seized control of the town of Wounded Knee. AIM and the Oglala tribe members declared Wounded Knee the Independent Oglala Nation "and said that as a sovereign nation it would negotiate directly only with the U.S. secretary of state" (Treuer, 2019, p. 322). Their purpose was to protest Wilson and the militarization of Pine Ridge.

Law enforcement immediately surrounded Wounded Knee and, at first, only intermittent gunfire was exchanged (Treuer, 2019). However, as the protest continued, the exchange of gunfire intensified.

> Despite the fact the 1878 Posse Comitatus Act forbade using the military against American citizens, even before the siege began on February 27, General Alexander Haig authorized the use of APCs [armored personnel carriers] and the U.S. Air Force at Pine Ridge. (Treuer, 2019, p. 324)

The AIM and the Oglala tribe members were armed with shotguns and deer rifles.

A series of negotiators met with members of AIM and the Oglala tribe to try to end the standoff. However, gunfights continued and the "cycle-violence, demands, negotiation, breakdown, more violence" continued (Treuer, 2019, p. 325). At the end, it was the Oglala tribe members who stopped the protest. Two leaders of AIM, Dennis Banks and Russell Means were arrested and charged with conspiracy and assault, but the charges were dismissed due to United States' officials mishandling of evidence and witnesses.

In total, the occupation of Wounded Knee lasted for 71 days. Two protestors were killed, and one was severely injured. One FBI agent was shot, possibly by friendly fire, and was paralyzed. Yet, Dick Wilson continued his corrupt reign over Pine Ridge (Treuer, 2019).

Pine Ridge – Part 2

In 1975, AIM members returned to the Pine Ridge Reservation and engaged in a gunfight that left three people dead (Treuer, 2019). Wilson and his GOONs had continued to terrorize Pine Ridge. Over 50 murders were committed between 1973 and 1976, many of which neither Wilson nor the FBI ever investigated. Some AIM members, including Leonard Peltier, continued to visit and live near Pine Ridge Reservation.

Peltier, along with some friends, was staying on the Jumping Bull Ranch located on the Pine Ridge Reservation (Treuer, 2019). Peltier was not only a member of AIM but also a federal fugitive. Two FBI agents, Jack Coler and Ron Williams, and two BIA Officers, Robert Ecoffey (Oglala) and Glen Little Bird (Nez Perce), were patrolling the area. The agents and officers thought they had located a suspect, and drove onto the Jumping Bull Ranch. Instead, they encountered Peltier. According to forensic reports, Coler and Williams

> didn't make it farther than the middle of a ten-acre pasture before the Indians ahead of them took position on higher ground and fired more than 125 rounds into the agents' cars. The agents fired a total of four times with their .38 service revolvers and once with the .308 rifle. (Treuer, 2019, p. 352)

Both FBI agents died. Peltier, who had fled to Canada, was extradited and charged with murder. Peltier was convicted and sentenced to two consecutive life sentences and remains in prison today (Treuer, 2019).

After the shootout at Jumping Bull, the majority of AIM leadership was either in prison or on the run. "The Jumping Bull incident was largely the end of AIM's efficacy as a prod to the nation's conscience" (Treuer, 2019, p. 356). By 1979, many Indigenous people wanted nothing to do with AIM or the violence that followed it.

Indigenous Female Activism

Many of the Red Power group members were young, urban males who were unaware of the matrilineal histories of their tribes. These men were highly acculturated to White society and often excluded women from the Red Power Movement (Gillio-Whitaker, 2019). In 1974, a group of female AIM members established the Women of All Red Nations (WARN) in response to the patriarchal structure of AIM.

WARN focused much of its efforts on Indigenous women's health issues, "especially exposing that the federal government had forcibly sterilized thousands of Indian women without their knowledge" (Gillio-Whitaker, 2019, p. 117). WARN focused national attention on the high rates of birth defects, cancer, and miscarriages caused by the uranium extraction of the Black Hills on the Pine Ridge Reservation.

WARN also brought national attention to the fact that up to 35% of Indigenous children were removed from their homes and placed in foster care, put up for adoption, or placed in institutions. In 1978, WARN's advocacy led to the Indian Child Welfare Act, which was created to

> protect the best interest of Indian Children and to promote the stability and security of Indian tribes and families by the establishment of minimum Federal standards for the removal of Indian children and placement of such children in homes which will reflect the unique values of Indian culture. (Indian Child Welfare, 1978)

Other Indigenous female activist groups were established to address a myriad of issues. In 2004, the Council of Thirteen Indigenous Grandmothers was founded as "an alliance of prayer, education and healing for our Mother Earth, all Her inhabitants, all the children, and for the next seven generations to come" (Gillio-Whitaker, 2019, p. 119). In 2012, the Idle No More Movement, specifically established to fight against a group of Canadian laws, caught on in the United States as an environmental rights movement. In 2015, a group of Indigenous women created the Indigenous Women of the Americas—Defenders of Mother Earth Treaty. "The treaty links the violence done to the Earth with the violence done to women, naming the crisis of missing, murdered, raped, and enslaved women in Indigenous communities worldwide" (Gillio-Whitaker, 2019, p. 120).

No DAPL Movement

In 2016, Indigenous activists, many of whom lived on the Standing Rock Reservation in North Dakota, began protesting the proposed Dakota Access Pipeline (DAPL). Part of the DAPL's route was to go underneath the Missouri River upstream of the Standing Rock Reservation (Treuer, 2019). This part of the route made the DAPL a violation of the 1868 *Fort Laramie Treaty* between the United States government and the Sioux Nation. In the treaty, the United States government recognized that the Black Hills were a part of the Great Sioux Reservation and, therefore, belonged exclusively to the Sioux people.

"Massive global resistance to Big Oil, decades of political organizing by Native people, networking across multiple spheres of interest, and sophisticated use of social media all account for the groundswell that made the Standing Rock convergence possible" (Gillio-Whitaker, 2019, p. 121). During the protest, crowds of protesters numbered up to 13,000 people (Gillio-Whitaker, 2019; Treuer, 2019). Indigenous people from over 300 tribes attended the protest and "it was the largest gathering of Indians in the United States since the same tribes…formed the tribal armies that defeated the U.S. Calvary at Little Bighorn" (Treuer, 2019, p. 435).

The Standing Rock protestors were non-violent. However, others were not. Private security teams hired by Energy Transfer Partners, the contracted developer of the DAPL, used violent methods on the protestors. The methods included pepper spray, the use of attack dogs, water cannons, and rubber bullets. Hundreds of protestors were arrested (Treuer, 2019).

The Standing Rock protest ended after ten months in February of 2017. Donald Trump took office as President and issued an executive order that construction of the DAPL was to resume. On May 14, 2017, the DAPL began carrying over 400,000 barrels of oil per day "…from the Bakken oil fields in northern North Dakota to Patoka, Illinois, over 1,172 miles, across four states, and under the Missouri and Mississippi Rivers" (Treuer, 2019, p.432).

Native Lives Matter

After the re-emergence of the Black Lives Matter (BLM) movement in 2020, some Indigenous people used the phrase Native Lives Matter to bring attention to the fact that "they, too were murdered by police and continued to suffer all sorts of violence related not just to racism but the ongoing forms of dispossession they experience every day" (Mays, 2021, p. 164). In fact, Indigenous people have been disproportionately murdered at the hands of police more than any other racial group in the United States. "For every one million people in the United States, an average of 2.9 Indigenous people were killed in an interaction with law enforcement, primarily police shootings, in the years between 1999 and 2015" (Mays, 2021, p. 164). That rate was 12% higher than for Black Americans during the same time.

Doctrine of Discovery – Part 2

In 1964, Vine Deloria, Jr. (Standing Rock Sioux) was elected as the head of the National Congress of American Indians (Lepore, 2018). In 1972, Deloria wrote *An Open Letter to the Heads of the Christian Churches in America* (Jones, 2023). In the letter, Deloria stated:

> We have been placed beyond the remedies of the Constitution of the United States because the Doctrine of Discovery has never been disclaimed by either the government of the Christian nations of the world or by the leaders of the Christian churches of the world. And more especially by the leaders of the Christian churches of this country...No effort has been made by Christians to undo the wrongs that were done, albeit mistakenly, and which are perpetuated because Christians refuse to...appraise the present situation in its true historical light (p 182).

In 2007, after 20 years, the United Nations passed the *Declaration on the Rights of Indigenous Peoples* (Jones, 2023). Article 8.1 of the *Declaration* (United Nations, 2007) states, "Indigenous peoples and individuals have the right not to be subjected to forced assimilation or destruction of their culture" (p. 10). The United States, Australia, Canada, and New Zealand were the only countries in the United Nations that voted against the *Declaration* (Jones, 2023).

Immediately after the *Declaration* passed, over 12 Christian organizations denounced the *Doctrine of Discovery*. In a released statement, the Episcopal Church in America repudiated the *Doctrine of Discovery* and asked that the United States change its vote against the *Declaration*. "On December 16, 2010, bowing to international and domestic pressure, President Barack Obama announced that the United States would reverse its position, becoming the last of the four holdout states to affirm the declaration" (Jones, 2023, p. 271).

Since 2010, the World Council of Churches (WCC), a group of more than 350 churches, the Evangelical Lutheran Church of the United States, and dozens of other Christian organizations have also denounced the *Doctrine of Discovery* (Jones, 2023). The Catholic Church nullified the Doctrine of Discovery back in the 1500s, but the damage was done as it seeped into colonialism in the Americas. In 2023, the Catholic Church again nullified the Doctrine of Discovery. Pope Francis stated, "Never again can the Christian community allow itself to be infected by the idea that one culture is superior to others, or that it is legitimate to employ ways of coercing others" (Chappell, 2023, para. 19).

The Contemporary Experience of Being Indigenous in the United States

Indigenous people have fought for their rights as sovereign nations and for their rights as individual human beings since the first White European explorer landed on the shores of North America. And Indigenous people continue to fight. According to Mays (2021), it is crucial "to understand the relationship between literal dispossession and symbolic dispossession through representations of Native people within popular culture" (p. 84). Nordel (2021) goes on to say, "The discrimination Native Americans face...often takes the form of not being considered at all" (p. 10).

In October of 2021, Joe Biden was the first sitting President to celebrate Indigenous Peoples' Day (Jones, 2023). Biden wrote:

> It is a measure of our greatness as a Nation that we do not seek to bury these shameful episodes of our past—that we face them honestly, we bring them to light, and we do all we can do to address them. (Jones, 2023, p. 265)

The Wabanaki Alliance was a tribal newspaper that was in print from 1977 – 1982. It was published in Orono, Maine by the Indian Resource Center. Once a month it featured articles about Passamaquoddy and Penobscot families, community events, and political news.

Being Latinx in the United States

Latinx history in the United States is both rich and complex, having been shaped by colonization, migration, and the westward expansion of the country. It is no wonder that the Latinx population's historical ties to the United States run so deep, when you consider that until the late 19th century states like Texas, New Mexico, and California were part of Mexico.. Over time, the Latinx population in the United States has continued to grow through migration, especially from Mexico, Puerto Rico, Cuba, and Central America. This migration was driven by economic opportunities, political upheavals, and labor demands, which still exist today. Despite marginalization and discrimination in the United States, the Latinx population has significantly influenced American culture, politics, and society.

> ### Activity 7.39 – Digging Deeper: Latinx statistics
>
> Below, find some statistics on the Latinx/Hispanic population in the United States.
>
> - As of 2023, 63.7 million people in the United States were classified as Hispanic by the United States Census Bureau (2023). This is 19.1% of the total population of the United States.
> - About one-third of that population are immigrants (Moslimani et al., 2023).
> - 72% of those classified as Hispanic in 2021 were English-proficient (Moslimani et al., 2023). Since 2010, the United States-born Hispanic population has grown by 10.7 million, while the immigrant population has only grown by 1.1 million.
> - In 2021, 81% of Hispanics living in the United States were U.S. citizens (Moslimani et al., 2023).
> - 78% of Hispanic immigrants have lived in the United States for more than 10 years (Moslimani et al., 2023).
> - As of 2022, the average age was 30.7 years old. (United States Census Bureau, 2023).
> - One in five Hispanics over 25 years old has a bachelor's degree or higher (Moslimani et al., 2023).
>
> Discussion Questions
>
> - What about these statistics surprised you?
> - What impact has the media had on your interaction with these statistics?

Inter-Group Diversity

According to Ramos (2020), the experience of being unsure of identity is common within the Latinx population. While she identifies strongly with the term Latinx and feels it is inclusive of her queerness, she also acknowledges that not all people of South American/Caribbean descent feel this term to be accurate. We will primarily use the term Latinx in this text due to the author's preference. However, this discussion of terminology mirrors the struggle of writing this section of text—the Latinx population is large, diverse, and growing in the United States.

> ### Activity 7.40 – Digging Deeper: Caribbean Countries
>
> Video: Here's Why Puerto Rico is Part of the U.S.- Sort Of (https://youtu.be/Bx_o1PWHdLA?si=YP2bavmRvuWMmIqK)
>
> *One or more interactive elements has been excluded from this version of the text. You can view them online here: https://milnepublishing.geneseo.edu/social-justice-in-human-services/?p=409#oembed-34 (#oembed-34)*
>
> Video: Afro Latinos Get DNA Tested (https://www.youtube.com/watch?v=xsmy3kYNDpI)
>
> *One or more interactive elements has been excluded from this version of the text. You can view them online here: https://milnepublishing.geneseo.edu/social-justice-in-human-services/?p=409#oembed-35 (#oembed-35)*
>
> **Discussion Questions**
>
> - How does Puerto Rico fit into our history as a country?
> - What did you learn from the DNA video? Why do the results of the DNA testing matter in a discussion of what Latinx is?
> - How do Afro-Latinx individuals navigate the complexities of race within the broader Latinx community? How does their experience differ from that of lighter-skinned Latinx individuals?

While many assume all Brown people or Latinx folks are Mexican and that they share a single distinct culture, the Latinx identity in the United States includes people from numerous other countries of origin such as Puerto Rico, Cuba, Dominican Republic, Guatemala, and Colombia. These groups each bring unique cultural traditions, histories, and languages to the broader Latinx community. For example, Puerto Ricans have a distinct history as United States citizens since the early 20th century. In contrast, Cubans have a long migration history shaped by political shifts such as the Cuban Revolution (Duany, 1999). In addition, a substantial portion of the Latinx population in the United States were born in the United States and thus consider themselves American nationals.

> **Activity 7.41 – Digging Deeper: Cultural Influences and Appropriation**
>
> Over the past two decades, Latinx representation in the media, television, film, music, and literature has increased. From the success of TV shows like *Jane the Virgin* and films like *Coco*, to the rise of Latin pop music, Latinx culture has become more visible and influential throughout United States popular culture. As a result, cultural appropriation, the act of borrowing or adopting cultural elements of a minority group in an exploitative, disrespectful or stereotypical way, has become a concern. Elements, such as Latinx clothing, hairstyles, music, art, food, language and religious practices are being used outside their original context, often without permission, or understanding, which results in commodifying or trivializing these cultural symbols and components of the Latinx identity. This is especially concerning when the group adopting them is in a position of privilege or power while the original culture is marginalized.
>
> **Article: Some say a 'Day of the Dead' Barbie is guilty of cultural appropriation. Its designer says it is celebrating tradition.** (https://www.cnn.com/2020/11/01/us/day-of-the-dead-barbie-cultural-appropriation-trnd/index.html)
>
> **Discussion Questions**
>
> - How might the creation and marketing of the Día De Muertos Barbie doll be seen as a form of cultural appropriation? Discuss the importance of authentic representation versus commodification.
> - Who benefits from the commercialization of Día De Muertos through products like the Barbie doll, and who is potentially marginalized?
> - Do you think Mattel, the creators of the Día De Muertos Barbie, had good intentions? Why or why not?
> - What is the difference between cultural exchange and cultural appropriation?

Language also plays a role in the Latinx identity. The embrace of Spanglish, a combination of English and Spanish, particularly used among younger generations, reflects the hybrid nature of modern Latinx identity while simultaneously challenging the traditional ideas of linguistic purity. The use of Spanish, Spanglish, and Indigenous languages continue to evolve, serving both as a symbol of cultural pride as well as identity. There is also a growing population of United States-born Latinx individuals who do not speak Spanish at all (Sanchez, 2018).

> ### Activity 7.42: Terminology
>
> I remember the first time I (Dr. DeJonge) visited Mexico. A really interesting tour guide discussed the term "Hispanic" and explained that "Hispanic" refers to Spain, the colonizers of Indigenous peoples, and is not how Indigenous people of Central and South America identify themselves. When I asked my Mexican American grandmother about this, she disagreed with the tour guide and said she identified as Hispanic. Fluent in Spanish and a devout Catholic, with little knowledge of her Indigenous roots, my grandmother's perspective showed how deeply colonization has shaped Mexican identity. Although both of these individuals are of Mexican heritage, the contrasting conversations revealed how differently people of Mexican descent relate to their country's history of colonization. This contrast also marked the beginning of my journey to explore my cultural identity.
>
> Interestingly, as I was working on this section, after doing my research, reading Paula Ramos's book, and choosing Latinx as the term for this section of text, my niece brought to my attention that Latine is now considered the proper term. She stated that this was because the "x" in Latinx is inconsistent with the Spanish language for pronouns. See a recent article by Lola Méndez on Latine vs Latinx Hispanic Executive magazine online (https://hispanicexecutive.com/latinx-latine-explainer/).
>
> **Discussion Questions**
>
> - How do terms like Latinx and Latine address issues of gender inclusivity within the Spanish language?
> - Where does not speaking Spanish fit into the experience of being Latinx?
> - How does colonization shape debates over terms like Hispanic and Latino?
> - How can individuals and institutions respectfully navigate these evolving terminologies?

Early History of Latinx Populations in the United States

Before the colonization of the United States, there were no borders between the Indigenous populations of what is currently the United States, Central America (Mexico), and South America. The borders that feel familiar today did not exist in the pre-Spanish colonization world. In 1492, Christopher Columbus landed in the Americas, marking the beginning of Spanish colonization. Spanish explorers, such as Juan Ponce de León (1513) and Hernan Cortes (1519), followed and began conquering and colonizing the Caribbean, Central America, and the current day United States Southwest (Gonzales, 2022).

When the English and Spanish arrived in the Americas in the 1500s, they encountered various Indigenous tribes each in different phases of civilization. Some, such as the Aztecs, had highly developed civilizations that rivaled those in England and Spain. Some, such as the Anasazi and Pueblo tribes, were less organized and were scattered among regions along the Gulf Coast and throughout what is now the Southwest United States. Indigenous tribes varied widely in their languages, traditions, alliances, and religious beliefs (Gonzales, 2022).

The Spanish established settlements, missions, and trade routes throughout current-day Mexico and the Southwestern part of the United States. Often these early settlers are seen historically as unsuccessful in their attempts to colonize the Americas. However, their influence and impact on Mexico and the Southwestern portion of the United States was significant. This colonization blended into the Latinx populations that exist in those areas today. The mixing of the Spanish and Indigenous populations led to Spanish becoming the predominant language in the area and influenced the naming of the towns, rivers, and other landmarks. In addition, the relentless pursuit of resources and conversion to Christianity led to the loss of Indigenous lives in astounding numbers (Gonzalez, 2022). Gonzales (2022) states that in the current United States, "An average of more than one million people perished annually for most of the sixteenth century" (p. 45). Causes of these deaths included direct massacre, enslavement, and diseases such as smallpox and measles, for which the Indigenous population had no immunity.

Activity 7.43 – Digging Deeper: Bartolome de las Casas

Video: Bartolome de las Casas: Changing Your Mind (https://www.youtube.com/watch?v=vH65erzQBkY)

One or more interactive elements has been excluded from this version of the text. You can view them online here: https://milnepublishing.geneseo.edu/social-justice-in-human-services/?p=409#oembed-36 (#oembed-36)

Resource: A Short Account of the Destruction of the Indies (https://nationalhumanitiescenter.org/pds/amerbegin/contact/text7/casas_destruction.pdf)

Discussion Questions

- How did Fray Bartolomé de las Casas' personal transformation reflect broader societal shifts in the Spanish Empire regarding the treatment of Indigenous peoples?
- In what ways do Casas' later views on African slavery complicate his legacy as an advocate for Indigenous rights?
- How can we reconcile Casas' early involvement in the encomienda system with his later critiques of colonial violence?

- How do Casas' arguments for Indigenous rights challenge the prevailing notions of the time about race, religion, and colonial authority?

Spanish settlements served as centers of government and military defense. The settlers' focus was twofold: to convert Indigenous populations to Christianity and to steal Indigenous resources (Gonzales, 2022). Spanish settlements facilitated the extraction of resources, most notably silver and gold. In addition, they were launching points for further resource exploitation. Notable Spanish settlements in North America included St. Augustine, Florida (1565), Santa Fe, New Mexico (1610), and San Diego, California (1769).

Activity 7.44 – Spanish Missions

Spanish missions were religious and cultural institutions established by Spanish settlers in the Americas, particularly in the southwestern United States, California, and parts of Central and South America. Their goal was to convert Indigenous peoples to Christianity, teach European farming techniques, and integrate them into Spanish colonial society. Spanish missions were established in the 16th century and remained in effect until Mexican independence from Spain in 1821. Military regimes brought priests with them who baptized Indigenous people into the Catholic faith by the thousands. In addition, unlike the European settlers who remained in separate family settlements and units, the Spanish colonizers intermixed with the Indigenous population generating a significant number of mixed-race children (Gonzales, 2022).

Video: Spanish Settlement of Texas (https://www.youtube.com/watch?v=Z1rEb3m3lIA)

 One or more interactive elements has been excluded from this version of the text. You can view them online here: https://milnepublishing.geneseo.edu/social-justice-in-human-services/?p=409#oembed-37 (#oembed-37)

Resource: We're Still Here: San Antonio Mission Descendant Stories (https://www.nps.gov/saan/learn/historyculture/we-re-still-here-san-antonio-mission-descendant-stories.htm)

Discussion Questions

- How did the establishment of the missions reflect the colonial power dynamics between Spanish settlers and Indigenous populations?
- In what ways did the mission system perpetuate social and economic inequalities for Indigenous communities?
- What role did missions play in the cultural assimilation of Indigenous peoples? How

> does this impact social justice discussions today?
> - What are the long-term effects of missionization on the social and economic status of Indigenous descendants?

In 1810, Father Miguel Hidalgo y Costilla delivered a speech entitled *Grito de Dolores* (Cry of Dolores) encouraging a revolt. This marked the start of the Mexican independence movement from Spain. Hidalgo rallied Indigenous peasant miners in the Bajío region of Mexico against the oppressive Spanish government and marched across central Mexico, capturing towns and gaining support. However, Hidalgo was not well organized and did not have the military experience to be successful. Spain captured and executed Hidalgo in 1811. Hidalgo's movement, however, was continued by other Mexican leaders utilizing decentralized guerilla tactics (Beezley, 2008).

In 1821, Augustin de Iturbide and Vicente Guerrero worked together to issue the *Plan of Iguala*, which outlined Mexico's independence from Spain. In addition, the plan designated Catholicism as the official religion of Mexico and included equal rights for Spaniards and Mexicans. This united many factions and generated a broad coalition of support for Mexican independence. On August 24, 1821, the Treaty of Cordoba was signed, and Spain recognized Mexico's independence (Beezley, 2008).

Following the revolution and independence, Mexico faced many challenges in establishing itself as a country. One was removing the emperor of Mexico, and adopting a federal constitution (modeled after the United States of America). This was accomplished by 1824. The first president of the United Mexican States was Guadalupe Victoria. Victoria struggled to unify the country, and power struggles between federalists and centralists marred the early decades of independence. In addition, Mexico faced significant economic challenges (Guardino, 2017).

Throughout the 1820s, many settlers from the United States moved to current-day Texas under the Mexican empresario system, which granted land to immigrants in exchange for them becoming both Mexican citizens and converting to Catholicism. Many of the settlers, who were primarily Protestant, resisted Mexican laws and did not integrate into Mexican culture. In particular, the settlers often brought enslaved Africans with them, which was illegal in Mexico (Guardino, 2017).

In 1834, Mexican President Antonio Lopez de Santa Anna established a centralized government. This further alienated Texans as disagreements over language, religion, and legal issues plagued Texan settlers. The first armed conflict between Texas and Mexico occurred in October, 1835, when Mexican troops attempted to retrieve a cannon from settlers in Gonzales, Texas. The settlers resisted. Texan forces captured San Antonio, driving out the Mexican troops. In March, 1836, Santa Anna led Mexican troops to reclaim Texas. They attacked the Alamo, which was being defended by approximately 200 Texans, and won the battle . Despite that defeat, Texas eventually won independence and declared itself an independent republic on March 2, 1836. The Republic of Texas existed for nine years before the United States approved the annexation of Texas amid fears of war with Mexico. Texas entered the United States as the 28th state on February 19, 1846, despite Mexico still claiming ownership of Texas (Guardino, 2017).

In 1846, the Mexican-American War began. The Mexican-American War was driven primarily by territorial disputes around both the annexation of Texas and westward expansion. Many in the United States felt it was the destiny of the United States to expand across the North American continent. Mexico disagreed. The United States even attempted to purchase California and New Mexico from Mexico. Mexican leaders refused. In April, 1846, Mexican troops ambushed a United States patrol in the disputed territory, sparking Congress to declare war on Mexico on May 13, 1846. The United States fought and won many battles against Mexico and eventually captured Mexico City. Ultimately, Mexico lost the war and ceded vast amounts of land to the United States. This included present-day California, Nevada, Utah, Arizona, New Mexico, Kansas, and parts of Wyoming and Colorado, resulting in the United States acquiring about 500,000 square miles of land. The Rio Grande was established as the official border between Texas and Mexico in 1848 (History.com, 2023; Guardino, 2017).

Activity 7.45 – Digging Deeper: Mexican History

Video: The History of Mexico (https://www.youtube.com/watch?v=ag7fpMIfJYA)

 One or more interactive elements has been excluded from this version of the text. You can view them online here: https://milnepublishing.geneseo.edu/social-justice-in-human-services/?p=409#oembed-38 (#oembed-38)

Discussion Questions

- Why is Mexican history important in discussing the Latinx population of the United States?
- How might the history of Mexico impact how people of Mexican descent experience being in the United States?

World Wars I and II

The Latinx population has always been involved in the wars fought by the United States. However, there are few records of how many actually fought, because, up through World War I, Latinx were considered white, not their own distinct race. However, "Ramirez, a history professor at Laredo College, said he's documented at least 5,000 men from Texas with Spanish surnames who served during the Great War" (Contreras, 2023, para. 13). Contreras (2023) states that returning veterans who were Latinx were essential to the Latinx civil rights movements which followed, as they brought home experiences of discrimination from the battlefields of World War I.

By World War II, there was a much higher population of Latinx people living in the United States, particularly those of Mexican descent. Approximately 500,000 Mexican American soldiers served in World War II. Many were in integrated units. However, they still faced significant discrimination which was primarily based on their skin tone. Puerto Ricans also served in both World War I and World War II in large numbers and also faced discrimination based on skin tone and were often sorted into Black and White regimens arbitrarily (Oropeza, n.d.).

Activity 7.46 – The Zoot Suit Riots

Video: Zoot Suit Riots Documentary (https://youtu.be/KxtThBTf0sI?si=yr-jpZe4tu1EHd5D)

One or more interactive elements has been excluded from this version of the text. You can view them online here: https://milnepublishing.geneseo.edu/social-justice-in-human-services/?p=409#oembed-39 (#oembed-39)

Discussion Questions

- How did the social, economic, and political conditions in Los Angeles during the 1940s contribute to the tensions that led to the Zoot Suit Riots?
- What role did racial and ethnic stereotyping play in the public perception of Mexican American youth and the "zoot suit" subculture during this period?
- What did the zoot suit symbolize for Mexican American youth, and why was it perceived as a threat by the dominant culture?
- Identify parallels between the Zoot Suit Riots and contemporary issues such as racial profiling, police violence, or cultural expression.

Legislation Impacting the Latinx Population

The Latinx population, like other marginalized communities, has endured significant systemic discrimination due to social policies, legislative actions, and legal frameworks in the United States. These measures have shaped their access to education, housing, employment, and healthcare, often reinforcing systemic inequalities and societal barriers.

Immigration Policy and Law

When the Mexican Revolution started, people from Mexico began crossing the border into Texas with El Paso serving as a gateway. The Library of Congress (n.d.-a) refers to El Paso at that time as the "Mexican Ellis Island" (para. 1). It is estimated that Mexican immigration tripled during the Mexican Revolution. However, counting the number of immigrants proved to be difficult as many travelled back and forth between the United States and Mexico, and there was a great deal of immigration that occurred illegally.

One of the first legislative acts which impacted the Latinx population was the Immigration Act of 1924, also called the Johnson-Reed Act. This legislation established quotas on immigration, which highly favored European immigration. The Immigration Act of 1924 was passed at the height of the eugenics movement, the belief and practice that certain groups had more desirable hereditary genes than others, and reinforced existing racial hierarchies and stereotypes about Latinx people. The Immigration Act of 1924 also established the visa requirement and the United States Border Patrol, significantly impacting Latinx immigration historically and today (Diamond, 2020).

Activity 7.47 – Latinx Immigration

Video: 100 Years of Immigration History (https://youtu.be/Nhz3u5aGIAY)

 One or more interactive elements has been excluded from this version of the text. You can view them online here: https://milnepublishing.geneseo.edu/social-justice-in-human-services/?p=409#oembed-40 (#oembed-40)

Resource: Slides for Lecture on 100 Years of Immigration History (https://www.sinbarrerascville.org/wp-content/uploads/2019/06/100-Yrs-of-Immigration-History.pdf)

Discussion Questions

- How does the video reflect the shifts in Latinx immigration policies? Identify specific eras or laws (e.g., Chinese Exclusion Act, Immigration Act of 1965) and discuss their impacts on the Latinx community.
- What role do you think public perception plays in legislation? How might those perceptions drive change?
- Advocacy and social movements are two ways we can advance immigrant rights. How does the video inspire advocacy or call for action? Where does learning about the history of immigration fit into this call for action?
- How do the historical policies and barriers described in the video resonate today? How can these historical events impact current immigration policy?

In 1920, the Immigration Act of 1924 was revised to criminalize undocumented entry into the United States. This led to the use of the term "illegal" to describe immigrants who came into the United States outside of the new visa system. By 1930, these policies resulted in repatriation drives, and between 1930 and 1940, 400,000 Mexicans and Mexican Americans were sent "back" or repatriated to Mexico. Approximately 40% of these individuals were American citizens (Morales, 2018).

As the United States entered World War II, following the bombing of Pearl Harbor, there were significant workplace shortages in the United States. To address this, the United States and Mexico negotiated to allow Mexicans to work in the United States on a temporary basis in order to fill jobs. This agreement, called the Bracero Program, brought over 4.5 million Mexican workers into the United States between 1942 and 1964. Laborers from Mexico, under the Bracero Program, were mainly used for agricultural work in California and Texas. These laborers faced brutal working conditions for low pay in the fields and lived under the constant stress of deportation. In addition, they faced discrimination and were often used to break picket lines when strikes occurred. The Bracero Program drove agricultural wages down and circumvented governmental labor policy by exploiting noncitizen workers well beyond World War II (Hernandez, 2006; National Park Service, 2024).

Following World War II, many workers from the Bracero Program remained in the United States. In addition, hundreds of thousands of undocumented workers had come to the United States outside of the Bracero Program (Hernandez, 2006). These individuals were working on farms throughout the American Southwest and California. In response to this, President Dwight D. Eisenhower and Commissioner Joseph Swing of the Immigration and Naturalization Service (INS) authorized Operation Wetback. Operation Wetback was a governmental policy initiative backed by the Immigration and Nationality Act of 1952, which authorized the deportation of undocumented immigrants (Hernandez, 2006).

Operation Wetback, implemented in 1954, was a military-style mass deportation that utilized the Border Patrol to deport upwards of one million Latinx individuals out of the United States, some of whom were United States citizens. Border Patrol Agents "engaged in a coordinated, tactical operation to remove immigrants. Along the way, they used widespread racial stereotypes to justify their sometimes brutal treatment of immigrants" (Blakemore, 2024, August 20, para. 5). Mass raids were conducted across the United States, and immigrants were often deported to unfamiliar cities. Family separation was common. During Operation Wetback, Mexican immigrants were deported by bus, plane, and boat. Often, boats sent individuals further into Mexico, assuming it would be harder for them to return that way. "In Texas, 25 percent of all of the immigrants deported were crammed into boats later compared to slave ships, while others died of sunstroke, disease and other causes while in custody" (Blakemore, 2024, August 20, para. 6).

Immigration policy has continued to be varied and complex for the Latinx population. The Immigration and Nationality Act of 1965 set an annual cap on immigration from the Western Hemisphere, creating new challenges for Latin American immigration. The 1980

Refugee Act established a system for admitting refugees into the United States. While some Latin American refugees were able to immigrate under this act, it has been and continues to be biased based on the status of United States allyship throughout the world. In 1986, the Immigration Reform and Control Act granted amnesty to around 2.7 million undocumented immigrants, many of whom were Latinx. However, ongoing labor demands influenced the continued unauthorized immigration into the United States, which persists today (Massey & Pren, 2012).

In 1996, there was a shift in immigration policy with the Illegal Immigration Reform and Immigrant Responsibility Act, which expanded grounds for deportation. It also established a punitive policy around detention and re-entry bans for those unlawfully caught in the United States. This act reinforced the negative stereotyping of undocumented immigrants as criminals, and undocumented life became further criminalized (Massey & Pren, 2012).

In 2001, the first of many Development, Relief, and Education for Alien Minors (DREAM) Acts was introduced. The goal of the DREAM Acts was to provide a pathway to citizenship for undocumented youth who had come to the United States as children. These youth, often called "Dreamers" in the proposed legislation, had not chosen to enter the United States but were instead brought there by their undocumented parents. In 2012, President Obama established the Deferred Action for Childhood Arrivals (DACA), which protects undocumented youth from deportation. DACA allows work permits for undocumented youth; however, it does not include a path to citizenship. It has benefitted over 800,000 individuals, primarily from Latin America (Rosenblum & Ruiz Soto, 2015).

Activity 7.48 – Deferred Action for Childhood Arrivals (DACA)

Video: WE ARE DREAMers Documentary (https://www.youtube.com/watch?v=jOdLqct0rmo)

One or more interactive elements has been excluded from this version of the text. You can view them online here: https://milnepublishing.geneseo.edu/social-justice-in-human-services/?p=409#oembed-41 (#oembed-41)

Resource: Consideration of Deferred Action for Childhood Arrivals (DACA) (https://www.uscis.gov/DACA)

Discussion Questions

- What is the significance of DACA in the broader context of United States immigration policy? How does it address (or fail to address) systemic issues faced by undocumented youth?
- How does DACA's temporary nature impact the stability and well-being of its recipients? What does this reveal about the broader challenges of immigration reform?
- DACA recipients are often referred to as "Dreamers." How does this label shape public

> perception of undocumented immigrants, and in what ways might it exclude or marginalize others within immigrant communities?
> - How does DACA fit within broader movements for social justice? What lessons can be drawn from other advocacy efforts to push for permanent protections for "Dreamers" and other undocumented immigrants?
> - How does the exclusion of DACA recipients from federal benefits and pathways to citizenship perpetuate systemic inequities?

From 2017 to 2021, policy again shifted with the Trump administration, and zero-tolerance policies led to highly publicized border incarceration and family separation. Videos of children in cages sparked outrage as the Trump administration increased deportation and attempted to repeal DACA (History.com, 2023). In addition, there was increased focus on building a border wall between the United States and Mexico to control immigration. These highly politicized policies, exacerbated by media coverage, led to increased fear and uncertainty among Latinx communities and to increased reports of discrimination towards Latinx people in the United States (Noe-Bustamante et al., 2021).

In 2021, Joe Biden was elected president, and policy towards immigration from the Southern Border again shifted. The Biden presidency worked to protect DACA and create a means for legal immigration from Latinx countries. In addition, the Biden administration focused on family reunification for those separated at the border (Krogstad & Gonzalez-Barrera, 2022). With the 2024 election and another Trump administration looming, many Latinx individuals are again facing discrimination and fear around promised mass deportation (Garsd, 2024).

Activity 7.49 – Digging Deeper: Managing the Southern Border

Video: Five Facts on the History of Border Patrol (https://www.youtube.com/watch?v=ufXKH-pMDDXk)

One or more interactive elements has been excluded from this version of the text. You can view them online here: https://milnepublishing.geneseo.edu/social-justice-in-human-services/?p=409#oembed-42 (#oembed-42)

Video: Riding 'The Death Train' to America's Border (https://www.youtube.com/watch?v=RSwwO00qeB0)

One or more interactive elements has been excluded from this version of the text. You can view them online here: https://milnepublishing.geneseo.edu/social-justice-in-human-services/?p=409#oembed-43 (#oembed-43)

Video: Understanding the Immigration System in 8 Minutes (https://www.youtube.com/watch?v=oqAnzGNfxCY)

One or more interactive elements has been excluded from this version of the text. You can view them online here: https://milnepublishing.geneseo.edu/social-justice-in-human-services/?p=409#oembed-44 (#oembed-44)

Discussion Questions

- All countries have entry rules, and the United States is no different. How do we decide who can come into the United States and who cannot?
- Do we have an ethical obligation to help people who are seeking asylum?
- How do current immigration policies at the southern border align with or contradict human rights principles?
- In what ways can border enforcement practices be reformed to uphold the dignity and safety of migrants?
- How can individuals contribute to creating a more equitable and humane immigration system?
- How does the portrayal of migrants in media and politics influence public opinion and policy?

Employment Law and Policy

As the United States grew, legislation impacted employment, and various employment laws were enacted. In 1935, the National Labor Relations Act, or the Wagner Act, established the right of workers to organize, unionize, and collectively bargain with employers. This act also generated the National Labor Relations Board, an independent agency tasked with enforcing labor laws, resolving employment disputes, and overseeing union elections. While the right to unionize was a decisive shift in United States employment law, the National Labor Relations Act had some very specific exclusions, which still impact the workforce today. One that was particularly impactful for Latinx populations was the exclusion of domestic and agricultural workers. At the time, the majority of Latinx workers in the United States were farmworkers or domestic workers, and this exclusion left them working difficult jobs with no federal protection (National Park Service, 2024).

The Fair Labor Standards Act of 1938 established additional protections for workers in the United States. It established a minimum wage for workers, overtime rules, and child labor protection. Once again, domestic workers and farmworkers were exempted. These exclusions, often lobbied for by owners of large farms, were deeply rooted in racism and bias, as they disproportionately affected individuals from marginalized populations (National Park Service, 2024).

Other Relevant Legislation

Mendez v. Westminster played a pivotal role in the desegregation of public schools in 1947. At the time, many school districts in California were exercising discriminatory practices of separating Latinx children from White children. Mendez, along with other parents, argued that the 14th Amendment's Equal Protection Clause made this segregation unconstitutional. In 1946, the United States district court ruled that school segregation based on national origin was indeed unconstitutional. This ruling was significant because it occurred before the more famous *Brown v. Board of Education* decision in 1954 setting a precedent for desegregating schools in California and paved the way for the later national movement to end school segregation (Hanigan, 2022).

The Fair Housing Act of 1968 aimed to criminalize discrimination in housing based on race, color, religion, sex, and national origin. Before the Fair Housing Act, many Latinx families faced discriminatory practices like redlining, racial covenants, and restrictive zoning laws, which prevented Latinx families from living in predominantly White neighborhoods. As a result, Latinx individuals often lived in substandard, overcrowded housing with limited access to services and education. The passage of the Fair Housing Act prohibited these exclusionary practices. While it provided legal recourse for discrimination in housing, the impacts of the Fair Housing Act were limited by enforcement issues and loopholes. For example, many landlords and real estate agents still found ways to circumvent the law through unofficial redlining practices. Over time, however, the changes sparked by the Fair Housing Act did increase housing access for many Latinx families. This led to a gradual integration of residential areas in cities like Los Angeles, New York, and Chicago (Yzaguirre et al., 1999).

The Bilingual Education Act of 1968 had a significant impact on the Latinx community. The Bilingual Education Act helped lay the foundation for bilingual education programs that would later be expanded in the 1970s and 1980s. These programs provided language support and cultural learning to Latinx children. For Latinx families, the Bilingual Education Act was a critical step toward gaining access to better educational opportunities. However, implementing the Bilingual Education Act faced challenges, such as limited resources, resistance from some educators, and political pushback (Garcia & Sung, 2018).

The Voting Rights Act of 1975 expanded the 1965 Voting Rights Act and was specifically aimed at improving the voting rights of minority communities, including Latinx voters. One significant feature of the 1975 amendment was the provision requiring bilingual ballots and election materials in areas with large populations of United States citizens who were non-English speakers. The law was a response to the growing consensus that language should not be a barrier to voting. The 1975 amendment profoundly impacted the Latinx community, as it led to the creation of bilingual election programs in jurisdictions with significant Latinx populations, particularly in the Southwest and parts of Florida, where many Puerto Rican communities were located (Cartagena, 2005).

Proposition 187, passed in California in 1994, was a highly controversial initiative aimed at restricting access to public services, including education and healthcare, for undocumented immigrants. Specifically, the measure denied public benefits to individuals not legally residing in the United States. Examples of these benefits included non-emergency healthcare and public schooling. The proposition was overwhelmingly supported by White voters and faced significant opposition from immigrant communities. The Latinx community, a substantial portion of California's immigrant population, viewed Proposition 187 as a form of racial and ethnic discrimination. Proposition 187 sparked widespread protests, activism, and a shift in political alignments among Latinx people. Proposition 187 galvanized Latinx political engagement in California as Latinx individuals formed advocacy groups to oppose the proposition and mobilize Latinx voters. Despite its support by White voters, the proposition was eventually ruled unconstitutional by a federal judge in 1997. Ultimately, Proposition 187 had the unintended effect of mobilizing a generation of Latino voters and activists, shaping the political discourse around immigration in the years that followed (Arellano, 2024).

The Personal Responsibility and Work Opportunity Reconciliation Act (PRWORA) of 1996, often referred to as "welfare reform," had a significant impact on low-income Latinx populations. This law, signed by President Bill Clinton, fundamentally altered the nation's welfare system by eliminating the Aid to Families with Dependent Children (AFDC) program and replacing it with Temporary Assistance for Needy Families (TANF). One of the critical aspects of the PRWORA was its emphasis on work requirements and time-limited assistance, which meant that individuals had to find employment to continue receiving benefits (Center for Public Impact, 2017). For the low-income Latinx community, the law's impacts were harsh. Latinx families, particularly immigrant populations, were disproportionately affected by PRWORA. While PRWORA's supporters argued that it encouraged self-sufficiency, advocacy groups and community leaders within the Latinx community criticized the law for being discriminatory, arguing that it unfairly targeted immigrant families, exacerbated poverty, and pushed many families into deeper economic hardship (Lovato & Abrams, 2023).

Activity 7.50 – Digging Deeper: Sonia Sotomayor

Video: Sonia Sotomayor (https://www.youtube.com/watch?v=BDzhYlOpW64)

 One or more interactive elements has been excluded from this version of the text. You can view them online here: https://milnepublishing.geneseo.edu/social-justice-in-human-services/?p=409#oembed-45 (#oembed-45)

Video: The Four Justices: Justice Sonia Sotomayor (https://www.youtube.com/watch?v=PDXrS5nnxsM)

 One or more interactive elements has been excluded from this version of the text. You can view them online here: https://milnepublishing.geneseo.edu/social-justice-in-human-services/?p=409#oembed-46 (#oembed-46)

Discussion Questions

- How has Sonia Sotomayor's background as a Latinx influenced her role as a justice on the Supreme Court?
- Why is Latinx representation in positions of power important?
- How do Sotomayor's childhood and life experiences inform her perspective on fairness and justice within the legal system?

Arizona's Senate Bill 1070 (SB 1070), passed in 2010, was one of the most controversial state-level immigration laws in recent United States history. Officially known as the "Support Our Law Enforcement and Safe Neighborhoods Act," SB 1070 required law enforcement officers to question individuals about their immigration status if there was reasonable suspicion that they were in the country illegally. For the Latinx community, SB 1070 had an immediate impact. Many in the community, including citizens and legal immigrants, feared racial profiling by law enforcement. The passage of SB 1070 sparked widespread national and international condemnation, including protests in Arizona and other parts of the United States. In 2012, the U.S. Supreme Court partially struck down SB 1070, ruling that certain provisions, including the "show me your papers" section, were unconstitutional. However, the court upheld the idea of allowing police to check immigration status during lawful stops, which left much of the law intact (Serratos, 2017).

Activity 7.50 – Digging Deeper: Knowledge Check

- How have legal decisions and laws, such as those related to education, housing, voting, and immigration, shaped the social, political, and economic experiences of the Latinx community in the U.S.?
- How have controversial policies such as California's Proposition 187 and Arizona's SB 1070 sparked political mobilization within the Latinx community?
- How does the Latinx community's experience with legal and political resistance mirror or differ from other marginalized groups in U.S. history?
- How have challenges in implementing these laws (such as enforcement issues or resistance from some sectors) affected their success or failure in achieving full equal-

> ity for Latinx populations?
> - How have these policies contributed to or hindered Latinx economic mobility, integration, and cultural inclusion within broader American society?

The Civil Rights Movement

The Civil Rights Movement of the 20th century represented more than just a quest for African American equality; it also significantly impacted the civil rights struggle of Latinx individuals. The 1964 Civil Rights Act catalyzed multiple civil rights movements within Latinx communities. Protests and activism erupted around systemic discrimination in housing, education, labor, and voting rights.

The Chicano Movement

The Chicano Movement, also known as "El Movimiento," was a civil rights movement that emerged in the 1960s and 1970s. It advocated for the rights and empowerment of Mexican Americans and was part of the broader wave of civil rights movements during this era. The Chicano Movement sought to address issues of inequality, discrimination, and cultural marginalization faced by Mexican Americans in the United States (Kraz, 2021).

Some of the key issues the Chicano Movement addressed were education reform, political empowerment, labor rights, land rights, anti-war activism, and cultural pride and identity. Some of the key individuals in the movement included César Chávez, Dolores Huerta, Reies López Tijerina, Rodolfo Gonzales, and José Ángel Gutiérrez. The Chicano Movement made a lasting impact. It led to reform in education, inspired the development of Chicano studies at universities, highlighted intersectional struggles for Latinx individuals, and cultivated a sense of pride in being Latinx (Kraz, 2021).

The Bracero Program, which began in the 1940s and 1950s, laid the foundation for the Chicano Movement. Farmers' unfair practices in utilizing labor from the Bracero Program led to consistent issues regarding fair labor and labor rights. Working conditions in the fields continued to be difficult. In the fields there were no toilets; water was often not provided or had to be shared; and farmworker housing had no cooking facilities or running water, despite the workers being required to pay rent (United Farm Workers, n.d.).

In 1962, Cesar Chavez and Dolores Huerta co-founded the National Farm Workers Association (NFWA), later renamed the United Farm Workers (UFW). Cesar Chavez, who was the son of farmworkers, spent three years going from farm to farm, talking to and recruiting farmworkers to organize. In 1965, the NFWA organized two small-scale strikes. Despite winning some wage demands, the NFWA still wanted to be recognized as a union, which the farmers refused. Around the same time, a similar organization, the Agricultural Workers

Organizing Committee (AWOC), led a walkout of grape pickers in the Coachella Valley. Again, the farmers gave in to demands regarding pay but refused to accept any attempts at unionizing (United Farm Workers, n.d.).

Dolores Huerta holding a Huelga ("strike") sign as a part of the Delano grape strike in 1966

Activity 7.52 – Digging Deeper: Women in the Labor Movement

Video: Latinas in the Labor Movement: The History You Didn't Learn
(https://www.youtube.com/watch?v=4LNzgpZ6_J8)

 One or more interactive elements has been excluded from this version of the text. You can view them online here: https://milnepublishing.geneseo.edu/social-justice-in-human-services/?p=409#oembed-47 (#oembed-47)

Discussion Questions

- How did societal conditions and labor exploitation drive Latinas to become leaders in the labor movement?
- What challenges did they face as women of color in predominantly male-led labor unions and broader social movements?

> - How did race, gender, and class intersect in the struggles faced by Latinas in the labor movement?
> - What leadership strategies did Latinas use to mobilize workers and communities? How did cultural values influence their approach to organizing?

As the summer of 1965 waned, the grapes were ripening in the Delano area of California. Propelled by their success in the walk-out at Coachella Valley, many migrant workers again demanded a fair wage. When their demands were not met, strikes organized by AWOC occurred at nine farms. As farmers began to bring in Chicano scabs, AWOC approached Cesar Chavez and asked the NFWA to join the strike, which mainly consisted of Filipino workers. While Chavez himself was apprehensive, the vote was overwhelming to join and the NFWA joined the strike. The NFWA brought many more members than the AWOC, and by late September, more than 30 farms were impacted by the strike. Again, the farmers attempted to concede on wages but refused to accept unionization. This time organizers were prepared for this, and any attempts at wage negotiation without unionization were rejected (United Farm Workers, n.d.).

The Civil Rights Movement of the time brought public attention to the issue of racism, and the timing of the strikes, which effectively used public outrage, bolstered its success. Chavez called upon the public to support the farmworkers by refusing to buy non-union grapes, and the public obliged.

> By 1970 the UFW got grape growers to accept union contracts and effectively organized most of that industry, claiming 50,000 dues-paying members—the most ever represented by a union in California agriculture. Gains included a health clinic and health plan, credit union, community center, cooperative gas station, higher wages as well as a union-run hiring hall The hiring hall meant an end to discrimination and favoritism by labor contractors. (United Farm Workers, n.d., para. 22)

Activity 7.53 – Digging Deeper: Cesar Chavez

Video: Cesar Chavez: American Civil Rights Activist (https://www.youtube.com/watch?v=Wznw9TA2jXk&t=47s)

 One or more interactive elements has been excluded from this version of the text. You can view them online here: https://milnepublishing.geneseo.edu/social-justice-in-human-services/?p=409#oembed-48 (#oembed-48)

Discussion Questions

- How did Chavez's work intersect with other civil rights movements of the 1960s and 1970s?
- How did Chavez address racial and economic injustices through his activism?
- What strategies used by Chavez and the UFW can be applied to modern labor movements?
- Do you think nonviolence is always the most effective strategy for social change? Why or why not?
- How might Chavez's movement have been different if social media existed during his time?

Current Experience of Being Latinx in the United States

The United States Census Bureau (2023) states that the Hispanic population in the United States reached 63.7 million in 2022. The Hispanic population is the nation's second-largest racial or ethnic group behind non-Hispanic White people. This racial group is also among the fastest-growing groups in the United States. Since 1970, the Hispanic population has grown more than sixfold (Funk & Lopez, 2022) and represents over 19% of the total population of the United States (U.S. Census Bureau, 2023).

A latinx family in Phoenix, AZ makes tamales together.

Discrimination

According to a 2021 Pew Research Study, more than half of the Latinx population reported experiencing discrimination in 2020. Examples cited included being criticized for speaking

Spanish, being told to go back to their country, fearing for their safety, being called offensive names, and being unfairly stopped by the police (Noe-Bustamante et al., 2021). Respondents also stated that they have experienced discrimination from both Hispanics and non-Hispanics alike and that younger Hispanics experience more discrimination than older individuals. In addition, Noe-Bustamante et al. found that often in the Hispanic population, darker skin usually equals increased discrimination, stating "Hispanics view skin color as a driver of advantage when it comes to getting ahead in the U.S." (para. 19).

In addition to the generalized discrimination discussed by Noe-Bustamante et al. (2021), Afro-Latinx individuals face unique challenges related to their African heritage and Latinx identity. They often navigate experiences of racial discrimination within their Latinx communities while also facing marginalization as people of color in broader society (Pujols, 2022).

Indigenous Latinx people also experience distinct discrimination challenges as they contend with the erasure of their culture and languages within both the larger Latinx community and the dominant society. Indigenous identity within the Latinx community is often overlooked. And because Indigenous populations frequently have darker skin and speak Indigenous languages, Indigenous Latinx individuals are often discriminated against within the general Latinx community (Urrieta & Calderon, 2019).

Discrimination and Mental Health

Studies show that Latinx youth experience higher levels of depression related to discrimination than their other marginalized counterparts (Ramos, 2020). According to Ramos (2020), depression is prevalent among Latinx youth, and 50% of Latinx youth feel perpetually sad or hopeless. This statistic has often been linked to the experience of racism despite 80% of Latinx youth under 35 being United States citizens. Ramos attributes these statistics to being labeled a "perpetual foreigner" (p. 82) in the United States. She argues that the experience of constantly being treated as if one does not belong where one was born and lives leads to some of the highest depression rates in the United States.

Activity 7.54 – Digging Deeper: Personal Experiences

"When I was in college, my husband (who is White) and I found a house that we wanted to rent. I had a new baby, and we needed more space. We found this house I really liked, so we arranged to meet with the landlord. He came out to meet us and took one look at me and said, "I don't rent to the likes of you." He didn't even bother to learn our names. I felt really hurt; someone would judge me like that- I remember feeling like I was dirty or something."

-Viola, Latinx American

Discussion Questions

- How does Viola's experience illustrate the intersection of race, ethnicity, and gender in shaping discriminatory practices?
- In what ways does housing discrimination reflect broader systemic inequalities?
- How might policies like the Fair Housing Act aim to address situations like the one described, and what limitations do they face?
- How does the landlord's refusal to "even bother to learn our names" highlight dynamics of power and dehumanization?
- Why is it important for landlords and others in positions of power to engage in cultural competence education?

While farmworker advocacy may feel like an issue rooted in the past, this is not the case. According to Ramos (2020), "There are approximately 2.5 million farmworkers across the country. More than half of them are undocumented, and more than 70 percent identify as Latino" (pg. 23). Being undocumented leaves many Latinx workers vulnerable to exploitation, poor working conditions, and limited access to legal protections. Addressing these challenges requires both policy reform and grassroots organizing. For example, contemporary efforts by organizations like the UFW and advocacy groups for undocumented immigrants emphasize securing better wages, working conditions, and pathways to citizenship (United Farm Workers, n.d.).

Activity 7.55 – Undocumented Workers and COVID-19

Video: 'Essential' Farmworkers Risk Infection and Deportation. Here's Why.
(https://www.youtube.com/watch?v=hmAxgI9HTWU)

One or more interactive elements has been excluded from this version of the text. You can view them online here: https://milnepublishing.geneseo.edu/social-justice-in-human-services/?p=409#oembed-49 (#oembed-49)

Discussion Questions

- How did the pandemic underscore the vulnerability of essential workers, particularly undocumented farmworkers?
- How can policy changes better protect undocumented farmworkers from health risks?
- What role does farmworkers' racial and immigrant status play in their ability to access healthcare and labor protections?
- What ethical considerations surround the classification of farmworkers as "essential"

yet providing them with minimal support?

Activity 7.56 – Digging Deeper: Child Labor

Video: Fingers to the Bone: Child Farmworkers in the United States (https://www.youtube.com/watch?v=NfEtO00DSvI)

 One or more interactive elements has been excluded from this version of the text. You can view them online here: https://milnepublishing.geneseo.edu/social-justice-in-human-services/?p=409#oembed-50 (#oembed-50)

Article: Children as young as 12 work legally on farms, despite years of efforts to change law (https://www.npr.org/2023/06/12/1181472559/child-labor-farms-agriculture-human-rights-congress)

Discussion Questions

- How do race, class, and immigration status intersect for Latinx children in the workforce?
- How has Latinx migration to the United States historically influenced the prevalence of child labor in agricultural sectors?
- What legal protections exist for Latinx children working in agriculture? How do these laws impact their safety and well-being? How are these laws enforced?
- How does the status of being undocumented exacerbate the challenges faced by Latinx children in the workforce?

Being Latinx in the United States is a complex, multifaceted experience shaped by a rich cultural heritage, systemic challenges, and enduring resilience. The persistence of stereotypes, such as the "perpetual foreigner" (Ramos, 2020, p. 82) narrative, highlights the need for a broader societal understanding of the Latinx community's historical and contemporary contributions to the United States. Despite these obstacles, the community has shown resilience and fostered solidarity by advocating for systemic change through grassroots activism, cultural expression, and political engagement.

Chapter Summary Questions

1. How do the intersections of race, ethnicity, and immigration status shape the lived

experiences of Asian, Indigenous, and Latinx communities in the United States? Provide specific examples that illustrate these dynamics.
2. What key historical events have influenced systemic inequities faced by each of the groups discussed in this chapter? How do these historical legacies continue to affect their social, political, and economic realities today?
3. How have stereotypes such as the "model minority" for Asians, the "noble savage" for Indigenous people, and the "perpetual foreigner" for Latinx individuals contributed to societal misconceptions and systemic oppression? What steps can be taken to combat these stereotypes?
4. Compare the impact of United States immigration policies on Asian and Latinx communities historically and in contemporary contexts. How have these policies shaped public perceptions and lived experiences?
5. How have individuals and organizations within these communities contributed to the broader social justice movement? Provide examples of notable leaders or movements that have made a significant impact.
6. Reflect on your positionality and the ways you can contribute to dismantling systems of oppression affecting Asian, Indigenous, and Latinx communities. What steps can you take to support social justice efforts in your personal or professional life?

Thoughts from the Author

The chapters on race were the last chapters that Dr. Golden and I worked on and they took a long time. There is just so much information on each population, and each population has a distinct experience worth exploring. Throw in the multiple intersecting identities that all individuals carry, and it ended up being a lot. We talked at great lengths about what to include and were surprised to find that we really wanted to include historical content, even more than we had thought when we started this project. Through this work, it has become clear how important and impactful the complex history of the United States is to the topic of social justice. We feel like we barely scratched the surface of so many things; we encourage you to learn more.

Sincerely,
Dr. DeJonge

References

Adams, D. W. (2020). *Education for extinction: American Indians and the boarding school experience, 1875-1928* (2nd ed. Rev.). University Press of Kansas.

Arellano, G. (2024, November 12). Column: We now live in a Prop. 187 America: What's next? *Los Angeles Times*. https://www.latimes.com/california/story/2024-11-12/proposition-187-donald-trump-victory

Atomic Heritage Foundation. (n.d.) *Potsdam: The crossroads of atomic science and international diplomacy*. Atomic Heritage Foundation. https://ahf.nuclearmuseum.org/ahf/history/potsdam-crossroads-atomic-science-and-international-diplomacy/

Beezley, W. H. (2008). *Mexican national identity: Memory, innuendo, and popular culture*. University of Arizona Press.

Blackhawk, N. (2023). *The rediscovery of America: Native peoples and the unmaking of U.S. history*. Yale University Press.

Blakemore, E. (2024, April 23). *Chinese Americans were once forbidden to testify in court. A murder changed that*. History.com. https://www.history.com/news/chinese-exclusion-act-yee-shun-legal-rights

Blakemore, E. (2024, August 20). *The largest mass deportation in American history*. History.com. https://www.history.com/news/operation-wetback-eisenhower-1954-deportation

Bonham, V. L. (2024, September 26). *Race*. National Human Genome Research Institute. https://www.genome.gov/genetics-glossary/Race

Brown, D. S. (2022). *The first populist: The defiant life of Andrew Jackson*. Scribner.

Budiman, A., & Ruiz, N. G. (2021, April 29). *Key facts about Asian Americans, a diverse and growing population*. Pew Research Center. https://www.pewresearch.org/short-reads/2021/04/29/key-facts-about-asian-americans/

Burton, L. M., Bonilla-Silva, E., Ray, V., Buckelew, R., & Freeman, E. H. (2010). Critical race theories, colorism, and the decade's research on families of color. *Journal of Marriage and Family, 72*, 440-459. https://doi.org/10.1111/j.1741-3737.2010.00712.x

Carasik, L., & Bachman, J. S. (2019). In J. S. Bachman (Ed.), *Cultural genocide: Law, politics, and global manifestations* (pp. 97-117). Routledge.

Cartagena, J. (2005). Latinos and section 5 of the Voting Rights Act: Beyond black and white. *National Black Law Journal, 18*(2), 201-223. https://www.national-consortium.org/__data/assets/pdf_file/0025/8467/latininos.pdf

Center for Public Impact. (2017, October 30). *The 1996 personal responsibility and work opportunity reconciliation act in the US*. https://centreforpublicimpact.org/public-impact-fundamentals/the-1996-personal-responsibility-and-work-opportunity-reconciliation-act-in-the-us/

Charles, M., & Rah., S. C. (2019). *Unsettling truths: The ongoing dehumanizing legacy of the Doctrine of Discovery*. InterVarsity Press.

Chappell, B. (2023, March 30). *The Vatican repudiates 'Doctrine of Discovery' which was used to justify colonialism*. NPR. https://www.npr.org/2023/03/30/1167056438/vatican-doctrine-of-discovery-colonialism-indigenous

Contreras, R. (2023, September 5). *Search for lost soldier shows how little we know about Latinos in World War I*. Doughboy Foundation. https://doughboy.org/search-for-lost-soldier-shows-how-little-we-know-about-latinos-in-world-war-i/

Cowie, J. (2022). *Freedom's dominion: A saga of white resistance to federal power*. Basic Books.

Cozzens, P. (2016). *The earth is weeping: The epic story of the Indian Wars for the American west*. Knopf.

Deer, S. (2015). *The beginning and end of rape: Confronting sexual violence in Native America*. University of Minnesota Press.

Diamond, A. (2020, May 19). The 1924 law that slammed the door on immigrants and the politicians who pushed it back open. *Smithsonian Magazine*. https://www.smithsonianmag.com/history/1924-law-slammed-door-immigrants-and-politicians-who-pushed-it-back-open-180974910/

Duany, J. (1999). Cuban communities in the United States: Migration waves, settlement patterns and socioeconomic diversity. *Pouvoirs dans la Caraibe, 11*, 69-103. https://doi.org/10.4000/plc.464

Funk, C., & Lopez, M. H. (2022, June 14). *A brief statistical portrait of U.S. Hispanics*. Pew Research Center. https://www.pewresearch.org/science/2022/06/14/a-brief-statistical-portrait-of-u-s-hispanics/

Garcia, O., & Sung, K. K. (2018). Critically assessing the 1968 Bilingual Act at 50 years: Taming tongues and Latinx communities. *Bilingual Research Journal, 41*(4), 318-333. https://doi.org/10.1080/15235882.2018.1529642

Garsd, J. (2024, November 19). *Trump's threats of mass deportations lead to hard discussions for families*. NPR. https://www.npr.org/2024/11/19/g-s1-34736/trumps-threats-of-mass-deportations-lead-to-hard-discussions-for-families

Gillio-Whitaker, D. (2019). *As long as the grass grows: The Indigenous fight for environmental justice, from colonization to Standing Rock*. Beacon Press.

Gonzalez, J. (2022). *Harvest of empire: A history of Latinos in America*. Penguin Books.

Grinde, D. A. (2004). Taking the Indian out of the Indian: U.S. policies of ethnocide through education. *Wicazo Sa Review, 19*(2), 25-32. https://www.jstor.org/stable/1409496

Grzanka, P. R., Gonzales, K.A., & Spanierman, L. B. (2019). White supremacy and counseling psychology: A critical-conceptual framework. *The Counseling Psychologist, 47*(4) 478-529. https://doi.org/10.1177/0011000019880843

Guardino, P. (2017). *The Dead March: A history of the Mexican-American War.* Harvard University Press.

Hämäläinen, P. (2019). *Lakota America: A new history of Indigenous power.* Yale University Press.

Hanigan, I. (2022, April 14). *Mendez v. Westminster, which ended forced school segregation, concluded 75 years ago today.* OCDE Newsroom. https://newsroom.ocde.us/the-final-ruling-in-mendez-v-westminster-which-ended-sanctioned-school-segregation-came-75-years-ago-today/

Hernandez, K. L. (2006). The crimes and consequences of illegal immigration: A cross-border examination of Operation Wetback, 1943-1954. *Western Historical Quarterly, 37*(4) 421-444. https://doi.org/10.2307/25443415

History.com. (2010, February 9). *World War II.* https://www.history.com/topics/world-war-ii/world-war-ii-history

History.com (2023). *Hispanic history milestones: Timeline.* https://www/topics/hispanic-history/hispanic-latinx-milestones

Hoffman, A., & Batalova, J. (2022, December 7). *Indian immigrants in the United States.* Migration Policy Institute. https://www.migrationpolicy.org/article/indian-immigrants-united-states-2021

Indian Child Welfare, 25 U.S.C. § 21 (1978). https://uscode.house.gov/view.xhtml?path=/prelim@title25/chapter21&edition=prelim

Jones, R. P. (2023). *The hidden roots of white supremacy and the path to a shared American future.* Simon & Schuster.

Kendi, I. X. (2016). *Stamped from the beginning: The definitive history of racist ideas in America.* Bold Type Books.

Kiel, D. (2017). *American expansion turns to official Indian removal.* National Park Service. https://www.nps.gov/articles/american-expansion-turns-to-indian-removal.htm

Kiilleen, A. (2021). Japan's victory in World War I. *Naval History, 35*(3). https://www.usni.org/magazines/naval-history-magazine/2021/june/japans-victory-world-war-i

Klein, C. (2023, July 12). *What happened at the Wounded Knee Massacre?* History.com. https://www.history.com/news/wounded-knee-massacre-facts

Kraz, J. (2021, September 23). *El Movimiento: The Chicano movement and Hispanic identity in the United States.* National Archives. https://prologue.blogs.archives.gov/2021/09/23/el-movimiento-the-chicano-movement-and-hispanic-identity-in-the-united-states/

Krogstad, J. M., & Gonzalez-Barrera (2022, January 11). *Key facts about U.S. immigration policies and Biden's proposed changes.* Pew Research Center. https://www.pewresearch.org/short-reads/2022/01/11/key-facts-about-u-s-immigration-policies-and-bidens-proposed-changes/

Lepore, J. (2018). *These truths: A history of the United States.* Norton.

Library of Congress. (n.d.-a). *A growing community.* https://www.loc.gov/classroom-materials/immigration/mexican/a-growing-community

Library of Congress. (n.d.-b). *Indian Citizenship Act.* https://www.loc.gov/item/today-in-history/june-02/

Library of Congress. (n.d.-c). *Legislation.* https://guides.loc.gov/american-indian-law/Legislation

Ling, H. (2023). *Asian American history.* Rutgers University Press.

Lovato, K., & Abrams, L. S. (2023). An examination of Latinx immigrant families' social service needs following a deportation. *Child Welfare, 100*(4) p 113-152. https://cimmcw.org/wp-content/uploads/Lovato_Abrams_pdf.pdf

Makos, I. (2021, April 13). *Roles of Native Americans during the Revolution.* American Battlefield Trust. https://www.battlefields.org/learn/articles/roles-native-americans-during-revolution

Massey, D. S., & Pren, K. A. (2012). Unintended consequences of US immigration policy: Explaining the post-1965 Surge from Latin America. *Population and Development Review, 38*(1), 1-29. https://doi.org/10.1111/j.1728-4457.2012.00470.x

Mays, K. T. (2021). *An Afro-Indigenous history of the United States.* Beacon Press.

Morales, D. (2018). *100 years of back-and-forth immigration policy.* Sin Barreras. https://www.sinbarrerascville.org/wp-content/uploads/2019/06/100-Yrs-of-Immigration-History.pdf

Moslimani, M., Lopez, M. H., & Noe-Bustamante, L. (2023, August 16). *11 facts about Hispanic origin groups in the U.S.* Pew Research Center. https://www.pewresearch.org/short-reads/2023/08/16/11-facts-about-hispanic-origin-groups-in-the-us/

National Archives. (2023). *Chinese Exclusion Act (1882).* https://www.archives.gov/milestone-documents/chinese-exclusion-act

National Archives. (n.d.). *Dawes Act (1887).* https://www.archives.gov/milestone-documents/dawes-act

National Library of Medicine. (n.d.). *1934: President Franklin Roosevelt signs the Indian Reorganization Act.* Native Voice. https://www.nlm.nih.gov/nativevoices/timeline/452.html

National Park Service. (2024, October 17). *Thirty years of farmworker struggle. Cesar E Chávez National Monument.* https://www.nps.gov/articles/000/a-new-era-of-farm-worker-organizing.htm

National Park Service. (n.d.). *Ely Parker.* https://www.nps.gov/people/ely-parker.htm

The National WWII Museum. (n.d.). *Japanese American incarceration.* https://www.nationalww2museum.org/war/articles/japanese-american-incarceration

Native American Rights Fund. (2019). *Trigger points: Current state of research on history, impacts, and healing related to the United States' Indian industrial/boarding school policy.* https://www.narf.org/nill/documents/trigger-points.pdf

Naval History and Heritage Command. (2023). *Naval bases in the Philippines.* https://www.history.navy.mil/browse-by-topic/organization-and-administration/historic-bases/philippine-bases.html

Newland, B. (2022). *Federal Indian boarding school initiative investigative report.* United States Department of the Interior, Bureau of Indian Affairs. https://www.bia.gov/sites/default/files/dup/inline-files/bsi_investigative_report_may_2022_508.pdf

Noe-Bustamante, L., Gonzales-Barrera, A., Edwards, K., Mora, L., & Lopez, M. H. (2021, November 4). *Half of U.S. Latinos experienced some form of discrimination during the first year of the pandemic.* Pew Research Center. https://www.pewresearch.org/race-and-ethnicity/2021/11/04/half-of-u-s-latinos-experienced-some-form-of-discrimination-during-the-first-year-of-the-pandemic/

Nordell, J. (2021). *The end of bias: A beginning: The science and practice of overcoming unconscious bias.* Metropolitan Books.

Office for Victims of Crime. (n.d.). *Laws & policies.* https://ovc.ojp.gov/program/victims-crime-act-voca-administrators/laws-policies

Office of the Historian. (n.d.). *Japanese-American relations at the turn of the century, 1900-1922.* U.S. Department of State. https://history.state.gov/milestones/1899-1913/japanese-relations

Oropeza, L. (n.d.). Fighting on two fronts: Latinos in the military. In National Park System Advisory Board (Ed.), *American Latino heritage theme study* (pp. 251-271). https://www.nps.gov/articles/latinothememilitary.htm

Pujols, J. S. (2022). 'It's about the way I'm treated': Afro-Latina Black identity development in the third space. *Youth & Society, 54*(4), 591-610. https://doi.org/10.1177/0044118X20982314

Ramos, P. (2020). *Finding Latinx: In search of the voices redefining Latino identity.* Vintage Books.

Richardson, H. C. (2010). *Wounded knee: Party politics and the road to an American massacre.* Basic Books.

Rosenblum, M. R., & Ruiz Soto, A. G. (2015). *An analysis of unauthorized immigrants in the United States by country and region of birth.* Migration Policy Institute. https://www.migrationpolicy.org/research/analysis-unauthorized-immigrants-united-states-country-and-region-birth

Rotondi, J. P. (2024, April 23). *Before the Chinese Exclusion Act, this anti-immigrant law targeted Asian women.* History.com. https://www.history.com/news/chinese-immigration-page-act-women

Ruiz, N. G., Im, C., & Tian, Z. (2023, November 30). *Asian Americans and the 'model minority' stereotype.* Pew Research Center. https://www.pewresearch.org/race-and-ethnicity/2023/11/30/asian-americans-and-the-model-minority-stereotype/

Sanchez, R. (2018). Spanglish and identity in modern Latinx communities. *Linguistic Studies, 24*(4), 455-471.

Serratos, O. (2017, November 17). *Generation SB1070: These Latino millennials grew up under controversial immigration law*. NBC News. https://www.nbcnews.com/news/latino/generation-sb1070-these-latino-millennials-grew-under-controversial-immigration-law-n821806

Smithers, G. D. (2022). *Reclaiming Two-Spirits: Sexuality, spiritual renewals, & sovereignty in Native America*. Beacon Press.

Tanaka, E. (n.d.). *Inconsistencies in the court (Ozawa v. Thind)*. H2O. https://opencasebook.org/casebooks/7606-asian-americans-and-us-law/resources/3.10-inconsistencies-in-the-court-ozawa-v-thind/

Treuer, D. (2019). *The heartbeat of Wounded Knee: Native America from 1890 to the present*. Riverhead Books

United Farm Workers. (n.d.). *UFW history*. https://ufw.org/research/history/ufw-history/

United Nations. (1951). *Convention on the prevention and punishment of the crime of genocide*. https://www.un.org/en/genocideprevention/documents/atrocity-crimes/Doc.1_Convention%20on%20the%20Prevention%20and%20Punishment%20of%20the%20Crime%20of%20Genocide.pdf

United Nations. (2007). *United Nations declaration on the rights of Indigenous Peoples*. https://www.un.org/development/desa/indigenouspeoples/wp-content/uploads/sites/19/2018/11/UNDRIP_E_web.pdf

Urrieta, L., Jr., & Calderon, D. (2019). Critical Latinx indigeneities: Unpacking indigeneity from within and outside of Latinized entanglements. *Association of Mexican American Educators Journal, 13*(2), 145-174. https://doi.org/10.24974/amae.13.2.432

U.S. Census Bureau. (2022). *About the topic of race*. https://www.census.gov/topics/population/race/about.html

U.S. Census Bureau. (2023, August 17). *Hispanic heritage month: 2023*. https://www.census.gov/newsroom/facts-for-features/2023/hispanic-heritage-month.html

U.S. Census Bureau. (2023a). *Facts for features: American Indian and Alaska Native heritage month: November 2023*. United States Census Bureau. https://www.census.gov/newsroom/facts-for-features/2023/aian-month.html

U.S. Census Bureau. (2023b). *Native American heritage day: November 24, 2023*. United States Census Bureau. https://www.census.gov/newsroom/stories/native-american-heritage-day.html

U.S. Commission on Civil Rights. (2023, September 26). U.S. commission on civil rights releases report: The Federal response to anti-Asian racism in the United States. https://www.usccr.gov/news/2023/us-commission-civil-rights-releases-report-federal-response-anti-asian-racism-united

Vinovskis, M. A. (1970). Horace Mann on the economic productivity of education. *The New England Quarterly, 43*(4), 550-571. https://doi.org/10.2307/363132

Wilkerson, I. (2023). *Caste: The origins of our discontent*. Random House.

Yzaguirre, R., Arce, L., & Kamasaki, C. (1999). The Fair Housing Act: A Latino perspective. *Cityscape: A Journal of Public Development and Research, 4*(3), 161-170. https://www.huduser.gov/portal/Periodicals/CITYSCPE/VOL4NUM3/yzaguirre.pdf

Zimbardo, P. (2008). *The Lucifer effect: Understanding how good people turn evil.* Random House.

Media Attributions

- Wong Chin Fu © National Portrait Gallery, Smithsonian Institution is licensed under a CC0 (Creative Commons Zero) license
- Mochida Family © Dorothea Lange is licensed under a Public Domain license
- Singh Yuba City is licensed under a Public Domain license
- Gintong Kasaysayan, Gintong Pamana Mural © art by Eliseo Art Silva | photo by Sampaiii is licensed under a CC BY-SA (Attribution ShareAlike) license
- Stop AAPI Hate logo © Stop AAPI Hate is licensed under a All Rights Reserved license
- Genoa students 1911 © Photographic print of students, 1910; 75-GS-10; Photographs of the Industrial School, Genoa, Nebraska, 1910-1910 (NAID 518933); Office of Indian Affairs; Record Group 75; National Archives and Records Administration-College Park, MD. is licensed under a Public Domain license
- Wabanaki Alliance © Passamaquoddy, Wabanaki Alliance Archive; This item is marked using Traditional Knowledge Labels: TK A, TK 0, & TK NC
- El_Malcriado,_No._21,_HUELGA
- Tamales © Ms. Phoenix is licensed under a CC BY (Attribution) license

8.
Being a Woman in the United States

Nikki Golden and Bernadet DeJonge

> **Learning Objectives**
>
> - The reader will understand the history of women's activism in the United States.
> - The reader will identify the progression of women's rights in the United States.
> - The reader will connect the women's rights movement to current social justice movements.

Being a woman in the United States of America is complex. American women are not monolithic in identity. They differ by ability, age, generation, geography, opportunity, race, relationship status, religion, socioeconomic status, and sexual orientation. Griffith (2022) states, "It's a risk to categorize or generalize because real people have multiple and individual identities" (p.xv). Recognizing this complexity when discussing women is an essential task of this chapter, as the experiences of American women throughout history have varied through their intersecting sociocultural identities.

This chapter starts with a brief history of Indigenous women before European colonization. It progresses chronologically through the women's rights movement, women's suffrage, and the various legislation and policies that impact women in the United States. There are entire books on women's history; thus, the choices about what to include in this chapter were complex and nuanced. These choices are intended to give an overview of the experience of being a woman in the United States throughout history, and to connect that experience to current events and social justice movements.

> **Activity 8.1 – Digging Deeper: Language Matters**
>
> What is the difference between the terms *woman* and *female*? *Female* is an assigned label given to those who are born with a visible vulva. *Woman* (or girl) is a sociocultural term denoting a gender identity. The gender identity of a woman (or girl) includes internal and external experience, expression, and role. For example, a duck can be female, but it cannot

be a woman. In general, we will use the term woman in this text to denote a more holistic definition of the gender identity of being a woman.

Discussion Questions:

- What are the key differences between the terms *woman* and *female*? How do these differences impact our understanding of gender identity?
- How might the distinction between *female* and *woman* influence discussions about gender equality and women's rights?
- How do internal and external experiences, expressions, and roles contribute to the gender identity of a woman? Can you provide examples of these internal and external factors?
- In what ways do societal and cultural factors shape the gender identity of a woman? How might these factors differ across cultures or historical periods?

Indigenous Women

From first contact, the Indigenous people's ways of expressing gender confounded European explorers and colonists. In Europe, gender and gender expression was defined within a patriarchal hierarchy, and European women had little to no power in private or public spheres. In contrast, many Indigenous women had power in both. Numerous Indigenous communities, such as the Cherokee, Iroquois, and Muscogee, were matriarchal in lineage, and children inherited their social status from their mothers (Faderman, 2022; Hämäläinen, 2022). In addition, it was often the Indigenous women that engaged with the European colonists. Indigenous women often understood the value of learning to read, speak, and write the colonists' languages, and would allow missionaries and priests to teach them to do so under the guise of religious conversion (Hämäläinen, 2022).

In some Indigenous communities, women participated in leadership roles and decided on consequences for captives (Dunbar-Ortiz, 2014; Zinn, 2003). For example, the Cherokee people engaged in inclusive decision-making, and Cherokee women held important advising roles in the tribe. Even when pregnant, some Cherokee women participated in battle and were known as "war women" (Hämäläinen, 2022, p. 198).

Activity 8.2 – Digging Deeper: Marriage in Indigenous Tribes

Many unmarried Indigenous women made autonomous decisions, including who they would and would not marry. If they no longer wanted to be with their husband, Indigenous

Untitled gelatin silver print circa 1910

women would put the man's belongings outside of their dwelling to signal that their relationship was over (Blackhawk, 2023).

Website: How Native American Women Inspired the Women's Rights Movement (https://www.nps.gov/articles/000/how-native-american-women-inspired-the-women-s-rights-movement.htm)

Discussion Questions:

- Describe how Indigenous marriage and divorce practices differed from those of European colonists. Why might the European colonists have felt threatened by this practice?
- How does the autonomy of Indigenous women in marriage decisions challenge or support modern feminist movements advocating for women's rights and gender equality? What parallels can be drawn between historical and contemporary struggles for women's autonomy?
- How might the practices of Indigenous women regarding marriage influence current discussions on the intersection of cultural traditions and women's rights? What balance should be struck between respecting cultural traditions and promoting universal women's rights?

- What lessons can contemporary societies learn from Indigenous women's practices in supporting and promoting women's rights and autonomy? How can these lessons be applied to improve gender equality and women's empowerment today?

Indigenous women entered the 18th century with positions of power, privilege, and respect. However, their positions were lost by the end of that same century due to European colonization and Christian conversion. Christian missionaries insisted that the equitable privilege Indigenous women experienced was sinful. As the United States expanded its territory westward, Indigenous women were expected to conform to the White European norms of womanhood. As a result, "they became as powerless as their White counterparts" (Faderman, 2022, p. 42).

Activity 8.3 – Digging Deeper: The Iroquois

Many Iroquois women had immense power within their communities. They chose the war chiefs, were heard first in community debates, and decided the fates of their enemies. Iroquois women proposed marriage and, at times, would take more than one husband. Iroquois matriarchs owned crops and homes, and controlled the wealth of their families (Faderman, 2022).

Discussion Questions

- How do you think the Iroquois and other Indigenous women influenced female European colonists?
- How do you think the Iroquois and other Indigenous women influenced male European colonists?
- Faderman (2022) states that colonists interpreted Indigenous women's equitable status as dominant and domineering behavior. How might this perception have influenced stereotypes about women today?

The Women's Rights Movement: The First Wave (1848-1920s)

The first wave of the women's rights movement began in the 19th century and continued throughout the early part of the 20th century. It included the women's suffrage movement as well as fights for higher education, equal citizenship, and reproductive rights for women

(Lepore, 2018). This first wave coincided with westward expansion, the continued genocide of Indigenous people, slavery, the Civil War, industrialization, and World War I.

During the first wave of the women's rights movement, women in the United States did not have the same power, privileges, or rights as men. Women were not allowed to vote, pursue education without permission, or, at times, choose their clothing. Married women were not allowed to inherit or own property, bring legal proceedings to court, run a business, divorce, or maintain custody of their children (Gallagher, 2021). According to Catt and Shuler (2020), the "legal existence of the wife was so merged in that of her husband that she was said to be dead in law" (p. 4).

The founders of the women's rights movement have often been stereotyped as White, middle-class, educated, and spinsters. While some fit those categories, women involved in the first wave were also Asian, Black, Indigenous, and Latinx. "For many Native American, Hispanic, Black, and Asian women political activism first and foremost meant ensuring their families survival in the systemic racism that menaced them" (Gallagher, 2021, p. xii). Some women were married, some lived in poverty, some were denied education, and some were part of the LGBTGEQIAP+ community.

Seneca Falls

In the late 1800s, most women understood that they did not have the same privileges and rights as men. Many women had been active in other social justice movements such as abolition and had learned to organize, raise money, and engage in public speaking (Griffith, 2022). As a result, some women individually railed against these inequities. However, they saw little sustainable change. In 1840, Lucretia Mott and Elizabeth Cady Stanton attended the World's Anti-Slavery Convention in London. On the Convention's first day, male delegates voted to ban women from participating. Mott and Stanton, who had not met before this event, "were thoroughly aroused by this experience" and "agreed to call a convention upon their return to the United States, to be devoted exclusively to the Rights of Women" (Catt & Shuler, 2020, p. 15). This was the beginning of the organized women's rights movement in the United States.

It took Mott and Stanton eight years, but on July 19, 1848, the first women's rights convention was held in Seneca Falls, New York. Mott and Stanton led the convention to launch the women's rights movement in the United States (Catt & Shuler, 2000). During its course, Stanton wrote and read the Declaration of Sentiments. This declaration was intentionally based on the Declaration of Independence. It was intended "to dramatize the denied citizenship claims of elite women during a period when the early republic's founding documents privileged white propertied males" (National Park Service, n.d., para 4). The Women's Rights Convention was so well attended that a second convention was held two weeks later in Rochester, New York (Catt & Shuler, 2020). The two conventions gained national attention and sparked the women's movement across the United States.

Elizabeth Cady Stanton

Activity 8.4 – What Happened at the Seneca Falls Convention?

Video: What Happened at the Seneca Falls Convention? (https://www.youtube.com/watch?v=TcYhuG1y3bc)

 One or more interactive elements has been excluded from this version of the text. You can view them online here: https://milnepublishing.geneseo.edu/social-justice-in-human-services/?p=159#oembed-1 (#oembed-1)

Discussion Questions:

- In what ways did the Seneca Falls Convention challenge the existing social and legal structures that oppressed women? What impact did it have on these structures?
- How did the women's rights convention contribute to the fight for women's rights and for social justice?
- How did the women's rights convention address issues of intersectionality, particularly the struggles faced by women of different races, classes, and backgrounds?
- What parallels can be drawn between the Women's Rights Convention and contemporary social justice movements? What can modern-day social justice movements learn from the strategies and approaches used by the convention?

> **Activity 8.5 – Digging Deeper: The Declaration of Rights and Sentiments.**
>
> Read through the Declaration of Rights and Sentiments by Elizabeth Cady Stanton, Susan B. Anthony, and M.J. Cag (https://www.womenshistory.org/resources/primary-source/declaration-sentiments-and-resolution)e as shared by the National Women's History Museum
>
> Discussion Questions:
>
> - What were the main grievances listed in the Declaration of Sentiments, and how did they reflect the social and political context of the time?
> - How did the Declaration of Sentiments frame the concept of women's rights, and what key demands did it make for achieving gender equality? Which of these demands have been addressed over time, and which are still relevant today?
> - What was the significance of the Declaration of Sentiments being modeled after the Declaration of Independence, and how did this influence its impact? How did this framing help to legitimize the demands for women's rights?
> - How might the principles outlined in the Declaration of Sentiments be applied to current issues facing women and marginalized groups? What modern issues could benefit from a similar approach to advocacy and reform?

Social Justice Movements

After the successes at Seneca Falls and Rochester, local women's suffrage societies were formed across the United States as women began to work in specific social justice movements. According to Catt and Shuler (2020),

Encouraged by the knowledge that other women were rising, organized groups sprang into being in all parts of the country with no other incentive than the ripeness of the time, and no other connection with the original movers than the announcements of the press. (p. 18)

While women participated in the suffrage movement, they also participated in many other social justice movements, including the social morality movement, the anti-slavery movement, and the labor reform movement.

Social Morality Movement

Starting in the late 19th century, White middle- and upper-class women in the United States began to be lauded as the moral "soul of the new nation" (Faderman, 2022, p. 87). During that time, women believed it was their responsibility to teach men to be good and moral. This cultural shift gave women a new sense of empowerment. Previously, women had been placed in a position inferior to men. Now, women were seen as morally superior to men.

Women took this role seriously and were ready to fight for the morality of the United States. The two most prevalent issues that women took a stand on during this time were prostitution and drunkenness (Faderman, 2022).

Prior to the early 1800s, many in the United States viewed prostitution as "a necessary evil" (D'Emilio & Freedman, 2012, p. 140). By the 1850s, it was estimated there were over six thousand prostitutes in New York City alone. However, as the social morality movement took hold, the American public was no longer willing to accept prostitution as necessary (Faderman, 2022; Lepore, 2018). Women, in particular, had genuine reason to despise prostitution because "[it] made a mockery of the widely cherished notion of women's innate modesty and purity" (Faderman, 2022, p. 89).

The evangelical revivalist movement, the Second Great Awakening, increased women's fervor for eradicating prostitution. Some evangelical women blamed men for being the "deliberate destroyers of female innocence" (Faderman, 2022, p. 92). These evangelical women, as well as others, established organizations to fight prostitution and to save women forced to prostitute. For example, Hetty Reckless, a free Black woman, established the Moral Reform Retreat, which focused on assisting free Black women who were prostitutes. Lydia Finney, an evangelical White woman, established the New York Female Moral Reform Society (NYFMRS), the first national organization of women. NYFMRS had its own journal, the *Advocate of Moral Reform*, with 17,000 subscribers (Faderman, 2022).

Activity 8.6 – Digging Deeper: Seduction Laws

In 1848, New York State passed the first seduction law in the United States. Seduction laws punished men for taking advantage of young women by promising, among other things, marriage, to obtain sex. The New York seduction laws were strongly influenced by the activism of the New York Female Moral Reform Society (NYFMRS). The NYFMRS was concerned about women coming from the countryside to the city to work. The concern was that, without parental supervision, women would be taken advantage of and fall into a life of sin and immorality, ultimately turning to prostitution. Other states followed this precedent and, by 1885, 27 states had seduction laws (Faderman, 2022). Seduction was punishable by up to five years in prison in New York State and up to 20 years in other states. Often, women of color, prostitutes, and women over the age of 37 years were excluded from the protection of the seduction laws (Knox, 2020).

Discussion Questions

- How did the seduction laws of the late 1800s reflect the societal attitudes towards gender and morality of the time? What do these laws say about how society tried to control women's sexuality?

- In what ways did seduction laws reflect or reinforce existing gender norms and expectations? How did these laws interact with other legal and social structures to regulate women's behavior?
- How did the exclusion of certain groups from the protections of seduction laws reflect broader patterns of discrimination and marginalization? What do these exclusions reveal about the intersection of gender, race, and socioeconomic status at that time?

Alcohol consumption was also rampant in the United States at this time, and became a focus of the Social Morality Movement. By the 1830s, the annual consumption of hard liquor was over seven gallons per capita. In comparison, the annual consumption in the 21st century is approximately two gallons per capita. Drunkenness, like prostitution, was considered a moral failing of men. Women, as well as some religious leaders, believed alcohol and men's drunkenness were ruining American families (Faderman, 2022).

For Black women, the issue of drunkenness was not just about family but about their quality of life in the United States. Black women advocated for temperance at the third annual Improvement of Free People of Color convention in 1833, and many Black women believed that if Black men were accused of or engaged in drunkenness, it would impact the social justice movements for equality and respectability in the United States. Many Black women promoted what was referred to as the politics of respectability, which entailed conforming to mainstream norms to gain rights (Faderman, 2022).

Activity 8.7 – Digging Deeper: Respectability Politics

Video: Respectability politics subjugate personal authenticity by Sarah Kelsey Hall (https://www.youtube.com/watch?v=KtgotrYHuqI)

 One or more interactive elements has been excluded from this version of the text. You can view them online here: https://milnepublishing.geneseo.edu/social-justice-in-human-services/?p=159#oembed-2 (#oembed-2)

Article: "Democracy Limited: The Politics of Respectability" by Brianna Nuñez-Franklin (https://www.nps.gov/articles/democracy-limited-the-politics-of-respectability.htm)

Discussion Questions

- What key arguments or themes do the resources present about respectability politics?
- How does respectability politics connect with the women's rights movement?
- What recommendations do you have for addressing the challenges associated with respectability politics, especially regarding women's rights? How practical and effective are these recommendations for current social justice efforts?

The Woman's Christian Temperance Union (WCTU), one of the largest national movements in the history of the United States, was a byproduct of the social morality movement (Gallagher, 2021). Established in 1874, the WCTU included Black and White women. Initially established to address the issues of alcohol consumption, the WCTU expanded its mission to become a comprehensive social reform program that included suffrage. The WCTU's leadership encouraged women to "take up an unusual line of work that forged new vocational paths" (Gallagher, 2021, p. 131), one of which was the new profession of social work.

> **Activity 8.8 – Women's Christian Temperance Union**
>
> **Video:** Women's Christian Temperance Union (https://youtu.be/WPczGnA7k9A?si=zDGAtEs6pRox3sMS)
>
> **Discussion Questions**
>
> - Discuss how the WCTU intersected with women's rights and women's safety.
> - How did the WCTU influence the women's rights movement?

Some women, such as Susan B. Anthony, left the social morality movement due to the sexist attitudes and behaviors of men in the movement. However, engagement in the social morality movement provided women with experience in leadership, organizing, and working together to advocate for a cause. The women of the social morality movement learned how to publish newsletters and journals, raise money, and lobby for support—skills that would all prove invaluable for the women's rights movement (Faderman, 2022; Griffith, 2022).

Anti-Slavery Movement

Slavery has existed in the world for millennia. Throughout history many people viewed slavery as a right or a necessary evil, but there have also been people who viewed slavery as unnecessary and cruel. In the United States and colonial America, those who were anti-slavery were in the vast minority for centuries, and it was not until the late 17th century that the anti-slavery movement gained momentum.

By the early 1800s, societal views on slavery were shifting as "most men and women recognized the incompatibility between America's founding principle of equality and at least some of its inherited structures" (Cobbs, 2023, p. 77). By the mid-1830s, women's anti-slavery societies were established across the northeastern areas of the United States. Black women participated in the anti-slavery movement, and former slaves such as Harriet Jacobs and Sojourner Truth shared their lived experiences. Other Black women, such as Nancy Remond, founded formal anti-slavery organizations (Cobbs, 2023; Faderman, 2022). Black women established anti-slavery societies in Connecticut, Massachusetts, and Pennsylvania, while White women established anti-slavery organizations in cities such as Boston, Cincinnati, and New York (Cobbs, 2023). Many of the women in the anti-slavery movement, such as Lucretia Mott, Susan B. Anthony, and Angelina Grimke, were Quakers. Traditionally, Quakers had been anti-slavery throughout the establishment of the American colonies and were later active in the underground railroad movement. Anthony, like many other White women in the anti-slavery movement, began her advocacy work in the social morality movement.

Not everyone welcomed women into the anti-slavery movement. Unlike other movements, women were not encouraged to be active participants or leaders in anti-slavery movements. Reverend Samuel Cornish, a free Black Man, believed if Black women were allowed to participate in the anti-slavery movement, their role should be limited to "raising money to support the activities of the men" and that they "must not pursue masculine views and measures" (Faderman, 2022, p. 108). In response, Maria W. Miller Stewart chastised Black men for not doing enough "to alleviate the woes of [their] brethren in bondage" (Faderman, 2022, p. 110).

After the Civil War, leaders of the anti-slavery movement shifted focus. Some leaders, such as William Lloyd Garrison, felt their work was done after the United States Congress passed the 13th Amendment. Other leaders, like Stanton and Anthony, believed it was time to shift the focus to universal suffrage. In 1866, Stanton and Anthony established the American Equal Rights Association (AERA) to support what they believed was a shared fight for universal suffrage. AERA was an integrated organization and Black women, such as Frances Harper and Sojourner Truth, were members (Faderman, 2022).

Despite the belief that Stanton and Anthony had that others shared their vision for universal suffrage, there continued to be dissension in the anti-slavery movement. Wendell Phillips, the president of the American Anti-Slavery Society, believed the interests of women and Black men needed to be divided to achieve political gains. In an editorial for the *National Anti-Slavery Standard*, Phillips wrote, "We cannot agree that the enfranchisement of women and enfranchisement of the blacks stand on the same ground or are entitled to equal effort at this moment" (Faderman, 2022, p. 183). Even Fredrick Douglass, a long-time supporter of women's rights and Anthony's friend, believed women should step aside so that Black men could attain their rights. During a debate at an AERA meeting, Douglass stated,

> When women, because they are women, are hunted down through the cities of New York and New Orleans, when they are dragged from their houses and hung upon lamp posts…when they are in danger of having their homes burnt down over their head…then they will have an urgency to obtain the ballot equal to our own. (Faderman, 2022, p. 183)

Many women, such as Anthony and Stanton, had worked tirelessly in the anti-slavery movement. They were devastated by the growing dissent and perceived statements such as these as a betrayal. Stanton believed that elevating "one oppressed group over another tempted it to abuse others lower on the ladder" (Cobbs, 2023, p. 106). Sojourner Truth stated,

> There is a great stir about colored men getting their rights, but not a word about the colored women; and if colored men get their rights, and colored women not theirs, the colored men will be masters over women, and it will be just as bad as it was before. (Gallagher, 2021, p. 53)

Some women agreed with Phillips and Douglass. Many Black women, such as Frances Harper, believed that some members of AERA ignored the genuine concerns of race and left the organization (Cobbs, 2023).

The 14th and 15th Amendments

In 1868, Congress passed the 14th Amendment. Its ratification meant that, for the first time, the word "male" was in the United States Constitution. The 14th Amendment granted birthright citizenship to all men born in the United States.

In 1870, the 15th Amendment was ratified, giving all citizens the right to vote. Because the 14th Amendment declared all men as citizens, the 15th Amendment then gave all men the right to vote. "The right of citizens of the United States to vote shall not be denied or abridged by the United States or by any State on account of race, color, or previous condition of servitude" (U.S. Const. amend. XV). Anthony and Stanton objected to the 14th and

Sojourner Truth, c. 1864.

15th Amendments not because they gave voting rights to all men, but because they did not do the same for all women. After four years of arguing that women's rights were of equal value to men's, Stanton made a series of divisive statements out of "damaging, white-hot outrage" (Cobbs, 2023, p. 106).

By 1870, the anti-slavery movement was victorious. Emancipation and the ratification of the 14th and 15th Amendments were clear indications that the anti-slavery movement had been successful. However, not all members of the anti-slavery movement were done fighting for the rights guaranteed to them by the United States Constitution. Women like Anthony and Stanton no longer believed the right to vote would be enough to challenge the systemic patriarchy of the United States. Even with equal rights, these women knew that prejudice against women was still embedded into the fabric of society (Cobbs, 2023).

Labor Reform Movement

By the early 19th century, it was not uncommon for women of lower economic status to contribute to their families' survival by working for wages. Most often, that work was done inside the home. For example, shop owners provided fabrics for weaving, and women were paid for the work they completed at home. However, with the opening of textile mills, young women moved out of their family homes and worked in the mills (Faderman, 2022).

Working conditions in the textile mills were challenging, and young women complained they were often penalized by having their wages reduced or losing their jobs. In 1834, a group of young women known as the Lowell Girls went on strike to protest a proposed wage reduction. Unfortunately, the strike failed as the young women needed more leverage to win. However, the strike resulted in the establishment of the first working women's union in the United States, the Factory Girls' Association (Faderman, 2022).

Activity 8.9 – The Lowell Girls

Video: The Lowell Girls (https://www.youtube.com/watch?v=s4iWOm5ZfTs)

Discussion Questions:

- What role did the Lowell Girls play in the early labor movement? How did their activism contribute to labor reform and workers' rights?
- What was the role of the Lowell Girls in the broader context of women's economic independence and empowerment? How did their work influence perceptions of women's roles in the economy?
- What is the legacy of the Lowell Girls in terms of labor rights and women's history? How are their contributions remembered or evident today?

During the early 1900s, "nearly one in five manufacturing jobs in the United States was held by a woman" (Lepore, 2018, p. 380), and many fought for labor protections and rights for women. The National Congress of Mothers, later known as the Parent Teacher Association (PTA), was one of the organizations that advocated for labor protection for women. The National Congress of Mothers wielded such respect that in 1908 Theodore Roosevelt referred to it by stating, "This is one body that I put even ahead of the veterans of the Civil War" (Lepore, 2018, p. 380).

Women, such as Jane Addams and Florence Kelly, led the fight for women's labor reform, including minimum wage laws, maximum hours worked laws, and child labor laws. Kelly, who had a law degree, noted that the court system treated women differently than men. Due to this, Kelly felt that some protections, such as maximum hour laws, would have a better chance of success if explicitly aimed at women laborers. Kelly argued that because they were physically more fragile than men, women needed special protections in the workplace (Lepore, 2018).

In 1906, Kelly hired attorneys Louis Brandeis and Josephine Goldmark to argue for protecting women laborers in the landmark case *Muller v. Oregon*. Muller, who owned a laundry business, was convicted of violation of Oregon labor laws because he had made his female employees work over ten hours a day. Muller challenged the conviction and took his case to

Julia Lathrop, Jane Addams and Mary McDowell in Washington, D.C. in 1913.

the Oregon State Supreme Court. The *Muller v. Oregon* case was, according to Kelly, representative of the need for protection for women laborers across the United States (Lepore, 2018).

Brandeis and Goldmark, who were instrumental in the labor reform movement, built their argument for *Muller v. Oregon* using other court cases from across the United States. Part of their argument was based on the premise that working long hours "is more disastrous to the health of women than of men and entails upon them more lasting injury" (Lepore, 2018, p. 381). Brandeis and Goldmark were victorious in *Muller v. Oregon*. The case provided the protections that Kelly wanted for women laborers.

Muller v. Oregon had positive and negative long-lasting effects that could not have been predicted. The most detrimental effect was that it opened the door to decades of gender discrimination in the workplace. Lepore (2018) states that:

> These laws rested on the idea that women were dependent, not only on men, but on the state. If women were ever to achieve equal rights, this sizable body of legislation designed to protect women would stand in their way. (p. 382)

One of *Muller v. Oregon*'s positive effects was that it created a legal precedent for the use of social science in court cases. This set the stage for the use of social science evidence to prove facts of racial inequality in *Brown v. Board of Education*.

> **Activity 8.10 – Digging Deeper: Labor Laws for Women**
>
> Between 1909 and 1917, maximum work hours labor laws for women existed in 39 states. By 1923, minimum wage laws for women existed in 15 states and, by 1920, laws that provided financial relief for women through mothers' and widows' pensions had been passed in 40 states (Lepore, 2018). Florence Kelly and others worked incredibly hard to get labor laws passed for women. This was a great accomplishment in protecting women who could not protect themselves.
>
> **Discussion Questions**
>
> - How did mothers' and widows' pensions contribute to the financial security of women? In what ways is this a women's rights issue?
> - Did labor laws for women impact every woman the same? Why or why not? Discuss disparities based on intersecting identities.
> - What were the long-term effects of the labor laws and pension systems established during this time?

Women's Rights in the West

During the mid-to-late 1800s, the Western region of the United States was very different from the East and South. White people in the West, including women, had different lifestyles and needs than those in the East and South. In many ways, women's rights progressed more quickly in the western United States. Women of the West, such as Clarina Nichols and Elizabeth Piper Ensley, fought for women's rights and, in many cases, won. An excellent example of this was divorce. Because married women could not inherit or own property, they were often destitute after a divorce in many areas of the United States. In addition, divorce was frowned upon in society, and usually, women would lose custody of their children if divorced. However, in the West, divorce was not seen as a stain on a woman's reputation in the same way. Judges "frequently rewarded the custody of children to mothers rather than father" (Gallagher, 2021, p. 48).

During the Civil War, women in the West gained even more rights. While President Lincoln signed the Homestead Act for political reasons and not to take a stand on women's rights, the Act allowed women who were heads of households to own property in the Western territories (Gallagher, 2021). "In addition to its economic benefits, the act enabled tens of thousands of women to realize the dream of land ownership that had been bound up with citizenship and status [and] set a powerful precedent for equalizing their legal status" (Gallagher, 2021, p. 50).

Another act, the Morrill Land-Grant Act, was passed within a few months of the Homestead Act. The Morrill Land-Grant Act allowed women to attend tuition-free higher education (Gallagher, 2021). Higher education gave women more choices regarding marriage and more potential for financial independence. Equally important, the Morrill Land-Grant Act created a legal precedent for women to be treated equally by the federal government of the United States (Gallagher, 2021).

As much as women's rights in the West improved over time, there was still little progress in the struggle for women's suffrage. This was equally true in the East and the South. By the end of the 19th century, it appeared as if the women's suffrage movement had stalled.

The 19th Amendment

At the turn of the 20th century, women still could not vote in the United States. As the founders of the women's rights movement aged and passed away, it felt like the suffrage movement had stalled. In time, new radical women activists stepped up to carry on the cause. Women like Mary Church Terrell and Carrie Chapman Catt infused new life and ideas into the women's suffrage movement (Cobbs, 2023).

Mary Church Terrell was a wealthy, upper-class, educated Black woman. As a young woman, she traveled in Europe and "tasted the joy of not thinking about color" (Cobbs, 2023, p. 140). In 1892, Terrell, with like-minded women, started the Colored Women's League (CWL). As an organization, the CWL focused on various issues faced by the Black community, including education, Jim Crow laws, and women's rights. In 1896, the CWL and Josephine St. Pierre Ruffin's Woman's Era Club joined forces to create one organization, the National Association of Colored Women (NACW). By 1924, the NACW had approximately 100,000 members (Cobbs, 2023). Terrell was praised for building bridges between people with shared interests. Terrell "believed that enduring progress could be achieved only through interracial cooperation" (Cobbs, 2023, p. 152). She was not alone. Susan B. Anthony continued to push for Black women to become members of the primarily White women's rights movement and asked Terrell to join the National American Women's Suffrage Association (NAWSA). Terrell agreed and, by 1901, began travelling across the United States to speak to integrated audiences. Terrell educated her audiences about "the progress of her gender and race, and violations of the Thirteenth, Fourteenth, and Fifteenth Amendments" (Cobbs, 2023, p. 155). In 1904, Terrell was invited to speak at the International Council of Women's Conference in Berlin and became an international sensation.

Activity 8.11 – Mary Church Terrell

Video: Mary Church Terrell's Advocacy & Impact on Voting Rights (https://www.youtube.com/watch?v=BtXx27RJS1I)

 One or more interactive elements has been excluded from this version of the text. You can view them online here: https://milnepublishing.geneseo.edu/social-justice-in-human-services/?p=159#oembed-3 (#oembed-3)

Speech Transcript: The Strongest for the Weakest – 1904 (https://awpc.cattcenter.iastate.edu/2019/12/20/the-strongest-for-the-weakest-1904/) by Mary Church Terrell

Discussion Questions

- What were Mary Church Terrell's critical contributions to the women's suffrage movement? How did she navigate the intersection of race and gender in her advocacy efforts?
- How did Mary Church Terrell's activism challenge or complement the work of other prominent suffragists and women's rights advocates of her time? In what ways did she agree with or differ from other leaders?
- How did Mary Church Terrell's activism contribute to the broader women's rights movement and the fight for racial equality? What lasting impact did her work have on these movements?

As Jim Crow laws continued to oppress Black people in the United States, tension increased between Black and White women in the suffrage movement. Some White women championed White supremacy by actively endorsing suffrage for White women only (Cobbs, 2023). "Rebecca Felton, a former slaveholder and the wife of a liberal Congressman from Georgia, advocated for both women's suffrage and the lynching of every 'Black fiend who lays unholy and lustful hands on a white woman'" (Cobbs, 2023, p. 157). Many Southern suffragists organized against women like Felton, but had little success in impacting the racist rhetoric.

Many White Women in the suffrage movement felt they needed to make difficult decisions to obtain the right to vote. They understood that if women won the suffrage battle in the United States, most Black women would not be allowed to exercise their right to vote, as the majority of Black Americans still lived in Southern states with oppressive Jim Crow laws (Cobbs, 2023). If the women's suffrage movement were successful and obtained the right to vote for all women, that "would inscribe a non-racist, non-sexist law in the Constitution that nominally doubled the number of Black voters" (Cobbs, 2023, p. 170). Most women's suffrage organizations took the middle path and continued to fight for all women but did not confront concerns about Jim Crow laws.

Mary Church Terrell, 1946.

Activity 8.12: Black Women in the Suffrage Movement

Video: Untold Stories of Black Women in the Suffrage Movement
(https://www.youtube.com/watch?v=Br6b9sIuIDU)

 One or more interactive elements has been excluded from this version of the text. You can view them online here: https://milnepublishing.geneseo.edu/social-justice-in-human-services/?p=159#oembed-4 (#oembed-4)

Discussion Questions:

- What was your initial reaction to the quote, "I am my ancestors' wildest dreams?" How does this quote resonate with you, and what emotions or thoughts does it evoke? How is the quote significant in a discussion of Black women's suffrage?
- How did Black women navigate the racial dynamics and exclusions within the mainstream suffrage movement? What strategies did they employ to assert their rights and advocate for racial and gender equality?
- How can we ensure that the contributions and stories of Black women in the suffrage movement are more fully recognized and integrated into historical narratives? What

> steps can be taken to address the historical erasure of their contributions?

In 1914, for the first time since 1887, the United States Congress agreed to allow a women's suffrage bill, the Susan B. Anthony Amendment, to be brought to the floor for a vote. In support of the Amendment, Terrell and other Black women of the NACW marched with White suffragists. A Black newspaper reported on the march, writing "No color line existed in any part of it. Afro-American women proudly marched right by the side of the white sisters" (Cobbs, 2023, p. 172).

Suffragists knew that the Susan B. Anthony Amendment would not pass. However, they needed to gain information on how Congress would vote and what barriers must be overcome for future success. After Congress engaged in a three-hour debate, it was clear that racism was the biggest obstacle to women obtaining the right to vote. Extremists like Senator James Vardaman went as far as to propose "trading Black male suffrage for women's suffrage" (Cobbs, 2023, p. 173).

As the United States entered World War I, American women were needed to fill jobs left by soldiers going overseas. Women, such as Carrie Chapman Catt, took advantage of this need. When asked by President Wilson to assist with promoting the war effort (Faderman, 2022; Griffith, 2022), Catt agreed to support Wilson's war efforts in exchange for his support of women's suffrage (Cobbs, 2023). In 1918, Wilson honored his agreement with Catt and supported the Susan B. Anthony Amendment. It is unclear if Wilson believed in women's rights or if he was concerned about the image of the United States. By 1918, 24 countries, including Germany, had already granted women the right to vote, and the United States was lagging behind the rest of the world (Catt & Shuler, 2020; Cobbs, 2023).

Even with President Wilson's support, there was no guarantee that Congress would pass the Susan B. Anthony Amendment or that the required number of states would ratify it. Suffragists, including Terrell and Paul, continued to fight hard. Anti-suffragists increased their rhetoric, claiming suffragists were anything from abnormal to socialists. "The omnipresent threat of Southern backlash constrained interracial cooperation among suffragists, regardless of their personal views or relationships" (Cobbs, 2023, p. 179). The United States Senate voted against women's suffrage four times: in 1887, 1914, 1918, and February, 1919. However, on June 4, 1919, the Senate passed the Susan B. Anthony Amendment. Ironically, the segregationist senators helped the Amendment pass by two votes (Cobbs, 2023).

On August 18, 1920, the Susan B. Anthony Amendment, known as the 19th Amendment, was ratified. It simply read, "The right of citizens of the United States to vote shall not be denied or abridged by the United States or by any state on account of sex" (Griffith, 2022, p. 19). The addition of one sentence to the Constitution took decades to achieve.

Not all states ratified the 19th Amendment. Mississippi, the last state to ratify, did not do so until 1984 (Griffith, 2022). Although the ratification of the 19th Amendment was finally successful, it had been a long and, in many ways, heartbreaking fight. Of the victory, Catt wrote,

> To get the word male in effect out of the constitution cost the women of the country fifty-two years of pause-less campaign thereafter. During that time they were forced to conduct fifty-six campaigns of referenda of male voters; 480 campaigns to get Legislatures to submit suffrage amendments to voters; 47 campaigns to get State constitutional conventions to write woman suffrage into State constitutions; 277 campaigns to get State party conventions to include women suffrage planks; 30 campaigns to get presidential party conventions to adopt woman suffrage planks in party platforms, and 19 campaigns with 19 successive Congresses …Young suffragists who helped forge the last links of that chain were not born when it began. Old suffragists who forged the first links were dead when it ended. (Cobbs, 2023, p. 181)

Limitations of the 19th Amendment

The ratification of the 19th Amendment was a milestone. However, it also had significant limitations. In the United States, racism still trumped the law. Although the 19th Amendment included Black women as United States citizens, it did not protect their right to vote. States had immense power over voting rules, and many did whatever they could to stop Black people, including women, from voting. Black women were subjected "to blatantly discriminatory practices, including unfairly administered literacy tests and 'grandfather' clauses that prevented descendants of enslaved people from voting while allowing illiterate whites to vote if their grandparents had" (Griffith, 2022, p. 23). Other tactics employed by states included White-only primaries and accusations of missed registration deadlines.

In addition to Black Americans being discriminated against in their right to vote, the 19th Amendment also failed to protect Indigenous women, women who lived in United States territories, or the District of Columbia (Griffith, 2022). Mary Church Terrell, who had fought tirelessly for women's suffrage, lived in the District of Columbia and "never did cast a ballot" (Griffith, 2022, p. 182). She died ten years before the District of Columbia passed suffrage in 1964 (Cobbs, 2023).

The 19th Amendment did not apply to Indigenous women because they were not citizens of the United States. However, not all Indigenous people desired United States citizenship. Some Indigenous leaders were concerned that if they obtained citizenship, the United States government would use that as a justification to negate the treaty and property rights guaranteed to Indigenous people (Blackhawk, 2023). Marie Louise Bottineau Baldwin, from the Turtle Mountain Chippewa community, and Zitkala-Sa, from the Yankton Sioux community, were both active in the women's suffrage movement and the movement for Indigenous rights (Griffith, 2022). Although Zitkala-Sa advocated for Indigenous citizenship, she did not believe it would resolve the systemic racism that Indigenous people faced in the United

States. Ultimately, Zitkala-Sa believed citizenship was "a necessary remedy for a broader illness" (Blackhawk, 2023, p. 385).

Activity 8.13 – Limitations of the 19th Amendment

Video: When Voting Rights Didn't Protect All Women (https://www.youtube.com/watch?v=ScU2oWfWReg)

 One or more interactive elements has been excluded from this version of the text. You can view them online here: https://milnepublishing.geneseo.edu/social-justice-in-human-services/?p=159#oembed-5 (#oembed-5)

Discussion Questions

- How did voting rights not protect all women?
- Do you see voting rights as a victory for suffragettes or a setback for the broader fight for racial equality? Explain your answer.
- How does the historical context of voting rights and racial inequality impact the current discourse on voting rights and representation for marginalized groups? What connections can be drawn between past and present struggles for voting rights?

Post-19th Amendment

After the ratification of the 19th Amendment, many suffragists split into special interest groups. Some women, such as Jane Addams and Ellen Starr, focused their energy and skills on working with immigrants to the United States. Addams and Starr established Hull House, the first settlement house in the United States to serve immigrants and working-class people (Griffith, 2022). Because of her work, Addams was the second woman to win the Nobel Prize for Peace in 1931 (Nobelprize.org, n.d.).

Some women, such as Mary Burnett Talbert, focused on the brutality of White supremacy. Talbert became the chair of the NAACP Anti-Lynching Committee and fought tirelessly to end the "legal terrorism of lynching, dismemberment, and burning in the Jim Crow South, where 90% of African Americans lived in 1920" (Griffith, 2022, pp. 34-35).

Some women, such as Alice Paul, remained focused on women's rights. On September 10, 1920, while giving a speech to the leaders of the National Woman's Party (NWP), Paul stated,

> It is incredible to me that any woman should consider the fight for full equality won. It is just the beginning. There is hardly a field, economic or political, in which the natural and accustomed policy is not to ignore women.... Unless women are prepared to fight politically, they must be content to be ignored politically. (Griffith, 2022, p. 40)

Paul's slogan, *Equality Not Protection*, expressed her belief that women deserved "political sameness" (Griffith, 2022, p. 43). Paul believed that gender-based protections, such as those in the labor reform movement, prohibited women's advancement toward equality.

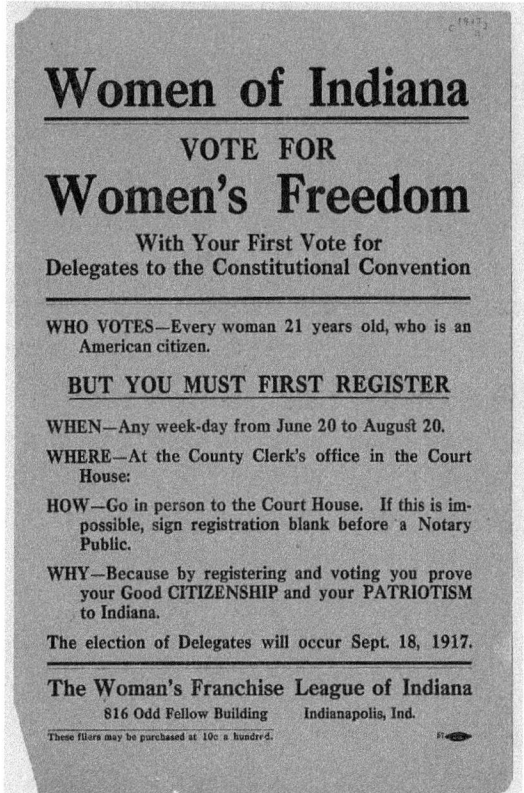

The Equal Rights Amendment

Alice Paul introduced the Equal Rights Amendment (ERA) at the National Women's Party (NWP) convention in 1921 (Griffith, 2022). The ERA, as written by Paul, declared: "No political, civil, or legal disabilities or inequalities on account of sex or on account of marriage, unless applying equally to both sexes, shall exist within the United States or any territory subject to its jurisdiction thereof" (Griffith, 2022, p. 43). Not everyone was a proponent of the ERA. Some women in the labor reform movement, such as Florence Kelly, believed the ERA would undo their accomplishments. Kelly called the ERA "miserable, monstrously stupid and deadly" (Griffith, 2022, p. 43).

The ERA, sponsored by the NWP, reached the floor of the United States Senate in 1946, where it was defeated (Faderman, 2022). The ERA had surprising opponents, such as women in the labor reform movement like Kelly and Eleanor Roosevelt, a Women's Trade Union League member. The NWP tried to revise the ERA in the early 1960s with little success. Although many women worked outside of the home, the social convention still saw women as primarily homemakers. Congressmember John F. Kennedy stated that a "woman's primary responsibility is in the home" (Faderman, 2022, p. 311).

Others, such as Congressmember Howard W. Smith, supported the ERA not because he supported women's rights but because "he was opposed to protective legislation for them" (Faderman, 2022, p. 311). Although Paul and Smith were not philosophically aligned in many ways, they worked together with some success. In 1963, the Civil Rights Act was presented to the House Rules Committee. Title VII of the Civil Rights Act "banned discrimination on the basis of race, color, religion, and national origin" (Faderman, 2022, p. 311). Paul asked Smith to add sex to Title VII, and Smith agreed. With Smith's endorsement, sex was successfully added to Title VII and signed into law on July 2, 1964 (Faderman, 2022).

In 1970, the ERA was again presented to Congress. Although there was continued opposition within Congress, the ERA was passed by the House of Representatives in 1971 and the Senate in 1972. However, for the ERA to be enacted into law, it needed to be ratified by 38 states. Members of Congress who opposed the ERA had set "an arbitrary time limit of seven years for ratification" (Faderman, 2022, p. 353). By 1973, 30 states had ratified the ERA.

During this time, the ERA gained a new opponent. Phyllis Schlafly and her STOP (Stop Taking Our Privileges) campaign rallied heavily against the ERA. Schlafly viewed the ERA as "a bottomless pit of horrors" (Cobbs, 2023, p. 295). She feared the ERA would make women subject to the military draft, damage labor protections for women, force happy homemakers to work, and negate women's rights to alimony and child support (Cobbs, 2023). Schlafly used her fears to motivate "an army of radical-right women followers" (Faderman, 2022, p. 355).

By 1977, the ERA was stalled, with only 35 of the necessary 38 states having ratified it. Congress granted a three-year extension of the ERA's ratification time limit. However, Schlafly's campaign was highly successful. Not only did her campaign stop some states from ratifying the ERA, but other states, such as Tennessee, withdrew their ratification (Faderman, 2022). By 1982, the ERA's time limit extension had expired, and the ERA was never ratified (Cobbs, 2023).

Women's Rights Movement: Second Wave (1960s to Current)

Just as the anti-slavery movement had inspired the first women's rights movement, the second wave of the women's rights movement was inspired by the civil rights movement. Many women in the second wave were also involved in the civil rights movement, where they learned how to advocate, march, and protest (Faderman, 2022).

In 1963, Betty Friedan wrote in *The Feminine Mystique* that women were unhappy due to "the problem that has no name" (Friedan, 2001, p. 10). Friedan theorized that because women had repressed their needs to do more than be a "happy housewife," they felt unhappy and worthless. Friedan's ideas resonated with many American women, and by 1966, she had sold over three million copies of *The Feminine Mystique*.

In 1966, at the third annual conference for the President's Commission on the Status of Women, Friedan, Aileen Hernandez, Inez Casiano, Shirley Chisholm, and Pauli Murray established the National Organization for Women (NOW; Berry & Gross, 2020; Faderman, 2022). NOW fought for the ERA. After its defeat, similar to the post-19th Amendment ratification, many women involved in NOW splintered to focus on other special interests. Some women like Marie Bass, Betsy Crone, and Ellen Malcom focused on the need for more women in political positions of power.

Activity 8.14 – Digging Deeper: Emily's List

Ellen Malcolm initially founded EMILY's (Early Money Is Like Yeast) List. EMILY's List is registered as a political action committee and operates as a donor network for women political candidates (Griffith, 2022).

Video: Ellen Malcolm, Founder of EMILY's list (https://www.youtube.com/watch?v=BSTU-WoTNnPc)

 One or more interactive elements has been excluded from this version of the text. You can view them online here: https://milnepublishing.geneseo.edu/social-justice-in-human-services/?p=159#oembed-6 (#oembed-6)

Discussion Questions:

- What impact has EMILY's List had on increasing the representation of women in politics?
- What role does money play in successful political campaigns? Why is this relevant to women's rights in the United States?
- In what ways has politics changed since Ellen Malcolm formed EMILY's List? How have these changes impacted the organization and its effectiveness?
- How can the principles and strategies of EMILY's List be applied to support other underrepresented groups in politics? What parallels can be drawn between supporting women and helping other marginalized communities?

By its second national convention, and partially due to Friedan's popularity and force of personality, NOW had become an organization of mostly middle-class White women. Before the term "intersectionality" was coined by Kimberlee Crenshaw in 1989, Black women lived the double jeopardy of being Black and being a woman (Berry & Gross, 2020; Griffith, 2022). While Black women benefited from some of NOW's initiatives, such as the protest against the Equal Employment Opportunities Commission (EEOC), they had additional challenges that middle-class White women did not share. Many Black women did not relate to Friedan's "problem with no name," as they had always had to work due to economic inequalities and systemic racism (Faderman, 2022; Griffith, 2022). "Black women were already ... roughly equal to Black men—just as they had been in the days of slavery, when their gender had not saved them from abuse" (Faderman, 2022, p. 321).

In 1973, Florence Kennedy, Margaret Sloan, and Eleanor Holmes established the National Black Feminist Organization (NBFO) in reaction to NOW, middle-class White feminists, and Black men. The NBFO's Statement of Purpose read,

> The women's liberation movement has been characterized as the exclusive property of so-called white middle-class women, and any Black women involved in this movement have been seen [by Black activists] as selling out, dividing the race, and an assortment of nonsensical epithets (such as lesbian, dyke, and bull dagger). (Faderman, 2022, p. 339)

While NBFO reflected some Black voices, Black lesbians, such as Audre Lorde and Gloria Hull, felt disconnected from NOW and NBFO. They worked together and formed the Combahee River Collective, intending to support women of all identities. They wanted to look beyond gender and race for inclusion. The women of the Collective were the first to define identity politics and interlocking systems of oppression.

Activity 8.15 – Black Feminist Organizations

Video: Black Feminist Organizations (https://www.youtube.com/watch?v=OSTPOoOIC6o)

 One or more interactive elements has been excluded from this version of the text. You can view them online here: https://milnepublishing.geneseo.edu/social-justice-in-human-services/?p=159#oembed-7 (#oembed-7)

Discussion Questions

- In what ways have Black feminist organizations contributed to the broader women's rights movement?
- How have Black feminist organizations navigated and challenged systemic racism and sexism within the broader feminist movement?
- What lessons can current social justice advocates take from the history and ongoing work of Black feminist organizations?

Ms. magazine, Fall 2009, featuring Alice Walker and Gloria Steinem

Reproductive Justice Movement

Reproductive justice is "the complete physical, mental, spiritual, political, social, and economic well-being of women and girls, based on the full achievement and protection of women's human rights" (Ross, 2006). The quest for women's reproductive justice has existed since European colonists first invaded America. Although reproductive injustice has affected and continues to affect all women, women of color have been disproportionately affected.

The history of Black women in the United States is fraught with reproductive injustice. During the many atrocities of the American slave trade, enslaved women's bodies were not ever their own, and "their gender was unacknowledged most of the time" (Faderman, 2022, p. 50). However, at the same time, slave owners were invested in enslaved women's reproductive functions as a financial investment. Enslaved women's economic value increased with each completed pregnancy, and slave owners often forced mating between slaves. However, pregnancy was not considered a reason to excuse enslaved women from work or punishment.

> If a pregnant woman did something to anger the overseer, he might dig a hole in the ground big enough to contain her stomach, force her to lie down, and then beat her—in that way protecting the unborn child, which was the master's property. (Faderman, 2022, p. 50)

Before the 1870s, midwives and other female healers assisted women through birth, contraception, and even abortion. By the 1870s, however, the practice of medicine was established as a male profession, and medical doctors lobbied for regulated qualifications, which disqualified midwives from practicing medicine (Griffith, 2022). In addition, at the time, women were not accepted into medical schools in the United States. Thus, for the first time in history, reproductive concerns in the United States were no longer in the control of women but, instead, in the control of men.

Childbirth

In the early 1900s, many medical professionals refused to use anesthesia during childbirth despite it having been available since 1831. "Aside from beliefs that anesthetics were dangerous, time-wasting, and likely to drive women erotically insane, most physicians still felt that they should be the judges of the pain of childbirth" (Cleghorn, 2021, p. 141). As part of the quest for reproductive justice, women challenged the idea that pain was a necessary and inevitable part of childbirth. "But the intention to have women reclaim their bodies from medical control was trampled in the obstetricians' race to transform childbirth into an illness that required drugs, instruments, and brutal procedures" (Cleghorn, 2021, p. 153).

Birth Control

In 1915, Mary Ware Dennett, inspired by the advocacy of Margaret Sanger, established the National Birth Control League. The National Birth Control League was "the first American organization to campaign to legalize contraception and release women from the wretchedness of unwilling parenthood" (Cleghorn, 2021, p. 153). Sanger, a strong advocate for access to birth control, published a newsletter, *The Woman Rebel*, where she "connected reproductive choice with women's economic emancipation" (Cleghorn, 2021, p. 154). Sanger, in her quest to provide birth control education, was a true advocate of women's choices.

In 1917, Margaret Sanger opened the first birth control clinic in the United States in Brooklyn, New York. Sanger believed that giving women access to birth control would reduce the need for abortions and would increase sexual pleasure (Cleghorn, 2021). Unfortunately, Sanger did not have the law on her side, and the clinic was raided and shut down. In addition, Sanger was arrested multiple times for being a public nuisance and for the distribution of lewd materials, which were materials about contraception. However, Sanger did not give up. In 1923, Sanger opened the first legal birth control clinic in the United States (Faderman, 2022)

Due to the advocacy of Sanger and others, contraceptive methods and education became available to women in the United States. Unfortunately, many of those contraceptive methods, including diaphragms, sponges, and condoms were unreliable, required advance planning, or required the cooperation of men. However, as eloquently stated by Cleghorn (2021), "[it] is an anger-inducing reality that the beginnings of reproductive justice were entangled with ideologies about how women-especially Black women, other ethnically diverse women, and vulnerable women-should be controlled and regulated" (p. 165).

By 1921, Sanger founded the American Birth Control League, eventually known as Planned Parenthood, and continued to support women's access to birth control and education about their bodies. By the late 1930s, approximately 400 birth control clinics existed in the United States (Cleghorn, 2021). In 1941, the National Council of Negro Women was the first national women's organization that officially endorsed contraceptives for women.

In the early 1950s, Sanger, both personally and through Planned Parenthood, provided partial funding to research an oral contraceptive for women. Sanger's friend, Katharine Dexter McCormick, provided the rest of the financing (Planned Parenthood, n.d.). By the mid-1950s, clinical trials began for an oral contraceptive (Cleghorn, 2021).

The first clinical trials for an oral contraceptive were held in Puerto Rico. The trial utilized racially biased, unethical, and unsafe methods. "The women of Puerto Rico were regarded as submissive enough to be coerced into continuously taking an uncharted drug" (Cleghorn, 2021, p. 272). Although Puerto Rican women, due to poverty, had a genuine need for birth control methods, they were not informed that they were being used as test subjects, nor were they informed of the potential side effects of the drug (Cleghorn, 2021).

On June 23, 1960, the United States Food and Drug Administration (FDA) approved the release of Enovid, commonly referred to as the Pill. Enovid was the first oral hormonal birth control for women (Cleghorn, 2021; Griffith, 2022). "Historical fears that women's sexual freedom would lead to the destruction of moral and societal values pervaded medical, religious, and governmental attitudes towards the pill from its very inception" (Cleghorn, 2021, p. 270). By its release date, it was illegal for doctors to prescribe Enovid in 30 states (Griffith, 2022).

In 1965, the United States Supreme Court ruled in *Griswold v. Connecticut* that married women had a constitutional right to privacy, which included the decision to use birth control. Because *Griswold* only applied to married women, there were still many women who could not use Enovid, including women under the age of 21 without parental consent (Cleghorn, 2021). It was not until 1972 when the United States Supreme Court ruled in *Baird v. Eisenstadt* that unmarried women, due to their constitutional right to privacy, could legally use birth control (Griffith, 2022).

Activity 8.16 – Birth Control

Video: Planned Parenthood: History of the Pill: Why Birth Control Matters (https://www.youtube.com/watch?v=f5pgO0VkGa0)

One or more interactive elements has been excluded from this version of the text. You can view them online here: https://milnepublishing.geneseo.edu/social-justice-in-human-services/?p=159#oembed-8 (#oembed-8)

> **Discussion Questions**
>
> - What role did birth control play in women's rights historically?
> - What role does birth control play in women's rights today?

People holding signs at a Planned Parenthood Rally, NYC 2011.

Eugenics and Forced Sterilization

While Sanger was fighting to give women access to birth control, eugenics gained popularity in the United States. Eugenics was a pseudoscience that postulated that deficits are genetic. Thus, it was believed that people with disabilities, people of certain races, and poor people should not be allowed to have children. Between 1907 and 1979, over 64,000 American women were forcibly sterilized based on their race, class, and intellectual disability.

In 1924, the State of Virginia passed a law that mandated the forced sterilization of women deemed intellectually disabled. That same year, Dr. Albert Priddy, who had performed hundreds of forced sterilizations, petitioned to sterilize Carrie Buck, an 18-year-old White woman who was institutionalized in the Virginia Colony for Epileptics and Feebleminded. According to Griffith (2022), Buck was raped by one of her relatives and had an illegitimate child. She was accused of being promiscuous and feebleminded. To guarantee that the Virginia law was legally sound, the Virginia Colony hired an attorney for Buck. In 1927, *Buck v. Bell* went to the United States Supreme Court. The Supreme Court upheld that the

State of Virginia had the right to sterilize Buck. In his majority rule, Justice Holmes wrote, "being swamped with incompetence...Three generations of imbeciles is enough." (Griffith, 2022, p. 56). The Supreme Court decision allowed the State of Virginia to sterilize Carrie Buck, and she underwent the procedure on October 19, 1927.

In the 1960s, during the civil rights fight, North Carolina (1961) and Mississippi (1964) passed forced sterilization laws. The forced sterilization of Black women occurred so often in southern states that the procedure was known as the "Mississippi appendectomy" (Griffith, 2022, p. 56). The Mississippi law, aptly dubbed the Genocide Bill, was initially written so that any woman who had a second illegitimate child would be charged with a felony punishable by either prison or sterilization. When the Mississippi law was passed, it changed the charge from a felony to a misdemeanor and reduced the sentence to 90 days in jail or sterilization (Griffith, 2022).

Unfortunately, in the United States, forced sterilization of women is not just history. According to a 2022 report from the National Women's Law Center (NWLC), 31 states and the District of Columbia currently have laws on the books that allow forced sterilization of disabled women. Only two states specifically ban forced sterilization, and the other 17 states have either statutes with loopholes or have had court rulings that have suggested forced sterilization may be possible (NWLC, 2022).

Abortion

Despite having access to birth control methods, millions of American women will experience an unplanned pregnancy in their lifetime. It is important to note that not all women in the United States will want or have an abortion. However, abortion has always existed in the United States regardless of legality. The most common reasons American women have abortions are "rape, incest, poverty, desperation, fatal fetal abnormalities, and risk to the mother" (Griffith, 2022, p. 363). Therefore, the most controversial issue in the women's reproductive justice movement is abortion.

Before the early 1800s, common law allowed free women to have abortions up until fetal movement, known as quickening, was detected. Thus, it was the pregnant woman who decided when and if they chose to abort, as only they could feel fetal movement (Griffith, 2022). Abortions were induced using herbs and some medications, usually given by midwives (Cleghorn, 2021). "For the most part, the persons who performed all manner of reproductive health care were women—female midwives. Midwifery was interracial; half of the women who provided reproductive health care were Black women. Other midwives were Indigenous and white" (Goodwin, 2020, para 5).

White male gynecologists viewed skilled Black and Indigenous midwives as an affront to their professional image (Goodwin, 2020) and, by the early 1800s, states had passed laws that limited or prohibited abortion. In 1821, the State of Connecticut passed the first law that limited access to abortion. Connecticut's law banned the use of herbs, a common way to induce abortion, and made their use punishable by a life sentence in prison. In 1845, the State of Massachusetts was the first to pass a law that prohibited abortion for any reason (Griffith, 2022). By 1857, the American Association of Medicine (AMA) "coordinated a national drive to outlaw abortion and midwifery, both to ensure women's safety and to eliminate competition for obstetrical patients" (Griffith, 2022, p. 193). The AMA succeeded in both goals.

Between 1821 and 1880, 40 states and territories had established anti-abortion laws and, by 1900, all 45 states had laws that made abortion illegal. Any exceptions to the law were decided by doctors (D'Emilio & Freedman, 2012; Griffith, 2022). "Doctors used their judgment in cases of rape or risk to the mental or physical health of the mother. If two psychiatrists and one physician agreed, a woman could have a therapeutic abortion" (Griffith, 2022, p. 194). Additionally, in many areas in the United States, hospitals and medical clinics were segregated by race, which meant that access to abortion was even more limited for women of color (Cleghorn, 2021; Griffith, 2022).

During the 1950s and 1960s, the number of illegal abortions performed was estimated from 200,000 to 1.2 million each year (Gold, 2003). As discussed above, birth control was not legal for single women until 1972. Therefore, women needed access to safe abortions. Many doctors provided abortions for women who had the necessary medical connections and the money to pay for the procedure. For women who had neither, often marginalized women, abortion was either not available or was unsafe (Garrow, 1999).

Activity 8.17 – The Jane Collective

Video: Abortion Was Illegal. This Secret Group Defied the Law (https://www.youtube.com/watch?v=b8NMhEcyJ_I)

 One or more interactive elements has been excluded from this version of the text. You can view them online here: https://milnepublishing.geneseo.edu/social-justice-in-human-services/?p=159#oembed-9 (#oembed-9)

In 1965, Heather Tobis Booth helped a friend find a doctor willing to perform an abortion. Booth, as a result of that experience, started the Jane Collective, a network of women that offered information about safe abortion providers, safe houses, and counseling. Because of their experiences with unlicensed abortion providers, some of the women of the Jane Collective learned how to perform abortions. Between 1969 and 1972, women in the Jane Collective performed 12,000 illegal abortions (Griffith, 2022).

Discussion Questions

- The Jane Collective is seen as an advocacy group. Do you agree that this work was advocacy?
- Where does the right to choose fit into the women's rights movement?

By the 1970s, "there was a distinct trend in the states...toward liberalization of abortion statutes" (Ginsburg, 1985, pp. 379-380). Some states, such as Alaska, Hawaii, and Washington, permitted first-trimester abortions with no restrictions. However, some states, such as Georgia and Texas, had highly restrictive abortion laws (Ginsburg, 1985). By 1970, approximately 20 constitutional cases were challenging restrictive abortion laws (Garrow, 1999).

In 1971, two abortion law cases, *Doe v. Bolton* and *Roe v. Wade*, were brought to the United States Supreme Court. *Doe v. Bolton* challenged a Georgia state law that only allowed abortions in cases of rape, fetal deformity, or potential of severe harm to a woman. The Georgia law also required abortions to be performed in hospitals after a woman was examined by three medical doctors and a committee approved the procedure. *Roe v. Wade* challenged an 1857 Texas state law that banned abortion unless determined to be lifesaving for a woman and punished participants of illegal abortion with up to five years in prison (Griffith, 2022).

In 1973, the United States Supreme Court ruled on *Doe v. Bolton* and *Roe v. Wade*. In *Doe v. Bolton*, the United States Supreme Court ruled in favor of Doe. The Court concluded that abortion rights should not be without specific parameters, but that the requirements in the State of Georgia were unduly burdensome. *Doe v. Bolton*, although a critical case, had limited impact because of its focus on the specific way the State of Georgia restricted abortion access (Griffith, 2022).

Roe v. Wade was a critical case because it challenged the right of states to ban abortion altogether, and the Court's ruling in *Roe* signified that women had control over decisions about their bodies. Specifically, the outcome of *Roe v. Wade* upheld the ideal of liberty derived from the 14th Amendment (Griffith, 2022). Although *Roe v. Wade* was challenged multiple times, the United States Supreme Court reaffirmed its decision in cases such as *Planned Parenthood of Southeastern Pennsylvania v. Casey*; that women had the essential liberty of bodily autonomy, and that individual states could not ban abortion before viability of a fetus (Faderman, 2022; Griffith, 2022). This changed in 2022 with the *Dobbs v. Jackson Women's Health Organization* Supreme Court decision (Griffith, 2022).

Roe v. Wade Backlash

In *Roe v. Wade*, the United States Supreme Court concluded that "access to abortion was a fundamental right" (Griffith, 2022, p. 196). However, the Court's ruling included a loophole for states' compelling interest, which "could justify restrictive state regulations" (Griffith, 2022, p. 196). An example of a compelling state interest was that in the second trimester of a pregnancy, "the state could regulate abortion in ways that are reasonably related to maternal health," as well as in the third trimester, "given its interest in the potentiality of human life, the state could justify regulating or banning abortion, except for the preservation of life or health of the mother" (Griffith, 2022, p. 196).

In creating these loopholes, the Court's ruling "created new gestational dividers, three-month increments, and a three-tiered legal framework" as well as making "viability, when a fetus could survive outside the womb, key to abortion law (Griffith, 2022, p. 196). According to Ginsburg (1985), Justice Sandra Day O'Connor described the Court's use of "the trimester approach as on a collision course with itself" (p. 381). Ginsburg believed that the Court "ventured too far in the change it ordered" because it generated a backlash from conservatives and "stimulated the mobilization of a right-to-life movement" (p. 381). Both O'Connor and Ginsburg would be proved right.

The backlash began as soon as the United States Supreme Court released its ruling on *Roe v. Wade*. "During the 1970s, a new set of right-wing organizations came into existence" (D'Emilio & Freedman, 2012, p. 348) determined to overturn *Roe v. Wade*. For anti-abortion activists, a major victory was needed. On September 30, 1976, in an attempt by Congress to limit abortions, the Hyde Amendment was passed as an attachment to the *Departments of Labor and Health, Education, and Welfare Appropriation Act of 1977* (D'Emilio & Freedman, 2012).

The Hyde Amendment restricted Medicaid funding for abortion except in cases of incest, rape, or if a woman's life was in jeopardy (Adashi & Occhiogrosso Abelman, 2017). After *Roe v. Wade* but before the Hyde Amendment, Medicaid funded approximately 25% of abortions in the United States. The Hyde Amendment drastically reduced Medicaid funding. The Centers for Disease Control and Prevention (CDC) reported that in 1977, before the Hyde Amendment was in full effect, 295,000 women had abortions covered by Medicaid. By 1979, only 2,400 women had abortions covered by Medicaid (Engstrom, 2016). "Though the constitutional right to abortion remained intact, anti-abortion forces had succeeded in sharply restricting the access that poor women had to it" (D'Emilio & Freedman, 2012, p. 348).

Because the Hyde Amendment is annually reviewed, Congress expanded it to restrict federal funding of abortions for women in the military and the Peace Corps, women with disabilities, women receiving care from Indian Health Services, and federal prisoners (Adashi & Occhiogrosso Abelman, 2017; Engstrom, 2016). In 2010, the enactment of the Affordable Care Act (ACA) facilitated the Hyde Amendment's extension "to federally subsidized private health insurance plans" (Adashi & Occhiogrosso Abelman, 2017, p. 1523). Between 2011 and 2020, historically conservative states passed over 480 restrictions on reproductive rights for women (Griffith, 2022).

On June 24, 2022, the United States Supreme Court overturned *Roe v. Wade* with their ruling on the *Dobbs v. Jackson Women's Health Organization*. In 2018, the State of Mississippi passed the Gestational Age Act, which banned abortion after 15 weeks, except if a woman's life was in danger or if there was fetal abnormality (Byron et al., 2022; Manninen, 2023). The *Dobbs v. Jackson Women's Health Organization* case challenged the act as unconstitutional based on prior abortion cases, including *Roe v Wade* and *Planned Parenthood v. Casey*.

The Court's ruling on *Dobbs* erased federal protections for women and gave decisions about abortion back to individual states. The Court ruled that the right to privacy "is controversial because such a right is not explicitly mentioned in the Constitution" (Manninen, 2023, p. 358). In its decision, the Court has set legal precedence to overturn other cases won based on the constitutional right to privacy argument. Included in those cases are *Lawrence v. Texas,* which deemed anti-sodomy laws unconstitutional, and *Obergefell v. Hodges,* which legalized same gender marriage in the United States (Manninen, 2023).

The Court's decision on *Dobbs* immediately affected the women's reproductive justice movement. By late 2022, 27 states had enacted laws to restrict or prohibit abortion. For example, the State of Oklahoma made abortion illegal from conception, the State of Ohio made abortion illegal six weeks post-gestation even in cases of incest or rape, and the State of Georgia has extended personhood rights to six-week-old fetuses (Byron et al., 2022). In 2024, Alabama passed a law granting personhood to embryos generated from in vitro fertilization (IVF) (Yousef, 2024).

Many American women believed that bodily autonomy was their guaranteed right in the United States after the *Roe v. Wade* decision. However, with the *Dobbs v. Jackson Women's Health Organization* decision, American women have learned that bodily autonomy was never their guaranteed right in the United States; it was only a law.

Activity 8.18 – Abortion Access

Video: Inequality and Abortion Access in the United States (https://www.youtube.com/watch?v=vdFtCizpedA&t=1s)

 One or more interactive elements has been excluded from this version of the text. You can view them online here: https://milnepublishing.geneseo.edu/social-justice-in-human-services/?p=159#oembed-10 (#oembed-10)

Discussion Questions

- What does unequal abortion access say about the women's rights movement?
- Where does access to abortion fit into a conversation about women's rights?

Anti-Rape Movement

The CDC (2014) defines sexual violence as "a sexual act that is committed or attempted by another person without freely given consent of the victim or against someone who is unable to consent or refuse" (p. 11). Although the dominant perception of sexual violence is men as perpetrators and women as victims, men are also victims of sexual violence. That said, in this section, the focus is on sexual violence perpetrated against women.

Indigenous Women

Historically, rape within Indigenous communities was forbidden and rare. Selling sex was non-existent as Indigenous people did not believe one could own another's sexuality, and that it could therefore not be purchased (D'Emilio & Freedman, 2012). European explorers and colonists sexually assaulted and raped Indigenous women and brought sexual oppression and terrorism to America. According to Griffith (2022), " [sexual] intimidation and violence against women were patriarchal prerogatives. That power was rooted in religious orthodoxy, white supremacy, territorial conquest, manifest destiny, frontier mythology, and masculine identity" (p. 365).

Black Women

Since the beginning of European colonization of the Americas, White men have used sexual violence to dehumanize and control enslaved Black women. According to Wilson (2021), enslaved Black women were forced to endure,

> public nudity; nude physical auction examinations to determine reproductive ability; rape for sexual pleasure and for economic purposes (reproducing children who could become slaves); intentional abortion to women who were pregnant as a result of rape generational poverty; and hypersexualization. (pp. 122-123)

However, sexual violence towards Black women did not end with slavery. "The rape of black women by white men continued, often unpunished, throughout the Jim Crow era. As reconstruction collapsed and Jim Crow arose, white men abducted and assaulted black women with alarming regularity" (McGuire, 2010, p. xviii). Black women testified about the systematic sexual violence they experienced from White men. "They launched the first public attacks on sexual violence as a systemic abuse of women in response to slavery and the wave of lynchings in the post-Emancipation South" (McGuire, 2010, p.xix).

1950s and 1960s

During the 1950s and early 1960s, rape was not acknowledged by victims, families, or the legal system. "Family, police, judges, and juries underestimated the prevalence of rape, and they faulted individual women for being in the wrong place at the wrong time" (Cobbs, 2023, p. 244). In North Carolina, only virgins were allowed to claim that they had been raped (D'Emilio & Freedman, 2012).

As the women's rights movement progressed, women identified acquaintance rape, marital rape, domestic abuse, and sexual harassment not as women's issues but as sociocultural problems (D'Emilio & Freedman, 2012). Laws, known as corroboration laws, required rape victims to prove that there was a rape. Therefore, rape victims needed to prove that force was used, that they resisted, that they did not consent, that there was penetration, and the identity of the rapist (Shelby, 2018). Force was proved by physical evidence such as "torn clothing or hysteria" (Shelby, 2018, p. 672), penetration was proved through medical evidence such as vaginal trauma or the presence of semen, and identity was proved by the victim's description of her rapist.

Women recognized the need for changes in both how evidence was collected in rape cases and how the criminal justice system perceived rape and rape victims. Evidence was not routinely collected in rape cases, and when it was collected, the evidence was not preserved appropriately. In the late 1970s, activist, sexual assault survivor, and founder of Citizens for Victims Assistance Martha Goddard co-developed the first comprehensive rape kit. Goddard visited hospitals and met with police, judges, and state legislators to learn what was needed to create the rape kits. Goddard's friend, Christie Hefner, funded the development of the first rape kits through Hugh Hefner's Playboy Foundation. Goddard's rape kits were first used in 1978 in Chicago's hospitals and, within two years, over 200 hospitals in Illinois were using the kits (Cobbs, 2023; Shelby, 2018).

Across the United States, women established self-defense groups and used the training to reconceptualize women not as potential victims but as powerful and in charge of their bodies (Jacquet, 2016). Women formed anti-rape squads that would act against male perpetrators. For example, the Contra Costa Anti-Rape Squad picketed the wedding of an accused rapist as well as put leaflets on wedding guests' cars detailing the alleged rape. Other anti-rape squads would find an alleged rapist and "jump him, shave his head, pour dye on him, take photographs and use them on a poster" that read, "This man rapes women" (Jacquet, 2016, p. 74).

In 1971, the first rape crisis centers were established in the United States and, by 1974, there were 61 centers in 27 states. In 1977, the National Coalition Against Sexual Assault was established by rape crisis centers, as was the National Center for the Prevention and Control of Rape in 1978. By 1982, feminist students were marching in Take Back the Night rallies on college campuses nationwide (Jacquet, 2016).

Activity 8.19 – Digging Deeper: Acquaintance Rape

In a landmark study published in 1987, psychologist Mary Koss surveyed 6,159 college women at 32 college campuses to find out about their experiences with sexual violence. Of the college women surveyed in Koss' study, 27.5% reported experiencing rape, with 84% raped by someone they knew. Koss went on to coin the phrases acquaintance rape and date rape (Driessen, 2020).

Discussion Questions

- How might being the victim of acquaintance or date rape be different than stranger rape? Why should there be a distinction?
- Where does a conversation about rape fit into a discussion about women's rights?
- What role do other intersecting identities play in violence against women?

In 1994, the United States Congress passed the Violence Against Women Act (VAWA), which was the first federal law that acknowledged domestic violence and sexual violence against women as crimes. The VAWA granted funding to support community resources such as domestic violence shelters and rape crisis centers. Additionally, VAWA granted federal prosecution of interstate domestic violence and sexual assault crimes, interstate enforcement of protection orders, and protections for women who did not have citizenship. However, the

VAWA was not permanent, as it requires reauthorization, generally every five years. Reauthorizations were passed in 2000, 2005, 2013 (Sacco & Hanson, 2019), and again in 2022 (Sacco, 2023).

In 2006, Tarana Burke started MeToo, a group for Girls of Color. Burke's MeToo group was in response to the sexual violence that girls and women experience, especially women of color in lower-income communities (Murphy, 2019). In 2017, sexual violence allegations against the powerful movie producer Harvey Weinstein became public, and actress Alyssa Milano asked her Twitter followers to tweet "me too" if they had experienced sexual abuse or violence; Milano received thousands of responses. In 24 hours, Facebook had 12 million "Me Too" posts from women across the globe. The #MeToo movement was the biggest social justice movement in the United States and possibly the largest to be spawned on social media. The #MeToo movement, much like the 1970s anti-rape squads, was determined to hold male predators accountable whether they ever saw the inside of a courtroom (Suk, 2023).

The #MeToo movement inspired other anti-sexual violence against women movements, such as the Time's Up movement. Women in the Time's Up movement raised over $22 million to support legal cases brought against powerful men in the entertainment industry. Famous women such as Gretchen Carlson, Rose McGowan, Simone Biles, Michelle Hurd, Evan Rachel Wood, and non-celebrities, such as Christine Blasey Ford, Morganne Picard, Juls Bindi, and Louise Godbold, went public with their experiences with sexual violence. Powerful men, such as Roger Ailes, Harvey Weinstein, Bill Cosby, Marilyn Mason, Brett Kavanaugh, and Larry Nassar, were publicly outed as sexual predators (Brodsky, 2021).

However, as important as the #MeToo and the Time's Up movements are, "there are many more not-famous people than famous ones" (Brodsky, 2021, p. 13). All American women are vulnerable to sexual violence, especially marginalized women. "Over and over again...abuse operates in the same ways: it targets the vulnerable and keeps them vulnerable. Inequality ensures its own survival through violence" (Brodsky, 2021, p. 24). According to the White House's *2023 U.S. National Plan to End Gender-Based Violence* report,

> Strategies for Action report collecting national and state-level data about the prevalence and nature of GBV in the United States is quite complex, and different from other crime victimization data collections. Many survivors do not share or disclose their experiences of victimization, and those who do disclose may not do so until years later. Moreover, the likelihood of survivors disclosing their victimizations to friends, family members, or other confidants is significantly higher than the likelihood of formal reporting to law enforcement, health care providers, school personnel, crisis centers or helplines, or other entities that may track and collect data. (p. 17)

Although the above statement is undoubtedly true, its implicit message is that it is the victims' fault that data collection is complex. The statement does not acknowledge the historical and systemic reasons why victims do not report their victimization immediately or ever. The statement does not acknowledge centuries of sexual violence experienced by women who have been repeatedly denied justice.

Conclusion

There is no happy ending to this chapter. Being a woman in the United States is still complex and fraught with difficulty. Many of the issues that women in the United States fought for in the 1800s are still concerns for women in 2024. Women are still paid less than men, are more likely to experience sexual violence than men, and have less power and privilege than men in the United States. However, as this chapter has hopefully made clear, women have fought and are willing to continue to fight for their equal rights as guaranteed by the United States Constitution.

Thoughts from the Author

As a woman, writing this chapter has been an amazing and heartbreaking experience. As a White woman, I had moments of shame because of what White women, including myself, have done to and not done for women of color. Yet, as eloquently stated by Griffith (2022), "[we] can condemn past actors and still consider their historical context" (p. xix). This does not change my core belief that genocide, oppression, and the enslavement of human beings are evil acts.

Suk (2023) argued that once patriarchal laws are repealed and other laws are put in place to protect women's equality, misogyny is "the vigilante punishment of women who challenge male power and endeavor to reset the presumed entitlements of a patriarchal society" (pp. 10-11). I agree. It is not enough to change laws; there needs to be a change of hearts and minds of those who continue to oppress others, including women.

My goal was to have this chapter read like a love letter to all the women who have come before me and to all the women who have and will come after me. I hope I was successful. We may be victimized, but we are not victims.

Sincerely,
Nikki

> **Chapter Summary Questions**
>
> 1. Describe and discuss the difference between being female and being a woman. Why is this important in a discussion of women's rights?
> 2. Early colonists discovered that Indigenous women had different cultural norms regarding gender roles. Compare and contrast the sexual practices of early colonists with those of Indigenous women.
> 3. Connect the women's rights movement to other social justice movements. What are the similarities? What are the differences?
> 4. Explore the historical and contemporary impact of United States laws and policies on women's rights.
> 5. What is reproductive justice?
> 6. What are the current social justice movements in women's rights? Describe two current movements that impact women today.

References

Adashi, E. Y., & Occhiogrosso Abelman, R. H. (2017). The Hyde Amendment at 40 years and reproductive rights in the United States: Perennial and panoptic. *JAMA: The Journal of the American Medical Association, 317*(15), 1523-1524. https://doi.org/10.1001/jama.2017.2742

Berry, D. R., & Gross, K. N. (2020). *A Black women's history of the United States: Revisioning American history.* Beacon Press.

Blackhawk, N. (2023). *The rediscovery of America: Native peoples and the unmaking of U.S. history.* Yale University Press.

Brodsky, A. (2021). *Sexual justice: Supporting victims, ensuring due process, and resisting the conservative backlash.* Metropolitan Books.

Byron, J. J., Avalos, M., Xiao, K., Klein, A. A., Leheste, J. R. (2022). Health equity in a post 'Roe versus Wade' America. *Cureus, 14*(12), 1-9. https://doi.org/10.7759/cureus.32100

Catt, C. C., & Shuler, N. R. (2020). *Woman suffrage and politics: The inner story of the suffrage movement.* Dover Publications.

Centers for Disease Control and Prevention. (2014). *Preventing sexual violence: An overview.* U.S. Department of Health and Human Services. https://www.cdc.gov/sexual-violence/prevention/

Cleghorn, E. (2021). *Unwell women: Misdiagnosis and myth in a man-made world.* Dutton.

Cobbs, E. (2023). *Fearless women: feminist patriots from Abigail Adams to Beyoncé.* Harvard University Press.

D'Emilio, J., & Freedman, E. B. (2012). *Intimate matters: A history of sexuality in America.* (3rd ed.). University of Chicago Press.

Driessen, M. C. (2020). Campus sexual assault and student activism, 1970-1990. *Qualitative Social Work, 19*(4), 564-579.

Dunbar-Ortiz, R. (2014). *An indigenous peoples' history of the United States.* Beacon Press.

Engstrom, A. (2016). The Hyde Amendment: Perpetuating injustice and discrimination after thirty-nine years. *S. Cal. Interdisc. LJ, 25,* 451.

Faderman, L. (2022). *Woman: The American history of an idea.* Yale University Press.

Friedan, B. (2001). *The feminine mystique.* Norton.

Gallagher, W. (2021). *New women in the old west: From settlers to suffragists, an untold American story.* Penguin.

Garrow, D. J. (1999). Abortion before and after Roe v. Wade: An historical perspective. *Albany Law Review, 62*(3), 883-852.

Ginsburg, R. B. (1985). Some thoughts on autonomy and equality in relation to Roe v. Wade. *North Carolina Law Review, 63*(2), 375-386.

Gold, R. B. (2003). Lessons from before Roe: Will past be prologue? *The Guttmacher Report on Public Policy.* https://www.guttmacher.org/sites/default/files/article_files/gr060108.pdf

Goodwin, M. (2020). *The racist history of abortion and midwifery bans.* ACLU. https://www.aclu.org/news/racial-justice/the-racist-history-of-abortion-and-midwifery-bans

Griffith, E. (2022). *Formidable: American women and the fight for equality: 1920-2020.* Pegasus.

Hämäläinen, P. (2022). *Indigenous continent: The epic contest for North America.* Liveright.

Jacquet, C. O. (2016). Fighting back, claiming power: Feminist rhetoric and resistance to rape in the 1970s. *Radical History Review, 126,* 71-83.

Knox, C. (2020). *Seduction: A history from the enlightenment to the present.* Pegasus.

Lepore, J. (2018). *These truths: A history of the United States.* Norton.

Manninen, B. A. (2023). A critical analysis of *Dobbs v. Jackson Women's Health Organization* and the consequences of fetal personhood. *Cambridge Quarterly of Healthcare Ethics, 32*(3), 357-367. https://doi.org/10.1017/S0963180122000809

McGuire, D. L. (2010). *At the dark end of the street: Black women, rape, and resistance—a new history of the civil rights movement from Rosa Parks to the rise of Black power.* Vintage.

Murphy, M. (2019). Introduction to "#MeToo movement". *Journal of Feminist Family Therapy, 31*(2-3), 63-65.

National Park Service. (n.d.). *The declaration of sentiments.* https://www.nps.gov/wori/learn/historyculture/declaration-of-sentiments.htm.

National Women's Law Center. (2022). *Forced sterilization of disabled people in the United States.* https://nwlc.org/resource/forced-sterilization-of-disabled-people-in-the-united-states/

Nobelprize.org. (n.d.). *Jane Addams: Facts.* https://www.nobelprize.org/prizes/peace/1931/addams/facts/

Planned Parenthood (n.d.). *Our history.* https://www.plannedparenthood.org/about-us/who-we-are/our-history

Ross, L. (2006). What is reproductive justice? *Reproductive justice briefing book: A primer on reproductive justice and social change.* SisterSong Women of Color Reproductive Health Collective.

Sacco, L.N., & Hanson, E.J. (2019). The Violence Against Women Act (VAWA): Historical overview, funding, and reauthorization (R45410). *Congressional Research Service.* https://crsreports.congress.gov/product/pdf/R/R45410

Sacco, L.N. (2023, May 23). The 2022 Violence Against Women Act (VAWA) reauthorization (R47570). *Congressional Research Service.* https://crsreports.congress.gov/product/pdf/R/R47570

Shelby, R. (2018). Whose rape kit? Stabilizing the Vitullo® Kit through positivist criminology and protocol feminism. *Theoretical Criminology, 24*(4), 669-688. https://doi.org/10.1177/1362480618819805

Suk, J. C. (2023). *After misogyny: How the law fails women and what to do about it.* University of California Press.

U.S. Const. amend. XIV

U.S. Const. amend. XV

The White House. (May, 2023). *U.S. national plan to end gender-based violence: Strategies for action.* https://www.whitehouse.gov/wp-content/uploads/2023/05/National-Plan-to-End-GBV.pdf

Wilson, D. (2021). Sexual exploitation of black women from the years 1619-2020. *Journal of Race, Gender, and Ethnicity, 10,* 122-129.

Yousef, O. (2024). *How 'fetal personhood' in Alabama's IVF ruling evolved from fringe to mainstream.* NPR. https://www.npr.org/2024/03/14/1238102768/fetal-personhood-alabama-ivf

Zinn, H. (2003). *A people's history of the United States.* Harper Collins.

Media Attributions

- Native American woman is licensed under a Public Domain license
- Elizabeth Cady Stanton is licensed under a Public Domain license
- World's Woman's Christian Temperance Union © WWCTU is licensed under a Public Domain license
- Sojourner Truth © National Portrait Gallery, Smithsonian Institution is licensed under a CC0 (Creative Commons Zero) license
- Julia Lathrop, Jane Addams and Mary McDowell is licensed under a Public Domain license
- Mary Church Terrell © Betsy Graves Reyneau is licensed under a Public Domain license
- Women of Indiana is licensed under a Public Domain license
- Ms. Magazine © Liberty Media for Women, LLC is licensed under a CC BY-SA (Attribution ShareAlike) license
- I Stand with Planned Parenthood © Charlotte Cooper is licensed under a CC BY (Attribution) license
- Keep Abortion Safe © Debra Sweet is licensed under a CC BY (Attribution) license

9.

Gender and Sexuality in the United States

Nikki Golden and Bernadet DeJonge

Learning Objectives

- The reader will gain an understanding of the influence of early Protestants on the sociocultural norms of gender and sexuality in the United States.
- The reader will gain knowledge of critical events in the history of the LGBTGEQIAP+ community in the United States.
- The reader will be introduced to state and federal discriminatory laws against the LGBTGEQIAP+ community in the United States.

Gender and sexual sociocultural norms in the United States have a multitude of influences. However, early English colonists and their Protestant religious beliefs remain the most decisive influence on gender and sexual norms in the United States. In this chapter, gender and sexuality in North American colonial and post-colonial periods are discussed. In addition, this chapter will address critical events in advancing social justice for the gay and transgender community, state and federal discriminatory laws against the gay and transgender community, and specific social justice movements in the gay and transgender community.

Activity 9.1 – Digging Deeper: What does LGBTGEQIAP+ mean?

- Lesbian
- Gay
- Bisexual
- Trans, Transgender, and Two-Spirit
- Gender-Expansive
- Queer and Questioning
- Intersex
- Agender, Asexual, & Aromantic

- Pansexual, Polygender, & Poly Relationships
- + Other related identities (SAIGE, n.d.)

Discussion Questions

- Did you know what all the letters in the LGBTGEQIAP+ acronym stood for?
- What might need to be added to the abbreviation?

Colonial Period

When English colonists arrived in North America, they brought strict religious and sociocultural beliefs. The Puritans, a sect of English Protestants, were some of the earliest colonists in North America. The Puritans rejected the Church of England and what they considered a decadent English society. In fact, they compared England to the biblical city of Sodom: traditionally recognized as a city destroyed by the sin of homosexuality. The Puritans believed that "England's corruption would be punished by God" (Cooke, 2014, p. 334). Faced with religious persecution, the Puritans fled England.

Since their introduction, Puritans' religious beliefs and system of law had, and continues to have, a tremendous influence on gender and sexual norms in the United States. The Puritans had a clear definition of what they considered appropriate gender expression and did not tolerate the blurring of gender roles (Smithers, 2022). Puritans idealized masculinity, and any man who engaged in behavior deemed as feminine, including having long hair, was judged as immoral. Similarly, Puritan women who stepped outside of their prescribed gender role were excommunicated or physically punished (Faderman, 2022).

Additionally, the Puritans had a rigid understanding of appropriate expressions of sexuality. For instance, sodomy was defined as any sexual acts deemed unnatural and included sexual acts between men, between men and women outside of marriage, and men with animals (D'Emilio & Freedman, 2012; Faderman, 2015). Puritans identified sodomy as a "sinne{sic} not once to be named" (Thompson, 1989, p. 31) and considered acts of sodomy to be worse than adultery. Not only were the acts of sodomy considered unnatural, but the Puritans believed that the people who engaged in sodomy were unnatural themselves (Bronski, 2011; D'Emilio & Freedman, 2012).

The Puritans utilized English laws, such as King Henry VIII's Buggery Act of 1533, as a template to create the first sodomy laws in North America (Bronski, 2011). However, the Puritans were not the only English colonists to enact sodomy laws. According to Bronski, all early English colonies had sodomy laws to regulate sexual behavior, though these laws varied due to differing religious beliefs and demographics. For instance, Chesapeake Bay colonists outlawed crimes of sin, which included adultery, rape, and sodomy, and equated such acts with offenses such as treason, murder, and witchcraft. Although sodomy laws technically concerned both men and women, the majority of those convicted and punished were men (D'Emilio & Freedman, 2012).

> **Activity 9.2 – Digging Deeper: English Buggery Laws**
>
> Oppression against gay male sex is documented throughout English history. For example, in 13th-century England, there was a legal document called the "Fleta," which punished sodomy by burying or burning men alive. In 1533, King Henry VIII criminalized gay male sex through the Buggery Act, which made sex between men punishable by death, typically by public hanging. This punishment was common across England for nearly 300 years of their history (Historic England, n.d.).
>
> **Discussion Questions**
>
> - How might these historic laws, which regulated sexual behavior, have influenced the Puritans who came to the colonies?
> - How might these historic laws, which regulated sexual behavior, influence the experience of LGBTGEQIAP+ individuals in the United States today?

As acts of sodomy challenged the paradigm of reproductive sexuality, colonial sodomy laws were strict, and punishments severe (D'Emilio & Freedman, 2012). According to D'Emilio and Freedman, it was not unusual for English colonies to prescribe "corporal or capital punishment, fines, and in some cases, banishment" (p. 18). However, as sexual mores had shifted by the late 1700s, Americans became less concerned about the sin of sodomy, instead worrying that sodomy "offended a natural order" (D'Emilio & Freedman, 2012, p. 122).

Sexual Identity Defined

Early English colonists did not recognize homosexuality as a personal identity. However, a new understanding of those who engaged in acts of sodomy had developed by the end of the American Revolutionary War (D'Emilio & Freedman, 2012). It was in the 1800s that the "binding of sexuality and identity" (Kunzel, 2018, p. 1563) occurred, and the concept of sexual identity emerged in the United States.

By the early 1800s, sexologists theorized that anyone who was sexually attracted to or engaged in sexual acts with someone of the same gender were "inverted" (Kunzel, 2018). Throughout the 1800s and the mid-1900s, medical professionals used the clinical term invert, but by the mid-1900s they began using the term homosexual to describe individuals who engaged in and preferred same-gender sexual behaviors.

Law enforcement used derogatory terms such as sexual psychopaths, before employing additional terms such as "degenerate or pervert" (Charles, 2015, p. 12) to describe homosexuality. Commonly used terms included pansy, fairy, and nancy boy for gay men and she-men or bulldagger for women. In the 1800s and early 1900s, gay men self-identified as fairies or as queer, though by the 1930s gay became the more acceptable term. However, women who identified as gay only used that term until the 1920s, when many began to self-identify as either bisexual or lesbian (Charles, 2015; Faderman, 2022).

By the mid-1900s, homosexuality was defined "less by a type of sexual relations than by a certain quality of sexual sensibility…the sodomite had been a temporary aberration; the homosexual was now a species" (Foucault, 1978, p. 43). Regardless of their gender, homosexuals were now considered a new category of humans.

Sexual Renaissance

During the 1920s, the United States "witnessed a permissiveness among the more sophisticated to experiment not only with heterosexuality but with bisexuality as well" (Faderman, 2022, p. 62) in certain parts of the country. Artists and bohemians were open to sexual experimentation, although "bisexuality was far more easily understood…particularly if it ended in heterosexuality" (Faderman, 2022, p. 85).

During this time, some women who identified as lesbians created their own subculture separate from gay men (Faderman, 2022). The Black lesbian subculture was established in Harlem, whereas the White lesbian subculture was established in Greenwich Village. Many believed that for women, bisexuality was a phase and that "it could be gotten out of a woman by a good psychoanalyst or a good man" (Faderman, 2022, p. 85).

Activity 9.3 – Digging Deeper: Harlem's Gay Renaissance

From 1918 to 1937, Harlem was considered a cultural mecca for not only Black Americans, but also for those in the larger gay community. At the same time, there was a cultural "renaissance in Harlem…there was also a burgeoning 'queer' renaissance, which was connected with the increased visibility of lesbian, gay, bisexual, and transgendered individuals" (Wilson, 2010, p. 28).

Black lesbian performers sang songs that "opened up a space for a variety of sexual identities to emerge" (Berry & Gross, 2020, p. 130). Nightclubs that catered explicitly to "the drag subculture, and acts featuring 'pansies' and 'bulldaggers' were not altogether uncommon" (Wilson, 2010, p. 39), and female impersonators were a consistent presence in the Harlem nightclub scene.

Video: The (Gay) Harlem Renaissance (https://www.youtube.com/watch?v=71fKS2SF-0U)

 One or more interactive elements has been excluded from this version of the text. You can view them online here: https://milnepublishing.geneseo.edu/social-justice-in-human-services/?p=167#oembed-1 (#oembed-1)

Video: The Queer History of the Harlem Renaissance (https://www.youtube.com/watch?v=DM7Qa_Xb8u0)

 One or more interactive elements has been excluded from this version of the text. You can view them online here: https://milnepublishing.geneseo.edu/social-justice-in-human-services/?p=167#oembed-2 (#oembed-2)

Discussion Questions

- What did you learn about the history of being gay from these videos?
- Why do you think you may not have been taught about the Harlem Renaissance in school?
- How do you think the gay renaissance of Harlem impacted what Harlem is today?

Activity 9.4 – Digging Deeper: The Hamilton Lodge Ball

Founded in 1869, The Hamilton Lodge Ball , was an annual masquerade and civil ball sponsored by a fraternity of Black men. Additionally, it served as a cross-dressing ball. By the 1920s, the Hamilton Lodge Ball recorded as many as 1,500 attendees. Due to its popularity, other drag balls were established; as many as 7,000 people attended them in Harlem. These balls included racially integrated audiences, contestants, and judges (Wilson, 2010).

Discussion Question

- Did you know about the drag balls in Harlem and beyond? Why do you think you may not have known about them?

Legislating Sexuality

Throughout the early 1900s, fear mongering about homosexuals—or, as they were often referred to in the media, sexual psychopaths—permeated American culture (Charles, 2015). As early as 1937, the United States Federal Bureau of Investigation (FBI) collected data on gay people under the guise that they were sex offenders. The director of the FBI, J. Edgar Hoover, justified this data collection as a means to keep the American public safe from sexual perverts.

Hoover and his contemporaries believed that gay people were a risk to national security. In fact, due to the state and federal laws that made homosexuality illegal in the United States, gay people or people who engaged in behavior deemed as homosexual were at risk of being blackmailed (Charles, 2015). As the United States entered World War II, paranoia about gay people increased.

Activity 9.5 – Digging Deeper: The Lavender Scare

Similar to McCarthy's hunt for communists during the Red Scare, the Lavender Scare was a hunt for gay people working in the United States government. However, unlike McCarthy's Red Scare, the Lavender Scare began in the late 1930s and lasted until the late 1970s. "Originating as a partisan political weapon in the halls of Congress, it sparked a moral panic within mainstream American culture and became the basis for a federal government policy that lasted nearly twenty-five years and affected innumerable people's lives" (Johnson, 2023, p. 9).

Video: The Lavender Scare (https://www.youtube.com/watch?v=2BXaXIAC_sI)

 One or more interactive elements has been excluded from this version of the text. You can view them online here: https://milnepublishing.geneseo.edu/social-justice-in-human-services/?p=167#oembed-3 (#oembed-3)

Discussion Questions

- Did you know about the Lavender Scare? Why do you think this might not have been taught as part of history like the Red Scare?
- Do these fears sound familiar? What kinds of issues are we facing today around gender identity and expression stemming from similar fears?
- What role does the media play in these fears? Compare how the media might have impacted the Lavender scare and how it represents LGBTGEQIAP+ people today.
- The FBI finally destroyed the files it had collected for Hoover's Sex Deviates program in 1978, five years after Hoover's death (Cervini, 2020). Why do you think it took so long for the FBI to destroy the files from the Sex Deviates program?

In spite of persecution, a gay subculture thrived in Washington, D.C. President Franklin D. Roosevelt's New Deal policies increased job opportunities and brought thousands of people to the United States capital to work in the federal government. The combination "of neutral civil service entrance examinations and a feminized work culture made government offices in Washington prior to the 1950s hospitable to gays and lesbians" (Johnson, 2023, p. 45).

As in the early years of industrialization within urban areas, the combination of employment and living in a new environment meant that gay people were able to be more open about their sexuality. In Lafayette Park—one block from the White House—gay men would meet, socialize, and occasionally engage in sexual activities. The neighborhoods surrounding Lafayette Park were the epicenter of gay social life. "Gay men and lesbians in the nation's capital in the 1930s and 1940s enjoyed a comfortable working environment in the federal government and a vibrant social life in a fast-growing city" (Johnson, 2023, p. 51).

After World War II, there was a backlash towards the gay community. The American public "had a growing sense that the country's moral codes were loosening and that homosexuality was becoming more prevalent or at least more visible" (Johnson, 2023, p. 53). The combination of the release of the Kinsey Report, increased publication of novels focused on gay desire, and sex crimes highlighted in the media all flamed the fears of gay people and homosexuality. Ultimately, the culmination of these concerns led to increased scrutiny on the gay subculture in Washington, D.C.

Activity 9.6 – Digging Deeper: The Kinsey Report

Read through a summary of **The Kinsey Report and related later surveys.** (https://kinseyinstitute.org/research/publications/historical-report-diversity-of-sexual-orientation.php#1948kinsey)

The Kinsey Report was a scientific publication that came out in 1948. It revealed research that stated that Americans were more sexually active than many expected in many ways. Additionally, it reported significant homosexual experiences. Scientists championed it as a much-needed educational and diagnostic tool, while others claimed it was an affront to American morality (PBS, n.d.).

Discussion Questions

- Discuss prevailing attitudes toward sex and gender when the Kinsey report was published. How did the prevailing attitudes towards sexuality influence the reception of the Kinsey Report?
- How did Kinsey's use of a scale (the Kinsey Scale) to measure sexual orientation challenge the binary view of sexuality prevalent at the time?
- How did the Kinsey Report affect the visibility and understanding of the gay community?
- How did Kinsey's findings challenge or reinforce existing stereotypes about homosexuality?

In 1948, the United States Congress held hearings on the need for a Sexual Psychopath Law in Washington, D.C. to control the gay community. "Beyond policing behavior...government officials wanted to contain what they saw as the increasing openness, even arrogance, of homosexuals" (Johnson, 2023, p. 58). The law was named after its sponsor, Congressmember Arthur Lewis Miller, who believed "the homosexual's instinct [for moral decency] breaks down, and he is driven into abnormal fields of sexual practice" (Faderman, 2015, p. 4).

Under the Miller Law, any individual charged with sodomy was required to be evaluated by a psychiatric team. If a psychiatric team deemed an individual as a sexual psychopath, they were committed to a psychiatric hospital until they recovered enough to stand criminal trial. If convicted in a court of law, individuals could face up to twenty years in prison (Faderman, 2015). In 1948, President Truman signed the Miller Sexual Psychopath Law in Washington, D.C.

The Miller Law gained support through inciting fears about the dangers of homosexuality to children. However, once it was passed, it was used to bolster the criminalization of gay sexuality (Johnson, 2023). The Miller Sexual Psychopath Law "prohibited taking 'into his or her mouth or anus the sexual organ of any other person or animal,' in addition to the reciprocal act" (Cervini, 2020, p. 38).

As the Miller Law was passed, the U.S. Park Police launched their "Pervert Elimination Campaign...that mandated the harassment and arrest of men in known gay cruising areas" (Johnson, 2023, p. 59). The campaign emboldened the U.S. Park Police to harass men, primarily gay men, without any restrictions. If a man was near a known gay cruising area, they could be stopped and interrogated by the U.S. Park Police. Hundreds of men were arrested, though most were not convicted due to a lack of evidence. However, their personal information—such as their names, occupations, and fingerprints—were collected.

As a consequence of the Red Scare and Lavender Scare, the media, and the collective fears of the American public, 29 states had sexual psychopathy laws by 1957. "In only a decade, homosexuals had graduated from criminals to merely incarcerated after homosexual activity to mentally ill criminals" (Cervini, 2020, p. 38). Individual states' sexual psychopathy laws, such as the Miller Act, outlawed anal and oral sex. Depending upon the state, punishment included "indefinite confinement" in a prison or mental institution (Duberman, 2019, p. xxiv). Gay people were sent to mental institutions and "treated" with shock therapy, lobotomies, and castration (Cervini, 2020). By the end of the 1960s, sodomy was illegal in all 50 states (Hagai & Crosby, 2016).

In the 1970s, some states repealed their sodomy laws. However, many of the old sodomy laws were replaced with more severe laws. For example, in 1971, Texas repealed its sodomy law, but by 1973 a new law was passed. Unlike Texas' old sodomy law, which concerned sodomy acts regardless of who engaged in them, the new law "targeted gays and lesbians only, whether they were caught having sex in public or in private, whether orally or anally, whether with mouth, penis, or dildo" (Faderman, 2015, p. 539). Gay activists attempted to challenge states' sodomy laws with little success.

A 1976 case, *Doe v. Commonwealth's Attorney,* challenged Virginia's sodomy law, arguing that it violated individuals' constitutional rights of privacy, freedom of speech, and due process, along with the prohibition against cruel and unusual punishment. Ultimately, this case failed, but it set a precedent for future legal challenges to similar laws and helped to raise awareness about the discrimination faced by gay individuals in the United States. "The ripple effects of the loss of *Doe v. Commonwealth's* Attorney were felt in Virginia for a long time" (Faderman, 2015, p. 540).

By 1979, 20 states had repealed their sodomy laws. Some states, such as Arkansas, reinstated their sodomy laws after the state's religious conservatives protested (Bronski, 2011). However, the remaining states' sodomy laws continued to be enforced. In 1986, 29-year-old Michael Hardwick was arrested under Georgia's sodomy laws for engaging in oral sex with another man; their legislation included a punishment of up to 20 years in prison. Though Hardwick was not prosecuted, he sued Georgia's Attorney General, claiming he could eventually be prosecuted for his consensual gay sex. In turn, his case went to the United States Supreme Court (Faderman, 2015). However, the United States Supreme Court ruled in *Bowers v. Hardwick* that Georgia's sodomy laws were constitutional (D'Emilio & Freedman, 2012). Chief Justice Burger wrote in his concurring opinion "To hold that the act of homosexual sodomy is somehow protected as a fundamental right would be to cast aside millennia of moral teaching" (Garretson, 2018, p. 88). Ultimately, in 1998—12 years after *Bowers v. Hardwick*—Georgia's Supreme Court repealed the 156-year-old sodomy law (Marcus, 2002).

In 2003, the United States Supreme Court ruled in *Lawrence v. Texas* that state sodomy laws violated an individual's right to privacy. Their ruling in *Lawrence v. Texas* represented the end of "an almost five-hundred-year tradition in Anglo-American law" (D'Emilio & Freedman, 2012, p. 374). Additionally, this ruling opened the door for other changes to law and legislation to protect the gay community's constitutional rights.

Activity 9.7 – Queer History

Video: Queer History is World History: Reframing Curriculum by Madeline English
(https://www.youtube.com/watch?v=oWTNBn1V8OI)

 One or more interactive elements has been excluded from this version of the text. You can view them online here: https://milnepublishing.geneseo.edu/social-justice-in-human-services/?p=167#oembed-4 (#oembed-4)

Discussion Questions

- How does the video define "queer history," and why is it essential to include it in the broader context of world history?
- How can educators effectively incorporate queer history into existing historical narratives? Why is this important?
- How has the exclusion of queer history affected the understanding of world history?
- How did the video challenge or change your perception of world history?
- What other resources or perspectives would you like to explore to deepen your under-

standing of queer history?

The plaque at the Stonewall Inn, New York City, NY

Stonewall Inn Riots

In the 1960s, the gay bar scene in New York City was controlled by the mafia and the police. As the only gay bars in New York City were owned and operated by the mafia, the proprietors had no incentive to cater to their customers. Instead, they spent as little money as possible and profited considerably; the greatest share was spent paying local police for protection (Duberman, 2019).

In 1966, the mafia opened the Stonewall Inn. The Stonewall Inn was, at best, a dive bar in Greenwich Village, New York. At the time, it had no running water and was semi-regularly raided by the police. Nevertheless, the Stonewall Inn had a diverse clientele and was a relatively safe place for the gay community. White gay men, gay people of color, and drag queens were regular patrons at the Stonewall Inn (Charles, 2015; Duberman, 2019). New York City's legal drinking age was 18 and customers' ages ranged from late teens to early thirties. Customers were primarily men, including White gay men, known as "the chino-penny loafer crowd" (Duberman, 2019, p. 234) as well as young drag queens, some of whom were homeless.

The Stonewall Inn was "a real dive, an awful, sleazy place" (Duberman, 2019, p. 224). Nevertheless it was the most popular gay bar in the area, primarily because it was the only gay bar in New York that allowed customers to dance. Although the mafia owners paid for protection at the Stonewall Inn, it was still regularly raided by police as all gay bars were. Police raids were tolerated by bar owners and customers alike because there was no other option. During a typical police raid, "the only people who would be arrested would be those without IDs, those dressed in the clothes of the opposite gender, and some or all of the employees" (Duberman, 2019, p. 237). As a courtesy, police usually notified owners when a raid was scheduled. However, on June 27, 1969, police conducted an unannounced raid at the Stonewall Inn.

The raid at the Stonewall Inn began as per usual; IDs were checked and some employees were arrested, as well as a few drag queens. However, eyewitness accounts contradict one another on the cause of the riots: some claimed it was because police were overly rough with a local drag queen, while others said it was because of the mood of the outside crowd (Duberman, 2019). "Several incidents were happening simultaneously. There was no one thing that happened or one person, there was just a a flash of group—of—anger" (Duberman, 2019, p. 243). Consequently, the crowd protested the treatment of the arrestees and the presence of the police—who were surprised by the ire of the crowd. "By now, the crowd had swelled to a mob, and people were picking up and throwing whatever loose objects came to hand—coins, bottles, cans, bricks " (Duberman, 2019, p. 244). Outnumbered, the police retreated into the Stonewall Inn and called for reinforcements. During the melee, a small fire started inside the Stonewall Inn while police were trapped inside.

The Tactical Patrol Force (TPF), "a highly trained, crack riot-control unit" (Duberman, 2019, p. 247) of the police, was summoned. Armed with billy clubs and tear gas, the TPF marched on the protestors. In turn, the protestors retreated, before doubling back on the TPF, and attacked them. This continued until the TPF responded with violence: "As they were badly beating up on one effeminate-looking boy, a portion of the angry crowd surged in, snatched the boy away, and prevented the cops from reclaiming him" (Duberman, 2019, p. 248).

Some protesting drag queens conducted a chorus line to taunt the TPF; "It was a deliciously witty, contemptuous counterpoint to the TPF's brute force that transformed an otherwise traditionally macho eye-for-eye combat and that provided at least the glimpse of a different and revelatory kind of consciousness" (Duberman, 2019, p. 248). Other protestors chased two police officers until they fled the scene. Police cars were damaged, and blood was spilled.

The TPF and fellow police had always used brute force and violence against the gay community. They expected the protestors to cower, but they did not. By the end of the first night,

13 protestors were arrested and many more were injured. "Four big cops beat up a young queen so badly—there is evidence that the cops singled out feminine boys—that she bled simultaneously from her mouth, nose, and ears" (Duberman, 2019, pp. 248-249). Four police officers sustained injuries. However, by 3:35 am, the area surrounding the Stonewall Inn was temporarily cleared.

The following day, the media began to cover the protests. Spurred by media reports, locals from the gay community gathered at the Stonewall Inn to witness the aftermath. An impromptu block party started; people shouted, "gay power," and drag queens resumed their chorus lines (Duberman, 2019). As more people gathered, the TPF returned to the Stonewall Inn and attempted to disperse the crowd. However, by the time the TPF arrived, thousands of people were celebrating gay power.

When the fearless chorus line of queens insisted on yet another refrain, kicking their heels high in the air, as if in direct defiance, the TPF moved forward, ferociously pushing their nightsticks into the ribs of anyone who didn't jump immediately out of their path (Duberman, 2019, p. 251).

The second night of the Stonewall Inn riots had begun. According to eyewitnesses, "all hell broke loose" (Duberman, 2019, p. 251). Protestors stopped cars and attacked police—throwing bottles, bricks, and concrete blocks at the police. "Twice the police broke ranks and charged into the crowd, flailing wildly with their nightsticks" (Duberman, 2019, p. 253) and clubbed protestors to the ground. The second night of the protests continued until 4 a.m. and only ended when the police withdrew their units from the area surrounding the Stonewall Inn. "After the second night of rioting, it had become clear to many that a major upheaval, a kind of seismic shift, was at hand..." (Duberman, 2019, p. 254). Gay activists called the media, created protest literature, handed out flyers, and called in reinforcements from gay organizations.

The following day—a Sunday—was mostly calm in the streets surrounding the Stonewall Inn. Police patrolled the area and "seemed spoiling for trouble" by yelling "faggots" out their car windows (Duberman, 2019, p. 256). The Stonewall Inn reopened for business and customers returned. Monday and Tuesday nights also remained quiet, but protestors returned to the streets surrounding the Stonewall Inn by Wednesday night.

Approximately 2,000 protestors gathered; they lit trash cans on fire, threw improvised projectiles, and shouted at the police. In response, the "TPF wielded their nightsticks indiscriminately, openly beating people up, left them bleeding on the street, and carted off four to jail on the usual charge of harassment" (Duberman, 2019, p. 257). Sunday night was the last night of the Stonewall Inn riots. By the end, it was estimated that approximately 400 police officers confronted approximately 2,000 protestors during the Stonewall Inn riots. "It was a full-fledged gay uprising" (Charles, 2015, p. 307).

Although the Stonewall Inn riots did not stop police harassment of the gay community, nor raids on gay bars, their demonstrations left a profound impact on the gay community. Media coverage of the riots exposed the public to gay people fighting for their rights as Americans.

Gay people across the United States felt empowered to resist police brutality and harassment (Duberman, 2019). Even the police recognized a power shift. Deputy Inspector Pine stated, "For those of us in public morals, things were completely changed...suddenly they were not submissive anymore" (Duberman, 2019, p. 257).

Activity 9.8 – Digging Deeper

Video: Stonewall at 50 from NYU (https://www.youtube.com/watch?v=31CX1Y0cen8&t=1s)

Discussion Questions

- What social, political, and legal conditions for LGBTGEQIAP+ individuals existed in the United States prior to the Stonewall Riots? How did these conditions contribute to the tensions leading up to the riots?
- How did the Stonewall Riots serve as a turning point for the LGBTGEQIAP+ rights movement?
- How did the Stonewall Riots highlight issues of intersectionality within the LGBTGEQIAP+ community, particularly regarding race, gender, and class?
- What is the significance of Pride Month, and how is it connected to the legacy of Stonewall?
- How does learning about the Stonewall Riots affect your understanding of LGBTGEQIAP+ history and the fight for civil rights?
- What actions can individuals and communities take today to honor the legacy of the Stonewall Riots and continue the fight for equality?

Organizing Gay Pride

After the Stonewall Inn riots, several new gay activist organizations were established. One group of young activists formed the Gay Liberation Front (GLF). According to Faderman (2015), the GLF "formed with the realization that sexual liberation for all people cannot come about unless existing social institutions are abolished" (p. 199). GFL's members wanted to create social change, not just a safe place for the gay community (Duberman, 2019).

Members of the GLF had been involved with other social justice movements, including the Civil Rights movement and the Women's Rights movement. They wanted to use more radical approaches to get the American public's attention (Duberman, 2019) and support other marginalized communities. Though many members appreciated the GLF's radical approach, they did not appreciate its diversified focus, such as supporting the Black Panther Party, which had often been overtly anti-gay (Faderman, 2015).

GENDER AND SEXUALITY IN THE UNITED STATES | 287

In December 1969, former members of the GLF established the Gay Activists Alliance (GAA; Bronski, 2011). The GAA was considered to be a bridge between the more conservative gay organizations and the radical GLF. GAA members "agreed that fighting for gay and lesbian rights didn't require tearing down the American system. They only wanted to open it up to gay people" (Federman, 2015, p. 214).

Logo of the Gay Liberation Front at Detroit, 1970

The AIDS Movement

The 1980s were a sociocultural backlash to the social justice-oriented 1960s and 1970s. Ronald Reagan was the President of the United States—conservatives were in power. During this time, the United States and the Soviet Union were engaged in the Cold War, and nuclear war was a tangible threat. However, another danger emerged during the 1980s: the AIDS epidemic.

AIDS Epidemic

On June 5, 1981, a Centers for Disease Control and Prevention (CDC) newsletter reported five cases of "unusual pneumonia" (Bronski, 2011, p. 224) in Los Angeles. A month later, the *New York Times* published an article about a rare cancer that was identified in 41 gay men. By the end of 1981, there had been at least 121 deaths attributed to a "gay-related immune deficiency" or the "gay plague" (Bronski, 2011, p. 224). The medical community was first baffled, then alarmed. It was not until 1983 that researchers were able to identify the virus ultimately known as the human immunodeficiency virus (HIV) as the cause of acquired immune deficiency syndrome (AIDS). By the end of 1982, 634 had been diagnosed—of those, 200 died. By 1990, over 31,000 people had died from AIDS-related illnesses.

Initially, AIDS was considered a gay disease because the first victims were gay men. Gay men, who already faced a great deal of discrimination, were now viewed as carriers of a deadly disease. The stigma of AIDS was intense, particularly before its transmission was understood. As a consequence, prejudiced views of the AIDS epidemic caused a great deal of harm to the gay community. In hospitals, medical professionals were afraid to touch AIDS patients, who were often left alone in their hospital beds unattended to. Even in death, the stigma of AIDS was devastating. After AIDS patients died, they were put into black trash bags; many funeral homes refused to care for their bodies (Faderman, 2015).

As the AIDS epidemic progressed, anyone who was found to be at high risk of contracting the disease was discriminated against, particularly those who used drugs intravenously. This individual discrimination led to discriminatory laws explicitly against people with HIV and/or AIDS. Furthermore the federal government, as well as individual state governments, did not apply additional resources to education or research to combat the disease. "The political and legal backlash engendered by the AIDS epidemic was tremendous" (Bronski, 2011, p. 230). By 1984, large cities closed the bathhouses and clubs that catered to gay men, as, according to officials, they were hazards to public health and safety. In a *New York Times* article, William F. Buckley Jr.—founder of the conservative journal *National Review*—suggested that "everyone detected with AIDS should be tattooed in the upper forearm, to protect common-needle users, and on the buttocks, to prevent the victimization of other homosexuals" (Bronski, 2011, p. 230).

By 1986, the AIDS epidemic continued to decimate the gay community. Although gay men were no longer the only known victims of AIDS, they remained the primary target of public fear, anger, and discrimination—"Brutal attacks on gay men were up everywhere" (Faderman, 2015, p. 424). Within the gay community's safe haven of San Francisco, there were 60 beatings of gay men reported to the police in one month; it is unknown how many occurred that were not reported. For gay activists, it felt as if all the progress that had been made toward acceptance by the American public was dying, as were many of their community members.

Activity 9.9 – The AIDS Crisis

Video: How The AIDS Crisis Changed The LGBT Movement (https://www.youtube.com/watch?v=zC1e9Zrb7cI)

 One or more interactive elements has been excluded from this version of the text. You can view them online here: https://milnepublishing.geneseo.edu/social-justice-in-human-services/?p=167#oembed-5 (#oembed-5)

Discussion Questions

- What were the immediate effects of the AIDS crisis on the LGBTGEQIAP+ community in terms of health, social stigma, and community cohesion?
- How did the government's initial response to the AIDS crisis affect the LGBTGEQIAP+ community?
- How did the AIDS crisis highlight issues of intersectionality within the LGBTGEQIAP+ community, particularly regarding race, gender, and socioeconomic status?
- In what ways did the AIDS crisis transform the goals and strategies of the LGBTGEQIAP+ rights movement?

AIDS Activism

By the early 1980s, the gay liberation movement had lost momentum and support (D'Emilio & Freedman, 2012). The emergence of the AIDS epidemic devastated the gay community as the disease killed many gay activists. Consequently gay activists who had not contracted AIDS shifted their focus from gay community rights to advocating for resources to combat the disease (Bronski, 2011; Marcus, 2002). The devastation of AIDS and the lack of federal funding and resources became the new driving force behind gay activists. Though the federal government and President Ronald Reagan ignored those suffering from the AIDS epidemic, others did not. Groups such as the Gay Men's Health Crisis (GMHC), AIDS Project LA (APLA), the Gay and Lesbian Alliance Against Defamation (GLAAD), and the Gay and Lesbian Latinos Unidos (GLLU) were formed (Bronski, 2011; Duberman, 2019).

Activity 9.10 – Digging Deeper: The Lavender Hill Mob

In 1986, Marty Robinson formed the Lavender Hill Mob. Known as the Mobsters, the group was active during the AIDS crisis. The Mobsters protested the Catholic Church and Senator Alfonse D'Amato of the State of New York. The Mobsters were the first gay group to reclaim the upside-down pink triangle that the Nazis used to label gay men in World War II, and they wore it when they went to protest the CDC (Faderman, 2015).

Discussion Questions

- The mobsters took on powerful opponents in their protests. What do you think led them to this?
- How did the social and political climate of the 1980s impact the formation of the Lavender Hill Mob?
- The mobsters reclaimed the upside-down pink triangle the Nazis used to label gay men. What does this mean? What other examples can you think of reclaiming something discriminatory?
- In what ways did the Lavender Hill Mob's protests contribute to the broader gay rights movement?

In 1982, Larry Kramer established the Gay Men's Health Crisis (GMHC). The GMHC was created to provide care for AIDS patients that the federal government, and sometimes even families, would not. GMHC gathered volunteers to visit AIDS patients, clean their apartments, take care of their pets, and help them navigate their medical needs (Faderman, 2015). GMHC created a 24-hour hotline, ran therapy groups, recruited lawyers, and raised money for the care of those with AIDS (Duberman, 2019; Faderman, 2015).

Activity 9.11 – Digging Deeper: ACT Up

Although Larry Kramer recognized that organizations like GMHC were doing good work, he knew it was not enough to stop the AIDS epidemic. In 1987, inspired by the Mobsters, Kramer established the AIDS Coalition to Unleash Power (ACT UP) group.

Video: How ACT UP Flipped the Script on AIDS and Gay Rights (https://www.youtube.com/watch?v=Y3rH8q9Q-mQ)

One or more interactive elements has been excluded from this version of the text. You can view them online here: https://milnepublishing.geneseo.edu/social-justice-in-human-services/?p=167#oembed-6 (#oembed-6)

Video: Larry Kramer 20th Anniversary ACT-UP AIDS Coalition Unleash Power (https://www.youtube.com/watch?v=S1hTZjObADg)

One or more interactive elements has been excluded from this version of the text. You can view them online here: https://milnepublishing.geneseo.edu/social-justice-in-human-services/?p=167#oembed-7 (#oembed-7)

> **Discussion Questions**
>
> - Discuss your thoughts on these videos. What impacted the organization? What were the impacts of these gay advocacy groups?
> - What might have happened to members of the gay community if these groups had not formed and advocated for them?

Chapters of ACT Up not only formed in major cities with large gay populations, such as Chicago, Los Angeles, New York City, and San Francisco, but also in cities that were not known as gay havens, including Oklahoma City, Orlando, and Shreveport (Faderman, 2015). ACT Up activists used the slogan *Silence = Death* and the upside-down pink triangle. Additionally, ACT Up also used picketing, protesting, and the tactic of Zaps: spontaneous public demonstrations designed to increase the visibility of their cause. ACT Up activists forced the office of the United States Food and Drug Administration to close, shackled themselves inside the headquarters of Burroughs Wellcome, a major pharmaceutical company, and caused commotion on the floor of the New York Stock Exchange (D'Emilio & Freedman, 2012).

Activity 9.12 – Digging Deeper: Zaps

Were you aware of the Zaps activist strategy? First used by gay activists in the early 1970s, Zaps combined protest with performance art. Gay activists used Zaps to disrupt and interrupt. Typically used to gain media coverage, Zaps were theatrical, active, and impossible to ignore. Often organized on short notice, Zaps were an effective way to confront discrimination directly and remind the American public of the existence of the gay community and, during the 1980s, the AIDS crisis (Bronski, 2011; Faderman, 2015).

Video: GAA Zaps (https://www.youtube.com/watch?v=16W20_QWjNM)

 One or more interactive elements has been excluded from this version of the text. You can view them online here: https://milnepublishing.geneseo.edu/social-justice-in-human-services/?p=167#oembed-8 (#oembed-8)

Reading: Out History Exhibit by Lindsay Branson (https://outhistory.org/exhibits/show/gay-liberation-in-new-york-cit/gaa/pg-2)

Discussion Questions

- How did the GAA ensure that Zaps were impactful and received widespread attention?
- How did the GAA use public demonstrations to put pressure on politicians and encourage other gays and lesbians to join their cause?

- What role did the media play in documenting and spreading the message of the GAA's Zaps?
- Why do you think Zaps are effective? What makes them different from other forms of protest?

In 1987, 600,000 gay activists held a weeklong conference in Washington, D.C. By this time, over 41,000 people had died of AIDS. Non-gay leaders, such as the Reverend Jesse Jackson and Cesar Chavez, spoke at the conference, demonstrating the universal concern of AIDS. According to D'Emilio & Freedman (2012):

> On Sunday, after an emotional unveiling of almost two thousand panels of the Names Project, a memorial quilt to those who died of AIDS, over half a million marched down Pennsylvania Avenue, past the White House, and toward the Capitol Building, in support of federal antidiscrimination legislation and a more concerted national response to AIDS. (p. 359)

Activity 9.13 – Digging Deeper: The AIDS Quilt

Video: First Unveiling AIDS Quilt 1987 (https://www.youtube.com/watch?v=lrVzjJ2e4hU)

 One or more interactive elements has been excluded from this version of the text. You can view them online here: https://milnepublishing.geneseo.edu/social-justice-in-human-services/?p=167#oembed-9 (#oembed-9)

Video: AIDS Memorial Quilt x Gilead: Honoring the Largest Living Memorial Project in the World (https://www.youtube.com/watch?v=QCOR6c2GaTI)

 One or more interactive elements has been excluded from this version of the text. You can view them online here: https://milnepublishing.geneseo.edu/social-justice-in-human-services/?p=167#oembed-10 (#oembed-10)

Website: The AIDS Memorial Quilt- Interactive (https://www.aidsmemorial.org/interactive-aids-quilt)

Discussion Questions

- What is the historical significance of the AIDS quilt, and how did it originate?
- How has the AIDS quilt evolved since its inception in 1987, and what does it represent today?
- What are the processes and criteria for adding a panel to the AIDS quilt?
- In what ways has the AIDS quilt served as a form of activism and awareness for the

> AIDS epidemic?

The United States government, led by the Reagan administration, was almost absent during the early years of the AIDS epidemic (Bronski, 2011). According to Faderman (2015):

> Reagan himself would not even utter the word AIDS until his good friend from Hollywood days, Rock Hudson, died of it in 1985. The year before, however, when three hundred thousand Americans had already been diagnosed with the disease, and Ronald Reagan was running for reelection, he told a group that kept tally of a presidential biblical scorecard that his administration would continue to resist all attempts to obtain any government endorsement of homosexuality. That seemed to include any effort to help save homosexual lives. (p. 418)

In a speech at the Third International Conference on AIDS on May 31st, 1987, President Reagan finally acknowledged the AIDS epidemic that had decimated the gay community. By that point, over 40,849 American deaths had been attributed to AIDS (Bronski, 2011; Faderman, 2015).

Activity 9.14 – Digging Deeper: Reagan's Response to the AIDS Crisis

Video: Reagan Administration's Chilling Response to the AIDS Crisis (https://www.youtube.com/watch?v=yAzDn7tE1IU)

 One or more interactive elements has been excluded from this version of the text. You can view them online here: https://milnepublishing.geneseo.edu/social-justice-in-human-services/?p=167#oembed-11 (#oembed-11)

Discussion Questions

- How did the silence and inaction of the Reagan administration in the early years of the AIDS epidemic affect the outcome of the crisis? How did it impact the spread and severity of the disease?
- How did funding decisions during the Reagan administration impact research, prevention, and treatment efforts for AIDS?
- How did political and social attitudes of the 1980s influence the Reagan administration's handling of the AIDS epidemic?
- How has Reagan's handling of the AIDS crisis been viewed in historical hindsight, and what lessons have been learned for public health policy?

- Compare and contrast the AIDS crisis to the COVID-19 pandemic.

ACT Up activists, alongside members of the National Gay Rights Advocates, declared October 11, 1988 to be the first National Coming Out Day in the United States. On the National First Coming Out Day, ACT UP activists, in front of the FDA headquarters, laid down on the lawns with cardboard tombstones with statements such as "Killed by the FDA" and wearing shirts that read "We Die and They Do Nothing" (Faderman, 2015, p. 431). ACT Up activists alerted every major media outlet about their upcoming National Coming Out Day celebration; their protest received international media coverage.

ACT UP activists held their National Coming Out Day celebration in front of the FDA offices in Maryland. The organization had a long-standing issue with the way the FDA was conducting AIDS medication trials. At the time, the FDA was using the same standard protocols for AIDS medications as it used for nasal sprays. The FDA's use of their standard protocols meant clinical trials would take 5 to 10 years, and 50 percent of trial participants would receive a placebo. ACT UP believed that the FDA, by using their standard protocols on potentially lifesaving AIDS medications, was allowing gay people to die (Faderman, 2015).

A small group of ACT UP activists, including Peter Staley and Mark Harrington, were frustrated by the handling of the AIDS crisis and did not trust the United States government, the FDA, or the medical community to learn about AIDS. Thus, they formed the Treatment and Data Committee of ACT UP (Faderman, 2015). The members of the Committee were:

> much more knowledgeable about AIDS than most doctors, who'd had neither the time nor the inclination to study the disease. To share what they'd learned, they published a comprehensive *Glossary of AIDS, Drug Trials, Testing, and Treatment*. They also put together a National AIDS Treatment Research Agenda that discussed, clearly and knowledgeably, past problems with AIDS drugs and treatments. (Faderman, 2015, pp. 436-437)

The Committee's Research Agenda featured a list of 30 promising medications that needed to be expedited through clinical trials. The Committee provided copies of its Research Agenda to the FDA and the National Institutes of Health (NIH) but received no response.

Activity 9.15 – Digging Deeper: Peter Staley

Video: The Life-Saving Legacy of HIV/AIDS Activist Peter Staley (https://www.youtube.com/watch?v=Eow4hcwoEjg)

One or more interactive elements has been excluded from this version of the text. You can view them online here: https://milnepublishing.geneseo.edu/social-justice-in-human-services/?p=167#oembed-12 (#oembed-12)

Discussion Questions

- In what ways did Peter Staley's work with ACT UP change public perception and policy around AIDS in the United States?
- In what ways did Peter Staley's activism intersect with other social and political movements of the 1980s and 1990s?
- Discuss how Peter Staley advocated for and impacted the HIV/AIDS epidemic.
- What are some of the critical lessons from Peter Staley's activism that can be applied to current public health crises or social justice movements?

In 1990, ACT Up activists tired of the plateaued progress of medications and the absence of a committed response from the FDA. They began to target the NIH and Dr. Anthony Fauci, the chief officer of the NIH's Institute of Allergy and Infectious Diseases. ACT Up targeted Fauci because of his influence over what medications were tested and what protocols were used. Additionally, his name was well known to the Committee members as Fauci had been actively publishing on AIDS (Faderman, 2015).

On May 21, 1990, ACT Up activists from across the United States gathered at the NIH campus and set off smoke bombs while yelling, "Fauci, you're killing us" and "the whole world is watching, Fauci" (Faderman, 2015, p. 438). The NIH's campus police arrived on the scene intending to remove the ACT UP activists from the NIH campus. However, Fauci intervened and asked the NIH campus police to escort the ACT UP leaders to a conference room to meet.

Members of the Committee, including Staley and Harrington, lectured Fauci on the FDA's inappropriate testing protocols "in the midst of a plague" (Faderman, 2015, p. 438). Staley—who was HIV positive—told Fauci that those who were positive did not have time to wait for the FDA's clinical trials, and that the practice of using placebos in those trials was unethical. Fauci was impressed by the Committee members' knowledge and the data they had gathered. Following their meeting, Fauci reported back to his NIH colleagues:

> These guys are extremely valuable. They can give us input into how to design the trials and the kinds of needs they see in their community. We have to listen to them. How can we work in partnership with them? (Faderman, 2015, p. 439)

The ACT UP Committee members meeting with Fauci changed the culture at the NIH. Their partnership:

brought about major changes in how the federal government tests and distributes experimental drugs, beginning with the Accelerated Approval process that the Treatment and Data Committee demanded. As a result of that partnership NIH advisory committees and counsels always include activists from communities that are directly affected by NIH's policy decisions. ACT Up changed America's scientific culture to profit everyone. (Faderman, 2015, p. 439)

Activity 9.16 – Digging Deeper: Dr. Fauci and the AIDS crisis

Video: How Dr. Fauci handled the AIDS crisis (https://www.youtube.com/watch?v=IDDhRpMA64I)

 One or more interactive elements has been excluded from this version of the text. You can view them online here: https://milnepublishing.geneseo.edu/social-justice-in-human-services/?p=167#oembed-13 (#oembed-13)

Discussion Questions

- Discuss the relationship between Dr. Fauci and AIDS activists, including moments of both conflict and collaboration. How did these interactions shape AIDS research and policy?
- How did Dr. Fauci balance his roles as a researcher, public health official, and policy advisor during the AIDS crisis?
- What criticisms did Dr. Fauci face from the scientific community and AIDS activists, and how did he respond to these critiques? Do you think Dr. Fauci handled the AIDS crisis well? Why or why not?
- Compare and contrast the public health responses to the AIDS crisis and the COVID-19 pandemic under Dr. Fauci's leadership. What lessons from the AIDS crisis were applied to the handling of COVID-19?

By 1986, "the emotions felt by many in the LGBT community shifted from despair to rage" (Garrettson, 2018, p. 88). Gay activist organizations such as ACT UP channeled the community's anger toward constructive action, focusing it on media figures and government authorities who downplayed or dismissed the AIDS crisis. (Garretson, 2018). During the AIDS movement, gay activists forever changed their community's perception of the government, the media, and—most importantly—themselves (Bronski, 2011; Garretson, 2018). One of those changes was the "development of a gay and lesbian community that took considerable pride in its identity" (Garretson, 2018, p. 96), which would consequently change how the gay community would advocate for their rights in the years to come.

In 2013, Peter Staley, a central figure in the AIDS movement, stated, "We're so caught up in the giddiness of the marriage-equality movement that we've abandoned the collective fight against HIV and AIDS" (Signorile, 2015, p. 41). Even as this text is written, HIV and AIDS are not controlled or eradicated. According to the World Health Organization (2023), HIV and AIDS continue to be global healthcare concerns. According to the World Health Organization, 40.4 million people globally have died from HIV/AIDS as of 2023—in 2022 alone, 630,000 people globally died from HIV-related causes. In 2021, 36,136 Americans received a new diagnosis of HIV, with a total of 1.2 million living with HIV in the United States (AIDS Foundation of Chicago, n.d.).

AIDS activist Peter Staley

Activity 9.17 – Digging Deeper: Gay Rights and the AIDS Epidemic

Video: LGBTQ+ Rights Movement and the AIDS Epidemic (https://www.youtube.com/watch?v=kWPQ_ArREKo)

 One or more interactive elements has been excluded from this version of the text. You can view them online here: https://milnepublishing.geneseo.edu/social-justice-in-human-services/?p=167#oembed-14 (#oembed-14)

Discussion Questions

- How do the LGBTGEQIAP+ rights movement and the AIDS epidemic impact and inform each other?

- Compare and contrast the LGBTGEQIAP+ rights movement with the civil rights movement of Black Americans. What social justice issues were/are present in both movements?

Conservative Backlash

AIDS was an ideal excuse for some conservatives to increase their level of hate speech towards the gay community. In 1990, conservative Republican Pat Buchanan wrote, "AIDS is nature's retribution for violating the laws of nature" (Bronski, 2011, p. 226). That same year, Jerry Falwell, a conservative Christian televangelist, stated, "AIDS is not just God's punishment for homosexuals. It is God's punishment for the society that tolerates homosexuals" (Bronski, 2011, p. 226). The American Family Association, a conservative organization, sent letters to fund their campaign to quarantine gay people with the following message:

> Since AIDS is transmitted primarily by perverse homosexuals, your name on my national petition to quarantine all homosexual establishments is crucial to your family's health and security...These disease carrying deviants wander the street unconcerned, possibly making you their next victim. What else can you expect from sex-crazed degenerates but selfishness? (Bronski, 2011, pp. 226-227)

Until 2015, the FDA banned gay and bisexual men, along with transgender women who have sex with men, from donating blood. In December 2015, the FDA removed the lifetime ban and changed their restrictions to allow gay and bisexual men to provide blood donations one year post sexual activity. Nevertheless, it was not until May 11, 2023 that the FDA finally removed their discriminatory restrictions for blood donations that specifically targeted gay and bisexual men (Human Rights Campaign, n.d.). However, according to the U.S. Food & Drug Administration (2023),

> All prospective donors who report having a new sexual partner, or more than one sexual partner in the past three months, and anal sex in the past three months, would be deferred to reduce the likelihood of donations by individuals with new or recent HIV infection who may be in the window period for detection of HIV by nucleic acid testing. (para. 5)

Legal and Political Social Justice Movements

By the 1990s, many gay rights activists had changed strategies: their focus was on changing specific anti-gay laws and expanding gay rights through legal and political means (Issenberg,

2021). Two primary issues, marriage equality and gay people's right to serve in the United States military dominated mainstream gay activism in the 1990s and 2000s. Both issues were fodder for politics, and both required change on a national level. Large-scale gay rights organizations, such as the Human Rights Campaign (HRC) and the Lambda Legal Defense and Education Fund (Lambda Legal), lobbied politicians—whereas private organizations, such as the Gill Foundation, funded campaigns (Issenberg, 2021). This next section details the fight for gay people's right to marry and to serve in the United States military.

Marriage-Equality Movement

Historically, in the United States, marriage was assumed to be a heterosexual union. In fact, it was not only assumed to be a heterosexual union; there was precedent in court cases that defined it as such. The heterosexual norm of marriage was so strong that before A, the notion of a same-sex couple entering into state-sanctioned marriage seemed culturally and legally implausible" (Eskridge, 1993, p. 1423).

Marriage has historically included specific financial, legal, and medical benefits and protections in the United States. Tax laws regarding inheritance, beneficiary rights of medical insurance and pensions, the ability to adopt a child, parental rights, and next of kin rights were limited to heterosexual marriage (Deitrich, 1994). Limiting those benefits and protections to only heterosexual marriage discriminated against anyone who was not heterosexual.

Although not all gay individuals sought marriage equality in the 1980s, many gay activists discovered that marriage inequality had widespread detrimental effects on the gay community during the AIDS crisis. During the AIDS crisis, gay people were denied marriage benefits and protections, such as the ability to make medical decisions for their partners, inherit shared property, and retain custody of their children (Hagai & Crosby, 2016). Post-AIDS crisis, marriage equality was an important cause for many in the gay community. Not only did the financial, legal, and medical benefits make marriage appealing, but marriage equality signified acceptance, which was critical for many in the gay community. According to Duberman (2018),

> Gays wanted in-wanted to hear, after all the suffering they'd been through that they were 'OK', wanted their unions officially sanctified, wanted public announcements posted on church doors declaring them decent human beings-not obscene sex maniacs-worthy of membership in the great American mainstream. (pp. 65-66)

Acknowledgment and validation of same-gender marriages would shift gay people's status from perpetual outsiders to insiders (Eskridge, 1993). Ultimately, "by denying gay and lesbian couples access to the sacred union, society proclaims them less worthy, less committed, insignificant" (Dietrich, 1994, p. 122).

Marriage Equality in Court

In the United States, the legal institution of marriage was left to individual states to decide. State laws, including those regarding marriage, must "pass constitutional muster" (Dietrich, 1994, p. 125). This means that any state law must meet the criteria set by the United States Constitution (Dietrich, 1994; Eskridge, 1993). Historically, the United States Supreme Court has used two clauses of the 14th Amendment, the Due Process Clause and the Equal Protection Clause, to uphold and overturn marriage laws in individual states. For example, in the 1967 case of *Loving v. Virginia*, the United States Supreme Court ruled that the Virginia law that prohibited marriage between "a white person and a colored person" was unconstitutional, because it violated both the Due Process Clause and the Equal Protection Clause of the 14th Amendment (Dietrich, 1994, p. 127).

Activity 9.18 – Digging Deeper: The 14th Amendment

Video: The 14 (https://www.youtube.com/watch?v=KWG8AcCty_I)th (https://www.youtube.com/watch?v=KWG8AcCty_I) Amendment of the U.S. Constitution: A History (https://www.youtube.com/watch?v=KWG8AcCty_I)

 One or more interactive elements has been excluded from this version of the text. You can view them online here: https://milnepublishing.geneseo.edu/social-justice-in-human-services/?p=167#oembed-15 (#oembed-15)

Discussion Questions

- Before watching this video, what was your understanding of the historical context in which the 14th Amendment was ratified? How did the social and political climate of the Reconstruction era influence its creation?
- What role does the 14th Amendment play in contemporary civil rights issues, such as voting rights, police reform, and anti-discrimination laws?
- How does the public understand the 14th Amendment compared to its actual legal and historical significance? What factors contribute to any gaps in understanding? How might these gaps impact the LGBTGEQIAP community?

By the 1990s, cases on gay equality had been both won and lost in the United States. However, legal cases regarding marriage equality, except for issues of race, had been lost. For example, in 1973, two women sued the state of Kentucky because their application for a marriage license was denied. The women lost their case, *Jones v. Hallahan*, because a Kentucky court used three dictionaries to conclude that marriage had "traditionally been defined as a union of a man and a woman" (Dietrich, 1994, p. 134).

On December 17, 1990, six same-gender couples went to Honolulu's Department of Health office and applied for marriage licenses; their applications were denied. The six couples sued the State of Hawaii arguing that because Hawaii's state constitution guaranteed all couples the right to marry: thus, it was unconstitutional to deny same-gender couples the right to marry. The case *Baehr v. Lewin* further intensified the fight for marriage equality in the United States (Issenberg, 2021). On May 7, 1993, the Supreme Court of Hawaii ruled in favor of *Baehr* (Faderman, 2015). The ruling was "the first time that any court on earth had acknowledged that a fundamental right to marriage could extend to gay couples" (Issenberg, 2021, p. 89). Although *Baehr v. Lewin* was a landmark win, it did not guarantee marriage equality in Hawaii or elsewhere in the United States.

Defense of Marriage Act

Conservatives across the United States feared that "if gay and lesbian marriage is legitimized in any state, other states would be forced to recognize gay marriages conducted in that state through the full faith and credit clause of the Constitution" (Dietrich, 1994, p. 146). After the *Baehr v. Lewin* ruling, other states enacted laws to prevent potential marriage equality cases (Issenberg, 2021). On February 2, 1995, South Dakota passed Bill 1184, which stated "that any marriage between persons of the same gender is null and void" (Faderman, 2015, p. 587). In March of 1995, both Alaska and Utah passed similar bills, and by 1996, 37 states had either passed bills denying marriage equality to same-sex couples or were in the process of doing so.

In 1996, conservative Congress members introduced the Defense of Marriage Act (DOMA) to bolster states' rights further. "DOMA was Congress' way of anticipatorily retrofitting the U.S. Code to withstand an orchestrated legal assault by homosexuals seeking access to the array of benefits, rights, and privileges its provisions make available to heterosexuals" (Koppelman, 2004, p. 2684). DOMA granted individual states the right "to ignore same-sex marriages contracted in other states" (Ruskay-Kidd, 1997, p. 1435) and created a federal definition of marriage that excluded same-gender couples—later applied to all federal programs and statutes. On September 21, 1996, President Clinton signed DOMA into law (Issenberg, 2021; Ruskay-Kidd, 1997).

Civil Unions

On April 26, 2000, Vermont enacted H.847, designed as a bill for civil unions (Issenberg, 2021). H.847 recognized domestic partnership as an equivalent structure to marriage. For Vermont politicians, H.847 was a compromise to appease the gay community and conservatives, providing many of the same benefits and protections of marriage without impeding on the sacred institution of marriage. "Vermont's legislature had created a legal classification that existed in no other jurisdiction in the world" (Issenberg, 2021, p. 298), though for many gay activists, H.847 was a loss. Domestic partnerships, although similar, were not tantamount to marriage.

The passing of Vermont's H.847 drew scrutiny from conservatives across the United States. "In various corners of the American right, political and legal strategists were already plotting whether to amend the U.S. Constitution—for the first time in a generation—to preempt...states from deviating from the historical definition of marriage" (Issenberg, 2021, p. 319). Conservatives no longer felt that a federal law such as DOMA was enough to protect heterosexual marriage. Groups such as the Institute for Family Values, the Alliance Defense Fund, and the Marriage Law Project actively worked to prohibit marriage equality efforts.

The late 1990s and early 2000s brought change to the American public's exposure to the gay community in popular culture. *Brides* magazine published an article on same-gender unions, and shows such as *Will & Grace* and *Queer Eye for the Straight Guy* were prominent television series (Issenberg, 2021). Nevertheless, opposition to same-gender marriage was still high. According to Issenberg,

> To the nongay world, and even within the less politically conscious corners of the gay and lesbian community, reaching for...the gold ring of marriage—especially as states remained within their power to outlaw gay sex between consenting adults—seemed so audacious as to mark any proponent as radical. (p. 392)

Activity 9.19 – Digging Deeper: Let California Ring

Marriage equality activists identified specific states with gay rights issues on their legislative agenda that a targeted campaign could impact. California was one of those states. In 2005, the Let California Ring project (the Project), supported by the HRC and the National Gay and Lesbian Task Force, was launched. The Project was a strategy for gay rights activists. "Never before had a gay-rights organization attempted to shift public opinion around same-sex unions in the absence of immediate political or legal action" (Issenberg, 2021, p. 465). The Project's public goal was to spark millions of conversations, while the practical goals were to increase public support for same-gender marriage by a minimum of two percentage points and to increase the number of supporters by 400,000.

Video: Let California Ring Campaign – Change Hearts and Minds (https://www.youtube.com/watch?v=YGXfj4DJ-Hw)

 One or more interactive elements has been excluded from this version of the text. You can view them online here: https://milnepublishing.geneseo.edu/social-justice-in-human-services/?p=167#oembed-16 (#oembed-16)

Discussion Questions

- Do you think Let California Ring was successful? Why or why not?
- Is this kind of advocacy manipulative or strategic? Discuss.

Civil rights equality celebration at the California State Capital after the U.S. Supreme Court ruled DOMA, the Defense of Marriage Act, to be unconstitutional.

Freedom to Marry

During the first decade of the 2000s, gay rights activists were losing the fight for marriage equality, both in court and with voters. By 2009, "thirty states had imposed constitutional amendments restricting marriage to heterosexual couples, and the majority of those amendments also blocked civil unions, domestic partnerships, or other recognition of same-sex relationships" (Issenberg, 2021, p. 533). Many opponents of marriage equality were in particular religious communities. The Church of Jesus Christ of Latter-Day Saints, evangelical Christians, and the Roman Catholic Church had immense power and resources to fight against marriage equality.

However, support for marriage equality shifted by 2012. Private donations from people as varied as Bill Gates, Jeff Bezos, and Brad Pitt contributed to marriage equality. Additionally, for the first time since President Clinton, the United States had a gay-friendly president, Barack Obama (Issenberg, 2021). During Obama's campaign, "Don't Ask, Don't Tell" (DADT) had been a straightforward issue—marriage equality was not. "As a candidate, Obama received few signals that marriage rights were a policy priority within the gay community, or liberal activists more broadly" (Issenberg, 2021, p. 636). From the beginning of his presidency, Obama made it clear he did not support DOMA, as he believed it to be a discriminatory policy and that it interfered with states' rights. Obama was not alone—by 2012, 120 Democrats in Congress co-sponsored the repeal of DOMA.

That said, Obama did not express explicit support for marriage equality. "For a decade he had been a gradualist on marriage, as a matter of principle and political contrivance" (Issenberg, 2021, p. 686). However, others surrounding Obama were ready to support marriage equality. In March 2012, Vice President Joe Biden supported marriage equality. During an interview for *Meet the Press*, Biden stated,

> The good news is that, as more and more Americans come to understand, what this is all about is a simple proposition: Who do you love and will you be loyal to the person you love? ...And that's what people are finding out is what all marriages at their root are about, whether their marriage is of lesbians or gay men or heterosexuals. (Issenberg, 2021, p. 693)

Obama stated many times that his view on same-gender marriage was evolving—by 2012, it had become one of support. On May 9, 2012, during an interview with Robin Roberts, President Obama became the first sitting president to state that he believed same-sex couples should be able to get married. This was an incredible risk for a president who was considered an underdog during his reelection campaign (Issenberg, 2021).

Activity 9.20 – Digging Deeper: President Obama and Gay Marriage

Video: President Obama – Gay Marriage: Gay Couples 'Should Be Able to Get Married' (https://www.youtube.com/watch?v=kQGMTPab9GQ)

Discussion Questions

- Why do you think it took so long for Obama to speak out for gay marriage?
- What were the political and social ramifications of Obama speaking out in support of gay marriage?

The Supreme Court

The fight for marriage equality in the United States has been punctuated by several landmark cases that have significantly impacted the rights of same-sex couples. Most cases were fought in individual states, as the United States Supreme Court chose not to hear arguments on same-sex marriage; in the early 2000s, that changed. The United States Supreme Court decided to engage in two cases, *Windsor v. The United States* and *Obergefell v. Hodges*. Ultimately, both changed the definition of marriage in the United States (Issenberg, 2021).

In 2007, Thea Spyer–who was diagnosed with multiple sclerosis in 1977–was told that she had less than a year to live. Thea Spyer and Edith Windsor had loved each other and lived together since 1965; they wanted to marry before Thea died. On May 22, 2007, Thea and Edith flew to Ontario, Canada to marry because they could not legally do so in New York. Thea died on February 5, 2009 (Faderman, 2015).

Although New York did not grant same-gender marriages, the state did recognize same-gender marriages performed elsewhere. However, due to DOMA, the federal government did not. Federal law deemed that Edith:

> inherited from Spyer half the value of the apartment and little cottage that the two women had shared in the Hamptons. To the federal government, she and Thea Spyer, despite their forty-plus-year history, despite their legal marriage, were no more than strangers to each other. (Faderman, 2015, p. 624)

The United States Internal Revenue Service (IRS) levied $363,000 in estate taxes against Edith. Edith, who was 81 years old, had no choice but to pay, which decimated her savings. Edith sued the United States government and won on June 6, 2012. The judge ruled that "section 3 of DOMA violated the plaintiff's rights of equal protection under the 5th Amendment" (Faderman, 2015, p. 626) and ordered the IRS to refund Edith her money plus interest. The United States government appealed the decision.

In 2012, the United States Supreme Court agreed to hear arguments in *Windsor v. United States*, and on June 26, 2013, the United States Supreme Court ruled that Section 3 of DOMA was unconstitutional. Justice Anthony Kennedy wrote:

> DOMA instructs all federal officials, and indeed all persons with whom same-sex couples interact, including their own children, that their marriage is less worthy than the marriages of others. The differentiation demeans the couple, whose moral and sexual choices the Constitution protects, and whose relationship the State has sought to dignify. And it humiliates tens of thousands of children now being raised by same-sex couples. (Issenberg, 2021, pp. 719-720)

The United States Supreme Court, with its ruling in *Windsor v. United States*, declared that same-gender couples had the rights to be treated by the IRS as their heterosexual counterparts were treated, but also that they could get social security and veteran's survivor benefits, they could hold on to their homes when widowed, they could get green cards for an alien spouse, they were eligible for over a thousand other benefits that only straight couples had enjoyed before. (Faderman, 2015, p. 628)

The *Windsor v. United States* ruling was a considerable victory for marriage equality. Although the ruling did not change states' rights to decide on other issues regarding same-gender marriages, states' courts did use the ruling for individual cases. Within 15 months, "an accelerated sequence of federal and state decisions had made same-sex marriage legal in thirty states" (Issenberg, 2021, p. 727).

In 2013, James Obergefell and John Arthur married in Maryland because it was not legal for them to do so in Ohio. John was dying, and he wanted James listed as his surviving spouse on his death certificate. As Ohio did not recognize John and James as legally married, James would not be listed on John's death certificate. Consequently, James filed a lawsuit, *Obergefell v. Hodges*, against the state of Ohio.

On December 23, 2013, an Ohio judge ruled in favor of *Obergefell*. In response, the state of Ohio appealed, and the United States Court of Appeals ruled against *Obergefell*. James then decided to take his case to the United States Supreme Court. On January 16, 2015, the Court announced that they would hear arguments in the case of *Obergefell v. Hodges*. On June 26, 2015, the United States Supreme Court ruled in favor of *Obergefell*; their ruling in *Obergefell v. Hodges* invalidated state laws that banned same-gender marriage (Issenberg, 2021). Justice Kennedy concluded:

> No union is more profound than marriage, for it embodies the highest ideal of love, fidelity, devotion, sacrifice, and family. In forming a marital union, two people become something greater than once they were. As some of the petitioners in these cases demonstrate, marriage embodies a love that may endure even past death. It would misunderstand these men and women to say they disrespect the idea of marriage. Their plea is that they do respect it, respect it so deeply that they seek to find its fulfillment for themselves. Their hope is not to be condemned to live in loneliness, excluded from one of civilization's oldest institutions. They ask for equal dignity in the eyes of the law. The Constitution grants them that right. (Murray, p. 1213)

Obergefell v. Hodges was the final case in the fight for marriage equality, but certainly not the only one. In many ways, the fight for marriage equality was hundreds of individual battles across the United States. Large-scale organizations, such as HRC, championed marriage equality, as did individual Americans, lawyers, judges, and politicians.

Activity 9.21 – Digging Deeper: Same Sex Marriage

Video: June 26, 2015: SCOTUS Same Sex Marriage Victory (https://www.youtube.com/watch?v=IQGD2bN_sc0)

One or more interactive elements has been excluded from this version of the text. You can view them online here: https://milnepublishing.geneseo.edu/social-justice-in-human-services/?p=167#oembed-17 (#oembed-17)

Video: Love Wins: June 26, 2015, Part 1 (https://www.youtube.com/watch?v=LQAFllfxrLw)

One or more interactive elements has been excluded from this version of the text. You can view them online here: https://milnepublishing.geneseo.edu/social-justice-in-human-services/?p=167#oembed-18 (#oembed-18)

Video: The Light of Progress: June 26, 2015, Part 3 (https://www.youtube.com/watch?v=1HEUJZsPtSk)

One or more interactive elements has been excluded from this version of the text. You can view them online here: https://milnepublishing.geneseo.edu/social-justice-in-human-services/?p=167#oembed-19 (#oembed-19)

Discussion Questions

- Why do you think it took so long for marriage equality to become federal law? What are the issues surrounding it?
- Do some research into marriage in other countries. What kind of same sex marriage laws do they have?

Don't Ask, Don't Tell

Elected in 1992, President Bill Clinton was the first prominent political figure in the United States to actively endorse gay rights. Clinton won the gay vote by promising to pass the Employment Non-Discrimination Act (ENDA) and to end the ban on gay people serving in the military, which was made illegal under Article 125 of the Uniform Code of Military Justice. Article 125 identified sodomy as a crime (Faderman, 2015). "There's no question that Clinton made his promise to gays and lesbians in good faith. As soon as he took office, he was ready to grab the pen and sign the executive order" (Faderman, 2015, p. 499).

Unfortunately for the gay community, Clinton had overestimated his power and the support of others in the government. Congress—particularly Senator Sam Nunn—was determined to stop any integration of gay people into the military. Clinton faced opposition from some members of Congress and the Joint Chiefs of Staff, who refused to support Clinton in ending the ban. General Colin Powell, along with other military leaders, was against gays in the military because he believed that they would be "distracting and destroy fighting readiness; they'd be divisive and would destroy unit cohesion and morale" (Faderman, 2015, p. 499).

Lastly, the Christian right mobilized to stop gay people from being in the military. Christians besieged congressional offices with thousands of letters requesting that the military ban remain in place. "During eight days in early February, soon after Clinton announced his intention to keep his promise to lesbians and gays, the Capitol switchboard logged 1,650,143 calls, mostly from people saying that his plan endangered the country" (Faderman, 2015, p. 500).

On March 29, 1993, the Senate Armed Services Committee began hearings to consider the matter—these hearings were "a disaster" (Faderman, 2015, p. 504). By the end, it was clear that Clinton would have to compromise. Ultimately, the two parties settled on the policy of *Don't Ask, Don't Tell* (DADT), which went into effect on July 19, 1993.

DADT allowed for gay people in the military if they did not speak about being gay or "get caught acting (or seeking to act) on it, on or off base" (Faderman, 2015, p. 504). Although Clinton tried to present DADT as "an honorable compromise" (Faderman, 2015, p. 504), the gay community was infuriated. DADT represented the idea that to be gay was wrong.

Ultimately, DADT did not work. In its time, over 14,000 gay service members were discharged after the military found them out. In 2001 alone, 1,273 service members were discharged under DADT. In its annual reports, the Servicemembers Legal Defense Network revealed that the persecution of gay service members had "gotten worse because the policy had 'stirred up a hornet's nest' of homophobia" (Faderman, 2015, p. 522). Over $1.3 billion was spent on investigations by the military to find out and justify the discharges of gay service members.

By 2007, views on gay people in the military had shifted in the United States. That year, 28 retired generals and admirals signed a letter to the United States Congress asking them to repeal DADT and allow gay people to serve in the military free of restrictions. In 2008, 104 retired generals and admirals reiterated the same sentiment. By 2009, a Washington Post survey reported that 75 percent of those polled believed that gay people should be allowed to openly serve in the military. That same year, General Colin Powell, who had been adamantly against lifting the ban against gay people in the military, changed his mind and stated, "it was time to reconsider the old policy" (Faderman, 2015, p. 512).

In 2009, President Obama resumed the fight that President Clinton had begun. Obama told members of the Joint Chiefs of Staff,

> I think Don't Ask, Don't Tell is wrong. So, I want you guys to understand that I want to work with the Pentagon, I want to figure out how to do this right, but I intend to repeal this policy. (Faderman, 2015, p. 514)

Almost immediately, Obama faced resistance; he agreed that he would allow Congress to be responsible for repealing the DADT.

During Obama's first year as president, another 428 gay military service members were discharged under DADT. "There's no doubt that Barack Obama genuinely wanted a military that was open to anyone willing and able to serve; yet he feared weakening his presidency" (Faderman, 2015, p. 517). In 2010, during his first State of the Union Address, Obama again stated his intention to repeal DADT.

Gay activists and community members were tired of waiting for Congress to decide to repeal DADT. Therefore, they went directly to the American public. Retired Admiral Alan Steinman, retired Brigadier General Virgil Richard, and retired Brigadier General Keith Kerr volunteered to have "a grand coming out" (Faderman, 2015, p.) in a *New York Times* article detailing their experiences as gay men being forced to lie about their identity while serving their country. The Call to Duty Tour:

> brought together young gay and lesbian vets and sent them out, especially to the red states, to tell their stories about how they'd served with devotion and faultless records and had been discharged only because they were gay, or had left before being kicked out because the stresses and strains or hiding were intolerable (Faderman, 2015, p. 524).

Some organizations, such as the Human Rights Campaign's Voices of Honor, followed the Call to Duty Tour's lead. Other organizations, such as Get Equal, took a more radical approach. Get Equal, founded by Robin McGehee and Kip Williams, engaged in activities reminiscent of ACT UP's effective Zaps (Faderman, 2015). On March 18, 2010, Get Equal members Dan Choi and James Pietrangelo, who had been discharged under DADT, allowed themselves to be chained to the White House fence by McGehee. Choi, Pietrangelo, and McGehee were arrested and fined. In both April and May of 2010, Get Equal members once again Zapped the White House by chaining themselves to a fence.

Meanwhile, the government sent surveys to 400,000 active and reserve service members and 150,000 military spouses to solicit their feelings about openly gay military service members. "More than 70 percent of respondents said the effect of repealing Don't Ask, Don't Tell would be positive, mixed, or nonexistent" (Faderman, 2015, p. 529). Cumulatively, 92 percent of active service members reported that the effect of having openly gay service members would have a very good, good, or neutral impact on unit cohesion.

In December 2010, both sides of Congress voted to repeal DADT. On December 22, after 17 years, DADT was repealed by President Obama (Faderman, 2015). Though this was a significant victory, DADT was only repealed: the Uniform Code of Military Justice still listed sodomy as a crime. It was not until 2014, when the National Defense Authorization Act for Fiscal Year 2014 passed, that Article 125 of the Uniform Code of Military Justice was revised and sodomy was removed as a crime.

Activity 9.22 – Repealing Don't Ask, Don't Tell

Video: President Obama Signs Repeal of Don't Ask, Don't Tell (https://www.youtube.com/watch?v=cS26CciE0VQ)

One or more interactive elements has been excluded from this version of the text. You can view them online here: https://milnepublishing.geneseo.edu/social-justice-in-human-services/?p=167#oembed-20 (#oembed-20)

Discussion Questions

- Why do you think it took over seventeen years to repeal DADT?
- Why do you think DADT was repealed under Obama instead of Clinton?

Gender

Sexuality and gender are both distinct aspects of individual identity. Although they differ, they are profoundly interconnected and often influence one another. Sexuality primarily concerns the attraction individuals experience, whereas gender encompasses the roles, behaviors, and identities that society deems appropriate for different sexes. Understanding sexuality offers valuable insight into the various ways people experience attraction and intimacy. However, to fully appreciate the complexities of identity, it is crucial to examine gender as well.

In the United States, gender has traditionally been determined by biological sex, limited to only two options: male or female. However, we now know that gender is a complex construct with biological, psychological, and social dimensions. The biological aspects of gender include physiological factors, such as genetics, hormones, and anatomy. Conversely, the psychological aspects of gender involve an individual's internal sense of their gender identity and their experience of it. The social aspects of gender include the perpetually evolving norms, roles, and expectations placed upon individuals based on their gender within the context of a specific culture and historical period (Barker & Iantaffi, 2019).

Gender identity is how people internally feel about who they are. Thus, gender identity is separate from sexual identity, just as it is apart from other sociocultural identities. However, the "experience of having one identity cannot be divorced or separated from the experience of embodying other identities" (Jourdan & Keenan, 2022, p. 17).

Gender expression is how people outwardly express their gender identity: it is how people move, speak, and dress. Gender roles are how people act upon their gender in the world and with other people (Iantaffi & Barker, 2018). However, the ideology of gender essentialism, dominant in Western cultures, claims that there are inherent ways gender should be expressed. For example, women should be accommodating and nurturing, whereas men should be aggressive and strong (Iantaffi, 2021).

Combining gender identity, expression, and roles creates how people experience gender. It is a multidirectional experience and "is the impact and manifestation of a range of intersections" (Iantaffi & Barker, 2018, p. 57). How individuals experience their gender can be validating or invalidating depending on how their external experiences align with their internal experiences. If an individual's internal and external experiences are misaligned, this may mean that they are transgender.

In the United States, transgressing gender sociocultural norms has never been easy, as European colonization brought rigid gender expectations and standards to the Americas. Although many of these gender expectations and norms are present today, some people have consistently challenged them. "In the United States, many trans people have resisted the institutional categorization of our bodies, arguably for as long as systemic categorization has taken place" (Jourdan & Keenan, 2022, p. 10).

Transgender

Initially coined by Virginia Prince in the 1970s, the term transgender was reclaimed by its respective community in the 1990s (Jourdan & Keenan, 2022). In the 21st century, the term transgender is used to describe "people who cross over (*trans-*) the boundaries constructed by their culture to define and contain that gender" (Stryker, 2017, p. 1). Prince's definition of transgender requires the socio-cultural construction of gender as two distinct entities, as well as a starting and ending place: transitioning from one place to another place. Others have defined transgender as "an active process of challenging the formal structures that govern how gender is defined" (Jourdan & Keenan, 2022, p. 3). Transgender practices include "cross-dressing, taking hormones to change the gendered appearance of the body, having genital or chest surgery, and living as a member of a gender other than one's birth assigned gender" (Stryker, 2017, p. 3). However, in the eloquent words of Jourdan and Keenan, "Perhaps the only simple truth about gender is that it is never simple" (p. 13).

Transgender Social Justice Movement

Through the late 1950s to the early 1960s, four events occurred that sparked awareness of the systemic discrimination that drag queens and transgender people experienced in the United States. These events were at different times and in various parts of the country. Though each were spontaneous, all four events had a unified effect on the transgender social justice movement.

The first event occurred at an all-night coffee shop, Cooper's Do-nuts, in Los Angeles. Cooper's was a hangout for gay people who lived and worked on the streets, including Black and Latinx drag queens. Police would frequently patrol the area around Cooper's, stop people for questioning, and demand: "identification—which for trans people whose appearance might not match the name or gender designation on their IDs, often led to an arrest on suspicion of prostitution, vagrancy, loitering, or many other so-called nuisance crimes" (Stryker, 2017, p. 82).

On a particular May night in 1959, Los Angeles police went to Cooper's and arrested a few of the customers. The customers "staged a mini-riot, with drag queens and hustlers assaulting the police" (Faderman, 2015, p. 116). The protestors threw coffee cups, doughnuts, and anything else they could get their hands on. Ultimately, police had to run out of Cooper's to call for backup. Several protestors were arrested, but others escaped.

The second event occurred in Philadelphia. Dewey's, an after-hours restaurant, had been a hangout for the gay community, drag queens, and sex workers since the 1940s. In April of 1965, Dewey's management refused service to the "gay kids" who wore "nonconformist clothing" (Stryker, 2017, p. 82) because they were interfering with their business. "Customers rallied to protest, and on April 25, more than 150 patrons were turned away by management" (Stryker, 2017, p. 82).

Three gender-transgressing street kids refused to leave Dewey's "in what appears to be the first act of civil disobedience over anti-transgender discrimination" (Stryker, 2017, pp. 82-83). The three teenagers, as well as one gay activist, were arrested and found guilty of disorderly conduct. During the next week, more protesters, including members of the gay community, picketed outside of Dewey's. On May 2, protesters had another sit-in; Dewey's management "backed down and promised an immediate cessation of all indiscriminate denials of service" (Stryker, 2017, p. 83).

The third event occurred in the Tenderloin neighborhood of San Francisco in an all-night restaurant: Compton's Cafeteria. In August of 1966, a group of young drag queens sat at a table and, according to Compton's management, were making too much noise and not spending enough money. Consequently, Compton's management called the police to have the young drag queens removed (Stryker, 2017).

A police officer, "accustomed to manhandling Compton's clientele with impunity, grabbed the arm of one of the queens and tried to drag her away. She unexpectedly threw her coffee in his face, and a melee erupted" (Stryker, 2017, pp. 85-86). Compton's customers turned tables upside down, smashed the windows, and went out into the streets. "Drag queens beat the police with their heavy purses and the sharp stiletto heels of their shoes" (Stryker, 2017, p. 86). The protest lasted through the night but was over by morning. The protest at Compton's "was long-lost to history…because the officers at the scene never filed a report. As such, most local media did not pick up the story, and the riot remained a fixture of local lore for decades" (Hart & Feng, 2022, p. 640).

The fourth event—discussed in detail above—was the 1969 New York City Stonewall Inn riots. It is important to note that drag queens and transgender people were critical during the Stonewall Inn riots. Although eyewitness accounts vary as to what triggered the riots, there is no doubt that many of the protestors were Black and Latinx drag queens and transgender people (Stryker, 2017).

These four events were triggered by discriminatory treatment of drag queens, gay people, and transgender people, many of whom were poor, Black, and Latinx. Thus, each event served as microcosmic representations of centuries of systemic injustice. The resulting protests sparked awareness in the gay community that change was needed. "That shift in awareness was a crucial step for contemporary transgender social justice movements" (Stryker, 2017, p. 98).

Street Transvestite Action Revolutionaries (STAR)

In 1970, not long after the Stonewall Inn riots, 19-year-old Sylvia Rivera described herself as " a man with a penis who liked to dress up as a woman" (Duberman, 2019, p. 293). Rivera was concerned for other young drag queens who, like her, engaged in sex work and lived on the streets. Rivera wanted to create " a place where these young queens not only could find emotional comfort but could maybe even learn enough skills to start another kind of life" (Duberman, 2019, p. 309). Rivera brought her concerns to her long-time friend, Marsha P. Johnson.

Johnson, a Black drag queen, had also lived on the streets of New York City and engaged in sex work. Johnson agreed with Rivera's concerns about trans street kids, and in 1970, Rivera and Johnson established the Street Transvestite Action Revolutionaries (STAR) group (Bronski, 2011; Duberman, 2019). Rivera and Johnson established their first STAR House in the back of an abandoned trailer truck. Approximately 24 young street queens joined STAR and moved in with Rivera and Johnson. STAR's rule was that "nobody had to go out and hustle her body, but that when they did, they had to kick back a percentage to help keep STAR

House going" (Duberman, 2019, p. 309). Both Rivera and Johnson hustled regularly to provide breakfast for the STAR House members.

Eventually, with help from other local drag queens, Rivera and Johnson were able to move themselves and the young street queens into a more permanent location. However, resources continued to plague STAR, and local gay groups were not supportive with money or time. Ultimately, STAR House closed its doors in July of 1971 (Duberman, 2019).

"STAR is often credited with being the first trans-women-of-color project" (Hart & Feng, 2022, p. 641) and the first transgender shelter in the United States. STAR leaders addressed the connected issues of transgender rights, homelessness, and housing inequality. "STAR called for an uprooting of transphobia in all the places from which it emanated-individual families, partners, and neighbors, but also systemic factors such as policing, incarceration, housing and job discrimination" (Hart & Feng, 2022, pp. 641-642).

Gains and Losses

During the 1970s, there were both gains and losses for the transgender community. The American medical community engaged in research that allowed many in the transgender community to receive free services as research participants. However, these services "became entangled with a socially conservative attempt to maintain traditional gender configurations in which changing sex was…permitted…to the extent that the practice did not trouble the gender binary" (Stryker, 2017, p. 118).

It was also during this time that a split occurred as the transgender community lost connection with the larger gay community. Many gay men sought to be accepted into the larger society and became "straight-looking and straight-acting" (Stryker, 2017 p. 120). Gay men's attempts to appease gender norms caused a rift with the transgender community, who celebrated transgressing those very norms. Moreover, the transgender community also lost ties to some feminist groups that believed transfeminine people were "by definition violators of women because they represented an unwanted penetration into women's space" (Styker, 2017, p. 129).

During the AIDS crisis, some mending of the rift between the gay and transgender communities occurred. According to Stryker (2017), the AIDS crisis "required gay men, and many lesbians, to rethink the cultural politics of homosexuality and the ways in which homosexual communities related to and intersected with broader social structures" (p. 166). Transgender women, especially those engaged in sex work, were especially vulnerable to contracting HIV. This prompted AIDS activists in the gay community to consider transgender issues seriously. "The name for this new kind of unabashedly pro-gay, nonseparatist, antiassimilationist alliance politics to combat AIDS…was queer" (Stryker, 2017, p. 166).

Modern Transgender Movements

As the mainstream gay community focused on issues of acceptance, such as marriage equality and ownership of property rights, many transgender people—especially trans People of Color (TPOC)—felt marginalized (Romero & Simms, 2022). Therefore, transgender activists focused on the issues of marginalization, including lack of access to safe places, healthcare equity, immigrant rights, mass incarceration, poverty, and sex workers' rights (Hart & Feng, 2022). TPOC, especially transwomen, "experience the multiplied effects of both transphobia and racism through increased police brutality, racial profiling, wealth disparities, and other forms of racism…including a disproportionate amount of violence " (Romero & Simms, 2022, p. 37).

Achieving social justice is an ongoing fight for the transgender and gender-expansive (T/GE) community. The transgender community continues to face systemic discrimination and oppression from the American people, media, and government. Transgender women, particularly those of color, have often "been disproportionately affected by denials of employment and housing, and by violent crimes against them, and have had greater needs to take political and self-protective action" (Stryker, 2017, p. 101). Sixteen percent of transgender Americans have been incarcerated in comparison to about 5 percent of the general population (Johnson, 2023).

The LGBTGEQIAP+ Community Today

In the United States, the LGBTGEQIAP+ community has fought for over 500 years to be recognized as human beings with inextricable rights: the right to exist, the right to work, the right to serve their country, and the right to love. Although there has been progress made in the pursuit of life, liberty, and happiness for the gay and transgender communities, there is still a long way to go. "In a spectacular transition of over the last seventy years, the federal government has gone from the most homophobic of workplaces to one of the most protective of LGBT rights" (Johnson, 2023, p. 226).

Backlash is—and always has been—a part of the social justice movement for the gay and transgender communities in the United States. The religious right in the United States, comprised of socially and politically conservative Christians, have continued to actively persecute the LGBTGEQIAP+ gay and transgender communities. From Reverend Jerry Falwell blaming the 9/11 terrorist attacks on "the gays and lesbians" to the Westboro Baptist Church members protesting outside of Matthew Shepard's memorial service, discrimination and violence continue to be a reality within the gay and transgender communities (Duberman, 2018; Garretson, 2018).

Thoughts from the Authors

As a Bisexual woman, it has been heart-wrenching to write this chapter. The amount of hate that has been poured onto the LGBTGEQIAP+ community, which I am a proud member of, is overwhelming. I am not sure I have ever cried as much writing anything else as I did while writing this chapter. I also experienced moments of awe, especially when reading the stories of so many LGBTGEQIAP+ people who have advocated, fought, and bled to be seen and treated as human beings. I have always been proud to be a member of the LGBTGEQIAP+ community, and after reading and writing about these amazing human beings, I am also grateful.

Sincerely,
Dr. Nikki Golden

Dr. Golden (Nikki) was the primary author of this chapter, and I learned so much from her in the process of writing it—so a shout-out to her for that. I realized through the reading and editing of the work Dr. Golden did how little I knew about the history of being gay in this country. I have many loved ones in my life who identify as gay. While I occasionally hear grumblings of losing rights and court cases, I think I started the process of this chapter without a thorough understanding of the fights it has taken to get there. I now see the reality of being gay in this country and the history of that fight in an entirely different way. For that learning, I am grateful.

Sincerely,

Dr. Bernie DeJonge

Chapter Summary Questions

1. What were some key historical events that significantly impacted LGBTGEQIAP+ rights and visibility?
2. What were some landmark legal cases that advanced LGBTGEQIAP+ rights?
3. What role did the AIDS crisis play in shaping LGBTGEQIAP+ activism?
4. How have intersectional issues influenced the LGBTGEQIAP+ rights movement?
5. What challenges remain in achieving full legal and social equality for LGBTGEQIAP+ individuals?

References

Adkins, J. (2016). "These people are frightened to death": Congressional investigations and the Lavender Scare. *Prologue Magazine, 48*(2). https://www.archives.gov/publications/prologue/2016/summer/lavender.html

AIDS Foundation of Chicago. (n.d.). *Facts about HIV/AIDS.* https://www.aidschicago.org/about-hiv/facts-about-hiv-aids/

Bhinder, J., & Upadhyaya, P. (2021). Brief history of gender affirmation medicine and surgery. In D. Nikolavsky & S.A. Blakely (Eds.), *Urological care for the transgender patient: A comprehensive guide* (pp. 249-254).

Blackhawk, N. (2023). *The rediscovery of America: Native peoples and the unmaking of U.S. history.* Yale University Press.

Bronski, M. (2011). *A queer history of the United States.* Beacon.

Cervini, E. (2020). *The deviant's war: The homosexual vs. the United States of America.* Picador.

Charles, D. M. (2015). *Hoover's war on gays: Exposing the FBI's "Sex Deviates" program.* University Press of Kansas.

Cleves, R. H. (2015). "What another female husband?": The prehistory of same-sex marriage in America. *The Journal of American History, 101*(4), 1055-1081.

Cooke, K. J. (2014). Generations and regeneration: "Sexceptionalism" and group identity among Puritans in colonial New England. *Journal of the History of Sexuality, 23*(3), 333-357. https://doi.org/10.7560/JHS23301

D'Emilio, J., & Freedman, E.B. (2012). *Intimate matters: A history of sexuality in America* (3rd ed.). The University of Chicago Press.

Duberman, M. (2019). *Stonewall: The definitive story of the LGBTQ rights uprising that changed America*. Plume.

Duberman, M. (2018). *Has the gay movement failed?* University of California Press.

Eskridge, W. N. (1996, March). *Law and the construction of the closet: American regulation of same-sex intimacy, 1880-1946*. [Lecture]. University of Iowa School of Law, Iowa City, IA. https://openyls.law.yale.edu/bitstream/handle/20.500.13051/3230/Law_and_the_Construction_of_the_Closet__American_Regulation_of_Same_Sex_Intimacy.pdf?sequence=2

Eskridge, W. N. (1997, November 20). *Hardwick and historiography*. [Lecture]. University of Illinois College of Law, Champaign, IL. https://openyls.law.yale.edu/bitstream/handle/20.500.13051/3234/Hardwick_and_History.pdf?sequence=2

Faderman, L. (2015). *The gay revolution: The story of the struggle*. Simon & Schuster.

Faderman, L. (2022). *Woman: The American history of an idea*. Yale University Press.

Fritz, M., & Mulkey, N. (2021). The rise and fall of gender identity clinics in the 1960s and 1970s. *Bulletin of the American College of Surgeons, 106*, 40-45. https://www.facs.org/for-medical-professionals/news-publications/news-and-articles/bulletin/2021/04/the-rise-and-fall-of-gender-identity-clinics-in-the-1960s-and-1970s/

Hagai, E. B., & Crosby, F. J. (2016). Between relative deprivation and entitlement: An historical analysis of the battle for same-sex marriage in the United States. In C. Sabbagh & M. Schmitt (Eds.), *Handbook of social justice theory and research* (pp. 477-489). Springer.

Hart, B., & Feng, K. (2022). Activism, politics, and organizing. In L. Erickson-Schroth (Ed.), *Trans bodies, trans selves: A resource by and for transgender communities* (2nd ed., pp. 638-658). Oxford University Press.

Historic England. (n.d.). *Law and oppression*. https://historicengland.org.uk/research/inclusive-heritage/lgbtq-heritage-project/law-and-oppression/

Human Rights Campaign. (n.d.). *Blood donations*. https://www.hrc.org/resources/blood-donations

Iantaffi, A. (2021). *Gender trauma: Healing cultural, social, and historical gendered trauma*. Kingsley.

Iantaffi, A., & Barker, M-J. (2018). *How to understand your gender: A practical guide for exploring who you are*. Kingsley.

Issenberg, S. (2021). *The engagement: America's quarter-century struggle over same-sex marriage*. Vintage Books.

Johnson, D. K.(2023). *The lavender scare: The cold war persecution of gays and lesbians in the federal government*. The University of Chicago Press.

Jourdan, M. C., & Keenan, H. B. (2022). Our selves. In L. Erickson-Schroth (Ed.), *Trans bodies, trans selves: A resource by and for transgender communities* (2nd ed., pp. 3-28). Oxford University Press.

Kirchick, J. (2022). *The secret city: The hidden history of gay Washington*. Holt.

Kunzel, R. (2018). The power of queer history. *The American Historical Review, 123*(5), 1560-1582.

Lemmey, H., & Miller, B. (2023). *Bad gays: A homosexual history*. Verso.

Lepore, J. (2018). *These truths: A history of the United States.* Norton.

Lopez, A. C., & Driskill, Q. (2022). U.S. history. In L. Erickson-Schroth (Ed.), *Trans bodies, trans selves: A resource by and for transgender communities* (2nd ed., pp. 585-613). Oxford University Press.

Manion, J. (2020). *Female husbands: A trans history*. Cambridge University Press.

Marcus, E. (2002). *Making gay history: The half-century fight for lesbian and gay equal rights.* Harper.

Margolin, L. (2021). Madman in the closet: "Homosexual panic" in nineteenth century New England. *Journal of Homosexuality, 68*(9), 1471-1488.

Morgensen, S. L. (2010). Settler homonationalism: Theorizing settler colonialism within queer modernities. *A Journal of Lesbian and Gay Studies, 16*(1-2), 105-131. https://doi.org/10.1215/10642684-2009-015

Oaks, R. F. (1978). "Things fearful to name": Sodomy and buggery in seventeenth-century New England. *Journal of Sexual History, 12*(2), 268-281.

PBS. (n.d.). *Kinsey in the news*. American Experience. https://www.pbs.org/wgbh/americanexperience/features/kinsey-news/

Robinson, M. (2020). Two-spirit identity in a time of gender fluidity. *Journal of Homosexuality, 67*(12), 1675-1690. https://doi-org.proxy.seattleu.edu/10.1080/00918369.2019.1613853

Romero, R., & Simms, S. (2022). Race, ethnicity, and culture. In L. Erickson-Schroth (Ed.), *Trans bodies, trans selves: A resource by and for transgender communities* (2nd ed., pp. 29-52). Oxford University Press.

SAIGE. (n.d.). *Initialism*. https://saigecounseling.org/initialism/

Smith, G. (2021). *About three-in-ten U.S. adults are now religiously unaffiliated.* Pew Research Center.

Smithers, G. D. (2014). Cherokee "Two Spirits": Gender, ritual, and spirituality in the native south. *Early American Studies: An Interdisciplinary Journal, 12*(3), 626-651. https://doi.org/10.1353/eam.2014.0023

Smithers, G. D. (2022). *Reclaiming Two-Spirits: Sexuality, spiritual renewal & sovereignty in Native America*. Beacon.

Stryker, S. (2017). *Transgender history: The roots of today's revolution* (rev. ed.). Seal Press.

Thompson, R. (1989). Attitudes towards homosexuality in the seventeenth-century New England colonies. *Journal of American Studies, 23*(1), 27-40.

U.S. Food & Drug Administration. (2023). *FDA finalizes move to recommend individual risk assessment to determine eligibility for blood donations.* https://www.fda.gov/news-events/press-announcements/fda-finalizes-move-recommend-individual-risk-assessment-determine-eligibility-blood-donations

Wilson, J. F. (2010). *Bulldaggers, pansies and chocolate babies: Performance, race, and sexuality in the Harlem Renaissance.* The University of Michigan Press.

World Health Organization. (2023). *HIV and AIDS fact sheet.* https://www.who.int/news-room/fact-sheets/detail/hiv-aids

Media Attributions

- Stonewall Inn plaque © Grace Mahony is licensed under a CC BY-SA (Attribution ShareAlike) license
- GLF logo © Kautr is licensed under a CC0 (Creative Commons Zero) license
- Peter Staley © Graham MacIndoe is licensed under a Public Domain license
- Pride © Robert Couse-Baker is licensed under a CC BY (Attribution) license
- Gay wedding © erin m is licensed under a CC BY-NC (Attribution NonCommercial) license
- DADT protest © Mary Slosson is licensed under a CC BY-SA (Attribution ShareAlike) license
- A trans couple taking a selfie in bed © Zackary Drucker, Vice Media, and the Gender Spectrum Collection is licensed under a CC BY-NC-ND (Attribution NonCommercial NoDerivatives) license

10.
Poverty in the United States

Bernadet DeJonge

> **Learning Objectives**
>
> - The reader will recognize how poverty exists in multiple contexts.
> - The reader will analyze how poverty in the United States is a form of discrimination.
> - The reader will connect poverty in the United States to social justice concepts.

This chapter will review core concepts of poverty, examine some of the history of poverty in the United States, and discuss how poverty is a social justice issue. It will also discuss legislation and policy around poverty, and how legislation, policy, and funding impact marginalized populations.

Defining Poverty

Living in poverty often means that essential resources are scarce or unobtainable, and the intersection of resources and living standards is stark and surprising in the United States. One in four Americans needs help to obtain essential resources such as food, water, and shelter. Other resources low-income Americans lack include money, mental and physical healthcare, childcare, and employment (Goldblum & Shaddox, 2021).

Many people in the United States see each other through value-laden lenses that focus on personal attributes such as values, personal decisions, and personality traits. However, poverty is much more than a personal attribute. Poverty is a systemic issue that stems from a history of racism, sexism, ableism, xenophobia, slavery, and an economic system that takes economic inequity for granted. Examples of these systems include criminal justice systems, housing systems, employment systems, healthcare systems, and safety net programs, which are often difficult to access (Assari, 2017; Desmond, 2023; Goldblum & Shaddox, 2021). In this chapter, we will frame poverty through this systemic lens, examining the factors that have influenced the United States to become a society that does not do enough to meet the income needs of its population.

Activity 10.1 – Systemic Roots of Poverty

Video: We can end poverty, but this is why we haven't by Teva Sienicki
(https://www.youtube.com/watch?v=vvlozhvQPJw)

 One or more interactive elements has been excluded from this version of the text. You can view them online here: https://milnepublishing.geneseo.edu/social-justice-in-human-services/?p=171#oembed-1 (#oembed-1)

Discussion Questions

- Examine the systemic factors that contribute to persistent poverty. How do these systems perpetuate a cycle of poverty?
- What implications arise from the assumption that poverty is a normal and unchangeable condition? How might this perspective influence policies and societal attitudes towards poverty?
- How does poverty affect the long-term brain development of children, and what are the broader implications for society?

Historical Aspects of Poverty

Elizabethan poor laws began in England in the 1600s to assist the poor. For the first time in Europe, these laws declared that the government was responsible for aiding poor citizens. These citizens were divided into three categories: able-bodied, impotent (not able-bodied), and children. Poor people were expected to work, and begging was prohibited. Local church leaders oversaw services, and a tax was levied on the population to fund the assistance (Kennedy, 2023).

As the colonists established themselves in the United States, they turned to Elizabethan laws to manage the poverty that inevitably followed them to the colonies. They also broke the poor into categories of "worthy" or "unworthy" (Kennedy, 2023, para. 7). Local leaders decided who was worthy of assistance and who was not. Early in colonial times, the poor were often contracted out for manual labor by farmers or homeowners, who agreed to take them in exchange for their labor and a fixed price. Geography mattered during this time, and people who sought assistance had to prove where they were from and were punished when they attempted to move from one geographic area to another to try and receive services (Kennedy, 2023).

In the early nineteenth century, the experience of the poor shifted as poorhouses came into favor. Poorhouses, also called workhouses or almshouses, were "designed to punish people for their poverty and, hypothetically, make being poor so horrible that people would continue to work at all costs" (Blakemore, 2023, para 8). Poorhouses were often kept out of public view as the plight of being poor carried a negative social stigma. Residents had to swear an oath that they were poor and were subjected to strict rules, harsh labor, pests, violence, poor housing, and inadequate food. Poorhouses later gave way to poor farms to move poor people further from public view. By the time the Great Depression began, poorhouses and poor farms were shut down as the federal government began implementing social safety net programs (Blakemore, 2023).

The Great Depression began with the stock market crash in 1929 and lasted until 1939 when World War II began. A combination of slowing of consumer demand, increased consumer credit, decreased industrial production, and the sudden stock market expansion triggered the Great Depression. Banks failed in large numbers. At the same time, industrial production plummeted. This led to unprecedented unemployment, with millions losing their jobs, homes, and savings. The agricultural sector was also severely impacted in the United States. The Dust Bowl, a period of severe drought and dust storms that struck the central United States during this time, exacerbated the suffering of farmers by destroying crops, degrading soil, and forcing many to abandon their land.

President Franklin D. Roosevelt implemented the New Deal in 1933 as a series of programs and reforms designed to revive the economy of the United States. However, it took the United States entering World War II and the need for manufacturing production due to war to end the Great Depression (History.com, 2023).

The War on Poverty

In January 1964, President Lyndon B. Johnson declared a "War on Poverty" (Matthews, 2014, para. 1) during his State of the Union address. He introduced multiple legislative acts to impact the state of poverty in the United States. This legislation included the creation of Medicare and Medicaid, made food stamps permanent, and included the Economic Opportunity Act and the Elementary and Secondary Education Act. Programs like Head Start, Job Corps, VISTA, and Title 1 also come from this legislation set (Matthews, 2014).

Statistics show that despite continued poverty in the United States, this legislation significantly impacted poverty levels and continues to do so today. Matthews (2014) states that "In 2012, food stamps (since renamed Supplemental Nutrition Assistance Program, or SNAP) alone kept 4 million people out of poverty" (para. 12).

Myths of Poverty

One of the biggest myths of poverty is that poverty is an individual problem and not a systemic issue. As a country that values hard work and individualism, many in the United States see those who remain in poverty as lazy, unmotivated, and uneducated (Assari, 2017). Thus, individuals struggling with poverty find themselves the victims of stereotyping and

Man on pier on New York City docks during Great Depression (1935)

judgment. Often, it is suggested that poor people should try harder, work harder, go back to school, etc., without thinking through the barriers inherent in those suggestions (Goldblum & Shaddox, 2021).

Another poverty myth is that poor people do not work. In actuality, the working poor make up much of the service industry, agricultural work, and factory work in the United States today. However, structural issues such as the cost of food, housing, daycare, and medical expenses make it impossible to get ahead on a minimum wage job (Goldblum & Shaddox, 2021). For example, a single mother of young children cannot just leave her children at home to return to work. If she does, then she could lose her children to Child Protective Services (CPS). Thus, if she does go back to work, she must make enough to cover daycare costs and living expenses, which many low-paying jobs do not do. Desmond (2023) describes this well, noting that "poverty is about money, of course, but it is also a relentless piling on of problems" (p. 13). Desmond highlights that financial hardship rarely exists in isolation, but is compounded by overlapping challenges such as housing instability, poor health, and limited access to services. Recognizing this complexity is essential for developing effective policies and interventions that address the root causes of poverty.

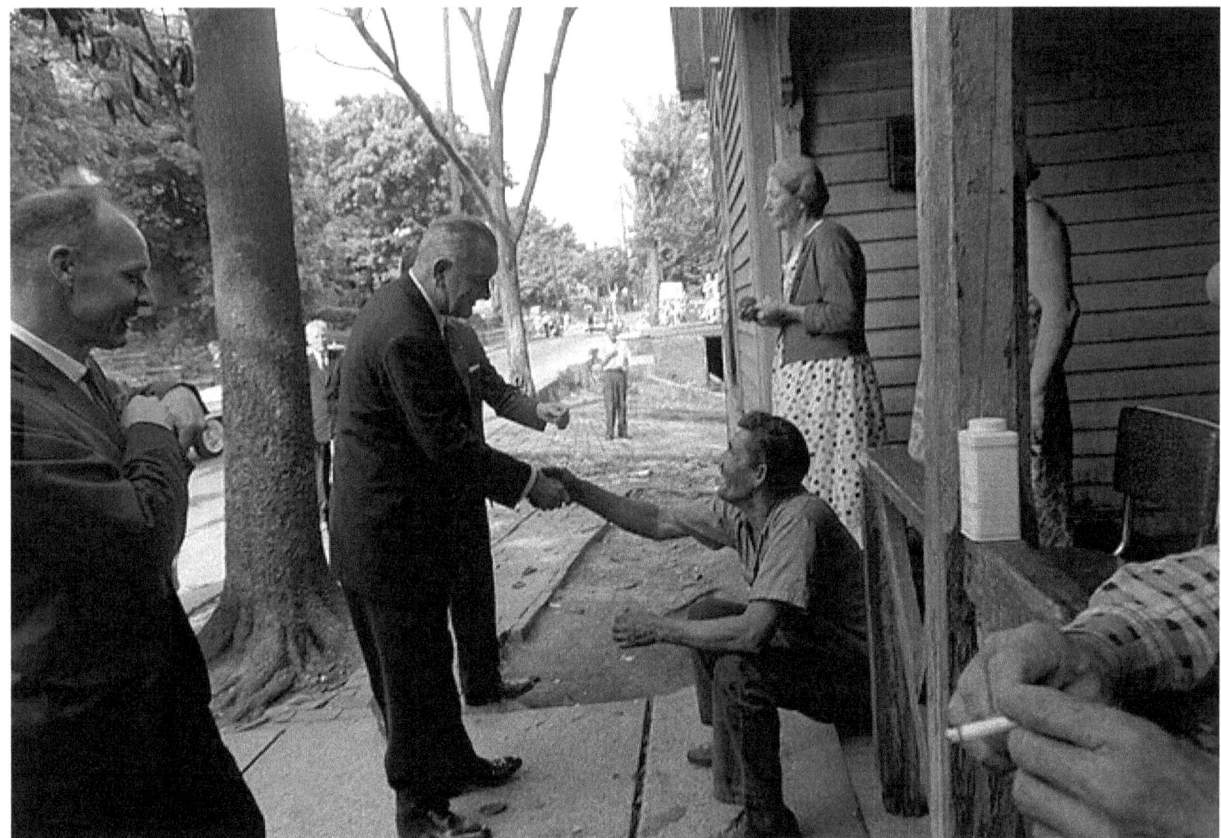

President Lyndon B. Johnson shakes the hand of one of the residents of Appalachia as Agent Rufus Youngblood (far left) looks on. May 1964.

The Welfare Queen

One of the most persistent myths about poverty is that of the welfare queen. Ronald Reagan coined this phrase when running for president in the late 1970s/early 1980s to reinforce his policies of cutting funding for welfare programs. The stereotypical welfare queen is a Black woman who hustles the welfare system and becomes wealthy from it. The welfare queen is flashy, promiscuous, well-dressed, and drives a nice car (Covert, 2019; Levin, 2021).

The welfare case that Reagan turned into the stereotype of the welfare queen was Linda Taylor, a woman who used multiple aliases to receive excessive welfare benefits fraudulently. Taylor was a complicated woman who also perpetuated multiple other crimes. Despite her criminal activity, including suspicion of murder, Taylor was only prosecuted for her fraudulent welfare claims. While Reagan claimed she made six figures a year as a welfare queen, court records show that she received a total of $8,865.67 in welfare payments. In addition to her criminal activity, it was also asserted that Taylor had significant mental health issues (Covert, 2019; Levin, 2021).

Following the prosecution of Linda Taylor for welfare fraud, the myth of the welfare queen became deeply ingrained in the national consciousness. In response, policies were implemented nationwide to combat perceived welfare system abuse. These crackdowns reinforced stereotypes that portrayed poor individuals as lazy and unmotivated, further stigmatizing those in need. In Chicago, the welfare department teamed up with the police to pursue welfare fraud cases. Those accused of welfare fraud then had exorbitant bail thrust upon them, and many were pushed into prison time. Fueled by the Taylor case, Reagan continued his crusade against welfare. Consequently, welfare eligibility and benefits saw cuts on both the state and national levels (Covert, 2019).

Activity 10.2 – Linda Taylor

Video: The True Story Behind the 'Welfare Queen' Stereotype (https://www.youtube.com/watch?v=mr_8B1IzFFY)

 One or more interactive elements has been excluded from this version of the text. You can view them online here: https://milnepublishing.geneseo.edu/social-justice-in-human-services/?p=171#oembed-2 (#oembed-2)

Discussion Questions

- Why did Linda Taylor's case become such a significant political issue? What factors contributed to this?
- How did poverty influence Linda Taylor's actions and experiences? What other factors might have played a role in shaping her behavior and circumstances?
- What is our responsibility in legislating social services? How do we decide who is entitled to assistance?

The Linda Taylor case generated a stereotype that continues to this day. Because she was a Black woman, the intersection of racism, sexism, and poverty combined with the political climate of the time to reinforce the public perception of who is poor. There are a variety of other poverty myths that continue today. These include the idea that those who live in poverty make poor financial decisions, do not care for their children, do not value education, and do not work hard. In addition, many believe that people choose to live on welfare and have more children because it is easier than working. This is far from true as access to safety net programs is often challenging and dehumanizing. One of the biggest of these myths is that poverty is inextricably intertwined with race. Statistics do not bear this out, and in 2015, 42 percent of those in poverty were White (Just Harvest, 2015).

Activity 10.3 – Terminology: Povertyism

People who are poor may also experience discrimination and stereotyping. Often, this treatment is based on the poverty myths discussed above. A 2022 United Nations report (https://www.ohchr.org/en/press-releases/2022/10/ban-povertyism-same-way-racism-and-sexism-un-expert) coined the term "povertyism" to describe this and argues that discrimination based on poverty will not resolve itself. The UN report states that poverty discrimination needs to be regulated like other kinds of discrimination such as racism, sexism, and ableism. The report cites examples such as judging job applicants by the address on their resume, landlords not accepting tenants on welfare programs, and poor children being discouraged from a college track (United Nations, 2022).

Article: Ban "povertyism" in the same way as racism and sexism: UN expert (https://www.ohchr.org/en/press-releases/2022/10/ban-povertyism-same-way-racism-and-sexism-un-expert)

Report: Extreme Poverty and Human Rights (https://docs.un.org/en/a/77/157)

Discussion Questions

- How might people who are poor be discriminated against?
- What role might discrimination against those in poverty play in the perpetuation of poverty?
- Do you agree with the United Nations report that povertyism should be regulated like we regulate racism, sexism, and ableism? Why or why not?

Poverty Measures

The question of how to measure poverty is a complicated one. The first poverty estimates were published in 1967 following President Johnson's State of the Union address (US Census Bureau, 2014). The United States government has been tracking poverty statistics ever since. Desmond (2023) states: "Technically, a person is considered 'poor' when they can't afford life's necessities like food and housing" (p. 10). While the definition posed by Desmond makes intuitive sense, this is not how the United States measures poverty. There are two ways that poverty is officially measured in the United States: the Official Poverty Measure (OPM) and the Supplemental Poverty Measure (SPM).

The OPM was developed by Mollie Oshansky in 1965 and frames poverty through the lens of food cost. Oshansky's equation looks at food cost in a given year and then compares that cost to how much income is devoted to paying for food. If a person or family pays more than one third of their income to food costs, then they are poor. The poverty threshold in 2022 was an income of $13,590 for a single person and $27,750 a year for a family of four (Desmond, 2023). The OPM examines all sources of cash income but does not take non-cash government assistance, such as food stamps or housing assistance, into account (Institute for Research on Poverty, n.d.). The OPM also does not consider geographic location, and Desmond (2023) points out that many families and individuals are living in poverty above the official poverty line, particularly in high cost of living areas.

The Supplemental Poverty Measure (SPM) was introduced in 2010 to provide an alternate view of poverty. The SPM is not meant to replace the OPM but to supplement it with pertinent information. The SPM balances the cost of basic needs, financial resources, and other expenses against an individual or family's resources. Resources include cash assets and non-cash assistance, such as food stamps or Medicaid (Kilduff, 2022). Cost includes food, shelter, medical expenses, work expenses, child support, and taxes. The SPM also considers unrelated people living in the home, geographic location, and whether an individual rents or owns their home (U.S. Census Bureau, 2022).

> ### Activity 10.4 – Digging Deeper: An example of the difference between the OPM and SPM
>
> When the OPM and the SPM are compared, the SPM often shows that individuals over 65 are more impoverished than when measured using the OPM. One reason might be that the SPM considers medical expenses and costs while the OPM does not. Many older Americans face crushing medical expenses as they age, and this is often not accounted for in official poverty measures.
>
> Discussion Questions
>
> - Which measure, the OPM or the SPM, makes the most sense to use in the example described above? Why?
> - Should it be a concern if one tool identifies an individual *below* the poverty level and another identifies that same individual as *not below* the poverty line? Why or why not? Does it help us better understand what poverty is? Why or why not?
> - How do you think poverty should be measured?

There are many critics of the way the United States government has chosen to identify and track poverty. Because it is well-known that the standard poverty measures do not accurately reflect the experience of the American population, many agencies use multipliers or adjust based on other factors when examining eligibility. For example, the US Department of Housing and Urban Development (HUD) looks at the median income of the state an applicant lives in to determine eligibility (Kilduff, 2022). One very critical voice in the debate about how to define poverty is Matthew Desmond (2023) who states that:

> Poverty isn't a line. It's a tight knot of social maladies. It is connected to every social problem we care about-crime, health, education, housing- and its persistence in American life means that millions of families are denied safety and security and dignity in one of the richest nations in the history of the world. (p. 23)

Safety Net Programs

Safety net programs are the public benefits and systems intended to assist those in need. Some examples of safety net programs include Temporary Assistance for Needy Families (TANF), Supplemental Nutrition Assistance Program (SNAP, previously called food stamps), housing assistance, cash assistance, child support, the earned income tax credit, Medicaid, Medicare, and social security (Gaines et al., 2021). In the United States, safety net programs have cut poverty by about half (Greenstein, 2015), and research consistently shows that safety net programs help people rise out of poverty and improve quality of life (Gaines et al., 2021). Despite this data, the United States government has continued to focus on cutting safety net programs.

Much of the cuts to safety net programs reflect a societal prejudice towards poverty that focuses on the individualistic, welfare queen rhetoric (Assari, 2017; Covert, 2019). In addition to funding cuts, safety net funding is often managed through state-run Medicaid programs with federal funding (Gaines et al, 2021). Thus, safety net programs vary significantly based on what state an individual lives in as well as the political climate of that state in any given year. In addition, Desmond (2023) points out that funding does not go directly to those in need. He states that "Nationwide, for every dollar budgeted for TANF in 2020, poor families directly received just 22 cents" (p. 28). Desmond argues that the rest of the money is spent in widely varying ways, much of which has nothing to do with impacting poverty in the United States.

Activity 10.5 – Poverty Myths

Video: Poverty in the USA: Being Poor in the World's Richest Country (https://www.youtube.com/watch?v=f78ZVLVdO0A)

 One or more interactive elements has been excluded from this version of the text. You can view them online here: https://milnepublishing.geneseo.edu/social-justice-in-human-services/?p=171#oembed-3 (#oembed-3)

Discussion Questions

- What poverty myths did you see present in the documentary?
- Most people featured in the documentary work. What does that help us to recognize about the state of poverty in the United States?
- Desmond (2023) talks about "the relentless piling up of problems" (p. 13). What problems do you see piling up in this documentary?

Intersectionality

Statistically, marginalized populations have been significantly impacted by poverty, particularly Black Americans. When slavery ended, many White Americans assumed that Black families were able to amass wealth in the same way that White families did. However, this is far from the truth. When slavery was abolished, other laws and policies were implemented to discriminate against former slaves and their families. While White families were amassing wealth, Black families suffered from discrimination, prejudice, and policies such as redlining, which made it impossible to accumulate wealth at the same rate. Sharecropping, forced prison labor, segregation laws, redlining, and voter discrimination continued to keep Black families poor and continue to impact the Black experience of poverty today (Jackson, 2021; PBS, n.d.; Race in America, n.d.).

> **Activity 10.6 – Digging Deeper: Home Ownership**
>
> One way that the working class can amass wealth is through home ownership, and research shows that having parents who own homes increases the likelihood that the next generation will also own homes (Goldblum & Shaddox, 2021). Because of historical racism and discrimination, it is far less likely that Black parents and grandparents were homeowners than White parents and grandparents (National Alliance to End Homelessness, 2021). The historical acts of slavery, discrimination, redlining, and racism have created an inequality that impacts Black individuals to this day.
>
> **Discussion Questions**
>
> - Why do you think homeownership is so important in amassing and passing on wealth?
> - How might poverty impact generational home ownership?
> - What solutions do you see to this historical, systemic issue?

Other contributing factors in Black poverty include lower employment rates, lower income, lack of access to healthcare (including racism in healthcare), poorer credit, higher levels of debt, and mass incarceration. Statistically, Black students have the highest level of student debt of any racial group and yet are disproportionately lower educated than the general population. In addition, Black children are six times more likely than White children to attend schools in high poverty areas (Bread of the World, 2017).

It is not only Black populations who experience poverty inequity. Many of the same issues that plague the Black population also affect other racial groups. While the history of racism may vary between the groups, that shared history has led to a country where marginalized people of color are more likely to be poor. As of 2021, the official poverty rate in the United States was 11.6%. This equates to 37.9 million impoverished people (Creamer et al., 2022). In 2021, the breakdown of poverty stats by race as cited by KFF (n.d.) were:

- White: 9.5%
- Black: 21.7%
- Hispanic: 17.6%
- Asian/Pacific Islander: 10.2%
- American Indian/Alaska Native: 25.9%
- Multiple races: 14.1%

Activity 10.7 – Poverty on Indigenous reservations

Video: Poorest Native American Reservation- What it Really Looks Like (https://www.youtube.com/watch?v=T9Nx3RQkAB0)

 One or more interactive elements has been excluded from this version of the text. You can view them online here: https://milnepublishing.geneseo.edu/social-justice-in-human-services/?p=171#oembed-4 (#oembed-4)

Discussion Questions

- What factors led to poverty on the Indigenous reservations?
- What role does United States history play in the poverty experience of the Oglala Lakota people?
- Desmond (2023) talks about poverty being a "relentless piling on of problems" (p. 13). What problems do you see piling in this video?
- What ideas do you have for solutions to poverty on the reservations?

Poverty affects people of all races; however, being White makes a person more likely to overcome poverty. Elliott (2016) argues that Black poverty is more persistent across generations than White poverty. In addition, Elliott (2016) states that:

> Among children who spent at least one year in poverty, a black child is twice as likely as a white child to also be poor as an adult (43 versus 20 percent). Perhaps more astonishingly, though, black adults have roughly the same chance of experiencing poverty (43 versus 41 percent) regardless of whether or not they were ever poor as children. (para. 5)

This may be partly because Black unemployment rates are 50% higher than those of White individuals in the United States (Gaines et al, 2021). Huang and Taylor (2019) share this disturbing statistic:

> If current trends continue, it will take the median Latino family over 2,000 years just to match the current wealth (financial and housing assets) of the median white household, and Black families will never catch up with white families' current level. (p. 9)

Activity 10.8 – Digging Deeper: Food Deserts

Only 8 percent of Black households live in an area with a supermarket. This is in comparison to 31 percent of White households. Food deserts are a significant concern for those living in both inner city and rural areas. Often, city dwellers pay higher prices at convenience or corner stores due to limited choices. These corner stores often have limited, if any, healthy food options such as fruit and vegetables and often charge significantly more for staple items, such as diapers and other hygiene supplies. Lower access to healthy food leads to a higher incidence of chronic diseases such as diabetes, heart disease, and obesity. Statistically, Black households are more likely to be in poor health, and often, this population chooses not to access healthcare due to healthcare costs (Bread of the World, 2017).

Activity 10.9 – Food Deserts

Video: Trying to Eat Healthy in a Food Desert (https://www.youtube.com/watch?v=dDbENx9c3Fg)

 One or more interactive elements has been excluded from this version of the text. You can view them online here: https://milnepublishing.geneseo.edu/social-justice-in-human-services/?p=171#oembed-5 (#oembed-5)

Discussion Questions

- How are food deserts both a cause and a symptom of poverty?
- How might living in a food desert make it hard for a family to amass wealth?
- Desmond (2023) talks about poverty being a "relentless piling on of problems" (p. 13). What problems pile on because of living in a food desert?

Disability and Poverty

Similar to what Black people in the United States have experienced, laws and policies have also kept people with disabilities from amassing wealth. Disabled individuals are twice as likely to live in poverty than individuals without a disability (Fessler, 2015). In addition, if this statistic is based on the standard measure of poverty, this number could be much higher as current poverty measures do not include individuals living in psychiatric wards, facilities, hospitals, or other supported living type environments (Desmond, 2023). There is an even bigger divide for an individual who is a person of color with a disability (Vallas et al., 2022).

Statistically, more people with disabilities struggle to afford to pay their rent and are more likely to have food insecurity. According to Vallas et al. (2022)

> disability remains both a cause and a consequence of poverty in the United States. Many of the persistent barriers to economic security facing Americans with disabilities are the result of policy failures that become visible when we center the perspectives and experiences of the disability community—from inadequate affordable, accessible housing and transportation to a long history of disinvestment in community living supports, and more. (para. 1)

Gender and Poverty

There is still a wage gap between women and men in the United States. As of 2023, women make 83.7 percent of what men do in the workforce (U.S. Department of Labor, 2023). Goldblum and Shaddox (2021) point out that "women's work" (p. 157) is often less profitable and has less upward mobility than more traditionally male jobs. One of these jobs is caregiving. Many nursing assistants care for the elderly and disabled and seldom get raises or move into more lucrative positions. In addition, many women who struggle with poverty provide informal caregiving for family—meaning they are unpaid. The Alzheimer's Association estimates that in 2022, 18 billion hours of unpaid help occurred in dementia care alone. This equates to nearly $340 billion in unpaid care. Of those caregivers, 41% make $50,000 or less (Sanchez, 2023).

Activity 10.10 – Case Study: Paying for Personal Care

While working as a contractor for the local Area Agency on Aging (AAA), I (Dr. DeJonge) had a client with dementia who was living with her daughter. The daughter worked at a convenience store full-time and barely made ends meet. As dementia progressed, Mom started wandering, becoming assaultive and was awake all hours of the night. They had no funds for placement. They applied for Medicaid and were approved. However, even with Medicaid funding, there were no placement options. The client continued to deteriorate, and she began to wander farther. She would go down the main road and walk along it quite unsafely. People would see her and call 911, which would then notify Adult Protective Services (APS). They visited and only had the suggestion of finding full-time care for the mother, either at home or in a dementia care facility. However, there were no placement options available for a Medicaid-funded client, as these facilities only take a small number of Medicaid-funded clients and often have lengthy waiting lists for state funding. The daughter started locking the home doors to keep mom in and safe. When APS came back out to check on the family, they cited her for inappropriately restraining her mother by locking her in the home.

Ultimately, the state offered the daughter 46 hours a month of pay to care for her mother at minimum wage. While this was significantly less than what the daughter made working full-time at the convenience store, she had to leave that job and accept the lower pay to stay home with her mother. Her biggest fear was that she would be arrested or somehow otherwise prosecuted for not caring for her mother properly.

Discussion Questions

- What role does poverty play in this scenario?
- Desmond (2023) talks about poverty being a "relentless piling on of problems" (p. 13). How does this apply in this example?
- What are the solution(s) to a situation like this? How do we put forth solutions in scenarios like this? Is there a solution?

Thoughts from the Author

I talk about poverty all the time. It is essential to understand how we have divided our society into classes based on wealth, which is often amassed in awful and unfair ways. I wonder how we move past that history as a nation. It is also so important to acknowledge stereotyping and discrimination as issues of poverty. My background is in working for Medicaid systems, and I have seen first-hand how poverty impacts people's lives. The quote by Desmond (2023) about poverty being "the relentless piling on of problems" (p. 13) stuck out to me so much that it informed much of my writing and, clearly, my questions in the activities and text boxes.

I used to do home visits. The conditions that many of our Medicaid clients live in are appalling. I have been in homes in the United States without running water or heat and with empty refrigerators. I have had clients choose between their medication and food based on cost. I have had clients who chose not to call an ambulance in an emergency because of cost. And when they made those decisions or reached out for safety net programs, they were discriminated against. It is so sad that we let people live in such awful conditions in one of the richest countries in the world.

I highly recommend reading the books *Evicted* and *Poverty, By America* by Matthew Desmond as well as *Broke in America* by Joanne Samuel Goldblum and Colleen Shaddox to learn more. They shaped my understanding of this complex issue so much. Hats off to them for putting some fantastic information into the world on this complex topic.

-Dr. DeJonge

Chapter Summary Questions

1. How would you define poverty?
2. What kinds of things "pile on" (Desmond, 2023, p. 13) in poverty situations?
3. What roles do history, law, and policy play in poverty in the United States?
4. What role does racism and marginalization play in poverty in the United States?
5. What ways can we impact poverty in the United States? What can you do to impact poverty in your immediate community?

References

Assari. S. (2017, June 30). *Why poverty is not a personal choice, but a reflection of society.* University of Michigan Institute for Healthcare Policy and Innovation. https://ihpi.umich.edu/news/why-poverty-not-personal-choice-reflection-society

Blakemore, E. (2023, September 14). Poorhouses were designed to punish people for their poverty. History.com. https://www.history.com/news/in-the-19th-century-the-last-place-you-wanted-to-go-was-the-poorhouse.

Bread of the World. (2017). *Hunger and poverty in the African-American community.* https://www.bread.org/sites/default/files/african-american-fact-sheet-february-2017.pdf

Covert, B. (2019, July 2). *The myth of the welfare queen.* The New Republic. https://newrepublic.com/article/154404/myth-welfare-queen

Creamer, J., Shrider, E., Burns, K., & Chen, F. (2022, September 13). *Poverty in the United States: 2021.* U. S. Census Bureau. https://www.census.gov/library/publications/2022/demo/p60-277.html

Elliott, D. (2016, July 21). *Two American experiences: The racial divide of poverty.* Urban Wire. https://www.urban.org/urban-wire/two-american-experiences-racial-divide-poverty

Desmond, M. (2023). *Poverty, by America.* Crown.

Fessler, P. (2015, July 23). *Why disability and poverty still go hand in hand 25 years after landmark law.* NPR. https://www.npr.org/sections/health-shots/2015/07/23/424990474/why-disability-and-poverty-still-go-hand-in-hand-25-years-after-landmark-law

Gaines, A. C., Hardy, B., & Schweitzer, J. (2021, September 22). *How weak safety net policies exacerbate regional and racial inequality.* https://www.americanprogress.org/article/weak-safety-net-policies-exacerbate-regional-racial-inequality/

Goldblum, J. S., & Shaddox, C. (2021). *Broke in America: Seeing, understanding, and ending US poverty.* BenBella.

Greenstein, R. (2015, November 3). *Examining the safety net.* Center on Budget and Policy Priorities. https://www.cbpp.org/research/poverty-and-inequality/examining-the-safety-net

History.com (2023). What caused the great depression? https://www.history.com/topics/great-depression/great-depression-history

Huang, C., & Taylor, R. (2019). *How the federal tax code can better advance racial equity: 2017 tax law took step backward.* Center on Budget and Policy Priorities. https://www.cbpp.org/sites/default/files/atoms/files/7-25-19tax.pdf

Institute for Research on Poverty. (n.d.). How is poverty measured? https://www.irp.wisc.edu/resources/how-is-poverty-measured

Jackson, C. (2021, Aug 17). *What is redlining?* The New York Times. https://www.nytimes.com/2021/08/17/realestate/what-is-redlining.html

Kennedy, L. (2023). *How 'poor laws' tried to tackle poverty in colonial America.* History.com. https://www.history.com/news/colonial-america-poor-laws

KFF. (n.d.). *Poverty rates by race and ethnicity.* https://www.kff.org/other/state-indicator/poverty-rate-by-raceethnicity/?currentTimeframe=0&sortModel=%7B%22colId%22:%22Location%22,%22sort%22:%22asc%22%7D

Kilduff, L. (2022, January 31). *How poverty in the United States is measured and why it matters.* PRB. https://www.prb.org/resources/how-poverty-in-the-united-states-is-measured-and-why-it-matters/

Levin, J. (2021). *The queen: The forgotten life behind an American myth.* Back Bay.

Matthews, D. (2014, January 8). *Everything you need to know about the war on poverty*. The Washington Post. https://www.washingtonpost.com/news/wonk/wp/2014/01/08/everything-you-need-to-know-about-the-war-on-poverty/

National Alliance to End Homelessness. (2021, February 26). *Homelessness and Black history: Poverty and income*. https://endhomelessness.org/blog/homelessness-and-black-history-poverty-and-income/

PBS. (n.d.). *Jim Crow Laws*. American Experience. https://www.pbs.org/wgbh/americanexperience/features/freedom-riders-jim-crow-laws/

Race in America. (n.d.). *Laws and race*. https://digitalgallery.bgsu.edu/student/exhibits/show/race-in-us/laws-and-race

Sanchez, V. (2023, March 15). *Unpaid dementia caregiving valued at $340 billion: Alzheimer's Association report*. ABC News. https://wjla.com/news/health/alzheimers-association-report-unpaid-dementia-caregiving-jobs-valued-340-billion-washington-metro-emotional-physical-financial-challenges-dementia-disease-2023-facts-figures-diagnosis-hospital-health-caregiving-expenses-dmv-virginia-maryland

U.S. Census Bureau. (2014, January). *Measuring America: Poverty: The history of a measure*. https://www.census.gov/library/visualizations/2014/demo/poverty_measure-history.html

U.S. Census Bureau. (2022). *Measuring America: How the U.S. Census Bureau measures poverty*. https://www.census.gov/library/visualizations/2021/demo/poverty_measure-how.html

U.S. Department of Labor. (2023). *Equal pay day 2023: Department of labor initiatives seek to close gender, racial wage gap, increase equity in federal programs*. https://www.dol.gov/newsroom/releases/osec/osec20230314

Vallas, R., Knackstedt, K., & Thompson, V. (2022, April 21). *7 facts about the economic crisis facing people with disabilities in the United States*. The Century Foundation. https://tcf.org/content/commentary/7-facts-about-the-economic-crisis-facing-people-with-disabilities-in-the-united-states/

Media Attributions

- Man on Dock © Franklin D. Roosevelt Presidential Library and Museum: photo by Lewis W. Hine is licensed under a Public Domain license
- Pres. Johnson's Poverty Tour © Cecil W. Stoughton is licensed under a Public Domain license
- SNAP © US Department of Agriculture is licensed under a Public Domain license

11.

Religion in the United States

Bernadet DeJonge; Nikki Golden; and Cailyn F. Green

> **Learning Objectives**
>
> - The reader will investigate the history of religion in the United States.
> - The reader will connect the history of religion in the United States to current social justice concepts.
> - The reader will identify current issues in antisemitism and Muslim hate in the United States.

The experience of religion in the United States is varied and complex. It is generally taught in school that the United States of America was founded by individuals fleeing religious persecution (Butler et al., 2007). People in the United States proudly declare that religious freedom is a foundation of this country. However, freedom of religion was not always as "free" as the story is told. This chapter will start with a discussion of United States law and religion, provide a brief historical context on religion in the United States, and discuss the current status of two religions facing significant discrimination in the United States today, Judaism and Islam.

United States Law and Religion

The phrase "separation of church and state" was coined by Thomas Jefferson in 1802 (Ryman & Elkhorn, 2009). The First Amendment of the United States Constitution states that

> Congress shall make no law respecting an establishment of religion or prohibiting the free exercise thereof; or abridging the freedom of speech, or of the press; or the right of the people peaceably to assemble, and to petition the Government for a redress of grievances. (Congress.gov, n.d., para. 1. n.d.)

The United States Supreme Court is responsible for upholding the constitution, and thus protecting the first amendment. However, the First Amendment has been interpreted in dif-

Symbols often used or associated with Hinduism, Buddhism, Jainism, Sikhism, Judaism, Christianity, and Islam.

ferent ways by different iterations of the Supreme Court. Thus, separation of church and state in the United States has historically had a rocky, complicated, and inconsistent implementation (Sarat, 2012).

Activity 11.1 – Digging Deeper: Religious Freedom

Sarat (2012), a scholar who studies the intersection of law and religion, discusses two different Supreme Court cases regarding religious freedom to point out how the implementation of the law is not always consistent.

The first case, *Reynolds v. United States* (1879), involved a Mormon man, George Reynolds, who was convicted of bigamy under federal law. The court did not side with the defendant, who was practicing polygamy. The Supreme Court justice who wrote the deciding opinion stated that the defendant was free to believe whatever he wanted, however, he was not free to act on this in a way that violated the law. This case established the belief-action distinction in First Amendment jurisprudence.

The second case, *Wisconsin v. Yoder* (1972) involved members of the Amish community who refused to send their children to public high school, citing their religious beliefs. In this case, the Supreme Court ruled on the side of the Amish community who did not want to adhere to compulsory education laws. The deciding opinion argued that because the Amish were generally law-abiding and had a religious justification for not wanting their children to go to high school, they were allowed an exemption to the law. In this decision, the state's interest in compulsory education did not outweigh the Amish families' First Amendment right to free exercise of religion.

Discussion Questions

> - Why do you think Sarat (2012) chose to highlight *Reynolds v. United States* (1879) and *Wisconsin v. Yoder* (1972)?
> - Are these cases the same? What are the similarities? What are the differences?
> - How do we explain the inconsistencies between these two cases?
> - Is the First Amendment open to interpretation? How?

The ramifications of the legal rulings regarding the First Amendment are significant. However, there are other laws that also impact religious freedoms. Some of the most important laws protecting religious freedom in the United States are labor laws.

In the United States, it is illegal to discriminate based on religion in the workplace. The US Equal Employment Opportunity Council (EEOC, n.d.) defines religious discrimination as

> treating a person (an applicant or employee) unfavorably because of his or her religious beliefs. The law protects not only people who belong to traditional, organized religions, such as Buddhism, Christianity, Hinduism, or Judaism, but also others who have sincerely held religious, ethical or moral beliefs. (p. 1)

The EEOC goes on to clarify that it is illegal to discriminate, harass, or segregate based on someone's religious beliefs and that there is a legal obligation to provide reasonable accommodation for religious practices.

Title VI of the Civil Rights Act is also used, at times, to protect religious freedom. The Civil Rights Act covers any entity or program which receives any federal funding (US Department of Health and Human Services, n.d.). Although Title VI does not protect specifically against religious discrimination, it does protect against discrimination based on ancestry, ethnic characteristics, or citizenship from a country with a dominant religion (US Department of Education, n.d.).

Activity 11.2 – Digging Deeper: Religious Discrimination

Video: Muslim Woman Sues Company After Facing Religious Discrimination
(https://www.youtube.com/watch?v=YUkEgb15e5E)

> *One or more interactive elements has been excluded from this version of the text. You can view them online here: https://milnepublishing.geneseo.edu/social-justice-in-human-services/?p=182#oembed-1 (#oembed-1)*

Discussion Questions

- Do you think the woman in the video was discriminated against? Why or why not?

- What did the employer do that was discriminatory?
- If you were a judge, how would you rule on this lawsuit?
- Which of the laws above apply here? Discuss.

Historical Aspect of Religion in the United States

Colonialism and Christianity are intertwined throughout the complex history of the United States. Understanding how religion is experienced in the United States today starts by understanding the history of how the United States was founded and how different political, religious, and cultural forces shaped United States history.

Early Religion in the United States

White settlers brought multiple branches of Christianity to the United States. In the original English colonies, those who did not belong to accepted Christian religions had less rights than those who did. In addition, non-Christian religions were often scorned and those who practiced them, such as Indigenous people, were persecuted, ostracized, converted, and killed. Davis (2010) described:

> In newly independent America, there was a crazy quilt of state laws regarding religion. In Massachusetts, only Christians were allowed to hold public office, and Catholics were allowed to do so only after renouncing papal authority. In 1777, New York State's constitution banned Catholics from public office (and would do so until 1806). In Maryland, Catholics had full civil rights, but Jews did not. Delaware required an oath affirming belief in the Trinity. Several states, including Massachusetts and South Carolina, had official, state-supported churches. (para. 10)

A Brief History of English Colonization in the United States

The Catholic Church had pervasive political and social influence throughout the Middle Ages. However, in the early 16th century, dissidents in England rose up, and brought new ideas to Christianity. As the Protestant Reformation took hold in England, conflict developed between the English monarchy and the Catholic Church as well as some smaller branches of Christianity. Many chose to leave England due to the religious uprising. Some went to other parts of Europe. Others came to America.

The Protestant Reformation is a significant piece of the United States's origin. America was considered a place where people could freely practice different faiths. Many people migrated from England in hopes that they could establish religious communities without interference from the Catholic Church, the English monarchy, or the Church of England. Those who emigrated across the Atlantic included Puritans, Quakers, Baptists, Shakers, and Jewish people (Gjelten, 2017).

A Brief History of Spanish Colonization in the United States

As the Spanish inquisition took hold in 1492, Queen Isabella of Spain ordered all Jews and Muslims to leave Spain or convert to Christianity. Many fled to America. This immigration expanded with the sailing of Christopher Columbus to the Americas and the Spanish began to occupy much of what are now the southern United States, Central America, and South America. Missionaries saw Indigenous peoples as opportunities to spread Christianity, and "Between 1500 and 1800, as many as 15,000 European priests arrived in the Americas" (Butler et al., 2007, p. 24).

The Spanish explorers and colonists did not allow Indigenous people to openly practice their own religion, and Spanish authorities destroyed whatever Indigenous religious objects they could. The Spanish also built Catholic churches on Indigenous religious sites. In this process, the Spanish created religious, educational, and medical institutions that cemented their presence in America. Many of these sites still exist today (Butler et al., 2007).

Conversion Tactics

The English, Spanish, and later French colonists used different tactics to convert Indigenous people to Christianity, with varying results. In many areas, conversion was violent and resistance was violently squelched. In other areas, such as modern-day Eastern Canada and parts of the Southwest, colonists worked to integrate themselves into Indigenous tribes as part of their conversion tactics (Butler et al., 2007).

No matter how colonists tried to convert them, Indigenous tribes continued to reject Christianity. However, with long-term exposure to Western religion, there was some integration of Indigenous and Christian practices. As time went by, Indigenous generations were born who were only exposed to Western religions and the colonists' way of life, and some second and third generations of Indigenous people adhered to Christian principles without the need for conversion (Butler et al., 2007).

Shifting Priorities

Religious influence decreased as priorities in the colonies shifted, and in some areas such as Boston, many did not affiliate with any specific religion. While more than 90% of English colonists were Congregationalist or Anglican before 1690, no single religion could claim more than 20% as members by 1770. In addition, magic and other kinds of folk religions were becoming fashionable amongst the colonists. Trade and economic growth slowly became more important than religion to many living in the United States. The Puritans, in particular, felt this decline as Baptist, Presbyterian, and Quaker congregations competed for followers (Butler et al., 2007).

Indigenous People and Religion

Indigenous people practiced their religions for centuries in the Americas prior to the arrival of European settlers. Much of the genocide of Indigenous people in what is now the United States, including the forcing of Indigenous children into boarding schools, occurred because of religious conversion efforts.

Activity 11.3 – Digging Deeper: Genocide

Did you react to the word genocide as a description of what happened to Indigenous populations? I use this word intentionally after listening to a speech by David Treuer, an Indigenous writer. He asked us to use the proper terminology for what happened to his people when we talk about the history of the United States. He specifically and intentionally called it genocide. I encourage you to reflect on this and consider changing your terminology, too.

Discussion Questions

- What kind of reaction do you have to the word genocide? Why do you think you have it?
- Did you learn differently about what happened to Indigenous people in this country?

Butler et al. (2007) states that less is known about historical Indigenous religious practices than Christianity. What is known is that many Indigenous religions were holistic and did not separate the secular and the sacred. Thus, Indigenous religious beliefs were integrated into day-to-day life. Many Indigenous religions focused on the relationship with nature and many Indiginous rituals included spirits, visions, and dreams (Martin, 1999). Keegan (2022) warns that many scholars oversimplify Indigenous religions, often because the written history we do have is from missionaries who perpetuated Indigenous stereotypes.

Activity 11.4 – Digging Deeper: Indian Boarding Schools

So-called Indian boarding schools were a primary factor in the decimation of Indigenous culture and religion. Beginning in the late 1800s, the United States government forced hun-

> dreds of thousands Indigenous children into Indian boarding schools. By 1926, 86% of Indigenous children were in some sort of boarding school. At these schools, Indigenous children were forced to learn and conform to Christianity and Western culture (The National Native American Boarding School Healing Coalition, n.d.). These boarding schools, most of which were in the Western part of the United States, were "the dominant form of Indian education in the United States for 50 years" (Waxman, 2022, p. 1).
>
> **Video:** PBS: Unspoken: America's Native American Boarding Schools (https://www.pbs.org/video/unspoken-americas-native-american-boarding-schools-oobt1r/)
>
> **Discussion Questions**
>
> - How did Indian boarding schools impact the perception White Americans had of Indigenous people's religious beliefs?
> - How do you think the religious beliefs of Indigenous people were impacted by the Indian Boarding Schools?

Historically, Indigenous tribes did not receive First Amendment protections of religious freedom because their belief systems did not fit into Christian definitions of religion (Pluralism.org, 2020b). As Indigenous communities were forced onto reservations and their children moved into boarding schools, laws and policies were implemented to continue to prohibit their freedom to practice religion. In 1883, the Code of Indian Offenses was implemented. The code established Western-style law on the reservations. However, it also prohibited Indigenous religious practices. Tatum (2018) points out that this law, along with harsh penalties for practicing Indigenous religions, violated the First Amendment right to free exercise of religion.

In 1933, the Code of Indian Offenses was amended to reinstate Indigenous people's right to dance. However, implementation was complex and intermittent. Often authorities on reservations withheld essential supplies, such as food, to coerce Indigenous people to not practice their religious ceremonies (Pluralism.org, 2020b). It was not until the passing of the American Indian Religious Freedom Act (AIRFA) in 1978 that the United States government acknowledged that federal policies were prohibiting Indigenous people from practicing their traditional religions. AIRFA protects the right of Indigenous people to practice traditional ceremonies, to access sacred ceremonial sites, and to possess sacred objects (Proctor, 2014). While AIRFA protects Indigenous religions on paper, the Supreme Court at the time of this writing has never ruled in the favor of Indigenous people when cases have been brought forth under AIRFA (Pluralism.org, 2020b; Tatum, 2018).

Two St. Benedict's Monastary sisters, Lioba Braun and Philomena Ketten with an Ojibwe child at White Earth Boarding School near the White Earth Ojibwe Reservation, Minnesota, USA. Estimated date of 1880.

Activity 11.5 – Recent Events: The Dakota Access Pipeline

In 2015, the Standing Rock Sioux Tribe stood their ground to stop the construction of the Dakota Access Pipeline arguing that the pipeline cut through their sacred ground and violated AIRFA. The Supreme Court did not agree. Find a timeline here: Key Moments in the Dakota Access Pipeline Fight (https://www.npr.org/sections/thetwo-way/2017/02/22/514988040/key-moments-in-the-dakota-access-pipeline-fight)

Video: Standing Rock Sioux Tribe Takes Pipeline Fight to U.N. (https://www.youtube.com/watch?v=TVN8cCMlxOE)

 One or more interactive elements has been excluded from this version of the text. You can view them online here: https://milnepublishing.geneseo.edu/social-justice-in-human-services/?p=182#oembed-2 (#oembed-2)

Discussion Questions

- Do you think the pipeline violated AIRFA? Why or why not?
- What factors do you think influenced the decision of the Supreme Court in this case?
- Did the Supreme Court decision perpetuate historical religious discrimination against Indigenous people? Why or why not?

Dakota Access Pipeline protesters against Donald Trump

In an effort to align with the dominant Christian framework of the time and to assert their First Amendment right to religious freedom, tribal leaders in Oklahoma established the Native American Church of Jesus Christ in 1918 (Hinton, 2018). The church is still active today as a "loose confederation" (Pluralism.org, 2020a, para. 6). Their leaders are called Road Men and they continue to integrate Christian and Indigenous belief systems, including the ceremonial use of peyote (Pluralism.org, 2020a). In 1990, the Supreme Court did not protect members of the Native American Church in their peyote rituals, instead deferring to the laws of the State of Oregon, which considered peyote to be an illegal substance. Many feel this was in direct violation of AIRFA (Pluralism.org, 2020a).

Current trends in Indigenous religious practices in the United States have proven difficult to study. Often, religious polling excludes Indigenous religions and people. That said, research shows that most Indigenous religions still have commonalities such as deep kinship ties, community connection, ties to geographic place, and ties to the cycles of nature (Garroutte et al., 2014).

Activity 11.6 – Knowledge Check: Indigenous People and Religion

Discussion Questions

- In writing this section, I struggled to find information on the current experience in Indigenous people and religion—why do you think that might be? Do some research. What can you find?
- Do you agree or disagree with the Supreme Court ruling that peyote use is to be considered illegal drug use when considering employment? Why? What factors might be important in such a decision?
- How do you think discrimination and religion intersect in this population?

African Slaves and Religion

While many Europeans emigrated to the United States to practice their religion unobstructed, the enslavement of African people was a different kind of immigration. Slaves were seen as a commodity in the early United States and there was little effort to convert African slaves to Christian religions. Slave owners feared that slaves would see themselves as equal and revolt if introduced to Christianity. Due to these fears, African slaves were not allowed to form congregations. However, many African slaves practiced both native religions and Christianity in secret (Butler et al., 2007).

Enslaved African people practiced many religions in the early United States. Many African slaves continued to practice their local and traditional religions of West Africa. The West African religious practices varied; however, many included a single deity who was supreme and incorporated herbal medicine and charms (Mohamed et al., 2021). Despite being regularly practiced, none of the traditional African religious practices were able to be sustained in the United States (Butler et al, 2007).

Some of the slaves who arrived in the United States were already Christian or Muslim due to African colonization. As they were not allowed to form congregations, African Christian congregations developed their own style of worship, including the development of Christian worship songs based on the plight of the Israelites' escapes from Egypt, which resonated with their slave experience (Mohamed et al., 2021).

Activity 11.7 – Black Religion

Video: How Slaves Became Christian (https://www.youtube.com/watch?v=HG9MebuJMEs)

> *One or more interactive elements has been excluded from this version of the text. You can view them online here: https://milnepublishing.geneseo.edu/social-justice-in-human-services/?p=182#oembed-3 (#oembed-3)*

Discussion Questions

- How do you think the experience of being a Christian as a slave was different from the experience of being Christian as a non-slave? Where did skin color or race fit into this experience?
- Describe another historical event where conversion happened in a similar way.

In the early 1800s, a freed Black slave, Richard Allen, started the first Black Protestant church, the African Methodist Episcopal (AME) Church. Allen had been a Methodist preacher, but did not feel welcome in the church, so he decided to start his own. Similarly, the AME Zion church was founded in 1821. After the United States Civil War, the AME churches sent missionaries to the southern states to bring Black Christians into the Black churches.

Attendance in the AME churches swelled throughout the 19th and 20th centuries. Beyond religious services, the AME church communities provided job training, insurance, reading materials, education, and athletic clubs. The AME churches were often the only places where Black people were allowed leadership roles (Mohamed et al., 2021).

The cornerstone on the First African Methodist Episcopal Church building, located in Pueblo, Colorado.

In 1930, the Nation of Islam was founded by Wallace D. Fard Muhammad which provided a foundation for Black nationalism in Islamic beliefs. Muhammad preached that God was Black and that the first man created in his image was also Black. Muhammad professed that Black people were the superior race (PBS, n.d.a). Throughout the 1950s and 1960s, the Nation of Islam actively built mosques in urban areas and recruited formerly incarcerated Black men. (National Archives, n.d.). The Nation of Islam has continued to be a religious presence in the United States and is currently led by Louis Farrakhan (Mohamed, 2021).

Activity 11.8 – Digging Deeper: Malcolm X

Malcolm Little, known as Malcolm X, converted to the Nation of Islam while in prison. Over time, Malcolm X shifted some of his beliefs, eventually splitting with the Nation of Islam in 1963. However, Malcolm X's experience with the Nation of Islam impacted his belief that White people could not be trusted and that Black people should establish their own communities (UShistory.org, n.d.).

Discussion Questions

- What do you think of the idea that Black people should establish their own communities?
- How might religion have influenced the beliefs of Malcolm X and other civil rights leaders of his time?

Malcolm X in 1964

In 1975, the Southern Christian Leadership Conference (SCLC) was established, led by Dr. Martin Luther King, Jr. King spoke out against racism and discrimination using both political and religious arguments. King believed that pluralism, or the coming together of many religions, was important to the civil rights movement (Whitaker, 2023). Although King is now viewed as a civil rights icon, at the time, many at the SCLC did not support his pluralistic ideals. Unsupported, King left the SCLC and, ultimately, founded the Progressive National Baptist Convention, which fully supported his civil rights efforts (Mohamed, 2021).

Activity 11.9 – Martin Luther King Jr. and the SCLC

Video: Crash Course Black American History #36 (https://www.youtube.com/watch?v=BmeUT7zH62E)

One or more interactive elements has been excluded from this version of the text. You can view them online here: https://milnepublishing.geneseo.edu/social-justice-in-human-services/?p=182#oembed-4 (#oembed-4)

Discussion Questions

- How did Dr. King contribute to the religious history of the United States?
- How did Dr. King contribute to the Social Justice movement through religion?

Martin Luther King, Jr. at freedom rally, Washington Temple Church, 1962

Currently, Black Americans are statistically more likely to be religious than non-Black Americans. However, religious affiliation is on the decline in all demographics. Of Black Americans who report that they do go to church, 60% say they do so in a predominantly Black church. This number is lower for younger Black Americans and higher for Black elders (Mohamed, 2021). "The research also shows that Black Protestants are the only Christian group in which a majority—63%—believes that congregations should get involved in social issues even if doing so means having difficult conversations" (DeRose, 2023, para. 9). DeRose reported this statistic is probably due to the historical involvement of Black churches in the civil rights movement.

Other Populations and Religion

While history often focuses on White, Christian settlers and religion, it must also be acknowledged that other cultures and religions came to the United States in a variety of ways. People other than Christian European settlers came to the United States in search of religious freedom as well. Borja (2021) states: "America has always been much more than a tri-faith nation of Protestants, Catholics and Jews" (p. 1). Their experiences were rich and complex, and these communities helped build the country the United States is today.

Borja (2021) points out that immigrants from Asian countries were present for much of the early history of the United States. "Chinese immigrants established the first Buddhist temple in the United States in San Francisco in 1853, and Sikhs built the first Gurdwara in the United States in nearby Stockton in 1912" (Borja, 2021, p. 1). The most often cited Eastern religions include Buddhism, Hinduism, Sikhism, Daoism, and Confucianism. As of 2020, around 1% of the population of the United States identifies as Buddhist and another 1% as Hindu. In addition, another 0.5%-1% of the US population identifies as "other," which may include Eastern religions (PRRI, 2020). Eastern religions date back over 2000 years and generally refer to religious and philosophical practices that began on the continent of Asia (Harrison, 2019). Eastern religions are often framed philosophically, and Harrison points out that despite the conventional approach of lumping Eastern religions together, they vary in philosophy, belief, and cultural context across a large geographic region.

Interestingly, the trajectory of Eastern religions in the United States has been different from many other religions. There is less literature that discusses discrimination based on Eastern religious practices and more literature on the concerns around cultural appropriation of Eastern religious practices. For example, though Buddhism has seen a surge in popularity in the United States since the 1960s, many scholars point out that it is a White-centric, "Hollywood" version of Buddhism. While more than two thirds of Buddhists in the United States are Asian American, White voices dominate the religion (Kandil, 2021). Deshpande (2017) agrees, pointing out that her Hindi yoga practices, which are more than 2000 years old, have become a White-centric fitness practice.

> ### Activity 11.10 – Cultural Appropriation
>
> **Video:** Cultural Appropriation (https://www.youtube.com/watch?v=vfAp_G735r0)
>
> *One or more interactive elements has been excluded from this version of the text. You can view them online here: https://milnepublishing.geneseo.edu/social-justice-in-human-services/?p=182#oembed-5 (#oembed-5)*
>
> **Discussion Questions**
>
> - Is Yoga/Buddhism as practiced in the United States cultural appropriation or cultural appreciation? Why?
> - Is US Buddhism cultural appropriation or cultural appreciation? Or is it something different?

The Church of Jesus Christ of Latter-day Saints differs from some of the other religions because it was founded in the United States. Historically referred to as Mormons, members of The Church of Jesus Christ of Latter-day Saints are Christians, yet its members have a history of being persecuted in the United States that continues today (PEW Research Center, 2012). The Church of Jesus Christ of Latter-day Saints believe in three levels of heaven and that the Father, Son, and Holy Ghost are three separate gods versus the more traditional Christian concept of the Trinity (Harris, 2012; History.com, 2021). In the mid- to late 1800s, followers of The Church of Jesus Christ of Latter-day Saints were driven out from their midwestern homes by anti-Mormon sentiment. In 1844, the founder of The Church of Jesus Christ of Latter-day Saints, Joseph Smith, was murdered by an anti-Mormon mob while incarcerated in Carthage, Illinois. In 1847, following Smith's murder, a large group of members of The Church of Jesus Christ of Latter-day Saints who had been driven from Illinois settled in Salt Lake City, Utah. They were led by Brigham Young (Harris; History.com). Currently, The Church of Jesus Christ of Latter-day Saints make up approximately 1.7% of the population of the United States and close to 50% of the population in Utah (Pew Research Center, 2009).

> ### Activity 11.11 – Terminology: Style Guide for The Church of Jesus Christ of Latter-day Saints
>
> The Church of Jesus Christ of Latter-day Saints has a Style Guide (https://newsroom.churchofjesuschrist.org/style-guide) that clearly outlines their official name and addresses the historical use of the word "Mormon" to describe their faith.
>
> **Discussion Questions**

- Review the style guide—what surprised you about it?
- Why is it important to acknowledge and respect terminology from different religious groups?
- I struggled to decide how to word my writing in this section after reading the style guide. Was my use of the word Mormon (where I did use it) appropriate and respectful based on the guide? Why or why not? How might you have written this section differently?

In 2012, the Pew Research Center did an extensive study on The Church of Jesus Christ of Latter-day Saints. They found that 62% of followers of The Church of Jesus Christ of Latter-day Saints felt that people in the United States are uninformed about their religion, and that nearly half felt that followers of The Church of Jesus Christ of Latter-day Saints face discrimination in the United States due to their religion. Two-thirds felt that people in the United States do not see The Church of Jesus Christ of Latter-day Saints as a part of mainstream American society (Pew Research Center, 2012).

Activity 11.12 – Current Events

Read an op-ed article: The Root: Is Broadway's 'Book Of Mormon' Offensive? by Janice C. Simpson (https://www.npr.org/2011/04/15/135437800/the-root-is-broadways-book-of-mormon-offensive)

Discussion Questions

- What do you think about parodying religion? Is this the same as discrimination? Why or why not?
- How do you think this musical contributes to stereotypes about followers of The Church of Jesus Christ of Latter-day Saints?
- How do you think the Church of Jesus Christ of Latter-day Saints reacted to *The Book of Mormon*? Do some research to find out.

The United States is becoming more secular, and church attendance has recently fallen below 50% (Glasze & Schmitt, 2018). Approximately 29% of the population of the United States does not identify with any religion. This statistic has increased from previous surveys and is anticipated to continue to rise. Non-religious individuals identify as agnostic, atheist, or just identify as "nothing in particular" in survey data (Smith, 2021, para. 7). Glasze and Schmitt found that nonbelievers experienced significant discrimination when they shared their views with others. In addition, Glasze and Schmitt found that nonbelievers are often

The Book of Mormon musical, Eugene O´Neill Theater, Broadway, New York, 2011

viewed with suspicion, seen as immoral or untrustworthy, and are perceived as pushing their nonbelief on others, particularly in workplace settings.

Activity 11.13 – Digging Deeper: Atheism and Agnostic

Atheism is the belief that God does not exist.

Agnosticism is the belief that we cannot know if there is a God. Because of this, most agnostics claim to neither believe nor disbelieve in God. (Mulhern, n.d.)

Video: Christian Discrimination for Praying in Public | What Would You Do? (https://www.youtube.com/watch?v=s4SkVFrQFW4)

 One or more interactive elements has been excluded from this version of the text. You can view them online here: https://milnepublishing.geneseo.edu/social-justice-in-human-services/?p=182#oembed-6 (#oembed-6)

Discussion Questions

- What do you think you would do in this scenario?
- What are the different sides of this issue?
- Where does the law fall on this issue?
- What are the ethics and morals of this issue?
- Do people have the *right* to pray in public?

Religion and Social Justice

While religious persecution has complicated history in the United States, religion has also played a significant role in social justice movements. The civil rights movement is an example (Cooper, n.d.). In addition, social justice is often seen as a moral imperative, and thus important in many religions. Religion often plays a role in social change and people like Dr. Martin Luther King Jr., Mother Teresa, and Mahatma Gandhi all viewed social change through a religious lens. Other examples include the anti-slavery movement, welfare reform, and women's suffrage (Cooper).

While religion is intertwined with social justice movements in many ways, it is difficult to separate out religious discrimination from other kinds of discrimination. The intersection of race, gender, ethnicity, and religion must be acknowledged. On the surface, the United States welcomes all religions; it is part of our Constitution and history as a country. Yet in examining the history of religion in the United States, the prominence of Christianity has clearly muddled the separation of church and state. Examples include our president swearing in on a Bible, Christmas as a national holiday, and "In God We Trust" being printed on our currency. Historically, there has not been equal treatment of religion under the law, and this is problematic in social justice movements.

In addition to the systemic issue of Christian influence in the United States, individual religious discrimination is also a complex experience. Again, intersecting identities make it hard to separate out religious discrimination versus other kinds of discrimination. Thus, someone who is Black may experience discrimination based on their race but not because they are Christian, and someone who is White may experience privilege because of their race but be discriminated against because they are a follower of The Church of Jesus Christ of Latter-day Saints.

Activity 11.14 – Example: Religious Discrimination

Last year, my friend's son finished his freshman year in a public high school. He is a good student, plays sports, is active in music programs, and is an overall good kid. Unbeknownst to his mom, her son has been the target of serious antisemitism for years.

When my friend's son was in 6th grade, he was getting ready for his bar mitzvah. He was exploring his Jewish identity and wanted to wear a yarmulke to school. His mom wasn't sure about this for a variety of reasons; however, she supported his choice. He wore it for about a week, and within days he became the target of antisemitism. It started out with taunts like being called "Jew," getting shoved in the hallway, and eventually being excluded from groups in gym class. Comments like "Don't ask him to join us, he's a Jew" were frequent. His mother contacted the school, and the antisemitic behavior stopped for a while, but would eventually start up again. He stopped telling her when it happened so she would stop calling the school.

Over the last few years, antisemitism towards him has increased and intensified into both verbal harassment and physical bullying. Comments like "Hitler was right," and "Where is your yellow star armband?" and "cheap Jew" were frequent throughout his school day. My friend's son got more and more anxious and depressed. He didn't tell his mom that things were getting bad because he did not want to burden her. He finally confided in a friend who encouraged him to tell his mother. His mother called the school and was told that one of the boys in question had been suspended months prior for antisemitic bullying. She could not believe the school administrators never notified her.

My friend's son just spent the summer in Israel, which was hopefully an empowering experience to get him through the rest of his high school experience. —Carrie, Jewish American

Discussion Questions

- How might the prolonged experience of antisemitism affect a young person's mental health and self-esteem? What coping mechanisms might be helpful for this student?
- What responsibilities do schools have in preventing and addressing bullying, particularly when it involves hate speech and discrimination?
- What long-term strategies can be implemented to foster a more inclusive and respectful school culture?
- How does antisemitism in schools reflect broader societal issues, and what can be done at a community level to address these?
- What are some ways to educate students about diversity, tolerance, and the harmful effects of discrimination?

Religious discrimination happens often in the United States. Much like other forms of discrimination, religious discrimination can be overt and systemic or covert and individualized. There are entire books dedicated to religion and religious discrimination. However, for the purposes of this text, a choice had to be made in terms of what to highlight. Thus, while acknowledging that there are many other stories and experiences in the United States around religion, we have chosen to focus this section on two religions that are currently and glaringly experiencing discrimination. These are the Jewish and Muslim faiths.

Judaism in the United States

Judaism is one of the oldest religions in the world. There are 14 million Jewish people worldwide (History.com, 2023) and Jewish people make up 1–2% of the population in the

United States (PRRI, 2021). Jewish people believe in one God who revealed Himself to ancient prophets and in the covenant between God and the Jewish people. Most Jewish people do not believe that Jesus was crucified and then raised from the dead three days later. Jewish people worship in synagogues and their spiritual leaders are referred to as rabbis. Their sacred text is the Tanakh. The Tanakh contains the same content as the Christian Bible's Old Testament, but some of it is in slightly different order (History.com, 2023).

The Spanish Inquisition led to significant Jewish migration to the United States starting in 1492. During Colonial times, most Jews in the English colonies were Sephardic Jews from the Iberian Peninsula. Jewish people settled in many metropolitan areas, such as New York City and Philadelphia, and began to establish synagogue-communities, which served the Jewish population in those cities. During the Civil War, there were Jewish people on both sides. However, xenophobic tensions increased during this time, and antisemitism and Jewish stereotyping surged. By the 1800s, the United States saw an infusion of Eastern European Jews, bringing the Yiddish language with them. Often these Ashkenazic immigrants had different religious tenets from the Jews already living in the developing United States, leading to some in-group discrimination (Sarna & Golden, n.d.).

The Holocaust Museum (n.d.) defines Antisemitism as "prejudice against or hatred of Jews" (para 1). Antisemitism has occurred since ancient times and scholars argue that the source of this antisemitism goes back to the role that Jewish people played in the crucifixion of Christ. This attitude shifted some in 1965 when, at a meeting of the Second Vatican Council, the Catholic Church repealed the theme of Jewish responsibility for the crucifixion. The term "Judeo-Christian tradition" resulted from this meeting (Anti-Defamation League, 2023).

National Menorah Lighting, Washington, DC

> **Activity 11.15 – Current Research: Jewish Holidays**
>
> In a recent survey (https://www.ajc.org/AntisemitismReport2022), 26% of Jewish college students and 10% of Jewish workers struggled to take time off for Jewish holidays (Huffnagle & Bandler, 2023).
>
> **Discussion Questions**
>
> - Is it fair that Jewish people do not officially get their holidays off? Why or why not?
> - Why do we celebrate Christmas as a national holiday and not Hanukkah?
> - How would you feel if we no longer recognized Christmas as a national holiday?

Hernandez (2021) states that nearly one quarter of Jewish Americans experienced antisemitism in 2020. The Anti-Defamation League (2023) states that in 2022 they recorded the highest number of antisemitic incidents since 1979 and, in 2022, a report by Tel Aviv University found that antisemitism is rising in the United States (Associated Press, 2023). Huffnagle and Bandler (2023) referred to this trend as "The mainstreaming of antisemitism in American society" (para. 3). Examples of antisemitic incidents include vandalism, harassment, and assault (Shveda, 2023). Interestingly, this trend only seems to be happening in the United States. Other countries with large Jewish populations, such as England and Canada, have seen a decrease in antisemitism (Associated Press, 2023).

Jewish people continue to feel unsafe in the United States. In a 2022 report, the American Jewish Committee (AJC) found that antisemitism is felt on a deeply personal level. Often, protecting oneself from antisemitism involves a suppression of personal identity, which in turn alters behavior. Examples cited included avoiding posting online content that clearly identified an individual as a Jew, avoiding wearing traditional Jewish clothing or accessories, and avoiding certain places or situations (Huffnagle & Bandler, 2023). Huffnagle and Bandler go on to state that American Jews feel less safe in America than they did the previous year, and that security at United States synagogues has increased.

The internet has become a place where antisemitism is a significant concern. Eighty-two percent of the population has observed antisemitism online. Huffnagle and Bandler (2023) state that

> The prevalence of antisemitism online has made the virtual communications sphere, with its limitless reach, the leading space for anti-Jewish prejudice, conspiracies, and hatred, and younger American Jews are more likely to be experiencing this form of hate. (para. 17)

Of those who reported experiencing antisemitism online, 72% did not report it to the online platform. Many of the participants who were younger Jews felt physically threatened in their online interactions (Huffnagle & Bandler, 2023).

> ### Activity 11.16 – Current Events: Antisemitism
>
> Research shows that visibly identifiable Jews—usually ultra-Orthodox Jews and younger Jews—are more targeted for antisemitism (Associated Press, 2023; Huffnagle & Bandler, 2023).
>
> Discussion Questions
>
> - What factors might contribute to the increased targeting of visibly identifiable Jews, particularly ultra-Orthodox and younger individuals, in acts of antisemitism?
> - How should communities and policymakers address the specific vulnerabilities faced by visibly identifiable Jewish populations while promoting broader efforts to combat antisemitism?

Personal contact with Jews makes one more aware of antisemitism and decreases the likelihood of engaging in antisemitic behavior (Huffnagle & Bandler, 2023). In addition, Davis (2022) recommends that individuals call out antisemitism when they see it. This may be in larger public and political spaces, such as cutting contracts with celebrities who make antisemitic remarks, or in personal settings, such as pointing out when someone makes antisemitic comments or jokes. In addition, Davis points out that when the media gives someone a platform for their antisemitic views through continuous news coverage, this may amplify those views. He recommends that those in power who make antisemitic statements be called out and publicly denounced.

> ### Activity 11.17 – Jewish Life in America
>
> **Video:** How Has Life Changed for Jews in America? (https://www.youtube.com/watch?v=gDZHNuS2L3o&t=375s)
>
> *One or more interactive elements has been excluded from this version of the text. You can view them online here: https://milnepublishing.geneseo.edu/social-justice-in-human-services/?p=182#oembed-7 (#oembed-7)*
>
> **Current Research:** Huffnagle and Bandler (2023) state that the more an individual knows about the Holocaust, the more likely they are to recognize antisemitism. In addition, having knowledge of the Holocaust increases recognition that antisemitism is rising.

Discussion Questions

- How did you learn about the Holocaust?
- Does your knowledge of the Holocaust increase your recognition of antisemitism? Why or why not?
- As history fades and the last of the Holocaust survivors die, how might this impact antisemitism in the United States?

Additional Resources: Videos

One or more interactive elements has been excluded from this version of the text. You can view them online here: https://milnepublishing.geneseo.edu/social-justice-in-human-services/?p=182#oembed-8 (#oembed-8)

One or more interactive elements has been excluded from this version of the text. You can view them online here: https://milnepublishing.geneseo.edu/social-justice-in-human-services/?p=182#oembed-9 (#oembed-9)

One or more interactive elements has been excluded from this version of the text. You can view them online here: https://milnepublishing.geneseo.edu/social-justice-in-human-services/?p=182#oembed-10 (#oembed-10)

Islam in the United States

Islam is also one of the dominant world religions. Those who practice Islam are called Muslims. It is not clear when the first Muslims arrived in the United States. Many point to African Muslims brought as slaves. However, some argue that small pockets of Muslims arrived in the Americas by the 14th century. Between 1878 and 1924, the United States saw a surge of Muslim immigrants from the Middle East, many of whom settled west of the original 13 colonies. By 1952, there were more than 1,000 mosques in the United States (PBS, n.d.b).

Muslims believe there is one God and many prophets, the last of which was Muhammad. In Islam, God is called Allah and the place of worship is called a mosque. Muslims have six major beliefs and five pillars (URI.org, n.d.).

The six major beliefs are

- Belief in one God—Allah
- Belief in the Angels
- Belief in three holy books—the Torah, the Bible, and the Qur'an.
- Belief in multiple prophets sent by God, which includes Jesus, who is seen as a prophet and not the son of God

- Belief in the day of judgment and life after death
- Belief in divine decree that everything happens with God's permission but God has given people free will; God will question everyone when they die about how they lived (URI.org, n.d.)

The five pillars are

- Shahadah—the declaration of faith
- Salat—the five daily prayers
- Zakah—almsgiving of 2.5% of wealth to the poor and needy
- Sawm—fasting during Ramadan
- Hajj—pilgrimage to Mecca at least once in their lifetime (URI.org, n.d.)

Muslims are about 1% of the total population of the United States. That said, Muslim population is forecasted to increase to 2.1% by the year 2025, which will equate to about 8.1 million Muslims in the United States. This anticipated increase is due to a combination of increased immigration from politically unstable Muslim countries and the generally young demographic of the Muslim population who are expected to have children in the United States (Constante, 2018). While Muslim and Middle Eastern or Arab are often used interchangeably, they are not interchangeable. Muslim communities in the United States include individuals from all ethnic groups. In addition, up to two thirds of all Arab Americans in the United States identify as Christian (Peek, 2011).

Activity 11.18 – Digging Deeper: What is Sharia?

Sharia is the legal system of Islam. Sharia law is a way of life for Muslims and is based on the Qur'an, the Sunnah, and Hadith–all religious texts. If a law cannot be found in the text, a crime is taken to religious scholars. A formal ruling under Sharia is called a *fatwa*. Sharia is not static–it has changed over time and continues to evolve. Muslims see Sharia as an integral part of their faith, thus when Sharia law is stereotyped as a threat, it makes no sense to them (Ali & Duss, 2011; BBC News, 2021)

Discussion Questions

- Did you already know what Sharia law is?
- Where have you learned about Sharia law?
- What biases might you have had towards Sharia law?
- How might the media have influenced your understanding of Sharia law?

Being Muslim has become intertwined with being Arab or Middle Eastern in the United States, and it is often difficult to pull that intersectionality apart. Peek (2011) describes this well:

> In the aftermath of 9/11, the media and public officials often used the terms "Muslim" and "Arab" interchangeably. This conflation of categories led to the perception among many that all Muslims are Arab and that all Arabs are Muslim. This is certainly not the case. Muslim is an identifier used to describe those who believe in the religion of Islam, and thus Muslims can come from any nation and be of any racial or ethnic background. An estimated 1.57 billion Muslims live in countries spanning the globe, and only about 20 percent of the world's Muslims reside in Arabic-speaking countries. (p. 11)

The Pre-9/11 Experience of Being Muslim in the United States

Muslims were in the Americas before the colonies were established and have been in what is now the United States since the 14th century (PBS, n.d.b). That said, finding history of the Muslim population is difficult due to dominant Puritan influences and the slave trade. Interestingly, there are hints that Muslim culture influenced the Spanish colonists and that while the Muslim faith was looked upon with some suspicion, it also was integrated into some of colonial life (Haselby, 2019).

In the early 20th century, many Muslim families in developing countries sent children to college in the United States. Some of these students remained in the United States, and pockets of American Muslim communities continued to grow in most major cities. As of 2011, nearly 60% of American Muslims had college degrees, including a significant portion of Muslim women. Thus, American Muslims are less likely to experience poverty and many work in well paying, professional jobs (Peek, 2011).

Despite this economic success, the stereotypes of Muslims were persistent even before the terrorist attacks of September 11, 2001. Many of these stereotypes were derived from film and television. Depictions of Muslims in the media included equating the Muslim daily prayer with guns and violence, the oppression of women, holy wars, and terrorism. Muslims were depicted as violent, primitive, and hateful (Peek, 2011).

Activity 11.19 – Knowledge Check: Muslims in Early America

Discussion Questions

- Did it surprise you to learn that Muslims were in the Americas before the original colonists? Why do you think that is not common knowledge?
- What role does education and income levels play in our assumptions about Muslim people?
- What kind of media depictions have you seen of the Muslim faith? How has this influenced your assumptions about people who practice Islam?

The Post-9/11 Experience of Being Muslim in the United States

Prior to the terrorist attacks on September 11, 2021, religious discrimination was the least reported type of discrimination (Dean, 2016). However, the terrorist attacks of September 11, 2001 changed the relationship between Muslim and non-Muslim Americans in a variety of ways. Peek (2011) points out the negative role the media played in the experience of American Muslims following the attacks: "In the aftermath of 9/11, religious leaders, politicians, media pundits, and self-proclaimed terrorism experts exploited the feelings of an already-terrified citizenry by offering gross overgeneralizations and blatantly incorrect depictions" (p. 5).

After the terrorist attacks of September 11, 2001, discrimination towards American Muslims intensified and religious discrimination claims to the U.S. Department of Justice more than doubled (Dean, 2016). Americans started to perceive Islam as a threat, and many believed that Muslims wanted to kill all Christians and Jews. Muslims endured racial profiling, arrest, threats, bullying, harassment, and calls for Muslim bans. Anti-Muslim hate included the federal government raiding mosques, Muslims being denied boarding on planes, Muslim children being bullied, and American Muslims being discriminated against in the workplace. In addition, Arab men were arrested, detained without council, and deported (Peek, 2011).

Islam continues to grow in the United States with the number of mosques in the United States doubling between 2000 and 2020. In 2006 the first Muslim was elected to the House of Representatives. However, even more than 20 years after the terrorist attacks of September 11, 2001, religious discrimination continues to be an issue for American Muslims, with 48% reporting they had personally experienced some sort of discrimination in 2017 (Mohamed, 2021).

> ### Activity 11.20 – Current Research: Middle Eastern College Students
>
> Abuelezam et al. (2022) compared the experience of White and Middle Eastern college students. They found that college students who identified as Middle Eastern and had experienced discrimination struggled with increased depression and anxiety. White students and Middle Eastern students who had not experienced discrimination had fewer mental health symptoms. That said, Abuelezam et al. also found that being religious was a protective factor against depression and anxiety. So, while students of Middle Eastern descent were often targeted due to their religious and ethnic backgrounds, those who had strong religious convictions were able to manage that discrimination more effectively.
>
> **Discussion Questions**
>
> - What does this research tell us about the current experience of Middle Eastern college students?
> - Why might religion be a protective factor for college students?
> - What other factors might be contributing to the experience of Middle Eastern college students?

When people in the United States who are non-Muslim know someone who is Muslim, they are more likely to view Muslim individuals favorably. Personal contact with Muslim peers leads to people being more likely to both see Muslims as nonviolent and object to violations of their civil liberties. Research has shown that many people in the United States do not understand the Muslim faith and that this lack of understanding leads to more discrimination (Muhamed, 2021; Peek, 2011).

Activity 11.21 – Knowledge Check: Discrimination Against American Muslims

Discussion Questions

- Do you know anyone who is Muslim? How might that impact your assumptions towards people who follow Islam?
- How can we defend the civil rights of American Muslims? Give some examples.
- What implications does the research cited about knowing people who are Muslim have? How might we use this research to impact the experience of American Muslims?

Additional Resources

Depictions of the Islamic Experience in the United States:

 One or more interactive elements has been excluded from this version of the text. You can view them online here: https://milnepublishing.geneseo.edu/social-justice-in-human-services/?p=182#oembed-11 (#oembed-11)

One or more interactive elements has been excluded from this version of the text. You can view them online here: https://milnepublishing.geneseo.edu/social-justice-in-human-services/?p=182#oembed-12 (#oembed-12)

 One or more interactive elements has been excluded from this version of the text. You can view them online here: https://milnepublishing.geneseo.edu/social-justice-in-human-services/?p=182#oembed-13 (#oembed-13)

 One or more interactive elements has been excluded from this version of the text. You can view them online here: https://milnepublishing.geneseo.edu/social-justice-in-human-services/?p=182#oembed-14 (#oembed-14)

Thoughts from the Author

This chapter was one of the hardest to write for a variety of reasons. It got written, edited, re-written, discussed, and debated more than any other among me and my peers as I worked on this chapter. And sometimes I simply avoided it all together. It was just so much to take in. Working on this chapter became a United States history lesson I didn't know I needed. I felt some strong feelings about the state of being Jewish or Muslim in the United States, and I hope you do too. And I found some of my biases that I need to work on, too. I learned so much in writing this chapter and couldn't fit all information and nuances I wanted to; I encourage students to learn more.

Sincerely,

Dr. DeJonge (Bernie)

Chapter Summary Questions

1. What did you learn about the history of religion in the United States? How might this learning impact how you view religion in the United States today?
2. How does religion connect with social justice?
3. How does your religious upbringing (or lack thereof) affect how you view people of different religions?

4. What are your thoughts on the inclusion of atheism and agnosticism in this chapter? Do they belong here? Why or why not?
5. How can we decrease antisemitism in the United States? How can you decrease it personally?
6. How can we decrease hatred against Muslims in the United States? How can you impact it personally?

References

Abuelezam, N. N., Lipson, S. K., Awad, G. H., Eisenberg, D., & Galea, S. (2022). Depression and anxiety symptoms among Arab/Middle Eastern American college students: Modifying roles of religiosity and discrimination. *PLOS One, 17*(11). https://doi.org/10.1371/journal.pone.0276907

Ali, W., & Duss, M. (2011, March 31). *Understanding Sharia law*. CAP. https://www.americanprogress.org/article/understanding-sharia-law/

Anti-Defamation League. (2023, Match 23). *Audit of antisemitic incidents 2022*. ADL. https://www.adl.org/resources/report/audit-antisemitic-incidents-2022

Associated Press. (2023, April 17). *Antisemitic incidents on rise across the U.S., report finds*. PBS. https://www.pbs.org/newshour/politics/antisemitic-incidents-on-rise-across-the-u-s-report-finds

BBC News. (2021, August 19). *What is Sharia law? What does it mean for women in Afghanistan?* https://www.bbc.com/news/world-27307249

Borja, M. (2021, May 3). *How Asian American religious history changes how we write American religious history*. Patheos. https://www.patheos.com/blogs/anxiousbench/2021/05/how-asian-american-religious-history-changes-how-we-write-american-religious-history/

Butler, J., Wacker, G., & Balmer, R. (2007). *Religion in American life: A short history*. Oxford University Press.

Congress.gov. (n.d.). *First Amendment explained*. https://constitution.congress.gov/constitution/amendment-1/

Constante, A. (2018, January 9). *Muslim projected to be the second-largest U.S. religious group by 2040*. NBC News. https://www.nbcnews.com/news/asian-america/muslims-projected-be-second-largest-u-s-religious-group-2040-n836191

Cooper, Z. (n.d.). Christianity's long history of social justice. *The Guardian*. https://www.theguardian.com/world/2021/jan/03/christianitys-long-history-in-fighting-for-social-justice

Davis, K.C. (2010, October). America's true history of religious tolerance. *Smithsonian Magazine*. https://www.smithsonianmag.com/history/americas-true-history-of-religious-tolerance-61312684/

Davis, W. (2022, December 1). *How to address antisemitic rhetoric when you encounter it.* NPR. https://www.npr.org/2022/12/01/1139929829/how-to-address-antisemitic-rhetoric-when-you-encounter-it

Dean, K. L. (2016, May 17). *Religious discrimination is "un-American."* [Video]. Tedx Talks. https://www.youtube.com/watch?v=7365IO9l-tw

DeRose, J. (2023, May 16). *The importance of religion in the lives of Americans is shrinking* [Radio broadcast]. NPR. https://www.npr.org/2023/05/16/1176206568/less-important-religion-in-lives-of-americans-shrinking-report

Deshpande, R. (2017, October 27). Yoga in America often exploits my culture-but you many not even realize it. *Self.* https://www.self.com/story/yoga-indian-cultural-appropriation

Garroutte, E. M., Anderson, H. O., Nez-Henderson, P., Croy, C., Beals, J., Henderson, J. A., Thomas, J., & Manson, S. M. (2014). Religio-spiritual participation in two American Indian populations. *Journal for the Scientific Study of Religion, 53*(1), 17-37. https://doi.org/10.1111/jssr.12084

Gjelten, T. (2017, June 20). *To understand how religion shapes America, look to its early days* [Radio broadcast]. NPR. https://www.npr.org/2017/06/28/534765046/smithsonian-exhibit-explores-religious-diversitys-role-in-u-s-history

Glasze, G., & Schmitt, T. M. (2018). Understanding the geographies of religion and secularity: On the potentials of a broader exchange between geography and the (post-) secularity debate. *Geographica Helvetica, 73,* 285-300. https://doi.org/10.5194/gh-73-285-2018

Harris, D. (2012). *What do Mormons believe?* ABC News. https://abcnews.go.com/US/mormons-%09/story?id=17057679.

Harrison, V. S. (2019). *Eastern philosophy: The Basics* (2nd ed.). Routledge.

Haselby, S. (2019, May 20). *Muslims of early America.* Aeon. https://aeon.co/essays/muslims-lived-in-america-before-protestantism-even-existed

Hernandez, J. (2021, October 26). *1 in 4 American Jews say they experienced antisemitism in the last year.* NPR. https://www.kcrw.com/news/shows/npr/npr-story/1049288223

Hinton, C. (2018, October 10). Native American church marks 100 years. *The Oklahoman.* https://www.oklahoman.com/story/news/religion/2018/10/10/native-american-church-marks-100-years/60496231007/

History.com. (2023, August 11). *Judaism.* https://www.history.com/topics/religion/judaism

History.com. (2021, October 7). *Mormons.* https://www.history.com/topics/religion/mormons

Huffnagle, H., & Bandler, K. (2023). *The state of antisemitism in America 2022: Insights and analysis.* American Jewish Committee. https://www.ajc.org/news/the-state-of-anti-semitism-in-america-2022-insights-and-analysis

Kandil, C. Y. (2021, July 9). *Young Asian American Buddhists are reclaiming narrative after decades of white dominance.* NBC news. https://www.nbcnews.com/news/asian-america/young-asian-american-buddhists-are-reclaiming-narrative-decades-white-rcna1236

Keegan, B. (2022). Contemporary Native American and Indigenous religions: State of the field. *Religion Compass, 16*(9). https://doi.org/10.1111/rec3.12448

Martin, J. W. (1999). *The land looks after us: A history of Native American religion.* Oxford University Press.

Mohamed, B. (2021, September 1). *Muslims are a growing presence in U.S., but still face negative views from the public.* Pew Research Center. https://www.pewresearch.org/short-reads/2021/09/01/muslims-are-a-growing-presence-in-u-s-but-still-face-negative-views-from-the-public/

Mohamed, B., Cox, K., Diamant, J., & Gecewicz, C. (2021, February 6). *A brief overview of Black religious history in the U.S.* Pew Research Center. https://www.pewresearch.org/religion/2021/02/16/a-brief-overview-of-black-religious-history-in-the-u-s/

Montana.gov. (n.d.). *ICWA history and purpose.* https://dphhs.mt.gov/cfsd/icwa/icwahistory#:~:text=The%20Indian%20Child%20Welfar%20e%20Act,placed%20in%20non%2DIndian%20families

Mulhern, K. (n.d.). *What is the difference between an atheist and an agnostic?* Patheos. https://www.patheos.com/answers/what-is-the-difference-between-an-atheist-and-an-agnostic

National Archives. (n.d.). *The Nation of Islam.* https://www.archives.gov/research/african-americans/black-power/nation-of-islam

PBS. (n.d.a). *Elijah Muhammad and the Nation of Islam.* https://www.pbs.org/wgbh/americanexperience/features/malcolmx-elijah-muhammad-and-nation-islam/

PBS. (n.d.b). *Islam in America.* https://www.pbs.org/opb/historydetectives/feature/islam-in-america/

Peek, L. (2011). *Becoming Muslim: The development of a religious identity.* Oxford University Press.

Pew Research Center. (2009). *A portrait of Mormons in the U.S.* https://www.pewresearch.org/religion/2009/07/24/a-portrait-of-mormons-in-the-us/

Pew Research Center. (2012). *Mormons in America-Certain of their beliefs, uncertain of their place in society.* https://www.pewresearch.org/religion/2012/01/12/mormons-in-america-executive-summary/

Pluralism.org. (2020a). *Native American church.* The Pluralism Project: Harvard University. https://pluralism.org/native-american-church

Pluralism.org. (2020b). *Religious freedom for Native Americans.* The Pluralism Project: Harvard University. https://pluralism.org/religious-freedom-for-native-americans

Proctor, E. (2014). *What is the Indian Religious Freedom Act of 1978?* MSU Extension. https://www.canr.msu.edu/news/what_is_the_indian_religious_freedom_act_of_1978

PRRI. (2020). *The American religious landscape in 2020.* https://www.prri.org/research/2020-census-of-american-religion/

Ryman, H. M., & Alcorn, J. M. (2009). *Establishment clause (Separation of church and state).* The First Amendment Encyclopedia. https://firstamendment.mtsu.edu/article/establishment-clause-separation-of-church-and-state/

Sarat, A. (Ed.) (2012). *Legal responses to religious practices in the United States: Accommodation and its limits.* Cambridge University Press.

Sarna., J. D., & Golden, J. (n.d.). *The American Jewish experience through the nineteenth century: Immigration and acculturation.* National Humanities Center. https://nationalhumanitiescenter.org/tserve/nineteen/nkeyinfo/judaism.htm

Shveda, K. (2023, March 23). *Antisemitic incidents in the US are at the highest level recorded since the 1970's.* CNN. https://www.cnn.com/2023/03/23/us/antisemitism-report-unprecedented-rise-dg/index.html

Smith, G. A. (2021, December 14). *About three-in-ten U.S. adults are now religiously unaffiliated.* Pew Research Center. https://www.pewresearch.org/religion/2021/12/14/about-three-in-ten-u-s-adults-are-now-religiously-unaffiliated/

Tatum, M. (2018, February 20). *No religious freedom for traditional native religions.* Berkley Center for Religion, Peace, and World Affairs. https://berkleycenter.georgetown.edu/responses/no-religious-freedom-for-traditional-native-religions

The Holocaust Museum. (n.d.). *What is antisemitism?* https://www.ushmm.org/antisemitism/what-is-antisemitism

The National Native American Boarding School Healing Coalition. (n.d.). *US Indian boarding school history.* https://boardingschoolhealing.org/education/us-indian-boarding-school-history/

U.S. Department of Education, Office of Civil Rights. (n.d.). *Know your rights: Title VI and religion.* https://www2.ed.gov/about/offices/list/ocr/docs/know-rights-201701-religious-disc.pdf

U.S. Department of Health and Human Services. (n.d.). *Civil Rights Requirements- A. Title VI of the Civil Rights Act of 1964, 42 U.S.C. 2000d et seq. ("Title VI").* https://www.hhs.gov/civil-rights/for-individuals/special-topics/needy-families/civil-rights-requirements/index.html

U.S. Equal Employment Opportunity Commission (EEOC). (n.d.) *Religious discrimination.* https://www.eeoc.gov/religious-discrimination

Ushistory.org. (n.d.). *Malcom X and the Nation of Islam.* https://www.ushistory.org/us/54h.asp

URI.org. (n.d.). *Islam: Basic beliefs.* https://www.uri.org/kids/world-religions/muslim-beliefs

Waxman, O. B. (2022, May 17). The history of Native American boarding schools is even more complicated than a new report reveals. *Time.* https://time.com/6177069/american-indian-boarding-schools-history/

Whitaker, R. (2023). *MLK's version of social justice included religious pluralism – a house of many faiths.* The Conversation. https://theconversation.com/mlks-vision-of-social-justice-included-religious-pluralism-a-house-of-many-faiths-197785

Media Attributions

- Religious Symbols © Shiva is licensed under a CC BY-SA (Attribution ShareAlike) license
- Ojibwe child is licensed under a Public Domain license
- Dakota Access Pipeline © Fibonacci Blue is licensed under a CC BY (Attribution) license

- First AME Church © Jeffrey Beall is licensed under a CC BY (Attribution) license
- Malcolm X © Library of Congress is licensed under a Public Domain license
- MLK Jr. © O. Fernandez is licensed under a Public Domain license
- Book of Mormon © André-Pierre du Plessis is licensed under a CC BY (Attribution) license
- Menorah © Ted Eytan is licensed under a CC BY-SA (Attribution ShareAlike) license
- Quran © Nina Zeynep Güler is licensed under a CC BY-NC (Attribution NonCommercial) license
- End Islamophobia © Fibonacci Blue is licensed under a CC BY (Attribution) license

12.

Ability in the United States

Bernadet DeJonge and Shannon Raybold

> **Learning Objectives**
>
> - The reader will examine the experience of disability in the United States.
> - The reader will explore historical events in the disability rights movement in the United States.
> - The reader will connect the disability rights movement to concepts of social justice.
> - This chapter will review core concepts of disability, the history of disability in the United States, and the disability rights movement. It will also discuss disability legislation and connect the disability rights movement to current social justice issues.

Definitions in Disability

Defining disability is a complex task. The Americans with Disabilities Act (ADA.gov, 2020) states:

> An individual with a disability is defined by the ADA as a person who has a physical or mental impairment that substantially limits one or more major life activities, a person who has a history or record of such an impairment, or a person who is perceived by others as having such an impairment. (para 2)

While this may be the legal definition of disability under this federal law, there are many different interpretations of what constitutes a disability. Many argue that all people exist on a spectrum and that differences are to be expected and valued. These individuals take issue with the definition of disability as being substantially different and feel the focus on an unsustainable cultural norm of what it is to be human is inappropriate. Other people identify with the label of disability as a significant part of who they are—they see it as a culture in and of itself. This divergence in perspectives has also contributed to the ongoing debate over language, particularly whether to use first-person ("I have a disability") or identity-first

("I am disabled") terminology, reflecting deeper questions of autonomy, pride, and the right to self-definition. An excellent example of this is the Deaf community. In between these two extremes lies a range of different definitions of disability, which is well beyond the scope of this introductory text.

> ### Activity 12.1 – Digging Deeper: Models of Disability
>
> Disability has been seen in different ways throughout history. Often, we refer to these as "models of disability." See below for some common models.
>
> The moral model: The moral model sees disability as stemming from God. Disability is somehow a mark of shame or wrongdoing. While this is often seen as a historical way of looking at disability, the attitude of morality is still very prevalent in the way that disability is perceived today, particularly globally (Olkin, 2022).
>
> The medical model: The medical model sees disability as something to be cured. The goal is to return the person to as close to "normal" as possible. Experts are professionals with specialized training and language is clinical. In this model, the problem is the person, and the goal is to seek a cure. Medical care is the prevalent need (Olkin).
>
> The social model: The social model sees disability as one aspect of a person's identity. In this way of viewing disability, the environment and society create the barriers, not the person or their disability. Thus, change needs to occur on a societal level versus changing the individual with a disability. Olkin goes on to say that, "Negative stereotypes, discrimination and oppression serve as barriers to environmental change and full inclusion" (para 5) in the social disability model.
>
> **Discussion Questions**
>
> - How do you think these models have evolved through time?
> - How might these models continue to impact people with disabilities today?
> - Do some research—what other models are out there?

Understanding the different definitions of disability and becoming familiar with several important terms in disability studies is crucial. These terms are fundamental to the study of disability:

- Acquired Disability: a disability that one acquires. For example, someone who loses a limb in a car accident or becomes quadriplegic from a diving accident.
- Congenital Disability: a disability someone is born with. For example, Down Syndrome or dwarfism.

- Invisible or Nonapparent Disability: a disability that is not clearly visible. For example, a mental illness, neurodiversity, or learning disability.
- Visible Disability: a disability that is clearly visible. For example, someone with Down syndrome or an amputation.

Activity 12.2 – Digging Deeper: Defining Disability

Website: Disability Definition (https://www.disabilitydatainitiative.org/method-briefs/disability-definition/)

Discussion Questions

- How would you define disability? Do some research and see the different ways people define disability.
- What is the role of the individual who identifies with a disability in defining disability?
- Can you think of an instance where it might be hard to tell if a disability is acquired or congenital?
- How do you think each kind of disability (acquired, congenital, invisible/non-apparent, visible) might differ in the experience of the individual?

Accessibility and Universal Design

Accessibility refers to the ability of people with varying abilities to access spaces, goods, education, and services with similar effort. Examples of accessibility include ramps, rails, ASL interpreters, and closed captioning. Accessibility is about equity and creates an environment where goods, education, and services are fair and equitable for everyone by eliminating barriers. Accessibility is about being person-centered and recognizing how someone's needs can be met in a given environment (SeeWriteHear.com, n.d.).

Universal design is a broader concept than accessibility. Universal design examines how environments, products, and services can be accessed, understood, and used by a wide spectrum of people who wish to use them (Center for Excellence in Universal Design, 2023). The term universal design was coined by Ron Mace, who was an architect and had polio as a child, which led him to be a wheelchair user. Mace's principles of universal design included equitable use, flexible use, simple and intuitive use, perceptible information, tolerance for error, low physical effort, and size and space for approach and use (Center for Universal Design, n.d.). The founding principle of universal design is that accessibility to all should be a right, not the privilege of the majority. Universal design assumes that a range of human abilities is typical and expected, not the exception. Therefore, products, spaces, and services should be designed to allow the broadest range of abilities to use them independently and with the same effort. This promotes dignity and respect. Universal design is a human-centered approach (Center for Excellence in Universal Design, 2023).

> ### Activity 12.3 – Current Issues: Accessibility and Universal Design
>
> Some stores and businesses include elements of universal design in their business practices. One example is businesses designating times for people with sensory processing differences. Some movie theaters, stores, and events have made "sensory-friendly" experiences for groups that need a quieter and calmer environment by opening early when the store is not crowded and leaving the overhead music off. Some movie theaters host special showings of movies with a lower volume, with the lights up, and allow people to move around and talk as needed during the film.
>
> Discussion Questions
>
> - How might movie theaters provide accessibility to movies?
> - How might movie theaters apply universal design to their theaters?
> - What is the difference between the two?

Early American History of Disability

During colonial times in the United States, people with disabilities were looked upon as God's punishment. This belief stemmed from European views on disability, and it was believed that people with disabilities and, by association, their families were morally corrupt (Ericsson, 2022). It was shameful to have a family member with a disability, and many kept their disabled relatives hidden away in their homes (Fox & Marini, 2024).

During this time, people with disabilities were seen as impetuous children who refused to conform to society's rules. Thus, fear and often abuse were used to change behavior. Treatment for disability was severe and included bleeding, corporal punishment, and confinement by chains (Ericsson, 2022). In addition, people with disabilities in the early United States were often persecuted or hanged as witches when they acted outside of social norms (Fox & Marini, 2024).

Early in American history, people with disabilities were also seen as a burden in the developing colonies. Being able-bodied was embedded in colonial culture, and every person was expected to contribute in a specific way. People with disabilities fell outside that narrow focus (Nielsen, 2012). Thus, people with disabilities were not permitted to immigrate to the colonies, and if they did arrive, they were often sent back to England (Ericsson, 2022; Fox & Marini, 2024; Reed, n.d.). This policy became official law with the Federal Immigration Act of 1882, which outlawed the immigration of people with disabilities to the United States. This law was used well into the 1900s to discriminate against people with disabilities (Fox & Marini, 2024).

As the colonies grew, Elizabethan poor laws, initially established in England, also migrated to the colonies. Anyone needing assistance would go to the Overseer of the Poor to be judged worthy of aid. Often, men with disabilities were deemed unworthy as it was expected that they would be able to work and support themselves (Wagner, n.d.). As the population in the United States swelled, poorhouses were established. People with disabilities intermixed with the poor in poorhouses regardless of their economic status and were subjected to overcrowding, abuse, and other maltreatment (The Disability Union, 2020).

Activity 12.4 – Digging Deeper: Cognitive versus Physical Disability

Nielsen (2012) points out that much of the colonial history of disability focuses on intellectual or cognitive disabilities and less on physical disability. She argues this through a social lens, stating that, at the time, having a physical disability was seen as less of a strain on society. Because of the dangers of living in the newly established colonies, physical disability was expected and was not viewed in the same way as psychological, intellectual, or cognitive disabilities were. Nielsen points out that many colonists with physical disabilities had jobs, married, had children, and were considered productive members of society.

Discussion Questions

- What does it mean to see disability through a social lens? How might this impact how we have seen disability throughout history?
- Do we still see people with physical disability differently than those with cognitive disability?

Into the 1800s, many in the upper and middle class saw poorhouses and, later, institutionalization as a method to cure or treat people with disabilities, including children. However, that was far from how they were run. Poorhouses were intentionally uncomfortable and overcrowded in order to encourage people to work by making accessing assistance miserable (Wagner, n.d.).

Activity 12.5

Video: The History of the Wayne County Poorhouse and Asylum-Eloise (https://www.youtube.com/watch?v=OEucvjNT2sg&t=366s)

Discussion Questions

- Many of the people who cared for Eloise's residents were not doctors but local politicians. What does this say about how people with disabilities were perceived?
- What concerns might you have about the idea that we can "cure" people with disabilities? What kind of consequences might there be to this attitude?
- There were often children in these asylums and poorhouses. What kind of impact might institutionalization have had on the children? What might the short- and long-term consequences of this be?

Following the Revolutionary War, many soldiers found themselves impoverished due to both disability and the low value of Continental currency. Before the war, people who acquired a disability were often sent back to England. However, post-revolution, public sentiment had changed, and many felt that veterans should be helped. For the first time in American history, the government stepped in and provided a pension to disabled soldiers, and the Continental Congress Pension Act was enacted on August 26, 1776 (The Disability Union, 2020). Four more acts followed in 1818, 1820, 1832, and 1836. The Act of 1836 also included widows of veterans (National Park Service, 2023).

Activity 12.6 – Digging Deeper: Did you know? There were people with disabilities involved

Central Indiana Hospital for the Insane from the Legislative and State Manual of Indiana, 1903

in the American Revolution.

Gouverneur Morris, an amputee, helped draft the constitution. He wrote the entire preamble, including the famous phrase "We the People." Gouverneur Morris had a severely burned and deformed right arm and had lost his left leg below the knee in a carriage accident. All historical depictions of Gouverneur Morris hide his leg and arm (de Groot, 2020).

Stephen Hopkins signed the Declaration of Independence and was active in the first Continental Congress. Medical historians believe he had Cerebral Palsy. He was famous for saying, "My hand trembles, but my heart does not." His signature is larger than all but John Hancock's (The Disability Union, 2020).

Signature of Stephen Hopkins on the Declaration of Independence.

Foundation of the American Government by John Henry Hintermeister. From the painting's copyright description: "Signing of the Constitution. At desk sits Washington watching Gouverneur Morris sign; behind Morris are Roger Sherman, Franklin, Robert Morris, Madison and others, and at right Hamilton and Randolf."

Discussion Questions

- In what ways do the stories of Morris and Hopkins provide a more inclusive and diverse understanding of American history? How can their inclusion in historical narratives impact contemporary views on disability and social justice?
- Considering the erasure or minimization of disabilities in historical depictions, what steps can historians and educators take to ensure a more accurate and inclusive representation of individuals with disabilities?
- When the authors did research on Stephen Hopkins in particular, they found historical websites that did not even mention his disability. What does this say about how we still see disability today?

After the Revolutionary War, public sentiment started to shift from seeing disability as a moral issue to seeing disability as a medical issue. Medical science was growing during this time, and many began to utilize physicians to diagnose and treat disability. In 1825, the U.S. Supreme Court started using the term "disease" instead of "madness" (Nielsen, 2012, p. 68) to define cognitive disabilities. As physician training became standardized, practitioners of folk medicine and midwives who had cared for people in the past were left behind. Physicians now control diagnosis and treatment (Nielsen, 2012).

Institutionalization

Treatments for those with disabilities continued to be varied and often cruel throughout the late 1800s. As treatment shifted from home-based care to physician-care, many experienced bloodletting, confinement, purging, labor, restraint, and immersion therapy in their homes at the hands of physicians. Those who were institutionalized also faced cruelty in their treatment and were often confined, chained, beaten, and starved. Often, institutions lacked heat, blankets, enough food, or appropriate bedding (Nielsen, 2012).

As the medicalization of disability took hold, institutionalization came into fashion to treat people with disabilities. The first hospital-style institution in the United States was the American Asylum for the Deaf, founded in 1817 (Nielsen, 2012). Many institutions were private initially, but by the mid-1800s, publicly funded institutions began to open for individuals with disabilities. Thus began the split between private care and public assistance in care. As happens today, as well, many who could not afford to pay for care ended up in homeless shelters (almshouses) and prisons (Wagner, n.d.).

The rise of institutionalization was a significant shift in the experience of individuals with disabilities in the United States. In the mid-1800s, most children and adults who had disabilities were generally integrated into society. Many went to school, worked, and married. However, as institutionalization took hold, societal views again shifted. Nielsen (2012) points out that "Family members of those with cognitive disabilities, once admired for their devotion and care, now experienced shame. With increased shame came increased institutionalization" (p. 72).

Institutionalization varied by location and more institutions were founded in the northern states than in the southern states. Those in the southern states tended to be of poorer quality unless they were specifically for the wealthy. Institutions were often self-sustaining as the concept of the almshouse or poorhouse shifted towards poor farms. Most institutions were in the country, away from the public eye, and many had working farms. These working farms are often cited as the start of vocational rehabilitation therapy (Ericsson, 2022).

Activity 12.7

Video: Institutionalized: The Story of State Hospitals (https://www.youtube.com/watch?v=wmAqPe65M5c)

> *One or more interactive elements has been excluded from this version of the text. You can view them online here: https://milnepublishing.geneseo.edu/social-justice-in-human-services/?p=199#oembed-1 (#oembed-1)*
>
> **Discussion Questions**
>
> - Were you aware of the history of institutionalization in the United States? What surprised you the most about this history?
> - In what ways do you think the legacy of institutionalization has contributed to societal perceptions and stigma surrounding disability?
> - Why is it important for the general public to be aware of the history of institutionalization of people with disabilities? How can increased awareness contribute to social justice and inclusion?
> - What kinds of impacts might the historical experience of institutionalization have on the experience of having a disability today?

Indigenous Populations and Disability

The Indigenous populations of the Americas had a different lens on disability than their European counterparts. In Indigenous tribes, disability was often seen as a normal part of life. Some tribes felt that disability was due to an imbalance or angering of the gods. However, most did not punish the individuals or families for this. They would do what was needed to right the imbalance, and the person would be integrated into society. Just as some people were better at hunting and some at making clothing, people with disabilities would be put to work utilizing their strengths to support the community (Nielsen, 2012).

As diseases brought from Europe decimated Indigenous tribes, being able to care for those with disability became more complex. Smallpox brought disability to the tribes, as those who survived were often blinded and scarred. Tribes no longer had solid and interconnected societies, and people with disabilities who did not perish in waves of epidemics could not be cared for in the same way. In addition, the shifting priorities of tribes to war with the colonists may have impacted the perception of people with disabilities who were not fit to battle their oppressors (Nielsen, 2012).

Activity 12.8 – Digging Deeper: Sign Language and Universal Design

Did you know that Indigenous people used sign language amongst tribes? This allowed tribes to communicate with each other, even when they did not speak the same language.

In addition, it created opportunities for those who were Deaf or hard of hearing to communicate. This is a great historical example of universal design (Nielsen, 2012).

Discussion Questions

- Were you aware that Indigenous tribes used sign language to communicate with each other? How does this change your understanding of the communication methods used by Indigenous peoples historically?
- How might the use of a shared sign language among tribes have impacted cultural exchange and the preservation of different languages and traditions? What are some potential benefits and drawbacks of this practice?
- In what ways did the use of sign language among Indigenous tribes provide opportunities for Deaf and hard-of-hearing individuals to participate in their communities? How does this compare to the inclusion of Deaf and hard-of-hearing individuals in other historical contexts?
- Are there stereotypes about Indigenous people using sign language? What tone do these stereotypes carry?

African Slavery and Disability

Nielsen (2012) states: "Disability permeated the ideology, experience, and practices of slavery in multiple and profound ways" (p. 42). She goes on to state that owning slaves who were perceived to be sound of mind and body was essential to slave traders and owners in the United States. As Black people were kidnapped from their homes in Africa, those who were not fit to work were often killed. Those who were captured endured disease, malnutrition, mental stress, and abuse on their journey to the United States. Frequently, this experience led to disability. Chattel slaves who arrived with disabilities in the United States did not have value and were often killed or left to die on their own when they did not sell for a high price (Nielsen, 2012).

Nielsen (2012) also points out that chattel slavery was justified by comparing Africans to people with disabilities. Enslaved people were said to lack intelligence in direct comparison to individuals with intellectual disabilities. It was believed that enslaved people could not survive without White supervision and care due to their physical and mental defects. Nielsen goes on to state that "The concept of disability justified slavery and racism—and even allowed many whites [sic] to delude themselves, or pretend to delude themselves, that via slavery they beneficially cared for Africans incapable of caring for themselves" (p. 57).

In addition to using the language of disability to justify chattel slavery, the experience of chattel slavery often led to disability. Chattel slavery involved heavy, repetitive labor as well as poor housing, poor working conditions, and emotional, physical, and sexual abuse. Enslaved people were often intentionally disabled or disfigured by cropped ears, scars, gunshot wounds, inadequate medical care, improperly healed fractures, and loss of fingers, toes, and limbs. When this occurred, enslaved people with disabilities had less value to their White enslavers. That said, they still labored. Often, disabled chattel slaves worked doing menial work. In addition, chattel slaves with disabilities were frequently utilized to care for both enslaved children and to work caring for White children. When chattel slaves with disabilities were deemed not useful, they were either killed or set "free" to die (Nielsen, 2012, p. 63).

Activity 12.9 – Digging Deeper: Abolitionist

Abolitionists (people who were anti-slavery) also used the language of disability to further their cause. Many argued that slavery had disabled the slaves by forcing them to be dependent on their White masters. To further their cause, they published detailed reports of disfiguring abuse and the impairments it caused. Abolitionists felt that emancipation would heal the disabling effects of slavery.

Discussion Questions

- Nielsen (2012) argues that the language of disability was used to justify chattel slavery. How did the language of the abolitionists contribute to assumptions about people with disabilities?
- How does the intersection of disability and race in the context of chattel slavery challenge or complicate traditional narratives of both disability history and African American/Black history?
- What are the long-term effects of the narratives created by abolitionists on the perception of African Americans and people with disabilities today?

The Industrial Revolution (1780-1870)

The Industrial Revolution changed how people worked in the United States. This included people with disabilities. Industrialization brought about mass production, which relied on able-bodied workers who could work long hours under poor working conditions. These conditions often excluded those with any mental or physical limitations (Fox & Marini, 2024). Individuals with disabilities had previously been able to work from home. However, they could not access the industrialized working environment in the same way. Nielsen (2012) describes this well:

This sign is just outside the Abington Quaker Meeting house, where Benjamin Lay and Sarah Lay are buried.

> The regulation and standardization of industrialization...had made it more difficult for people with impairments to earn a living. A young woman unable to walk had easily worked in her family's shoemaking industry. She could not, however, continue to make shoes as shoemaking slowly transferred from home industries to the factories of New England. She would not be able to live in the inaccessible dormitories available to female factory workers...she would not be able to walk the distances demanded of her; nor would other factory workers be as willing as her family members to make food available to her nearby her residence or aid in emptying her chamber pot. (p. 74)

In addition to changing work environments, industrialization led to an increase in individuals with acquired disabilities. Accidents were common in the fast-paced workshops, and workers had no legal protections. Generally, when individuals were injured, they were fired and lost their ability to make a living. Employees could sue. However, they typically lost based on the assumption that the accident was negligence by themselves or their coworkers (not the company) and that they knew the risks when they took the job (Fox & Marini, 2024).

Activity 12.10 – Digging Deeper: Industrialization and Public Schools

The public school system rose out of industrialization, and the industrialized "one size fits all" workplace format of the industrial period is also what public schools in the United States

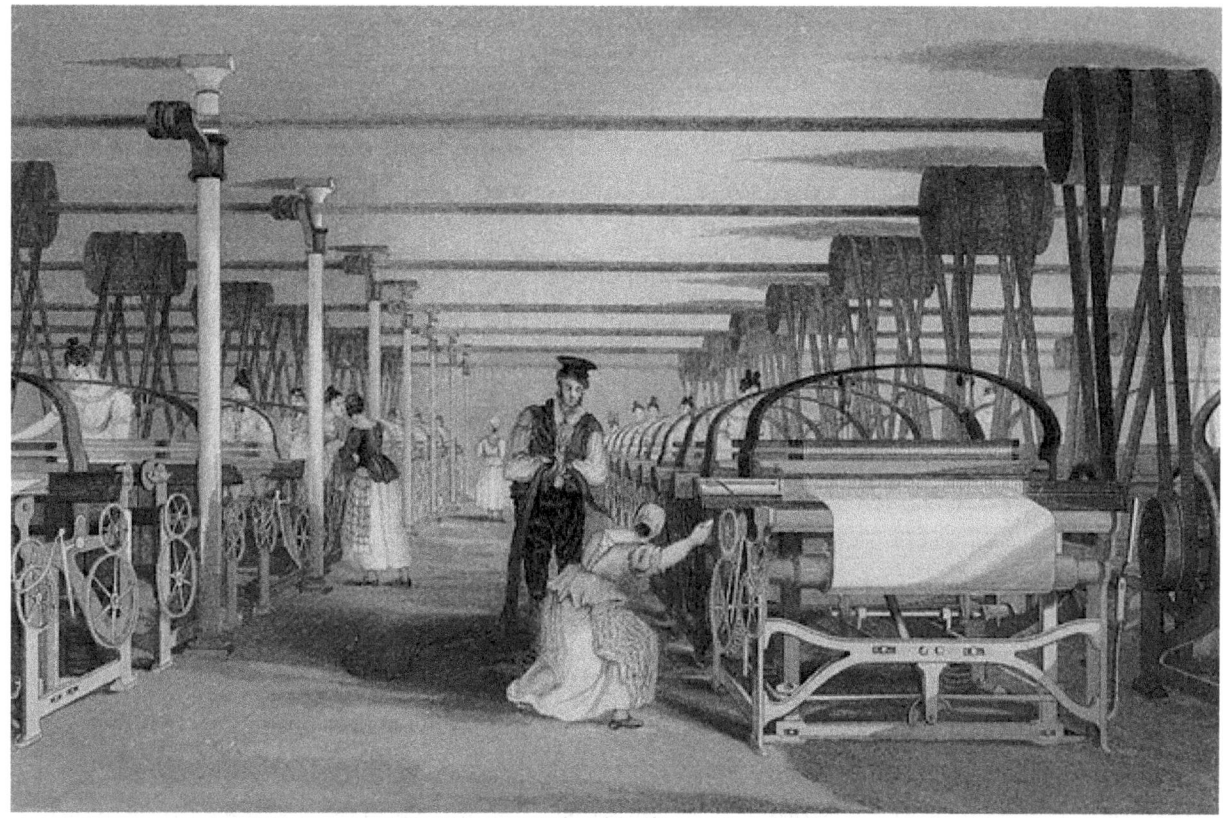

Powerloom weaving in 1835.

were modeled after. Thus, children with disabilities experienced a similar shift in their day-to-day experience as their adult counterparts as schools emulated the work environment (Schrager, 2018). Many argue that this experience of building public schools during industrialization has continued to impact how schools are run today.

Discussion Questions

- How did the rise of industrialization influence the development of the public school system in the United States? What aspects of the industrial workplace were emulated in the school environment?
- What are the potential benefits and drawbacks of an education system modeled after industrial workplaces? How do these aspects specifically affect students with disabilities?
- What are some alternative education models that challenge the traditional industrial approach? How might these models better serve students with disabilities?

The Civil War 1861-1865

Much like the Revolutionary War, the United States Civil War had significant consequences around the experience of disability. While people were more likely to die than survive substantial injury at the time, some did survive, and again, war brought about the need for wounded soldiers to return home. Pensions continued to be expanded for veterans, and homes were established for returning soldiers who needed care. In addition, the advent of photography meant that veterans with disabilities were more visible to the public (Nielsen, 2012).

Activity 12.11 – Digging Deeper: The Invalid Corps

In 1863, President Abraham Lincoln established the Invalid Corps. The Invalid Corps was meant to release able-bodied men from more menial tasks by giving those tasks to disabled veterans. This allowed able-bodied men to return to the front lines. Tasks included guarding prisoners, warehouses, and railways; enforcing the draft; supply runs; cooking and cleaning; clerical work; and marching in parades. The Invalid Corps was renamed the Veteran Reserve Corps in 1864 to boost morale as the initials IC were also used for rotten food stamped as "Inspected-Condemned." This, plus discrimination against people with disabilities, led to ridicule of the men in the Invalid Corps. Despite the intention that the Invalid Corps would not fight on the front lines, many ended up in battle as a part of their service (McQuade, 2023; Nielsen, 2012).

Discussion Questions

- Why do you think the Invalid Corps is not commonly taught in history classes?
- How might the Invalid Corps have fit into the narrative of disability at the time? How does it fit into the narrative of disability that we have today?

Many Black soldiers also fought in the Civil War and acquired disabilities from their service. However, due to racism, it was much more difficult for Black soldiers to receive the pensions owed them. Often, they had to travel long distances to apply for the pensions. Once they did this, they also needed to be literate enough to fill out extensive forms or find someone to do it. Even if they overcame these obstacles, the agents who managed the programs were overtly racist and denied claims regularly (Nielsen, 2012).

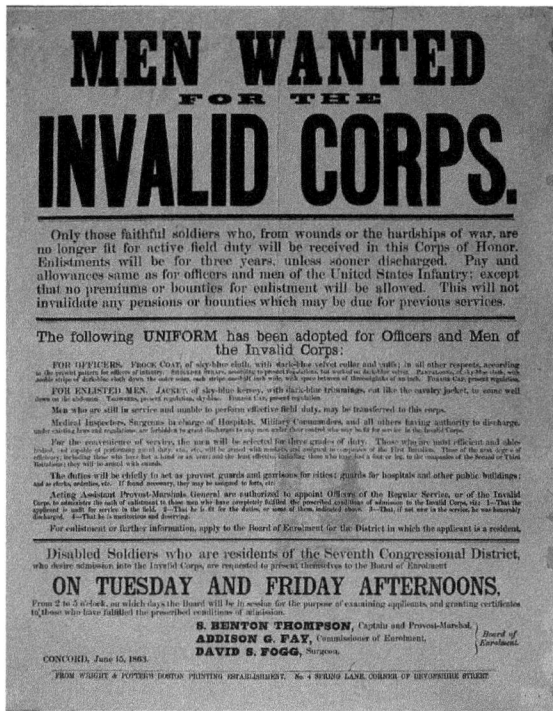
Men wanted for Invalid Corps notice, 1863

The Progressive Era to the New Era (1890-1927)

The late 1800s and early 1900s brought new experiences to those with disabilities. As the 1800s ended, the polio epidemic was in full swing. Not only did people who were already disabled acquire polio, but people who did not previously have a disability became disabled from the disease. Institutionalization, family structure, and the social perception of people with disabilities were all influenced by the polio epidemic. In addition, eugenics, forced sterilization, and institutionalization became prevalent issues in the disabled community.

Activity 12.12 – Digging Deeper: The 1916 Polio Epidemic

The first wide-scale epidemic in European settlers in the United States was the polio epidemic of 1916. Polio left many people disabled, particularly those who had it as children, as it causes paralysis and weakness in muscles. Many children were removed from their homes and institutionalized due to polio and its aftereffects. This often led to the formation of a community among survivors.

Discussion Questions

- How do you think the polio epidemic changed public perception of disability?
- In some ways, the polio epidemic created community amongst survivors; in other

> ways, it ripped families apart when children/family members were institutionalized. How do you think this experience impacted the families left at home and their view of disability?

Eugenics and Forced Sterilization

The eugenics movement started in the early 1900s and continues to be a concern for disability rights today. Eugenicists of the early 1900s argued that success was genetic and that selective breeding would lead to a superior race of humans. The eugenics movement of the 1900s was spurred by the popularization of Darwin's theory on the survival of the fittest and the rise of formalized medicine as doctors began to philosophize on the origins of illness and disability. Proponents of the eugenics movement believed that people who were wealthy and successful should have children to propagate successful humans, and those who were poor and disabled should not (Fox & Marini, 2024). The advent of salpingectomy (tying tubes in women) and vasectomy combined with eugenics led to the forced regulation of individual reproduction in the United States (Nielsen, 2012).

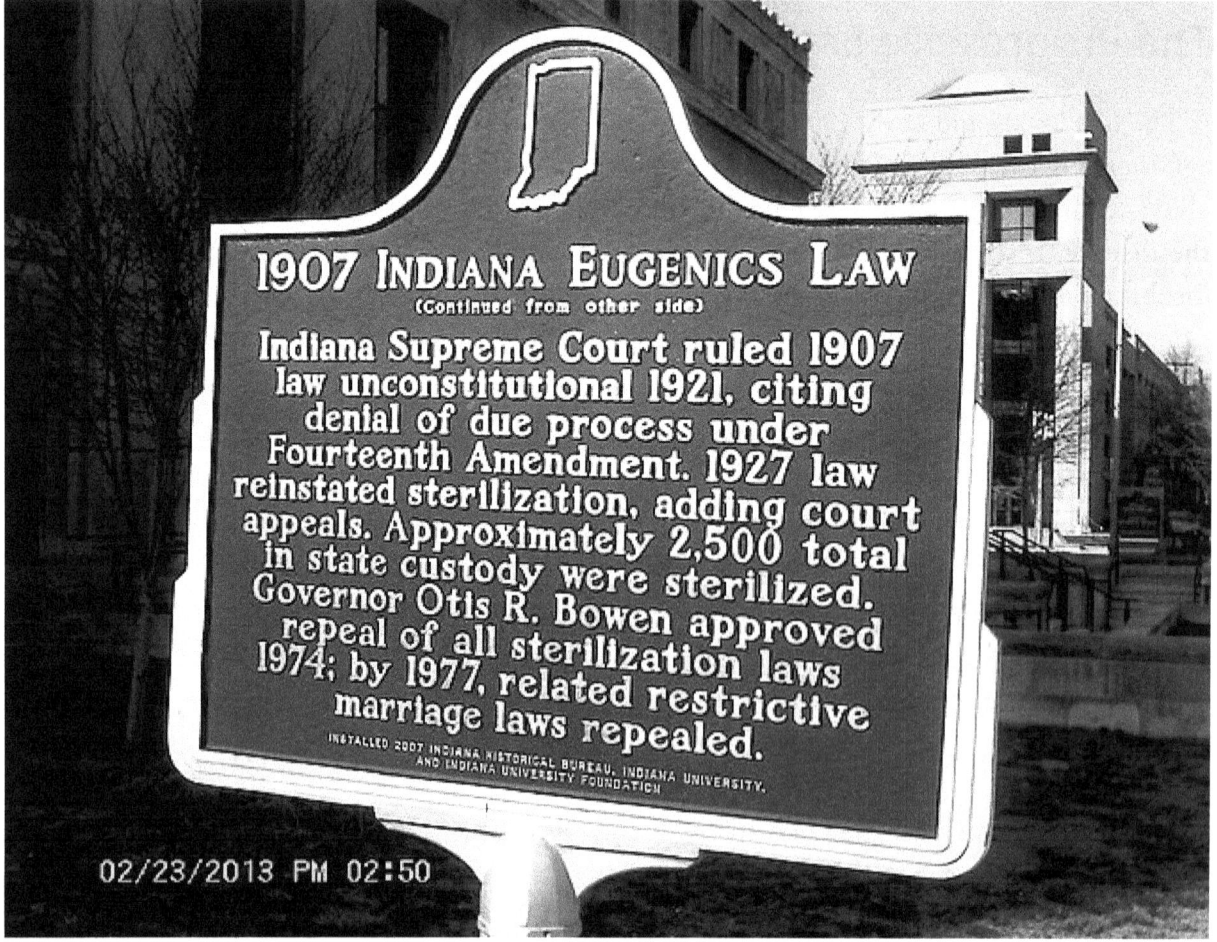

In 1896, Connecticut was the first state to forbid people with disabilities to marry or have sexual relations, and other states followed suit. Public support for these laws was high, and they soon expanded into forced sterilization. The first sterilization law was passed in Indiana in 1907. By 1926, 24 states had sterilization laws on the books. Of these states, 17 still had forced sterilization laws well into the 1980s. It is estimated that by 1950, 60,000 people had been forcibly sterilized in the United States (Fox & Marini, 2024).

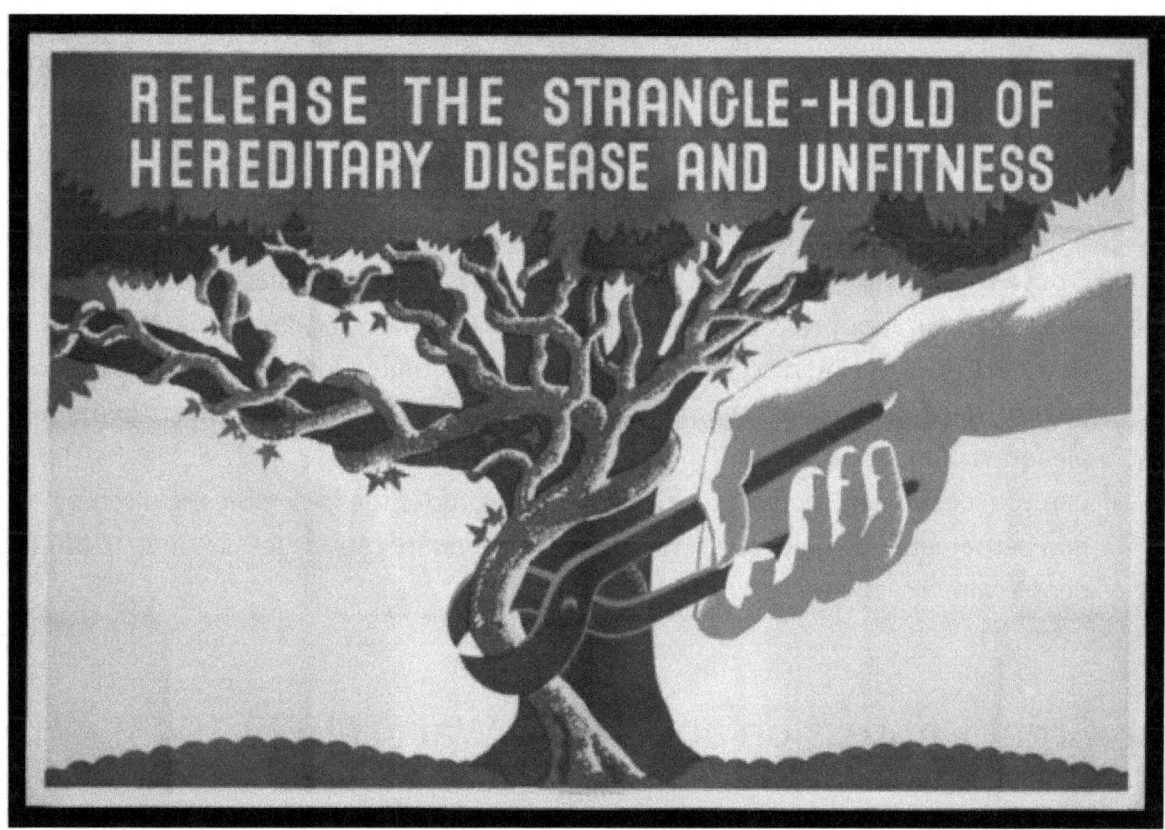

Eugenics Society Poster (1930s).

World War II significantly impacted the public perception of eugenics in the United States. Once America took sides in the war, Nazi Germany was seen as barbaric and something to rally against. The Nazis murdered an estimated 300,000 German citizens who were deemed disabled throughout World War II, and eugenics as an overt science fell out of fashion in the United States as people began to associate eugenics with Nazi concentration camps (Fox & Marini, 2024). Despite this change in public perception, forced sterilization and reproductive justice continue to be a conversation in the disability rights movement to this day (National Women's Law Center, 2022).

> **Activity 12.13 – Digging Deeper: Ugly Laws**
>
> Ugly Laws were enacted to keep unsightly beggars and people with apparent deformities and scarring off the streets of cities in the United States. The first Ugly Law was passed in San Francisco in 1867. Other western states followed, and these laws became common in many states (Fox & Marini, 2024). The last arrest for an Ugly Law violation was in Omaha, Nebraska, in 1974, when a homeless man was arrested for having scars. The arrest was not prosecuted (Manoukian, 2023).
>
> **Discussion Questions**
>
> - What do Ugly Laws and eugenics have in common?
> - From a social justice perspective, how do Ugly Laws highlight issues of discrimination and marginalization? How did these laws perpetuate inequality and social exclusion?
> - How did Ugly Laws intersect with other forms of discrimination, such as those based on race, gender, or socioeconomic status? Discuss the compounded effects of multiple forms of marginalization.
> - Can you identify any modern policies or social attitudes that resemble the discrimination perpetuated by Ugly Laws? How do these contemporary issues continue to affect people with disabilities?

The Great Depression and World War II (1929-1945)

The stock market crash of 1929 started the biggest economic downturn in United States history—the Great Depression. Banks failed, and the life savings of millions of Americans were lost (SSA.gov, n.d.). The eugenics movement continued to impact the lives of those with disabilities as eugenicists shifted their argument to economics instead of genetics as jobs became scarcer (LEAP, n.d.). People with disabilities were again seen as worthless and a burden. In addition, people with disabilities faced crushing unemployment rates, with some estimating it to be more than 80 percent (Rosenthal, n.d.).

Franklin Delano Roosevelt (FDR) was elected president in 1932. FDR believed that the federal government needed to rescue the American people from the Great Depression. He implemented policies known as the New Deal, which encompassed bank reform, agricultural programs, emergency relief, work relief, union protection, social security, and programs for tenant and migrant farmers (Library of Congress, n.d.). Many programs brought about by the New Deal excluded people with disabilities. This exclusion led to some of the first advocacy protests for disability rights in the United States (Nielsen, 2012).

Activity 12.14 – Digging Deeper: Franklin Delano Roosevelt

Did you know we had a president with a disability? FDR had post-polio syndrome and was paralyzed from the waist down. This was hidden from the public because he did not want to be seen as weak. Interestingly, even the Press Corps and those closest to him, such as Secret Service agents, conspired to hide the extent of his disability, and there were only two times during his presidency that he was shown as clearly disabled (Fleischer & Zames, 2011).

Discussion Questions

- Were you aware of FDR's disability? Why do you think FDR's disability was not emphasized during his presidency and beyond?
- The eugenics movement and discrimination towards people with disabilities was at an all-time high during the Great Depression. How do you think someone with a disability was able to be elected president during these times? What factors may have contributed to this?

President Roosevelt in his wheelchair on the porch at Top Cottage in Hyde Park, NY with Ruthie Bie and Fala. February 1941. This photograph was taken by his friend, Margaret "Daisy" Suckley.

As the United States entered World War II in 1941, there was a need to fill jobs as able-bodied men left to fight overseas. Many women stepped up to work during this time through the popular Rosie the Riveter campaign. Less well known is that the employment of people with disabilities surged during this time, as well. By 1945, 300,000 individuals with disabilities were placed through government agencies in workplace settings. By 1950 that number was almost 2 million (Nielsen, 2012).

Workplace accidents also increased during this time. The increased pace of industry was dangerous to workers, who were often undertrained and overworked. Speed was often more important than safety, and many were disabled in industrial accidents during World War II. Nielsen (2012) suggests it was safer to be on the battlefield during this time than to work in industry on the home front.

Activity 12.15 – Digging Deeper: World War II and Rationing

Many goods were rationed during World War II, including gas and rubber for tires. Early advocates for individuals with disabilities argued that rationing unfairly impacted those who could not access public transportation, such as those with physical disabilities. People who relied on personal transportation to get to work and other commitments found themselves suddenly stuck and unable to receive accommodation. This rationing then excluded individuals with disabilities from filling much-needed jobs during World War II (Nielsen, 2012).

Discussion Questions

- How might rationing have impacted people with disabilities more than those without?
- How might the experience of rationing be different for people with disabilities in the current day? How might it be the same?
- Compare this experience of people with disabilities during World War II to that of people with disabilities during the COVID-19 pandemic. What are the similarities? What are the differences?

World War II also impacted the institutions housing people with disabilities. Many institutions faced staffing shortages and crises as staff left to fight in the war. Men went to war, and women left to fill their jobs in factories and other arenas (Nielsen, 2012). Nielsen goes on to say that:

> At the same time, the federal government sought placements for the nearly twelve thousand World War II conscientious objectors assigned to public service. Nearly three thousand were assigned to state mental hospitals and training schools containing an array of people with cognitive and developmental disabilities. (p. 144)

These conscientious objectors found harsh working conditions, long days, and severe abuse of the patients they were charged with caring for. This led many to speak out against the conditions of institutions. They reached out to community leaders, the media, academics, and other influential Americans with a plea to improve institutional conditions. The influence of media, including photographs, brought the brutality of institutionalization to the masses (Nielsen, 2012).

> ### Activity 12.16 – Digging Deeper: The Impact of War
>
> Both World War I and World War II resulted in soldiers returning home with disabilities. As these soldiers were seen as war heroes, there was support for rehabilitation and support for them as they were disabled while serving the United States. Both wars led to advances in rehabilitation and technology and more government funding for such developments (Anti-Defamation League, 2024).
>
> **Discussion Questions**
>
> - Is there a bias toward acquired disability versus a congenital one in our society? Why?
> - What are the implications of war equating to a surge in advances in disability technology and rehabilitation? Discuss.
> - Do we perceive veterans who have acquired disabilities differently than those who acquired disabilities outside of war? Why?

Vocational Rehabilitation

The concept of vocational rehabilitation was born out of war. Soldiers from both World Wars I and II had come home disabled, and society felt a need to support them as heroes. This support led to the Smith-Hughes Vocational Education Act in 1917 and the Smith-Sears Veterans Rehabilitation Act in 1918. Both acts provided funding for veterans' training, jobs, and follow-up services. In 1920, the Smith-Fess Act established federal vocational rehabilitation for civilian citizens (Fleischer & Zames, 2011).

> ### Activity 12.17 – Digging Deeper: Soldiers and Civilians
>
> Despite the passing of vocational rehabilitation acts for soldiers, soldiers found accessing services to be complicated. This led to the formation of advocacy groups. One of the largest and most prominent was the Disabled American Veterans of the World War (DACWW), which advocated for veterans with disabilities. The DACWW lobbied to disassociate soldiers

needing vocational rehabilitation and civilians. Thus, the legislation that was passed in the 1920s through the 1940s was separate for disabled civilian citizens and veterans.

Discussion Questions

- FDR advocated for rehabilitation to include both soldiers and civilians and the DACWW rallied against this. What are the two sides to this argument?
- Why might it make sense to combine soldiers and civilians? Why might it not?

By the 1920s, vocational rehabilitation had taken hold for civilians and soldiers. While some laws separated specific rehabilitation services for veterans, public support was in favor of vocational rehabilitation for all. While this was an advance in the experience of individuals with disabilities, attitudes towards individuals with disabilities were often paternalistic. People with disabilities were not given choices but instead were told what to do by vocational rehabilitation specialists who claimed they knew better and could guide their clients in the right direction. Client choice and self-determination were not a part of the early rehabilitation experience (Fleming et al., 2024).

Activity 12.18 – Digging Deeper: The Social Security Act

In 1935, FDR signed the Social Security Act into law. Initially, it only provided benefits to the elderly. However, as paradigms started to shift, legislators began discussing how to support individuals with disabilities as well. In 1950, it was expanded to include individuals over 55 with a disability, and in 1960, the age requirement for people with disabilities was dropped altogether (Reed, n.d.).

Discussion Questions

- Why do you think the first version of the Social Security Act only provided benefits to the elderly? Do some research on this.
- Subsequent expansion has made Social Security one of the most likely ways for individuals with disabilities to receive income if they are not working. What do you know about this process and how it works? Is it fair to individuals with disabilities?
- What are the current implications of receiving Social Security benefits as an individual with a disability?

In 1944, Dr. Howard Rusk opened the first medical rehabilitation facility for veterans—the Air Force Rehabilitation Center at Pawling, New York. Dr. Rusk had spent time with airmen and discovered that disabled veterans needed more than job training. Dr. Rusk found that airmen needed holistic care, such as emotional, educational, and social support, including working with families to ensure integration back into the family system. At the time, Dr. Rusk was ridiculed by his medical peers for delving into social services. That said, Dr. Rusk is now credited with beginning the consumer-driven movements that followed, such as the Independent Living Movement (Fleischer & Zames, 2011).

The Post-War United States (1945-1968)

Following the Depression and World War II, many parents still found themselves being pressured to institutionalize their children with disabilities. However, in the 1940s, Laura Blossfield, a parent of a child considered to be "mentally retarded" (Nielsen, 2012, p. 142), reached out to fellow parents and began to network. As time went on, more parents banded together. In addition, famous people spoke out, arguing that children with cognitive disabilities were not a punishment from God. These roots of advocacy culminated in the National Association for Retarded Children, which formed as a merger of multiple local groups into a national group in 1952. By 1974, the organization had changed its name to the National Association for Retarded Citizens. And in 1992, the organization, still active in disability rights, changed its name to The Arc (Nielsen, 2012).

Major Disability Legislation

After the Civil Rights movement, the Disability Rights movement emerged. People with disabilities fought for equal rights to live independent lives with dignity and freedom of choice. As awareness grew about the challenges faced by disabled individuals, there was a demand to safeguard their rights through laws and legislation. Over the past 50 years, several important pieces of legislation have played a key role in shaping the protections that exist today.

The Rehabilitation Act of 1973

The Rehabilitation Act of 1973 is a civil rights law that prohibits discrimination based on disability in any federally-funded program. It has multiple sections. Section 501 protects federal workers with disabilities from discrimination. Section 503 prohibits employers with federal contracts from discriminating against applicants or employees and requires that they actively hire people with disabilities as an affirmative action provision. Section 504 prohibits discrimination by any program that receives federal funding. Section 508 addresses information technology.

Section 504

Section 504 of the Rehabilitation Act is the most cited and has two primary purposes. Section 504 was intended to grant educational access to children with disabilities and to protect people with disabilities from discrimination. Section 504 of the Rehabilitation Act requires schools receiving federal funds to assess and accommodate children with disabilities. If a disability is identified, the school must provide appropriate services and support to that student. All of this happens at no cost to their parents or families. Essentially, schools are required to meet the needs of disabled children the same way that they meet the needs of any other child. This is done through a 504 Plan, which outlines the required services to remove disability-related barriers (Lee, n.d.).

The second piece of section 504 prohibits discrimination against people with disabilities in any program or activity that receives federal funding. Thus, Section 504 covers places like national parks, hospitals, universities, and airports if they receive federal monies (Lee, n.d.).

Interestingly, President Nixon vetoed the Rehabilitation Act twice over funding disagreements. There was a fundamental disagreement about the federal government's role versus state/local governments in providing funding to support the added costs of educating children with additional learning needs. During the 1970s, this disagreement led to multiple protests in the disability rights movement (Heumann, 2020).

The IDEA Act

The U.S. Department of Education (2023) estimated that in 1970, only 1 in 5 children with disabilities received public education. In addition, they reported that many states had discriminatory laws excluding children with a variety of disabilities from attending school. The Education for All Handicapped Children Act (EHA; Public Law 94-142) was signed into law in late 1975. This legislation guaranteed free and appropriate public education to any child with a disability in the United States. According to the U.S. Department of Education, "In the 1976-77 school year, 3,694,000 students aged 3 through 21 were served under the EHA" (para. 18). The U.S. Department of Education states that the purposes of the EHA was:

- to assure that all children with disabilities have available to them…a free appropriate public education which emphasizes special education and related services designed to meet their unique needs,
- to assure that the rights of children with disabilities and their parents…are protected,
- to assist States and localities to provide for the education of all children with disabilities, and
- to assess and assure the effectiveness of efforts to educate all children with disabilities. (para. 15)

In 1986, Part C of EHA was added. Part C provided a grant program for early intervention services for children ages birth to three. Children identified with developmental delays or disabilities and their families work with a team to develop an Individualized Family Service Plan (IFSP). The EHA required Local Education Agencies to conduct Child Find activities, which involve identifying, locating, and evaluating children with disabilities, to raise awareness of the availability of early intervention programs and evaluations in the community. Due to the evidence supporting the effectiveness of early intervention, new parents must be made aware of what to do if they have concerns about their child's development before they are kindergarten-aged (U.S. Department of Education, 2023).

In 1990, the EHA was reauthorized and renamed the Individuals with Disabilities Education Act (IDEA). The reauthorization of IDEA provided services for children identified with special learning needs from birth to 21 years old. This reauthorization also added brain injury and autism as coverable disabilities to the legislation. It mandated Individualized Educational Programs (IEPs) and Individual Transition Plans (ITPs) in schools (U.S. Department of Education, 2023).

Before the passage of the EHA in 1975, most children with disabilities were educated in separate classrooms and, often, separate schools. Thus, children with disabilities were not allowed to have contact with nondisabled peers in an educational setting. This segregation limited their ability to develop age-appropriate social and academic skills. When the EHA was renamed IDEA in 1990, the legislation identified this as a concern and required school-aged children with an identified disability to be educated in the least restrictive environment (LRE). Thus, children with disabilities now have the right to be with their same-aged peers if their IEP team determines that is the LRE for that learner. This shift in educational practice created a momentous shift in how children with disabilities are served in the classroom. Because of this legislation, children with disabilities are allowed to attend and participate in their local public school classrooms (Lambert, 2008).

Having children with a wider variety of educational needs in the same classroom had positive impacts on learning for all students—both disabled and non-disabled. However, it also challenged educators to adequately meet the needs of all students, particularly students with moderate to severe disabilities. Numerous research studies show that the impact of teacher and administrator perception on the successful inclusion of a child with a disability is a critical factor (Lambert, 2008). Thus, some of the success of inclusion lies in the attitude of those teaching the students. In 2019, the U.S. Department of Education (2022) noted that children ages 5–21 who received special education services in inclusive classrooms was 64.8 percent. This is a significant increase from 2000, when the percentage was 46.5 percent (Cole et al., 2021; National Center for Education Statistics, 2019).

Though progress with inclusion has been made in the last 20 years, many children are still educated in segregated settings. Disability advocates continue to work toward acceptance from the broader public that people with disabilities belong in all places and spaces, including the public school classroom.

The Americans with Disabilities Act (ADA)

To Justin Dart. Without your drive, your 'believing' and your leadership this day would not have been possible. With respect + friendship, G. Bush

President George H. W. Bush signing the Americans with Disabilities Act, 1990

The Americans with Disabilities Act (ADA) of 1990 is a landmark federal civil rights law that established comprehensive civil rights protections for individuals with disabilities. Prior to the ADA, Section 504 of the Rehabilitation Act of 1973 prohibited discrimination based on disability within programs and activities receiving federal financial assistance. While Section 504 was groundbreaking in setting a precedent for disability rights, its scope was limited to federally-funded entities (Fleischer & Zames, 2011).

In addition to Section 504 of the Rehabilitation Act, various state laws and provisions from the Civil Rights Act of 1964 provided some protection for people with disabilities prior to 1990. However, there was no unified federal legislation specifically guaranteeing civil rights to people with disabilities. The ADA expanded upon the foundation laid by Section 504, becoming the first comprehensive federal law to ensure equal opportunities and prohibit discrimination based on disability in a wide range of areas, including employment, public services, public accommodations, transportation, and telecommunications (Fleischer & Zames, 2011). The ADA has multiple sections:

Title I—Employment. Title I applies to any employer with 15 or more employees and requires employers not to ask about disability status when interviewing a potential employee. It also requires reasonable accommodation for employees with disabilities and equal access to recruitment, hiring, pay, training, and promotion.

Title II—State and Local Government Activities. Requires that state and local governments provide equal access to people with disabilities. Entities covered include public education, places of employment, transportation, recreation, health care, social services, justice services, and voting. Title II includes architectural standards in new construction for accessibility and reasonable accommodation for people with disabilities receiving services. Title II also covers public transportation such as city buses, railways, and subways.

Title III—Public Accommodations. This section of the ADA stems from the Civil Rights Act and prohibits discrimination based on disability in any public business or service. Title III states that any building built after January 26, 1993, must be accessible, and any older building needs to make any accessibility changes that are "readily achievable" (Fleischer & Zames, 2011, p. 96).

Title IV—Telecommunications and Relay Services. This section of the ADA addresses access to telephone and television for people with disabilities and established interstate and intrastate telecommunication relay services such as TTY for Deaf individuals. Title IV also requires closed captioning of any federally funded public service announcements (ADA.gov, 2020; Fleischer & Zames, 2011).

Activity 12.19 – Digging Deeper: ADA

Video: How the ADA Changed the Built World (https://www.youtube.com/watch?v=5aiFVhXSvgc)

Discussion Questions

- How has the Americans with Disabilities Act (ADA) changed the physical environment and accessibility of public spaces since its enactment in 1990?
- What role did advocacy and activism play in the passage of the ADA?
- Despite the ADA, what ongoing challenges do people with disabilities face in accessing public spaces and services? How can these be addressed?
- Compare the impact of the ADA with other civil rights legislation, such as the Civil Rights Act of 1964. How do these laws collectively work to promote equality?

The Disability Rights Movement

Disability rights movements have been active since the 1930s. One of the first advocates for disability rights was Dorthea Dix, who famously exposed the horrific experiences of people with disabilities in institutions in the 1840s and 1850s. Dorthea Dix impacted legislation at the state level but fell short of her goal of establishing federal funding to fix the systems of institutions (Disability History Museum, n.d.). In addition to Dorthea Dix, there were other pioneers in disability rights early on, such as Elizabeth Ware Packard, Agatha Tiegel Hanson, and Helen Keller.

> **Activity 12.20 – Digging Deeper: Eunice Kennedy Shriver**
>
> Eunice Kennedy (Shriver) was one of the nine Kennedy children of Rose and Joseph P. Kennedy. Of the nine siblings, many went on to influential social and political roles, including a future president of the United States (John F. Kennedy) and two future U.S. Senators (Edward and Robert Kennedy). The Kennedy's oldest daughter, Rosemary, had an intellectual disability. In 1941, she underwent a lobotomy organized by Mr. Kennedy, but without her mother's knowledge. This procedure had disastrous consequences. After the procedure, her self care skills deteriorated to that of a toddler despite being in her early 20s. Rosemary was institutionalized and disappeared from family life. She would live in an institution for the next six decades. Eunice was closest with Rosemary throughout her life and tried to support her sister. Eunice and her other sister, Jean Kennedy Smith, became lifelong supporters of people with intellectual and physical disabilities. Eunice founded the Special Olympics. She believed sports could unite everyone (Special Olympics, n.d.). Jean founded Very Special Arts, an organization that helped people with intellectual disabilities access the arts (John F. Kennedy Presidential Library & Museum, n.d.).
>
> **Discussion Questions**
>
> - How did Rosemary Kennedy's condition affect the dynamics within the Kennedy family? What role did her family play in her care and public representation?
> - How does Rosemary Kennedy's story compare to other prominent individuals with disabilities in history? What similarities or differences can be observed in their experiences and societal responses?
> - What kind of support can the Special Olympics provide to people with disabilities? Is this inclusive, or does it exclude people with disabilities?

There was a lull in disability rights activism in the 1930s and 1940s, probably due to the polio pandemic as well as the two World Wars. However, by the late 1950s and early 1960s,

Eunice Kennedy, c. 1931

disability was back on activists' radars as the shift toward deinstitutionalization began. This shift was brought on by advancements in medical science and the introduction of the first effective antipsychotic medication in 1955, Thorazine (Torrey, 1997). With these advancements, a movement toward transitioning people with mental health issues out of institutions and back into the community started. Torrey (1997) states:

> The magnitude of deinstitutionalization of the severely mentally ill qualifies it as one of the largest social experiments in American history. In 1955, there were 558,239 severely mentally ill patients in the nation's public psychiatric hospitals. In 1994, this number had been reduced by 486,620 patients, to 71,619. (para 3)

Torrey goes on to say that most of the individuals released from institutions in the 1950s and 1960s had severe mental illness and estimates that 60% of those individuals were diagnosed with schizophrenia.

In addition to individuals with mental health diagnoses being deinstitutionalized, individuals with physical disabilities who were living in institutions were also impacted by deinstitutionalization. In 1958, Anne Emerman asked to go to college following high school and was a "test case" (Fleischer & Zames, 2011, p. 33) for deinstitutionalization from Goldwater Memorial Hospital in New York City. Emerman had an acquired physical disability from polio and was a wheelchair user. Emerman went on to receive a master's in social work, start a family, and work in the mayor's office on disability. Emerman also became a significant figure in the disability rights movement (Fleischer & Zames). She died on November 3, 2021.

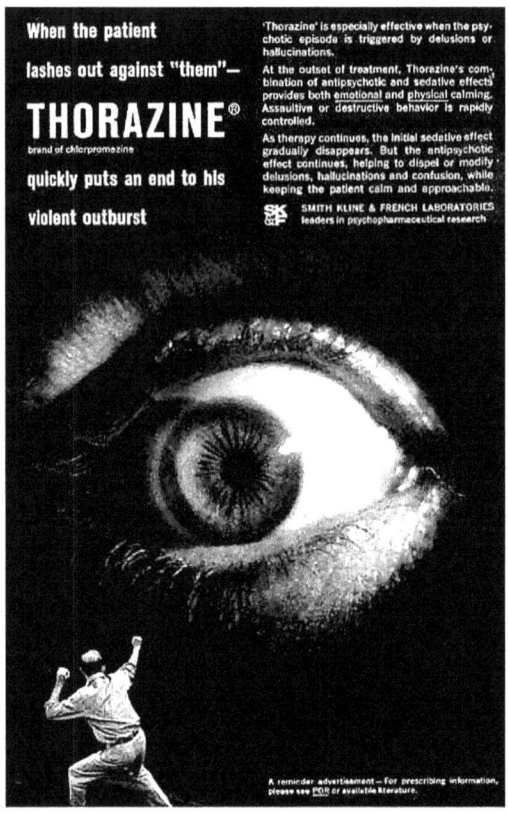

Advert from ca. 1962 for Thorazine (trade-name of chlorpromazine in the U.S.). An antipsychotic (neuroleptic, major tranquilizer, antischizophrenic, actaractic).

Activity 12.21 – Digging Deeper: Marilyn Saviola

Marilyn Saviola was a disability rights advocate who lived at Goldwater Memorial Hospital. When she was not allowed to move from the facility, she advocated within the facility for a separate ward for young adults. The ward looked more like a dorm, and social connections were made between residents. Saviola advocated for herself to attend college and became the first person to do so while institutionalized at Goldwater. Saviola went on to leave the institution in 1973. In 1983, she became the executive director of the Center for Independence of the Disabled in New York City, founded in 1978 and the first independent living center in New York State.

Discussion Questions

- What can current institutions learn from what Saviola did at Goldwater?
- Saviola talked about having to continue to live at a poverty level to maintain her benefits. This contributed to her ability to work or not work. How might this continue to be

an issue today?

Edward Roberts and the Independent Living Movement

Accessibility on college campuses was one of the first issues in the 1950s and 1960s to spur the disability rights movement. There had been several small victories on college campuses; however, Edward Roberts' experience at the University of California, Berkeley, is often cited as the start of the independent living movement. Roberts was disabled by polio at the age of 14 and used an iron lung. Due to this, he completed high school from home. He then decided he wanted to go to college. He chose the University of California, Berkeley, to get his degree in political science. They did not agree to admit him, so in 1962, Roberts sued the University of California, Berkeley, for admission. He was successful (Fleischer & Zames, 2011).

At the University of California, Berkeley, Roberts lived at the Berkeley Infirmary at Cowell Hospital. His needs were met by orderlies doing public service to avoid military service in Vietnam. As time passed, more students in wheelchairs joined him at the hospital, and Berkeley became a haven for disabled students. Eventually, Roberts obtained a grant to help people with disabilities and began to work on political change at the college. Roberts and other students formed a political group called the Rolling Quads. The Rolling Quads were a disability pride group that advocated for independence on the college campus by decreasing physical barriers and increasing self-reliance (Nielsen, 2012). Through the advocacy of the Rolling Quads, the experience of being a disabled student on campus at Berkeley in the 1970s became one of inclusivity and access (Fleischer & Zames, 2011).

Roberts and other disability activists began to develop independent living centers nationwide. These centers focused on self-determination, consumer control, choice, and deinstitutionalization and provided services such as caregiving, wheelchair repair, counseling, legal assistance, training in self-advocacy, and community. In addition, the founders of the centers advocated for architectural and transportation accessibility for people with disabilities (Nielsen, 2012).

Activity 12.22 – Digging Deeper: Disability Rights and Civil Rights

Roberts acknowledged the influence of other civil rights movements, such as the women's rights movement, Native American activists, and the Black Power movement in his work. He saw connections between the disability rights movement and other civil rights movements. That said, he was often dismissed when trying to build connections with them (Fleischer & Zames, 2011).

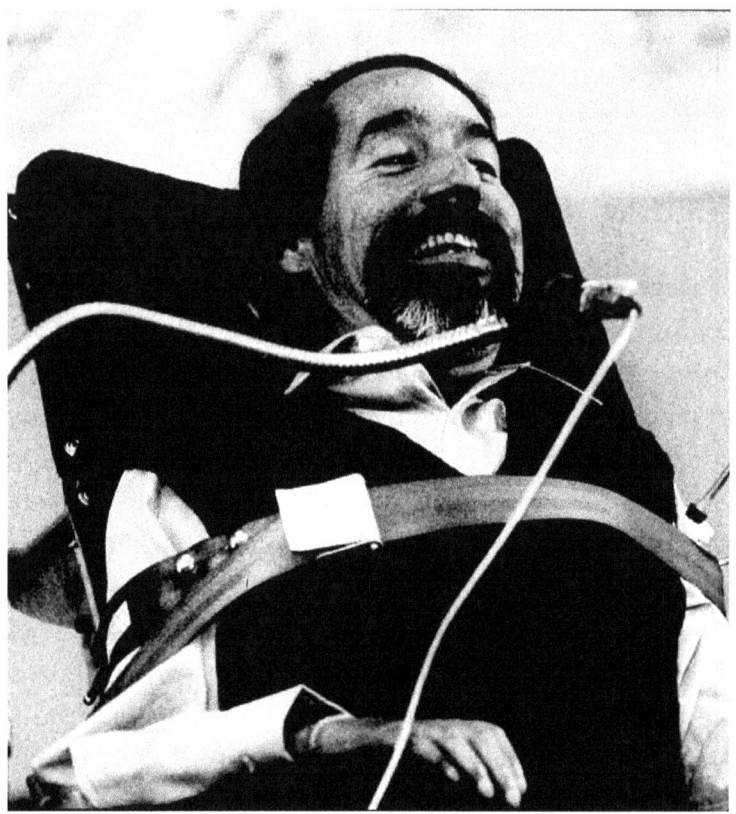

Edward V. Roberts was the Director of the California Department of Rehabilitation and the host of the conference "Consumer Unity: New Platforms for Progress in the 1980s," a leadership planning session for persons with disabilities.

Discussion Questions

- What connections do you think Roberts saw between the different civil rights movements and the disability rights movement?
- Why do you think he was shunned when he tried to work with other civil rights movements? How might they have seen Roberts and his movement as different from theirs?
- Do you think the disability rights movement is still shunned by some of the other civil rights movements, such as Black Lives Matter or #MeToo? Why might this continue to happen today?

Roberts earned his bachelor's and master's degrees in political science from the University of California, Berkeley. He was then appointed to a position at his alma mater. In 1975, he became the director of the State Department of Rehabilitation in California. He went on to have a career in disability advocacy, raising public awareness and lobbying throughout his life. Roberts died at the age of 56 in 1995 of cardiac arrest (Fleischer & Zames, 2011).

Influential Events and People of the 1960s and 1970s

The civil rights movements of the 1960s and 1970s significantly impacted the disability rights movement. Much like other movements, the disability rights movement began to coalesce nationally late in the 1960s. People with disabilities began to challenge the medical model of disability, which focused on hierarchical constructs of physical and mental fitness. Nielsen (2012) states:

> The disability rights movement was energized by, overlapping with, and similar to other civil rights movements across the nation, as people with disabilities experienced the 1960s and 1970s as a time of excitement, organizational strength, and identity exploration. Like feminists, African Americans, and gay and lesbian activists, people with disabilities insisted that their bodies did not render them defective. Indeed, their bodies could even be sources of political, sexual, and artistic strength. (p. 160)

In 1968, the Architectural Barriers Act (ABA) passed. This act required that all newly built buildings be accessible, and that accessibility be built into any new construction. However, this legislation had inconsistent implementation due to a lack of oversight and uniform accessibility standards (U.S. Access Board, n.d.). In addition, it paid no attention to public transportation, housing, recreational facilities, or any privately owned buildings. In general, the ABA was not seen as successful legislation, but it set the stage for the disability rights movement (Nielsen, 2012).

In the 1970s, there was a conversation in the United States government about where disability rights fit into the civil rights movement. In 1972, Senator Hubert Humphrey and Congressman Charles Vanik introduced legislation to amend the Civil Rights Act of 1964 to include disability, which did not pass. However, the drafted language was taken and built into Section 504 of the Rehabilitation Act, which is a critical part of that legislation today. Interestingly, when the Rehabilitation Act went up for discussion and debate in Congress and public hearings, only one person commented on Section 504's anti-discrimination language (Nielsen, 2012).

The discussions surrounding the Rehabilitation Act and its two vetoes by President Nixon sparked protests from disability activists. Much like the ABA, the initial implementation of the Rehabilitation Act did not include enforcement or enactment. That had to be done by the head of the Health Education and Welfare (HEW) department in Washington, D.C. His name was Joseph Califano, and he showed little interest in advancing disability rights. He did nothing to move Section 504 forward. To combat this, disability advocates took 504 enactment to court. However, despite a judge saying that the government needed to move forward with enactment, nothing happened (Nielsen, 2012). As enactment stalled, protests began to erupt around the country. In April of 1977, disability rights activists worked together to stage demonstrations at HEW offices nationwide. Protests and subsequent sit-ins occurred in Denver, Washington, D.C., and Los Angeles HEW buildings. In San Francisco, protesters occupied the HEW building for a 25-day sit-in (Heumann, 2020).

Judy Heumann, a disability rights advocate and woman with a disability, describes the experience of the 25-day sit-in at the HEW building in San Francisco in her memoir, *Being Heumann* (Heumann, 2020). Heumann led the protest with fellow disability rights advocate Kitty Cone, demanding that Section 504 of the Rehabilitation Act be enacted. As the sit-in continued, the government turned off the hot water, refused to allow people or goods (including medicine) in and out of the building and cut the phone lines. Every time the government tried to cut access, the people protesting organized to manage the complex process of remaining onsite at the HEW building (Heumann. 2020).

Judy Heumann at the conference "Consumer Unity: New Platforms for Progress in the 1980s"

The San Francisco protesters had multiple well-known supporters. Ed Roberts, who was running the California Department of Rehabilitation, gave a speech at the protest encouraging the implementation of Section 504. The Glide Memorial Church, under Reverend Cecil Williams, organized a vigil outside the HEW building to maintain visibility. Organizers in other movements, such as labor unions, churches, and civil rights groups, urged President Carter to end the protests and enact the legislation. The Butterfly Brigade, a gay rights group, smuggled walkie-talkies into the building when the phone lines were cut (Nielsen, 2012). On day three of the sit-in, the Black Panthers forced their way into the building and, in solidarity, brought hot food to the protesters daily. Twenty-four days after the sit-in started, the enabling regulations were signed in Washington, DC. The protesters spent one more night in the HEW building to celebrate and left the building on Saturday, April 30th, singing "*We Have Overcome*" (Heumann, 2020, p. 147).

Following the enactment of Section 504, disability advocacy became about implementing the law. Heumann (2020) points out that desegregation was a lot simpler in terms of implementation than the Rehabilitation Act and uses the example of access on a public bus. It is easy enough for Black people without disabilities to access the bus once the law changed, however those with disabilities need a different kind of structural changes, such as adding lifts to the bus, for access to occur (Heumann, 2020).

Activity 12.23 – Digging Deeper: The Capitol Crawl

Video: Disabled Activists Crawl Up the Steps of the Capitol (https://www.youtube.com/watch?v=WHWcJiNQZEw)

One or more interactive elements has been excluded from this version of the text. You can view them online here: https://milnepublishing.geneseo.edu/social-justice-in-human-services/?p=199#oembed-2 (#oembed-2)

The Capitol Crawl, which took place on March 12, 1990, was a powerful and symbolic act of protest led by disability rights activists, particularly those from the organization American Disabled for Accessible Public Transit (ADAPT). In a bold demonstration of the barriers people with disabilities face, protesters—many of whom used wheelchairs or other mobility aids—crawled up the steps of the U.S. Capitol building to highlight the lack of accessibility in public spaces, including government buildings. The Capitol Crawl played a crucial role in galvanizing support for disability rights and was instrumental in the eventual passage of the ADA, signed into law later that year on July 26, 1990.

Discussion Questions

- How did the Capitol Crawl serve as a turning point in the disability rights movement, and what role did it play in the passage of the Americans with Disabilities Act (ADA)?
- What impact did the visual symbolism of the Capitol Crawl—particularly the image of people with disabilities physically crawling up the Capitol steps—have on public perception of disability rights and accessibility issues?
- In what ways does the Capitol Crawl highlight the tension between individual rights and societal responsibility in creating accessible public spaces? How can this protest inform current debates on accessibility and inclusion?

Current Issues in Disability

As many anticipated, implementing the Rehabilitation Act, IDEA, and ADA has been complex and intermittent. The Disability Rights Movement now clearly identifies itself as a civil rights movement and continues to advocate for the civil rights of individuals with disabilities. Issues that are currently being faced include but are not limited to funding, vocational rights, parental rights, reproductive healthcare, institutionalization, and physician-assisted suicide (Fleischer & Zames, 2011; Nielsen, 2012).

Activity 12.24

Video: The Changing Reality of Disability in America (https://www.youtube.com/watch?v=lHK7wjPXHH8)

One or more interactive elements has been excluded from this version of the text. You can view them online here: https://milnepublishing.geneseo.edu/social-justice-in-human-services/?p=199#oembed-3 (#oembed-3)

Discussion Questions

- How does the video address shifts in societal attitudes towards disability? In what ways have these attitudes changed, and what factors have contributed to these changes?
- What are some of the ongoing challenges faced by people with disabilities despite progress made? How does the video suggest addressing these challenges?
- How has the information presented in the video changed your understanding of disability? What new perspectives or insights have you gained?

Ability Privilege and Ableism

Ability privilege refers to the experience of having privilege based on ability. In our society, people have advantages because they have abilities. Much like being White has certain privileges in our society, the experience of being traditionally able-bodied also carries privileges. Harveston (2019) states: "Able-bodied privilege, in a nutshell, means living under the assumption that everybody else on earth can speak, hear, see, and get around, more-or-less the same way we do, with a similar amount of ease." (para 7). She goes on to state that: "Able-bodied privilege is less about who you are and more about the things you don't have to worry about in life. And through no fault of their own, a lot of people have a lot more worries than others" (Harveston, 2019, para 8).

There are many examples of ability privilege, partly because there are many kinds of identified disabilities. Some examples include not having to consider the physical environment for a work or social event, being able to move freely away from uncomfortable things, being able to easily use credit card machines in the store, representation in the media, reproductive freedom, appropriate medical care, and housing access (Riolriri, 2009).

Activity 12.25 – Digging Deeper: Ability Priviledge

Article: Examples of Ability Privilege (https://sites.lsa.umich.edu/inclusive-teaching-2/wp-content/uploads/sites/732/2017/08/Examples-of-Ability-Privilege.pdf)

Discussion Questions

- Have you ever considered yourself privileged because of ability? Why or why not?
- After reviewing this extensive list, what stood out to you? Why?
- Is there anything missing from this list?

In addition to ability privilege, the experience of living with a disability often involves regular and systemic discrimination. While accessibility is the law of the land, ask any wheelchair user about accessibility, and they will have an entirely different story to tell. As Sligh (2019) points out, there is a significant difference between accessible and disability friendly. Sligh has a daughter with a physical disability and gives examples of elevators in buildings. While they are often present, placement rarely makes sense. Thus, having to find and access elevators reinforces her daughter's social isolation. She also points out that there is often an assumption of intellectual disability whenever there is an apparent physical disability present, which impacts her daughter in many ways (Sligh, 2019).

Activity 12.26 – Digging Deeper: Access as a Civil Right

Is access a privilege, or is it a civil right? Niziolek (n.d.) argues that access to healthcare, in-home assistance, employment, housing, transportation, and marriage should not be considered a privilege for people with disabilities—they should be regarded as civil rights. This reframe is often met with resistance as there is a pervasive social attitude that people with disabilities should be grateful for the services they receive.

Video: Disabled Americans Are Punished for Getting Married (https://www.youtube.com/watch?v=0q-gJXauP3Y)

One or more interactive elements has been excluded from this version of the text. You can view them online here: https://milnepublishing.geneseo.edu/social-justice-in-human-services/?p=199#oembed-4 (#oembed-4)

Discussion Questions

- How does reframing access from a privilege to a right change the conversation about disability access?
- Why might some people still see access for people with a disability as a privilege? Where does this attitude stem from?
- Do people with disabilities have the right to get married without it impacting their benefits? Why or why not?

In addition to discrimination, people with disabilities often find themselves faced with myths or stereotypes of disability. Examples of myths about disability include (a) that people with disabilities are somehow partial or not whole people; (b) that the successful disabled person is a superhuman triumphing over adversity; (c) that the burden of disability is unending, that the life of a disabled person is one of sorrow and sadness; (d) that the families of people with disabilities sacrificed nobly; (e) that disability needs to be fixed or corrected; (f) that people with disabilities are somehow a menace or dangerous to society; and (g) that people with disabilities are somehow innocent and endowed with some sort of special grace meant to inspire (Block, n.d.). Block goes on to point out that these stereotypes permeate the individual experience of being disabled in the United States, as well as impacting public policy and legislation.

Activity 12.27

Video: Inspiration Porn and the Objectification of Disability by Stella Young (https://www.youtube.com/watch?v=SxrS7-I_sMQ)

 One or more interactive elements has been excluded from this version of the text. You can view them online here: https://milnepublishing.geneseo.edu/social-justice-in-human-services/?p=199#oembed-5 (#oembed-5)

Discussion Questions

- How does inspiration porn affect people with disabilities personally and socially? What are some potential psychological and emotional impacts?
- In what ways does inspiration porn contribute to or detract from social justice efforts for individuals with disabilities? How does it affect the broader goals of equity and inclusion?

- What are some positive and empowering ways to represent disability that avoid inspiration porn? How can media and advocacy shift towards more respectful and accurate portrayals?
- Have you seen/heard inspiration porn about people with disabilities? Where?

Deinstitutionalization

Deinstitutionalization remains a concern for the disabled community. In many places, people with disabilities continue to be housed in group homes, nursing homes, and other congregate care facilities despite the deinstitutionalization movement. In addition, what is legally considered institutionalization versus what feels like institutionalization can be two very different things. For example, a nursing home is legally viewed as an institution in the State of Washington. However, an adult family home or assisted living is not. That said, clients often feel institutionalized in those settings, as well. For those who want to live in their own homes, funding for care can be complex and challenging to access. In addition, it often varies from state to state as most caregiving services are funded through Medicaid dollars. In some states, institutionalization is the only option for 24-hour care for individuals who need it (DaSilva, 2018). As an offshoot of the independent living movement, many current disability advocates focus on where individuals with disabilities live and receive services.

Activity 12.28

Video: How Health Care Makes Disability A Trap (https://www.youtube.com/watch?v=7LfxIe9UwCI)

 One or more interactive elements has been excluded from this version of the text. You can view them online here: https://milnepublishing.geneseo.edu/social-justice-in-human-services/?p=199#oembed-6 (#oembed-6)

Discussion Questions

- What are the pros and cons of different states treating people with disabilities differently?
- How do policies within the healthcare system contribute to the stigmatization of disability? What changes in policy could help mitigate this?
- What kind of policy change is needed to fix Jason DaSilva's dilemma?
- What are some effective strategies for advocating for systemic change within the healthcare system to better support individuals with disabilities? How can individuals and organizations work toward reform?

- Is it fair that Jason DaSilva must live so far from his son because he cannot receive care? Is this discrimination? Why or why not?

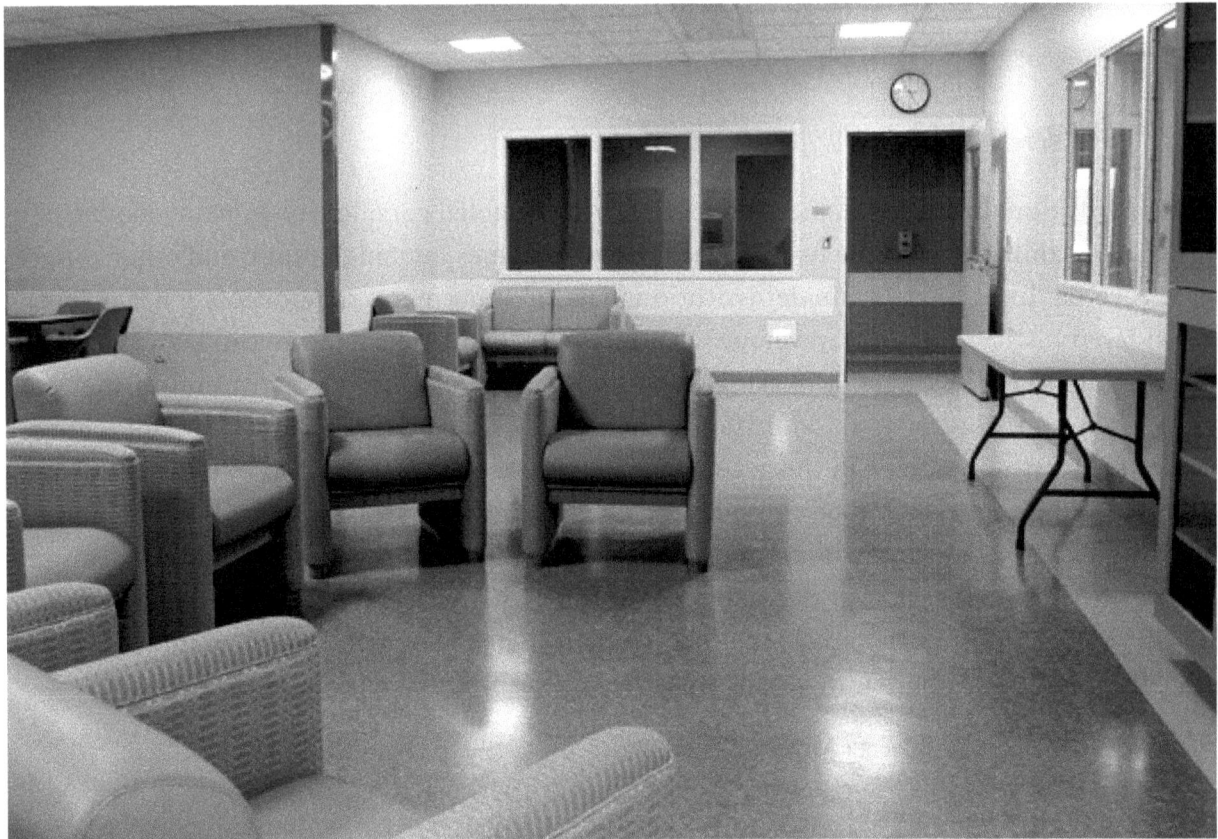

Day room inside the Oregon State Hospital – Junction City

Activity 12.29

Video: Institutionalized as a Teen with Jensen Caraballo (https://www.youtube.com/watch?v=r17OfF8_r1w)

 One or more interactive elements has been excluded from this version of the text. You can view them online here: https://milnepublishing.geneseo.edu/social-justice-in-human-services/?p=199#oembed-7 (#oembed-7)

Discussion Questions

- Jensen Caraballo is talking about current day institutionalization—is deinstitutionalization failing?
- What kind of options are there for someone like Jensen Caraballo? What kind of

options should there be?

The other side of the deinstitutionalization coin has been the lack of services available for people with disabilities in the community who need them. Access to caregiving and other healthcare services can be a significant barrier to success for people with disabilities who need personal care and other kinds of services. Staffing shortages, high staff turnover, and a lack of education often result in poor or absent care for people who need it.

Nielsen (2012) points out that historically, the individuals who were successful in deinstitutionalization were, and continue to be, those with privilege. Individuals with disabilities with strong family advocacy, financial resources, access to independent living centers, and access to well-run community group homes and community-based mental health centers have had positive outcomes from deinstitutionalization. However, those without financial means or familial support and advocacy have not had the same experience of deinstitutionalization. A lack of services for those without resources has led to mass incarceration of people with disabilities, particularly for those with mental health issues. Nielsen goes on to say, "The vast majority of those [people with disabilities] incarcerated are poor and people of color" (p. 164).

Activity 12.30 – Digging Deeper: Deinstitutionalization and Mental Illness

Torrey (1997) argues that the deinstitutionalization of mental health institutions without providing medication and services has led to a mental health crisis. He argues that a lack of services and medication management outside the institution, as well as the loss of hospital beds for those having mental health crises, have negatively impacted those living in the United States with severe mental health issues. Nielsen (2012) agrees and argues that the failure of deinstitutionalization was not providing sufficient support for people who needed it, even when this support is significantly cheaper than institutionalization.

Discussion Questions

- Do you agree with Torrey (1997) and Nielsen (2012) that this is a downside of deinstitutionalization?
- What kind of funding and programs are needed to successfully deinstitutionalize people who continue to need support?
- What assumptions are being made when we discharge people without services to the community? What do these assumptions say about how we see people with mental health disabilities in our society?

Access to Healthcare

Not only do individuals with disabilities face concerns when needing care at home, but inequity in healthcare access also permeates the experience of this community. From inaccessible healthcare to discrimination in reproductive healthcare and rights, people with disabilities face complex issues when interacting with the healthcare system.

Krahn et al. (2015) state that "Adults with disabilities are 4 times more likely to report their health to be fair or poor than people with no disabilities" (p. 1). Research shows that people with disabilities experience more preventable health conditions such as obesity, pain, depression, high blood pressure, and type 2 diabetes than those without disability. This inequity in healthcare is often attributed to issues with access to healthcare for people with disabilities. Accessibility issues in healthcare include inaccessible buildings, equipment, transportation issues, poor health literacy, poverty, and lack of knowledge on the provider's part (U.S. Centers for Disease Control and Prevention, 2024).

> **Activity 12.31**
>
> Video: Bridging the Gap Improving Healthcare Access for People with Disabilities (https://www.youtube.com/watch?v=h307701-b-c)
>
> *One or more interactive elements has been excluded from this version of the text. You can view them online here: https://milnepublishing.geneseo.edu/social-justice-in-human-services/?p=199#oembed-8 (#oembed-8)*
>
> **Discussion Questions**
>
> - What gaps in healthcare are discussed in the video?
> - What solutions can you come up with for the issues of health disparity for people with disabilities?
> - Why do you think these gaps in care persist? What do these gaps have to do with social justice?

Access to reproductive healthcare is complicated for individuals with disabilities. As people with disabilities are often seen as "sexless" or "undesirable," it is frequently assumed that people with disabilities will not need sexual education or healthcare. This discriminatory practice begins in the public school system. Research has shown that comprehensive sexual education for children with disabilities can decrease abuse, decrease rates of STI infection, decrease unintended pregnancy, and increase healthy, consensual sexual activity. However, students with disabilities are often excluded from sexual education courses, particularly those that promote healthy sexual behavior (National Partnership for Women & Families, 2021).

As adults, many women with disabilities often encounter similar attitudes towards reproductive healthcare. DiMatteo et al. (2022) identify a multitude of access issues, including access to abortion care, contraceptives both for pregnancy prevention and menstruation control, preventative care, and maternal health services as issues faced by women with disabilities. They go on to cite the eugenics movement as a concern for women with disabilities as well, pointing out the social implications of aborting disabled fetuses and the overarching social belief, which still exists, that people with disabilities should not have children. Forced sterilization continues to be a legitimate and real fear in the disabled population. DiMatteo et al. go on to say that,

> According to the National Women's Law Center, 31 states and the District of Columbia currently allow forced sterilization—and only three states explicitly prohibit forced sterilization of disabled children. Such laws work in tandem with other barriers to inhibit the full autonomy of disabled women... forced sterilization is not only part of historical violence against marginalized communities, but likely continues to this day. As Mia Mingus notes, 'eugenic 'science' is still a vibrant part of U.S. culture that interacts with and shapes the reproductive lives of disabled women in many ways. (para 13)

Activity 12.32

Video: AcessSex: How to Deliver Sexual and Reproductive Healthcare to Women with Disabilities (https://www.youtube.com/watch?v=mv-MgvNat-0)

One or more interactive elements has been excluded from this version of the text. You can view them online here: https://milnepublishing.geneseo.edu/social-justice-in-human-services/?p=199#oembed-9 (#oembed-9)

Discussion Questions

- What kind of prejudice and ableist perspectives impact the access of people with disabilities to reproductive services?
- What kinds of system changes need to be made to provide good reproductive healthcare for people with disabilities?
- What kinds of individual changes need to be made to provide good reproductive healthcare for people with disabilities?

When people with disabilities have children, their ability to parent is often questioned. According to Nielson (2012), "almost two-thirds of US states continue to list 'parental disability' as possible grounds for terminating parental rights, and parents with disabilities lose custody of their children at disproportionately high rates" (p 172).

> **Activity 12.33 – Digging Deeper: Parenting as an Individual with a Disability**
>
> **Video:** Disabled Parenting in an Ableist World by Kara Ayers (https://www.youtube.com/watch?v=STtI5wXxErY)
>
> *One or more interactive elements has been excluded from this version of the text. You can view them online here: https://milnepublishing.geneseo.edu/social-justice-in-human-services/?p=199#oembed-10 (#oembed-10)*
>
> **Video:** Being Disabled Doesn't Stop Us Being Great Parents (https://www.youtube.com/watch?v=EzOzJirP_68)
>
> *One or more interactive elements has been excluded from this version of the text. You can view them online here: https://milnepublishing.geneseo.edu/social-justice-in-human-services/?p=199#oembed-11 (#oembed-11)*
>
> **Discussion Questions**
>
> - How do societal attitudes and stereotypes about disability affect the experiences of parents with disabilities? What impact do these perceptions have on their parenting and family dynamics?
> - What legal rights and protections are in place for parents with disabilities? How effective are these policies in ensuring fair treatment and support?
> - How does ableism impact how we perceive people with disabilities and their parenting skills?
> - What changes or advancements would you like to see in terms of supporting parents with disabilities? How can ongoing advocacy and policy work address these needs?

Abuse and Mistreatment of People with Disabilities

According to Sanctuary for Families (2022), 70 percent of disabled people experience some form of abuse in their lifetime. They go on to say that people with disabilities experience higher rates of domestic violence and sexual assault than non-disabled individuals and that these statistics are exceptionally high for women and children with disabilities. According to the Office for Victims of Crime (2012),

> Persons with disabilities are particularly vulnerable to abuse and victimization due to their physical, intellectual, and emotional challenges and, in some cases, their dependence on others for basic needs. Success in identifying and intervening in situations that place persons with disabilities at risk requires an understanding of

what makes them more vulnerable to becoming victims of crime, abuse, and neglect. (para 1)

They go on to identify a lack of control over their care, dependency on others, socialization to touch, lack of sexual education, lack of ability to communicate, and lack of credibility when abuse is reported as common in this population.

Sanctuary for Families (2022) identifies power in caregiving relationships as a concern for people with disabilities. Examples include the care provider's control over food, medication, personal care, finances, and transportation. Often, the individual involved in the abuse is a family member or someone who is supposed to be caring for the individual with a disability, making the experience of abuse even more complex. Because of the isolating experience of disability, many victims of abuse have no one to report the abuse to, and fewer people are in their lives who might report for them. Often, abuse in disabled populations is overlooked, and when it is reported, it is less likely to be prosecuted than other crimes (Sanctuary for Families, 2022).

Activity 12.34 – Digging Deeper: Abuse and Disability

Video: Everyone's Responsibility: Preventing Abuse Against People with Disabilities (https://www.youtube.com/watch?v=Ps0Rt9TU3ao)

One or more interactive elements has been excluded from this version of the text. You can view them online here: https://milnepublishing.geneseo.edu/social-justice-in-human-services/?p=199#oembed-12 (#oembed-12)

Video: Living with Disabilities (https://www.youtube.com/watch?v=3fbUqcc2bGs)

One or more interactive elements has been excluded from this version of the text. You can view them online here: https://milnepublishing.geneseo.edu/social-justice-in-human-services/?p=199#oembed-13 (#oembed-13)

Discussion Questions

- How does the social construct of disability impact how we see abuse in disability?
- In what ways are people with disabilities more vulnerable to abuse?
- Can a system perpetuate abuse? Alex's story occurs in the United Kingdom, but people with disabilities in the United States live similar experiences. Is this abuse by the system? What is the responsibility of the system in these situations?

If domestic violence or abuse is reported, this can cause upheaval in the lives of people with disabilities. If someone must leave their home due to abuse, many shelters are not accessible, and the staff do not have the appropriate training to intake and support disabled individuals. Often, domestic violence shelters focus on women, so male victims may struggle even more to find suitable shelter placement. In addition, many shelters cannot provide necessary care or accommodate caregivers needed for an individual with a disability (Sanctuary for Families, 2022).

Activity 12.35 – Digging Deeper: Prioritizing Care

Video: Why are People with Disabilities Left out of Disaster Planning? (https://www.youtube.com/watch?v=Fu_ifvFaz7M&t=35s)

 One or more interactive elements has been excluded from this version of the text. You can view them online here: https://milnepublishing.geneseo.edu/social-justice-in-human-services/?p=199#oembed-14 (#oembed-14)

Article: Ventilators limited for the disabled? Rationing plans are slammed amid coronavirus crisis. (https://www.nbcnews.com/news/us-news/ventilators-limited-disabled-rationing-plans-are-slammed-amid-coronavirus-crisis-n1170346)

Discussion Questions

- What do these resources say about how we see people with disabilities today?
- Is this systemic abuse? Why or why not?

Intersectionality

The relationship between disability, race, and poverty is complex and interconnected. Historically, children from non-white racial groups have been overidentified for special education services (Morgan, 2020). This over-identification begins and perpetuates a lifetime of marginalization within the school system and is a significant contributing factor in the preschool-to-prison pipeline. Factors such as poverty, native language, cultural differences, and lack of exposure to high-quality early learning environments can all be contributing factors to the over-identification of Black and Brown children as having a disability and needing special education services. However, an actual disability may not be present.

Activity 12.36 – Digging Deeper: Intersectionality

Video: Intersectionality and Disability (https://www.youtube.com/watch?v=p2XN0CQazr0)

One or more interactive elements has been excluded from this version of the text. You can view them online here: https://milnepublishing.geneseo.edu/social-justice-in-human-services/?p=199#oembed-15 (#oembed-15)

Video: Disability and Poverty in America (https://www.youtube.com/watch?v=RT0IACLhk5M)

One or more interactive elements has been excluded from this version of the text. You can view them online here: https://milnepublishing.geneseo.edu/social-justice-in-human-services/?p=199#oembed-16 (#oembed-16)

Discussion Questions

- What did you learn about intersectionality in these videos?
- Why is it important to look at intersectionality and disability?
- How do public benefits impact the experience of poverty for people with disabilities?

Thoughts from the Authors

I have worked with people with disabilities my entire career. It is a population I have passion for. Writing this chapter was hard for me because it was so difficult to pick out what was important, to leave some things behind, and to really delve into the history of disability in this country. I got sidetracked by so many rabbit trails! And yet I learned so much in doing this work, too. I already see it impacting my teaching, and for that opportunity I am grateful. One in four people will experience some kind of disability in their lifetime. We need to shift how our culture interacts with people with disabilities. I have loved ones with disabilities—multiple types. My family has seen what prejudice and lack of caring can do to someone's life. Advocacy, voice, policy, and culture all have to be pieces of the puzzle in working with people with disabilities and I hope this chapter gave you at least a taste of some of those complex issues in working with this complex, often overlooked population.

Sincerely,
Dr. DeJonge (Bernie)

As a lifelong special educator, I have watched the students and families who I work with be ignored, marginalized, and disrespected because of their learning or physical differences. I entered the field of special education to be a part of the solution by educating children in a respectful and dignified way. ALL children have the right to learn at school. ALL children have the right to be with peers. ALL children deserve to have their voices heard and needs met. It is the responsibility of the adults in our community to have an inclusive mindset and understand that there is a wide spectrum of human experience, all of which is valid and valued. My life's work is opening hearts and minds to understand and listen to the experiences of people in our community experiencing a disability. Human nature is to feel secure with the familiar and predictable, but life is not predictable and would be very boring if everything was familiar so my hope is to challenge others to step into spaces where they can listen to those with different experiences and perspectives on the world. It will make our views richer, more colorful, and more inclusive if we do.

-Shannon Raybold, M.Ed.

Chapter Summary Questions

1. How do you define disability?
2. How do other identities intersect with disability?
3. Describe accessibility and universal design. Why are these concepts important?
4. How has history impacted the experience of people with disabilities today?
5. How do cultural and social norms impact how people interact with disability?
6. Do we still practice eugenics and forced sterilization of people with disabilities? Discuss both sides of these topics.
7. Describe the disability justice movement and ability privilege. How do these things impact the experience of being disabled in the United States today?

References

ADA.gov. (2020, February 28). *Guide to disability rights laws*. U.S. Department of Justice, Civil Rights Division. https://www.ada.gov/resources/disability-rights-guide/

Anti-Defamation League. (2024, November 22). *A brief history of the disability rights movement*. ADL Education. https://www.adl.org/resources/backgrounder/brief-history-disability-rights-movement

Block, L. (n.d.) *Stereotypes about people with disabilities.* Disability History Museum. https://www.disabilitymuseum.org/dhm/edu/essay.html?id=24

Cole, S. M., Murphy, H. R., Frisby, M. B., Grossi, T. A., & Bolte, H. R. (2021). The relationship of special education placement and student academic outcomes. *Journal of Special Education, 54*(4), 217-227. https://doi.org/10.1177/0022466920925033

Centre for Excellence in Universal Design. (2023). *About universal design.* https://universaldesign.ie/about-universal-design

DaSilva, J. (2018, July 29). *How health care makes disability a trap.* [Video]. YouTube. https://www.youtube.com/watch?v=7Lfxle9UwCI&t=7s

de Groot, K. (2020, August 4). *Gouverneur Morris: Founding father, disabled American.* Penn Today. https://penntoday.upenn.edu/news/gouverneur-morris-founding-father-disabled-american

DiMatteo, E., Ahmed, O., Thompson, V., & Ives-Rublee, M. (2022, April 13). *Reproductive justice for disabled women: Ending system discrimination.* American Progress. https://www.americanprogress.org/article/reproductive-justice-for-disabled-women-ending-systemic-discrimination/

Disability History Museum (n.d.). *Dorthea Dix and the gendered Politics of advocacy.* https://www.disabilitymuseum.org/dhm/edu/lesson_details.html?id=2#:~:text=During%09%20the%201840s%20and%201850s,world%20of%20home%20and%20family

Ericsson, A. (2022, May 28). *Institutionalized: The story of state hospitals.* [Video]. YouTube. https://www.youtube.com/watch?v=wmAqPe65M5c&t=31s

Fleischer, D. Z., & Zames, F. (2011). *The disability rights movement.* Temple University Press.

Fleming, A. R., Roundtree, S. M., & Pierce, K. L. (2024). The evolution of laws and policies in the United States and their impact on disabled people. In I. Marini, A. R. Fleming, & M. Bishop (Eds.), *The psychosocial and social impact of illness and disability* (8th ed., pp. 85-101). Springer.

Fox, D. D., & Marini, I. (2024). History of treatment toward persons with disabilities in America and abroad. In I. Marini, A. R. Fleming, & M. Bishop (Eds.), *The psychosocial and social impact of illness and disability* (8th ed., pp. 5-16). Springer.

Harveston, K. (2019, June 6). *All-access pass: What is able-bodied privilege?* Headstuff.org. https://headstuff.org/topical/able-bodied-privilege/

Heumann, J. (2020). *Being Heumann: An unrepentant memoir of a disability rights activist.* Beacon Press.

John F. Kennedy Presidential Library & Museum. (n.d.). *Rosemary Kennedy.* https://www.jfklibrary.org/learn/about-jfk/the-kennedy-family/rosemary-kennedy

Krahn, G. L., Walker, D. K., & Correa-De-Araujo, R. (2015). Persons with disabilities as an unrecognized health disparity population. *American Journal of Public Health, 105*(suppl 2), 198-206. https://doi.org/10.2105/AJPH.2014.302182

Lambert, L. (2008). Inclusive education. *Journal of the American Academy of Special Education Professionals, Fall,* 67-71. https://files.eric.ed.gov/fulltext/EJ1139241.pdf

Lee, A.M.I. (n.d.). *Section 504 of the Rehabilitation Act of 1973: What you need to know.* Understood. https://www.understood.org/en/articles/section-504-of-the-rehabilitation-act-of-1973-what-you-need-to-know

LEAP. (n.d.). *History of disability rights.* https://www.leapinfo.org/advocacy/history-of-disability-rights/1930s

Library of Congress. (n.d.). *President Franklin Delano Roosevelt and the New Deal.* https://www.loc.gov/classroom-materials/united-states-history-primary-source-timeline/great-depression-and-world-war-ii-1929-1945/franklin-delano-roosevelt-and-the-new-deal/

Manoukian, M. (2023, August 23). *The untold history of ugly laws.* Grunge. https://www.grunge.com/664678/the-untold-history-of-ugly-laws/

McQuade, T. (2023, May 22). *Ready and able to serve: The "Invalid Corps" in the Civil War.* Emerging Civil War. https://emergingcivilwar.com/2023/05/22/ready-and-able-to-serve-the-invalid-corps-in-the-civil-war/

Morgan, H. (2020). Misunderstood and mistreated: Students of color in special education. *Voices of Reform: Educational Research to Inform and Reform, 3*(2), 71-81. https://doi.org/10.32623/3.10005

National Center for Education Statistics. (2019). *Percentage distribution of students 6 to 21 years old served under IDEA* (No. 204.60). U. S. Department of Education, Digest of Education Statistics. https://nces.ed.gov/programs/digest/d18/tables/dt18_204.60.asp

National Park Service. (2023, August 8). *Revolutionary war veterans and widow pensions.* https://www.nps.gov/articles/000/revolutionary-war-veteran-and-widow-pensions.htm

National Partnership for Women & Families. (2021). *Access, autonomy, and dignity: Comprehensive sexuality education for people with disabilities.* https://nationalpartnership.org/wp-content/uploads/2023/02/repro-disability-sexed.pdf

Nielsen, K. E. (2012). *A disability history of the United States.* Beacon Press.

Niziolek, J. (2010, January 1). *Civil rights, not disability privilege.* https://www.abilities.com/community/civil-rights.html

Office for Victims of Crime. (2012). *Risk factors for abuse.* https://ovc.ojp.gov/sites/g/files/xyckuh226/files/pubs/victimswithdisabilities/stateguide/risk-factors.html

Olkin, R. (2022, March 29). *Conceptualizing disability: Three models of disability.* American Psychological Association. https://www.apa.org/ed/precollege/psychology-teacher-network/introductory-psychology/disability-models

Reed, G. (n.d.) *Attitudes towards and support for those with disabilities has been an evolving process in the United States. History of Disability in America.* https://www.brrlaw.com/history-of-disability-in-america-part-1/

Riolriri. (2009, April 23). *The invisible crutch.* She Dances on the Sand. [Blog.] http://rioiriri.blogspot.com/2009/04/invisible-crutch.html

Rosenthal, K. (n.d.). Pioneers in the fight for disability rights: The League of the Physically Handicapped. *International Socialist Review*, (90). https://isreview.org/issue/90/pioneers-fight-disability-rights/index.html

Sanctuary for Families. (2022, July 28). *The links between disability and domestic violence.* https://sanctuaryforfamilies.org/disability-domestic-violence/

Schrager, A. (2018, June 29). *The modern education system was designed to teach future factory workers to be 'punctual, docile, and sober.'* Quartz. https://qz.com/1314814/universal-education-was-first-promoted-by-industrialists-who-wanted-docile-factory-workers

SeeWriteHear.com. (n.d.). *What is accessibility?* https://www.seewritehear.com/learn/what-is-accessibility/

Sligh, A. (2019, June 20). *What I want you to know about able-bodied privilege.* Bringing the Sunshine. https://www.bringingthesunshine.com/2019/06/what-i-want-you-to-know-about-able-bodied-privilege/

SSA.gov. (n.d.). *The Depression.* Social Security History. https://www.ssa.gov/history/bank.html

Special Olympics. (n.d.). *Eunice Kennedy Shriver's story.* https://www.specialolympics.org/eunice-kennedy-shriver/bio

The Disability Union. (2020, September 19). *Know your disability history: Early America.* Disability Union.

Torrey, E. F. (1997). *Out of the shadows: Confronting America's mental illness crisis.* Wiley.

U.S. Access Board. (n.d.). *History of the U.S. Access Board.* https://www.access-board.gov/about/history.html

U.S. Centers for Disease Control and Prevention CDC. (2024). *Disability and health information for healthcare providers.* CDC Disability and Health. Retrieved January 13th, 2024, from https://www.cdc.gov/ncbddd/disabilityandhealth/hcp.html

U.S. Department of Education. (2022). *43rd Annual report to congress on the implementation of the Individuals with Disabilities Act, 2021.* Office of Special Education and Rehabilitative Services, Office of Special Education Programs. https://sites.ed.gov/idea/files/43rd-arc-for-idea.pdf

U.S. Department of Education. (2023). *A history of the Individuals with Disabilities Education Act.* https://sites.ed.gov/idea/IDEA-History#1980s-90s

Wagner, D. (n.d.). *Poor relief and the almshouse.* Disability History Museum. https://www.disabilitymuseum.org/dhm/edu/essay.html?id=60

Media Attributions

- Happy hour © Elevate is licensed under a CC BY-NC (Attribution NonCommercial) license
- Central Indiana Hospital © Legislative and State Manual of Indiana, 1903 is licensed under a Public Domain license
- Foundation of the American Government © Henry Hintermeister is licensed under a Public Domain license
- Stephen Hopkins Signature is licensed under a Public Domain license
- Benjamin Lay plaque © J. Nathan Matias is licensed under a CC BY-SA (Attribution ShareAlike) license
- Looms © Illustrator T. Allom, Engraver J. Tingle is licensed under a Public Domain license
- Men Wanted for the Invalid Corps © War Department is licensed under a Public Domain license

- 1907 Indiana Eugenics Law Marker © Gbauer8946 is licensed under a CC BY-SA (Attribution ShareAlike) license
- "Release the strange hold" © Wellcome Collection is licensed under a All Rights Reserved license
- FDR © FDR Presidential Library & Museum photograph by Margaret Suckley is licensed under a CC BY (Attribution) license
- Americans with Disabilities Act © National Museum of American History Smithsonian Institution is licensed under a CC BY-SA (Attribution ShareAlike) license
- Eunice Kennedy © Photograph by Richard Sears in the John F. Kennedy Presidential Library and Museum, Boston. is licensed under a Public Domain license
- Thorazine Ad © Unknown
- Edward V. Roberts © William Bronston is licensed under a Public Domain license
- Judy Heumann © William Bronston is licensed under a Public Domain license
- Day room © Oregon State Hospital is licensed under a Public Domain license

13.

Community Action and Activism

Bernadet DeJonge; Nikki Golden; and Cailyn F. Green

> **Learning Objectives**
>
> - The reader will explain different kinds of activism.
> - The reader will describe how activism impacts social change.
> - The reader will analyze theories of social change.

Systemic racism, discrimination, power, and privilege impact our society in various ways. Marginalized individuals may only sometimes be aware of how their experiences are connected to larger systems of discrimination. However, it is essential to recognize that, over time, individual marginalization can become a structural problem that affects entire communities. Individual and systemic factors contributing to discrimination must be addressed to create a more equitable and just society.

As people learn about systemic social justice issues, they often want to do something to impact injustice. Social movements such as the women's rights movement, the civil rights movement, the disability justice movement, and the Black Lives Matter movement all confronted individual and systemic injustice. Countless individuals, including Martin Luther King Jr., Elizabeth Cady Stanton, and Judy Heumann, have dedicated their lives to fighting for social justice causes. While the United States still struggles with systemic inequity, social change through activism has occurred throughout the complex history of the United States. This chapter examines how social change comes about and discusses people's different roles in social change.

Activism and Social Change

The Oxford English Dictionary (n.d.) defines *activism* as "the policy or action of using vigorous campaigning to bring about political or social change." Appadurai (2013) defines *activism* as "...the practice of addressing an issue, any issue, by challenging those in power" (2:25). Activism occurs both in personal and structural ways. According to Appadurai, Rosa

428 | COMMUNITY ACTION AND ACTIVISM

Parks became an individual activist when she refused to move to the back of the bus. Additionally, the 1999 WTO protests in Seattle exemplified structural activism by challenging the global economic systems and institutions that reinforce inequality.. While these two events differed in scope and scale, both shaped social change for generations. Appadurai states that anyone can be an activist.

Activity 13.1

Video: Danger of a Single Story by Chimamanda Ngozi Adichie (https://www.youtube.com/watch?v=D9Ihs241zeg)

 One or more interactive elements has been excluded from this version of the text. You can view them online here: https://milnepublishing.geneseo.edu/social-justice-in-human-services/?p=204#oembed-1 (#oembed-1)

Discussion Questions

- How does the video *The Danger of a Single Story* reflect the concepts of activism and social justice?
- Discuss the importance of a single story and the importance of collective stories. How do these concepts impact the experience of activism?

Activists work towards social change in various ways, including conventional and radical activism (Harvey, 2023; Human Rights Careers, n.d.). Conventional activism usually occurs through more traditional, legal means and often outside the public view. Conventional activism includes work in policy matters, media promotion, and networking with other advocacy groups. Radical activism is usually more extreme and, sometimes, through non-legal means. Radical activism is often more visible, generally through media coverage. Examples include sit-ins and protests (Johnston & Gulliver, 2022).

The heart of activism is people. Activists fight for their beliefs in various social, political, and cultural climates. Being an activist does not require protesting, subject expertise, or a naturally loud voice (Witter, 2023). Other ways to be a social activist include boycotting, running for office, policy advocacy, social media campaigns, fundraising, letter writing, and volunteer work (Anti-Defamation League, 2017; Harvey, 2023).

Activity 13.2 – What is Activism?

Video: What is Activism? by Anjali Appadurai (https://www.youtube.com/watch?v=zDVA7r7r0d0)

 One or more interactive elements has been excluded from this version of the text. You can view them online here: https://milnepublishing.geneseo.edu/social-justice-in-human-services/?p=204#oembed-2 (#oembed-2)

Discussion Questions

- Discuss the differences between conventional activism and radical activism. Is there a place for both? When might they conflict?
- What kind of activism have you participated in?

Moyer (2001) identified four individual activist roles during the change process. Social movements require all four roles: citizen, reformer, rebel, and change agent.

Citizen: To be effective, citizen activists must gain the community's respect. Effective citizen activists promote values such as freedom and non-violence while being willing to resist unethical or unfair institutional policy and practice. Ineffective citizen activists do not recognize the privilege held by the elite or corrupt power structures. Ineffective citizen activists often believe whatever they are told and give automatic obedience to those in power (Moyer, 2001).

Reformer: Reformer activists work within systems like government and corporations to enact change. Effective reformer activists enact change through lobbying, legal action, support for political candidates, and organizing rallies and protests. Ineffective reformer activists utilize a more patriarchal leadership model and struggle to remain flexible with a social movement. Ineffective reformer activists' leadership style does not promote actual democratic values, and they often take a middle ground or promote minor changes. Ineffective reformer activists frequently identify more with status quo power structures than proposed just changes (Moyer, 2001).

Rebel: Rebel activists stand up to institutions of power. They say "no" to current power structures. Effective rebel activists recognize systemic power issues and put those issues at the forefront of their action. Effective rebel activists are individuals who often take risks and find rebelling against power to be exciting. They believe truth is relative and are mindful of the best strategies for change. Ineffective rebel activists act without strategy. They are often disruptive and take an "any means necessary" approach to change. Ineffective rebel activists are often on the fringe of social movements. They have an attitude of absolute truth and usually put themselves and their ego before social movements (Moyer, 2001).

Change Agent: Change agent activists promote shifting paradigms towards social issues. They bring others into social movements. Effective change agent activists provide education and participatory opportunities for others, often striving to connect existing social structures. Ineffective change agent activists do not understand how sustainable system change occurs and instead promote a perfect, utopian version of social change. Ineffective change agent activists often focus on a singular issue without considering the overlap of multiple systems. In addition, they may promote more minor changes instead of large-scale paradigm shifts and have a patriarchal philosophy of leadership (Moyer, 2001).

> ### Activity 13.3 – Knowledge Check: Moyer's Roles
>
> **Discussion Questions**
>
> - Which of Moyer's (2001) roles in social change movements aligns best with your strengths and personality?
> - Which of Moyer's (2001) roles least aligns with your strengths or personality, and why?
> - Why is it important to understand and identify different roles in social change movements?
> - How can recognizing these roles enhance the effectiveness and cohesion of a social change movement?

Tension Between Roles

Hammond (2019) defines an activist as someone who "sees a problem in the world, believes the situation could be different, and takes action in the direction of the change they want to see" (p. 1). Each activist has an individual worldview and often acts on similar issues differently, even when the end goal is the same. These differences can lead to tension within social movements. Hammond argues that this tension must be resolved for activism to be effective. Activists must work to communicate with each other to avoid inter-activist conflict. Some suggestions to relieve this tension include increasing self-awareness, understanding the process of a social movement, connecting to other activists, having a strength-based approach, and collaborating through the conflict (Hammond).

Hammond (2019) utilizes Moyer's activist roles to exemplify inter-activist tension. Citizen and change agent activists often have tension regarding paradigm shifts, and reformer and rebel activists often have tension regarding strategies to enact change. For example, a reformer activist working on a policy change may find a rebel activist organizing a large-scale protest ineffective or detrimental to impacting change. Moyer (2001) argues that all roles must be present for activism to be effective. Thus, tension between roles must be acknowledged and managed as part of social change (Hammond, 2019).

> ### Activity 13.4 – Knowledge Check: Tension Between Roles
>
> **Discussion Questions**
>
> - What role tension might you experience based on your preferred role from above?
> - How can you mitigate tension between roles?

Social Change Theory

Social change theories examine the social changes in human interactions, cultures, and social institutions over time. Social change is complex and often slow (Human Rights Careers, n.d.).

Moyer argued that there are eight stages of social movements (Rose, 2012). They are:

- Normal Times—politically quiet times. Violations of freedom and beliefs exist, but no action is taken.
- Prove the Failure of Institutions. The public realizes that institutional and governmental policies violate their core beliefs and values and that government power is being used unfairly.
- Ripening Conditions. As the public becomes more discontent about societal conditions, more significant historic developments occur. Grassroots organizations form, which increases the public's discontentment and encourages the public to believe change can happen.
- Social Movement Take-Off. The social movement receives the public spotlight. Issues previously not at the forefront are suddenly headlines in the news. The public has conversations about the issues. A triggering event often fuels social movement take-off.
- Identify Crisis of Powerlessness. Activists worry that their efforts could be more effective and that they are futile. Activists believe those in power are too strong and that the movement has failed.
- Majority Public Support. The issue shifts from a short-term novelty to a long-term one and gains public support. The longer-term process of political and policy change begins.
- Success. Activists can envision the long-term success of a social movement. Success can take three forms: dramatic showdown, quiet showdown, or attrition.
- Continuing the Struggle. With success comes a return to normalcy, and the process begins again.

Discussion Questions

- Where do you think we are in the stages of social movement?
- Do you foresee a change in where we are in the stages of social movement? Discuss this.

Radical Flank Effect

The radical flank effect (RFE) considers how radical activists impact social movements. According to the RFE framework, there can be positive or negative flank effects. A positive flank effect occurs when the moderate activists look less extreme compared to the more radical ones. This may happen during a crisis, and the authorities work with the more moderate activists on potential solutions. A negative flank effect occurs when radical activists discredit a social movement. A negative flank effect can lead to collaboration with authorities, such as policyholders and politicians, which is less effective for more moderate activists. Many social movement activists fear the negative flank effect and thus often overlook the power of the positive flank effect (Hammond, 2019).

Momentum in Social Movement

In examining past social movements, Engler and Engler (2014) identified a difference between the initial momentum of a popular social movement and the long-term policy and structural change made through steady work on organizational structure, politics, and policy. There are four stages through which social movements progress: emergence, coalescence, bureaucratization, and decline. At times, movements can experience a lull due to widespread discouragement. This differs from individualized burnout. Some examples of social movements that have experienced lulls include Occupy Wall Street and the Climate Change Movement (Engler & Engler).

Both individual and systemic changes impact long-term cultural shifts. Hebert-Dufrense et al. (2022) theorize that achieving social change requires individual and policy change. In their research, Hebert-Dufrense et al. suggest that the best way to enact social change is for individuals and institutions to make simultaneous changes. This is a parallel process in which an individual impacts policy and, at the same time, policy impacts an individual.

Activity 13.5 – Digging Deeper: Bringing it All Together

Video: The Civil Rights Movement (https://www.youtube.com/watch?v=9ppTiyxFSs0)

One or more interactive elements has been excluded from this version of the text. You can view them online here: https://milnepublishing.geneseo.edu/social-justice-in-human-services/?p=204#oembed-3 (#oembed-3)

Video: Occupy Wall Street (https://www.youtube.com/watch?v=KFOWci6yrSs)

One or more interactive elements has been excluded from this version of the text. You can view them online here: https://milnepublishing.geneseo.edu/social-justice-in-human-services/?p=204#oembed-4 (#oembed-4)

Video: The #MeToo Movement (https://www.youtube.com/watch?v=u1Rb7TGgsp4)

One or more interactive elements has been excluded from this version of the text. You can view them online here: https://milnepublishing.geneseo.edu/social-justice-in-human-services/?p=204#oembed-5 (#oembed-5)

Video: Black Lives Matter Movement (https://www.youtube.com/watch?v=YG8GjlLbbvs)

One or more interactive elements has been excluded from this version of the text. You can view them online here: https://milnepublishing.geneseo.edu/social-justice-in-human-services/?p=204#oembed-6 (#oembed-6)

Video: The Disability Rights Movement (https://www.youtube.com/watch?v=2PnUza4FPz8)

One or more interactive elements has been excluded from this version of the text. You can view them online here: https://milnepublishing.geneseo.edu/social-justice-in-human-services/?p=204#oembed-7 (#oembed-7)

Discussion Questions

- What are some examples of conventional activism in these videos?
- What are some examples of radical activism in these videos?
- What examples do you see of the four stages of social movement in these videos?
- What might be the unintended consequences of these movements?
- What tensions exist in these movements?

- How have social movements of the past influenced each of these movements?

Thoughts from the Author

A book (Goldblum & Shaddox, 2021) I read while writing this text gave specific, actionable, and individual things that an individual can do to impact change. This format stuck with me throughout the writing of this text and continues to do so today. It led me to think a lot about how social change comes to be. In political commentary, we hear about community organizers, and we hear on social media and TikTok videos about people who are standing up to systemic racism, ableism, heterosexism, sexism, power, and privilege. I wanted to take some time in this text to make sure we addressed how social change occurs. It has been an exciting exercise in personal activism to think about my efforts and where and how I can continue to be an activist to impact social issues I care about. Increasingly, I realize how much my actions help me feel like I can make a difference. I try to shop locally, boycott stores that conflict with my ethical beliefs, call out "isms" when I see them, frame my work through a social justice lens, and have considered running for local office. These small things, even while systemic issues loom, might impact social change in some small ways. I like to think I can be an activist.

Sincerely,

Bernadet DeJonge

Chapter Summary Questions

1. What do you do that might be considered activism?
2. What new ways can you be an activist?
3. What actions can you take to advocate for social justice?
4. Considering Moyer's eight stages of social change, think about different social movements you have experienced in your lifetime. Does this model ring true?
5. How might understanding social change theory impact your ability to make a difference?

6. Describe your personal theory of social change. How do individuals make change?
7. How does this chapter on social change connect to different social justice movements?
8. Use the video examples provided to think about social change. Identify the roles and stages of social change in each movement.

References

Anti-Defamation League. (2017). *Ten ways youth can engage in activism*. ADL Education. https://www.adl.org/resources/tools-and-strategies/10-ways-youth-can-engage- activism

Appadurai, A. (2013, May 25). *What is activism?* [Video]. TedxYouth. https://www.youtube.com/watch?v=zDVA7r7r0d0

Engler, M., & Engler, P. (2014). *Surviving the ups and downs of social movement*. The Commons: Social Change Library. https://commonslibrary.org/surviving-the-ups-and-downs-of-social-movements/

Hammond, H. (2019). *Exploring roles in social change*. The Commons: Social Change Library. https://commonslibrary.org/exploring-roles-in-social-change-movements/

Harvey, B. (2023, January 1). *26 types of activism to know (plus examples)*. Good Resources. https://www.goodgoodgood.co/articles/types-of-activism

Hebert-Dufrense, L., Waring, T. M., St-Onge, G., Niles, M. T., Corlew, L. K., Dube, M. P., Miller, S. J., Gotelli, N., & McGill, B. J. (2022). Source-sink cooperation dynamics constrain institutional evolution in a group structured society. *Royal Society Open Science*, 9(3). https://doi.org/10.1098/rsos.211743

Human Rights Careers. (n.d.). *13 types of activism*. https://www.humanrightscareers.com/issues/types-of-activism/

Human Rights Careers. (n.d.). *What is social change?* https://www.humanrightscareers.com/issues/what-is-social-change/

Johnston, J., & Gulliver, R. (2022). *Activism and advocacy in public interest communication*. University of Queensland Press.

Moyer, B. (2001). *The four roles of social activism*. The Commons: Social Change Library. https://commonslibrary.org/the-four-roles-of-social-activism/

The Oxford English Dictionary. (n.d.). Activism. In *OED.com*. Retrieved August 30th, 2023 from https://www.oed.com/search/dictionary/?scope=Entries&q=activism

Rose, A. (2012). *Bill Moyer's movement action plan*. The Commons: Social Change Library. https://commonslibrary.org/resource-bill-moyers-movement-action-plan/

Witter, A. (2023). *What is activism? Here are 5 misconceptions*. ONE. https://www.one.org/international/blog/what-is-activism-misconceptions/

Media Attributions

- Black Lives Matter © Luis Morera is licensed under a CC BY-NC (Attribution NonCommercial) license
- Time for Change © Duncan Shaffer is licensed under a CC BY-NC (Attribution NonCommercial) license
- Denver protest © Colin Lloyd is licensed under a CC BY-NC (Attribution NonCommercial) license

14.

Social Justice Practice in Human Services: An Individual Approach

Cailyn F. Green; Kim Brayton; Carrie Steinman; and Bernadet DeJonge

Learning Objectives

- The reader will understand the role ethics play in working in the human service field.
- The reader will analyze how different types of personal bias impact human service professionals working in the field.
- The reader will describe how diversity issues exist within assessment practices.

The human services profession has always served culturally diverse populations in the United States. Early involvement in social issues demonstrates a commitment to social justice and advocacy to end discrimination, oppression, poverty, and other forms of injustice throughout the country's history (Sue & Sue, 2016). As human services professionals, we must recognize how individual and historical power and privilege may prevent us from understanding our clients' experiences and views.

In the human services field, professionals work with clients on various levels. Often, these levels are viewed through a systems lens. Bronfenbrenner's (1979) systems theory, also known as the ecological systems theory, posits that different environmental systems influence the people we serve in the human services field. This theory identifies five systems that interact to shape individual development: the microsystem (immediate surroundings like family and school), the mesosystem (interactions between microsystems), the exosystem (external environmental settings that indirectly affect the individual), and the macrosystem (broader cultural and societal influences). The chronosystem (the dimension of time encompassing life transitions and historical events) was recently added to the model. Bronfenbrenner's framework emphasizes the dynamic interplay between these systems and highlights the importance of considering multiple environmental contexts in understanding human growth and development (Bronfenbrenner, 1979).

Understanding the interactions between systems is essential in identifying the roles of power, privilege, and oppression in human services. Once we have identified how power,

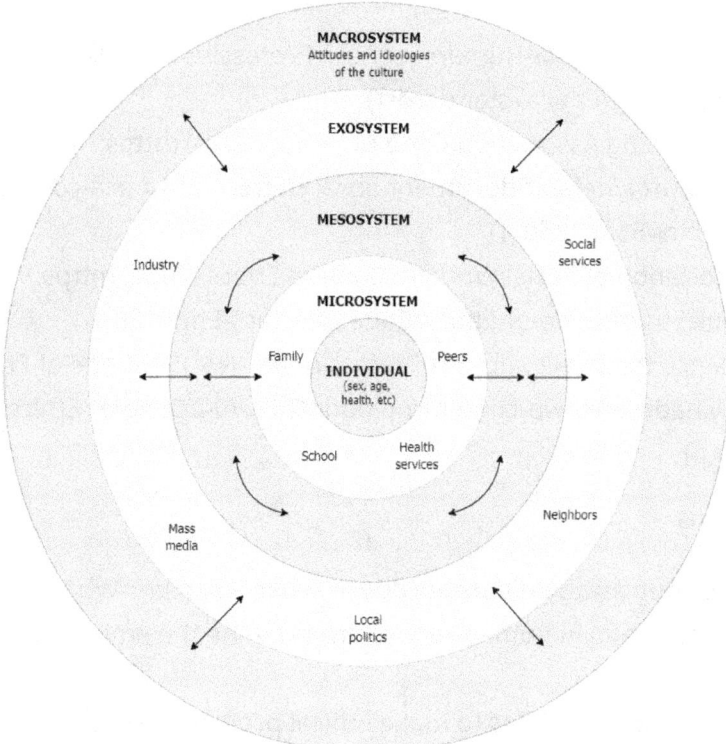

Bronfenbrenner's Ecological Theory of Development

privilege, and oppression impact clients, we can look toward equitable change in the field. This chapter will focus on the microsystem and examine individual social justice experiences in human services.

Ethics and Social Justice

One of the core foundations of the human services profession is understanding our ethical responsibilities. Ethics is the study of what is right and wrong and how we make decisions when that choice is unclear. Many professions, such as counseling, social work, direct support professionals, and human services, have established ethical codes of conduct to help. The National Organization for Human Services (NOHS) provides an ethical code of conduct for those working in the Human Services field to follow (NOHS, 2024).

Activity 14.1 – Digging Deeper: Ethical Codes

There are different ethical codes for various helping professions. As this is a chapter for human services students, we will focus on the National Organization for Human Services (NOHS) code. However, we are sharing some that might also be applicable as students continue in their helping careers.

- NOHS Ethical Standards for Human Services Professionals (2024) (https://www.nationalhumanservices.org/ethical-standards/)
- American Counseling Association Code of Ethics (2014) (https://www.counseling.org/docs/default-source/default-document-library/ethics/2014-aca-code-of-ethics.pdf?sfvrsn=55ab73d0_1)
- National Association of Social Workers Code of Ethics (2021) (https://www.socialworkers.org/About/Ethics/Code-of-Ethics/Code-of-Ethics-English)
- National Alliance for Direct Support Professionals (NADSP) Code of Ethics (2000) (https://www.nadsp.org/wp-content/uploads/2017/04/Code-of-Ethics-fillable-form-2016.pdf)

Discussion Questions

- Compare and contrast the different codes—what is similar? What is different?
- Why might it be useful in human services to examine the ethical codes of different professions?
- How can you use ethical codes to make ethical professional decisions?

NOHS Ethical Code in Practice

The National Organization for Human Services (NOHS) has developed an ethical code of conduct for human services professionals (NOHS, 2024). The Ethical Standards for Human Services Professionals outlines standards for human services work to establish professional boundaries and facilitate healthy, appropriate client relationships.

Multiple NOHS ethical codes apply to social justice in human services. Standard seven states: "Human service professionals ensure that their values or biases are not imposed upon their clients" (NOHS, 2024, para 11). Additionally, the NOHS ethical code calls out the responsibility of human services workers to be self-aware. This includes awareness of how social and political issues may disenfranchise and impact clients. Standard 14 states: "Human service professionals are aware of social and political issues, comprehend their effects on clients, and recognize how the impact of such issues vary among individuals from diverse backgrounds," (NOHS, 2024, para 18).

As ethical practitioners, human service professionals must examine their values and how they impact client relationships. Most ethical decision-making starts with an examination of values. This foundation for personal and professional choices profoundly impacts client services. All human service professionals have personal and professional values that can affect their work, and recognizing the similarities and differences between personal, professional, and client values is an important skill (Kenyon, 1999). In addition, boundaries are essential in the professional relationship, and if a human services worker does not maintain appropriate professional boundaries with their clients, power differentials become more apparent.

> ### Activity 14.2 – Digging Deeper: Values
>
> Can you identify what your values are? Having a solid sense of values is essential in the human services field. One of the ways human services workers can examine our values is by completing a card sort. Look at the cards listed at motivationalinterviewing.org (https://www.motivationalinterviewing.org/sites/default/files/valuescardsort_0.pdf) and sort out what cards are Important, Very Important, and Not Important to you. Then, choose your top five values from the choices.
>
> **Discussion Questions**
>
> - Did you find any values missing from the sort? What were they?
> - Was it hard to choose a top five? Why do you think that is?
> - What do the values you chose say about who you are as a human services worker?
> - What do the values you did not choose say about who you are as a human services worker?
> - How might knowing your values help when you conflict with someone else?

The human service professional has multiple responsibilities to their clients around social justice issues. The NOHS ethical code clearly states that supporting and developing a relationship with a client should be based on social justice principles. It outlines that human services workers must understand cultural norms within the client's community and integrate them into their practice (Hays & Erford, 2018). Ethical human services workers acknowledge the impact of social justice issues by respecting diversity and difference and ensuring inclusion and accessibility to all. Human services workers make a transparent and open effort to foster equity in all client interactions (NOHS, 2024).

Human service professionals also have a responsibility to their employers. Statements 33 and 34 discuss providing clients with high-quality services. Workload issues are a common problem in human services, and it is unethical to allow excessive workload to result in poor services, particularly since the clients we serve are often marginalized. Additionally, statement 34 states: "When a conflict arises between fulfilling the responsibility to the employer and the responsibility to the client, human service professionals advise both and work conjointly with all involved to manage the conflict" (NOHS, 2024).

Activity 14.3 – Digging Deeper: Case Example OASAS

The Office of Addiction Services and Supports (OASAS, 2020) in New York State uses policy to ensure equitable services. They developed a policy that their substance use treatment outpatient facility will monitor and assign cases to "ensure that all clients can expect quality treatment" (pg. 8). OASAS outlines how the intensity of treatment for each case should be a determining factor in assigning cases amongst the case managers. As human service workers, our workload requirements and high caseload often affect our client work. Our ethical obligation is to resolve this issue if it negatively impacts our clients.

Note from the author:

While evidence-based best practices and clinical standards exist to maintain equity amongst treatment, there is also a reality outside these guidelines. When I was working in an outpatient substance use treatment facility, the reality was that we had such a high number of clients seeking support that we had to take on cases that might have been intense for our already high caseload. Since many of our fellow outpatient facilities in the area had similar issues, we worked together to move clients around the best we could, but sometimes, there needed to be somewhere to refer to them. In these situations, we followed evidence-based best treatment practices in our groups and individual sessions to provide each client the highest quality of treatment. Sometimes the reality is a human service professional gets bigger caseloads than they can realistically handle. When this happens, what should we do as human service professionals?

-Dr. Green

Activity 14.4 – Burnout

Video: Service with a Smile (https://www.youtube.com/watch?v=6g09eRbouQg) by Laura Hockenbury, TEDxBoulder

> *One or more interactive elements has been excluded from this version of the text. You can view them online here: https://milnepublishing.geneseo.edu/social-justice-in-human-services/?p=206#oembed-1 (#oembed-1)*

Discussion questions

- How does this video connect to how we, as human service professionals, can properly distribute our time without burning out?
- How may burnout impact our ability to work effectively with clients who present with unique diverse situations that we are not personally aware of?

Personal Bias in Human Service Practice

Human services professionals are responsible for cultivating inclusivity and must be aware of personal biases and how they impact professional interaction (Hays & Erford, 2018). Biases are ingrained thoughts or feelings stemming from past experiences that significantly influence our actions and decisions. In general, biases are unconscious or implicit, and people are unaware of them. As Ross (2020) articulates in his book *Everyday Bias*, "If you are human, you are biased" (p. 1). This statement underscores the universality of bias, highlighting that everyone harbors some form of bias regardless of their background. Ross further elaborates that these biases can manifest in various ways, both constructive and detrimental. He explains that positive biases can sometimes lead to favorable outcomes, while negative biases can result in harmful consequences. Thus, the impact of bias is multifaceted, influencing our personal and professional perceptions and interactions in various ways (Ross, 2020). Understanding this dual nature of biases is crucial for fostering greater self-awareness and promoting fairer, more equitable services in the human services field.

Activity 14.5 -Digging Deeper

Discussion Questions

- Ross (2020) states, "If you are human, you are biased." How do you interpret this statement, and what implications does it have for self-awareness and personal growth in pursuing social justice in human services?
- Can you think of a situation where a positive bias had a constructive outcome in advancing social justice? Conversely, can you provide an example where a positive bias led to negative consequences that hindered social justice efforts?
- What strategies can individuals employ to identify and mitigate their own biases, both

> positive and negative, to promote social justice and more equitable interactions in human services?

Types of Bias

Before discussing how biases impact the human services field, let us define a few biases. Here are a few of the primary types of biases we regularly experience:

Affinity bias—We tend to prefer people more like us. If the group you identify yourself to be in is one with power or privilege, the affinity bias is stronger. When a decision is made which was impacted by affinity bias, it can interfere with people's work lives, personal situations, education settings, and social situations (Ricee, 2023).

Attribution Bias—Making judgments or assumptions about someone based on their appearance or behavior. This often occurs when we evaluate other people's behaviors based on our behaviors or cultural norms (Hurd, 2018).

Beauty bias – When an individual prioritizes others with cultural beauty characteristics (Maccarone, 2003). As beauty is defined by culture, what everyone defines as "beautiful" may differ.

Conformity Bias—This is "group think," the idea that when we are in a group, we are more likely to do things we may not do on our own (The University of Texas, 2024). Thus, we conform to the norm of the group.

Confirmation Bias—The tendency to favor and seek out evidence that supports preexisting beliefs, while ignoring or dismissing contradictory information. This often leads to individuals giving more weight to evidence that supports their views and downplaying evidence that does not (Casad & Luebering, 2023).

Contrast Effect—This bias occurs when people are compared to each other (Caccavale, 2020). Rather than seeing an individual based on their own merits, they are seen only in comparison to others. "Our perception is altered once we start comparing things to one another" (Caccavale, 2020, para. 2). This contrast effect can occur in two ways, positive and negative. A positive contrast effect is when someone is seen as better than someone else. A negative effect is when someone is seen as worse than someone else (Caccavale, 2022).

Gender Bias – This bias favors one gender over another, often resulting in unfair treatment towards individuals based on their gender. Unconscious gender bias can present itself in subtle ways (American Psychological Association, 2023). For example, assuming that some professions are for males and some are for females.

Geographical bias – This bias occurs when a person has a distorted opinion or judgment based on geographical location (Kowal, Sorokowski, Kulczycki, & Zelazniewicz, 2022). The geographical location may be where someone was previously living, is currently living, or will be moving to in the future.

The Halo Effect—This bias occurs when we focus on one perceived good feature about someone to the exclusion of everything else. It is also sometimes referred to as the "physical attractiveness stereotype" (Cherry, 2022, para. 3). Attractiveness is a significant part of the Halo Effect; people who are considered attractive by cultural standards are often seen to be more important in society than others (Cherry, 2022).

Sexism, Heterosexism, and Trans bias—These biases appear when individuals are biased toward those who deviate from traditional gender norms and expectations. These biases often lead to heterosexism, a prejudice that factors opposite-sex relationships and the belief that heterosexuality is superior to homosexuality (Centers for Disease Control, 2023).

Social class biases—This occurs when individuals experience negative feelings about a client based on their socio-economic background and social class. This kind of bias supports inequality based on economic and social status (Durante & Fiske, 2017).

Unconscious Bias – That first thought, any feeling you may get or preconceived notions we have are all personal biases. This may be based on a client's clothing, skin color, smell, language spoken, or the family members they may have with them (Veesart, 2020). Having them does not make us bad people; it simply makes us human. The goal is not to allow these unconscious, personal biases to influence the way we interact and make decisions for our clients.

Activity 14.6 – Overcoming Bias

Video: How to Overcome Our Bias (https://www.ted.com/talks/verna_myers_how_to_overcome_our_biases_walk_boldly_toward_them) by Verna Myers

 One or more interactive elements has been excluded from this version of the text. You can view them online here: https://milnepublishing.geneseo.edu/social-justice-in-human-services/?p=206#oembed-2 (#oembed-2)

Discussion Questions

- What does it mean to "walk boldly towards" our biases, and why is this approach important in overcoming them?
- According to the video, why do biases persist even when we consciously try to avoid them? How can awareness of this phenomenon help in addressing biases effectively?

- Discuss the concept of "bias literacy" introduced in the video. How can developing this literacy help us to be better human services professionals?
- In what ways does the concept of "walking boldly towards biases" align with principles of social justice? How can addressing biases contribute to advancing social justice goals in human services?
- Considering the insights from the video, what steps can individuals take today to start addressing their biases and fostering a more inclusive mindset? How can these actions create ripple effects in promoting fairness and equality in human services?

Assessment and Social Justice

One of the tasks of human services is to administer standardized assessments and screening tools. Examples of screening tools used in human services include the PHQ-9 for depression, the GAD-7 for anxiety, the ACES questionnaire to look at childhood trauma, the CAGE questionnaire to identify drug and alcohol use, and the Mini-Mental Status Exam, which looks at cognitive functioning in adults. These screening tools help human services professionals in various fields, such as social work, counseling, healthcare, and education, to identify potential issues, assess client needs, and guide appropriate interventions and treatment plans. Screenings in human services are selected based on the population being served and should be informed by evidence-based best practices. Screening and assessment play a crucial role in developing personalized treatment plans and ensuring that individuals receive the support and services required to improve their quality of life (Mulvaney-Day. et al, 2017).

Assessment and screening tools often contain significant biases. Social justice issues arise not only from the personal bias of human service professionals in interpreting answers but also from bias in the screening tools themselves. Some contextual factors that have the potential to cause bias in a screening or assessment tool include racialized identity and ethnicity, discrimination, neighborhood context, trauma, immigration status, gender identity, sexual orientation, and a client's age (Bridgwater, 2023).

Reynolds and Suzuki (2012) identify seven specific categories when it comes to potential consequences of bias in screening tools:

1. Inappropriate content. Tests are geared to majority experiences and values or are scored arbitrarily according to majority values. Correct responses or solution methods depend on material that is unfamiliar to minority individuals.
2. Inappropriate standardization samples. Minorities' representation in norming samples is proportionate but insufficient to allow them any influence over test development.
3. Examiners' and language bias. White examiners who speak standard English intimidate

minority examinees and communicate inaccurately with them, spuriously lowering their test scores.
4. Inequitable social consequences. Ethnic minority individuals, already disadvantaged because of stereotyping and past discrimination, are denied employment or relegated to dead-end educational tracks. Labeling effects are another example of invalidity of this type.
5. Measurement of different constructs. Tests largely based on majority culture are measuring different characteristics altogether for members of minority groups, rendering them invalid for these groups.
6. Differential predictive validity. Standardized tests accurately predict many outcomes for majority group members, but they do not predict any relevant behavior for their minority counterparts. In addition, the criteria that tests are designed to predict, such as achievement in White, middle-class schools, may themselves be biased against minority examinees.
7. Qualitatively distinct aptitude and personality. This position seems to suggest that minority and majority ethnic groups possess characteristics of different types, so that test development must begin with different definitions for majority and minority groups. (Reynolds & Suzuki, 2012, p. 87)

Some contextual factors which have potential to cause bias in a screening or assessment tool include racialized identity and ethnicity, discrimination, neighborhood context, trauma, immigration status, gender identity, sexual orientation, and a clients age (Bridgwater, 2023).

> ### Activity 14.7 – Knowledge Check: CAGE screening tool
>
> The CAGE screening tool is a common 4-question tool used to screen clients for alcohol abuse. CAGE stands for:
>
> - C—Cutting down
> - A—Annoyance by criticism
> - G—Guilty feeling
> - E—Eye-openers
>
> CAGE screening questions:
>
> - Have you ever felt you should cut down on your drinking?
> - Have people annoyed you by criticizing your drinking?
> - Have you ever felt bad or guilty about your drinking?
> - Have you ever had a drink first thing in the morning to steady your nerves or get rid of a hangover (eye-opener)?

> **Discussion Questions**
>
> - Which question do you think could have an issue with cultural bias? Explain your reasoning.
> - What are the advantages and disadvantages of using this 4-question screening tool?
> - Is there room for cultural differences to be explained by the client when answering this screening tool?

Human service professionals can take a variety of steps to mitigate the harmful consequences of bias in screening tools. These steps include utilizing updated and culturally sensitive and inclusive assessments, incorporating feedback from clients on assessments into best practice, and regularly reviewing screening tools to ensure they continue to meet best practice in the field. One of the most important steps is to facilitate the use of screening tools through an interactive dialogue with the client (McClintock et al., 2021). In this, the human services professional asks the questions and discusses the answers given, versus just writing down the answers or leaving the client in a room to fill out a form. By treating assessment as a conversation, the human service professional offers the client the opportunity to explain their answers. This allows the client to incorporate their cultural differences into their explanations.

Another important step in addressing bias in screening tools and assessments is training. Staff training is essential prior to using any screening tools. Training should include discussions about cultural bias in assessment, including the specific tool being implemented (McClintock et al., 2021). This approach allows professionals to consider these issues before using the screening tool.

Bias in Assessment and Documentation

Completing an intake assessment, also known as a biopsychosocial assessment, is often one of the first tasks in setting up services. This intake assessment forms the basis for developing, implementing, and evaluating a client's goals and progress. The human services professional collects information relevant to the client's background and needs during intake. Biases can impact the client's intake experience. For example, if a human service professional assumes an answer to a question and skips it, the client information in their chart or file may be incomplete. This may occur because of personal biases and preconceived notions and will result in an inaccurate assessment.

> **Activity 14.8 – Note from the author: Skipping Information**
>
> I am half White and half Mexican. However, I present as White. Many times, when forms have been filled out for me, people assume—based on appearance, education, and lack of accent—that I am White and mark that box. Thus, some of my records do not indicate my mixed-race status.
>
> -Dr. DeJonge (Bernie)
>
> **Discussion Questions**
>
> - What kind of important details might a human services professional overlook in a scenario like the one described? How could this affect service delivery?
> - What challenges might arise when administrative forms or records inaccurately reflect an individual's racial or ethnic identity? How could this impact the quality of services or support human service professionals provide?
> - How can human services professionals foster environments that validate and honor individuals' self-identified racial and ethnic identities, regardless of how they may be perceived externally?

To promote equity and inclusivity, human services professionals must ensure that they provide clients with an environment conducive to genuine responses. Often, biases are evident in both the questions asked of a client and those that are not. Examples of this include not asking about military service if the client is female, assuming someone's sexuality when they have stated they are married, or not asking a young student whether they have used substances or are sexually active. Additionally, documentation is a vital component for both the client and the agency, and often, reimbursement for services and accountability for the organization depends on appropriate documentation.

Charting

Human services professionals are responsible for recording client's employment, family, medical, social, socioeconomic, and mental health information. Documentation should be balanced, nonjudgmental, and objective. A chart should always be current and contain reliable information so that any agency professional can read and understand it (Silvestre et al., 2017). The chart should also explain why the client sees the human service professional. Case notes should be written about every interaction between the professional and the client. Strong case notes allow other human services professionals to read about the client's process thus far (Summers, 2016). The client's chart should not contain personal feelings about the client or any judgmental comments.

> ### Activity 14.9 – Digging Deeper: Case Examples
>
> Some examples of judgmental notes in a chart:
>
> - A human services worker conducts a home visit and writes notes about how the home does not feel comfortable or 'homey.'
> - A human services worker notes that a client's family members were "uncooperative" or "hostile" during a home visit.
> - A human service professional meets with a client and makes a case note about the client's hair being unfashionable or out of style.
> - A human services worker writes in a progress note that a client's religious practices are "strange" or "unusual."
> - A human services professional writes in a report that a client's neighborhood is "sketchy" or unsafe.
> - A human services worker notes that a client's behavior is "loud" or "boisterous."
> - A healthcare provider notes in a medical chart that a patient's weight or appearance is "unhealthy" or "unattractive."
>
> Discussion Questions
>
> - What kind of biases are present in the examples provided?
> - Discuss the potential consequences of human services professionals making subjective assessments about a client's appearance, living conditions, or cultural practices in writing. How can these judgments affect the clients being served?
> - What strategies can human services professionals employ to ensure that their documentation remains objective and free from personal biases?
> - How can professionals ensure that their notes accurately reflect the experiences and perspectives of clients, particularly those from diverse cultural backgrounds or communities?

Client Biases

It is important to recognize that clients also harbor unconscious biases that may affect their perceptions of us as professionals. Clients often feel anxious or uneasy about sharing their medical, mental health, employment, social, or familial information with providers (Summers, 2016), and this may be in part due to their assumptions and biases about both the individual they are working with or the human services field in general. It is the responsibility of the human services worker to identify when a client seems uncomfortable and work to establish rapport. It is also important to remember that sharing personal information and details about one's life can be a complicated process for many. This could be for personal, professional, or cultural reasons. In addition, many clients are in new and vulnerable situations. Even when clients feel a strong rapport with an individual human services worker, they may have negative biases around the systems they are navigating. These can develop from past negative events, things they have heard in the community, and/or biases they hold around what kind of people receive or are entitled to help when they are struggling. At times, these biases can present as hostility or frustration, making building rapport difficult. It is our responsibility to be aware of this and mitigate it professionally and within the bounds of our employment agency's parameters.

Activity 14.10 – Case Study: Selina

Selina is an experienced addiction counselor and a Credentialed Alcoholism and Substance Abuse Counselor (CASAC) with a master's degree in mental health counseling who works at a local outpatient treatment facility. Hunter is her court-mandated client. Hunter is a 26-year-old Black male who was assigned to be on Selina's caseload after he was pulled over and cited for driving while intoxicated (DWI). Hunter faces potential jail time for noncompliance with treatment. After completing a comprehensive biopsychosocial assessment with Hunter, Selina presented his case to the treatment team. The team recommended that Hunter engage in intensive outpatient treatment, which would consist of three hours of group therapy, three days a week. Hunter strongly disagreed with this treatment recommendation. During their discussion in Selina's office, Hunter expressed skepticism about Selina's expertise due to her lack of personal addiction experience. Hunter said directly to Selina, "You are a pretty little White girl who has never seen any problem in your whole life because daddy always got you out of every problem you ever encountered. I want a counselor like me, who has lived where I live and who has been through issues like this. That is the only way I will get a fair treatment recommendation."

Discussion Questions

- How might racial differences between Hunter and Selina influence their interactions and perceptions of each other's expertise?
- What steps can be taken to address potential racial biases or cultural misunderstandings in therapeutic settings? What strategies can build culturally responsive therapeutic alliances?
- Reflecting on Hunter's skepticism toward Selina's expertise, how might racial stereo-

types or historical mistrust impact his willingness to engage in treatment?
- Considering Selina's role as a White counselor and Hunter's experience as a Black client, how might cultural competence and humility contribute to effective treatment outcomes? How can counselors educate themselves about the impact of systemic racism on addiction treatment and recovery?
- Discuss the importance of cultural humility in Selina's response to Hunter's criticism of her expertise. How can counselors acknowledge their own limitations and biases while fostering an environment of mutual respect and collaboration?

Activity 14.11 – Digging Deeper: Proxemics: The Study of Personal Space

The amount of personal space we provide between ourselves, and others varies depending on our relationship status with them (Mehta, 2020). The video linked here gives a great outline of the study of proxemics: Proxemics (https://players.brightcove.net/268012963001/Sy9lbkRKl_default/index.html?videoId=ref:V807648&secureConnections=true&secureHTMLConnections=true&autoStart=false)

Discussion Questions

- How does personal bias or your power as a human service professional impact your personal space with a client?
- How would you respond if a client is not respecting your personal space?

Equitable Distribution of Services

Triage, derived from the French verb "trier" meaning "to sort" (Christian, 2019), plays a crucial role not only in emergency room settings but also in human services agencies. Triage guides the prioritization of client services, starting during intake or initial assessments and continuing throughout the client's service journey. Triage often follows policies established by funding sources, legislation, and human services agencies. As human services agencies are often underfunded, triage allocates limited resources efficiently and ensures timely access to care. However, concerns related to social justice arise as the triage process can inadvertently perpetuate systemic inequalities, affecting marginalized communities who may face barriers to accessing timely and appropriate services. These disparities highlight the importance of implementing equitable triage protocols prioritizing fairness, inclusivity, and respect for diverse client needs and circumstances (Christian, 2019).

The human service field also faces challenges related to wait times. From mental health visits to emergency departments, Black Americans experience the longest waiting times and are less likely to be transferred to another facility compared to White Americans (Macias-Konstantopoulos, 2023). Wait times are often influenced by over-triaging. This occurs when the human services worker identifies a high number of clients needing immediate care. When over-triaging occurs, already stretched resources are stretched even tighter, and human services agencies start to experience extended wait times for treatment, extended treatment times, errors in triaging, and overcrowding (Hitchcock et al., 2013).

An example of this is the scheduling of initial appointments. Often, there are same-day or similar appointment slots set aside for emergency intake cases. However, when clients have been over-triaged, those slots may be filled, and more urgent needs may still need to be met. A crucial step in addressing this issue is to ensure that intake specialists receive thorough training in triage protocols, encompassing a comprehensive understanding of policy regarding initial appointments, emergency cases, and triage procedures (Christian, 2019).

Access and Barriers to Resources

Human service workers assist clients in accessing essential resources. These resources can be tangible, such as housing, medicine, textbooks, transportation, or wheelchairs, or intangible, such as emotional support or education. When human service professionals strategize to provide clients with access to these resources, they must consider their circumstances and ability to utilize them effectively. Human service professionals must also consider realistic accessibility before referring clients to resources (Martin, 2018).

For example, we can tell a client, "If you go to the pharmacy, you can pick up your prescription." However, it may not be that simple. Barriers to picking up a prescription include lack of transportation, the pharmacy's limited hours, prescription coverage, and cost. Lee et al. (2021) identified that "non-Hispanic Whites had the highest health insurance coverage at 94.6%, followed by Asians at 93.2%, Blacks at 90.3%, and Hispanics at 82.2%" (2011, p. 1). In addition to these barriers, there may also be a language barrier or issues with health literacy that can impact medication adherence. It is a probability that all clients will experience some roadblocks in obtaining services. It is the responsibility of a human services worker to recognize these obstacles and assist clients in navigating around them.

Creating accessibility to resources requires creativity and brainstorming. Often, human services workers must think outside the box when it comes to generating access. Examples of this include contacting vendors who can provide resources at a lower cost, negotiating with community organizations to secure donated goods or services, coordinating with local transportation providers to arrange reliable travel options, leveraging social media and community networks to find support groups or educational opportunities, and partnering with businesses to create job opportunities or internships. By employing creative and resourceful strategies, human services workers can better meet the diverse needs of their clients. A bonus to identifying and managing barriers to resources is that increasing access to one resource often creates a path for future resources. For example, if we support clients in obtaining employment and stable housing, we open the door for them to access education (Martin, 2018).

Human service professionals must balance the quality of the resources against reasonability and accessibility (Martin, 2018). If the best resource is an hour's drive away, but the client does not have access to transportation, then it is not the best resource for them. When this occurs, it is the responsibility of the human services worker to work with the client to determine what is accessible to the client. Sometimes, a lesser quality resource is better than the client not getting any resource due to lack of accessibility.

> **Activity 14.12 – Knowledge Check: Access to Resources**
>
> 1. What are some common barriers that clients from marginalized communities might face in accessing tangible resources such as housing, medicine, and transportation? How can human service professionals help clients overcome these barriers while advocating for social justice?
> 2. Discuss the importance of understanding a client's specific circumstances when strategizing to provide access to resources. How can human service professionals ensure they are aware of systemic inequalities that may affect their clients?
> 3. How can human service workers balance the quality of resources against their accessibility? Consider the social justice implications of making these decisions and ensuring fair resource distribution.
> 4. Discuss the importance of continuous assessment and adaptation in helping clients access resources. How can human service professionals ensure they remain responsive to the changing needs and circumstances of clients, particularly those from marginalized communities?
> 5. What strategies can you employ when no accessible resources are available to clients?

Education of the Human Services Professional

Effective social justice and diversity education prepares competent practitioners (Olcon et al., 2020), and human services educators set the tone and direction for professional discourse and practice. However, theoretical frameworks and strategies for teaching social justice and diversity in education have increasingly been criticized. Sue and Sue (2016) suggest that the educational focus on cultural competence and skills such as self-awareness and personal knowledge have become the focus in higher education as opposed to anti-racist practice (Dominelli, 2008). While many human service professionals call for eliminating racism and oppression, the field has remained mostly silent on the role that Whiteness and Eurocentrism play in systemic racism and structural injustice (Olcon et al., 2020).

Human service courses in social justice that teach students about power, privilege, and oppression are essential additions to professional education. Jeyasingham (2012) explains that White human service professionals should consider engaging with "Whiteness studies" because they provide insight into the invisible and dominant ways power operates (p. 682). Social justice-focused education allows human service professionals to understand White Privilege and its potential impact on their relationships with clients. This approach to incorporating social justice education into human services must include anti-racist pedagogy (Abrams and Gibson, 2007). It is the responsibility of the human services worker to introspect and consider individual and institutional causes of inequalities that may affect their relationships with clients.

One way for human services professionals to continue their education on social justice and diversity is through obtaining licenses and credentials. Many licensing entities require professionals to complete continuing education credits, which can include specific training, classes, or conferences. By maintaining an active license or credential, human services workers remain current on the latest research and best practices in their field. Since social justice is a field that is constantly evolving, these training sessions are essential for human service professionals.

Activity 14.13 – Digging Deeper: Research a credential or license you are interested in working towards obtaining.

Some example credentials include (but aren't limited to):

- Certified Case Manager (https://ccmcertification.org/get-certified)
- Mental Health Counselor in New York State (https://www.op.nysed.gov/professions/mental-health-counselors/license-requirements)
- CASAC Credential in New York State (https://oasas.ny.gov/credentialing/casac)
- Certified Rehabilitation Counselor (CRC) Guide (https://crccertification.com/wp-content/uploads/2021/01/CRCCertificationGuide-2021.pdf)
- Licensed Clinical Social Worker in New York State (https://www.op.nysed.gov/professions/licensed-clinical-social-worker/license-requirements)

Discussion Questions

- What credential or license are you interested in obtaining, and why did you choose it?
- What are the specific educational and experiential requirements needed to qualify for

> this credential? How might these be easy or difficult to obtain? What social justice concerns might be present in this requirement?
> - Are there any ethical considerations or professional standards associated with holding this credential? Discuss the ethical code associated with this credential.
> - Are there any financial considerations associated with pursuing this credential such as application fees, exam costs, or continuing education expenses? Why might cost be an issue of social justice?
> - What are the requirements for social justice or diversity continuing education for this credential? If there are none, why do you think this is so? Should there be?

Thoughts from the Authors

I have worked hands-on in the human service field for many years. I worked as a New York State Credentialed Alcoholism and Substance Abuse Counselor (CASAC) in outpatient, inpatient, long-term, and short-term facilities. My specialty was working closely with the recently incarcerated who were court-mandated to substance use treatment. While working with this population, I had to learn quite a bit about my personal biases and how to address them to be the best counselor possible. I had to check my preconceived notions about the recently incarcerated. While I have put in significant work to move toward eliminating my bias from my clinical interactions, there will never be a time when my personal bias is *Poof* gone. My personal bias is part of what makes me unique as a human and a counselor. As long as I keep them in the forefront of my mind so I do not let them interfere with my clinical practices, I am working towards creating a stable and safe environment for my clients.

While writing this chapter, I researched current social justice issues. At first, I read the most commonly discussed topics (e.g., George Floyd, how our prisons have a disproportionate population of minorities, etc.). However, as I dove down some internet rabbit holes, I learned about many more that have yet to be widely known or discussed. We must discuss these situations to gather the strength to make the necessary changes. Here is a short list of current social justice issues that need to be discussed and paid more attention to (please note this list is not exhaustive; instead, it is a jumping-off point to entice you to fall some of those research rabbit holes):

- How COVID-19–induced poverty has disproportionately impacted the Latino and Black communities:
  - Income inequality
  - Food insecurity
  - Housing insecurity
  - Gender-based violence
  - Political extremism
  - Reproductive rights

-Dr. Green

Like Dr. Green, I have worked in the human service field for many years now. I feel like I am learning a new way my biases affect my perceptions every day. How many times have you heard the older people in your lives say something like: "Kids these days…"? I find myself falling into that thinking more as I age. This is where my daughters help me to recognize how even biases based on my generation impact my interactions.

A great example is accessibility. Both of my daughters dread calling someone on the phone. They would much rather text or go online to make a reservation or send a message. When they are now at the age where they need to call to set up their own doctor's appointments and procedures, they have shared how challenging it is and that it is something they avoid, therefore putting off getting seen by their doctors. At first, my reaction was to dismiss this and minimize the issue. Then, I stopped to think that the upcoming generation has a very different experience with communication. Just because I can easily make that phone call, are we limiting accessibility for those without that ability? I guess this is where those patient portals I still do not use come in handy. While I believe there are some beautiful traditions and lots to learn from others who have been doing things for some time, assuming that the younger generation has to do everything the way we have always done things is a potentially dangerous bias.

A few words of advice from someone who has worked in this field for many years and has learned some lessons that apply across all situations. I want to share a couple here. Your role does not matter; there are two key things to integrate into any intake in this field. First, LISTEN. There is a saying: "We have two ears and one mouth because it is twice as important to listen as it is to talk." Actively listening means you are present, attentive, and engaged in what that person is sharing. Second, when in doubt, ask. Never assume you know someone's experience. Even if the person looked like you and grew up in the same neighborhood as you, you have no idea what they experienced. Never be afraid to ask.

-Dr. Brayton

Chapter Summary Questions

1. Why must human service professionals be in tune with social justice and equity movements in their community?
2. Why is it important that we not allow our personal biases to be shown in our work with clients? What might the consequences of this be?
3. What are some examples of personal biases that have come up for you as a human services professional?
4. How does connecting with culture help us recognize our biases?
5. How do we decide how to distribute our time amongst our clients? What are some things we should consider?

References

Abrams, L. S., & Gibson, P. (2007). Teaching notes: Reframing multicultural education: Teaching White privilege in the social work curriculum. *Journal of Social Work Education*, 43(1), 147–160. doi:10.5175/JSWE.2007.200500529

American Counseling Association. (2014). Code of Ethics. ACA 2014 Code of Ethics (counseling.org)

Andreassen, R. A. (2016). Professional intervention from a service perspective. In Gubrium, J. F., Andreassen, T. A., Solvang, P., & Hamm, L. (eds), *Reimagining the human service relationship* (pp 33–58). Columbia University Press. https://doi.org/10.7312/gubr17152

Bridgwater, M. A., Petti, E., Giljen, M., Akouri-Shan, L., DeLuca, J. S., Rakhshan Rouhakhtar, P., Millar, C., Karcher, N. R., Martin, E. A., DeVylder, J., Anglin, D., Williams, R., Ellman, L. M., Mittal, V. A., & Schiffman, J. (2023). Review of factors resulting in systemic biases in the screening, assessment, and treatment of individuals at clinical high-risk for psychosis in the United States. *Frontiers in Psychiatry, 14*, 1117022–1117022. https://doi.org/10.3389/fpsyt.2023.1117022

Buggs, M. D., Catalano, C. J., & Wagner, R. (2023). Sexism, heterosexism, and trans oppression: An integrated perspective. In M. Adams (Ed.), *Teaching for diversity and social justice* (4th ed., pp. 176–213). Routledge. https://doi.org/10.4324/9781003005759

Casad, B. J., & Luebering, J. E. (2023, August 18). *Confirmation bias*. Britannica. https://www.britannica.com/science/confirmation-bias

Caccavale, J. (2020, October, 12). *What is contrast effect? And how it impacts recruitment.* Applied. https://www.beapplied.com/post/what-is-contrast-effect-and-how-it-impacts-recruitment

Centers for Disease Control. (2023). Genderism, Sexism, and Heterosexism. Genderism, Sexism, and Heterosexism | CDC

Cherry, K. (2022, October 24). *The halo effect in psychology: Attractiveness is more than looks.* VeryWell Mind. https://www.verywellmind.com/what-is-the-halo-effect-2795906

Christian, M. D. (2019). Triage. *Critical Care Clinics, 35*(4), 575–589. https://doi.org/10.1016/j.ccc.2019.06.009

Crandall, A., Powell, E. A., Bradford, G. C., Magnusson, B. M., Hanson, C. L., Barnes, M. D., Novilla, M. L. B., & Bean, R. A. (2020). Maslow's hierarchy of needs as a framework for understanding adolescent depressive symptoms over time. *Journal of Child and Family Studies, 29*(2), 273–281. https://doi.org/10.1007/s10826-019-01577-4

Dominelli, L. (2008). *Anti-racist social work* (3rd ed). Palgrave Macmillan.

Durante, F., & Fiske, S. T. (2017). How social-class stereotypes maintain inequality. Current Opinion Psychology. 18:43–48. doi: 10.1016/j.copsyc.2017.07.033.

Hays, D. G., & Erford, B. T. (2018). *Developing multicultural counseling competence: A systems approach.* 3rd edition. Pearson.

Hitchcock, M., Gillespie, B., Crilly, J., & Chaboyer, W. (2013). Triage: An investigation of the process and potential vulnerabilities. *Journal of Advanced Nursing, 70*(7), 1532–1541. doi.org/10.1111/jan.12304

Hoskovec, J. M., Bennett, R. L., Carey, M. E., DaVanzo, J. E., Dougherty, M., Hahn, S. E., LeRoy, B. S., O'Neal, S., Richardson, J. G., & Wicklund, C. A. (2018). Projecting the supply and demand for certified genetic counselors: A workforce study. *Journal of Genetic Counseling, 27*(1), 16–20. https://doi.org/10.1007/s10897-017-0158-8

Hughes, C. (2020). *Critical employment, ethical, and legal scenarios in human resource development.* University of Arkansas.

Hurd, S. (2018, September 29). *What is attribution bias and how it secretly distorts your thinking.* Learning Mind. https://www.learning-mind.com/attribution-bias/

Jeyasingham, D. (2012). White noise: A critical evaluation of social work education's engagement with Whiteness studies. *British Journal of Social Work, 42*(4), 669–686. doi:10.1093/bjsw/bcr110

Kenyon, P. (1999). *What would you do? An ethical case workbook for human service professionals* (1st ed) Cengage.

Kowal, M., Sorokowski, P., Kulczycki, E.,& Żelaźniewicz, A. (2022). The impact of geographical bias when judging scientific studies. *Scientometrics, 127*(1), 265-273.

Lee, D.C., Liang, H., & Shi, L. (2021). The convergence of racial and income disparities in health insurance coverage in the United States. *International Journal Equity Health, 20*(1):96. doi: 10.1186/s12939-021-01436-z.

Macias-Konstantopoulos, W. L., Collins, K.A., Diaz, R., Duber, H.C., Edwards, C.D., Hsu, A.P., Ranney, M.L., Riviello, R.J., Wettstein, Z.S., & Sachs, C.J. (2023). Race, healthcare, and health disparities: A critical review and recommendations for advancing health equity. *Western Journal of Emergency Medicine, 24*(5):906-918. doi: 10.5811/westjem.58408.

Maccarone, D. (2003). The beauty bias. *Psychology Today.* The Beauty Bias | Psychology Today

Marsden, J., Newton, M., Windle, J., & Mackway-Jones, K. (2013). *Emergency triage: telephone triage and advice.* John Wiley & Sons.

Martin, M., (2018). *Through the eyes of practice settings.* Pearson.

McClintock, A. H., Fainstad, T., Jauregui, J., & Yarris, L.M. (2021). Countering bias in assessment. *Journal of Graduate Medical Education,13*(5):725-726. doi: 10.4300/JGME-D-21-00722.1.

McElroy, K., Moore, D., Hilterbrand, L., & Hindes, N. (2017). Access services are human services: Collaborating to provide textbook access to students. *Journal of Access Services, 14*(2), 80-91. https://doi.org/10.1080/15367967.2017.1296769

Myer, R. A., Whisenhunt, J. L., & James, R. K. (2022). *Crisis intervention ethics casebook.* American Counseling Association.

Office of Addiction Services and Supports. (2020). Part 822 Outpatient Services Clinical Standards. Clinical Standards (ny.gov)

Olcoń, K., Gilbert, D. J., & Pulliam, R. M. (2020). Teaching about racial and ethnic diversity in social work education: A systematic review. *Journal of Social Work Education, 56*(2), 215-237. https://doi.org/10.1080/10437797.2019.1656578

Reynolds, C. R., & Suzuki, L. A. (2012). Bias in psychological assessment. Assessment Psychology. In Weiner, I. B (Eds.), *Handbook of Psychology.* (82-113). John Wiley & sons, Inc. https://doi.org/10.1002/9781118133880.hop210004

Ricee, S. (2023, July 13). *What is affinity bias?* Diversity for Social Impact. https://diversity.social/affinity-bias-definition/

Ross, H. J. (2020). *Everyday bias: Identifying and navigating unconscious judgements in our daily lives.* Rowman & Littlefield.

Schippers, M. (2007). Recovering the feminine other: Masculinity, femininity, and gender hegemony. *Theory and Society, 36*(1), 85-102. https://doi.org/10.1007/s11186-007-9022-4

Silvestre, C. C., Santos, L. M. C., de Oliveira-Filho, A. D., & de Lyra, D. P. (2017). 'What is not written does not exist': The importance of proper documentation of medication use history. *International Journal of Clinical Pharmacy, 39*(5), 985–988. https://doi.org/10.1007/s11096-017-0519-2

Stiffler, M. C., & Dever, B. V. (2015). *Mental Health Screening at School Instrumentation, Implementation, and Critical Issues* (1st ed.). Springer International Publishing. https://doi.org/10.1007/978-3-319-19171-3

Substance Abuse and Mental Health Services Administration. (2018). *Crisis intervention team (CIT) methods for using data to inform practice: A step-by-step guide.* HHS Pub. No. SMA-18-5065.

Sue, D. W., & Sue, D. (2016). *Counseling the culturally diverse: Theory and practice* (7th ed.). Wiley & Sons.

Sue, D. W., Rasheed, M. N, & Rasheed, J. M. (2016). *Multicultural social work practice* (2nd ed.). Wiley & Sons.

Summers, J. (2019). Theory of healthcare ethics. In E.E. Morrison & B. Furlong (Eds.), *Health Care Ethics: Critical Issues for the 21st Century* (4th ed., pp. 3–39). Jones & Bartlett.

Veesart, A., & Barron, A. (2020). Unconscious bias: Is it impacting your nursing care? *Nursing Made Incredibly Easy!, 18*(2), 47–49. doi: 10.1097/01.NME.0000653208.69994.12.

Walker, P. (2020). Triage in a pandemic; equity, utility, or both? *Ethics & Medicine, 36*(3), 147–131.

Media Attributions

- Bronfenbrenners Ecological Theory of Development © Abbeyelder is licensed under a CC BY-SA (Attribution Share-Alike) license

15.

Social Justice Practice in Human Services: A Systems Approach

Cailyn F. Green; Kim Brayton; Carrie Steinman; and Bernadet DeJonge

> **Learning Objectives**
>
> - The reader will understand the history and current issues regarding systematic barriers to clients receiving human services.
> - The reader will analyze the systems behind addressing housing emergencies, disaster planning, and intimate partner violence in an equitable way.
> - The reader will describe how historical human service theories guide professionals working in the field today.

Introduction

A system is a combination of resources, people, institutions, and processes working towards a similar goal (Clarkson et al., 2018). Systems are created to help people and entities complete work more efficiently. Human service professionals often work within systems regarding intake processes, documentation, billing, and other logistics. Human service professionals should recognize that the environment and culture of a social service organization/system may be an inherent obstacle to clients' successes. Additionally, workers must recognize that the problems clients face when accessing services are due to organizational or systemic issues. Multicultural organizational development is an approach to ending organizational oppression and discrimination (Sue et al., 2016). This chapter will examine the intersection of human services systems and social justice.

Power Structures

Human service organizations depend on the rules and regulations set by different stakeholders to succeed. This is a common practice of all service agencies, governmental or nonprofit. Human service professionals often become accustomed to following these rules and may forget the power their role gives them. When the human service professionals assess the level of care the client needs, formulate the treatment plan, and interact with the insurance companies, the client can feel as if they have no control over the outcome (Andreassen, 2016). Human service professionals should always remember that their clients are human and may be in vulnerable situations (Nesoff, 2022). While this power dynamic between the worker and client may be challenging, a client-centered, collaborative approach to working together is crucial to demonstrating respect (Spencer et al., 2019).

Power Roles

Human service professionals must recognize that the environment and culture of a social service organization may be an inherent obstacle to client success. The human services worker/client relationship is power-centric, and clients may perceive that human services professionals have the power to provide them with access to resources and services. However, it is often the agency itself that has the most power in human service organizations.

Many social service organizations support monocultural policies and practices in their agencies where only one way of doing things is supported and enforced. An example of a monoculture would be a substance use treatment facility choosing not to practice harm reduction techniques even though harm reduction is identified as an evidence-based best practice. The agency, and subsequently the human services workers, see this as "we just don't do it that way here." Monocultural attitudes often result in outdated methods being used at an agency, as change is rejected in favor of the status quo (Sue et al., 2016).

Progressing from a monocultural to a multicultural organization requires agencies to understand both mono- and multicultural strategies and analyze whether the agency's policies and procedures promote an organizational culture of access and equity. Multicultural Organizational Development (MOD) is a theory that examines organizations through a social justice framework. MOD is an approach to ending organizational oppression and discrimination, and can be used to analyze and change monocultural attitudes at the organizational level. MOD investigates the power imbalance between management and employees and how that relationship impacts clients of human services (Sue et al., 2016).

Human service workers must recognize that issues with client access to services are often due to organizational or systemic issues. According to Sue et al. (2016), monocultural organizations have policies and procedures that may impede a worker's attempt to provide their diverse clients with "culturally appropriate services" (p. 345). For an agency, and, consequently, a worker, to provide culturally competent services, the organization must have workers who practice cultural competence, and the organization itself must have a culture of competence and proficiency around DEI issues (Sue et al., 2016).

> **Activity 15.1 – Knowledge Check**
>
> 1. If you have experience in a human service organization as a client or a worker, would you rate that agency as monocultural or multicultural? How do you decide if an agency is monocultural or multicultural?
> 2. What social justice issues might emerge from policies or practices at human services agencies?
> 3. What interventions can be used by organizations to meet the needs of diverse clients?
> 4. What are the supports and barriers to implementing anti-oppressive practices in human services organizations? How do we overcome these barriers?

Systemic Barriers to Service

When a human service provider is tasked with identifying a client's needs, the first step is to undertake a comprehensive needs assessment. This needs assessment provides information to help connect clients with the resources that address their needs. While each client has different needs, there are some common systemic barriers to receiving services. Examples include access to identification or documentation, internet access, and language barriers.

Many marginalized populations do not have access to identification. Research shows that 21% of Black Americans, 23% of Latin Americans and 68% of Transgender Americans do not have a valid form of identification (Hesano, 2023). Lack of identification creates an immediate social justice issue as many government and privately funded resources require identification for clients to receive benefits. Some government organizations have acknowledged the systemic racism and inequities in their policies and are working to improve access and remove obstacles for clients, yet many have not. It is the task of the worker and the client together to identify and resolve potential issues before the client is sent to receive services.

Internet access is another systemic issue of equity when considering human service clients. Access to services usually starts online where applications, program requirements, costs, and intake forms are found. While this is convenient for the agency and individuals with reliable internet access, many clients lack stable, reliable internet access. Before assuming that a client has stable internet, the human services worker should assess this as a potential barrier (Bauerly et al., 2019). If a client does not have access to the internet, it is the responsibility of the human service worker to problem-solve this with the client. This may look like helping them find a local library or community program that offers internet access, or, if your role permits, assisting them to access the internet. Human service workers must also be aware that some clients may struggle not only with internet access but also lack the computer skills to utilize it, even when access is provided.

If a client experiences a language barrier, it is important for the human service provider to acknowledge this and find ways to assist the client. Supporting monolingual habits, where an agency only provides resources in one language or does not offer language interpretation support, leads to social exclusion. This becomes a social justice issue when a client cannot communicate effectively with their treatment provider (Papa, 2020). Many human service professional agencies contract with interpreters, which can be accessed via phones. This looks like a client being in a session with the human service provider, calling the interpreter and putting them on speaker. They support the professional in communicating with the client.

Activity 15.2 – Digging Deeper: Utilizing an Interpreter

Dr. DeJonge (Bernie) here. I have worked extensively with interpreters in a variety of settings and have had my share of good, bad, and everything in between. Here are some real-world examples from my work.

I had a client from Iraq who had a crippling depression and would only sit on the floor in a corner. The Farsi interpreter, who was a woman, explained the cultural significance of this, walked me through appropriate vs. inappropriate questions on my assessment to ask in front of the men present, and cued me for cultural considerations like taking off my shoes. Because of her contextual information, I was able to build a solid rapport with the client and her family support system.

I had a Muslim caregiver from the Middle East who needed an interpreter to complete her paperwork and training. The interpreting agency sent a male interpreter. She got very upset and refused to meet with him, particularly since I wanted to leave them alone to watch a required video. The male interpreter explained to me it was not socially appropriate for him to be alone with her. The next visit, I ensured the agency sent a female interpreter.

I had a Spanish interpreter who was interpreting for an Adult Protective Services case I was investigating. I would ask questions, and he would give short one-to-two-word interpretations to the client. I speak a little bit of Spanish, so I was able to follow along and knew he was not providing good interpretation services. The family member who was present also said he was being rude with the client. I terminated the session and completed my interview via phone with a different interpreter later.

I did assessment work in a large Russian/Ukrainian population area. It was a rural area, and there was only one certified interpreter in the entire county. She and I saw countless families together. She taught me many cultural expectations (such as never turning down food) and helped me to learn how to do my assessments in a culturally competent fashion. In addition, I had strong trust in her and she often could tell me when things did not seem right or if there were issues I was not capturing in my assessment. I learned how effective good interpreters can be through that experience.

Video: Best Practice in Using Interpreters (https://www.youtube.com/watch?v=-taVYZrpgqY)

One or more interactive elements has been excluded from this version of the text. You can view them online here: https://milnepublishing.geneseo.edu/social-justice-in-human-services/?p=208#oembed-1 (#oembed-1)

Video: Working with Interpreters in the Healthcare Setting (https://www.youtube.com/watch?v=GmNGX0EWpfY)

One or more interactive elements has been excluded from this version of the text. You can view them online here: https://milnepublishing.geneseo.edu/social-justice-in-human-services/?p=208#oembed-2 (#oembed-2)

Discussion Questions

- Why is it important for interpreters to provide cultural context in addition to linguistic translation?
- How can professionals assess the quality of interpretation services during a session?
- Why is building trust between interpreters and social service professionals crucial for effective service delivery?
- What strategies can be employed to handle interpreter shortages in rural or underserved areas?
- What are the ethical considerations involved in using interpreters?

Safety Net Services

Safety net services refer to government or community programs designed to provide a minimum level of support to individuals and families facing financial hardship or other vulnerabilities. Generally, safety net services are government-funded. Safety net services aim to ensure that basic needs are met, particularly for those who are unemployed, underemployed, or otherwise unable to support themselves. Examples of safety net services include Electronic Benefits Cards (EBT, previously known as food stamps), Supplemental Security Income (SSI), Social Security Disability Insurance (SSDI), housing benefits, Medicaid, Medicare, childcare, and transportation assistance.

Accessing safety net services is often frustrating for human services clients. Often, there is a lengthy paperwork process to gain access to one or more of these services. Researching eligibility requirements, required documentation, language barriers, hours of operation, walk-ins or appointments only, and contacting someone at the location before referring clients to the agency is essential. These steps can help clients avoid frustration and save time and money. In addition, many social services offices that provide safety net services struggle with staffing and resource management. Thus, wait times both in person and on the phone can be significant. For example, it is not uncommon to wait on hold for over an hour when trying to call the Social Security Office. Although frustrating, this is sometimes preferable to going in person to an office where the wait might be longer.

Often, these offices do not allow for drop-in appointments, and clients should be warned if they need an appointment ahead of time to speak to someone. Following the COVID-19 pandemic, many programs now require reservations or appointment times to meet with agency workers. Once contact is made, intake and paperwork can be overwhelming. Intake forms are a way to collect a client's contact information and presenting issues or needs. Most questions on this form will focus on gathering eligibility information, and a file will be started. Information gathered may include medical history, social support, mental health background, and financial status. The intake form will typically ask questions to identify if the client is experiencing dangerous living situations or needs immediate food support. This intake form will also inquire if the client is experiencing any self-harming or suicidal behaviors and thoughts.

Suppose the client does not have any medical or mental health, dangerous living situations, or lack of food emergencies. In that case, they will most likely be given an appointment time and date to come back and formally meet with a case manager who is best suited to address their expressed areas of concern. Suppose the client expresses concerns regarding safety in their living situations, food availability, or self-harming or suicidal thoughts. In that case, they will be transferred to a case manager that day to address these areas of concern. No client should ever be left alone to deal with a life-threatening or unsafe situation.

Activity 15.3 – Human Services Traffic Jam

Video: Human Services Traffic Jam by Erine Gray (https://www.youtube.com/watch?v=nus-GQs-qXBY)

 One or more interactive elements has been excluded from this version of the text. You can view them online here: https://milnepublishing.geneseo.edu/social-justice-in-human-services/?p=208#oembed-3 (#oembed-3)

Discussion Questions

- How do you find resources in your community? Is the website or phone number easy to access? Why or why not?
- What are some ways you can help your clients troubleshoot and avoid potential challenges when accessing these resources?
- What are some ways human service and community resource agencies can save money?

Housing Emergencies

The issue of homelessness and housing insecurity has always been a severe problem in the United States. Housing insecurity, from affordability to homelessness, is a problem that increased after the COVID-19 pandemic. When Americans are having difficulty accessing affordable, safe housing, this escalates the need for emergency shelters and other emergency housing services (Joint Center for Housing Studies of Harvard University, 2019). These emergency shelters and other emergency resources are funded and distributed by state and local government entities.

People of color are almost twice as likely as White individuals to experience housing insecurity (Joint Center for Housing Studies of Harvard University, 2019). Structural racism has been a longstanding problem in the United States housing system and is only more evident today. Pre-pandemic rates consistently showed that more than half of the homeless population was typically found in major cities in the United States. According to the State of Homelessness in America report put out in 2023 by the National Alliance to End Homeless, there are an estimated 421,392 people (about half the population of Maine) experiencing homelessness on any given night; the majority (65%) stay in sheltered venues (including emergency shelters), with 35% in unsheltered locations (on the streets or in encampments). Six percent are veterans, and 22% are chronically homeless individuals. This report identifies that the majority of our homeless population are native Hawaiian, Pacific Islander, Black or Brown people.

> **Activity 15.4 – Digging Deeper: Case Example: Migrants in New York**
>
> Recently, in New York City and other cities, the immigration crisis has made the shortage of shelter beds and housing for people with low incomes even more acute. In 2023, New York City opened 186 emergency shelters to cope with the large influx of homeless migrants (Hogan et al., 2023), but it was not without controversy.
>
> Large amounts of money and resources go towards systems to house the large influx of migrant individuals, which has been met with controversy. One side argues that the individuals who live in New York City need those resources, and the other advocates for aiding the migrant individuals. According to the Coalition for the Homeless (2024), in March 2024 there were an estimated 350,000 homeless individuals living in New York City. Further controversy stems from whether New York City supports its own homeless population before spending money on an additional homeless population being brought in.
>
> **Discussion Questions**
>
> - How should New York City prioritize its resources between existing homeless residents and the incoming migrant population?
> - What factors should be considered when allocating shelter beds and housing resources?
> - What ethical dilemmas arise from allocating resources to migrants versus existing homeless individuals?
> - What long-term solutions can be proposed to handle both the existing homelessness crisis and the needs of new migrants?
> - What best practices from other cities can New York City adopt to improve its response to homelessness and migrant influxes?

Working with clients with housing insecurity or homelessness is a very challenging intervention. Contacting county or city Emergency Housing Services is the entry point in locating and securing emergency and long-term housing. Human service professionals advocating for their clients should know the eligibility and documentation required to apply before sending them directly for assistance. Safe housing is a highly scarce resource, and some of the options provided to clients are so unsafe that they choose to be homeless instead of staying in shelters. Human service professionals must convey empathy and understanding if a client chooses this.

> ### Activity 15.5 – Homelessness
>
> **Video: So you think you understand homelessness by Marisa A. Zapata**
> (https://www.youtube.com/watch?v=8AMy3UR-77U)
>
> > *One or more interactive elements has been excluded from this version of the text. You can view them online here: https://milnepublishing.geneseo.edu/social-justice-in-human-services/?p=208#oembed-4 (#oembed-4)*
>
> **Discussion Questions**
>
> - What has changed with the homelessness issue?
> - What is happening in the community you live in regarding homelessness?
> - How are communities addressing homelessness? Is it working?
> - How does your community address homelessness?
> - How does homelessness impact your community?

Intimate Partner Violence

Intimate Partner Violence (IPV) is a complex scenario in human service systems. IPV is complicated as the human services worker must work within their system to balance safety, human rights, personal decision-making, and their potential personal bias. The first ethical responsibility of the human services worker is to offer safety and resources to our clients when they disclose IPV (Warshaw, 2019). That said, clients will not always accept this support for a variety of reasons. It is also the ethical responsibility of the human service worker to respect a client's choice. Clients have the basic human right to make their own choices, including staying in an IPV situation. This may look like a person going back to an IPV living situation against their case manager's advice. Managing a case with IPV involved is a difficult situation for any human service professional. The human service professional must keep their personal bias and feelings out of the interaction and focus only on offering resources and respecting the client's decisions (Warshaw, 2019).

> ### Activity 15.6 – Digging Deeper: IPV on College Campuses
>
> **Video: What's Love Gotta Do With It? from the OMH Resource Center**
> (https://www.youtube.com/watch?v=mBGIc0vwv5Y&t=1918s)
>
> > *One or more interactive elements has been excluded from this version of the text. You can view them online here: https://milnepublishing.geneseo.edu/social-justice-in-human-services/?p=208#oembed-5 (#oembed-5)*

> **Discussion Questions**
>
> - What factors contribute to the prevalence of IPV on college campuses?
> - What strategies can be used to change campus culture regarding IPV?
> - How does IPV impact a student's academic performance and mental health?
> - What innovative approaches could be developed to combat IPV on college campuses?
> - How can research on IPV in college settings inform broader societal efforts to address the issue?

Disaster Planning and Response

The World Health Organization's disaster model includes vulnerability, hazards, and trigger events, including storms, earthquakes, floods, and fires (Morrison & Bawel-Brinkley, 2019). When different individuals, communities, or cultures go through a devastating disaster, their needs can be drastically different depending on the community's trauma. Part of applying human rights as human service professionals is ensuring all people involved in the disaster are offered the support they need, prioritizing physiological and safety needs, following Maslow's hierarchy of needs (Crandall et al., 2020). For example, if a tornado hits a community in Kansas, the first responders will be there as soon as possible to offer universal support like first aid, food, and clothing. What if Family A does not need first aid or food? They may need housing as they have a sick child who should not be out in the cold weather. Family B may need more food, but no shelter as they have friends they can go to stay with. Applying human rights to this situation will involve the human service professionals identifying what resources each unique family needs and doing their best to provide them. It is much easier to think "we just offer everyone the same things," but that is not what being a human service advocate looks like. We must advocate for our clients to receive the resources they each need.

Human service professionals walk a very thin line in our work, and it is their responsibility to utilize evidence-based best practices to make daily decisions. The professionals job is first to identify resources uniquely needed by each client. It is then their responsibility to help support clients in obtaining these resources. However, they must keep their personal bias out of the conversation and respect our clients' decisions in these life-changing events.

> **Activity 15.7 – Digging Deeper: Disaster Response**
>
> Video: How to organise social services during and after a natural disaster? (https://www.youtube.com/watch?v=ctWhIglYFhE)

One or more interactive elements has been excluded from this version of the text. You can view them online here: https://milnepublishing.geneseo.edu/social-justice-in-human-services/?p=208#oembed-6 (#oembed-6)

Video: 4 nursing home residents die after Ida evacuation (https://www.youtube.com/watch?v=XHfD8Vikcmc)

One or more interactive elements has been excluded from this version of the text. You can view them online here: https://milnepublishing.geneseo.edu/social-justice-in-human-services/?p=208#oembed-7 (#oembed-7)

Discussion Questions

- How can human service organizations ensure they are adequately prepared for different types of disasters?
- How can agencies ensure that vulnerable populations receive timely and appropriate emergency services?
- How can human service agencies support individuals and communities in rebuilding their lives post-disaster?
- What ethical dilemmas might arise during disaster interventions, and how can they be addressed?
- Discuss what went wrong in the nursing home video. How would you have done things differently for these vulnerable residents? What kind of advocacy work still needs to be done around disaster and vulnerable populations?

How Theories Impact Human Service Practices

It is important to create ethical and equitable resources for human service clients. Often, this is framed through a human rights lens. Below are a few theories as to how human rights are interwoven into human services, including (a) authority-based theories, (b) natural law-based theory, (c) teleological theories, and (d) virtue ethics theory.

Authority-based theories in human service typically refer to theories that emphasize the role of authority figures, structures, or systems. Authority-based theory posits that the right thing to do is based on what an authority figure has decided (Summers, 2019). Authority-based theories can be faith-based, as, historically, religions and faiths have told us what is right versus wrong. An example of authority-based theory impacting human services is the decision-making chain of command. When a clinical supervisor tells the human service professional what to do, they expect follow-through. In this case, the authority figure is the clinical supervisor, and they are deciding on what is ethically right or wrong.

Authority-based theories underlie many ethical codes in human services. This can be a challenge, as ethics, by definition, often involves difficult grey areas. In addition, many human service workers and organizations have a governing body that provides direction in treatment that can be seen as authority-based. Organizations develop policies and procedures, or written rules, that their employees must follow, and they are expected to do so without question.

Natural law-based theory is a philosophical and ethical perspective that asserts that universal principles govern human behavior and morality. These principles are believed to originate from nature or a higher order of reality rather than from human-made laws or social conventions (Summers, 2019). The governing religion or political beliefs often influence the perception of natural laws. This may be demonstrated in human services when agencies have a political or religious agenda. This agenda may impact the ability of human services workers to serve clients ethically. One example of a natural law is that people are not allowed to kill each other. We saw this being enforced differently while going through the COVID-19 pandemic. The life threatening nature of the illness provoked governments, agencies, and communities to adopt practices like mask-wearing and social distancing due to how this natural pandemic spread, and the damage it caused.

Teleological theories, often referred to in philosophy, focus on the consequences of decisions (Summers, 2019). These theories aim to maximize the potential good outcomes from a given situation. Theories about what is right and wrong are standardly divided into two kinds: those that are teleological and those that are not. Teleological theories first identify what is good in states of affairs and then characterize right acts entirely in terms of that good. (Encyclopedia of Philosophy, 2019, para 1). This may look like a human service professional deciding on a treatment plan based on the best outcomes for a client's living, family, work, and financial situations.

Virtue ethics theory stems from Plato and Aristotle. Virtue theory posits that all people are virtuous at their core (Summers, 2019). Virtue ethics suggests that everyone wants to follow the best possible ethical standards. In human services, this can look like a human service professional thinking about how a client's life can benefit and become better with their involvement. This is the very basis of the Hippocratic Oath—"above all, do not harm." This overarching belief relates to the thought that the intentions of those working in the human service sectors are all based on wanting to help others and the commitment that what we do will not hurt another.

Strategies for Systemic Change

Promoting systemic change in favor of our social justice climate will not come easy. These changes will require work that will need to start from the bottom and rise up through the systems, this is challenging work. Some ways people can make systemic change is by leading with evidence based policy (Mears, 2022). This happens when individuals educate their system officials with acts and policies that have been proven to create direct positive impact on the community (Mears, 2022).

Interventions are also a way to promote systemic change in a positive way. When human service works implement interventions to better support social justice causes, they are integrating systemic changes (Mears, 2022). As these interventions show themselves to be helpful, they should become ingrained in the system and promote long term change.

Dr. Courtney Harris, M. Ed is an experienced language arts educator located in Texas. She has spent her professional career focused on fostering positive learning environments for students from diverse backgrounds. She has created a workbook for people to use to help learn how they can advocate for social justice in their own communities. This workbook focuses on 20 specific ways one can impact social justice issues from a systemic approach. These vary from supporting products and services that align with your positive social justice mindset to writing letters or calling local politicians to seek reform.

Activity 15.8 – Digging Deeper: Advocating for Change

Article: 20 Ways to Be An Advocate for Social Change and Transformation (https://courtney-harriscoaching.com/20-ways-to-be-an-advocate/)

Discussion Questions

- Which one of Dr. Harris' ways to be a systemic advocate for social change have you practiced? Please explain.
- Which one of Dr. Harris' ways to be a systemic advocate for social change do you think you could incorporate into your daily routine? Please explain.
- Which one of Dr. Harris' ways to be a systemic advocate for social change can you engage in to make a large systemic change? Please explain.
- How can you encourage others to engage in the practices to create more advocates for systemic social change?

Thoughts from the Authors

I had to do a significant quantity of background research before I could even think about starting to write this chapter. This chapter included many topics that I thought I was knowledgeable about... However, I found that I was not as savvy as I thought. I always placed the "human rights" concept in international affairs or public policy. Learning about human rights' role in everyday interactions with clients was eye-opening. Writing this chapter reminds me of how I am always learning, expanding my knowledge base, and growing to become a more robust human service professional.

-Dr. Green

As for me, one thing that has enhanced my appreciation for our role in respecting human rights is my advanced studies in trauma. In this field, there is a practice called Trauma-Informed Care. The premise of this practice is that we approach people in a way that considers that we may not know what potentially traumatizing experiences have happened to them. Because others have hurt many people, I want their interactions with me to be safe, consistent, and predictable. This is why I am on time for appointments. I stop listening to what someone is saying, and I try to empower others by allowing them to choose what steps they want to pursue. Remember, though you may be a professional, you are still human and will never be perfect, so it is also important to acknowledge when we make mistakes. Something as small as saying "I am sorry" goes a long way to show how much we respect that other person. Not only does it create a safe experience for someone with a trauma history, but it is also the ultimate way to respect human dignity.

-Dr. Brayton

Chapter Summary Questions

1. In your own words, explain the role the government plays in allocating resources to human service clients and the role social justice can play in this action.
2. What are some examples of screenings that can be used for substance use? Suicide? Mental Health? How can screening be adjusted to support social justice concepts?
3. Why must human service workers utilize evidence-based best practices when deciding how to deal with specific situations?
4. How can the natural power struggle between a human service worker and client hinder the treatment process?

References

Andreassen, R. A. (2016). Professional intervention from a service perspective. In Gubrium, J. F., Andreassen, T. A., Solvang, P., & Hamm, L. (eds), *Reimagining the human service relationship* (pp 33-58). Columbia University Press. https://doi.org/10.7312/gubr17152

Bauerly, B. C., McCord, R. F., Hulkower, R., & Pepin, D. (2019). Broadband access as a public health issue: The role of law in expanding broadband access and connecting underserved communities for better health outcomes. *The Journal of Law, Medicine & Ethics, 47*(2_suppl), 39-42. https://doi.org/10.1177/1073110519857314

Christian, D. M. (2019). Triage. *Critical Care Clinics, 35*(4), 575-589. https://doi.org/10.1016/j.ccc.2019.06.009

Clarkson, J., Dean, J., Ward, J., Komashie, A., & Bashford, T. (2018). A systems approach to healthcare: From thinking to practice. *Future Healthcare Journal. 5*(3), 151-155. doi: 10.7861/futurehosp.5-3-151.

The Coalition for the Homeless. (2024). Basic facts about homelessness: New York City. https://www.coalitionforthehomeless.org/basic-facts-about-homelessness-new-york-city/

Crandall, A., Powell, E. A., Bradford, G. C., Magnusson, B. M., Hanson, C. L., Barnes, M. D., Novilla, M. L. B., & Bean, R. A. (2020). Maslow's hierarchy of needs as a framework for understanding adolescent depressive symptoms over time. *Journal of Child and Family Studies, 29*(2), 273-281. https://doi.org/10.1007/s10826-019-01577-4

Hesano, D. (2023, November 16). *How ID requirements harm marginalized communities and their right to vote*. Democracy Docket. https://www.democracydocket.com/analysis/how-id-requirements-harm-marginalized-communities-and-their-right-to-vote

Hogan, B., Crane, E., & Hicks, N. (2023, July 11). *Major Adams warns that NYC is still 'dealing with a silent crisis' as two new mega migrant shelters open*. New York Post. https://nypost.com/2023/07/11/adams-opens-two-new-emergency-relief-centers-as-migrants-surpass-54k/

Joint Center for Housing Studies of Harvard University. (2019) . *The state of the nation's housing: 2019*. Harvard Graduate School of Design and Harvard Kennedy School.

King, N. B. (2019). Health inequalities and health inequities. In E.E. Morrison & B. Furlong (Eds.), *Health care ethics: Critical issues for the 21st century* (4th ed., pp. 197-209). Jones & Bartlett.

McClintock, A. H., Fainstad, T., Jauregui, J., & Yarris, L.M. (2021). Countering bias in assessment. *Journal of Graduate Medical Education.13*(5), 725-726. doi: 10.4300/JGME-D-21-00722.1.

Mears, D. P. (2022). Escaping the sisyphean trap: Systemic criminal justice system reform. *American Journal of Criminal Justice, 47*(6), 1030–1049. https://doi.org/10.1007/s12103-022-09711-7

Morrison, E. E., & Bawel-Brinkley, K. J. (2019). Ethics of disasters: Planning and response. In E.E. Morrison & B. Furlong (Eds.), *Health care ethics: Critical issues for the 21st century* (4th ed., pp. 221-239). Jones & Bartlett.

National Alliance to End Homeless. (2023). *2023 state of homelessness.* https://endhomelessness.org/state-of-homelessness/

Nesoff, I. (2022). *Human service program planning through a social justice lens.* Routledge. https://doi.org/10.4324/9781003148777

Papa. R. (Eds.). (2020). Handbook on promoting social justice in education. Springer Publishing Company. https://doi.org/10.1007/978-3-030-14625-2_111

Spencer, J., Goode, J., Penix, E. A., Trusty, W., & Swift, J. K. (2019). Developing a collaborative relationship with clients during the initial sessions of psychotherapy. *Psychotherapy, 56*(1), 7–10. https://doi.org/10.1037/pst0000208

Sue, D. W., Rasheed, M. N, & Rasheed, J. M. (2016). *Multicultural social work practice* (2nd ed.). Wiley & Sons.

Summers, N. (2016). *Fundamentals of case management practice: Skills for the human services* (5th ed.). Cengage.

Walker, P. (2020). Triage in a pandemic; equity, utility, or both? *Ethics & Medicine, 36*(3), 147–131.

Warshaw, C. (2019). Domestic violence: Changing theory, changing practice. In E.E. Morrison & B. Furlong (Eds.), *Health care ethics: Critical issues for the 21st century* (4th ed., pp. 237-258). Jones & Bartlett.

World Health Organization & United Nations. High Commissioner for Human Rights. (2008). Human rights, health, and poverty reduction strategies. https://iris.who.int/handle/10665/43962

Media Attributions

- PNG counselling service for women © Department of Foreign Affairs and Trade is licensed under a CC BY (Attribution) license

PEER REVIEWER STATEMENT

Social Justice and Advocacy in Human Services was produced with support from SUNY OER Services and Milne Open Textbooks, a Milne Library, SUNY Geneseo publishing initiative offering a collaborative model for publishing open textbooks. Critical to the success of this approach is including mechanisms to ensure that open textbooks produced with the community are high quality and meet the needs of all students and learners.

Each chapter received two rounds of peer review between Spring 2023 and Spring 2025. The entire text was reviewed by one peer reviewer and each chapter was individually reviewed by a subject matter expert in that area. Finally, an APA expert reviewed the entire textbooks for formatting and citations.

The chapter reviews were structured around considerations of the intended audience of the book, and examined the comprehensiveness, accuracy, and relevance of content, as well as longevity and cultural relevance. Further review by the editors and the project manager focused on clarity, consistency, organization structure flow, and grammatical errors. Changes suggested by the reviewers were incorporated by chapter authors.

Lead authors Cailyn F. Green, Ph.D., M-CASAC and Bernadet DeJonge, Ph.D., CRC would like to thank all authors and peer reviewers for the time, care, and commitment they contributed to the project. We recognize that peer reviewing is a generous act of service on their part. This book would not be the robust, valuable resource that it is if not for their feedback and input.

Reviewers:

- Jeanette Alvarez MS, CASAC-M
- Elizabeth A. Boland, Ph.D., CRC, affiliated with Western Washington University Not only served as a peer reviewer for the OER as a whole, but also served as an APA formatting a citation expert.
- Kari Carrol, MS, SUNY Empire State University
- Vincent Chirimwami, PhD ,Oregon Research Institute
- Sarah Eickhoff, MA, LMHC, MHP
- Matthew Jeffries, Ph.D., Washington State University
- Kasuni T. Kotelawala, M.D.
- Debra Kram-Fernandez, Ph. D, LCSW, SUNY Empire State University
- Lauren Lestremau Allen, Ph.D., BCBA-D, NCSP, LBA, LP, SUNY Empire State University

- Alan Mandell, Ph.D., SUNY Empire State University
- Michael McGeown-Walker, J.D., M.S.
- Maureen McLeod, Ph.D
- Shannon Raybold, MS
- Nadine Wedderburn Ph.D, SUNY Empire State University

ACKNOWLEDGEMENTS

It takes a village to produce an ambitious project such as this; we are deeply grateful for the support of a generous community that came together to edit and proofread this text.

Editors

- Robin Ambrosino
- David Brandt
- Dina Bruun
- Carolyn Connors
- Samantha Dannick
- Jennifer DeVito
- Megan Gadke
- Flynn Hams
- Ellen Heddendorf
- Emma Johnson-Rivard
- April Jupe
- Allison Richard
- Paul Spalletta
- Olympia Stewart-Willis
- Zoe Wake Hyde

Proofreaders

- Anna G
- April Jupe
- Shruti Mehta
- Shannon Pritting
- Allison Richard
- Danielle Walkup

ABOUT THE AUTHORS

Cailyn F. Green

Cailyn F. Green is a Certified Alcoholism and Substance Abuse Counselor- Masters Level (CASAC-M) through New York State. She is the Addiction Studies Professor at the State University of New York: Empire State University. She earned her BA from Western New England University in Springfield, MA and her MS in Forensic Mental Health from Sage Graduate School in Albany, NY. Her Ph.D is in Criminal Justice, specializing in Substance Use from Walden University in Minneapolis, MN. Dr. Green has over 10 years of experience teaching both in online and in-person college-level settings in substance use, human service, criminal justice and clinical counseling topics. She won the Scholars Across the University award in 2024 for her research in substance use topics and this social justice-focused textbook. She has 9 journal article publications to date and her other published textbooks include *Evidence-Based Substance Use Treatment* and the *Group Counseling Workbook*.

Bernadet DeJonge

Bernadet (Bernie) DeJonge, PhD, CRC, LMHC, has her BA in psychology (1999) and MA in Rehabilitation Counseling (2007) from Western Washington University. Her PhD is from Oregon State University in Counseling (2022). She is currently an Assistant Professor in the School of Human Services at Empire State University. Bernie's areas of interest include DEIB, the integration of counseling into medical services, online pedagogy, and disability.

Nikki Golden

Dr. Nikki Golden, LMFT, SUDP, MAC, CMHS is currently an assistant professor at Seattle University in the Counseling Program. She is a licensed Marriage and Family Therapist (LMFT), a Substance Use Disorder Professional (SUDP), a Masters of Addiction Counselor (MAC), and a Child Mental Health Specialist (CMHC). Dr. Golden has extensive clinical experience in both the mental health and substance use disorder fields. Dr. Golden's areas of clinical expertise include addictions, clinical supervision, co-occurring disorders, relationships, sexuality, trauma and working with the LGBTGEQIAP+ population. Dr. Golden's research interests include sociocultural identities and relationships, burnout as a systemic issue, sexuality, and trauma.

Kim Brayton

Dr. Brayton received a joint law and clinical psychology doctorate in California at Palo Alto University and Golden Gate School of Law. She is a professor at Russell Sage College where she heads the program working with students in forensic mental health. Additionally, she has a private practice where she specializes in treating adult survivors of trauma and forensic assessment. In her spare time she enjoys golf, reading and the various exotic locations she bikes through on her stationary bike.

Carrie Steinman

Carrie Steinman, Ph.D., LMSW, MS, has been a faculty member in the School of Human Services at SUNY Empire State University since 2016. She holds a Ph.D. in Social Welfare from

Stony Brook University, an LMSW from Hunter College School of Social Work, and a Master of Science in Counseling and Development from Long Island University. With a Ph.D. in Social Welfare and as a New York State Licensed Social Worker (LMSW), Dr. Steinman brings extensive practical experience to her academic role. She has worked with a range of vulnerable populations, with expertise in child welfare, including foster care, juvenile offenders, and homeless and at-risk youth. Her professional background includes work as both a clinician and an administrator across various agency settings. At SUNY Empire, Dr. Steinman has contributed to curriculum development and revision as a member of the School of Human Services Curriculum Committee. She currently serves as co-chair of the school's Diversity, Equity, Inclusion, and Social Justice (DEISJ) Committee, which she joined at its inception in 2020. In this role, she has helped integrate anti-racist practices and DEISJ principles into the curriculum.

Shannon Raybold

Shannon Raybold is a Program Administrator for Multnomah Early Childhood Program, which provides special education services to over 3,000 children ages birth-5 years old in the Portland, OR metro area. She has a BA in Special and Elementary Education from Western Washington University, a master's degree from the University of Washington specializing in Autism and low incidence disabilities, and is currently completing her EdD from Portland State University in Special Education Leadership. Shannon has been a practitioner in the field of special education for over 20 years, working with children from birth through adulthood. She has supported children in public and private schools around the world, in addition to founding a private educational consulting practice. Shannon has provided professional development for teachers and administrators at local, national, and international conferences on a wide variety of topics related to supporting students with special learning needs. In addition, she has written courses for SENIA Academy and MiniPD to build the capacity of educators and administrators globally. She also serves as an Associate Director for SENIA International and is a tireless advocate for children who experience the world in diverse ways.

www.ingramcontent.com/pod-product-compliance
Lightning Source LLC
Chambersburg PA
CBHW062136160426
43191CB00014B/2299